If you're looking for more study aids, make sure you check out the Online Learning Center at

www.mhhe.com/mcshane2e

Where you can find

- Additional Chapter Quizzes
- Internet Exercises
- Video Cases
- Additional Readings
- Career Corner
- a Guide to Electronic Research

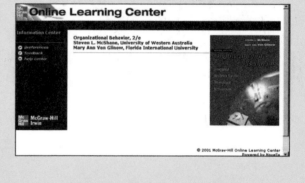

And introducing our new

- OB Online Interactive Exercises

and much more!

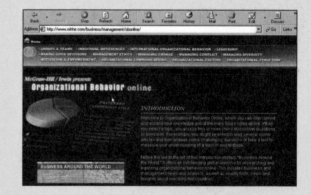

FEB 2005

Organizational Behavior

Implications for Organizational Behavior   Diversity presents both opportunities and challenges in organizations. It can become a competitive advantage by improving decision making and team performance on complex tasks.[27] For many businesses, a diverse workforce is also necessary to provide better customer service in the global marketplace. "We go out of our way to recruit from a melting pot of nationalities," says an executive at Amadeus, a developer of worldwide airline reservation software near Nice, France. "We believe that our product is superior because of the different cultures of the people developing it."[28]

Along with its benefits, workforce diversity presents new challenges. For instance, women have represented a large portion of the workforce for the past two decades, yet they are still underrepresented in senior positions. Most ethnic minorities in the United States also believe that discrimination in the workplace is still common.[29] Various organizational behavior topics, including perceptual distortions (Chapter 3) and organizational politics (Chapter 12) address these issues. Diversity also influences team development (Chapter 8) and the potential for conflict among employees (Chapter 13).

Organizations need to address these potential problems and adapt to emerging workforce needs. For instance, the global consulting firm Cap Gemini Ernst & Young distributes a monthly planning calendar that identifies various religious holidays or ethnic/national celebrations. J. C. Penney executives attend special classes to learn what motivates younger-generation employees. When Siemens AG's nuclear power division in Germany and French nuclear giant Framatome SA merged, executives at the two firms attended cross-cultural sensitivity and team-building classes to minimize cross-cultural conflict.[30]

Emerging Employment Relationships

The workforce isn't the only thing that's changing. After more than 100 years of relative stability, employment relationships are being redefined. Replacing the implied guarantee of lifelong employment in return for loyalty is a "new deal" called **employability.** Employees perform a variety of work activities rather than hold specific jobs, and they are expected to continually learn skills that will keep them employed. Corporate leaders claim that employability is necessary so that organizations can adapt to the rapidly changing business environment. However, as we shall learn throughout this book, employability also has implications for job design, organizational loyalty, career dynamics, and workplace stress.[31]

Another employment shift is the increasing percentage of the workforce in **contingent work**—any job in which the individual does not have an explicit or implicit contract for long-term employment, or one in which the minimum hours of work can vary in a nonsystematic way.[32] By some estimates, more than 15 percent of the U.S. workforce is employed in some sort of contingent work arrangement. Several experts predict that this trend will continue. "We are moving into the age of contractualization where everyone is their own boss," claims a consultant who believes the concept of "employee" is a throwback to industrial revolution servitude.[33]

A new breed of free agents is thriving on the independence and reliance on knowledge that contingent work demands.[34] But contrasting with this optimistic view is the reality that many contingent workers would rather be

employability
An employment relationship in which people are expected to continually develop their skills to remain employed.

contingent work
Any job in which the individual does not have an explicit or implicit contract for long-term employment, or one in which the minimum hours of work can vary in a nonsystematic way.

employed in stable, well-paying jobs. We will learn that contingent work affects organizational loyalty, career dynamics, and other aspects of organizational behavior.

Telecommuting   It's 9 A.M., the beginning of another busy day for Paolo Conconi, the Italian-born owner of Hong Kong electronic-parts maker MPS Electronics. But Conconi doesn't worry about fighting Hong Kong traffic to get to work. His office is at home, far away on the Indonesian island of Bali. Conconi's office is a table by the swimming pool, where he checks e-mail and calls staff and clients in Europe and Asia. "I've organized my work so that I can do it from anywhere," he says. "As long as I have electricity and one or two phone lines, that's all I need."[35]

Paolo Conconi is among the tens of millions of people who have altered their employment relationship through **telecommuting** (also called *teleworking*)—working from home, usually with a computer connection to the office. Technology has untethered some employees so completely from the employer's physical work space that clients and co-workers are oblivious to their true location. For instance, call center operators in Kansas work at home during snowstorms without clients' knowing the difference.[36]

As we move from an industrial to a knowledge-based economy, the number of people who take the information highway to work each day will continue to increase. However, telecommuting poses a number of challenges for organizations and employees.[37] Employers who previously evaluated employees for their "face time"—the amount of time they were physically in the workplace—need to develop outcome-based measures of performance. Evaluating telecommuters is particularly difficult in some Asian cultures where company loyalty is measured by the number of hours at the office.

Employees accustomed to direct supervision need to learn how to manage themselves through self-leadership (see Chapter 6). Many employees complain that telecommuting can be a lonely experience, whereas working at the office is more likely to fulfill a person's social needs. Another problem is that telecommuting creates risks in office politics, a topic we discuss in Chapter 12. As telecommuting increases, employees must also learn how to get things done through **virtual teams**—cross-functional groups that operate across space, time, and organizational boundaries with members who communicate mainly through electronic technologies (see Chapter 8).[38]

Information Technology and OB

By day, Nana Frimpong is the official wood-carver for King Otumfuo Osei Tutu II in the royal Asante court of Ghana, West Africa. But when he isn't carving stools for the king, Frimpong sells his wares over the Internet. Demand from international buyers is so strong that he now employs a staff of 15 carvers. In this country of 19 million people and only 100,000 telephones, Frimpong is somewhat of a celebrity and a role model for the country's potential prosperity. "There are a lot of Nana Frimpongs in the Asante nation," says King Tutu. "Many can be helped through the Internet."[39]

Whether we make fiber-optic routers in California or wooden stools and masks in Ghana, the Internet is changing our lives. It has created opportunities to connect people around the planet and allow small businesses in developing

---

telecommuting
Also called teleworking, it is working from home, usually with a computer connection to the office.

virtual teams
Cross-functional groups that operate across space, time, and organizational boundaries with members who communicate mainly through electronic technologies.

"Can't talk now. I'm in a seminar about improving communication with technology."

(Copyright © 1996. Ted Goff www.tedgoff.com.)

countries to compete in the global marketplace. Information technology is also shaking up traditional organizational behavior concepts within organizations. We have already noted how this technology has given rise to virtual teams and has made it possible for knowledge workers to carry on their business from home or from an Indonesian island. It also increases communication among people with diverse cultural backgrounds and creates new ways to acquire knowledge. In general, information technology challenges traditional business logic regarding how employees interact, how organizations are configured, and how they relate to customers.

network organization

An alliance of several organizations for the purpose of creating a product or serving a client.

Information technology also makes it easier to create a **network organization**—an alliance of several organizations for the purpose of creating a product or serving a client. Cisco Systems, which makes routers and other technology for the Internet, is really a constellation of suppliers, contract manufacturers, assemblers, and other partners connected through an intricate web of information technology. Cisco's network springs into action as soon as a customer places an order (usually through the Internet). Suppliers send the required materials to assemblers, who ship the product directly to the client, usually the same day. Seventy percent of Cisco's product is outsourced this way. In many cases, Cisco employees never touch the product.[40]

Workplace Values and Ethics

At the beginning of this chapter, we read that The Container Store is very careful about hiring the right people. The Dallas-based retailer isn't particularly looking for the job applicant's technical skills. Rather, company founders Kip Tindell and Garrett Boone have emphasized that the best employees bring the same values to the workplace that The Container Store holds up as its corporate values. In other words, the company looks for alignment of values.

values

Stable, long-lasting beliefs about what is important in a variety of situations.

The Container Store and other organizations are paying a lot more attention these days to values in the workplace. **Values** represent stable, long-lasting beliefs about what is important in a variety of situations. They are evaluative standards that help us define what is right or wrong, or good or bad, in the world.[41] Values dictate our priorities, our preferences, and our desires. They influence our motivation and decisions. "Ninety-nine percent of what we say is about values," advises Anita Roddick, founder of the Body Shop.[42]

Cultural, personal, and organizational values have been studied by organizational behavior scholars for several decades.[43] *Cultural values*, which we discuss in Chapter 4 (along with personal and ethical values) represent the dominant prescriptions of a society. They are usually influenced by religious, philosophical, and political ideologies. *Personal values* incorporate cultural values, as well as other values socialized by parents, friends, and personal life events. *Organizational values*, discussed in Chapter 15, on **organizational culture,** are widely and deeply shared by people within the organization.[44]

organizational culture

The basic pattern of shared assumptions, values, and beliefs governing the way employees within an organization think about and act on problems and opportunities.

Importance of Values and Ethics   If values have been studied for so long, why are they just now becoming an emerging issue? One reason is globalization. As organizations expand across cultures, differences in values become more pronounced.[45] Such differences lead to both personal and organizational challenges. At the individual level, employees may find that their personal values conflict with organizational and cross-cultural values.[46] At the organizational level, leaders are looking for ways to integrate (or, at least, coordinate) people with diverse personal and cultural value systems.

Another reason for the recent attention to values is that the old command-and-control system of direct supervision is expensive and incompatible with today's more independently minded workforce. Organizational values represent a subtle, yet potentially effective, alternative. Corporate culture is a deeply embedded form of social control that guides employee decisions and behavior so that they are consistent with the organization's success. For example, The Container Store wants to hire people who value mutual support and customer focus.

A third reason why values have become so important is that many societies are putting more pressure on organizations to engage in ethical practices. **Ethics** refers to the study of moral principles or values that determine whether actions are right or wrong and outcomes are good or bad. We rely on our ethical values to determine the right thing to do. Throughout this textbook, you will discover numerous topics that relate to business ethics, such as monitoring employee performance, rewarding people equitably, stereotyping employees, using peer pressure, engaging in organizational politics, and applying organization development practices. Ethics is also discussed in Chapter 4 and is related to corporate culture in Chapter 15.

ethics

The study of moral principles or values that determine whether actions are right or wrong and outcomes are good or bad.

THE FIVE ANCHORS OF ORGANIZATIONAL BEHAVIOR

Globalization, the changing workforce, emerging employment relationships, information technology, and workplace values are just a few of the issues that we will explore in this textbook. To understand these and other topics, organizational behavior scholars rely on a set of basic beliefs or knowledge structures (see Exhibit 1.3). These conceptual anchors represent the way that OB researchers think about organizations and how they should be studied. Let's look at each of these five beliefs that anchor the study of organizational behavior.

The Multidisciplinary Anchor

Organizational behavior is anchored around the idea that the field should develop from knowledge in other disciplines, not just from its own isolated research base.[47] In other words, OB should be multidisciplinary. The top part of Exhibit 1.4 identifies the traditional disciplines from which organizational behavior knowledge has developed. For instance, the field of psychology has aided our understanding of most issues relating to individual and interpersonal behavior. Sociologists have contributed to our knowledge of team dynamics, organizational socialization, organizational power, and other aspects of the social system.

The bottom part of Exhibit 1.4 identifies some of the emerging fields from which organizational behavior knowledge is acquired. The communications field helps us understand the dynamics of knowledge management, electronic mail, corporate culture, and employee socialization. Information systems scholars are exploring the effects of information technology on team dynamics, decision making, and knowledge management. Marketing scholars have enhanced our understanding of job satisfaction and customer service, knowledge management, and creativity. Women's studies scholars are studying perceptual biases and power relations between men and women in organizations.

The MONY Group's ethics and social responsibility practices strengthen its relationship with both the community and its own employees. The New York–based financial services firm donates $100 to employees who volunteer at least five hours over six months to a nonprofit organization of their choice. MONY employees also volunteer to brighten up school yards (shown in photo) and help students with their reading. "Volunteerism is one element that goes into retaining a good employee," says Lynn Stekis of the MONY Foundation. Carla Cohn, MONY's director of information technology and a volunteer reader to schoolchildren, agrees. "It's another indication of how MONY is not just a company, but also a place that cares about its people and the community," she says.[48] Why do an organization's ethical and social responsibility practices affect its ability to attract and retain employees? *(Courtesy of* Training *magazine)*

EXHIBIT 1.3

Five conceptual anchors of organizational behavior

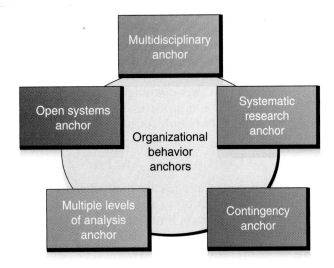

EXHIBIT 1.4

Multidisciplinary anchor of organizational behavior

Discipline	Relevant OB topics
Traditional	
Psychology	Motivation, perception, attitudes, personality, job stress, job enrichment, performance appraisals, leadership
Sociology	Team dynamics, roles, socialization, communication patterns, organizational power, organizational structure
Anthropology	Corporate culture, organizational rituals, cross-cultural dynamics, organizational adaptation
Political science	Intergroup conflict, coalition formation, organizational power and politics, decision making, organizational environments
Economics	Decision making, negotiation, organizational power
Industrial engineering	Job design, productivity, work measurement
Emerging	
Communications	Knowledge management, electronic mail, corporate culture, employee socialization
Information systems	Team dynamics, decision making, knowledge management
Marketing	Knowledge management, creativity, decision making
Women's studies	Organizational power, perceptions

The true test of OB's multidisciplinary anchor is how effectively OB scholars continue to transfer knowledge from traditional and emerging disciplines. History suggests that fields of inquiry tend to become more inwardly focused as they mature.[49] It is our hope that OB will avoid this tendency by continuing to recognize ideas from other disciplines.

The Systematic Research Anchor

A second anchor is that organizational behavior researchers believe in the systematic collection of data and information about organizations. In other words, they rely on a set of principles and practices that minimize personal biases and distortions about organizational events. For the most part, they rely on the scientific method by forming research questions, systematically collecting data, and testing hypotheses against those data. OB scholars are also turning to qualitative research methods to make sense of organizations. Qualitative researchers rely on grounded theory and other systematic practices to ensure that they document shared meaning of organizational events. Appendix A at the end of this book provides an overview of research design and methods commonly found in organizational behavior studies.

The Contingency Anchor

contingency approach
The idea that a particular action may have different consequences in different situations.

"It depends" is a phrase that OB scholars often use to answer a question about the best solution to an organizational problem. The statement may frustrate some people, yet it reflects an important way of understanding and predicting organizational events, called the **contingency approach.** This anchor states that a particular action may have different consequences in different situations. In other words, no single solution is best in all circumstances.[50]

Many early OB theorists proposed universal rules to predict and explain organizational life, but there are usually too many exceptions to make these "one best way" theories useful. For example, in Chapter 14 we will learn that leaders should use one style (e.g., participation) in some situations and another style (e.g., direction) in other situations. Thus, when faced with a particular problem or opportunity, we need to understand and diagnose the situation, and select the strategy most appropriate *under those conditions*.[51]

Although contingency-oriented theories are necessary in most areas of organizational behavior, we should be wary about carrying this anchor to an extreme. Some contingency models add more confusion than value over universal ones. Consequently, we need to balance the sensitivity of contingency factors with the simplicity of universal theories.

The Multiple Levels of Analysis Anchor

This textbook divides organizational behavior topics into three levels of analysis: individual, team, and organization (see Exhibit 1.5). The individual level includes the characteristics and behaviors of employees as well as the thought processes that are attributed to them, such as motivation, perceptions, personalities, attitudes, and values. The team level of analysis looks at the way people interact. This level includes team dynamics, decisions, power, organizational politics, conflict, and leadership. At the organizational level, we focus on how people structure their working relationships and on how organizations interact with their environments.

Although an OB topic is typically pegged into one level of analysis, it usually relates to all three levels.[52] For instance, communication is located in this book as a team process, but we also recognize that it includes individual and organizational processes. Therefore, you should try to think about each OB topic at the individual, team, and organizational levels, not at just one of these levels.

The Open Systems Anchor

Hewlett-Packard may have lots of buildings and equipment, but CEO Carly Fiorina says that her job is to nurture something that is alive. "I think that a

EXHIBIT 1.5

Three levels of analysis in organizational behavior

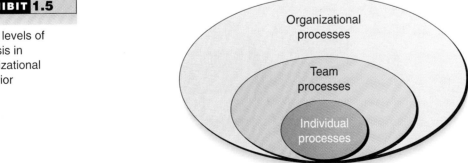

open systems
Organizations that take their sustenance from the environment and, in turn, affect that environment through their output.

company is a living system," says Fiorina. "It is an organism, it is operating in other living systems, and a leader has to think about the company as a living, breathing system."[53] Carly Fiorina is describing the <u>fifth anchor of organiza</u>tional behavior—the view that organizations are **open systems.**

Organizations are open systems because they take their sustenance from the environment and, in turn, affect that environment through their output. A company's survival and success depend on how well employees sense environmental changes and alter their patterns of behavior to fit those emerging conditions.[54] In contrast, a closed system has all the resources needed to survive without dependence on the external environment. Organizations are never completely closed systems, but monopolies operating in very stable environments can ignore customers and others for a fairly long time without adverse consequences.

As Exhibit 1.6 illustrates, organizations acquire resources from the external environment, including raw materials, employees, financial resources, information, and equipment. Inside the organization are numerous subsystems, such as processes (communication and reward systems), task activities (production, marketing), and social dynamics (informal groups, power dynamics). With the aid of technology (such as equipment, work methods, and information), these subsystems transform inputs into various outputs. Some outputs (e.g., products and services) may be valued by the external environment, whereas other outputs (e.g., work stress, employee layoffs) have adverse effects. The organization receives feedback from the external environment regarding the value of its outputs and the availability of future inputs. This process is cyclical and, ideally, self-sustaining, so that the organization may continue to survive and prosper.

stakeholders
Shareholders, customers, suppliers, governments, and any other groups with a vested interest in the organization.

External Environment and Stakeholders   The external environment consists of the natural and social conditions outside the organization. For example, companies depend on physical space, natural resources, and a knowledgeable workforce. Probably the most important component of the external environment is the organization's **stakeholders.** These are the shareholders, customers, suppliers, governments, and any other groups with a vested interest in the organization.[55] Stakeholders influence the firm's access to inputs and

Open systems view of organizations

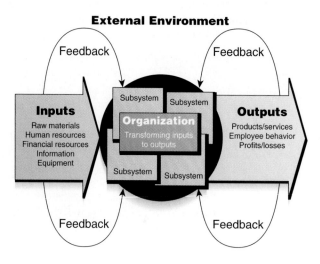

ability to discharge outputs. Some scholars suggest that each organization's distinctiveness depends on the stakeholders it emphasizes. And unless they pay attention to the needs of stakeholders, organizational leaders may find their business in trouble.

Because organizations operate in a much more complex and turbulent environment than a few decades ago, careful analysis of corporate decisions may be a waste of precious time.[56] Organizations remain responsive by giving employees more freedom to make decisions, allowing them to experiment, and viewing mistakes as learning opportunities. In other words, corporate change occurs more quickly when the people on the frontlines of the changing environment are empowered to make decisions.

Systems as Interdependent Parts   Organizational systems consist of many internal subsystems that need to be continually aligned with each other. As companies grow, they develop more and more complex subsystems that must coordinate with each other in the process of transforming inputs to outputs.[57] These interdependencies can easily become so complex that a minor event in one subsystem may amplify into serious unintended consequences elsewhere in the organization.

British Airways taught its employees about the interdependence of subsystems through a computer simulation. The task involved making "Granny" a happy British Airways passenger while getting her from her home to a particular destination. It isn't as easy as it sounds. When participants use frequent flyer plan incentives to lure Granny onto a particular flight, for example, the computer program quickly points out that this action affects other customers and requires the marketing department to communicate the incentive. Through this exercise, British Airways employees learn how decisions and actions in one subsystem affect not just Granny, but also other people in other parts of the organization.[58]

The open systems anchor is an important way of viewing organizations. However, it has traditionally focused on physical resources that enter the organization and are processed into physical goods (outputs). This outlook was representative of the industrial economy, but not of the new economy, where the most valued input is knowledge. The final section of this chapter introduces the key features of this emerging perspective in organizational behavior.

knowledge management
Any structured activity that improves an organization's capacity to acquire, share, and utilize knowledge in ways that improves its survival and success.

KNOWLEDGE MANAGEMENT

Organizational behavior scholars have built on the open system anchor to create an entire subfield of research dedicated to the dynamics of **knowledge management.** Knowledge management is any structured activity that improves an organization's capacity to acquire, share, and use knowledge in ways that improve its survival and success.[59] The knowledge that resides in an organization is called its **intellectual capital.** Intellectual capital is the sum of an organization's human capital, structural capital, and relationship capital.[60]

intellectual capital
The sum of an organization's human capital, structural capital, and relationship capital.

- *Human capital* is the knowledge that employees possess and generate, including their skills, experience, and creativity.
- *Structural capital* is the knowledge captured and retained in an organization's systems and structures. It is the knowledge that remains after all the human capital has gone home.

- *Relationship capital* is the value derived from an organization's relationships with customers, suppliers, and other external stakeholders who provide added value for the organization. It includes customer loyalty as well as mutual trust between the organization and its suppliers.[61]

Knowledge Management Processes

Intellectual capital represents the *stock* of knowledge held by an organization. This stock of knowledge is so important that some companies try to measure its value.[62] But knowledge management is much more than the organization's stock of knowledge. It is a *process* that develops an organization's capacity to acquire, share, and use knowledge more effectively. This process is often called *organizational learning* because companies must continually learn about their environments in order to survive and succeed through adaptation.[63] The capacity to acquire, share, and use knowledge means that companies have established systems, structures, and organizational values that support the knowledge management process. Let's look more closely at some of the strategies companies use to acquire, share, and use knowledge.

Knowledge Acquisition   Knowledge acquisition includes the organization's ability to extract information and ideas from its environment as well as through insight. One of the fastest and most powerful ways to acquire knowledge is through **grafting**—hiring individuals or buying entire companies.[64] For instance, Nortel Networks quickly moved from telecommunications into fiber-optic gear by acquiring Bay Networks, Qtera Corporation, and other organizations with leading-edge knowledge. Knowledge also enters the organization when employees learn about the external environment. Wal-Mart executives do this by systematically shopping at competitor stores every week. A third knowledge acquisition strategy is experimentation. Companies receive knowledge through insight as a result of research and other creative processes (see Chapter 10).[65]

Knowledge Sharing   Many organizations are reasonably good at acquiring knowledge but waste this resource by not effectively disseminating it. As several executives have lamented: "I wish we knew what we know." Studies report that knowledge sharing is usually the weakest link in knowledge management.[66] Valuable ideas sit idly—rather like unused inventory—or as hidden "silos of knowledge" throughout the organization. One organizational unit might apply useful ideas to improve performance or customer service, whereas a nearby unit has not discovered these better procedures.

Organizations need to improve communication to improve knowledge sharing (see Chapter 11). Global Connections 1.1 describes how Ericsson, the Swedish electronics firm, encourages knowledge sharing mainly through information technology. Some companies encourage knowledge sharing through **communities of practice.** These are informal groups bound together by shared expertise and passion for a particular activity or interest.[67] Great Harvest Bread Company applies this idea by encouraging its 140 highly autonomous franchisees to participate in the company's learning community. This community consists of casual visits, telephone calls, and e-mails to other Great Harvest franchisees. "We had an epiphany a long time ago," says Tom

---

grafting
The process of acquiring knowledge by hiring individuals or buying entire companies.

communities of practice
Informal groups bound together by shared expertise and passion for a particular activity or interest.

Ericsson Shares the Knowledge

Ericsson values knowledge sharing, but the giant Swedish electronics company is a highly decentralized business spread across many business units and countries. To overcome these distance and functional barriers, Ericsson applies several knowledge-sharing strategies.

A cornerstone of Ericsson's knowledge sharing is providing free Internet access to its employees and their families. The service connects users to Zopps, a virtual community site filled with Ericsson information. The Zopps website invites users to comment on the Ericsson technology and information content, thereby receiving market testing and structured knowledge transfer. "We are really interested in their opinions," says an Ericsson business development executive in Stockholm. "Not so much the technical opinions of our engineers, but their teenage children's ideas of what is good or bad about network technology, content and multimedia."

A second knowledge-sharing venue is Knack, an internal website focused on competence development. To some extent, Knack is an online learning center. However, it is also a place for knowledge transfer through a virtual "coffee shop," where discussion groups and specialist forums are maintained. In this respect, Knack becomes the meeting place of communities of practice. It also provides a knowledge map by listing competence inventories of experts in different fields.

To help the Web-based knowledge connections flow more smoothly, Ericsson brings together project man-

Ericsson, the Swedish electronics giant, relies on several strategies to share knowledge throughout its decentralized business units. *(©Reuters NewMedia Inc./CORBIS)*

agers at the Ericsson Project Management Institute. The explicit objective of these sessions is for project managers to learn new methods and the best practices. Implicitly, the gatherings improve networking, which, in turn, increases knowledge sharing through information technology.

Sources: Based on T. Hellström, "Knowledge and Competence Management at Ericsson: Decentralization and Organizational Fit," *Journal of Knowledge Management* 4 (2000); M. Van Niekerk, "Ericsson Employees Are One Big Internet Family," *The Age (Melbourne),* July 21, 1998, p. 2.

McMakin, chief operating officer of the Dillon, Montana, company. "Owners profit more from each other's experiences than from the 'wisdom' of a central world headquarters."[68]

Knowledge Use Acquiring and sharing knowledge are wasted exercises unless knowledge is effectively put to use. To do this, employees must realize that the knowledge is available and that they have enough freedom to apply it. Effective use of knowledge requires a culture that supports experiential learning (see Chapter 2).

Organizational Memory

organizational memory
The storage and preservation of intellectual capital.

Intellectual capital can be lost as quickly as it is acquired. Corporate leaders need to recognize that they are the keepers of an **organizational memory.** This metaphor refers to the storage and preservation of intellectual capital. It includes information that employees possess as well as knowledge embedded in the organization's systems and structures. It includes documents, objects, and anything else that provides meaningful information about how the organization should operate.

How do organizations retain intellectual capital? One way is by keeping good employees. While many high-tech companies laid off an unprecedented number of people to cut costs during the recent "tech wreck," Apple Computer held on to its talent. "Our main asset is human talent, and we cannot afford to lose it," explains Apple's chief financial officer, Fred Anderson.[69] A second strategy is to systematically transfer knowledge before employees leave. This process occurs when new recruits apprentice with skilled employees, thereby acquiring knowledge that is not documented.

Rod Willcox didn't know how to turn on the lights, let alone operate the equipment, when he first walked into this cracker bakery that Nabisco had shut down a year earlier. Fortunately, Willcox quickly recaptured the lost memory when his company, the Atlantic Baking Group, reopened the East Liberty, Pennsylvania, plant. Willcox simply rehired 40 former Nabisco employees who had worked at the bakery. The former Nabisco workers have been invaluable in redesigning the manufacturing layout and eliminating some kinks in the way things worked under the former owner.[70] Along with keeping (or rehiring) knowledgeable employees, how else can an organization retain organizational memory? (©AP/Wide World)

A third organizational memory strategy is to transfer knowledge into structural capital.[71] This strategy includes bringing out hidden knowledge, organizing it, and putting it in a form that can be available to others. This is what the organizing committee for the Sydney Olympics (SOCOG) did. SOCOG received mostly informal and anecdotal information from the Atlanta Olympics on how to run this type of event. To ensure that future Olympics organizers would have more knowledge, all divisions and functional areas within SOCOG completed extensive templates of how they set up their operations. This effort resulted in 90 manuals that document everything from organizational structure and stakeholders to staffing and budgets.[72]

Before leaving the topic of organizational memory and knowledge management, you should know that successful companies also *unlearn*. Sometimes it is appropriate for organizations to selectively forget certain knowledge.[73] This means that they should cast off the routines and patterns of behavior that are no longer appropriate. Employees need to rethink their perceptions, such as how they should interact with customers and which is the best way to perform a task. As we shall discover in Chapter 16, unlearning is essential for organizational change.

THE JOURNEY BEGINS

This chapter gives you some background about the field of organizational behavior. But it's only the beginning of our journey. Throughout this book, we will challenge you to learn new ways of thinking about how people work in and around organizations. We will also rely on a broad range of firms across the United States and around the planet. You will recognize some companies—such as Ericsson, Boeing, and Southwest Airlines. But we also introduce you to many firms that you probably haven't heard about. Some, such as IDEO and Agilent Technologies, are emerging forces in today's fast-paced world of work. Still others, such as Ipswitch and Animal Logic, are small organizations. Chances are that you will work in a small business, so it makes sense that you should learn about organizational behavior in these operations.

CHAPTER SUMMARY

Organizational behavior is a relatively young field of inquiry that studies what people think, feel, and do in and around organizations. Organizations are groups of people who work interdependently toward some purpose.

OB concepts help us predict and understand organizational events, adopt more accurate theories of reality, and control organizational events more effectively. They let us make sense of the work world, test and challenge our personal theories of human behavior, and understand ways to manage organization activities.

There are several emerging issues and changes in organizational behavior. Globalization requires corporate decision makers to be more sensitive to cultural differences. The workforce is becoming increasingly diverse. Companies and employees must adjust to emerging employment relationships. Information technology has created virtual teams and network organizations. Corporate leaders are paying more attention to values in the workplace.

Organizational behavior scholars rely on a set of basic beliefs to study organizations. These anchors include beliefs that OB knowledge should be multidisciplinary and based on systematic research, that organizational events usually have contingencies, that organizational behavior can be viewed from three levels of analysis (individual, team, and organization), and that organizations are open systems.

The open systems anchor suggests that organizations have interdependent parts that work together to continually monitor and transact with the external environment. They acquire resources from the environment, transform them through technology, and return outputs to the environment. The external environment consists of the natural and social conditions outside the organization. This environment includes stakeholders—any group with a vested interest in the organization. External environments are generally much more turbulent today, so organizations must become adaptable and responsive.

Knowledge management develops an organization's capacity to acquire, share, and use knowledge in ways that improve the organization's survival and success. Intellectual capital is knowledge that resides in an organization, including its human capital, structural capital, and relationship capital. It is a firm's main source of competitive advantage. Organizations acquire knowledge through grafting, individual learning, and experimentation. Knowledge sharing occurs mainly through communication. Knowledge use occurs when employees realize that the knowledge is available and that they have enough freedom to apply it. Organizational memory refers to the storage and preservation of intellectual capital.

KEY TERMS

communities of practice, p. 20
contingency approach, p. 16
contingent work, p. 11
employability, p. 11
ethics, p. 14
globalization, p. 8
grafting, p. 20

intellectual capital, p. 19
knowledge management, p. 19
network organization, p. 13
open systems, p. 18
organizational behavior (OB), p. 4
organizational culture, p. 14

organizational memory, p. 21
organizations, p. 5
stakeholders, p. 18
telecommuting, p. 12
values, p. 14
virtual teams, p. 12

DISCUSSION QUESTIONS

1. A friend suggests that organizational behavior courses are useful only to people who will enter management careers. Discuss the accuracy of your friend's statement.
2. Look through the list of chapters in this textbook; then discuss how information technology could influence each organizational behavior topic.
3. Comment on the accuracy of this statement: Organizational theories should follow the contingency approach.
4. Employees in the water distribution unit of a large city were put into teams and encouraged to find ways to improve efficiency. The teams boldly crossed departmental boundaries and areas of management discretion in search of problems. Employees working in other parts of the city began to complain about these intrusions. Moreover, when some team ideas were implemented, the city managers discovered that a dollar saved in the water distribution unit may have cost the organization two dollars in higher costs elsewhere. Use the open systems anchor to explain what happened here.
5. After attending a seminar on knowledge management, a mining company executive argues that this perspective ignores the fact that that mining companies could not rely on knowledge alone to stay in business. They also need physical capital (such as digging and ore processing equipment) and land

(where the minerals are located). In fact, those two factors may be more important than what employees carry around in their heads. Do you agree with the mining executive's statement? Why or why not?
6. Fully describe intellectual capital, and explain how an organization can retain this capital.
7. At a recent seminar on information technology, you heard a consultant say that over 30 percent of U.S. companies use software to manage documents and exchange information, whereas firms in Europe are just beginning to adopt this technology. On the basis of this information, the consultant concluded that knowledge management in Europe is at its beginning stages. In other words, few firms in Europe practice knowledge management. Comment on this consultant's statement.
8. BusNews Corporation is the leading stock market and business news service. Over the past two years, BusNews has experienced increased competition from other news providers. These competitors have brought in Internet and other emerging computer technologies to link customers with information more quickly. There is little knowledge within BusNews about how to use these computer technologies. Based on the knowledge acquisition processes for knowledge management, explain how BusNews might gain the intellectual capital necessary to become more competitive in this respect.

ANCOL CORPORATION

Paul Sims was delighted when Ancol Corporation offered him the job of manager at its Lexington, Kentucky, plant. Sims was happy enough managing a small metal stamping plant with another company, but the invitation to apply to the plant manager job at one of the leading metal fabrication companies was irresistible. Although the Lexington plant was the smallest of Ancol's 15 operations, the plant manager position was a valuable first step in a promising career.

One of Sims's first observations at Ancol's Lexington plant was that relations between employees and management were strained. Taking a page from a recent executive seminar that he attended on building trust in the workplace, Sims ordered the removal of all time clocks from the plant. Instead, the plant would assume that employees had put in their full shift. This symbolic gesture, he believed, would establish a new level of credibility and strengthen relations between management and employees at the site.

Initially, the 250 production employees at the Lexington plant appreciated their new freedom. They felt respected and saw this gesture as a sign of positive change from the new plant manager. Two months later, however, problems started to appear. A few people began showing up late, leaving early, or take extended lunch breaks. Although this represented only about 5 percent of the employees, others found the situation unfair. Moreover, the increased absenteeism levels were beginning to have a noticeable effect on plant productivity. The problem had to be managed.

Sims asked supervisors to observe and record when the employees came or went and to discuss attendance problems with those abusing their privileges. But the supervisors had no previous experience with keeping attendance, and many lacked the necessary interpersonal skills to discuss the matter with subordinates. Employees resented the reprimands, so relations with supervisors deteriorated. The additional responsibility of keeping track of attendance also made it difficult for supervisors to complete their other responsibilities. After just a few months, Ancol found it necessary to add another supervisor position and reduce the number of employees assigned to each supervisor.

But the problems did not end there. Without time clocks, the payroll department could not deduct pay for the amount of time that employees were late. Instead, a letter of reprimand was placed in the employee's personnel file. However, this required yet more time and additional skills from the supervisors. Employees did not want these letters to become a permanent record, so they filed grievances with their labor union. The number of grievances doubled over six months, which required even more time for both union officials and supervisors to handle these disputes.

Nine months after removing the time clocks, Paul Sims met with union officials, who agreed that it would be better to put the time clocks back in. Employee–management relations had deteriorated below the level when Sims had started. Supervisors were overworked. Productivity had dropped due to poorer attendance records and increased administrative workloads.

A couple of months after the time clocks were put back in place, Sims attended an operations meeting at Ancol's headquarters in Cincinnati. During lunch, Sims described the time clock incident to Liam Jackson, Ancol's plant manager in Portland, Oregon. Jackson looked surprised, then chuckled. He explained that the previous manager at his plant had done something like that with similar consequences six or seven years ago. The manager had left some time ago, but Jackson heard about the earlier time clock incident from a supervisor during his retirement party two months ago.

"I guess it's not quite like lightning striking the same place twice," said Sims to Jackson. "But it sure feels like it."

Discussion Questions

1. Use the systems theory model to explain what happened when Ancol removed the time clocks.

2. What changes should occur to minimize the likelihood of these problems in the future?

STAYING PUT IN INDONESIA

BusinessWeek Many of the largest and best-known companies operate on an international scale. Corporations such as General Electric, Coca-Cola, and Exxon Mobil employ people on all continents. They bring to their employers a wide diversity of talents, experience, and cultural norms. A complete understanding of organizational behavior must be able to account for such variation.

This *Business Week* case study describes how organizations remain competitive in international markets. Specifically, it describes the challenges and opportunities facing several businesses with operations in Indonesia, which underwent a great deal of political turmoil following the ouster of President Suharto in 1998. Read through this *Business Week* case study at www.mhhe.com/mcshane2e and prepare for the discussion questions below.

Discussion Questions

1. Apply the open systems model to describe with what elements of the environment the companies described in this article interact. Give an example of how one of these elements might affect organizational behavior in one of the companies mentioned.

2. According to the article's author, why do the companies operate in Indonesia and employ managers from India? What are some management challenges related to this international arrangement?

3. What aspects of knowledge management would be particularly relevant to the organizations described in this article?

Source: Michael Shari, "Staying Put in Indonesia," *Business Week*, September 17, 2001.

HUMAN CHECKERS

Purpose This exercise is designed to help students understand the importance and application of organizational behavior concepts.

Materials Chairs (optional). The instructor has information about the teams' task.

Instructions

- *Step 1*—Form teams with six students. If possible, each team should have a private location where team members can plan and practice the required task without being observed or heard by other teams.

- *Step 2*—All teams will receive special instructions in class about the teams' assigned task. All teams have the same task and will have the same amount of time to plan and practice the task. At the end of this planning and practice period, each team will be timed while completing the task in class. The team that completes the task in the least time wins.

- *Step 3*—Other than chairs, no special materials are required or allowed for this exercise. Although the task is not described here, students should learn the following rules for planning and implementing the task:

Rule 1—You cannot use any written form of communication or any props other than chairs to assist in the planning or implementation of this task.

Rule 2—You may speak to other students on your team at any time during the planning and implementation of this task.

Rule 3—When performing the task, you must move only in the direction of your assigned destination. In other words, you can only move forward, not backward.

Rule 4—When performing the task, you can move forward to the next space, but only if it is vacant (see Exhibit 1).

Rule 5—When performing the task, you can move forward two spaces, if that space is vacant. In other words, you can move around a student who is one space in front of you to the next space if that space is vacant (see Exhibit 2).

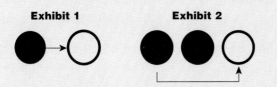

Exhibit 1   **Exhibit 2**

■ *Step 4*—When all teams have completed their tasks, the class will discuss the implications of this exercise for organizational behavior.

Discussion Questions

1. Identify organizational behavior concepts that the team applied to complete this task.

2. What personal theories of people and work teams were applied to complete this task.

3. What organizational behavior problems occurred, and what actions were (or should have been) taken to solve them?

T E A M   E X E R C I S E   1.4

DEVELOPING KNOWLEDGE FROM MISTAKES

Purpose   The problem that people make from their mistakes isn't so much the mistake itself. Rather, it's that they do not take the time to learn from the mistake. This exercise is designed to help you understand how to gain knowledge from past mistakes in a specific situation.

Instructions

■ *Step 1*—The class will be divided into small teams of four to six people. The instructor will identify a situation that students probably have experienced and in which they probably made mistakes. This situation could be the first day at work, the first day of classes, or a social event, such as a first date.

■ *Step 2*—After the topic has been identified, each team member writes down an incident in which something went wrong in that situation. For example, if the topic is the first day of classes, someone might note how he or she was late for class as a result of forgetting to set the alarm clock.

■ *Step 3*—Each student describes the mistake to other team members. As an incident is described, students should develop a causal map of the incident. They should ask why the problem happened, what the consequences were of this incident, whether it happened again, and so on. The knowledge might not be as obvious as you think. For example, in the incident of being late, the learning might not be that we should ensure the alarm clock is set. It might be a matter of changing routines (going to bed earlier), rethinking our motivation to enroll in a program, and so on.

■ *Step 4*—As other incidents are analyzed, the team should begin to document specific knowledge about the incident. Think of this knowledge as a road map for others to follow when they begin their first day of class, first day at work, first date, and the like.

Source: This exercise was developed by Steven L. McShane, based on ideas in P. LaBarre, "Screw Up, and Get Smart," *Fast Company* 19 (November 1998), p. 58.

IT ALL MAKES SENSE?

Purpose This exercise is designed to help you understand how organizational behavior knowledge can help you understand life in organizations.

Instructions Read each of the statements below and circle whether each statement is true or false, in your opinion. The class will consider the answers to each question and discuss the implications for studying organizational behavior. After reviewing these statements, the instructor will provide information about the most appropriate answer. (Note: This exercise may be done as a self-assessment or a team activity.)

1. True   False   A happy worker is a productive worker.

2. True   False   Decision makers tend to continue supporting a course of action even though information suggests that the decision is ineffective.

3. True   False   Organizations are more effective when they prevent conflict among employees.

4. True   False   It is better to negotiate alone than as a team.

5. True   False   Companies are most effective when they have a strong corporate culture.

6. True   False   Employees perform better without stress.

7. True   False   Effective organizational change always begins by pinpointing the source of the organization's current problems.

8. True   False   Female leaders involve employees in decisions to a greater degree than do male leaders.

9. True   False   Thomas Edison is a classic example of the fact that creative people are lone geniuses.

10. True   False   Top-level executives tend to exhibit Type A behavior patterns (i.e., hard-driving, impatient, competitive, and short-tempered; rapid talkers with a strong sense of time urgency).

11. True   False   Employees usually feel overreward inequity when they are paid more than co-workers performing the same work.

After studying the preceding material, be sure to check out our website at
www.mhhe.com/mcshane2e
for more in-depth information and interactivities that correspond to this chapter.

Individual Behavior and Processes

Individual Behavior and Learning in Organizations

Bob Garland was taken aback when executive coach Kathy Lubar suggested he should improve his speaking style. "Why should I have to do that?" wondered the senior manager at accounting firm Deloitte and Touche. "I'm a good speaker already. I've given 300 to 400 speeches over the last 20 years." But after a role-play session with Lubar, Garland realized his speeches were too cerebral and boring. "I thought I was a good speaker," Garland said. "Now, I realize that was not the case at all."

Bob Garland was a skeptic when he started using an executive coach. Now he is a convert, as are a lot of other people. One recent survey estimates that 25 percent of Fortune 500 companies use executive coaches. IBM says it has a competitive advantage by retaining 30 leadership consultants to work with its top 300 executives. At Merrill Lynch, executive coach Don Greene works with stockbrokers and executives, using the same techniques he has applied to Grand Prix drivers, Olympic divers, and Metropolitan Opera divas.

Executive coach Nancy Gerber (left) helps Liz Sanford with her leadership skills after Liz opened her own planning firm in Decatur, Georgia.
(© *Jean Shifrin*, The Atlanta Journal-Constitution)

Executive coaches offer accurate feedback, open dialogue, and constructive encouragement to improve the client's performance and personal well-being. They ask provocative questions, offer perspective, and help clients clarify choices. Experts suggest that coaching is an excellent way to improve a person's emotions and interpersonal skills.

Liz Sanford turned to an executive coach when she realized her skills as a boss needed work. "I didn't set clear expectations for people, and I had trouble with the whole facade of being in charge," says the founder of a city and transportation planning firm in Decatur, Georgia. Sanford's leadership skills and confidence improved dramatically after working with personal coach Nancy Gerber. "Coaching is simply a relationship with someone who is paid to tell you the absolute truth," says Gerber.[1]

Executive coaching is a booming business because it potentially addresses some of the drivers of individual behavior and performance that we discuss in this chapter. We begin by introducing a model of individual behavior and performance as well as the main types of work-related behavior. Most elements of the individual behavior model are influenced by individual learning, so the latter part of this chapter discusses the concept of learning and describes four perspectives of learning in organizational settings: reinforcement, feedback, observation, and experience.

MARS MODEL OF INDIVIDUAL BEHAVIOR AND PERFORMANCE

A useful model for understanding the drivers of individual behavior is the MARS model of individual behavior and performance. Exhibit 2.1 illustrates the MARS model, which represents the four factors that directly influence an employee's voluntary behavior and resulting performance—motivation, ability, role perceptions, and situational factors. These four factors are represented by the acronym "MARS" in the model's name.

The MARS model shows that these four factors have a combined effect on individual performance. If any factor weakens, employee performance will decrease. For example, highly qualified salespeople who understand their job duties and have sufficient resources will not perform their jobs as well if they aren't motivated to market the company's products or services. Companies that excel in customer service and employee performance pay attention to all four factors. Global Connections 2.1 describes how paying attention to employee abilities, motivation, role perceptions, and situational factors has helped Singapore Airlines become the world's top-rated airline.

EXHIBIT 2.1   MARS model of individual behavior and performance

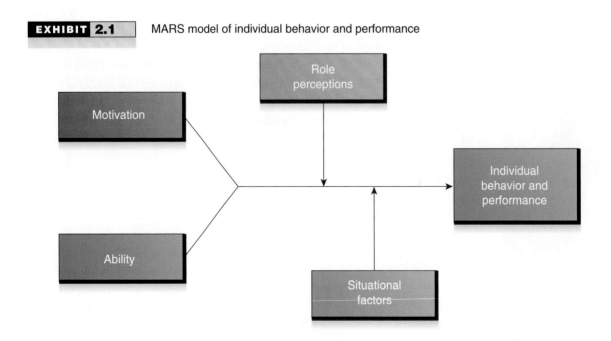

The MARS Model Helps Singapore Airlines Soar in Customer Service

Singapore Airlines (SIA) is obsessed with providing exceptional customer service. The island-state's national airline has a limited domestic market, so it competes directly with other airlines for passengers. "Excellent service has been the foundation stone of our success," says a senior SIA executive.

SIA starts its customer service journey by carefully selecting job applicants. Flight attendants are specially screened for their customer-orientation values and other competencies. Prospective managers must pass a series of tests and two interviews. Overall, only 1 in 50 applicants receives a job offer. "Quality people are the company's most important resource, and the most rigorous quality control process we apply is for staff selection," says a former SIA chief executive.

Extensive training is another strategy SIA uses to achieve its high customer service standards. The airline spends 12 percent of payroll on training, compared with 2.3 percent in the average Singaporean firm. Cabin crew complete a five-month course where they learn every possible element of service, from social etiquette to emergency procedures. SIA's most recent training initiative, called Transforming Customer Service, encourages staff to go beyond the routines to serve customers uniquely. "The most important thing that you can do for customers is to make them feel cared for as individuals," explains an SIA executive.

Selection and training guide SIA skills and role perceptions, but the airline also pays attention to employee motivation through companywide financial rewards and a customer-focused culture. As for support through situational factors, SIA, the premier customer for Boeing

Singapore Airlines applies the MARS model of individual behavior to provide exceptional customer service. *(Courtesy of Singapore Airlines)*

777 jets, has one of the world's most modern fleets. The result is an organization that consistently leads the global airline industry in customer service ratings and profitability.

Sources: R. Rosen, P. Digh, M. Singer, and C. Phillips, *Global Literacies* (New York: Simon & Schuster, 2000), pp. 247–48; L. McCauley, "How May I Help You? Unit of One," *Fast Company*, March 2000, p. 93; J. B. Cunningham and P. Gerrard, "Characteristics of Well-Performing Organizations in Singapore," *Singapore Management Review* 22 (January 2000), pp. 35–64; J. Pfeffer, "Seven Practices of Successful Organizations," *California Management Review* 40 (1998), pp. 96–124; B. Davis, "Why Singapore Airlines Is the World's Most Profitable Airline," *Asian Business Review*, December 1996, pp. 34–36.

Employee Motivation

motivation
The forces within a person that affect his or her direction, intensity, and persistence of voluntary behavior.

Motivation represents the forces within a person that affect the direction, intensity, and persistence of his or her voluntary behavior.[2] *Direction* refers to the fact that motivation is goal-oriented, not random. People are motivated to arrive at work on time, finish a project a few hours early, or aim for many other targets. *Intensity* is the amount of effort allocated to the goal. For example, two employees might be motivated to finish their project a few hours early (direction), but only one of them puts forth enough effort (intensity) to achieve this goal. Finally, motivation involves varying levels of *persistence*, that is, continuing the effort for a certain amount of time. Employees may sustain their effort until they reach their goal, or they may give up beforehand. Chapter 5 looks more closely at the conceptual foundations of employee motivation, while Chapter 6 considers some applied motivation practices.

Ability

A second influence on individual behavior and performance is the person's ability. **Ability** includes both the natural aptitudes and learned capabilities required to successfully complete a task. *Aptitudes* are the natural talents that help employees learn specific tasks more quickly and perform them better. For example, you cannot learn finger dexterity; rather, some people have a more natural ability than others to manipulate small objects with their fingers. There are many different physical and mental aptitudes, and our ability to acquire skills is affected by these aptitudes. *Learned capabilities* are the skills and knowledge that you have actually acquired—including the physical and mental skills you possess as well as the knowledge you acquire and store for later use.

Employee Competencies   The external environment is changing so rapidly that many organizations prefer to hire people for their generic competencies rather than for job-specific skills. **Competencies** are the characteristics of people that lead to superior performance.[3] Along with natural and learned abilities, competencies include the person's values and personality traits.

Many firms have identified generic competencies that distinguish outstanding performers across the organization or in broad job groups. Other competencies apply to specific jobs or job groups. Ericsson, the Swedish telecommunications giant, has a competence triangle consisting of three sets of generic and job-specific competencies: technical/professional competence, human competence, and business competence. Technical/professional competence is specific to a particular task or position, such as the person's product knowledge. In its human competence category, Ericsson identifies teamwork, communications, cultural awareness, and other competencies necessary for social interaction. Business competence refers to understanding the business; it includes language skills, customer skills, and general knowledge about the organization.[4]

Person–Job Matching   There are three basic ways to match individuals and their competencies with job requirements.[5] One strategy is to select applicants whose existing competencies best fit the required tasks. This approach includes comparing each applicant's competencies with the requirements of the job or work unit. A second approach is to provide training so that employees develop required skills and knowledge. Canadian Tire, a leading Canadian retailer of automobile and home improvement products, estimates that $50 invested in customer service and related training programs can yield paybacks of $500 a year in increased profits. Academic research also suggests that job-related training improves organizational effectiveness.[6]

The third person job matching strategy is to redesign jobs so employees are given only those tasks that are within their capabilities. MediaOne adopted this strategy after introducing e-mail as a form of customer communication at its call centers. Executives at the U.S. cable television systems company realized that call center staff with strong verbal communication skills aren't necessarily good at written communication. "Many people who can carry on a good conversation on the phone could not put a cogent thought down in

ability
Both the natural aptitudes and learned capabilities required to successfully complete a task.

competencies
The abilities, values, personality traits, and other characteristics of people that lead to superior performance.

writing if they tried," says a MediaOne executive. The company identified employees with strong written communication skills and redesigned their tasks so that they would be responsible for answering e-mail questions.[7]

Role Perceptions

A February cold snap turned a rainy weekend into a citywide skating rink on Monday morning in Madison, Wisconsin. Within hours, emergency crews were scrambling to make the roads safer, while hospital staff worked at full speed to handle the large numbers of emergency room visitors. One hospital spokesperson called it the worst day of ice injuries he had seen. Still, the emergency room staff worked smoothly throughout the day. "The emergency room was a well-oiled machine between nursing staff, medical imaging, and emergency physicians," says Meriter Hospital spokesperson Mae Knowles.[8]

> **role perceptions**
> A person's beliefs about what behaviors are appropriate or necessary in a particular situation, including the specific tasks that make up the job, their relative importance, and the preferred behaviors to accomplish those tasks.

Emergency room staff at Meriter Hospital acted like a "well-oiled machine" not just because they had learned the appropriate skills. They had also developed accurate **role perceptions.** Employees have accurate role perceptions when they understand the specific tasks assigned to them, the relative importance of those tasks, and the preferred behaviors to accomplish those tasks. Role perceptions clarify the preferred direction of effort. For example, retail salespeople need to remember to stock shelves, not just to serve customers. Otherwise, sales are lost if the product isn't on the shelves.[9]

How do organizations improve role perceptions? One strategy is to clearly describe each employee's required responsibilities and to show how those goals relate to organizational goals. Second, employees clarify their role perceptions as they work together over time and receive frequent and meaningful performance feedback.

Situational Factors

Job performance depends not just on motivation, ability, and role perceptions. It is also affected by the situation in which the employee works. Situational factors include conditions beyond the employee's immediate control that constrain or facilitate his or her behavior and performance.[10] Some factors—such as time, people, budget, and physical work facilities—are controlled by others in the organization. Corporate leaders need to carefully arrange these conditions so that employees can achieve their performance potential. Lockheed Martin's jet fighter production facility does this by asking employees to identify obstacles created by management that prevent them from performing effectively.[11]

Other situational characteristics—such as consumer preferences and economic conditions—originate from the external environment and, consequently, are beyond the employee's and organization's control. A sales representative may have more difficulty selling the product or service when the economy enters a recession or if the demographics of the sales area indicate fewer people would purchase the item. Rather than create a defeatist attitude, some companies encourage employees to focus on things they can control rather than on the external situational factors.

Motivation, ability, role perceptions, and situational factors affect all conscious workplace behaviors and performance outcomes. In the next section, we introduce the five categories of behavior in organizational settings.

TYPES OF WORK-RELATED BEHAVIOR

People engage in many different types of behavior in organizational settings. Exhibit 2.2 highlights five types of behavior discussed most often in the organizational behavior literature: joining the organization, remaining with the organization, maintaining work attendance, performing required tasks, and exhibiting organizational citizenship.

Joining the Organization

At Dell Computer Corporation, success doesn't sound like a cash register. It sounds more like the clang of a cowbell. Whenever someone with valuable knowledge or experience joins Dell's headquarters, employees ring a bell that symbolically signals the good news. Dell employees celebrate the arrival of key employees because they—and employees of other organizations—need qualified people to perform tasks and acquire knowledge. In fact, attracting and retaining talented employees is one of the top 5 (from a list of 39) nonfinancial factors used by Wall Street's decision makers to pick stocks.[12]

The importance of hiring qualified people is obvious when we consider the consequences of staff shortages. Richcolor, a professional photo lab in Puget Sound, Washington, closed its doors and laid off 50 people because one of the company's two color correctors quit on doctor's orders, and a national search firm couldn't find a replacement. Color correctors look at each frame manually to ensure the colors and shades are just right. "We do not choose to watch Richcolor perform poorly and slowly [lose] its customers and reputation," Richcolor owner Jerry Saunders wrote to customers and employees.[13]

Along with avoiding shortages, effective organizations constantly search for the most qualified people. As consulting firm McKinsey and Company highlighted in its report "The War for Talent," organizations need to acquire knowledge by hiring the best employees. A more recent McKinsey report concludes that successful companies win the talent war by applying many of the

EXHIBIT 2.2

Types of work-related behavior

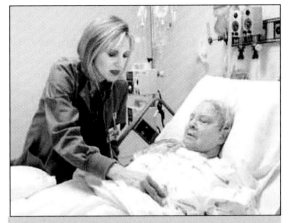

Hospitals across the United States are struggling to find enough nurses to keep beds open. Nursing school enrollment has fallen by 20 percent over the past five years, just as hospitals are expanding capacity to handle the aging population. Hospitals make up for the shortfall by hiring nurses from agencies, but that isn't a long-term solution. "We're all competing for the same shrinking pool of nurses," admits the president of a large nursing agency in Cleveland. Many hospitals provide bonus incentives so that nurses will work overtime. Ironically, the nursing shortage feeds on itself by causing active nurses to leave the profession as a result of burnout. "I think nurses are very frustrated," says Denise Borgman (shown in photo), a charge nurse at Providence Hospital in Southfield, Michigan.[16] What actions would you recommend to a large hospital that faces this shortage of nurses? (© Detroit News/*David Coates*)

ideas in this book—building trust and loyalty, having visionary leaders, offering enriched jobs, financially rewarding performance.[14]

Remaining with the Organization

The war for talent includes keeping the best people, not just hiring them. As we learned in Chapter 1, much of an organization's intellectual capital is the knowledge employees carry around in their heads. Long-service employees, in particular, have valuable information about work processes, corporate values, and customer needs. Very little of this information is documented anywhere. Thus, knowledge management involves keeping valuable employees with the organization. "At 5 p.m., 95% of our assets walk out the door," says an executive at SAS Institute, a leading statistics software firm. "We have to have an environment that makes them want to walk back in the door the next morning."[15]

The problem is that many employees don't return the next morning. The U.S. Bureau of Labor Statistics estimates that the typical American employee holds nine jobs by the age of 32. One large-scale survey reports that nearly half of those currently employed say they are looking around for another job. Over half of the 500 executives recently surveyed worldwide identified retaining talented employees as the top people issue in the company. Even with recent layoffs in some industries, the emerging employability attitude toward work and continuing shortages in some occupations (e.g., information technology, nursing) will keep turnover rates near record levels.[17]

Why do people quit their jobs? The main cause of turnover is low **job satisfaction**—a person's attitude regarding his or her job and work context (see Chapter 4). Employees become dissatisfied with their employment relationship, which motivates them to search for and join another organization with better conditions. Job dissatisfaction, which "pushes" employees out of their current jobs, has a greater effect on turnover than incentives that "pull" them into new jobs. In other words, the main cause of high turnover isn't that other firms lure away good employees. The main problem is that their current jobs don't motivate good employees to stay.[18]

job satisfaction
A person's attitude regarding his or her job and work content.

Maintaining Work Attendance

Along with attracting and retaining employees, organizations need everyone to show up for work at scheduled times. Situational factors—such as a car breakdown, family illness, or a snowstorm—represent a major cause of absenteeism. Recognizing this fact, Xerox minimizes absenteeism by giving all employees free flu shots and health screenings. When the car breaks down or a child is sick, Xerox employees are encouraged to do their work from home. To minimize absenteeism on snowy days, ARO, a call center in Kansas City, also relies on telecommuting.[19]

Motivation is another influence on absenteeism. Employees desiring to temporarily withdraw from stressful or dissatisfying working conditions are more often absent or late for work. Absenteeism is also higher in organizations with generous sick leave because this benefit limits the negative financial impact of taking time away from work.[20]

Performing Required Tasks

task performance
Goal-directed activities that are under the individual's control.

People are hired to perform tasks above a minimum standard. **Task performance** refers to goal-directed activities that are under the individual's control.[21] These include physical behaviors as well as mental processes leading to behaviors. For example, foreign exchange traders make decisions and take actions to exchange currencies. These traders have certain *performance standards;* that is, their behaviors and the outcomes of those behaviors must exceed minimum acceptable levels.

In most jobs, employees are evaluated on several performance dimensions.[22] Foreign exchange traders, for example, must be able to identify profitable trades, work cooperatively with clients and co-workers in a stressful environment, assist in training new staff, and work on special telecommunications equipment without error. Each of these performance dimensions requires specific skills and knowledge. Some are more important than others, but only by considering all performance dimensions can we fully evaluate an employee's contribution to the organization.

Exhibiting Organizational Citizenship

Rick Boomer, head porter at the Empress Hotel in Victoria, Canada, happened to be in the hotel on his day off when a busload of tourists left for the ski resort of Whistler, leaving behind 100 pieces of luggage. Boomer rented a large truck, loaded it himself, took the two-hour ferry ride from Victoria to Vancouver, fought Vancouver's rush-hour traffic, negotiated twisting mountain roads for another two hours, and delivered the luggage to Whistler Mountain ski resort. He took a quick nap, then returned to Victoria for his regular work shift![23]

organizational citizenship
Behaviors that extend beyond the employee's normal job duties.

For the past 60 years, management writers have known that organizations depend on employees who, like Rick Boomer, are willing to "go the extra mile." **Organizational citizenship** refers to behaviors that extend beyond the employee's normal job duties.[24] They include avoiding unnecessary conflicts, helping others without selfish intent, gracefully tolerating occasional impositions, being involved in organizational activities, and performing tasks that extend beyond normal role requirements.[25] Good organizational citizens work cooperatively with co-workers and share resources. They forgive others for mistakes and help co-workers with their problems.

How do employees become good organizational citizens? Rewards and recognition may encourage these behaviors. For example, the New Mexico state government has an "Extra Mile" award for employees who perform beyond the call of duty.[26] However, research has identified two conditions that are essential for organizational citizenship. One of these is the perceived

A traveler from the Middle East had an unusual request when he recently took his family to the Four Seasons hotel in Washington, D.C. "My kids haven't seen Santa Claus since we've arrived," he lamented to the Four Seasons staff. Going beyond the call of duty, assistant front-office manager Liliana Vidal-Quadras (shown in photo) found a costume and an employee to play Santa for a few hours. It's this extra effort that makes the Four Seasons one of the top luxury hotels in the world. Although the pay is adequate, Four Seasons employees engage in organizational citizenship mainly because they are carefully selected for their strong sense of social responsibility and conscientiousness. Vidal-Quadras also says she's treated fairly and has good career opportunities at the hotel chain. In what other ways could Four Seasons employees demonstrate organizational citizenship?[29] (© Mario Tama)

fairness of the company's treatment of employees. Organizations encourage organizational citizenship by correcting perceptions of injustice in the workplace. Employees feel a higher sense of obligation to go the extra mile when organizations distribute rewards fairly and have a process in place to correct problems when employees feel unfairly treated. One way to improve organizational citizenship through perceived fairness is to involve employees in decisions that affect them.[27]

The second condition contributing to organizational citizenship is the degree to which employees hold strong ethical values, particularly a sense of social responsibility.[28] **Social responsibility** refers to a person's or an organization's moral obligation toward others who are affected by his or her actions. People with a strong social responsibility norm are more motivated to assist others, whether or not this assistance will ever be repaid, and to avoid behaviors that interfere with others' goals. It is a value learned through lifelong socialization, so organizations might try to hire people with this value.

The five types of workplace behavior and the MARS model of individual performance are related to many topics in this book. One of the more important topics is individual learning because it affects employee ability, role perceptions, and motivation. The rest of this chapter examines the topic of learning in organizational settings.

LEARNING IN ORGANIZATIONS

social responsibility
A person's or organization's moral obligation toward others who are affected by his or her actions.

learning
A relatively permanent change in behavior that occurs as a result of a person's interaction with the environment.

Most employees appreciate a good paycheck, but an increasing number of them place at least as much value on the opportunity to learn new things at work. "I'm here because I keep learning," says John Waterman, a thirty-something employee. "Whenever I start to get a little bored, a new project comes along with opportunities for learning."[30] **Learning** is a relatively permanent change in behavior (or behavior tendency) that occurs as a result of a person's interaction with the environment.[31] We learn through our senses, such as through study, observation, and experience. Learning becomes evident when the learner behaves differently. For example, we can see that you have learned computer skills if you are operating the keyboard and windows more quickly than before.

Learning influences individual behavior and performance through three elements of the MARS model. First, people acquire skills and knowledge through learning opportunities, which gives them the competencies to perform tasks more effectively. Second, learning clarifies role perceptions. Employees develop a better understanding of their tasks and relative importance of work activities. Third, learning motivates employees. Employees are more motivated to perform certain tasks because they learn that their effort will result in desired performance. Moreover, as in John Waterman's experience, learning generates feelings of accomplishment and other forms of need fulfillment. Learning is also essential for knowledge management—the organization's capacity to acquire, share, and utilize knowledge in ways that improves its survival and success (see Chapter 1).[32]

Learning Explicit and Tacit Knowledge

When employees learn, they acquire both explicit and tacit knowledge. Explicit knowledge is organized and can be communicated from one person to another. The information you receive in a lecture is mainly explicit knowledge because the instructor packages and consciously transfers it to you. Explicit knowledge can be written down and given to others.

However, explicit knowledge is really only the tip of the knowledge iceberg. Most of what we know is **tacit knowledge.**[33] You have probably said to someone: "I can't tell you how to do this, but I can show you." Tacit knowledge is not documented; rather, it is action-oriented and known below the level of consciousness. Some writers suggest that tacit knowledge also includes the organization's culture and a team's implicit norms. People know these values and rules exist, but they are difficult to describe and document.[34]

Tacit knowledge is acquired through observation and direct experience.[35] For example, airline pilots do not learn how to operate a commercial jet through lectures. They master the necessary skills by watching the subtle details as others perform the tasks, and by directly experiencing this complex interaction of behavior with the machine's response. Because most knowledge in organizations is tacit, an important challenge in knowledge management is to make tacit knowledge more explicit so that it may be more easily stored and shared.

Learning tacit and explicit knowledge occurs in many ways. The rest of this chapter introduces four perspectives of learning: reinforcement, feedback, social learning (observation), and direct experience. These activities are not completely separate. For example, feedback can be viewed as a form of reinforcement. Rather, they provide different views of the learning process, and by understanding each of these perspectives, we can more fully appreciate the dynamics of learning.

tacit knowledge
Knowledge embedded in our actions and ways of thinking, and transmitted only through observation and experience.

BEHAVIOR MODIFICATION: LEARNING THROUGH REINFORCEMENT

behavior modification
A theory that explains learning in terms of the antecedents and consequences of behavior.

One of the oldest perspectives on learning, called **behavior modification** (also known as *operant conditioning* and *reinforcement theory*), takes the rather extreme view that learning is completely dependent on the environment. Behavior modification does not question the notion that thinking is part of the learning process, but it views human thoughts as unimportant intermediate stages between behavior and the environment.[36] Our experience with the environment teaches us to alter our behaviors so that we maximize positive consequences and minimize adverse consequences.[37]

Behavior modification emphasizes voluntary behaviors. Researchers call them *operant behaviors* because they "operate" on the environment—they make the environment respond in ways that we want.[38] For example, you put a certain amount of money in a machine and press a certain button so that a particular can of soft drink comes out. You learned from past experience how to cause the environment (the soft drink machine) to deliver that brand of soft drink. Operant behaviors are different from *respondent behaviors*. Respondent behaviors are involuntary responses to the environment, such as automatically withdrawing your hand from a hot stove or automatically contracting your eyes when you turn on a bright light. This book looks at operant behaviors because most learned behaviors in organizational settings are voluntary.

A-B-C's of Behavior Modification

Behavior modification recognizes that behavior is influenced by two environmental contingencies: the antecedents that precede behavior and the consequences that follow behavior. These principles are part of the A-B-C model of behavior modification shown in Exhibit 2.3. The central objective of behavior modification is to change behavior (B) by managing its antecedents (A) and consequences (C).[39]

Antecedents are events preceding the behavior, informing employees that certain behaviors will have particular consequences. An antecedent may be a sound from your computer signaling that an e-mail has arrived or a request from your supervisor to complete a specific task by tomorrow. These antecedents let employees know that a particular action will produce particular consequences. Notice that antecedents do not cause operant behaviors. The computer sound doesn't cause us to open our e-mail. Rather, the sound is a cue telling us that certain consequences are likely to occur if we engage in certain behaviors.

law of effect
A principle stating that the likelihood that an operant behavior will be repeated depends on its consequences.

Although antecedents are important, behavior modification focuses mainly on the *consequences* of behavior. Consequences are events following a particular behavior that influence its future occurrence. This concept is based on the **law of effect,** which says that the likelihood that an operant behavior will

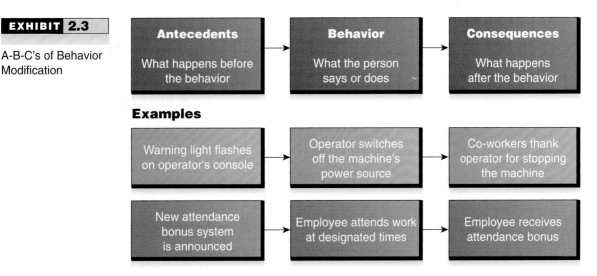

EXHIBIT 2.3

A-B-C's of Behavior Modification

Sources: Adapted from T. K. Connellan, *How to Improve Human Performance* (New York: Harper & Row, 1978), p. 50; F. Luthans and R. Kreitner, *Organizational Behavior Modification and Beyond* (Glenview, IL: Scott, Foresman, 1985), pp. 85–88.

be repeated depends on its consequences. If a behavior is followed by a pleasant experience, then the person will probably repeat the behavior. If the behavior is followed by an unpleasant experience or by no response at all, then the person is less likely to repeat it. The law of effect explains how people learn to associate behaviors with specific environmental responses. Organizational behavior scholars have identified four types of consequences and five schedules to administer those consequences.

Contingencies of Reinforcement

Behavior modification identifies four types of consequences, collectively known as the *contingencies of reinforcement*, that strengthen, maintain, or weaken behavior. Exhibit 2.4 describes these contingencies: positive reinforcement, negative reinforcement, punishment, and extinction.[40]

▪ **Positive reinforcement** occurs when the *introduction* of a consequence *increases or maintains* the frequency or future probability of a behavior. Receiving a bonus after successfully completing an important project usually creates positive reinforcement because it typically increases the probability that you use those behaviors in the future.

▪ **Negative reinforcement** occurs when the *removal or avoidance* of a consequence *increases or maintains* the frequency or future probability of a behavior. Supervisors apply negative reinforcement when they stop criticizing employees whose substandard performance has improved. When supervisors withhold criticism, employees are more likely to repeat behaviors that improved their

positive reinforcement
Occurs when the introduction of a consequence increases or maintains the frequency or future probability of a behavior.

negative reinforcement
Occurs when the removal or avoidance of a consequence increases or maintains the frequency or future probability of a behavior.

EXHIBIT 2.4   Contingencies of reinforcement

	Consequence is introduced	No consequence	Consequence is removed
Behavior increases or is maintained	**Positive reinforcement** Example: You receive a bonus after successfully completing an important project.		**Negative reinforcement** Example: Supervisor stops criticizing you when your job performance improves.
Behavior decreases	**Punishment** Example: You are threatened with a demotion or discharge after treating a client badly.	**Extinction** Example: Co-workers no longer praise you when you engage in dangerous pranks.	**Punishment** Example: You give up your "employee of the month" parking spot to this month's winner.

performance.[41] Negative reinforcement is sometimes called avoidance learning because employees engage in the desired behaviors to avoid unpleasant consequences (such as being criticized by your supervisor or being fired from your job).

■ **Punishment** occurs when a consequence *decreases* the frequency or future probability of a behavior. It may involve introducing an unpleasant consequence or removing a pleasant consequence (see Exhibit 2.4). An example of the former would be when an employee is threatened with a demotion or discharge after treating a client badly. The latter form of punishment would occur when a salesperson must give a cherished parking spot to another employee who has higher sales performance for the month.

■ **Extinction** occurs when the target behavior decreases because no consequence follows it. For example, if an employee makes practical jokes that are potentially dangerous or costly, such behavior might be extinguished by discouraging others from praising the employee when he or she engages in these pranks. Behavior that is no longer reinforced tends to disappear; it becomes extinct. In this respect, extinction is a do-nothing strategy.[42]

Comparing Reinforcement Contingencies In most situations, positive reinforcement should follow desired behaviors and extinction (do nothing) should follow undesirable behaviors, because there are fewer adverse consequences when applying these contingencies compared with punishment and negative reinforcement. However, some form of punishment (dismissal, suspension, demotion, etc.) may be necessary for extreme behaviors, such as deliberately hurting a co-worker or stealing inventory. Indeed, research suggests that, under certain conditions, punishment maintains a sense of equity.[43] Co-workers are often eager to hear about an employee's discipline because it fulfills their need for social justice.

Unfortunately, organizations tend to be inconsistent in their administration of punishment, so justice through discipline is an elusive goal.[44] Moreover, punishment is usually an emotionally charged event that creates negative feelings and undermines the employee's ability to learn from the punishment.[45] In extreme cases, employees develop hostilities toward the organization that may result in aggression and other forms of dysfunctional behavior.

Schedules of Reinforcement

Along with the types of consequences, behavior modification identifies the schedule that should be followed to maximize the reinforcement effect. In fact, some evidence suggests that scheduling the reinforcer affects learning more than the size of the reinforcer does.[46] Behavior modification theorists have identified five schedules of reinforcement. One of these is **continuous reinforcement**—reinforcing every occurrence of the desired behavior. Continuous reinforcement is most effective for learning new behaviors. Employees learn desired behaviors quickly, and when the reinforcer is removed, extinction also occurs very quickly.

The other four schedules of reinforcement are intermittent. They apply the reinforcer after a fixed or variable time (interval) or number of target behaviors (ratio). As illustrated in Exhibit 2.5, a fixed schedule means that the reinforcer occurs after the same number of behaviors or time units, whereas a

punishment
Occurs when a consequence decreases the frequency or future probability of a behavior.

extinction
Occurs when the target behavior decreases because no consequence follows it.

continuous reinforcement
Reinforcing every occurrence of a desired behavior.

EXHIBIT 2.5

Schedules of reinforcement

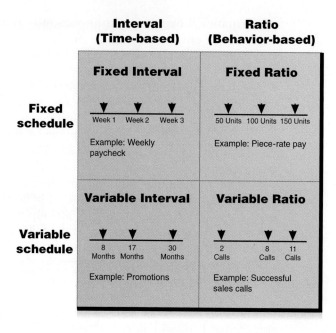

	Interval (Time-based)	Ratio (Behavior-based)
Fixed schedule	**Fixed Interval** ▼ ▼ ▼ Week 1 Week 2 Week 3 Example: Weekly paycheck	**Fixed Ratio** ▼ ▼ ▼ 50 Units 100 Units 150 Units Example: Piece-rate pay
Variable schedule	**Variable Interval** ▼ ▼ ▼ 8 Months 17 Months 30 Months Example: Promotions	**Variable Ratio** ▼ ▼ ▼ 2 Calls 8 Calls 11 Calls Example: Successful sales calls

fixed interval schedule
Reinforcing behavior after a fixed time.

variable interval schedule
Reinforcing behavior after it has occurred for a varying length of time around some average.

fixed ratio schedule
Reinforcing behavior after a fixed number of times.

variable ratio schedule
Reinforcing behavior after it has occurred a varying number of times around some average.

variable schedule means that the reinforcer occurs randomly around an average number of behaviors or time units.

The **fixed interval schedule** occurs when behavior is reinforced after a fixed time. Most people get paid on a fixed interval schedule—their paychecks are received every week or two weeks. As long as the job is performed satisfactorily, a paycheck is received on the appointed day. The **variable interval schedule** involves administering the reinforcer after a varying length of time. Promotions typically follow this schedule—they occur at uneven time intervals. The first promotion might be received after two years of good performance, the next after four years, and the third after 18 months.

The **fixed ratio schedule** reinforces behavior after a fixed number of times. Some piece-rate systems follow a schedule in which employees get paid after they produce a fixed number of units. The **variable ratio schedule** reinforces behavior after a varying number of times. Salespeople experience variable ratio reinforcement—they make a successful sale (the reinforcer) after a varying number of client calls. They might make four unsuccessful calls before receiving an order on the fifth one. This might be followed by 15 unsuccessful sales calls before another sale is made. One successful sale might be made after 10 calls on average, but this does not mean that every 10th call will be successful.

The variable ratio schedule is a low-cost way to reinforce behavior because employees are rewarded infrequently. It is also highly resistant to extinction. Suppose your boss walks into your office at varying times of day. Chances are that you will work consistently better throughout the day than if your boss visits at exactly 11 A.M. every day. If your boss doesn't walk into your office at all on a particular day, you would still expect a visit right up to the end of the day if previous visits were random.

Behavior Modification in Practice

Everyone practices behavior modification in one form or another. We thank people for a job well done, are silent when displeased, and sometimes try to punish those who go against our wishes. Some companies, such as an International Paper plant in Moss Point, Mississippi, provide training programs where supervisors learn about the power of positive reinforcement. David Sulik took one of these courses. Now, the International Paper manager criticizes less and finds many more ways to praise staff for their performance. He can already see the results. "I think they trust me more than in the past," says Sulik.[47]

Behavior modification also occurs in various formal programs to reduce absenteeism, minimize accidents, and improve task performance. When such programs are implemented correctly, the results are generally impressive.[48] For instance, VJS Foods, a British food company, reduced absenteeism by giving employees with perfect attendance each month two chances to win $500. Electric Boat also uses behavior modification principles to minimize sick time among salaried employees at the Groton, Connecticut, shipyard. Top prizes of $2,500 were recently awarded to each of 20 winners drawn from a pool of 955 employees who have not called in sick for at least two years. Auto parts manufacturer Dana Corporation applies behavior modification to reinforce safe work behaviors through a game called safety bingo. Employees can draw a number for their bingo card for every day that the plant has no accident. The employee who fills a bingo card first wins a television set.[49]

NOVA Chemicals introduced a million-dollar "Recruitment and Retention Program" to reinforce good attendance and continued employment at its construction site in Alberta, Canada. Absenteeism had reached 20 percent on some Fridays before long weekends, threatening the project's completion deadline. NOVA Chemicals' solution was to reward employees who achieved perfect attendance with a chance to win one of ten $1,300 prizes each week. A final draw of four $65,000 grand prizes encouraged employees to stay until the end of their contract. NOVA's behavior modification program cut absenteeism rates by 25 percent and dramatically improved employment levels.[52] Would this type of reinforcement work as effectively for employees in long-term jobs, such as assembly line workers?
(Courtesy of NOVA Chemicals)

Limitations of Behavior Modification In spite of these favorable results, behavior modification is more difficult to apply to conceptual activities than to observable behaviors. For example, it's much easier to reward employees for good work attendance than for good problem solving.[50] A second problem is reward inflation, in which the reinforcer is either quickly forgotten or is eventually considered an entitlement. A bonus that was once an unexpected surprise becomes an expected part of the employment relationship. Withholding the reinforcer may represent extinction, but it feels like punishment.[51]

Behavior modification programs also raise ethical concerns. One issue is that the variable ratio schedule is sometimes viewed as a form of gambling because employees are essentially betting that they will win a lottery or some other reinforcer. A forest products firm that applied this schedule discovered that some employees held strong antigambling beliefs and were upset with the company's behavior modification practices.[53] The other ethical concern is that behavior modification is sometimes viewed as a form of manipulation. It alters human behavior by rearranging incentives and other environmental conditions while ignoring human thoughts and feelings.[54] Behavior modification experts point out that any attempt to change employee behavior is a form of manipulation. No matter how valid this counterargument, behavior modification has an image problem that is difficult to overcome.

LEARNING THROUGH FEEDBACK

feedback

Any information that people receive about the consequences of their behavior.

Feedback is any information that people receive about the consequences of their behavior. Feedback may be an antecedent or a consequence, if we look at it from a behavior modification perspective. However, our discussion of learning through feedback will take a broader view by considering the effects on employee thoughts as well as behaviors.

Feedback influences behavior and task performance through role perceptions, ability, and motivation.[55] It clarifies role perceptions by communicating what behaviors are appropriate or necessary in a particular situation. Feedback improves ability by frequently providing information to correct performance problems.[56] This *corrective feedback* makes people aware of their performance errors and helps them correct those errors quickly. Lastly, feedback is a source of motivation. It fulfills personal needs and makes people more confident that they are able to accomplish certain tasks (see Chapter 5).

Feedback Sources

360-degree feedback

Performance feedback received from a full circle of people around an employee.

Feedback can originate from social or nonsocial sources.[57] Social sources include supervisors, clients, co-workers, and anyone else who provides information about the employee's behavior or results. An increasingly popular strategy is for employees to receive performance feedback from several people. This multisource feedback is called **360-degree feedback** because feedback is received from a full circle of people around the employee, including subordinates, co-workers, project leaders, and customers.[58] Performance reviews are sometimes submitted directly to the employee through an anonymous computer program, or they may be integrated into a single report by the supervisor.

Research suggests that multisource feedback provides more complete and accurate information than that from a supervisor alone.[59] It is particularly useful when the supervisor is unable to observe the employee's behavior or performance throughout the year. Lower-level employees also feel a greater sense of fairness and open communication when they are able to provide upward feedback about their boss's performance.

Multisource feedback also creates challenges.[60] Having several people review so many other people can be expensive and time-consuming. With multiple opinions, the 360-degree process can also produce ambiguous and conflicting feedback, so employees may require guidance to interpret the results. A third concern is that peers may provide inflated rather than accurate feedback to avoid conflicts over the forthcoming year. Connections 2.2 describes a fourth concern, namely, the emotional consequences of giving and receiving critical feedback involving people who work with you.

Personal Challenges of 360-degree Feedback

Multisource feedback systems are spreading like wild-fire across the corporate landscape. According to a recent Towers Perrin survey, one-quarter of large U.S. firms rely on 360-degree feedback, up from just 4 percent of these firms five years ago.

But some firms may quickly discover that 360-feedback is not for the faint of heart. "Everybody is a little apprehensive the first time they do this," says Russell Huerta, a senior accounts manager at software maker Autodesk. Even in firms with a supportive culture and in which the feedback is anonymous, employees tend to worry about the repercussions of submitting critical comments.

Receiving feedback is even more difficult than giving it, which creates concerns about interpersonal relations at work. "Initially you do take it personally," admits Huerta. "It's meant to be constructive, but you have to internally battle that." Huerta manages his emotional reaction to the feedback by pretending the advice is about someone else, then learning how to improve his own behavior from that information. "It's almost an out-of-body experience, to take your mind and your emotions out of it," he recommends.

Partners at Baker Botts had plenty of opportunity to practice Huerta's advice. The Houston-based law firm recently started asking nonpartners at the 600-lawyer firm to evaluate the partners. The evaluation form asks associates to rate a partner on office demeanor and approachability, feedback and development, and work assignments and project management. The form also asks for an overall assessment of whether the associate would want to work with that partner in the future.

Richard Johnson, Baker Botts's managing partner, says there was plenty of candid feedback during the first round of upward evaluation. "They were not all positive comments, as you might imagine. Frankly, it smarted a bit, but it's supposed to." He adds that the multisource feedback process is already having a positive effect. "I think we've seen some behavioral change," says Johnson.

Sources: S. Watkins, "Ever Wanted to Review the Boss?" *Investor's Business Daily*, August 10, 2001, p. A1; B. S. Jeffreys, "Lone Star Firms Try Out 360-degree Job Reviews," *The Recorder*, June 22, 2001, p. 3.

Nonsocial Feedback Sources Along with social sources, employees usually receive nonsocial sources of feedback. With a click of the computer mouse, many executives can look at the previous day's sales and compare them with sales of previous dates. The job itself can also be a source of feedback. Many employees see the results of their work effort while they are making a product.

The preferred feedback source depends on the purpose of the information. To learn about their progress toward goal accomplishment, employees usually prefer nonsocial feedback sources, such as computer printouts or feedback directly from the job,[61] because such information is considered more accurate than that from social sources. Corrective feedback from nonsocial sources is also less damaging to self-esteem, because social sources tend to delay negative information, leave some of it out, and distort the bad news in a positive way.[62]

When employees want to improve their self-image, they seek out positive feedback from social sources. It feels better to have co-workers say that you are performing the job well than to discover this information from a computer printout.[63] Positive feedback from co-workers and other social sources motivates mainly because it fulfills social (relatedness) as well as growth needs (see Chapter 5).

Giving Feedback Effectively

Whether feedback is received from a supervisor or from a computer printout, it should be specific, sufficiently frequent, timely, credible, and relevant.

▨ *Specific feedback*—Feedback should include specific information, such as "you exceeded your sales quota by 5 percent last month," rather than subjective and general phrases, such as "your sales are going well." Specific information helps employees redirect their efforts and behavior more precisely and gives them a greater sense of accomplishment when the feedback is positive. Also, notice that specific feedback focuses on the task, not the person, thereby reducing the person's defensiveness when receiving negative feedback.

▨ *Frequent feedback*—Ideally, employees should be able to monitor their own performance from nonsocial feedback sources. If that isn't possible, then the feedback provider needs to consider the employee's task cycle (how long it takes to complete each task) and task experience. Grocery store cashiers, for instance, have very short task cycles (they finish working with a customer within a few minutes), so they should receive feedback more often than people with long cycles (executives, salespeople). Employees working on new tasks should also receive more frequent feedback because they require more behavior guidance and reinforcement.

▨ *Timely feedback*—Feedback should be available as soon as possible so that employees see a clear association between their behavior and its consequences. Computers and other electronic equipment can provide timely feedback, but usually only for routine or standardized information.[64]

▨ *Credible feedback*—Employees are more likely to accept feedback (particularly corrective feedback) from trustworthy and credible sources.[65] Multisource feedback has higher credibility because it comes from several people. Employees are also more likely to accept corrective feedback from nonsocial sources (e.g., computer printouts, electronic gauges) because it is not as judgmental.

▨ *Relevant feedback*—Feedback must relate to the individual's behavior rather than to conditions beyond the individual's control to ensure that the feedback is not distorted by situational factors.[66] Feedback is also relevant when it is linked to goals. Goals establish the benchmarks (i.e., what ought to be) against which feedback is judged.

Seeking Feedback

So far, we have presented the traditional view that supervisors and others give feedback to employees. However, employees do not just passively receive feedback; they also actively seek it.[67] The most obvious way is through *inquiry*—asking other people about performance and behavior. This feedback-seeking tactic tends to be used when individuals have high self-esteem, expect to receive positive feedback, and work in an organization that values openness.

One of the most common ways to receive feedback is *monitoring*. This approach involves scanning the work environment and the behavior of others for information cues. Executives monitor corporate data to determine whether their strategies have worked. Salespeople monitor the nonverbal cues of customers during a transaction. Monitoring occurs at any time and can be more efficient than relying on others to transmit the information. For instance, production employees can continuously monitor the quality of their work quickly and independently. Although monitoring nonverbal cues of clients and co-workers creates the risk of misinterpreting meaning (see Chapter 11), it has the advantage of avoiding problems with saving face.

Another feedback-seeking strategy is *direct inquiry*. This can be a powerful form of learning in a private setting and when the person providing the feedback communicates the information clearly, yet diplomatically. However, many people have difficulty with direct inquiry when someone has performed a task poorly. Supervisors and co-workers are more likely to provide inaccurate feedback when the information is negative. Moreover, it is more difficult to save face when receiving negative feedback in response to a direct request. A third problem is that inquiry is possible only when someone else is available and has time to answer questions. One solution to these concerns is to retain a coach whose job is to provide candid feedback and guidance to improve performance. The opening vignette in this chapter describes how executive coaches offer honest feedback. They are trained to provide feedback constructively and to build on the employee's strengths rather than criticize his or her weaknesses.

Ethics of Employee Monitoring

From the time you wake up to the time you retire for the day, you leave behind a trail of data for others to gather, merge, analyze, massage, and even sell—often without your knowledge or consent. This type of monitoring applies not just to consumers but also to employees in most organizations. Feedback requires some form of monitoring employee behavior or performance. But technology has raised monitoring to such an advanced science that we need to recognize and respect its ethical implications.[68]

According to a recent survey of 1,600 large and midsize firms, 78 percent of employers monitor their staff by videotaping them on the job or by checking their e-mail, Internet use, or telephone conversations. A few employees at Continental Airlines sued the airline for secretly videotaping them while they worked in an international concierge office. Ameritech Corporation, Bell-South, and other firms have installed global positioning tracking systems in repair vans that can let the company know exactly where drivers are at all times. A Fort Lauderdale construction company places several video surveillance cameras at each building site to monitor the work in case of workers' compensation claims and for other legal protection. Executives at Taco Bell franchises in Southern California can use a password-protected Internet connection to monitor employees and customers. "I could go on vacation and still watch my restaurants," says one vice president at the franchise.[69]

Critics argue that monitoring is an invasion of employee privacy. It symbolizes a lack of trust that undermines the employment relationship. Employers, on the other hand, point out that they need to monitor the workplace to protect company assets, provide a safer work environment, and give employees more accurate feedback about their performance. AT&T Corporation claims that its high-quality customer service is partly due to employee monitoring. "Our quality is quite high, and that's why," says AT&T spokesman Jim McGee. "We keep quite an eye on them."[70] Some research indicates that employees see monitoring as a necessary evil. Although concerned about invasion of privacy, most employees are willing to be monitored when the information is used only for developmental feedback.[71] Still, as technology leads to more sophisticated surveillance, debate about the ethics of employee monitoring will become more intense.

"My boss will monitor our meeting to insure that you receive excellent customer service."

(Copyright © 2001 Ted Goff. www.tedgoff.com)

SOCIAL LEARNING THEORY: LEARNING BY OBSERVING

social learning theory

A theory stating that much learning occurs by observing others and then modeling the behaviors that lead to favorable outcomes and avoiding behaviors that lead to punishing consequences.

Feedback and behavior modification consider learning mainly through direct experience with the environment. However, we also learn by observing the behaviors of other people and the consequences of those behaviors. **Social learning theory** states that much learning occurs by observing others and then modeling the behaviors that lead to favorable outcomes and avoiding behaviors that lead to punishing consequences.[72] There are three related features of social learning theory: behavioral modeling, learning behavior consequences, and self-reinforcement.

Behavioral Modeling

People learn by observing the behaviors of a role model on the critical task, remembering the important elements of the observed behaviors, and then practicing those behaviors.[73] Behavioral modeling works best when the model is respected and the model's actions are followed by favorable consequences. For instance, recently hired college graduates could learn by watching a previously hired college graduate who successfully performs the task.

Behavioral modeling is a valuable form of learning because tacit knowledge and skills are acquired from others mainly in this way. Earlier in this chapter, we explained that tacit knowledge is the subtle information about required behaviors, the correct sequence of those actions, and the environmental consequences (such as a machine response or customer reply) that should occur after each action. The adage that a picture is worth a thousand words applies here. It is difficult to document or explain verbally how a master baker kneads dough better than someone less qualified. Instead, we must observe the subtle actions to develop a more precise mental model of the required behaviors and the expected responses. Behavioral modeling also guides role perceptions, for example, when leaders model the behavior that they expect from others.

Behavioral Modeling and Self-Efficacy   Behavioral modeling is valuable because it also enhances the observer's **self-efficacy.** Self-efficacy refers to a person's belief that he or she has the ability, motivation, and resources to complete a task successfully.[74] People with high self-efficacy have a can-do attitude toward a specific task and, more generally, toward other challenges in life.

Behavioral modeling increases self-efficacy because people gain more self-confidence after seeing someone else do a task than if they are simply told what to do. This result is particularly likely when observers identify with the model, such as someone who is the same gender and similar in age, experience, and related features. You might experience self-efficacy when working in a student support group. You form a can-do attitude when another student similar to you describes how he or she was able to perform well in a course that you are now taking. You learn not only what has to be done but also that others like you have been successful at this challenge.

Self-efficacy is also affected by initial experiences when practicing the previously modeled behavior. Observers gain confidence when the environmental cues follow a predictable pattern and there are no surprises when practicing the behavior.[75] For example, computer trainees develop a stronger self-efficacy when they click the mouse and get the same computer response as the model did when performing the same behavior. The expected response gives trainees a greater sense of control over the computer because they can predict what will happen following a particular behavior.

Learning Behavior Consequences

A second element of social learning theory says that we learn the consequences of behavior in ways other than through direct experience. In particular, we learn by logically thinking through the consequences of our actions and by observing the consequences that other people experience following their behavior. First, we logically expect either positive reinforcement or negative reinforcement after completing an assigned task and either punishment or extinction after performing the job poorly.

Second, we learn to anticipate consequences by observing the experiences of other people. Civilizations have relied on this principle for centuries, by punishing civil disobedience in public to deter other potential criminals.[76] Learning behavior consequences occurs in more subtle ways in contemporary organizations. Consider the employee who observes a co-worker receiving a stern warning for working in an unsafe manner. This event would reduce the observer's likelihood of engaging in unsafe behaviors because he or she has learned to anticipate a similar reprimand following those behaviors.[77]

Self-Reinforcement

The final element of social learning theory is *self-reinforcement*. Self-reinforcement occurs whenever an employee has control over a reinforcer but doesn't "take" the reinforcer until having completed a self-set goal.[78] For example, you might be thinking about taking a work break after you finish reading the rest of this chapter—and not before! You could take a break right now, but you don't use this privilege until you have achieved your goal of reading the chapter. The work break is a form of positive reinforcement that is self-induced. You use the work break to reinforce completion of a task.

---

self-efficacy

A person's belief that he or she has the ability, motivation, and resources to complete a task successfully.

Numerous consequences may be applied in self-reinforcement, ranging from raiding the refrigerator to congratulating yourself for completing the task.[79] Self-reinforcement has become increasingly important because employees are given more control over their working lives and are less dependent on supervisors to dole out positive reinforcement and punishment.

LEARNING THROUGH EXPERIENCE

Mandy Chooi is about to meet with a promising manager who has botched a new assignment. She is also supposed to make a strategy presentation to her boss in three hours, but the telephone won't stop ringing and she is deluged with e-mail. It's a stressful situation. Fortunately, Chooi isn't at her office. Instead, the Motorola human resources executive from Beijing is sitting in a simulation to develop and test her leadership skills. "It was hard. A lot harder than I had expected," says Chooi. "It's surprising how realistic and demanding it is."[80]

Many organizations are discarding the notion that learning is measured by the number of hours employees spend in the classroom. Classrooms transfer explicit knowledge that has been documented, but most tacit knowledge and skills are acquired through experience as well as observation. Much of what we learn in organizations takes place through experience.[81]

Experiential learning has been conceptualized in many ways, but one of the most enduring perspectives is Kolb's experiential learning model, shown in Exhibit 2.6.[82] This model illustrates experiential learning as a cyclical four-stage process. Concrete experience involves sensory and emotional engagement in some activity. It is followed by reflective observation, which involves listening, watching, recording, and elaborating on the experience. The next stage in the learning cycle is abstract conceptualization. This is the stage in which we develop concepts and integrate our observations into logically sound theories.

EXHIBIT 2.6

Kolb's experiential learning model

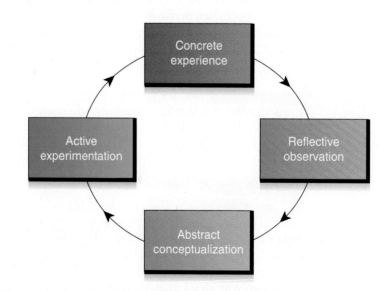

Sources: Based on information in J. E. Sharp, "Applying Kolb Learning Style Theory in the Communication Classroom," *Business Communication Quarterly* 60 (June 1997), pp. 129–34; D. A. Kolb, *Experiential Learning* (Englewood Cliffs, NJ: Prentice Hall, 1984).

The fourth stage, active experimentation, occurs when we test our previous experience, reflection, and conceptualization in a particular context.

Notice from this model that experiential learning includes the polar opposites of concrete and abstract conceptualization. We need to experience concrete reality as well as form abstract concepts from that reality. Experiential learning also involves the polar opposites of active experimentation and passive reflection. People tend to prefer and operate better in some stages than in others as a result of their unique competencies and personality. Still, experiential learning requires all four stages in proper balance.

Experiential Learning in Practice

learning orientation
The extent that an organization or individual supports knowledge management, particularly opportunities to acquire knowledge through experience and experimentation.

Learning through experience works best where there is a strong **learning orientation.**[83] Organizations with a strong learning orientation value knowledge management and, in particular, the generation of new knowledge as employees achieve their goals. If an employee initially fails to perform a task, the

The tranquil Auburn Hills campus of Oakland Community College in Michigan is about to be transformed into a place with arsonists, bound hostages, and terrified bank tellers. It's the site of a mock city designed to provide real-life instruction for police, fire, and emergency medical personnel. Instructors intend to test participants with car crashes, narcotics searches, hostage situations, bank robberies, toxic spills, and fires in the city. The idea behind the $16 million center is that emergency crews need experiential learning to acquire tacit knowledge. "Trying to explain what it's like dealing with a hot fire is like trying to explain what chocolate ice cream tastes like," explains Pontiac fire Battalion Chief Michael Nye. "You have to try it in order to know what it's like."[84] How does this emergency training center apply Kolb's experiential learning model?
(Courtesy of the Combined Regional Emergency Services Training Center)

experience might still be a valuable learning opportunity. In other words, organizations encourage employees to appreciate the process of individual and team learning, not just the performance results. Organizations achieve a learning orientation culture by rewarding experimentation and recognizing mistakes as a natural part of the learning process. They encourage employees to take reasonable risks to ultimately discover new and better ways of doing things. Without a learning orientation, mistakes are hidden and problems are more likely to escalate or reemerge later. It's not surprising, then, that one of the most frequently mentioned lessons from the best-performing manufacturers is to expect mistakes. "[Mistakes] are a source of learning and will improve operations in the long run," explains an executive at Lockheed Martin. "[They] foster the concept that no question is dumb, no idea [is] too wild, and no task or activity is irrelevant."[85]

Action Learning   The fastest-growing form of experiential learning in the workplace is called **action learning.** Action learning refers to a variety of experiential learning activities in which employees are involved in a "real, complex, and stressful problem," usually in teams, with immediate relevance to the company.[86] In action learning, the task becomes the source of learning.

> **action learning**
> A variety of experiential learning activities in which employees are involved in a "real, complex, and stressful problem," usually in teams, with immediate relevance to the company.

Kolb's experiential learning model is usually identified as the main template for action learning.[87] Action learning requires concrete experience with a real organizational problem. The process includes learning meetings, in which participants reflect on their observations regarding the problem or opportunity. The action learning team is responsible for conceptualizing or applying a model to solve the problem or opportunity. Then the team tests the model through experimentation in the real setting. For example, an action learning team at Carpenter Technology was given the challenge to investigate the steel manufacturer's strategy for entry into India. The team investigated the opportunity, wrote up its recommendation, and participated in its implementation.[88]

Action learning is considered one of the most important ways to develop executive competencies.[89] It involves both tacit and explicit learning, forces employees to diagnose new situations, and makes them rethink current work practices. At the same time, the results of action learning potentially add value to the organization in terms of a better work process or service. For example, one of Motorola's action learning teams spent several months learning how to create and manage a software business.[90]

In this chapter, we introduced the behavioral side of organizational behavior, such as the MARS model and types of workplace behaviors. Organizational behavior, however, recognizes that a lot more goes on in organizations beyond behaviors. Over the next two chapters, we look at the fundamental concepts that operate beneath the surface of behavior, including perceptions, personality, values, and emotions.

CHAPTER SUMMARY

Individual behavior is influenced by motivation, ability, role perceptions, and situational factors (MARS). Motivation consists of internal forces that affect the direction, intensity, and persistence of a person's voluntary choice of behavior. Ability includes both the natural aptitudes and learned capabilities to perform a task. Role perceptions are a person's beliefs about what behaviors are appropriate or necessary in a particular situation. Situational factors are environmental conditions that constrain or facilitate employee behavior and performance. These four factors influence various types of behavior, including joining the organization, remaining with the organization, maintaining work attendance, performing required job duties, and exhibiting organizational citizenship.

Learning is a relatively permanent change in behavior (or behavior tendency) that occurs as a result of a person's interaction with the environment. Learning influences ability, role perceptions, and motivation in the MARS model of individual performance. The four main perspectives of learning in organizations are behavior modification (reinforcement), feedback, social learning, and direct experience.

The behavior modification perspective of learning states that behavior change occurs by altering its antecedents and consequences. Antecedents are environmental stimuli that provoke (not necessarily cause) behavior. Consequences are events following behavior that influence its future occurrence. Consequences include positive reinforcement, negative reinforcement, punishment, and extinction. The schedules of reinforcement also influence behavior.

Feedback is any information that people receive about the consequences of their behavior. It affects role perceptions, learning (through corrective feedback), and employee motivation. Employees prefer nonsocial sources of feedback to learn about their goal progress. They prefer positive feedback from social sources to improve their self-image. Effective feedback is specific, frequent, timely, credible, and relevant. Employees seek out feedback, rather than just passively receive it. Although employee monitoring is usually necessary for feedback, it raises ethical concerns.

Social learning theory states that much learning occurs by observing others and then modeling those behaviors that seem to lead to favorable outcomes and avoiding behaviors that lead to punishing consequences. It also recognizes that we often engage in self-reinforcement. Behavioral modeling is effective because it transfers tacit knowledge and enhances the observer's self-efficacy.

Many companies now use experiential learning because employees do not acquire tacit knowledge through formal classroom instruction. Kolb's experiential learning model is a cyclical four-stage process that includes concrete experience, reflective observation, abstract conceptualization, and active experimentation. Action learning refers to a variety of experiential learning activities in which employees solve problems or opportunities, usually in teams, with immediate relevance to the organization.

KEY TERMS

ability, p. 34
action learning, p. 54
behavior modification, p. 40
competencies, p. 34
continuous reinforcement, p. 43
extinction, p. 43
feedback, p. 46
fixed interval schedule, p. 44
fixed ratio schedule, p. 44

job satisfaction,, p. 37
law of effect, p. 41
learning, p. 39
learning orientation, p. 53
motivation, p. 33
negative reinforcement, p. 42
organizational citizenship, p. 38
positive reinforcement, p. 42
punishment, p. 43

role perceptions, p. 35
self-efficacy, p. 51
social learning theory, p. 50
social responsibility, p. 39
tacit knowledge, p. 40
task performance, p.38
360-degree feedback, p. 46
variable interval schedule, p. 44
variable ratio schedule, p. 44

DISCUSSION QUESTIONS

1. An insurance company has high levels of absenteeism among the office staff. The head of office administration argues that employees are misusing the company's sick leave benefits. However, some of the mostly female staff members have explained that family responsibilities interfere with work. Using the MARS model, as well as your knowledge of absenteeism behavior, discuss some of the possible reasons for absenteeism here and how it might be reduced.

2. Organizational citizenship behaviors occur in a variety of settings. Identify specific organizational citizenship behaviors that you have encountered when working with other students on team projects and assignments.

3. You notice that sales representatives in the Pacific Northwest made 20 percent fewer sales to new clients over the past quarter than salespeople located elsewhere in the United States. Use the MARS model to provide possible explanations for

the low performance of the Pacific Northwest sales reps.

4. Customer service reps at Cisco Systems, a major Internet equipment manufacturer, receive 50 points every time they convince a client to click through an online demo rather than place an order over the telephone. If the employees reach a minimum number of sales, they receive at least 1,500 points. These points are later traded in for music CDs (900 points), coffeemakers (2,500 points), and other rewards. What contingency and schedule of reinforcement is Cisco Systems using here?

5. When do employees prefer feedback from non-social rather than social sources? Explain why nonsocial sources are preferred under those conditions.

6. Senior officials in a manufacturing firm are increasingly concerned about the liability they face if any of their supervisory staff engage in sexual harassment. The company's attorney says that this risk may be minimized by monitoring supervisory staff with hidden cameras. Discuss the dilemmas that this company might face with employee monitoring in this situation. What is the best solution here?

7. The person responsible for training and development in your organization wants to build a new training center where all employees can receive classroom instruction in new skills and knowledge. Why might this idea be an ineffective approach to learning?

8. A consulting firm has recommended that Big Rock Mining Company should rely on action learning to prepare its technical staff for leadership positions in the organization. The executives complain that action learning takes too long, whereas they could have consultants provide several classroom sessions in less time and at less expense. Discuss the merits of the executives' arguments against action learning.

CASE STUDY 2.1

PUSHING PAPER CAN BE FUN

A large American city government was putting on a number of seminars for managers of various departments throughout the city. At one of these sessions, the topic discussed was motivation—how we can get public servants motivated to do a good job. The plight of a police captain became the central focus of the discussion:

> I've got a real problem with my officers. They come on the force as young, inexperienced rookies, and we send them out on the street, either in cars or on a beat. They seem to like the contact they have with the public, the action involved in crime prevention, and the apprehension of criminals. They also like helping people out at fires, accidents, and other emergencies.
>
> The problem occurs when they get back to the station. They hate to do the paperwork, and because they dislike it, the job is frequently put off or done inadequately. This lack of attention hurts us later on when we get to court. We need clear, factual reports. They must be highly detailed and unambiguous. As soon as one part of a report is shown to be inadequate or incorrect, the rest of the report is suspect. Poor reporting probably causes us to lose more cases than any other factor.
>
> I just don't know how to motivate them to do a better job. We're in a budget crunch and I have absolutely no financial rewards at my disposal. In fact, we'll probably have to lay some people off in the near future. It's hard for me to make the job interesting and challenging because it isn't—it's boring, routine paperwork, and there isn't much you can do about it.
>
> Finally, I can't say to them that their promotions will hinge on the excellence of their paperwork. First of all, they know it's not true. If their performance is adequate, most are more likely to get promoted just by staying on the force a certain number of years than for some specific outstanding act. Second, they were trained to do the job they do out in the streets, not to fill out forms. All through their career it is the arrests and interventions that get noticed.
>
> Some people have suggested a number of things, like using conviction records as a performance criterion. However, we know that's not fair—too many other things are involved. Bad paperwork increases the chance that you lose in court, but good paperwork doesn't necessarily mean you'll win. We tried setting up team competitions based upon the excellence of the reports, but the officers

caught on to that pretty quickly. No one was getting any type of reward for winning the competition, and they figured, why should they bust a gut when there was no payoff?

I just don't know what to do.

Discussion Questions

1. What performance problems is the captain trying to correct?

2. Use the MARS model of individual behavior and performance to diagnose the possible causes of the unacceptable behavior.

3. Has the captain considered all possible solutions to the problem? If not, what else might be done?

Source: T. R. Mitchell and J. R. Larson, Jr., *People in Organizations*, 3rd ed. (New York: McGraw-Hill, 1987), p. 184. Used with permission.

CASE STUDY 2.2

OFFICE DEPOT'S E-DIVA

BusinessWeek An organization's success follows many individual success stories of the organization's people. For example, Office Depot's winning record in e-commerce has been driven by the actions of its chief of e-commerce, Monica Luechtefeld. Her behavior and knowledge have made Luechtefeld an important strategic asset of Office Depot. She has applied lessons learned from customers and career experiences to develop and implement an unconventional strategy that has moved Office Depot's Internet operations far ahead of those of other online businesses.

This *Business Week* case study describes how Monica Luechtefeld has combined abilities and behaviors to achieve a series of ambitious goals. It identifies significant experiences in Luechtefeld's life and tells how she has learned from them. Read through this *Business Week* case study at www.mhhe.com/mcshane2e and prepare for the discussion questions below.

Discussion Questions

1. Apply the MARS model of individual performance (see Exhibit 2.1) to Luechtefeld's performance at Office Depot. On the basis of the information in the article, how would you rate Luechtefeld's motivation, ability, role perceptions, and situational factors, as defined in the model?

2. The article describes Luechtefeld as an active learner. What kinds of learning has Luechtefeld engaged in? Give an example of each.

3. What lessons has Luechtefeld learned from her experiences? How do these lessons contribute to her performance?

Source: "Office Depot's E-Diva," *Business Week e.biz,* August 6, 2001.

TEAM EXERCISE 2.3

A QUESTION OF FEEDBACK

Purpose This exercise is designed to help you understand the importance of feedback, including problems that occur with imperfect communication in the feedback process.

Materials The instructor will distribute a few pages of exhibits to one person on each team. The other students will require a pencil with eraser and blank paper. Movable chairs and tables in a large area are helpful.

Instructions

- *Step 1*—The class is divided into pairs of students. Ideally, each pair is located in a private area away from other students and where one person can write. One student is given the pages of exhibits from the instructor. The other student in each pair is not allowed to see these exhibits.
- *Step 2*—The student holding the materials will describe each of the exhibits, and the other student's task is to replicate each exhibit accurately. The pair of students can compare the replication with the original at the end of each drawing. They may also switch roles for each exhibit, if they wish. If roles are switched, the instructor must distribute exhibits separately to each student so that they are not seen by the other person. Each exhibit has a different set of limitations, as described below:

    Exhibit 1—The student describing the exhibit cannot look at the other student or his or her diagram. The student drawing the exhibit cannot speak or otherwise communicate with the person describing the exhibit.

    Exhibit 2—The student describing the exhibit may look at the other student's diagram. However, he or she may say only yes or no when the student drawing the diagram asks a specific question. In other words, the person presenting the information can use these words only for feedback and only when asked a question by the writer.

    Exhibit 3 (optional, if time permits)—The student describing the exhibit may look at the other student's diagram and may provide any feedback at any time to the person replicating the exhibit.

- *Step 3*—The class will gather to discuss this exercise. In particular, the class should consider the importance of feedback, the characteristics of effective feedback for individual learning, and the ways in which feedback is a form of reinforcement in behavior modification.

Copyright © 2001. Steven L. McShane.

TEAM EXERCISE 2.4

TASK PERFORMANCE

Purpose This exercise is designed to help you understand how specific behaviors are associated with job performance and how people may have different standards or expectations about which behaviors constitute good performance.

Instructions The instructor will identify a job that all students know about, such as a bank teller or course instructor. Students will focus on one performance dimension, such as service skills among cafeteria cashiers, technical skills of computer lab technicians, or lecture skills of professors. Whichever performance dimension or job is chosen for your team, the following steps apply:

- *Step 1*—The instructor identifies a specific job and students are placed into teams (preferably four or five people).
- *Step 2*—Working alone, each student writes down five specific examples of effective or ineffective behavior for the selected job and performance dimension. Each incident should clearly state the critical behavior that made it effective or ineffective (e.g., "instructor sat at desk during entire lecture"; "bank teller chewed gum while talking to client"). The statements should describe behaviors, not attitudes or evaluations.
- *Step 3*—Members of each team jointly number each statement and delete duplicates.

Each behavior statement is read aloud to the team and, without any discussion, each team member privately rates the statement using the seven-point behaviorally anchored rating scale accompanying this exercise. When all statements have been rated, the ratings for each statement are compared. Discard statements about which team members significantly disagree (such as when ratings are two or three points apart).

■ *Step 4*—Average the ratings of the remaining statements, and write them at the appropriate location on the accompanying seven-point behaviorally anchored rating scale. An arrow or line should point to the exact place on the scale where the statement's average score is located. (You may want to put the seven-point rating scale and your results on an overhead transparency or flip chart if your results will be shown to the class.)

■ *Step 5*—Each team presents its results to the class and describes areas of disagreement. Other class members will discuss their agreement or disagreement with each team's results, including the quality of the state-ments (e.g., behavior-oriented) and their location on the performance scale.

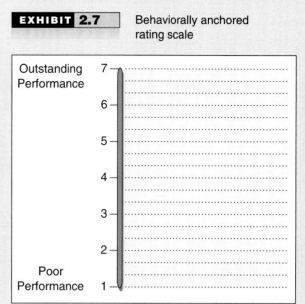

EXHIBIT 2.7 Behaviorally anchored rating scale

Outstanding Performance — 7

6

5

4

3

2

Poor Performance — 1

S E L F - A S S E S S M E N T   E X E R C I S E   2.5

ASSESSING YOUR SELF-EFFICACY

Purpose This exercise is designed to help you understand the concept of self-efficacy and to estimate your general self-efficacy.

Overview Self-efficacy refers to a person's belief that he or she has the ability, motivation, and situational contingencies to complete a task successfully. Self-efficacy is usually conceptualized as a situation-specific belief. You may believe that you can perform a certain task in one situation, but are less confident with that task in another situation. However, there is also evidence that people develop a more general self-efficacy that influences their beliefs in specific situations. This exercise helps you estimate your general self-efficacy.

Instructions Read each of the statements below and circle the response that best fits your personal belief. Then use the scoring key in Appendix B of this book to calculate your results. This self-assessment is completed alone so that students rate themselves honestly without concerns of social comparison. However, class discussion will focus on the meaning of self-efficacy, how this scale might be applied in organizations, and the limitations of measuring self-efficacy in work settings.

General self-efficacy scale

To what extent does each statement describe you? Indicate your level of agreement by marking the appropriate response on the right.

Statement	Strongly Agree	Agree	Neutral	Disagree	Strongly Disagree
1. When I make plans, I am certain I can make them work.	☐	☐	☐	☐	☐
2. One of my problems is that I cannot get down to work when I should.	☐	☐	☐	☐	☐
3. If I can't do a job the first time, I keep trying until I can.	☐	☐	☐	☐	☐
4. When I set important goals for myself, I rarely achieve them.	☐	☐	☐	☐	☐
5. I give up on things before completing them.	☐	☐	☐	☐	☐
6. I avoid facing difficulties.	☐	☐	☐	☐	☐
7. If something looks too complicated, I will not even bother to try it.	☐	☐	☐	☐	☐
8. When I have something unpleasant to do, I stick to it until I finish it.	☐	☐	☐	☐	☐
9. When I decide to do something, I go right to work on it.	☐	☐	☐	☐	☐
10. When trying to learn something new, I soon give up if I am not initially successful.	☐	☐	☐	☐	☐
11. When unexpected problems occur, I don't handle them well.	☐	☐	☐	☐	☐
12. I avoid trying to learn new things when they look too difficult for me.	☐	☐	☐	☐	☐
13. Failure just makes me try harder.	☐	☐	☐	☐	☐
14. I feel insecure about my ability to do things.	☐	☐	☐	☐	☐
15. I am a self-reliant person.	☐	☐	☐	☐	☐
16. I give up easily.	☐	☐	☐	☐	☐
17. I do not seem capable of dealing with most problems that come up in life.	☐	☐	☐	☐	☐

Source: Reproduced with permission of authors and publisher from M. Sherer, J. E. Maddux, B. Mercandante, S. Prentice–Dunn, B. Jacobs, and R. W. Rogers, "The Self–Efficacy Scale: Construction and Validation." *Psychological Reports* 51 (1982), pp.663-71. Copyright © *Psychological Reports* (1982).

After studying the preceding material, be sure to check out our website at

www.mhhe.com/mcshane2e

for more in-depth information and interactivities that correspond to this chapter.

3

Perception and Personality in Organizations

AFTER READING THIS CHAPTER, YOU SHOULD BE ABLE TO:

- Outline the perceptual process.

- Explain how we perceive ourselves and others through social identity.

- Discuss the accuracy of stereotypes.

- Describe the attribution process and two attribution errors.

- Diagram the self-fulfilling prophecy process.

- Discuss the objectives and limitations of diversity initiatives.

- Explain how the Johari Window can help improve our perceptions.

- Identify the Big Five personality dimensions.

- Discuss the psychological dimensions identified by Jung and measured in the Myers-Briggs Type Indicator.

The arrest of nuclear scientist Dr. Wen Ho Lee for allegedly stealing secrets at Los Alamos Nuclear Laboratory raised more than national security concerns. It also opened a long-simmering issue regarding bias against Asian Americans. Government officials deny that Lee, a naturalized U.S. citizen born in Taiwan, was singled out because of his ethnicity, whereas two counterintelligence officers claim Lee's race was a factor.

The U.S. Energy Department says that China recruits ethnic Chinese in the United States for espionage purposes. Others point out that this incident is one more example of the perpetual-foreigner syndrome—that Asian Americans are viewed by others as forever non-American.

Anne Xuan Clark frequently experiences the misperception that she is a foreigner. "I've been told a million times, 'Your English is so good! Where are you from?'" says Clark, a Seattle resident whose ancestors are Vietnamese and Irish. Clark comes from California, but that doesn't satisfy some acquaintances. "No, where are you *really* from?" they ask again.

U.S. Representative David Wu recently experienced perpetual-foreigner bias when he was detained entering the Energy Department building in Washington, D.C. Wu was repeatedly asked if he was an American citizen, even after showing his congressional pass. A recent survey also found that one-third of Americans believe Chinese Americans are more loyal to China than to the United States. "We always knew there was an element of some negative bias . . . but we were startled by the results," says Henry Tang, chairman of a group of prominent Chinese Americans who sponsored the survey.

The arrest of nuclear scientist Dr. Wen Ho Lee for allegedly stealing secrets at Los Alamos raised concerns about the perpetual-foreigner syndrome as a perceptual bias. *(© AFP/ CORBIS)*

"For years, a lot of these things have festered, and it was typical of the Asian way to say nothing," says Kalina Wong, an American-born scientist of Chinese and Hawaiian descent who works at the Livermore nuclear lab. "The whole Chinese spy allegation has set us back further." Wong and eight other Asian-American scientists and engineers at Livermore recently filed a racial discrimination complaint against their employer.[1]

perception
The process of selecting, organizing, and interpreting information in order to make sense of the world around us.

The Greek philosopher Plato wrote long ago that we see reality only as shadows reflecting against the rough wall of a cave.[2] In other words, reality is filtered through an imperfect perceptual process. **Perception** is the process of receiving information about and making sense of the world around us. It involves deciding which information to notice, how to categorize that information, and how to interpret it within the framework of our existing knowledge.

The opening vignette illustrates how perceptions shape opinions, decisions, and actions. Many automatically assume that people who look Chinese must be new to the United States. A few are convinced that Chinese Americans are more Chinese than American in terms of their allegiance. These and other perceptions shape our opinions about people from different backgrounds, as well as our decisions and actions toward them. In this world of increasing cultural diversity and globalization, we need to be particularly aware of the perceptual process and how we can minimize misperceptions of others.

This chapter begins by describing the perceptual process, that is, the dynamics of selecting, organizing, and interpreting external stimuli. Social identity theory is introduced, including how the perceptual process influences our self-perceptions and our perceptions of others. Social identity theory lays the foundation for our coverage of stereotyping, prejudice, and discrimination. The perceptual processes of attribution and self-fulfilling prophecy are described next, followed by an overview of strategies to minimize perceptual problems. Our perceptions of others, as well as most other organizational behavior processes, are influenced by our personality. The final section of this chapter introduces that important concept and its relevance to organizational behavior.

THE PERCEPTUAL PROCESS

As Exhibit 3.1 illustrates, the perceptual process begins when environmental stimuli are received through our senses. Most stimuli are screened out; the

EXHIBIT 3.1

Model of the perceptual process

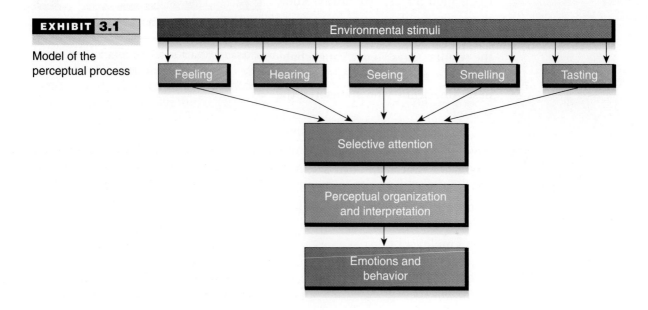

EXHIBIT 4.5   Job satisfaction across cultures

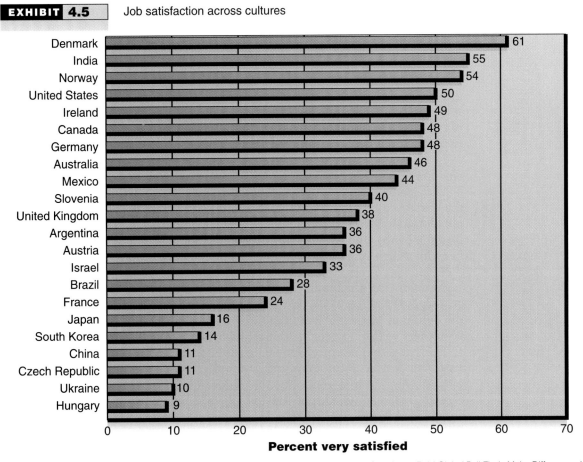

Source: Based on Ipsos-Reid survey of 9,300 employees in 39 countries in middle of 2000. See "Ipsos-Reid Global Poll Finds Major Differences in Employee Satisfaction around the World," Ipsos-Reid News Release, January 8, 2001.

their jobs, be absent or late for work, steal from their employer, or engage in acts of violence.[77]

Job satisfaction is also an ethical issue. People spend a large portion of their time working in organizations, and many societies now expect companies to provide work environments that are safe and enjoyable. This moral obligation is apparent when an organization has low job satisfaction. The company tries to hide this fact, and when morale problems become public, corporate leaders are usually quick to improve the situation.

But what about job satisfaction and job performance? Is it true that "happy workers are productive workers"? The answer is that researchers have found a weak or negligible association between job satisfaction and task performance.[78] One reason for the weak relationship is that general attitudes (like job satisfaction) don't predict specific behaviors very well. Instead, they affect different people in different ways. One dissatisfied employee may decide to put in less work effort, whereas another dissatisfied employee works productively while looking for employment elsewhere. Another explanation is that job performance leads to job satisfaction (rather than vice versa), but only when performance is linked to valued rewards. High performers receive more rewards and, consequently, are more satisfied than low-performing employees who receive fewer rewards. This connection between job satisfaction and performance is weak because many organizations do not reward good performance.[79]

Job Satisfaction and Customer Satisfaction   Job satisfaction may have a fuzzy effect on job performance, but its influence on customer satisfaction seems to be strong and clear. Marketing experts have developed a model that relates the job satisfaction of employees to customer satisfaction and profitability. As shown in Exhibit 4.6, this employee–customer–profit chain model suggests that increasing employee satisfaction and loyalty results in higher customer perceptions of value, which improves the company's profitability.[80]

The opening vignette in this chapter describes how The Warehouse applies the employee–customer–profit chain model through its "people first" principle. Founder Stephen Tindall believes that companies have happy customers through happy employees. Sears, Roebuck and Company also follows this philosophy. A few years ago, the retail giant calculated that a 5-point improvement on the Sears job satisfaction survey scale would increase customer satisfaction ratings by 1.3 points, which, in turn, would improve revenue growth by 0.5 percent. Gordon Bethune, CEO of Continental Airlines, sums up the equation this way: "We treat our people well, and in turn, they treat our customers well. Happy employees equal customer satisfaction."[81]

There are two main reasons why job satisfaction has a positive effect on customer service. First, job satisfaction affects a person's general mood. Employees who are in a good mood are more likely to display friendliness and positive feelings, which puts customers in a better mood. Second, satisfied employees are less likely to quit their jobs, and longer-service employees have more experience and better skills to serve clients. Lower turnover also gives

EXHIBIT 4.6

The employee–customer–profit chain model

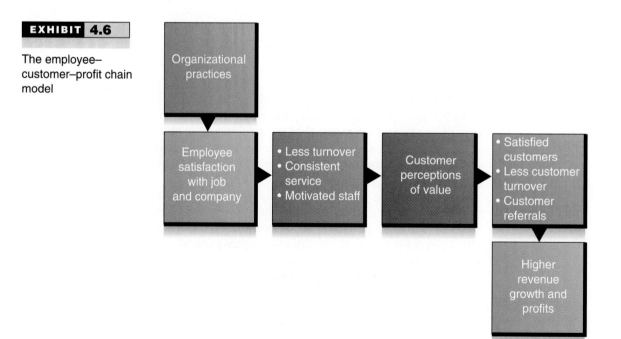

Roger Greene (wearing goggles in photo) isn't taking any chances on poor customer service. The CEO and founder of Ipswitch Inc. has taken all 130 employees—plus one guest each—on a four-day cruise in the Bahamas. The cruise is the Lexington, Virginia, software maker's way of thanking employees for steady financial performance. It's also consistent with Greene's larger objective to keep employees happy so that they will continue to provide exceptional customer service. Ipswitch employees also get five weeks of paid time off, child and elder care, domestic partner benefits, and a concierge service. "If employees are treated well," Greene explains, "they will treat the customers well, and then the profits will come."[82] Along with job satisfaction, what other work attitude described in this chapter might explain why a trip to the Bahamas increases customer satisfaction? *(© John Wilcox, Boston Herald)*

customers the same employees to serve them, so there is more consistent service. There is some evidence that customers build their loyalty to specific employees, not to the organization, so keeping employee turnover low tends to keep customer turnover low.[83]

Improving Job Satisfaction Given the importance of job satisfaction, how can companies ensure that they have happy workers? The job satisfaction concept is so broad—remember, there are many facets of job satisfaction—that the answer comes from every part of this textbook. Feedback, equity, rewards, leadership, corporate culture, change management, and other topics all implicitly or explicitly refer to job satisfaction as a possible outcome. We must also remember that individual differences, such as personality and personal beliefs, moderate the effects of the work environment on job satisfaction.

Organizational Commitment

organizational commitment
The employee's emotional attachment to, identification with, and involvement in a particular organization.

Organizational commitment refers to the employee's emotional attachment to, identification with, and involvement in a particular organization.[84] It is the person's *affective commitment*—his or her loyalty to the organization.[84] Affective commitment can also refer to loyalty toward co-workers, customers, or a profession.[85] In this book, we will concentrate mainly on the employee's overall commitment to the organization.

Along with affective commitment, employees have varying levels of *continuance commitment*.[86] Continuance commitment occurs when employees believe it is in their own personal interest to remain with the organization. In other words, this form of commitment is a calculative bond with the organization rather than an emotional attachment. For example, you may have met people who do not particularly identify with the organization where they work but feel bound to remain there because it would be too costly to quit. Continuance commitment is this motivation to stay because of the high cost of leaving.[87]

Is organizational loyalty declining? Some surveys suggest that organizational commitment has fallen considerably over the past decade, whereas others see no change. Some writers argue that employees are still loyal, but their loyalty is directed more toward their profession, their immediate work unit, or their immediate boss rather than the overall organization.[88]

Consequences of Organizational Commitment   Research suggests that a loyal workforce can be a significant competitive advantage. Employees with high levels of affective commitment are less likely to quit their jobs and be absent from work. Organizational commitment also improves customers' satisfaction because long-tenure employees have better knowledge of work practices and clients like to do business with the same employees. Employees with high affective commitment also have higher work motivation and organizational citizenship.[89]

However, there are potential problems where employees have too much organizational commitment. One potential problem with a highly loyal workforce is that the organization may have very low turnover. This limits the organization's opportunity to hire new employees with new knowledge and fresh ideas. Another concern is that loyalty results in conformity, which holds back creativity. Some critics also argue that organizational commitment is a vestige of the ancient "master–servant" relationship that should be replaced by more professional relationships between employer and employee.[90]

Building Organizational Commitment   Although there are almost as many ways to build organizational loyalty as topics in this textbook, the following activities have been most prominent in the literature:[91]

▨ *Fairness and satisfaction*—The most important ingredients for a loyal workforce are positive and equitable work experiences. New employees must believe that the company is fulfilling its obligations.[92] Organizational commitment seems to suffer when people face increased workloads in companies with record profits and senior executives earning lucrative bonuses. Other companies have built commitment by sharing profits and distributing company shares to employees.

▨ *Job security*—Layoff threats are one of the greatest blows to employee loyalty, even among those whose jobs are not immediately at risk.[93] Building commitment doesn't require lifetime employment guarantees, but employees should have enough job security to feel some permanence and mutuality in the employment relationship.

▨ *Organizational comprehension*—Affective commitment is a person's identification with the company, so it makes sense that this attitude is strengthened when employees have a solid comprehension of the company. Employees feel disconnected when they don't know what's going on. This uncertainty calls for improved communication processes (see Chapter 11) as well as opportunities to work in various parts of the organization. It also requires more social interaction, particularly where employees are often separated from each other.

▨ *Employee involvement*—Employees feel that they are part of the organization when they make decisions that guide the organization's future. Through participation, employees begin to see how the organization is a reflection of their decisions. Employee involvement also builds loyalty because giving this power is a demonstration of the company's trust in its employees.

▨ *Trusting employees*—**Trust** occurs when we have positive expectations about another party's intentions and actions toward us in risky situations.[94] Trust means putting faith in the other person or group. It is also a reciprocal activity; to receive trust, you must demonstrate trust. Trust is important for organizational commitment because it touches the heart of the employment relationship (see Chapter 18). Employees identify with and feel obliged to work for an organization only when they trust its leaders.

trust

Positive expectations about another party's intentions and actions toward us in risky situations.

Aside from these practices, some firms try to build commitment by tying employees financially to the organization through low-cost loans and stock options. Many knowledge-based firms offer stock options that are vested (withheld) for two or more years. Anglo Irish Bank uses loyalty bonuses to reduce turnover of new staff. People who are hired at the Irish bank receive half of their bonus—which can range up to 50 percent of base salary—after 12 months of employment and the other half 6 months later. "The hope," says an Anglo Irish Bank executive, "is to keep them a little longer."[95]

These "golden handcuffs" do tend to reduce turnover, but they also increase continuance commitment, not affective commitment. Evidence suggests that employees with high levels of continuance commitment have *lower* performance ratings and are *less* likely to engage in organizational citizenship behaviors.[96] Although vested options may be necessary, continuance commitment should not be a substitute for strategies to build and maintain employee loyalty. Employers still need to win employees' hearts (affective commitment) beyond tying them financially to the organization (continuance commitment).

CHAPTER SUMMARY

Values represent stable, long-lasting beliefs about what is important to us. They influence our decisions and interpretation of what is ethical. Some values are terminal, whereas others are instrumental. We also need to distinguish espoused values from enacted values. There are also different levels of values (personal, organizational, professional, and cultural).

Values have become more important in organizations because of globalization, the need to replace command-and-control systems, and the increasing pressure for organizations to engage in ethical practices. Organizations are more effective when they align the company's values with those held by individuals and the society in which they operate.

Five values that differ across cultures are individualism versus collectivism, power distance, uncertainty avoidance, achievement versus nurturing orientation, and long- versus short-term orientation.

Three values that guide ethical conduct are utilitarianism, individual rights, and distributive justice. Three other factors that influence ethical conduct are the extent to which an issue demands ethical principles (moral intensity), the person's sensitivity to the presence and importance of an ethical dilemma, and situational factors that cause people to deviate from their moral values.

People from different cultures tend to act differently when faced with an ethical issue. Although ethical values differ somewhat across cultures, most of this variation is explained by the fact that unique cultural experiences cause people to see different levels of moral intensity.

Emotions are feelings experienced toward an object, person, or event that create a state of readiness. They differ from attitudes, which represent the cluster of beliefs, feelings, and behavioral intentions toward an object. Beliefs are a person's perceptions about an attitude object. Feelings are judgments about our emotional experiences associated with the target. Behavioral intentions represent a motivation to engage in a particular behavior with respect to the target. Emotions usually affect behavior through beliefs, feelings, and behavioral intentions.

Emotional labor refers to the effort, planning, and control needed to express organizationally desired emotions during interpersonal transactions. Emotional labor is more common in jobs with frequent and lengthy customer interaction, where the job requires a variety of emotions displayed, and where employees must abide by the display rules. Emotional labor creates problems because true emotions tend to leak out, and conflict between expected and true emotions (emotional dissonance) causes stress and burnout.

Emotional intelligence is the ability to monitor your own and others' emotions, to discriminate among them, and to use the information to guide your thinking and actions. Emotional intelligence includes self-awareness, self-regulation, self-motivation, empathy, and social skill.

Job satisfaction represents a person's evaluation of his or her job and work context. Job satisfaction affects absenteeism and turnover, and reflects the ethical standards of the organization. Although it has a weak association with task performance, job satisfaction is a strong and clear factor in customer satisfaction.

Affective organizational commitment (loyalty) refers to the employee's emotional attachment to, identification with, and involvement in a particular organization. Affective commitment contrasts with continuance commitment, which is a calculative bond with the organization. Companies build loyalty through fairness and satisfaction, some level of job security, organizational comprehension, employee involvement, and trust. Some companies rely on golden handcuffs, but this approach produces continuance commitment, which tends to reduce job performance.

KEY TERMS

attitudes, p. 107
cognitive dissonance, p. 110
emotional dissonance, p. 112
emotional intelligence (EQ), p. 112
emotional labor, p. 111
emotions, p. 106

ethical sensitivity, p. 105
individualism versus collectivism, p. 101
moral intensity, p. 104
negative affectivity (NA), p. 110
organizational commitment, p. 119

positive affectivity (PA), p. 110
power distance, p. 101
trust, p. 121
uncertainty avoidance, p. 101
utilitarianism, p. 104

DISCUSSION QUESTIONS

1. An American company is beginning to expand operations in Japan and wants you to form working relationships with Japanese suppliers. Considering only the values of individualism and uncertainty avoidance, what should you be aware of or sensitive to in your dealings with these suppliers? You may assume that your contacts hold typical Japanese values along these dimensions.

2. Not long ago, Microsoft set up a program whereby computer science professors would receive $200 for mentioning Microsoft's products at public presentations. The money is used to offset travel costs to attend these sessions. Discuss the ethical implications of this incentive.

3. Compare and contrast moral intensity and ethical sensitivity.

4. After a few months on the job, Susan has experienced several emotional episodes ranging from frustration to joy toward the work she is assigned. Use the model of emotions, attitudes, and

behaviors to explain how these emotions affect Susan's level of job satisfaction with the work itself.

5. The latest employee attitude survey in your organization indicates that employees are unhappy with some aspects of the organization. However, management tends to pay attention to the single-item question asking employees to indicate their overall satisfaction with the job. The results of this item indicate that 86 percent of staff members are very or somewhat satisfied, so management concludes that the other results refer to issues that are probably not important to employees. Explain why management's interpretation of these results may be inaccurate.

6. A recent study reported that college instructors are frequently required to engage in emotional labor. Identify the situations in which emotional labor is required for this job. In your opinion, is emotional labor more troublesome for college instructors or for telephone operators working at a 911 emergency call center?

7. If a co-worker told you that he or she had a high level of emotional intelligence, what would you look for to confirm that statement?

8. Universal Broadcasting Corporation is concerned about losing some of its best technical staff to competitors. Senior executives have decided that the best way to build a loyal workforce is to introduce a deferred profit-sharing plan. Employees would receive half of each year's profit share at the end of the year, but the other half would be paid out over the next two years as trailers. Anyone who leaves, other than as a result of retirement or layoffs, would forfeit some or all of the deferred payments. Explain what effect this plan may have on organizational commitment and employee behaviors.

CASE STUDY 4.1

ROUGH SEAS ON THE LINK650

Professor Suzanne Baxter was preparing for her first class of the semester when Shaun O'Neill knocked lightly on the open door and announced himself: "Hi, Professor, I don't suppose you remember me?" Professor Baxter had large classes, but she did remember that Shaun was a student in her organizational behavior class two years earlier. Shaun had decided to work in the oil industry for a couple of years before returning to school to complete his diploma.

"Welcome back!" Baxter said as she beckoned him into the office. "I heard you were working on an oil rig in the United Kingdom. How was it?"

"Well, Professor," Shaun began, "I had worked two summers in the Texas oil fields and my family's from Ireland, so I hoped to get a job on the LINK650. It's that new WestOil drilling rig that arrived with so much fanfare in the North Sea fields two years ago. The LINK650 was built by LINK, Inc., in Texas. A standard practice in this industry is for the rig manufacturer to manage its day-to-day operations, so employees on the LINK650 are managed completely by LINK managers with no involvement from WestOil.

We all know that drilling rig jobs are dangerous, but they pay well and offer generous time off. A local newspaper there said that nearly a thousand people lined up to complete job applications for the 50 nontechnical positions. I was lucky enough to get one of those jobs.

"Everyone hired on the LINK650 was enthusiastic and proud. We were one of the chosen few and were really pumped up about working on a new rig that had received so much media attention. I was quite impressed with the recruiters—so were several other hires—because they really seemed to be concerned about our welfare out on the platform. I later discovered that the recruiters came from a consulting firm that specializes in hiring people. Come to think of it, we didn't meet a single LINK manager during that process. Maybe things would have been different if some of those LINK supervisors had interviewed us.

"Working on LINK650 was a real shock, even though most of us had some experience working in the oil fields. I'd say that none of the 50 nontechnical people hired was quite prepared for the brutal jobs on the oil rig. We did the dirtiest jobs in the biting cold winds of the North Sea.

Still, during the first few months most of us wanted to show the company that we were dedicated to getting the job done. A couple of the new hires quit within a few weeks, but most of the people hired with me really got along well—you know, just like the ideas you mentioned in class. We formed a special bond that helped us through the bad weather and grueling work.

"The LINK650 supervisors were another matter. They were mean taskmasters who had worked for many years on oil rigs in the Gulf of Mexico or North Sea. They seemed to relish the idea of treating their employees the same way they had been treated before becoming managers. We put up with their abuse for the first few months, but things got worse when the LINK650 was completely shut down twice to correct mechanical problems. These setbacks embarrassed LINK's management and they put more pressure on the supervisors to get us back on schedule.

"The supervisors started to ignore equipment problems and pushed us to get jobs done more quickly without regard to safety procedures. They routinely shouted obscenities at employees in front of others. A couple of my workmates were fired and a couple of others quit their jobs. I almost lost my job one day just because my boss thought I was deliberately working slowly. He didn't realize—or care—that the fittings I was connecting were damaged. Several people started finding ways to avoid the supervisors and get as little work done as possible. Many of my co-workers developed back problems. We jokingly called it the 'rigger's backache' because some employees faked their ailment to leave the rig with paid sick leave.

"On top of the lousy supervisors, we were always kept in the dark about the problems on the rig. Supervisors said that they didn't know anything, which was partly true, but they said we shouldn't be so interested in things that didn't concern us. But the rig's problems, as well as its future contract work, were a major concern to crew members who weren't ready to quit. Their job security depended on the rig's production levels and whether WestOil would sign contracts to drill new holes. Given the rig's problems, most of us were concerned that we would be laid off at any time.

"Everything came to a head when Bob MacKenzie was killed because someone secured a hoist improperly. Not sure if it was mentioned in the papers here, but it was big news around this time last year. A government inquiry concluded that the person responsible wasn't properly trained and that employees were being pushed to finish jobs without safety precautions. Anyway, while the inquiry was going on, several employees decided to unionize the rig. It wasn't long before most employees on LINK650 had signed union cards. That really shocked LINK's management and the entire oil industry because it was, I think, just the second time that a rig had ever been unionized there.

"Since then, management has been doing everything in its power to get rid of the union. It sent a 'safety officer' to the rig, although we eventually realized that he was a consultant the company hired to undermine union support. Several managers were sent to special seminars on how to manage a unionized workforce, although one of the topics was how to break the union.

"So you see, Professor, I joined LINK as an enthusiastic employee and quit last month with no desire to lift a finger for them. It really bothers me, because I was always told to do your best, no matter how tough the situation. It's been quite an experience."

Discussion Questions

1. Identify the various ways that employees expressed their job dissatisfaction on the LINK650.

2. Shaun O'Neill's commitment to the LINK organization dwindled over his two years of employment. Discuss the factors that affected his organizational commitment.

REVENGE OF THE DOWNSIZED NERDS

BusinessWeek The economic slowdown of 2001 hit the high-tech sector especially hard. Although some people had thought e-commerce would be immune from the punishing downturns of business cycles, many of the layoffs occurred at dot-coms. Newly unemployed high-tech workers in California's Silicon Valley reacted in vastly different ways. Some looked for traditional jobs; others joined the Peace Corps. Some of the most dramatic reactions involved retaliation

This *Business Week* case study discusses the laid-off dot-com workers who sought revenge. It provides several anecdotes of high-tech workers who sabotaged their employers or extorted favorable severance packages. Read through this *Business Week* case study at www.mhhe.com/mcshane2e and prepare for the discussion questions at right.

Discussion Questions

1. From an employer's standpoint, what are the ethical issues in handling an economic downturn by laying off employees? Are the issues different in the case of skilled workers, such as computer experts at a high-tech firm? What values does a company demonstrate when it lays off employees?

2. From the perspective of the employees described in this article, were these forms of retaliation justifiable? Why or why not? What values are they demonstrating?

3. What were the likely emotions underlying the behavior described in the article? Do you think these emotions represented a high level of emotional intelligence? Why or why not?

Source: Michelle Conlin, "Revenge of the Downsized Nerds," *Business Week,* July 30, 2001.

RANKING JOBS ON THEIR EMOTIONAL LABOR

Purpose This exercise is designed to help you understand the jobs in which people tend to experience higher or lower degrees of emotional labor.

Instructions

■ *Step 1*—Individually rank the jobs listed on the next page according to the extent that they require emotional labor. In other words, assign a 1 to the job you believe requires the most effort, planning, and control to express organizationally desired emotions during interpersonal transactions. Assign a 10 to the job you believe requires the least amount of emotional labor. Mark your rankings in column (1).

■ *Step 2*—The instructor will form teams of four or five members, and each team will rank the items based on consensus (not simply averaging the individual rankings). These results are placed in column (2).

■ *Step 3*—The instructor will provide expert ranking information. This information should be written in column (3). Then students will calculate the differences and record the results in columns (4) and (5). Students then sum the total absolute difference in each of these columns.

■ *Step 4*—The class will compare the results and discuss the features of jobs with high emotional labor.

Occupational emotional labor scoring sheet					
Occupation	(1) Individual ranking	(2) Team ranking	(3) Expert ranking	(4) Absolute difference between (1) and (3)	(5) Absolute difference between (2) and (3)
Bartender					
Cashier					
Dental hygienist					
Insurance adjuster					
Lawyer					
Librarian					
Postal clerk					
Registered nurse					
Social worker					
Television announcer					
			Total		
				Your score	Team score

SELF-ASSESSMENT EXERCISE 4.4

ETHICS CHECK

Purpose This exercise is designed to help you assess your ethical response to various business and nonbusiness situations.

Instructions Read each of the scenarios on the next page and indicate how you would likely respond in each scenario. There is no scoring key for this scale. Instead, the instructor will present the results of other students who have completed this instrument. This exercise is completed alone so that students assess themselves honestly without concerns of social comparison. However, class discussion will focus on business ethics and the issue of ethical sensitivity.

Ethics check scale					
Please indicate the probability that you would take the action indicated at the end of each scenario.	Yes ▼	Probably yes ▼	Unsure ▼	Probably no ▼	No ▼

1. At work you use many different software packages. Several weeks ago your supervisor ordered a new package for you that several of your colleagues are currently using. The software is now late in arriving. The package would aid you tremendously in completing your current project but is not absolutely necessary. Earlier today your supervisor brought her copy of the software over to you and suggested that you copy it onto your computer for use until your copy arrives. You know that the software is licensed to be installed onto only one computer. Do you copy the software? .... ☐ ☐ ☐ ☐ ☐

2. While at lunch with several of your colleagues last week, you overheard a discussion about a client company's financial situation. An accountant working closely with the company noticed significant decreases in sales and receivables. He wasn't sure exactly how bad it was until he heard a rumor at the company about the possibility of filing for bankruptcy. You're now worried because you own a significant block of shares in the company. Do you sell the shares based on this inside information? .... ☐ ☐ ☐ ☐ ☐

3. Yesterday you drove to the store with your neighbor and her young son. When you got back out to the car, your neighbor noticed that her son picked up a small item from the store worth about $5 that wasn't paid for. Your neighbor reprimanded the child and then turned to you and said she was ready to go. You asked her if she was going to go back into the store to pay for the item. She said it's not worth the hassle. Do you refuse to drive her home unless she goes back to the store and pays for the item? .... ☐ ☐ ☐ ☐ ☐

4. While on a trip out of town on business, you had dinner with your sister. Your company has a policy of reimbursing dinner expenses up to $50 per meal. The total cost for this meal for both you and your sister was $35.70. The cost of your meal alone was $16.30. You know that others in your company routinely submit claims for dinner expenses for nonbusiness parties. Do you claim the entire amount for reimbursement? .... ☐ ☐ ☐ ☐ ☐

Source: Adapted from R. R. Radtke, "The Effects of Gender and Setting on Accountants' Ethically Sensitive Decisions," *Journal of Business Ethics* 24 (April 2000), pp. 299–312.

INDIVIDUALISM–COLLECTIVISM SCALE

Purpose This self-assessment is designed to help you identify your level of individualism and collectivism.

Instructions Read each of the statements below and circle the response that you believe best indicates how well each statement describes you. Then use the scoring key in Appendix B to calculate your results for each scale. This exercise is completed alone so that students assess themselves honestly without concerns of social comparison. However, class discussion will focus on the individualism–collectivism values.

Individualism–collectivism scale					
Circle the number that best indicates how well each statement describes you.	Does not describe me at all ▼	Does not describe me very well ▼	Describes me somewhat ▼	Describes me well ▼	Describes me very well ▼
1. I often do "my own thing."	1	2	3	4	5
2. The well-being of my co-workers is important to me.	1	2	3	4	5
3. One should live one's life independently of others.	1	2	3	4	5
4. If a co-worker gets a prize, I would feel proud.	1	2	3	4	5
5. I like my privacy.	1	2	3	4	5
6. If a relative were in financial difficulty, I would help within my means.	1	2	3	4	5
7. I prefer to be direct and forthright when discussing issues with people.	1	2	3	4	5
8. It is important to maintain harmony within my group.	1	2	3	4	5
9. I am a unique individual.	1	2	3	4	5
10. I like sharing little things with my neighbors.	1	2	3	4	5
11. What happens to me is my own doing.	1	2	3	4	5
12. I feel good when I cooperate with others.	1	2	3	4	5
13. When I succeed, it is usually because of my abilities.	1	2	3	4	5
14. My happiness depends very much on the happiness of those around me.	1	2	3	4	5
15. I enjoy being unique and different from others in many ways.	1	2	3	4	5
16. To me, pleasure is spending time with others.	1	2	3	4	5

Source: T. M. Singelis, H. C. Triandis, D. P. S. Bhawuk, and M. J. Gelfand, "Horizontal and Vertical Dimensions of Individualism and Collectivism: A Theoretical and Measurement Refinement," *Cross-Cultural Research* 29 (August 1995), pp. 240–75. Copyright © 1995 by Sage Publications. Reprinted by permission of Sage Publications, Inc.

After studying the preceding material, be sure to check out our website at
www.mhhe.com/mcshane2e
for more in-depth information and interactivities that correspond to this chapter.

CHAPTER 5

Foundations of Employee Motivation

AFTER READING THIS CHAPTER, YOU SHOULD BE ABLE TO:

- Define *motivation* and distinguish between content and process theories.

- Compare the four content theories of motivation.

- Discuss the practical implications of content motivation theories.

- Explain how each component of expectancy theory influences work effort.

- Discuss the implications of expectancy theory.

- Explain how employees react to inequity.

- Describe the characteristics of effective goal setting.

Mark Hawkins knows what it's like to be challenged. The senior business analyst joined Capital One a few years ago and has been pushing his potential ever since. "The first few weeks you are playing catch-up, learning about a new industry and organization," says Hawkins, who works at the credit card company's British operations. "But pretty soon you are making decisions about how to take the company forward. There are so many opportunities and you are free to pick up as many projects as you can run with."

Capital One knows how to motivate employees. The Falls Church, Virginia–based firm starts by carefully screening job applicants and selecting those with an inherent entrepreneurial need for achievement. Then, as Mark Hawkins discovered, the company stretches them with challenging goals. "We expect associates to get out of their comfort zones and look for those 'stretch assignments,'" explains a Capital One executive.

Employees are formally evaluated twice each year by supervisors and peers against specific behavioral competencies. They also receive plenty of informal feedback and encouragement. "You have to spend a lot of time working with people and giving them constant feedback," says a Capital One executive. "It makes people feel valued and involved." Employees are also motivated by financial incentives based on individual and organizational performance.

But Capital One's dramatic growth over the past decade creates a challenge for co-founders Richard Fairbank and Nigel Morris. "As we become bigger, we have to make sure we preserve the spirit and the magic of Capital One," Fairbank says. "Now we're at 20,000 [employees], and it still has that entrepreneurial spirit. But it won't be easy."[1]

Motivated employees are one reason why Capital One is so successful. In this photo, Dawna DePollo (right) and another Capital One employee are signing their names to the last steel beam on the credit card firm's new building in Richmond, Virginia.
(© Joe Mahoney/Richmond Times Dispatch)

motivation

The forces within a person that affect his or her direction, intensity, and persistence of voluntary behavior.

content theories of motivation

Theories that explain the dynamics of employee needs, such as why people have different needs at different times.

process theories of motivation

Theories that describe the processes through which needs are translated into behavior.

needs

Deficiencies that energize or trigger behaviors to satisfy those needs.

apital One employees are high performers partly because the company has found ways to keep everyone motivated. **Motivation** refers to the forces within a person that affect his or her direction, intensity, and persistence of voluntary behavior.[2] Motivated employees are willing to exert a particular level of effort (intensity), for a certain amount of time (persistence), toward a particular goal (direction). Even when people have clear work objectives, the right skills, and a supportive work environment, they must have sufficient motivation to achieve work objectives.

Most employers (92 percent of them, according to one recent survey) agree that motivating employees has become more challenging.[3] One reason is that many firms have dramatically changed the jobs that people perform, reducing layers of hierarchy, and jettisoned large numbers of employees throughout the process. These actions have significantly damaged the levels of trust and commitment necessary for employees to put out effort beyond the minimum requirements.[4] Some organizations have completely given up on motivation from the heart and, instead, rely on pay-for-performance approaches and lay-off threats. These strategies may have some effect (both positive and negative), but they do not capitalize on the employee's motivational potential.

A second problem is that as companies flatten their hierarchies to reduce costs, they can no longer rely on supervisors to practice the old command-and-control methods of motivating employees. This is probably just as well, because direct supervision is incompatible with the values of today's educated workforce. Still, many businesses have not discovered other ways to motivate employees.

Lastly, employee needs are changing. Younger generations of employees are bringing different expectations to the workplace than their baby boomer counterparts.[5] Workforce diversity and globalization have added to this complexity because diverse employees typically have diverse values. Recall from the previous chapter that values represent stable, long-lasting beliefs about what is important in a variety of situations.[6] These values influence what we want, what we need, and what organizations should and should not do to fulfill those needs.

In this chapter, we look at the foundations of employee motivation. Motivation theories fall into two main categories: content theories and process theories. **Content theories of motivation** explain the dynamics of employee needs, such as why people have different needs at different times. By understanding an employee's needs, we can discover the conditions that motivate that person. **Process theories of motivation** do not directly explain how needs emerge. Instead, they describe the processes through which needs are translated into behavior. Process theories of motivation help explain why people behave the way they do. In doing so, they help us understand, predict, and influence employee performance, attendance, work satisfaction, and other outcomes.

CONTENT THEORIES OF MOTIVATION

Most contemporary theories recognize that motivation begins with individual needs. **Needs** are deficiencies that energize or trigger behaviors to satisfy those needs. At some point in your life, you might have a strong need for food and shelter. At other times, your social needs may be unfulfilled. Unfulfilled

needs hierarchy theory
Maslow's content motivation theory of five instinctive needs arranged in a hierarchy, whereby people are motivated to fulfill a higher need as a lower one becomes gratified.

needs create a tension that makes you want to find ways to reduce or satisfy those needs. The stronger your needs, the more motivated you are to satisfy them. Conversely, a satisfied need does not motivate.[7] In this section, we will look at the four content theories of motivation that dominate organizational thinking today.

Maslow's Needs Hierarchy Theory

One of the earliest and best-known content theories is **needs hierarchy theory.** Developed by psychologist Abraham Maslow, this theory condenses the numerous needs that scholars have identified into a hierarchy of five basic categories.[8] At the bottom are *physiological needs*, which include the need to

7.5.3 Core Project Team: Bala Akella, Wendy Chiou, Doug Clarke, Mike Crawford, Micha H.

Computer programmers like a good paycheck, but they love the recognition found in Easter eggs. Easter eggs are nuggets of graphical graffiti left behind by programmers in most software programs. Click in the right place or type in a special command, and a special message or image will appear. Some Easter eggs are inspired by individual programmers who gain respect by cleverly sneaking them by the quality inspectors. Other Easter eggs are created by the entire development team to fulfill their need for public recognition. For example, this hidden image of Apple Computer's headquarters, complete with a flag that waves in the direction of the user's mouse, scrolls the names of the team that developed the operating system. Software engineers have also introduced Easter eggs in some DVD-formatted movies. What needs are fulfilled when software engineers secretly insert Easter eggs into their programs?[9]

satisfy biological requirements for food, air, water, and shelter. Next come *safety needs*—the need for a secure and stable environment and the absence of pain, threat, or illness. *Belongingness* includes the need for love, affection, and interaction with other people. *Esteem* includes self-esteem through personal achievement as well as social esteem through recognition and respect from others. At the top of the hierarchy is *self-actualization*, which represents the need for self-fulfillment—a sense that the person's potential has been realized.

Maslow recognized that an employee's behavior is motivated simultaneously by several need levels, but behavior is motivated mostly by the lowest unsatisfied need at the time. As the person satisfies a lower-level need, the next higher need in the hierarchy becomes the primary motivator. This concept is known as the **satisfaction-progression process.** Even if a person is unable to satisfy a higher need, he or she will be motivated by it until it is eventually satisfied. Physiological needs are initially the most important, and people are motivated to satisfy them first. As they become gratified, safety needs emerge as the strongest motivator. As safety needs are satisfied, belongingness needs become most important, and so forth. The exception to the satisfaction-progression process is self-actualization; as people experience self-actualization, they desire more rather than less of this need.

Although Maslow's needs hierarchy is one of the best-known organizational behavior theories, the model is much too rigid to explain the dynamic and unstable characteristics of employee needs.[10] Researchers have found that individual needs do not cluster neatly around the five categories described in the model. Moreover, gratification of one need level does not necessarily lead to increased motivation to satisfy the next higher need level. Although Maslow's model may not predict employee needs as well as scholars initially expected, it provides an important introduction to employee needs and has laid the foundation for Alderfer's ERG theory, which has better research support.

Alderfer's ERG Theory

ERG theory was developed by organizational behavior scholar Clayton Alderfer to overcome the problems with Maslow's needs hierarchy theory.[11] ERG theory groups human needs into three broad categories: existence, relatedness, and growth. (Notice that the theory's name is based on the first letter of each need.) As Exhibit 5.1 illustrates, existence needs correspond to Maslow's physiological and safety needs. Relatedness needs refer mainly to Maslow's belongingness needs. Growth needs correspond to Maslow's esteem and self-actualization needs.

Existence needs include a person's physiological and physically related safety needs, such as the need for food, shelter, and safe working conditions. **Relatedness needs** include a person's need to interact with other people, receive public recognition, and feel secure around people (i.e., interpersonal safety). **Growth needs** consist of a person's self-esteem through personal achievement as well as the concept of self-actualization presented in Maslow's model.

ERG theory states that an employee's behavior is motivated simultaneously by more than one need level. Thus, you might try to satisfy your growth needs (such as by completing an assignment exceptionally well) even though your relatedness needs aren't completely satisfied. ERG theory applies the satisfaction-progression process described in Maslow's needs hierarchy model,

satisfaction-progression process
A process whereby people become increasingly motivated to fulfill a higher need as a lower need is gratified.

ERG theory
Alderfer's content motivation theory of three instinctive needs arranged in a hierarchy, in which people progress to the next higher need when a lower one is fulfilled, and regress to a lower need if unable to fulfill a higher one.

existence needs
A person's physiological and physically related safety needs, such as the need for food, shelter, and safe working conditions.

relatedness needs
A person's need to interact with other people, receive public recognition, and feel secure around people.

growth needs
A person's self-esteem through personal achievement as well as the concept of self-actualization.

customer. The employee who signs up the most new customers wins a $2,500 shopping spree; a dozen runners-up each receive $1,000. Bank One's reward plan is part of a trend toward more performance-based rewards. Performance-based rewards have existed since Babylonian days in the twentieth century B.C.[24] Today, they come in more varieties than ever before. Exhibit 6.2 lists the most common types of individual, team, and organizational performance-based rewards.

Individual Rewards One of the oldest performance-based rewards is the *piece rate*, which calculates pay by the number of units the employee produces. *Commissions* pay people on the basis of sales volume rather than units produced. For example, sales associates at department store chain Hudson Belk earn commissions in addition to their salary for the value of merchandise they sell to customers.[25] *Royalties* pay individuals a percentage of revenue from the resource or work ascribed to them. Some mining companies pay their exploration geologists royalties from the mineral deposits they discover. *Merit pay*—increasing the individual's pay on the basis of performance appraisal results—was common during times of high inflation, but most organizations now offer re-earnable *bonuses* for accomplishing specific tasks or achieving certain goals.

Team Rewards A decade ago, most institutional brokers on Wall Street were paid individual commissions. Today, the top dozen firms have shifted to salary and bonuses determined by team and organizational performance. Similar changes are occurring in retail brokerages as Merrill Lynch and other firms move brokers into teams.[26]

Companies across the United States are shifting from individual to more team-based reward systems.[27] One of the most popular team-based rewards is the **gainsharing plan.** Gainsharing motivates team members to reduce costs and increase labor efficiency in their work process. Typically, the company shares the cost savings with employees for one or two years.[28] An unusual example of gainsharing was recently introduced at St. Joseph's Hospital in Atlanta, Georgia. Cardiac surgeons can cut about $2,000 out of the $15,000 cost

gainsharing plan
A reward system that rewards team members for reducing costs and increasing labor efficiency in their work process.

Types of performance-based rewards

Team and organizational incentives keep Steel Dynamics profitable at a time when many American steel mills are in trouble. "You'll rarely see people standing around doing nothing," says Bob Soden, manager of engineering and services at the Butler, Indiana–based mini-mill. "Everyone is motivated by the pay systems to get in there and lend a hand when something breaks." Steel Dynamics production employees can double their $10 per hour base pay when the mill achieves production level targets. They earn another bonus by reducing input costs during production. Everyone from office assistants to workers running furnaces gets stock options twice a year. The company also hands out profit sharing bonuses across the workforce. Thanks to these financial incentives, the average Steel Dynamics employee (excluding officers) earns nearly $65,000 each year."[29] Why would Steel Dynamics rely on team and organizational rewards rather than individual rewards to motivate employees? *(Courtesy of Steel Dynamics, Inc.)*

of a heart bypass surgery operation by using less expensive sutures and avoiding opening supplies that aren't used. St. Joseph encourages this cost savings by paying surgeons 50 percent of the cost savings. Because of the emphasis on safety, this particular application of gainsharing required a special ruling from the U.S. government. "We're not withholding (services)," explains the surgeon who devised the pay plan. "We're just reducing waste."[30]

Gainsharing plans tend to improve team dynamics and pay satisfaction. They also create a reasonably strong E→P expectancy (see Chapter 5) because much of the cost reduction and labor efficiency is within the team's control. In other words, team members quickly learn that their work efficiencies increase the size of the gainsharing bonus.[31] One concern, however, is that gainsharing plans may increase workloads and reduce customer service in the long run as employees find ways to cut costs in the short term.

Organizational Rewards IKEA's Big Thank You Bonus, described at the beginning of this chapter, is typical of the emerging trend toward organizational rewards. The most common organizational rewards are employee stock ownership plans, stock options, and profit sharing plans.

employee stock ownership plans (ESOPs)
A reward system that encourages employees to buy shares of the company.

stock options
A reward system that gives employees the right to purchase company stock at a future date at a predetermined price.

profit sharing
A reward system that pays bonuses to employees based on the previous year's level of corporate profits.

■ **Employee stock ownership plans (ESOPs)** encourage employees to buy shares in the company, usually at a discounted price or with a no-interest loan from the company. Employees are subsequently rewarded through dividends and market appreciation of those shares. There are currently 10,000 ESOP plans representing 10 million employees throughout the United States. Most of these are in privately held companies, but you will also find ESOPs at Procter & Gamble, Home Depot, and other publicly traded firms.[32]

■ **Stock options** are a variation of ESOPs that give employees the right to purchase company stock at a future date at a predetermined price.[33] For example, your employer might offer you the right to purchase 100 shares at $50 two years or more from now. If the stock price two years from now is above $50, you could exercise your options by purchasing the shares from the company at $50 and selling them at a profit. If the price is below $50, you would wait until the stock price rises above that amount or let the options expire. Most North American high-technology firms offer stock options because they instantly connect new employees to the organization's success. As Global Connections 6.1 describes, stock options are also gaining popularity throughout Asia.

■ **Profit sharing** plans pay bonuses to employees on the basis of the previous year's level of corporate profits. These plans are most often found in firms that use teams and face plenty of competition, such as Southwest Airlines and Steel Dynamics. Tien Wah Press, a Malaysian printing company, also has a profit sharing plan that annually distributes a percentage of pretax profits to its 3,000 employees in Malaysia, Singapore, and Indonesia.[34]

How effective are organizational rewards? The evidence is mixed. The positive news is that ESOPs and stock options tend to align employee behaviors more closely with organizational objectives. In other words, they create an ownership culture in which employees feel aligned with the organization's success. According to one study, productivity rises by 4 percent annually at ESOP firms, compared with only 1.5 percent at non-ESOP firms. Profit sharing tends to create less of this ownership culture effect. However, it has the advantage of automatically adjusting employee compensation with the firm's prosperity, thereby reducing the need for layoffs or negotiated pay reductions during recessions.[35]

The main problem with organizational-level rewards is that employees often perceive a weak connection between individual performance and corporate profits or the value of company shares. Even in small firms, the company's stock price or profitability is influenced by economic conditions, competition, and other factors beyond the employee's immediate control. These organizational-level rewards also fail to motivate employees when

The Stock Option Generation Arrives in Asia

Most of the 3,000 staff at Micron Semiconductor's production plant in Singapore are keeping a close watch on the company's stock price. That's because the U.S.-based high-technology company recently gave every employee around the world options to buy 25 shares per year over the next four years at the fixed price of US$28.56 per share. If the stock price on the market is higher, employees immediately earn the difference. Micron's Singapore staff keep track of the company's stock performance with a scrolling electronic board on the cafeteria wall.

Micron employees are the latest group to become "Soggies"—the stock option generation. PepsiCo, the U.S. soft drink company, first granted stock options to employees worldwide back in 1989, making it a Soggie pioneer in Asia. Lucent Technologies granted 100 stock options to each of its 100,000 employees when it split away from AT&T in 1996. By 2000, the shares were worth nearly 10 years of wages for most Lucent employees in Thailand. "I still can't believe it," says Khun Taen, who works at Lucent's manufacturing plant near Bangkok.

Singapore Press Holdings and Singapore Airlines, two of the island-state's largest companies, have followed the American trend by distributing stock options to all employees. So did Cable & Wireless HKT, Hong Kong's telephone company, to replace the "thirteenth month" paycheck that all employees traditionally received. HKT's employees complained about losing their guaranteed bonus but are now seeking more stock options. "[HKT employees] will be actively seeking stock options—unlike our passive response before," says a union representative.

Sources: H. Chow, "All Micron Staff Get Stock Options," *Straits Times (Singapore),* November 14, 2000; Y. Cohen, "Stock Options Trickle Down to Thai Workers," *Christian Science Monitor,* March 27, 2000; Y. Ghahremani, "In the Company of Millionaires," *Asiaweek,* March 17, 2000, pp. 42ff.

profits are negligible or in bear markets, when stock prices decline. Indeed, morale may suffer in companies with these plans.[36]

Improving Reward Effectiveness

Performance-based rewards have been criticized for a variety of reasons.[37] One concern is that they distract employees from the motivation that comes from serving customers or achieving challenging objectives. Rewards also potentially create relationship problems. One study of performance-based pay reported that conflict increased between supervisors and staff when performance appraisal results were used to determine pay increases. It also created tensions between "star" employees and those with lower performance.[38]

A third criticism of performance-based pay systems is that they discourage creativity and risk taking because employees are less likely to explore new opportunities outside the realm of rewarded behavior or results. Lastly, many corporate leaders use rewards as quick fixes, rather than carefully diagnosing the real causes of the undesirable behavior. For example, one company hands out cash to employees who arrive early at company meetings and fines those who arrive late.[39] The company would be better off identifying the causes of lateness and changing the conditions, rather than using money to force a solution to the problem.

These concerns do not necessarily mean that we should abandon performance-based pay. On the contrary, evidence indicates that the top-performing companies around the world are more likely to have performance-based rewards.[40] Reward systems do motivate most employees, but only under the right conditions. Here are some of the more important strategies to improve reward effectiveness.

Link Rewards to Performance   Employees with better performance should be rewarded more than those with poorer performance.[41] This simple principle is a logical conclusion of both behavior modification (Chapter 2) and expectancy theory (Chapter 5), yet it seems to be unusually difficult to apply. A recent survey reported that one-third of the 770 U.S. and Canadian firms studied paid rewards to people who didn't meet minimum performance standards. This situation occurs partly because it is difficult to measure the many elements of job performance and organizational citizenship. Moreover, research suggests that performance-pay decisions are biased by organizational politics.[42]

How can we improve the pay-for-performance linkage? First, bias in pay systems can be minimized by introducing gainsharing, ESOPs, and other plans that rely on objective performance measures. Second, where subjective measures of performance are necessary, companies should rely on multiple sources of information. In other words, use 360-degree feedback to minimize biases from any single source (see Chapter 2). Third, companies need to apply rewards soon after the performance occurs, and in a large enough dose (such as a bonus rather than a pay increase) that employees can see the reward.[43]

Ensure That Rewards Are Relevant   Companies need to align rewards with performance within the employee's control. The more employees see a direct connection between their daily actions and the reward, the more they are motivated to improve performance.[44] Sears, Roebuck and Company rewards senior executives for corporate performance because they have some control over the Chicago-based retail giant's overall success. Bonuses for department sales managers, on the other hand, are on the basis of profits and customer satisfaction in their departments, but not for Sears's overall corporate performance.[45] Reward systems also need to correct for situational factors. Salespeople in one region may have higher sales because the economy is stronger there than elsewhere, so sales bonuses need to be adjusted for those economic factors.

Use Team Rewards for Interdependent Jobs   Organizations should use team (or organizational) rewards rather than individual rewards when employees work in highly interdependent jobs.[46] One reason is that individual performance is difficult to measure in these situations. For example, you can't determine how well one employee in a chemical processing plant contributes to the quality of the liquid produced. It is a team effort. A second reason is that team rewards tend to make employees more cooperative and less competitive. People see that their bonuses or other incentives depend on how well they work with co-workers, and they act accordingly.

The third reason for having team rewards is that they support employee preferences for team-based work arrangements. This result was found in a study of Xerox customer service representatives. The Xerox employees assigned to teams with purely team bonuses eventually accepted and preferred a team structure, whereas those put in teams without team rewards did not adapt as well to the team structure.[47]

Ensure Rewards Are Valued   It seems obvious that rewards work best when they are valued. Yet recall from Chapter 5 that companies sometimes make false assumptions about what employees want, with unfortunate consequences. The solution, of course, is to ask employees what they value. Campbell Soup did this when it introduced a special team reward program at one of its distribution centers. Executives at the food company thought distribution staff would want money as the top reward. Instead, employees said they wanted leather jackets with the Campbell Soup logo on the back as the winning team's prize.[48]

Watch Out for Unintended Consequences   Performance-based reward systems sometimes have unexpected—and undesirable—effects on employee behaviors.[49] Consider the pizza company that decided to reward its drivers for on-time delivery. The plan got more hot pizzas to customers on time, but it also increased the accident rates of its drivers because the incentive motivated them to drive recklessly.[50] Connections 6.2 describes a few other examples where reward systems had unintended consequences. The solution here is to carefully think through the consequences of rewards and, where possible, test incentives in a pilot project before applying them across the organization.

Beyond Money and Other Financial Rewards

At the beginning of this chapter, we said that money and other financial rewards have a complex effect on the needs, emotions, and self-identity of employees. Money also seems to have become a top priority when forming the employment relationship. "Show me the money"—the often repeated phrase from the film *Jerry Maguire*—captures this emerging reality as companies offer more signing bonuses, stock options, and BMWs.

But money isn't the only thing that motivates people to join an organization and perform effectively. "High performers don't go for the money," warns William Monahan, CEO of Oakdale, Minnesota–based Imation Corporation. "Good people want to be in challenging jobs and see a future where they can get even more responsibilities and challenges." Rafik O. Loutfy, a Xerox research center director, agrees with this assessment. "Our top stars say they want to make an impact—that's the most important thing," he says. "Feeling they are contributing and making a difference is highly motivational for them."[51] In other words, Imation, Xerox, and other companies motivate employees mainly by designing interesting and challenging jobs, which we discuss next.

JOB DESIGN

job design

The process of assigning tasks to a job, including the interdependency of those tasks with other jobs.

Organizational behavior scholars generally agree that the deepest passion for performing a job well comes from the work itself. **Job design** refers to the process of assigning tasks to a job, including the interdependency of those tasks with other jobs. A *job* is a set of tasks performed by one person.[52] Some jobs have very few tasks, each requiring limited skill or effort. Other jobs involve very complex tasks requiring highly trained tradespeople or professionals.

Information technology has transformed many jobs over the past couple of decades. It has increased responsibility and autonomy for many employees by improving direct access to information. Yet these same computer networks

When Rewards Go Wrong

There is an old saying that "what gets rewarded, gets done." But what companies reward isn't always what they had intended for employees to do. Here are a few dramatic examples:

- Toyota rewards its dealerships on the basis of customer satisfaction surveys, not just car sales. What Toyota discovered, however, is that this strategy motivates dealers to increase satisfaction scores, not customer satisfaction. One Toyota dealership received high ratings because it offered free detailing to every customer who returned a "Very Satisfied" survey. The dealership even had a special copy of the survey showing clients which boxes to check off. This tactic increased customer ratings, but not customer satisfaction.

Customer service incentives may have rewarded the wrong behavior at Toyota dealerships. *(© John Thoeming)*

- A building design company implemented an incentive plan that encouraged its engineers to design buildings so that they would be built below budget. One creative employee achieved this goal by simply scaling down the building's walls and ceilings by an inch or two. This approach saved thousands of dollars for the company and earned the engineer a sizable bonus, until the company and client discovered the shrunken results.

- Some investment analysts warn that stock options motivate executives to improve the value of the company's stock, not necessarily the company's long-term success. At IBM, stock-optioned executives have spent almost $39 billion repurchasing IBM stock from the market over the past five years. This amount is significantly more than the $33 billion IBM invested in its entire research and development budget over that same time span. The buyback rewarded IBM executives through improved stock prices, but probably didn't help IBM's development of new products and services for future profitability.

- Donnelly Mirrors introduced a gainsharing plan that motivated employees to reduce labor but not material costs. Employees at the automobile parts manufacturer knew they worked faster with sharp grinding wheels, so they replaced the expensive diamond wheels more often. This action reduced labor costs, thereby giving employees the gainsharing bonus. However, the labor savings were easily offset by much higher costs for diamond grinding wheels.

Sources: D. S. Hilzenrath, "Financial 'Performance' Options Getting a Second Look," *Washington Post*, April 1, 2001, p. H1; C. Teasdale, "Not All Firms Find Variable Pay Plans Pay Off," *St. Louis Business Journal*, September 28, 1998; F. F. Reichheld, *The Loyalty Effect* (Boston, MA: Harvard University Press, 1996), p. 236; D. R. Spitzer, "Power Rewards: Rewards That Really Motivate," *Management Review*, May 1996, pp. 45–50.

have reduced personal control in other jobs by monitoring employee actions, keystrokes, and whereabouts. The amount of personal control available to employees depends on how the technology is implemented.[53] Employability is another influence on job design. Employees are no longer hired into specific, narrowly defined jobs. Instead, they hold generic titles (associates, team members) and are expected to perform several clusters of tasks.[54]

Whether the change occurs through information technology or workforce flexibility, job design often produces an interesting conflict between the employee's motivation and ability to complete the work. To explain this issue more fully, we begin by describing early job design efforts aimed at increasing work efficiency through job specialization.

Job Design and Work Efficiency

Cindy Vang sits in a blue vinyl chair at Medtronic's assembly line in Minneapolis, Minnesota. Using a pair of tweezers, she loads 275 feedthroughs—tiny needlelike components for pacemakers and neurostimulators—onto a slotted storage block. She fills a block in about 15 minutes, then places the completed block on a shelf, and loads the next block.[55]

Cindy Vang works in a job with a high degree of **job specialization.** Job specialization occurs when the work required to build a pacemaker—or any other product or service—is subdivided into separate jobs assigned to different people. Each resulting job includes a very narrow subset of tasks, usually completed in a short cycle time. Cycle time is the time required to complete the task before starting over with a new work unit. For Cindy Vang, the cycle time for loading each feedthrough is a few seconds.

The economic benefits of dividing work into specialized jobs have been described and applied for at least two centuries. Over 2,300 years ago, the Chinese philosopher Mencius and the Greek philosopher Plato noted that division

job specialization
The result of division of labor in which each job now includes a subset of the tasks required to complete the product or service.

These sewing machine operators on the main assembly floor of the United International Corporation garment plant in Saipan (a U.S. territory in the Pacific Ocean) have a high degree of job specialization. An employee might complete each work unit (a piece of clothing) in a few minutes. This specialization improves work efficiency, but it can also lead to boredom and repetitive strain injuries. Some garment plants have introduced team-based work and job rotation to offset these problems, but some sewing jobs involve specialized work. How does job specialization improve work efficiency for sewing machine operators? (© AP/Wide World)

EXHIBIT 6.3

Horizontal and vertical
job specialization

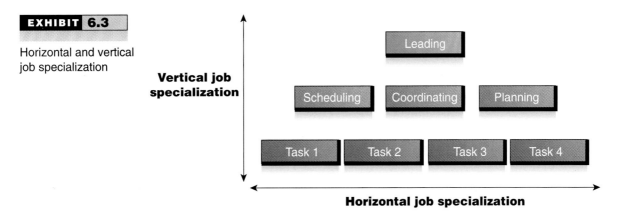

of labor improves work efficiency. In 1436 A.D., the waterways of Venice became an assembly line loading 10 galleons in just six hours. Over 200 years ago, economist Adam Smith described how 10 pin makers working alone could each produce no more than 20 pins per day. But Smith also described a factory where 10 pin makers collectively produced as many as 48,000 pins per day because they performed specialized tasks, such as straightening, cutting, sharpening, grinding, and whitening the pins.[56]

Why does job specialization potentially increase work efficiency? One reason is that employees have fewer tasks to juggle and therefore spend less time changing activities. They also require fewer physical and mental skills to accomplish the assigned work, so less time and fewer resources are needed for training. A third reason is that employees practice their tasks more frequently with shorter work cycles, so jobs are mastered quickly. Lastly, work efficiency increases because employees with specific aptitudes or skills can be matched more precisely to the jobs for which they are best suited.[57]

Adam Smith's example of pin manufacturing mainly describes *horizontal job specialization,* in which the basic physical behaviors required to provide a product or service are divided into different jobs (see Exhibit 6.3). With horizontal job specialization, employees perform fewer tasks. *Vertical job specialization,* on the other hand, refers to separating physical tasks from the administration of those tasks (planning, organizing, scheduling, etc.). In other words, vertical job specialization divorces the "managing" job functions from the "doing" job functions.

Scientific Management   One of the strongest advocates of job specialization was Frederick Winslow Taylor, an industrial engineer who introduced the principles of **scientific management** in the early 1900s.[58] Scientific management involves systematically partitioning work into its smallest elements and standardizing tasks to achieve maximum efficiency. Taylor advocated vertical job specialization so that detailed procedures and work practices are developed by engineers, enforced by supervisors, and executed by employees. He also applied horizontal job specialization, such as narrowing the supervisor's role to such a degree that one person manages operational efficiency, another manages inspection, and another is the disciplinarian. Through scientific management, Taylor also popularized many organizational practices that are commonly found today, such as goal setting, employee training, and incentive systems.

scientific management
Involves systematically partitioning work into its smallest elements and standardizing tasks to achieve maximum efficiency.

There is ample evidence that scientific management has improved efficiency in many work settings. One of Taylor's earliest interventions was at a ball bearing factory where 120 women each worked 55 hours per week. Through job specialization and work efficiency analysis, Taylor increased production by two-thirds using a workforce of only 35 women working fewer than 45 hours per week. Taylor also doubled the employees' previous wages. No doubt, some of the increased productivity can be credited to improved training, goal setting, and work incentives, but job specialization also contributed to the success of scientific management.

Problems with Job Specialization   Job specialization tries to increase work efficiency, but it doesn't necessarily improve job performance because job specialization ignores the effects of job content on employees.[59] Some jobs—such as Cindy Vang's task of loading feedthroughs—are so specialized that they are tedious, trivial, and socially isolating. Job specialization was supposed to let companies buy cheap, unskilled labor. Instead, many have to offer higher wages—some call it *discontentment pay*—to compensate for the job dissatisfaction of narrowly defined work.[60] Job specialization also costs more in terms of higher turnover, absenteeism, sabotage, and mental health problems. Work quality is often lower with highly specialized jobs because employees see only a small part of the process. As one observer of automobile assembly line work reports: "Often [employees] did not know how their jobs related to the total picture. Not knowing, there was no incentive to strive for quality—what did quality even mean as it related to a bracket whose function you did not understand."[61]

Perhaps the most important reason job specialization has not been as successful as expected is that it ignores the *motivational potential of jobs.* As jobs become specialized, the work tends to become easier to perform, but it is less motivating. As jobs become more complex, work motivation increases, but the ability to master the job decreases. Maximum job performance occurs somewhere between these two extremes, where most people can eventually perform the job tasks efficiently, yet the work is interesting.

Job Design and Work Motivation

Industrial engineers may have overlooked the motivational effects of job characteristics, but these effects are now the central focus of many job design changes.[62] Frederick Herzberg cast a spotlight on the motivational potential of job content with his motivator–hygiene theory, described in Chapter 5.[63] It might seem rather obvious to us today that the job itself is a source of motivation, but it was radical thinking when Herzberg proposed the idea in the 1950s.

Herzberg's writing and subsequent research by organizational behavior scholars has led to the **job characteristics model,** shown in Exhibit 6.4. This model details the motivational properties of jobs as well as specific personal and organizational consequences of these properties.[64] The job characteristics model identifies five core job dimensions that produce three psychological states. Employees who experience these psychological states tend to have higher levels of internal work motivation (motivation from the work itself), job satisfaction (particularly, satisfaction with the work itself), and work effectiveness.

job characteristics model
A job design model that relates the motivational properties of jobs to specific personal and organizational consequences of these properties.

EXHIBIT **6.4**   The job characteristics model

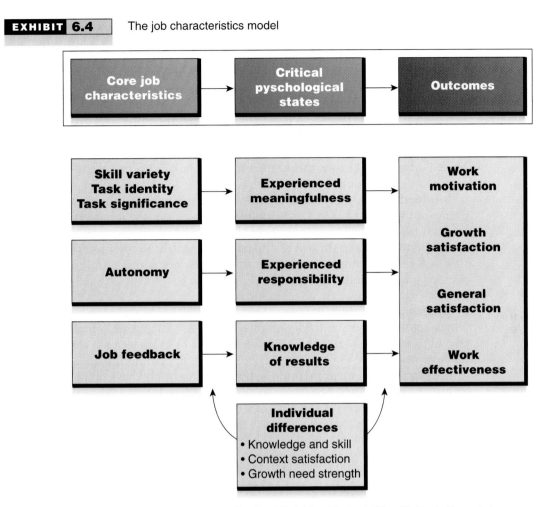

Source: J. R. Hackman and G. Oldham, *Work Redesign* (Reading, MA: Addison-Wesley, 1980), p. 90. Used with permission.

Core Job Characteristics   The job characteristics model identifies five core job characteristics (see Exhibit 6.4). Under the right conditions, employees are more motivated and satisfied when jobs have higher levels of these characteristics.

skill variety
The extent to which employees must use different skills and talents to perform tasks within their job.

▪ **Skill variety** refers to using different skills and talents to complete a variety of work activities. For example, salesclerks who normally only serve customers might be assigned the additional duties of stocking inventory and changing storefront displays.

▪ **Task identity** is the degree to which a job requires completion of a whole or identifiable piece of work, such as doing something from beginning to end, or where it is easy to see how one's work fits into the whole product or service. An employee who assembles an entire computer modem rather than just soldering in the circuitry would develop a stronger sense of ownership or identity with the final product.

▪ **Task significance** is the degree to which the job has a substantial impact on the organization and/or larger society. For instance, Medtronic executives

task identity
The degree to which a job requires completion of a whole or identifiable piece of work.

task significance
The degree to which the job has a substantial impact on the organization and/or larger society.

autonomy
The degree to which a job gives employees the freedom, independence, and discretion to schedule their work and determine the procedures used in completing it.

job feedback
The degree to which employees can tell how well they are doing based on direct sensory information from the job itself.

realize that Cindy Vang (described earlier) and many other employees have low skill variety, so they have special sessions where patients give testimonials to remind staff of their task significance. "We have patients who come in who would be dead if it wasn't for us," says a Medtronic production supervisor. Little wonder that 86 percent of Medtronic employees say their work has special meaning and 94 percent feel pride in what they accomplish.[65]

▪ **Autonomy** is the degree to which the job provides employees with freedom, independence, and discretion in scheduling the work and determining the procedures to be used to complete the work. In autonomous jobs, employees make their own decisions rather than relying on detailed instructions from supervisors or procedure manuals.

▪ **Job feedback** is the degree to which employees can tell how well they are doing on the basis of direct sensory information from the job itself. Airline pilots can tell how well they land their aircraft, and physicians can see whether their operations have improved the patient's health. Some research suggests that task feedback has an important effect on reducing role ambiguity and improving job satisfaction.[66]

Critical Psychological States   The five core job characteristics affect employee motivation and satisfaction through three critical psychological states.[67] One of these is *experienced meaningfulness*—the belief that one's work is worthwhile or important. Skill variety, task identity, and task significance contribute directly to the job's meaningfulness. If the job has high levels of all three characteristics, employees are likely to feel that their job is highly meaningful. Meaningfulness drops as the job loses one or more of these characteristics.

Work motivation and performance increase when employees feel personally accountable for the outcomes of their efforts. Autonomy directly contributes to this feeling of *experienced responsibility*. Employees must be assigned control of their work environment to feel responsible for their successes and failures. The third critical psychological state is *knowledge of results*. Employees want information about the consequences of their work effort. Knowledge of results can originate from co-workers, supervisors, or clients. However, job design focuses on knowledge of results from the work itself.

Individual Differences   Job redesign doesn't increase work motivation for everyone in every situation. Employees must have the required skills and knowledge to master the more challenging work. Otherwise, job redesign tends to increase stress and reduce job performance. A second condition is that employees must be reasonably satisfied with their work environment (e.g., working conditions, job security, salaries) before job redesign affects work motivation. A third condition is that employees must have strong growth needs. People with strong growth needs have satisfied their relatedness or existence needs, and are looking for challenges from the work itself (see Chapter 5). In contrast, improving the core job characteristics will have little motivational effect on people who are focused primarily on existence or relatedness needs.[68]

Increasing Work Motivation through Job Design

Three main strategies are used to increase the motivational potential of jobs: job rotation, job enlargement, and job enrichment. This section also identifies several ways to implement job enrichment.

Police officers in Pulaski, Tennessee, are feeling plenty of task significance, thanks to a unique video program that shows them at work. For nine months, a reserve officer videotaped staff in field assignments, office work, meetings, and organized events of fellowship. With inspirational background music, the final program featured each officer in the course of his or her duties. Officers were clearly moved when the tape was presented for the first time at the year-end holiday party. Everyone received a copy with thanks for her or his contribution to the community. Pulaski's recently retired assistant police chief sums up the video's effect: "The video allows officers to see themselves through the eyes of others; realize how important their work appears to others; understand how integral their contribution is to accomplishing the goals of the agency; and recognize how vital they are to the everyday operations of the department."[70] In what other ways might a police department increase officer perceptions of the task significance among police officers and other staff? *(Carl Sutton, © 1999 Almost Life Size Productions)*

Job Rotation   **Job rotation** is the practice of moving employees from one job to another. Consider a large one-hour photo finishing retail outlet where one employee interacts with customers, another operates the photo finishing machine, and a third puts the finished product into envelopes and files them for pickup. Job rotation would occur where employees move around those three jobs every few hours or days.

Moving employees around different jobs might reduce job boredom, but most organizations introduce job rotation mainly to develop a flexible workforce. Employees become multi-skilled, so they can fill in vacancies and staff shortages. A third reason for introducing job rotation is to reduce the incidence of repetitive strain injuries. Carrier Corporation uses job rotation for this reason. The air conditioning manufacturer identified complementary jobs so that employees move around to different jobs to use different muscles, thereby reducing strain on one muscle.[69]

Job Enlargement   Rather than rotating employees through different jobs, **job enlargement** combines tasks into one job. This approach might involve combining two or more complete jobs into one, or just adding one or two more tasks to an existing job. Either way, the job's skill variety has increased because there are more tasks to perform. A recent example of job enlargement is video journalists who perform tasks previously handled by a three- or four-person news crew. As Exhibit 6.5 illustrates, a traditional news team consists of a camera operator, a sound and lighting specialist, and the journalist who writes and presents or narrates the story. Video journalists perform all these tasks. Some are even using notebook computers with video software to edit the final report in the field, then upload the story to the television network using wireless technology.

Job enlargement significantly improves work efficiency and flexibility. However, research suggests that simply giving employees more tasks only minimally improves motivation, performance, and job satisfaction. Instead, these benefits result only when skill variety is combined with more autonomy and job knowledge.[71] In other words, employees are motivated when they have a variety of tasks *and* have the freedom and knowledge to structure their work to achieve the highest satisfaction and performance. These job characteristics are at the heart of job enrichment, which we discuss next.

Job Enrichment   **Job enrichment** occurs when employees are given more responsibility for scheduling, coordinating, and planning their own work.

job rotation
The practice of moving employees from one job to another.

job enlargement
Increasing the number of tasks employees perform within their job.

Job enlargement of
video journalist

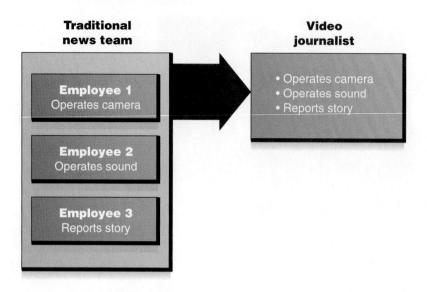

job enrichment
Employees are given
more responsibility
for scheduling, coor-
dinating, and plan-
ning their own work.

empowerment
A feeling of control
and self-efficacy that
emerges when
people are given
power in a previously
powerless situation.

Although some writers suggest that job enrichment is any strategy that increases one or more of the core job characteristics, Herzberg strongly argued
that jobs are enriched only through autonomy and the resulting feelings of
responsibility.[72] Notice that this definition of job enrichment relates directly to
vertical job loading because it reverses vertical job specialization, which was described earlier. There are numerous ways to enrich jobs, but we will discuss the
three most popular methods: empowering employees, forming natural work
units, and establishing client relationships.

Empowering employees   Karl Heid keeps a laminated card in his wallet
signed by the CEO of Ford Motor Company. It says: "Don't ask, just do it." The
miniature agreement gives the material handling supervisor the right to put
his good ideas into action and the responsibility to be accountable for the results. DaimlerChrysler is doing the same thing right down to the plant floor. "A
trend has been to give more responsibility to the [plant] floor and to cascade
that responsibility down to empower our people," says a DaimlerChrysler
spokesperson.[73]

Ford, DaimlerChrysler, and many other organizations are trying to empower
employees. The definition of **empowerment** is still under discussion, but we
will cautiously define empowerment as a feeling of control and self-efficacy
that emerges when people are given power in a previously powerless situation.[74]
Karl Heid and other empowered employees are given autonomy—freedom, independence, and discretion over their work activities. They are assigned work
that has high levels of task significance—importance to the organization and society. Empowered employees also have control over performance feedback,
which guides their work. Notice from the definition that empowered employees
have feelings of self-efficacy; that is, they believe that they are capable of successfully completing the task (see Chapter 2). When these ingredients are in
place, empowerment can have a noticeable effect on employee motivation and
performance.[75]

Forming natural work units   Another way to enrich jobs is to group tasks
into a natural grouping, such as completing a whole task. An example of forming a natural work unit would be assembling an entire computer modem

Traditionally, television networks required up to four people to shoot a news clip: a reporter, camera operator, sound operator, and lighting person. Now, CNN and other companies want one video journalist to perform all four jobs. "Look for the quick introduction of small, high-quality DV cameras and laptop editing equipment, enabling us to deploy smaller reporting teams, one or two people at a time, when it makes sense," CNN executives wrote in a recent memo to employees. "[C]orrespondents would do well to learn how to shoot and edit . . . and smart shooters and editors will learn how to write and track." The memo continues by saying that "CNN will always value exceptional ability, [but] the more multi-talented a newsgatherer, the more opportunity the News Group will provide that person."[77] According to the job characteristics model, how would the video journalist job have more motivational potential than each of the more specialized jobs?
(© Ted Thai/TimePix)

rather than just some parts of it. Or it might involve assigning employees to a specific client group, such as managing entire portfolios for specific clients rather than taking random client calls from a customer service pool. Forming natural work units gives jobholders stronger feelings of responsibility for an identifiable body of work. They feel a sense of ownership and, therefore, tend to increase job quality. Forming natural work units increases task identity and task significance because employees perform a complete product or service and can more readily see how their work affects others.

Establishing client relationships As mentioned, some natural work units assign employees to a specific client group. However, establishing client relationships takes this process one step further by putting employees in *direct contact* with their clients rather than using the supervisor as a go-between. The key factor is direct communication with clients. These clients submit work and provide feedback directly to the employee rather than through a supervisor. By being directly responsible for specific clients, employees have more information and can make decisions affecting those clients.[76]

Brooklyn Union, a New York gas company, has enriched the jobs of field distribution crews by establishing client relationships. At one time, these crews would only install pipes from the main lines to the house. A customer service representative would then come into the house to finish the work. Now, the distribution employees do the entire job and work directly with customers. After the distribution employees have installed the pipes, they clean off their shoes and enter the house to unlock the gas, relight the pilot light, and check the results. The customer deals with one person or crew, and the field staff feel a stronger sense of obligation to their client.[78]

Job Design Prospects and Problems

Job rotation, enlargement, and enrichment are now common in the United States. Research suggests that job design interventions have a much higher survival rate than most other work interventions and are generally effective. In particular, employees with high growth needs in enriched jobs have higher job satisfaction and work motivation, along with lower absenteeism and turnover. Productivity is also higher when task identity and job feedback are improved. Product and service quality tend to improve because job enrichment increases the jobholder's felt responsibility and sense of ownership over the product or service. Quality improvements are most apparent when employees complete a natural work unit or establish client relationships.[79]

Obstacles in Job Design   In spite of these potential benefits, job design is not easy to implement. Objective measures of job characteristics are expensive, and the *perceived* job characteristics measures typically used by scholars and consultants may be distorted by the employee's attitudes regarding other aspects of the job.[80] Job design interventions also face resistance to change. Some supervisors don't like job redesign interventions because they change their roles and may threaten job security.[81] Labor union leaders have been bitter foes of job specialization and scientific management, yet many are concerned that job enrichment programs are management ploys to get more work out of employees for less money. Unskilled employees may lack the confidence or growth need strength to learn more challenging tasks. Skilled employees are known to resist job redesign because they believe the intervention will undermine their power base and force them to perform lower-status work.[82]

Lastly, an ongoing dilemma with job design is finding the ideal balance between job enrichment and specialization. There are several competing factors to consider. Specialized jobs may improve work efficiency, but performance may fall if this specialization reduces employee motivation. Job enrichment may increase motivation, but performance may fall if employees lack the skills necessary to perform these challenging tasks. Job enrichment may increase recruiting and training costs, whereas job specialization may increase payroll costs if companies provide discontentment pay to entice people into boring jobs.[83] Job enrichment improves product quality, but error rates may increase when tasks become so challenging that employees lack the necessary skills or experience stress.[84] Of course, job specialization also increases stress if employees do not make effective use of their talents in narrowly defined jobs.

MOTIVATING YOURSELF THROUGH SELF-LEADERSHIP

While most companies are busy finding new "carrots" to motivate employees, Key Resources is teaching its employees to motivate themselves. On their first day of work at the Atlanta-based company, new recruits are brought to a quiet room and asked to write down what they want to do and achieve, from personal to professional goals. "The intention is to give them a process, a formula to set and achieve goals," explains Key Resources chief executive Jeff Moore. "People are self-motivated."[85]

Jeff Moore recognizes that employees motivate themselves and direct their own behavior most of the time. According to a recent survey, corporate leaders also identify self-motivation as one of the most important features to look for in new hires.[86] This is probably because direct supervision is becoming too expensive and is incompatible with the values and expectations of today's workforce.

self-leadership
The process of influencing oneself to establish the self-direction and self-motivation needed to perform a task.

The emerging view is that employees should manage themselves most of the time through **self-leadership**—the process of influencing oneself to establish the self-direction and self-motivation needed to perform a task.[87] This concept includes a tool kit of behavioral activities borrowed from social learning theory (Chapter 2) and goal setting (Chapter 5). It also includes constructive thought processes that have been studied extensively in sports psychology. Overall, self-leadership takes the view that individuals mostly regulate their own actions through these behavioral and cognitive (thought) activities.

Although we are in the early stages of understanding the dynamics of self-leadership, the five main elements of this process have been identified

EXHIBIT 6.6   Elements of self-leadership

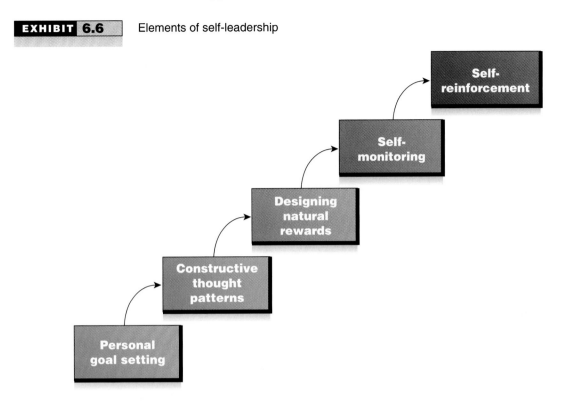

(Exhibit 6.6). These elements, which generally follow each other in a sequence, include personal goal setting, constructive thought patterns, designing natural rewards, self-monitoring, and self-reinforcement.[88]

Personal Goal Setting

The first step in self-leadership is to set goals for your own work effort. This step applies the ideas we learned in Chapter 5 on goal setting, such as identifying goals that are specific, relevant, and challenging. The main difference between personal goal setting and our previous discussion is that goals are set alone, rather than assigned by or jointly decided with a supervisor. According to the self-leadership literature, effective organizations establish norms whereby employees have a natural tendency to set their own goals to motivate themselves.[89]

Constructive Thought Patterns

Before beginning a task and while performing it, employees should engage in positive (constructive) thoughts about that work and its accomplishment. In particular, employees are more motivated and better prepared to accomplish a task after they have engaged in positive self-talk and mental imagery.

Positive Self-Talk   Do you ever talk to yourself? Most of us do, according to a recent study of undergraduate students.[90] **Self-talk** refers to any situation

self-talk
Talking to ourselves about our own thoughts or actions for the purpose of increasing our self-efficacy and navigating through decisions in a future event.

in which we talk to ourselves about our own thoughts or actions. Some of this internal communication assists the decision-making process, such as weighing the advantages of a particular choice. Self-leadership is mostly interested in evaluative self-talk, in which you evaluate your capabilities and accomplishments.

The problem with most evaluative self-talk is that it is negative; we criticize much more than encourage or congratulate ourselves. Negative self-talk undermines our self-efficacy, which, in turn, undermines our potential for performing a particular task.[91] In contrast, positive self-talk creates a can-do belief and thereby increases motivation by raising our E→P expectancy. We often hear that professional athletes psych themselves up before an important event. They tell themselves that they can achieve their goal and that they have practiced enough to reach that goal. They motivate themselves through self-talk.

Mental Imagery   You've probably heard the phrase "I'll cross that bridge when I come to it." Self-leadership takes the opposite view. It suggests that we need to practice a task mentally and imagine performing it successfully beforehand. This process is known as **mental imagery**.[92]

As you can see from this definition, mental imagery has two parts. One part involves practicing the task mentally, anticipating obstacles to goal accomplishment, and working out solutions to those obstacles before they occur. By mentally walking through the activities required to accomplish the task, we

mental imagery
Mentally practicing a task and visualizing its successful completion.

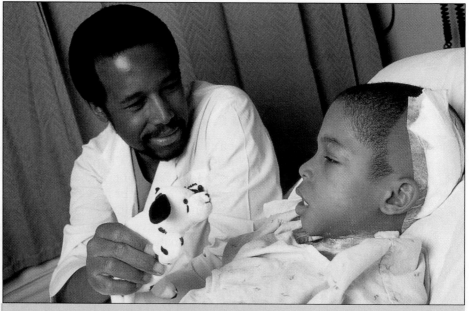

As one of the world's leading neurosurgeons, Dr. Ben Carson uses mental imagery to visualize each medical operation he performs—up to 500 of them each year. "I think through every procedure: how I expect it to go, how long each phase will last, when I can move on to the next one," explains the chief of pediatric neurosurgery at Johns Hopkins Hospital in Baltimore. Carson also imagines the worst thing that could happen, and what he should do if it does. "I always anticipate the worst-case scenario," says Carson.[93] How might Dr. Carson apply other elements of the self-leadership model in his work? *(Courtesy of Carson Scholars Fund)*

begin to see problems that may occur. We can then imagine what responses would be best for each contingency.[94]

While one part of mental imagery helps us anticipate things that could go wrong, the other part involves visualizing successful completion of the task. We imagine the experience of completing the task and the positive results that follow. Everyone daydreams and fantasizes about being in a successful situation. You might imagine yourself being promoted to your boss's job, receiving a prestigious award, or taking time off work. This visualization increases goal commitment and motivates us to complete the task effectively.

Designing Natural Rewards

Self-leadership recognizes that employees actively craft their jobs. To varying degrees, they can alter tasks and work relationships to make the work more motivating.[95] One way to build natural rewards into the job is to alter the way a task is accomplished. People often have enough discretion in their jobs to make slight changes to suit their needs and preferences. For instance, you might try out a new software program to design an idea, rather than sketching the image with pencil. By using the new software, you are adding challenge to a task that may have otherwise been mundane.

Self-Monitoring

Self-monitoring is the process of keeping track of one's progress toward a goal. In the section on job design, we learned that feedback from the job itself communicates whether we are accomplishing the task successfully. Self-monitoring includes the notion of consciously checking that naturally occurring feedback at regular intervals. It also includes designing artificial feedback where natural feedback does not occur. Salespeople might arrange to receive monthly reports on sales levels in their territory. Production staff might have gauges or computer feedback systems installed so that they can see how many errors are made on the production line. Research suggests that people who have control over when they receive performance feedback perform their tasks better than those with feedback assigned by others.[96]

Self-Reinforcement

Self-leadership includes the social learning theory concept of self-reinforcement. Self-reinforcement occurs whenever an employee has control over a reinforcer but doesn't take the reinforcer until completing a self-set goal (see Chapter 2).[97] A common example is taking a break after reaching a predetermined stage of your work. The work break is a self-induced form of positive reinforcement. Self-reinforcement also occurs when you decide to do a more enjoyable task after completing a task that you dislike. For example, after slogging through a difficult report, you might decide to spend time doing a more pleasant task, such as catching up on industry news by scanning websites.

Self-Leadership in Practice

It's too early to say that every component of self-leadership is useful, but evidence suggests that these practices generally improve self-efficacy, motivation, and performance. Studies in sports psychology indicate that self-set goals and constructive thought processes improve individual performance. For example, young ice-skaters who received self-talk training improved their performance one year later. Self-talk and mental imagery have also improved performance of tennis players and female college swimmers. Indeed, studies show that almost all Olympic athletes rely on mental rehearsal and positive self-talk to achieve their performance goals.[98]

One of the few studies in organizational settings reported that new employees who practiced self-set goals and self-reinforcement had higher internal motivation. Another study found that airline employees who received constructive thought training experienced better mental performance, enthusiasm, and job satisfaction than co-workers who did not receive this training.[99]

People with a high degree of conscientiousness and internal locus of control are more likely to apply self-leadership strategies. However, one of the benefits of self-leadership is that it can be learned. Training programs have helped employees improve their self-leadership skills. Organizations can also encourage self-leadership by providing sufficient autonomy and establishing rewards that reinforce self-leadership behaviors. Employees are also more likely to engage in self-monitoring in companies that emphasize continuous measurement of performance.[100] Overall, self-leadership promises to be an important concept and practice for improving employee motivation and performance.

Self-leadership, job design, and rewards are valuable approaches to motivating people in organizational settings. However, they are not the only ways to motivate. Motivation is derived from a person's unique combination of natural and learned needs. Each of these needs can be fulfilled in many ways and from various sources. In some respects, many of the topics covered later in this book—such as team cohesiveness and corporate culture—also affect employee motivation.

CHAPTER SUMMARY

Money and other financial rewards are a fundamental part of the employment relationship. They also potentially fulfill existence, relatedness, and growth needs. People experience various emotions and hold many attitudes toward financial rewards. They also tend to identify themselves in terms of how much money they have acquired and dispersed.

Organizations reward employees for their membership and seniority, job status, competencies, and performance. Membership-based rewards may attract job applicants, and seniority-based rewards reduce turnover. However, they are more likely to discourage turnover among those with the lowest performance. Rewards on the basis of job status try to maintain internal equity and motivate employees to compete for promotions. However, job status-based rewards can lead to organizational politics and create a psychological distance between employees and management.

Competency-based rewards are becoming increasingly popular because they improve workforce flexibility and are consistent with the emerging idea of employability. However, competency-based rewards tend to be measured subjectively and can result in higher costs as employees spend more time learning new skills.

Piece rates, commissions, and other individual performance-based rewards have existed for centuries and are widely used. Many companies are shifting to team-based rewards, such as gainsharing plans, and to organizational rewards, such as employee stock ownership plans (ESOPs), stock options, and profit sharing. ESOPs and stock options create an ownership culture, but employees often perceive a weak connection between individual performance and the organizational reward.

Financial rewards have been criticized for being used as quick fixes. There is also a risk that they distract employees from the motivational potential of the work, create a psychological distance between the person giving and the person receiving the reward, and discourage creativity and risk taking. To improve reward effectiveness, organizational leaders should ensure that rewards are linked to work performance, are aligned with performance within the employee's control, are valued by employees, and do not have unintended consequences. Additionally, leaders should ensure that team rewards are used where jobs are interdependent.

Job design involves assigning tasks to a job and distributing work throughout the organization. Job specialization, which subdivides work into separate jobs for different people, increases work efficiency because employees master the tasks quickly, spend less time changing tasks, require less training, and can be matched more closely with the jobs best suited to their skills. However, job specialization may reduce work motivation, create mental health problems, lower product or service quality, and increase costs through discontentment pay, absenteeism, and turnover.

Contemporary job design strategies reverse job specialization through job rotation, job enlargement, and job enrichment. The job characteristics model is a template for job redesign that specifies core job dimensions, psychological states, and individual differences. Companies often enrich jobs through empowering employees, forming natural work units, and establishing client relationships.

Self-leadership is the process of influencing oneself to establish the self-direction and self-motivation needed to perform a task. This process includes personal goal setting, constructive thought patterns, designing natural rewards, self-monitoring, and self-reinforcement. Constructive thought patterns include self-talk and mental imagery. Self-talk refers to any situation in which a person talks to him- or herself about his or her own thoughts or actions. Mental imagery involves practicing a task mentally and imagining performing it successfully beforehand.

KEY TERMS

autonomy, p. 180

employee stock ownership plans (ESOPs), p. 171

empowerment, p. 183

gainsharing plan, p. 169

job characteristics model, p. 178

job design, p. 174

job enlargement, p. 181

job enrichment, p. 183

job evaluation, p. 167

job feedback, p. 180

job rotation, p. 181

job specialization, p. 176

mental imagery, p. 186

profit sharing, p. 171

scientific management, p. 177

self-leadership, p. 184

self-talk, p. 185

skill variety, p. 179

skill-based pay, p. 168

stock options, p. 171

task identity, p. 180

task significance, p. 180

DISCUSSION QUESTIONS

1. As a consultant, you have been asked to recommend either a gainsharing or a profit sharing plan for employees who work in the four regional distribution and warehousing facilities of a large retail organization. Which reward system would you recommend? Explain your answer.

2. Some city councils pay bonuses to parking contractors when they issue more than a predetermined minimum number of parking fines each month. Discuss the benefits and potential problems associated with this reward system.

3. Yakka Tire Corporation has redesigned its production facilities around a team-based system. However, the company president believes that employees will not be motivated unless they receive incentives on the basis of their individual performance. Give three explanations why Yakka Tire should also introduce team-based rewards in this setting.

4. Under what conditions would job specialization be most appropriate?

5. Most of us have watched pizzas being made while we are waiting to pick one up from a pizza shop. What level of job specialization do you usually notice in these operations? Why does this high or low level of specialization exist? If some pizza shops have different levels of specialization than others, identify the contingencies that might explain the differences.

6. In a large grocery store, cashiers spend most of their time at the cash register, stock handlers focus on moving goods from the storeroom onto the shelves, and cleaners keep the area clean. But Aldi, a German-based company, has opened grocery superstores where cashiers are asked to bring stock from storage areas, stock shelves, and clean the floors at the end of the day. Use the job characteristics model to explain the implications of Aldi's revised job description for cashiers.

7. Tomorrow, you present your first report to senior management to extend funding for your unit's special initiative. All the materials are ready for the

presentation. Following the five steps in self-leadership, describe how you can prepare for that meeting.

8. Several elements of self-leadership are derived from concepts presented earlier in this book.

Identify those concepts and explain how they are applied in self-leadership.

C A S E   S T U D Y   6.1

KEEPING SUZANNE CHALMERS

Thomas Chan hung up the telephone and sighed. The vice president of software engineering at Advanced Photonics Inc. (API) had just spoken to Suzanne Chalmers, who called to arrange a meeting with Chan later that day. She didn't say what the meeting was about, but Chan almost instinctively knew that Suzanne was going to quit after working at API for the past four years. Chalmers is a software engineer in Internet Protocol (IP), the software that directs fiber-optic light through API's routers. It is very specialized work, and Suzanne is one of API's top talents in that area.

Thomas Chan had been through this before. A valued employee would arrange a private meeting. The meeting would begin with a few pleasantries; then the employee announces that he or she wants to quit. Some employees say they are leaving because of the long hours and stressful deadlines. They say they need to decompress, get to know the kids again, or whatever. But that's not usually the real reason. Almost every organization in this industry is scrambling to keep up with technological advances and the competition. They would just leave one stressful job for another one.

Also, many of the people who leave API join a start-up company a few months later. These start-up firms can be pressure cookers where everyone works 16 hours each day and has to perform a variety of tasks. For example, engineers in these small firms might have to meet customers or work on venture capital proposals rather than focus on specialized tasks related to their knowledge. API has over 1,000 employees, so it is easier to assign people to work that matches their technical competencies.

No, the problem isn't the stress or long hours, Chan thought. The problem is money—too much money. Most of the people who leave are millionaires. Suzanne Chalmers is one of them. Thanks to generous stock options that have skyrocketed on the stock markets, many employees at API have more money than they can use. Most are under 40 years old, so they are too young to retire. But their financial independence gives them less reason to remain with API.

The Meeting

The meeting with Suzanne Chalmers took place a few hours after the telephone call. It began like the others, with the initial pleasantries and brief discussion about progress on the latest fiber-optic router project. Then, Suzanne made her well-rehearsed statement: "Thomas, I've really enjoyed working here, but I'm going to leave Advanced Photonics." Suzanne took a breath, then looked at Chan. When he didn't reply after a few seconds, she continued: "I need to take time off. You know, get away to recharge my batteries. The project's nearly done and the team can complete it without me. Well, anyway, I'm thinking of leaving."

Chan spoke in a calm voice. He suggested that Suzanne should take an unpaid leave for two or maybe three months, complete with paid benefits, then return refreshed. Suzanne politely rejected that offer, saying that she needs to get away from work for a while. Thomas then asked Suzanne whether she was unhappy with her work environment—whether she was getting the latest computer technology to do her work and whether there were problems with co-workers. The workplace was fine, Susanne replied. The job was getting a bit routine, but she had a comfortable workplace with excellent co-workers.

Chan then apologized for the cramped work space, due mainly to the rapid increase in the number of people hired over the past year. He suggested that if Suzanne took a couple of months off, API would give her special treatment with a larger work space with a better view of the park behind the campuslike building when she returned. She politely thanked Chan for that offer, but it wasn't what she needed. Besides, it wouldn't be fair to have a large work space when other team members work in smaller quarters.

Chan was running out of tactics, so he tried his last hope: money. He asked whether Suzanne had higher offers. Suzanne replied that she regularly received calls from other companies, and some of them offered more money. Most were start-up firms that offered a lower salary but higher potential gains in stock options. Chan knew from market surveys that Suzanne was already paid well in the industry. He also knew that API couldn't compete on stock option potential. Employees working in start-up firms sometimes saw their shares increase by five or ten times their initial value, whereas shares at API and other large firms increased more slowly. However, Chan promised Suzanne that he would recommend that she receive a significant raise—maybe 25 percent more—and more stock options. Chan added that Chalmers was one of API's most valuable employees and that the company would suffer if she left the firm.

The meeting ended with Chalmers promising to consider Chan's offer of higher pay and share options. Two days later, Chan received her resignation in writing. Five months later, Chan learned that after a few months traveling with her husband, Chalmers joined a start-up software firm in the area.

Discussion Questions

1. Do financial rewards have any value in situations such as this, where employees are relatively wealthy?

2. If you were Thomas Chan, what strategy, if any, would you use to motivate Susan Chalmers to stay at Advanced Photonics Inc.?

3. Of what importance is job design in this case?

Copyright © 2001. Steven L. McShane.

CASE STUDY 6.2

SAVAGED BY THE SLOWDOWN

BusinessWeek During the business boom of the 1990s, many companies used stock options to attract and reward employees. A stock option gives its owner the right to buy a specified amount of stock at a specified price during a specified time period. When stock prices were soaring, the value of an employee's stock options might rise along with the market to a million dollars or more. When stock prices peaked and fell, however, the value of the options could fall to zero—and sometimes stock ownership involved hefty tax bills in spite of its worthlessness. Worse yet, many employees who were used to being courted by employers began to experience shrinking bonuses and even layoffs. In this environment, what can an employer offer the remaining employees to keep them motivated, even as they shoulder the responsibilities of their laid-off colleagues?

This *Business Week* case study describes the challenges of motivating employees in a slowing economy. The examples of worried, debt-burdened employees illustrate the need for motivational tools that are appropriate for this situation. Read through this *Business Week* case study at www.mhhe.com/mcshane2e and prepare for the discussion questions below.

Discussion Questions

1. How have changing income levels affected the employees described in this article? Consider the effects on their motivation at work, as well as the effects on them personally.

2. According to the examples in this article, what are some disadvantages of rewards linked to a company's profits or stock price? How might an employer address these disadvantages?

3. What do you think are appropriate ways to motivate the employees described in this

article? Consider both rewards and job-related sources of motivation.

Source: Michelle Conlin, "Savaged by the Slowdown," *Business Week*, September 17, 2001.

TEAM EXERCISE 6.3

IS STUDENT WORK ENRICHED?

Purpose This exercise is designed to help students learn how to measure the motivational potential of jobs and to evaluate the extent that jobs should be further enriched.

Instructions Being a student is like being an employee in several ways. You have tasks to perform, and someone (such as your instructor) oversees your work. Although few people want to be students most of their lives (the pay rate is too low!), it may be interesting to determine how enriched your job is as a student.

- ■ *Step 1*—Students are placed into teams (preferably four or five people).
- ■ *Step 2*—Working alone, each student completes both sets of measures in this exercise.

Then, using the guidelines below, they individually calculate the score for the five core job characteristics as well as the overall motivating potential score for the job.

- ■ *Step 3*—Members of each team compare their individual results. The group should identify differences of opinion for each core job characteristic. They should also note which core job characteristics have the lowest scores and recommend how those scores could be increased.
- ■ *Step 4*—The entire class will then discuss the results of the exercise. The instructor may ask some teams to present their comparisons and recommendations for a particular core job characteristic.

Job Diagnostic Survey						
Circle the number on the right that best describes student work.	**Very little** ▼		**Moderately** ▼			**Very much** ▼
1. To what extent does student work permit you to decide on your own how to go about doing the work? .. 1	2	3	4	5	6	7
2. To what extent does student work involve doing a whole or identifiable piece of work, rather than a small portion of the overall work process? 1	2	3	4	5	6	7
3. To what extent does student work require you to do many different things, using a variety of your skills and talents? 1	2	3	4	5	6	7
4. To what extent are the results of your work as a student likely to significantly affect the lives and well-being of other people (e.g., within your school, your family, society)? 1	2	3	4	5	6	7
5. To what extent does working on student activities provide information about your performance? 1	2	3	4	5	6	7
Circle the number on the right that best describes student work.	**Very inaccurate** ▼		**Uncertain** ▼			**Very Accurate** ▼
6. Being a student requires me to use a number of complex and high-level skills. 1	2	3	4	5	6	7

(continued)	Very inaccurate ▼			Uncertain ▼			Very Accurate ▼
7. Student work is arranged so that I do *not* have the chance to do an entire piece of work from beginning to end.	7	6	5	4	3	2	1
8. Doing the work required of students provides many chances for me to figure out how well I am doing.	1	2	3	4	5	6	7
9. The work students must do is quite simple and repetitive.	7	6	5	4	3	2	1
10. How well the work of a student gets done can affect a lot of other people.	1	2	3	4	5	6	7
11. Student work denies me any chance to use my personal initiative or judgment in carrying out the work.	7	6	5	4	3	2	1
12. Student work provides me the chance to completely finish the pieces of work I begin.	1	2	3	4	5	6	7
13. Doing student work by itself provides very few clues about whether or not I am performing well.	7	6	5	4	3	2	1
14. As a student, I have considerable opportunity for independence and freedom in how I do the work.	1	2	3	4	5	6	7
15. The work I perform as a student is *not* very significant or important in the broader scheme of things.	7	6	5	4	3	2	1

Source: Adapted from the Job Diagnostic Survey, developed by J. R. Hackman and G. R. Oldham. The authors have released any copyright ownership of this scale (see J. R. Hackman and G. Oldham, *Work Redesign* [Reading, MA: Addison-Wesley, 1980], p. 275).

Scoring Core Job Characteristics Use the following set of calculations to score the core job characteristics for the job of being a student. Use your answers from the Job Diagnostic Survey that you completed above.

Skill variety (SV) $\quad \dfrac{\text{Question } 3 + 6 + 9}{3} = \underline{\hspace{2cm}}$

Task identity (TI) $\quad \dfrac{\text{Question } 2 + 7 + 12}{3} = \underline{\hspace{2cm}}$

Task significance (TS) $\quad \dfrac{\text{Question } 4 + 10 + 15}{3} = \underline{\hspace{2cm}}$

Autonomy $\quad \dfrac{\text{Question } 1 + 11 + 14}{3} = \underline{\hspace{2cm}}$

Job feedback $\quad \dfrac{\text{Question } 5 + 8 + 13}{3} = \underline{\hspace{2cm}}$

Calculating Motivating Potential Score (MPS) Use the formula on p.194 and the results above to calculate the motivating potential score. Notice that skill variety, task identity, and task significance are averaged before being multiplied by the scores for autonomy and job feedback.

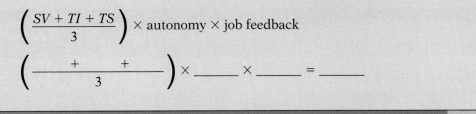

$$\left(\frac{SV + TI + TS}{3}\right) \times \text{autonomy} \times \text{job feedback}$$

$$\left(\frac{\underline{} + \underline{} + \underline{}}{3}\right) \times \underline{} \times \underline{} = \underline{}$$

SELF-ASSESSMENT EXERCISE 6.4

WHAT IS YOUR ATTITUDE TOWARD MONEY?

Purpose This exercise is designed to help you understand the types of attitudes toward money and to assess your attitude toward money.

Instructions Read each statement below and circle the response that you believe best reflects your position regarding that statement. Then use the scoring key in Appendix B to calculate your results. This exercise is completed alone so that students assess themselves honestly without concerns of social comparison. However, class discussion will focus on the meaning of money, including the dimensions measured here and other aspects of money that may have an influence on behavior in the workplace.

Money Attitude Scale					
Circle the number that best reflects the extent you agree or disagree with each statement.	Strongly Agree ▼	Agree ▼	Neutral ▼	Disagree ▼	Strongly Disagree ▼
1. I sometimes purchase things because I know they will impress other people.	1	2	3	4	5
2. I regularly put money aside for the future.	1	2	3	4	5
3. I tend to get worried about decisions involving money.	1	2	3	4	5
4. I believe that financial wealth is one of the most important signs of a person's success.	1	2	3	4	5
5. I keep a close watch on how much money I have.	1	2	3	4	5
6. I feel nervous when I don't have enough money.	1	2	3	4	5
7. I tend to show more respect to people who are wealthier than I am.	1	2	3	4	5
8. I follow a careful financial budget.	1	2	3	4	5
9. I worry about being financially secure.	1	2	3	4	5
10. I sometimes boast about my financial wealth or how much money I make.	1	2	3	4	5
11. I keep track of my investments and financial wealth.	1	2	3	4	5
12. I usually say I can't afford it, even when I can afford something.	1	2	3	4	5

Sources: Adapted from J. A. Roberts and C. J. Sepulveda, "Demographics and Money Attitudes: A Test of Yamauchi and Templer's (1982) Money Attitude Scale in Mexico," *Personality and Individual Differences* 27 (July 1999), pp. 19–35; K. Yamauchi and D. Templer, "The Development of a Money Attitudes Scale," *Journal of Personality Assessment* 46 (1982), pp. 522–28.

SELF-ASSESSMENT EXERCISE 6.5

ASSESSING YOUR SELF-LEADERSHIP

Purpose This exercise is designed to help you understand self-leadership concepts and to assess your self-leadership tendencies.

Instructions Read each statement below and circle the response that you believe best reflects your position regarding that statement. Then use the scoring key in Appendix B to calculate your results. This exercise is completed alone so that students assess themselves honestly without concerns of social comparison. However, class discussion will focus on the meaning of each self-leadership concept, how this scale might be applied in organizations, and the limitations of measuring self-leadership in work settings.

Self–leadership questionnaire					
Circle the number that best reflects your position regarding each statement.	Describes me very well ▼	Describes me well ▼	Describes me somewhat ▼	Does not describe me well ▼	Does not describe me at all ▼
1. I try to keep track of how I am doing while I work. . . .	5	4	3	2	1
2. I often use reminders to help me remember things I need to do.	5	4	3	2	1
3. I like to work toward specific goals I set for myself. . .	5	4	3	2	1
4. After I perform well on an activity, I feel good about myself.	5	4	3	2	1
5. I seek out activities in my work that I enjoy doing. . . .	5	4	3	2	1
6. I often practice important tasks before I do them. . . .	5	4	3	2	1
7. I usually am aware of how I am performing an activity.	5	4	3	2	1
8. I try to arrange my work area in a way that helps me positively focus my attention on my work.	5	4	3	2	1
9. I establish personal goals for myself.	5	4	3	2	1
10. When I have successfully completed a task, I often reward myself with something I like.	5	4	3	2	1
11. When I have a choice, I try to do my work in ways that I enjoy rather than just trying to get it over with.	5	4	3	2	1
12. I like to go over an important activity before I actually perform it.	5	4	3	2	1
13. I keep track of my progress on projects I am working on.	5	4	3	2	1
14. I try to surround myself with objects and people that bring out my desirable behaviors.	5	4	3	2	1
15. I like to set task goals for my performance.	5	4	3	2	1
16. When I do an assignment especially well, I like to treat myself to something or an activity I enjoy.	5	4	3	2	1
17. I try to build activities into my work that I like doing. . .	5	4	3	2	1
18. I often rehearse my plan for dealing with a challenge before I actually face the challenge.	5	4	3	2	1

Source: C. C. Manz, *Mastering Self-Leadership: Empower Yourself for Personal Excellence* (Englewood Cliffs, NJ: Prentice Hall, 1992). Used with permission of the author. The scale presented here excludes the self-punishment dimension found in the SLQ1 instrument because it is not calculated in the SLQ1 total score. The designing natural rewards dimension presented here is measured by items in the third dimension of the SLQ2 instrument.

After studying the preceding material, be sure to check out our website at

www.mhhe.com/mcshane2e

for more in-depth information and interactivities that correspond to this chapter.

Stress Management

AFTER READING THIS CHAPTER, YOU SHOULD BE ABLE TO:

- Define *stress* and describe the stress experience.

- Outline the stress process from stressors to consequences.

- Identify the different types of stressors in the workplace.

- Explain why the same stressor might produce different stress levels in different people.

- Discuss the physiological, psychological, and behavioral effects of stress.

- Identify five ways to manage workplace stress.

Sammy Fong has coped with floods, earthquakes, and other crises for the California Department of Water Resources. But nothing compares with the intensity of his new job as an energy buyer for the State of California. "It's hard to convey the stress," says Fong, who must buy up enough energy supply to meet California's energy demand. "Your adrenaline's flowing, your senses are alive . . . and the gravity of everything is hanging over you."

Power shortages and sudden spikes in energy prices have put added pressure on Fong and his co-workers in Sacramento to make the right decisions. Wrong choices can cost millions or result in rolling blackouts. Trading room supervisors try to alleviate the stress by scrawling humorous messages on the wall or offering fun prizes, such as riding the boss's Harley-Davidson. They also watch for symptoms of burnout. "With the long hours, people start to get rummy after a while, and that's when it's time to rotate them out," says Fong.

On Louisiana Street in Houston, America's center for energy trading, many energy traders wear out within 10 years. They are replaced by energetic newcomers, but it doesn't take long before they also feel stressed from the intense bartering and 24/7 schedule. "The money is so good, it's worth being obsessed and not taking vacations," says Robin Conner, a 30-year-old trader at Reliant Energy. "But it can wear you out. You get home at night and you don't even want to talk anymore. I want to soak in a tub for five hours."

These energy traders at Houston-based Reliant Energy experience intense stress that wears out many of them within 10 years. (© Smiley N. Pool/ The Houston Chronicle)

Axia Energy trader Ken Merideth has the same feelings. "I am so burned out at the end of the day, I don't even want to make a decision about what to eat for dinner," he admits.[1]

The stress associated with energy trading has both short- and long-term effects on employees in this industry. But work-related stress is becoming an epidemic in almost every organization. According to a major survey by the Families and Work Institute, 28 percent of employees often or very often feel overworked or overwhelmed by work. Another recent survey suggests that over half of American employees say they work under a great deal of stress. The American Institute of Stress estimates that work-related stress costs American businesses about $300 billion each year in lower productivity and higher absenteeism, turnover, alcoholism, and medical costs.[2]

Chronic work-related stress is not just an American affliction. Japan's Institute of Life and Living reports that 68 percent of Japanese often feel worried and anxious, up from 37 percent a decade earlier. A study sponsored by the Canadian Heart and Stroke Foundation found that almost one-third of employees in that country regularly have difficulty coping with the demands of their jobs. Nearly two-thirds of Australian employees say they are under extreme stress at work. An international study reported that people born after 1955 are up to three times as likely to experience stress-related disorders as were their grandparents. At the Escorts Heart Institute in Delhi, India, routine cardiac screenings indicate that most executives are in the advanced stages of stress. "Corporate India is finally waking up to the fact that a lot of human potential is being drained away because of stress and burnout," says Shekhar Bajaj, CEO of the Indian consumer electronics manufacturer Bajaj Electricals.[3]

In this chapter, we look at the dynamics of work-related stress and how to manage it. The chapter begins by describing the stress experience. Next, the causes and consequences of stress are examined, along with the factors that cause some people to experience stress when others do not. The final section of this chapter looks at ways to manage work-related stress from either an organizational or an individual perspective.

WHAT IS STRESS?

stress
An individual's adaptive response to a situation that is perceived as challenging or threatening to the person's well-being.

Stress is an adaptive response to a situation that is perceived as challenging or threatening to the person's well-being.[4] As we shall see, stress is the person's reaction to a situation, not the situation itself. Moreover, we experience stress when something is perceived to interfere with our well-being, that is, with our need fulfillment. Stress has both psychological and physiological dimensions. Psychologically, people perceive a situation and interpret it as challenging or threatening. This cognitive appraisal leads to a set of physiological responses, such as higher blood pressure, sweaty hands, and faster heartbeat.

We often hear about stress as a negative consequence of modern living. People are stressed from overwork, job insecurity, information overload, and the increasing pace of life. These events produce *distress*—the degree of physiological, psychological, and behavioral deviation from healthy functioning.[5] There is also a positive side of stress, called *eustress*, that refers to the healthy, positive, constructive outcome of stressful events and the stress response. Eustress is the stress experience in moderation, enough to activate and motivate people so that they can achieve goals, change their environments, and succeed in life's challenges. In other words, we need some stress to survive. However, most research focuses on distress, because it is a significant concern in organizational settings.[6] Employees frequently experience enough stress to hurt their job performance and increase their risk of mental and physical health problems. Consequently, our discussion will focus more on distress than on eustress.

General Adaptation Syndrome

The stress experience was first documented 50 years ago by Dr. Hans Selye, a pioneer in stress research.[7] Selye determined that people have a fairly consistent physiological response to stressful situations. This response, called the **general adaptation syndrome,** provides an automatic defense system to help us cope with environmental demands. Exhibit 7.1 illustrates the three stages of the general adaptation syndrome: alarm reaction, resistance, and exhaustion. The line in this exhibit shows the individual's energy and ability to cope with the stressful situation.

Alarm Reaction   In the alarm reaction stage, the perception of a threatening or challenging situation causes the brain to send a biochemical message to various parts of the body, resulting in increased respiration rate, blood pressure, heartbeat, and muscle tension, as well as other physiological responses. At first, the individual's energy level and coping effectiveness decrease in response to the initial shock. Extreme shock, however, may result in incapacity or death because the body is unable to generate enough energy quickly enough. In most situations, the alarm reaction alerts the person to the environmental condition and prepares the body for the resistance stage.

Resistance   The person's ability to cope with the environmental demand rises above the normal state during the resistance stage because the body has activated various biochemical, psychological, and behavioral mechanisms. For example, we have a higher than normal level of adrenaline during this stage, which gives us more energy to overcome or remove the source of stress. However, our resistance is directed to only one or two environmental demands, so we become more vulnerable to other sources of stress. This

---

general adaptation syndrome

A model of the stress experience, consisting of three stages: alarm reaction, resistance, and exhaustion.

EXHIBIT 7.1

Selye's general adaptation syndrome

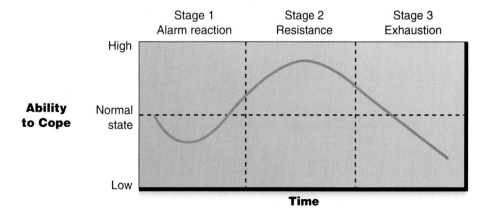

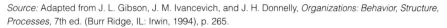

Source: Adapted from J. L. Gibson, J. M. Ivancevich, and J. H. Donnelly, *Organizations: Behavior, Structure, Processes,* 7th ed. (Burr Ridge, IL: Irwin, 1994), p. 265.

Janice Howell experienced all three stages of the general adaptation syndrome from teaching 28 students, 11 of them with learning or behavioral difficulties, at a primary school in Wales. She initially had the assistance of an English-language teacher, but that teacher took long-term leave and was not replaced. Unable to cope with the additional workload, Howell had a nervous breakdown. After recovering several months later, Howell complained to the school about the intolerable stress. Rather than providing support, the school added two more troubled kids to Howell's class. One new student to Wales ran away one morning and was seen playing near dangerous mudflats. Although he was taken home safely, no one told Howell until the end of the day. This incident led to Howell's second breakdown, effectively ending her career. "From being a confident, well-adjusted teacher who enjoyed her job, I became depressed and dysfunctional," says Howell, who was awarded U.S.$180,000 in compensation for her stress. "It got to the stage that I was physically unable to enter the classroom."[10] How does the exhaustion stage of the general adaptation syndrome relate to the consequences of stress discussed later in this chapter? *(Ian Nicholson/PA Photos)*

situation explains why people are more likely to catch a cold or other illness when they have been working under pressure.

Exhaustion   People have a limited resistance capacity, and if the source of stress persists, they will eventually move into the exhaustion stage as this capacity diminishes. In most work situations, the general adaptation syndrome process ends long before total exhaustion. Employees resolve tense situations before the destructive consequences of stress become manifest, or they withdraw from the stressful situation, rebuild their survival capabilities, and return later to the stressful environment with renewed energy. However, people who frequently experience the general adaptation syndrome have increased risk of long-term physiological and psychological damage.[8]

The general adaptation syndrome describes the stress experience, but this is only part of the picture. To effectively manage work-related stress, we must understand its causes and consequences as well as individual differences in the stress experience.

STRESSORS: THE CAUSES OF STRESS

Stressors, the causes of stress, include any environmental conditions that place a physical or emotional demand on the person.[9] There are numerous stressors in organizational settings and other life activities. Exhibit 7.2 lists the four main types of work-related stressors: physical environment, role-related, interpersonal, and organizational stressors.

Physical Environment Stressors

Some stressors, such as excessive noise, poor lighting, and safety hazards, are found in the physical work environment. For example, a study of textile workers in a noisy plant found that their levels of stress measurably decreased when they were supplied with ear protectors. Another study reported that clerical employees experience significantly higher stress levels in noisy open offices than in quiet areas.[11] Physical stressors also include poorly designed office space, lack of privacy, ineffective lighting, and poor air quality.

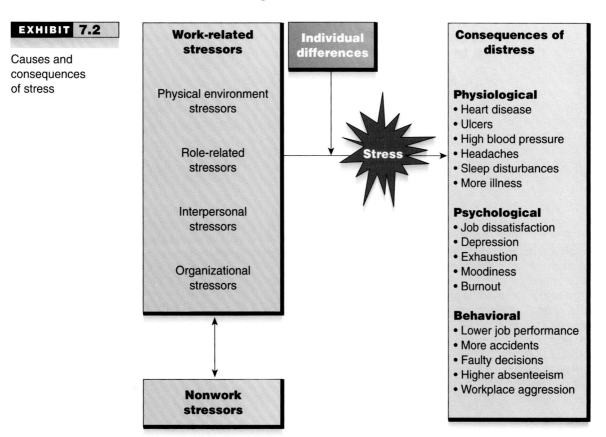

EXHIBIT 7.2

Causes and consequences of stress

stressors
The causes of stress, including any environmental conditions that place a physical or emotional demand on the person.

Role-Related Stressors

Role-related stressors include conditions where employees have difficulty understanding, reconciling, or performing the various roles in their lives. The four main role-related stressors are role conflict, role ambiguity, workload, and task control.

role conflict
Conflict that occurs when people face competing demands.

■ *Role conflict*—**Role conflict** occurs when people face competing demands.[12] *Interrole conflict* exists when employees have two roles that conflict with each other. For example, sales staff in the U.S. banking industry experience interrole conflict trying to balance the needs of their bank and the needs of customers.[13] Role conflict also occurs when an employee receives contradictory messages from different people about how to perform a task (called *intrarole conflict*) or work with organizational values and work obligations that are incompatible with his or her personal values (called *person-role conflict*).[14]

role ambiguity
Uncertainty about job duties, performance expectations, level of authority, and other job conditions.

■ *Role ambiguity*—**Role ambiguity** exists when employees are uncertain about their job duties, performance expectations, level of authority, and other job conditions. This ambiguity tends to occur when people enter new situations, such as joining the organization or taking a foreign assignment, because they are uncertain about task and social expectations.[15]

■ *Workload*—Work underload, receiving too little work or having tasks that do not sufficiently use your talents, is a possible stressor. However, work overload

Karoshi: Death by Overwork in Japan

Nobuo Miuro was under a lot of pressure from his employer to get a new restaurant ready for its launch. The interiors fitter from Tokyo worked late, sometimes until 4:30 in the morning. After one such marathon, Miuro caught a few hours of sleep, then returned for another long day. But he didn't get very far. The 47-year-old suddenly took ill and keeled over while picking up his hammer and nails. He died a week later. The coroner's verdict was that Miuro died of *karoshi*—"death by overwork."

Karoshi accounts for nearly 10,000 deaths each year in Japan. Research indicates that long work hours cause unhealthy lifestyle behaviors, such as smoking, poor eating habits, lack of physical exercise, and insufficient sleep. This lifestyle results in weight gain, which, along with stressful working conditions, damages the cardiovascular system and leads to strokes and heart attacks.

Karoshi came to the public spotlight in the 1970s when Japan's economy was booming, but the country's current recession is making matters worse. Companies are laying off employees and loading the extra work onto those who remain. Performance-based expectations are replacing lifetime employment guarantees, putting further pressure on employees to work long hours. Many also blame Japan's "samurai spirit" culture, which idealizes long work hours as the ultimate symbol of company loyalty and personal fortitude. "Being exhausted is considered a virtue," explains a Japanese psychiatrist.

So far, only 17 percent of Japanese firms offer overstressed employees some form of counseling. However, the Japanese government has launched an advertising campaign encouraging people to call a "karoshi hotline" for anonymous help. The families of deceased workaholics, including Nobuo Miuro's relatives, are also taking action by suing the employers for lack of due care.

Sources: "Trend of Caring for Employees Waning among Japan's Companies," *Japan Weekly Monitor*, May 14, 2001; C. Fukushi, "Workplace Stress Taking Toll on Women's Health," *Daily Yomiuri (Japan)*, April 21, 2001; S. Efron, "Jobs Take a Deadly Toll on Japanese," *Los Angeles Times*, April 12, 2000, p. A1; M. Millett, "Death of a Salaryman," *The Age (Melbourne)*, April 11, 2000, p. 15; E. Addley and L. Barton, "Who Said Hard Work Never Hurt Anybody?" *The Guardian (UK)*, March 13, 2001; M. Shields, "Long Working Hours and Health—1994–1997 Data," *Health Reports* 11 (Fall 1999), pp. 3–48.

is a far more common stressor these days. Employees have either too much to do in too little time, or they work too many hours on the job. Long work hours lead to unhealthy lifestyles, which, in turn, cause heart disease and strokes. As Global Connections 7.1 describes, work overload is such a problem in Japan that death from overwork has its own name—*karoshi*.

Task control—Employees are more stressed when they lack control over how and when they perform their tasks as well as the pace of work activity.[16] Work is potentially more stressful when it is paced by a machine or involves monitoring equipment, or when the work schedule is controlled by someone else. Information technology has this effect on office workers because they are always on call through e-mail, pagers, and cell phones. "I resent the fact that you can't get away today," says Pat Boyce, a medical equipment installer in Ohio who relies on his cell phone. "It's always there. You can be found at any time."[17]

Interpersonal Stressors

Interpersonal stressors include ineffective supervision, office politics, and other conflicts we experience with people. Call center employees are stressed from uncooperative customers and high productivity quotas. "260 calls a day from rude and angry people . . . it's hard to deal with at times," concludes one call center employee.[18] The trend toward teamwork also seems to generate more interpersonal stressors because employees must interact more with co-workers.[19]

Sexual Harassment   Laura Flannery was experiencing a lot of stress at the small Long Island manufacturing plant where she worked. The stress wasn't from her sales job; it was from an older male co-worker who would frequently drop by her office to boast about his sexual prowess and proposition her. Flannery recorded some of his lewd remarks so that the company owner would stop the problem, but no action was taken. "I was miserable whenever I saw him," says Flannery, "but I needed the job."[20]

Laura Flannery has experienced the stress of **sexual harassment**—unwelcome conduct of a sexual nature that detrimentally affects the work environment or leads to adverse job-related consequences for its victims. One form of sexual harassment, called *quid pro quo*, includes situations in which a person's employment or job performance is conditional on unwanted sexual relations (e.g., a male supervisor threatens to fire a female employee if she does not accept his sexual advances). Laura Flannery experienced the second and more common form of sexual harassment, called *hostile work environment*. This form of harassment includes sexual conduct that interferes unreasonably with an individual's work performance or creates an intimidating, hostile, or offensive working environment.[21]

However, sexual harassment is more than a legal issue. It is a serious interpersonal stressor.[22] Victims of sexual harassment experience trauma (especially from rape or related exploitation) or must endure tense co-worker relations in a hostile work environment. Moreover, they are expected to endure more stress while these incidents are investigated. This is particularly true in Japan and other countries where women who complain of harassment are sometimes stigmatized by friends and co-workers. "Companies don't want to hire 'dangerous women,' who make a fuss about sexual harassment," says Moeko Tanaka, the pen name of a Japanese woman who won a case of harassment against a prefecture governor.[23]

Workplace Violence   Another serious interpersonal stressor is the rising wave of physical violence in the workplace.[24] In the United States, 1,000 employees are murdered on the job each year and 2 million others experience lesser forms of violence. For instance, the National Institute of Occupational Safety and Health (NIOSH) estimates that more than 9,000 nurses and other health care workers are injured or verbally or physically attacked on the job *every day*.[25] But workplace violence isn't highest in the United States. According to research published by the International Labor Organization, employees in France, Argentina, Romania, Canada, and England have a higher incidence of workplace assaults and sexual harassment.[26]

Employees who experience violence usually have symptoms of severe distress after the traumatic event.[27] It is not uncommon for these primary victims to take long-term disability. Some never return to work. Workplace violence is also a stressor to those who observe the violence. After a serious workplace incident, counselors assist many employees, not just the direct victims. Even employees who have not directly experienced or observed violence may show signs of stress if they work in high-risk jobs. For example, one study reported that the greatest cause of work-related stress among British bus drivers was their perceived risk of physical assault.[28]

Workplace Bullying   Although less dramatic than violence, workplace bullying is becoming so common that it is considered a more serious interpersonal

---

sexual harassment

Unwelcome conduct of a sexual nature that detrimentally affects the work environment or leads to adverse job-related consequences for its victims.

stressor. **Workplace bullying** refers to offensive, intimidating, or humiliating behavior that degrades, ridicules, or insults another person at work.[29] The incidence of bullying reported in university studies ranges from 5 percent among hospital workers in Finland to 40 percent of federal court employees in Michigan (within the past five years). People with higher authority are more likely to engage in bullying or incivility toward employees in lower positions. Women are more likely than men to be targets of bullying.[30] Research indicates that most victims experience stress and its consequences following incidents of bullying. They also have more absenteeism and, back on the job, have impaired decision making, lower work performance, and more work errors.[31]

Bullying has become enough of a concern that Scandinavian countries have passed laws against it.[32] Some organizations have also taken steps to minimize the incidence of incivility. For example, Quaker Oats explicitly advises in its code of conduct that employees must treat each other with consideration, respect, and dignity. Past behavior is the best predictor of future behavior, so companies should carefully screen applicants in terms of past incidents. Feedback, particularly the 360-degree variety (see Chapter 2), lets employees know when their behavior is out of line. Lastly, organizations should have a grievance, mediation, or other conflict resolution process that employees trust when they become victims of workplace bullying.[33]

Organizational Stressors

Organizational stressors come in many forms. As we shall learn in Chapter 16, most forms of organizational change are stressful. Mergers and acquisitions are increasingly common organizational stressors, as are most other forms of organizational change. Downsizing (reducing the number of employees) is extremely stressful to those who lose their jobs. Layoff survivors also experience stress. For example, the company nurse at one high-tech firm discovered that the percentage of employees suffering from high blood pressure doubled after the company laid off 10 percent of its workforce. A study in Finland reported that long-term sick leave taken by surviving government employees doubled after a major downsizing.[34] As Connections 7.2 describes, the stress experienced by layoff survivors is due mainly to higher workloads, feelings of guilt, increased job insecurity, and the loss of friends at work.

Nonwork Stressors

Work is usually the most stressful part of our lives, but it's not the only part. We also experience numerous stressors outside organizational settings. Employees do not park these stressors at the door when they enter the workplace. The stressors carry over and ultimately affect work behavior. Moreover, the stress model shown earlier in Exhibit 7.2 has a two-way arrow, indicating that stressors from work spill over into nonwork and conflict with each other. The three main work–nonwork stressors are time-based, strain-based, and role behavior conflict.[35]

Time-Based Conflict   Jennifer Kelly knows all about the stress of trying to balance time at work with family. The graphic designer in New Jersey works 52 hours a week, sleeps about 6 hours a night and, in her words, is "frazzled

The Stress of Surviving Layoffs

Janet Driscoll enjoyed her job as marketing manager at Sega Software in Reston, Virginia—until the company laid off most of her staff. Sega was acquired by a large corporation, which slashed Driscoll's budget and left her to do the work of several people. But the toughest part of the downsizing was seeing her staff leave. As employees cleaned out their desks, Driscoll retreated to her office and cried. The experience was so heart-wrenching that Driscoll quit her job and moved to Colorado.

People who are laid off experience considerable stress, but so do the layoff survivors. Some of the stress is simply from the chaos of change. "Most people have their heads down, they're in shell shock during layoffs," says Dick Fincher, a consultant in Phoenix, Arizona, and survivor of 20 layoffs at various large employers. Others, such as Janet Driscoll, experience stress from losing friends and co-workers.

Patricia Baccus, who has 28 years of seniority at Virginia-based Viasystems Technologies Corporation, experienced layoff survivor stress from her feelings of guilt. "You felt a little guilty because you still had a job and there were those that didn't," she says after the circuit board manufacturer slashed half of its workforce. "I think it's going to be a long time before the hurt goes away."

For Mike Hewitt, being a layoff survivor meant coping with the stress of overwork. "When we were really busy and had a tough time keeping up with all the work coming in, I was probably working 40 hours a week," recalls the director of client services for Renaissance Worldwide in Cary, North Carolina. Following the layoffs at the information technology consulting firm, he was given tasks performed by former co-workers. "Now that business is down 15 percent, I'm working 60 hours a week," he says.

Janet Driscoll (shown here saying good-bye to a co-worker) quit her job at Sega Software because the stress of being a layoff survivor was too much. (© Paul Corbit Brown)

Sources: K. S. Rives, "Tired, Overworked and Stressed Out," Raleigh (NC) News and Observer, July 15, 2001, p. E1; J. Magruder, "Pink-Slip Blues Touch Entire Office," Arizona Republic, July 4, 2001, p. E1; S. Schafer, "Moving Up, Then Moving Out," Washington Post, May 8, 2001, p. E1; M. McCance, "Post-Layoff Workplace Stress," Richmond (VA) Times Dispatch, February 11, 2001, p. E1.

and tired." With clients all over the world, Kelly has a 24/7 schedule, leaving little time for family. "When I'm with them [the children], I'm so tired sometimes that I can't take them anywhere or do anything fun," admits Kelly.[36]

Jennifer Kelly has to contend with *time-based conflict*—the challenge of balancing the time demanded by work with family and other nonwork activities. This stressor is particularly noticeable in employees who hold strong family values. Time-based conflict largely explains why stress increases with the number of hours of paid employment and the amount of business travel or commuting time. Inflexible work schedules and rotating shift schedules also take a heavy toll because they prevent employees from effectively juggling work and nonwork.[37] Time-based conflict is more acute for women than for men because housework and childcare represent a "second shift" for many women in dual-career families.[38] Until men increase their contribution to homemaking and business learns to accommodate the new social order, many of these "supermoms" will continue to experience "superstress."

Strain-Based Conflict   *Strain-based conflict* occurs when stress from one domain spills over to the other. Relationship problems, financial difficulties, and loss of a loved one usually top the list of these nonwork stressors. New responsibilities, such as marriage, birth of a child, and a mortgage, are also stressful to most of us. Stress at work also spills over to an employee's personal life and often becomes the foundation of stressful relations with family and friends. One study found that fathers who experience stress at work engage in dysfunctional parenting behaviors, which then lead to their children's behavior problems in school.[39]

Role Behavior Conflict   A third work–nonwork stressor, called *role behavior conflict*, occurs when people are expected to enact different work and nonwork roles. People who act logically and impersonally at work have difficulty switching to a more compassionate behavioral style in their personal lives. For example, one study found that police officers were unable to shake off their professional role when they left the job. This role conflict was confirmed by their spouses, who reported that the officers would handle their children in the same manner as they would people in their job.[40]

Stress and Occupations

Several studies have attempted to identify which jobs have more stressors than others.[41] These lists are not in complete agreement, but Exhibit 7.3 identifies a representative sample of jobs and their relative levels of stress. You should view this information with some caution, however. One problem with rating occupations in terms of their stress levels is that a particular occupation may have considerably different tasks and job environments across organizations

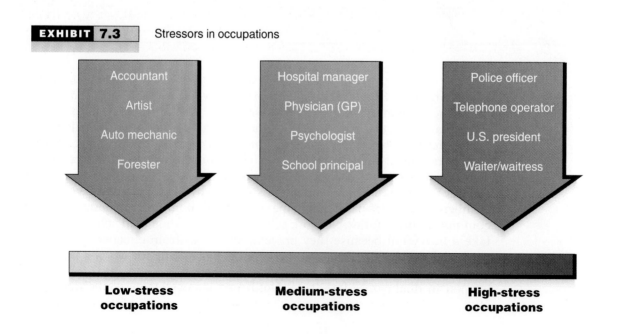

EXHIBIT 7.3   Stressors in occupations

Accountant	Hospital manager	Police officer
Artist	Physician (GP)	Telephone operator
Auto mechanic	Psychologist	U.S. president
Forester	School principal	Waiter/waitress

Low-stress occupations   **Medium-stress occupations**   **High-stress occupations**

and societies. A police officer's job may be less stressful in a small town, for instance, than in a large city where crime rates are higher and the organizational hierarchy is more formal.

Another important point to remember when looking at Exhibit 7.3 is that a major stressor to one person is insignificant to another. In this respect, we must be careful not to conclude that people in high-stress occupations actually experience higher stress than people in other occupations. Some jobs expose people to more serious stressors, but careful selection and training can result in stress levels no different from those experienced by people in other jobs. The next section discusses individual differences in stress.

INDIVIDUAL DIFFERENCES IN STRESS

As indicated earlier in this chapter (see Exhibit 7.2), individual characteristics moderate the extent to which people experience stress or exhibit a specific stress outcome in a given situation. Two people may be exposed to the same stressor, such as having too many deadlines, yet they experience different stress levels or different stress symptoms.[42]

People exposed to the same stressors might have different stress symptoms for three reasons. One reason is that each of us perceives the same situation differently. People with high self-efficacy, for instance, are less likely to experience stress consequences in that situation because the stressor is less threatening.[43] Self-efficacy refers to a person's belief that he or she has the ability, motivation, and situational contingencies to complete a task successfully (see Chapter 2). Similarly, some people have personalities that make them more optimistic, whereas others are more pessimistic (see Chapter 3). Those with pessimistic dispositions tend to develop more stress symptoms, probably because they interpret the situation in a negative light.[44]

A second reason some people have more stress symptoms than others in the same situation is that people have different thresholds of resistance to a stressor. Younger employees generally experience fewer and less severe stress symptoms than older employees because they have a larger store of energy to cope with high stress levels. This explains why exercise and healthy lifestyles, discussed later in this chapter, are one way to manage stress. People who exercise regularly and have other healthy lifestyle behaviors are also less likely to experience negative stress outcomes.

A third reason people may experience the same level of stress and yet exhibit different stress outcomes is that they use different coping strategies.[45] Some employees tend to ignore the stressor, hoping that it will go away. This is usually an ineffective approach, which would explain why they experience higher stress levels. There is some evidence (although still inconclusive) that women cope with stress better than their male counterparts. Specifically, women are more likely to seek emotional support from others in stressful situations, whereas men try to change the stressor or use less effective coping mechanisms.[46] However, we must remember that these coping strategies are not true for all women or men.

Type A and Type B Behavior Patterns

A 52-year-old systems analyst collapsed on a downtown sidewalk. An ambulance crew discovered he had blood flow problems to his heart, so they strapped him to a gurney and hooked him up to a heart monitor. In spite of his confinement and health condition, the systems analyst tried to make business calls on his mobile telephone while the ambulance was racing him to the nearest hospital.[47]

This systems analyst probably has a **type A behavior pattern.** Type A people are hard-driving, competitive individuals with a strong sense of time urgency. They tend to be impatient, lose their temper, talk rapidly, and interrupt others during conversations (see Exhibit 7.4).[48] In contrast, those with a **type B behavior pattern** are less competitive and less concerned about time limitations. They tend to work steadily, take a relaxed approach to life, and be even-tempered. Type B people may be just as ambitious to achieve challenging tasks, but they generally approach life more casually and systematically than do type A people. The important distinction, however, is that type B people are less likely than type A people to experience distress and its physiological symptoms (such as blood flow problems to the heart) when exposed to a stressor.

Regarding job performance, type A people tend to work faster than type B people, choose more challenging tasks, have higher self-motivation, and be more effective in jobs involving time pressure. On the other hand, type A people are less effective than type B people in jobs requiring patience, cooperation, and thoughtful judgment.[49] Type A people tend to be irritable and aggressive, so they generally have poorer interpersonal skills.

type A behavior pattern

A behavior pattern associated with people having premature coronary heart disease; type A's tend to be impatient, lose their temper, talk rapidly, and interrupt others.

CONSEQUENCES OF DISTRESS

The general adaptation syndrome introduced at the beginning of this chapter describes how chronic stress diminishes the individual's resistance, resulting in adverse consequences for both the employee and the organization. This results in a variety of physiological, psychological, and behavior consequences.

EXHIBIT 7.4   Characteristics of type A and type B behavior patterns

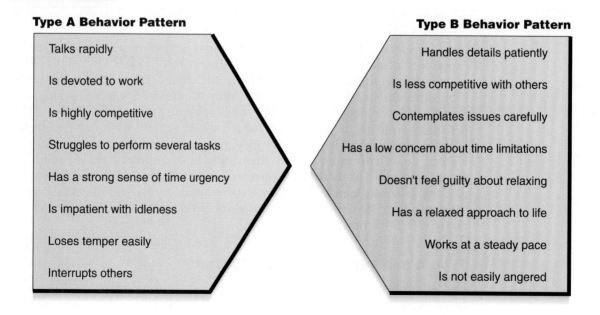

Type A Behavior Pattern

Talks rapidly

Is devoted to work

Is highly competitive

Struggles to perform several tasks

Has a strong sense of time urgency

Is impatient with idleness

Loses temper easily

Interrupts others

Type B Behavior Pattern

Handles details patiently

Is less competitive with others

Contemplates issues carefully

Has a low concern about time limitations

Doesn't feel guilty about relaxing

Has a relaxed approach to life

Works at a steady pace

Is not easily angered

Physiological Consequences

Stress takes its toll on the human body. Studies have found that medical students who are anxious about their exams are more susceptible to colds and other illnesses.[50] Many people experience tension headaches due to stress. Others get muscle pain and related back problems. These physiological ailments are attributed to muscle contractions that occur when people are exposed to stressors.

Cardiovascular disease represents one of the most disturbing effects of stress in modern society.[51] Strokes and heart attacks were rare a century ago but are now the leading causes of death among American adults. Stress also influences hypertension (high blood pressure). Hypertension has decreased in recent years as a result of better lifestyles and medical treatment. Still, nearly one-quarter of all American adults are treated for this condition.[52]

Medical researchers believe that the long-term effect of stress on the heart goes something like this: Whenever people are stressed, their blood pressure goes up and down. That frequent pressure change causes injury to the blood vessel walls, which eventually makes them constrict and function abnormally. Over time, this sequence leads to heart disease. Unfortunately, we often can't tell when we are physiologically stressed. For example, researchers have found that people think they are in a low-stress state when, in fact, their palms are sweating and their blood pressure has risen.[53]

Psychological Consequences

Stress produces various psychological consequences, including job dissatisfaction, moodiness, and depression.[54] Emotional fatigue is another psychological consequence of stress and is related to job burnout.

Job Burnout   **Job burnout** refers to the process of emotional exhaustion, depersonalization, and reduced personal accomplishment resulting from prolonged exposure to stress.[55] The phrase "job burnout" didn't exist 40 years ago; now it's heard in everyday conversations. Job burnout is a complex process that includes the dynamics of stress, coping strategies, and stress consequences. Burnout is caused by excessive demands made on people who serve or frequently interact with others. In other words, burnout is mainly due to interpersonal and role-related stressors.[56] For this reason, it is most common in helping occupations (e.g., nurses, teachers, police officers).

Exhibit 7.5 diagrams the relationship among the three components of job burnout. *Emotional exhaustion*, the first stage, plays a central role in the burnout process.[57] It is characterized by a lack of energy and a feeling that one's emotional resources are depleted. Emotional exhaustion is sometimes called compassion fatigue because the employee no longer feels able to give as much support and caring to clients.

Depersonalization follows emotional exhaustion and is identified by the treatment of others as objects rather than people. Burned-out employees become emotionally detached from clients and cynical about the organization. This detachment reaches the point of callousness, far beyond the level of detachment normally required in helping occupations. For example, a burned-out nurse might coldly label a patient as "the kidney in room 307."

type B behavior pattern
A behavior pattern of people with low risk of coronary heart disease; type B's tend to work steadily, take a relaxed approach to life, and be even-tempered.

job burnout
The process of emotional exhaustion, depersonalization, and reduced personal accomplishment resulting from prolonged exposure to stress.

EXHIBIT 7.5

The job burnout process

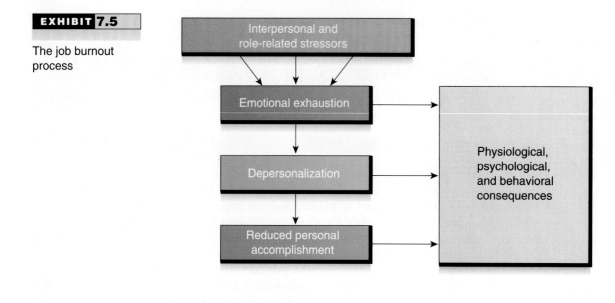

Depersonalization is also apparent when employees strictly follow rules and regulations rather than try to understand the client's needs and search for a mutually acceptable solution.

Reduced personal accomplishment, the final component of job burnout, refers to the decline in one's feelings of competence and success, and becomes evident in feelings of diminished competency. In other words, the person's self-efficacy declines (see Chapter 2). In these situations, employees develop a sense of learned helplessness as they no longer believe that their efforts make a difference.

"It's a smoke detector. The boss thinks I might be headed for a burnout."

(Copyright © Randy Glasbergen. Reprinted with special permission from www.glasbergen.com)

Behavioral Consequences

When stress becomes distress, job performance falls and workplace accidents are more common. High stress levels impair our ability to remember information, make effective decisions, and take appropriate action.[58] You have probably experienced this level of distress in an exam or emergency work situation. You forget important information, make mistakes, and otherwise draw a blank under intense pressure.

Overstressed employees also tend to have higher levels of absenteeism. One reason is that stress makes people sick. The other reason is that absenteeism is a coping mechanism. At a basic level, we react to stress through fight or flight. Absenteeism is a form of flight—temporarily withdrawing from the stressful situation so that we have an opportunity to re-energize. Companies may try to minimize absenteeism, but it sometimes helps employees avoid the exhaustion stage of the stress experience (see Exhibit 7.1).[59]

Workplace Aggression   Workplace aggression is more than the serious interpersonal stressor described earlier. It is also an increasingly worrisome consequence of stress.[60] Aggression represents the fight (instead of flight) reaction to stress. In its mildest form, employees engage in verbal conflict. They fly off the handle and are less likely to empathize with co-workers. Occasionally, the combination of an individual's background and workplace stressors escalate this conflict into more dangerous levels of workplace hostility.

Co-worker aggression represents a relatively small proportion of workplace violence, but these behaviors are neither random nor inconsequential. Like most forms of organizational behavior, co-worker aggression is caused by both the person and the situation.[61] Although certain individuals are more likely to be aggressive, we must remember that employee aggression is also a consequence of extreme stress.[62] In particular, employees are more likely to engage in aggressive behavior if they believe they have been treated unfairly, experience other forms of frustration beyond their personal control, and work in physical environments that are stressful (e.g., hot, noisy).

MANAGING WORK-RELATED STRESS

A recent Christmas holiday season was a nail-biter for Sharon Milligan. The 28-year-old retail director for New York fashion house Nicole Miller agonized as daily sales of the company's 14 stores fell below the previous year's numbers. She had to personally tell employees at the store in Scottsdale, Arizona, that the boutique there would be closed. A store scheduled for opening in Florida was delayed, missing a crucial weekend of holiday sales. Three days before Christmas, Milligan sat in the doctor's office with a fever and sore throat. "I just crashed," she says. Milligan flew to Jamaica the day after Christmas and slept through the first three days of her long-awaited vacation.[63]

Sharon Milligan was fortunate. She was able to manage her stress before matters got worse. Unfortunately, many of us deny the existence of our stress until it is too late. This avoidance strategy creates a vicious cycle because the failure to cope with stress becomes another stressor on top of the one that created the stress in the first place. The solution is to discover the tool kit of effective stress management strategies identified in Exhibit 7.6, and to

EXHIBIT 7.6

Stress management strategies

determine which ones are best for the situation.[64] As we look at each approach, keep in mind that the organization and the employees have joint responsibility for effective stress management. Moreover, managing stress often includes more than one of these strategies.

Remove the Stressor

From this list of stress management strategies, some writers argue that the *only* way companies can effectively manage stress is by removing the stressors that cause unnecessary tension and job burnout. Other stress management strategies may keep employees "stress-fit," but they don't solve the fundamental causes of stress.[65]

One way for organizations to manage stress is to investigate the main causes of stress in their workplace. Good Hope Hospital in the United Kingdom is conducting such an audit by asking staff to complete confidential questionnaires to identify when and how they experience stress.[66] In general, research has found that one of the most powerful ways to remove workplace stressors is to empower employees so that they have more control over their work and work environment (see Chapter 6).[67] Role-related stressors can be minimized by selecting and assigning employees to positions that match their competencies. Noise and safety risks are stressful, so improving these conditions would also go a long way to minimize stress in the workplace. Workplace bullying can be minimized through clear guidelines for behavior and feedback to those who violate those standards.

Employees can also take an active role in removing stressors. If stress is due to ambiguous role expectations, for example, we might seek out more information from others to clarify these expectations. If a particular piece of work is too challenging, we might break it into smaller sets of tasks so that the overall project is less threatening or wearing. We can minimize workplace violence by learning to identify early warning signs of aggression in customers and co-workers and by developing interpersonal skills that dissipate aggression.

Family–Friendly and Work–Life Initiatives   As a consultant with a major firm, David Peterson worked on a long-term assignment in another city and flew home on weekends. But on one of those weekends, he overheard one of his two-year-old twin daughters ask his wife, "Does Daddy live here anymore?" That question changed Peterson forever. His children were growing up fast, and he didn't want to miss out on those special moments. So Peterson decided to form the North Highland Company, an independent management and technology consulting firm with a unique policy. The Atlanta-based company makes work-related travel completely voluntary. In fact, when work started coming in from other cities, North Highland set up separate offices with local consultants so that no one had to travel. "Consulting work is very stressful and travel is an additional strain, especially when you get to the point where you have a family and lots of responsibilities at home," says Peterson.[68]

North Highland and many other organizations have applied specific policies to help employees maintain a work–life balance. Many companies claim to offer a work–life balance, yet Americans are working more hours than ever and some employees complain that much of the rhetoric doesn't match corporate practices. Five of the most common work–life balance initiatives are flexible

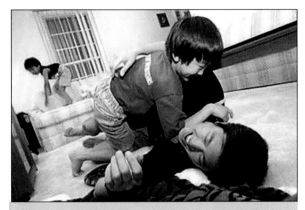

On this workday afternoon, when many auto executives aren't even thinking about heading home, Mark-Tami Hotta is engaged in a rousing game of Daddy Elephant–Baby Elephant with his kids. The chief program engineer for the Ford Windstar minivan leaves work early three days each week as part of the company's effort to improve work–life balance. Hotta is starting to change Ford's culture away from one that praises long work hours as a badge of honor. For example, Hotta initiated an event where 250 people on the Windstar team agreed to get their assignments completed and be out of the building by 3 P.M. on Valentine's Day. The exercise was so successful that Ford's entire North America car group did the same on the Friday before Memorial Day.[71] What other activities would encourage busy Ford executives to balance their work with nonwork? *(© D. Guralnick/* Detroit News*)*

work time, job sharing, telecommuting, personal leave programs, and child care support.

▪ *Flexible work time*—Many firms are flexible with regard to the hours, days, and amount of time employees want to work.

▪ *Job sharing*—Job sharing splits a career position between two people so that they experience less time-based stress between work and family. They typically work different parts of the week, with some overlapping work time in the weekly schedule to coordinate activities.[69]

▪ *Telecommuting*—Chapter 1 described how an increasing number of employees are telecommuting. This reduces the time and stress of commuting to work and makes it easier to fulfill family obligations, such as temporarily leaving the home office to pick up the kids from school. Research suggests that telecommuters experience a healthier work–life balance.[70] However, telecommuting may increase stress for those who crave social interaction. It also isn't a solution for child care.

▪ *Personal leave programs*—Employers with strong work–life values offer extended maternity, paternity, and personal leaves to care for a new family or take advantage of a personal experience. The U.S. Family and Medical Leave Act gives expectant mothers (and anyone considered to have an illness) 12 weeks of unpaid, job-protected leave. However, almost every other developed nation requires employers to provide paid maternity leave.[72] Increasingly, employees require personal leave to care for elderly parents who need assistance.

▪ *Child care support*—Nearly one-quarter of American employees have on-site or subsidized child care facilities. Child care support reduces stress because employees are less rushed to drop off their children and less worried during the day about how well they are doing.[73]

Withdraw from the Stressor

Removing the stressor may be the ideal solution, but that option is often not feasible. An alternative strategy is to permanently or temporarily remove employees from the stressor. Permanent withdrawal occurs when employees are transferred to jobs that better fit their competencies and values.

Temporary Withdrawal Strategies   Temporarily withdrawing from stressors is the most frequent way that employees manage stress. Nortel Networks has a relaxation room complete with comfy chairs and comedy videos where employees can temporarily escape from the hassles of work. Washrooms are becoming increasingly popular retreats for American employees, particularly as

Keep the Stress-Busting Siesta in Modern Spain

María José Mateo is defying a force that has ruled Spain for centuries. The 29-year-old bank employee is trying to stay awake during the afternoon. She and many other Spaniards are giving up their siesta—a two- or three-hour mid-afternoon break when employees head home for a hot meal, followed by a restful nap.

Customers in other European countries increasingly expect Spanish employees to answer the telephone throughout the day. Companies are also discouraging these long breaks in an attempt to increase productivity. TotalFina, the French oil company, gives its Spanish managers and salespeople coupons for nearby fast-food outlets—a hint that they should have a power lunch, not a power nap. Commuting is also killing siestas. Employees don't have time to commute twice each day through traffic-clogged Madrid and Barcelona.

Ironically, the siesta is disappearing just when people in other countries are discovering the health benefits of a midday snooze. American studies report that the nervous system needs a long break at night and a shorter one somewhere between 2 P.M. and 5 P.M. A smattering of American firms, such as Burlington Northern Santa Fe Railway, have established napping policies. Kodak, PepsiCo, IBM, and Pizza Hut offer courses teaching employees how to take power naps at work. Deloitte Consulting has gone as far as setting up nap rooms.

Fede Busquet, a former tanning salon owner, may have found a solution to Spain's siesta dilemma. Busquet realized that Spaniards still need their siesta when he noticed rows of parked cars along Barcelona's streets with men sleeping inside around midday. He thought these people might prefer a more comfortable place for a power nap near their office.

Busquet set up two dozen parlors where, for 1,000 pesetas (U.S.$7), customers get a 10-minute massage in an ergonomic chair, then an hour in that same chair to

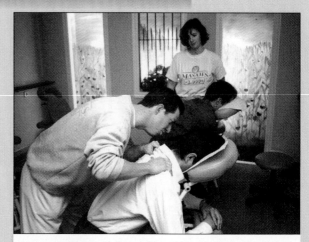

Masseurs Remco Rafina, left, and Eva Pacheco give two people a special siesta massage in a newly opened massage parlor in Madrid, Feb. 3, 1999. For 1,000 pesetas ($7, 6 euros) customers get a 10-minute massage in an ergonomic chair, then an hour in that same chair to sleep or rest. Those in a hurry can stay half as long for half the price. *(AP Photo/Paul White)*

sleep or rest. Those in a hurry can stay half as long for half the price. Business is booming. It seems that Spaniards still need their midday siesta, but something quicker and closer to the office.

Sources: L. Stevens, "Believers in the Midday Doze Are Stripping Away Stigma of Siestas," *Fort Worth (TX) Star-Telegram*, March 24, 2001; R. Hogan, "A Daytime Nap Could Make You More Productive," *Los Angeles Times,* January 15, 2001; S. M. Handelsblatt, "Stressed Out and Stranded in Barcelona?" *Wall Street Journal Europe*, August 4, 2000, p. 32; R. Boudreaux, "Spaniards Are Missing Their Naps," *Los Angeles Times*, March 28, 2000; D. Woolls, "Spanish Entrepreneur Finds Market Niche in Siesta Deprived," *Deseret News (Salt Lake City, UT)*, March 22, 1999.

open work spaces replace private offices.[74] Siestas provide midday sleep breaks for employees in Spain and other Mediterranean countries. However, as Global Connections 7.3 describes, Spanish employees are under pressure to give up their cherished siesta because of globalization and urbanization, just as other countries discover the benefits of these power naps.

Vacations represent somewhat longer temporary withdrawals from stressful conditions. Richer Sounds has eight holiday homes around the world, and all 300 employees at the U.K. hi-fi retailer are entitled to one week each year in one of these properties at no charge. "I'd far rather someone was using these places than being at home," says Richer Sounds managing director David Robinson. "That way, when they come back, they're relaxed and firing on all cylinders."[75] Nearly one-third of the best 100 companies to work for in America offer sabbaticals to long-service employees.[76] Sabbaticals represent an extended version of vacations, whereby employees take a few months of paid leave after several years of service.

Change Stress Perceptions

Employees often experience different levels of stress in the same situation because they perceive it differently. Consequently, stress can be minimized by changing perceptions of the situation. This strategy does not involve ignoring risks or other stressors. Rather, it involves strengthening our self-efficacy and self-esteem so that job challenges are not perceived as threatening.

Humor can help in this regard. Consider Shirley Cayton, director of nursing at Presbyterian Hospital in Matthews, North Carolina. When work gets tense, colleagues encourage Cayton to put on fuzzy kitty slippers—the ones that are three sizes too large and have jingly bells. "I feel silly, all dressed up in a business suit and wearing the slippers," she admits. But this little silliness breaks the sober business pressure and provides a little levity in the office.[77]

Several elements of self-leadership described in Chapter 6 can alter employee perceptions of job-related stressors. For example, mental imagery can reduce the uncertainty of future work activities. A study of newly hired accountants reported that personal goal setting and self-reinforcement can reduce the stress that people experience when they enter new work settings.[78] Positive self-talk can potentially change stress perceptions by increasing our self-efficacy and by helping us develop a more optimistic outlook, at least in that situation.

Control the Consequences of Stress

Coping with workplace stress also involves controlling its consequences. Research indicates that physical exercise reduces the physiological consequences of stress by helping employees lower their respiration, muscle tension, heartbeat, and stomach acidity.[79] Beyond fitness programs, some companies offer wellness programs that educate and support employees in better nutrition and fitness, regular sleep, and other good health habits.[80] Another way to control the physiological consequences of stress is through relaxation and meditation. Generally, these activities decrease the individual's heart rate, blood pressure, muscle tension, and breathing rate.[81]

employee assistance programs (EAPs)
Counseling services that help employees overcome personal or organizational stressors and adopt more effective coping mechanisms.

Many large employers offer **employee assistance programs (EAPs).** EAPs are counseling services that help employees overcome personal or organizational stressors and adopt more effective coping mechanisms. Most EAPs are broad-brush programs that counsel employees on any work or personal problems. Family problems often represent the largest percentage of EAP referrals, although this varies with industry and location. EAPs can be one of the most effective stress management interventions where the counseling helps employees understand the stressors, acquire stress management skills, and practice those skills.[82]

Receive Social Support

Social support from co-workers, supervisors, family, friends, and others is one of the more effective stress management practices.[83] Social support refers to the person's interpersonal transactions with others and involves providing either emotional or informational support to buffer the stress experience.

Employees at Homestake's Darlot gold mine are running for their lives. Each week, Fleta Solomon (center) and other exercise physiologists are flown into the mine site in Australia's outback to help the 190 miners and other staff improve their health and fitness. Along with organizing training runs, the physiologists check employee posture on the job, test cholesterol levels, and give lunchtime lectures on nutrition and coping with shift work. Darlot's mine manager hopes this health and fitness campaign will result in healthier employees who, in turn, experience less stress and have fewer accidents.[86] In your opinion, what else could Homestake do to help the Darlot mine employees minimize stress? *(© R. Taylor/West Australian)*

Social support reduces stress in at least three ways.[84] First, employees improve their perception that they are valued and worthy. This, in turn, increases their self-esteem and perceived ability to cope with the stressor (e.g., "I can handle this crisis because my colleagues have confidence in me"). Second, social support provides information to help employees interpret, comprehend, and possibly remove the stressor. For instance, social support might reduce a new employee's stress because co-workers describe ways to handle difficult customers. Finally, emotional support from others can directly help buffer the stress experience. This last point reflects the idea that misery loves company. People seek out and benefit from the emotional support of others when they face threatening situations.[85]

Everyone can practice social support by maintaining friendships. This important way to cope with stress includes helping others when they need a little support from the stressors of life. Organizations can facilitate social support by providing opportunities for social interaction among employees as well as their families. People in leadership roles should also practice a supportive leadership style when employees work under stressful conditions and need this social support. Mentoring relationships with more senior employees may also help junior employees cope with organizational stressors.

CHAPTER SUMMARY

Stress is an adaptive response to a situation that is perceived as challenging or threatening to the person's well-being. Distress represents high stress levels that have negative consequences, whereas eustress represents the moderately low stress levels needed to activate people. The stress experienc, called the general adaptation syndrome, involves moving through three stages: alarm reaction, resistance, and exhaustion.

The stress model shows that stress is caused by stressors. However, the effect of those stressors depends on individual characteristics. Stress affects a person's physiological and psychological well-being, and is associated with several work-related behaviors.

Stressors include any environmental conditions that place a physical or emotional demand on the person. Stressors are found in the physical work environment, the employee's various life roles, interpersonal relations, and organizational activities and conditions. Conflicts between work and nonwork obligations represent a frequent source of employee stress.

Two people exposed to the same stressor may experience different stress levels because they perceive the situation differently, have different threshold stress levels, or use different coping strategies. Employees with type A behavior patterns tend to experience more stress than those exhibiting type B behaviors.

High levels of stress or prolonged stress can cause physiological symptoms, such as high blood pressure, ulcers, sexual dysfunction, headaches, and coronary heart disease. Psychologically, stress reduces job satisfaction and increases moodiness, depression, and job burnout. Job burnout refers to the process of emotional exhaustion, depersonalization, and reduced personal accomplishment resulting from prolonged exposure to stress. It is mainly due to interpersonal and role-related stressors and is most common in helping occupations. Behavioral symptoms of stress include lower job performance, poorer decisions, more workplace accidents, higher absenteeism, and more workplace aggression.

Many interventions are available to manage work-related stress. Some directly remove unnecessary stressors or remove employees from the stressful environment. Others help employees alter their interpretation of the environment so that it is not viewed as a serious stressor. Wellness programs encourage employees to build better physical defenses against stress experiences. Social support provides emotional, informational, and material resource support to buffer the stress experience.

KEY TERMS

employee assistance programs (EAPs), p. 215

general adaptation syndrome, p. 199

job burnout, p. 209

role ambiguity, p. 201

role conflict, p. 201

sexual harassment, p. 203

stress, p. 198

stressors, p. 201

type A behavior pattern, p. 208

type B behavior pattern, p. 209

workplace bullying, p. 204

DISCUSSION QUESTIONS

1. Use your favorite browser to find one of the many websites on managing stress. Which of the stress management strategies discussed in this chapter receives the most attention? Why, in your opinion, is that particular strategy highlighted more than others?

2. Sally works as an attorney for a leading Washington, D.C., law firm. She was married a few years ago and is currently pregnant with her first child. Sally expects to return to work full-time a few months after the baby is born. Describe two types of work–nonwork conflict that Sally will likely experience during the first year after her return to work.

3. Police officer and waiter are often cited as high-stress jobs, whereas accountant and forester are low-stress jobs. Why should we be careful about describing these jobs as high- or low-stress occupations?

4. Two recent graduates join the same major newspaper as journalists. Both work long hours and have tight deadlines to complete their stories. They are under constant pressure to scout out new leads and be the first to report new controversies. One journalist is increasingly fatigued and despondent, and has taken several days of sick leave. The other is getting the work done and seems to enjoy the challenges. Use your knowledge of stress to explain why these two journalists are reacting differently to their jobs.

5. Do people with type A personalities make better managers? Why or why not?

6. A friend says that he is burned out by his job. What questions might you ask this friend to determine whether he is really experiencing job burnout?

7. How might fitness programs help employees working in stressful situations?

8. A senior official of a labor union stated: "All stress management does is help people cope with poor management. [Employers] should really be into stress reduction." Discuss the accuracy of this statement.

JIM BLACK: SALES REPRESENTATIVE

Jim Black impatiently drummed the steering wheel and puffed on a cigarette as his car moved slowly northbound along the parkway. Traffic congestion was normal in the late afternoon, but it seemed much heavier today. In any event, it was another irritation that was going to make him late for his next appointment.

As a sales representative at Noram Corporation, Jim could not afford to keep clients waiting. Sales of compressed oxygen and other gases were slow during this prolonged recession. Other compressed gas suppliers were eager to grab new accounts, and it was becoming more common for clients to switch from one supplier to another. Jim pressed his half-finished cigarette against the ashtray and accelerated the car into another lane.

Buyers of compressed gases knew that the market was in their favor, and many were demanding price discounts and shorter delivery times. Earlier in the week, for example, one of Jim's more demanding customers telephoned for another shipment of liquid oxygen to be delivered the next morning. To meet the deadline, Jim had to complete an expedited delivery form and then personally convince the shipping group to make the delivery in the morning rather than later in the day. Jim disliked making expedited delivery requests, even though this was becoming increasingly common among the reps, because it often delayed shipment of Noram's product to other clients. Discounts were even more troublesome because they reduced his commission and, except for very large orders, were frowned upon by Noram management.

Meanwhile, at Noram headquarters where Jim worked, senior managers were putting more pressure on sales reps to produce. They complained that the reps weren't aggressive enough, and area supervisors were told to monitor each sales rep's monthly numbers more closely. Jim fumbled for another cigarette as the traffic stopped momentarily.

Two months ago, the area sales supervisor had "a little chat" (as he called it) with Jim about the stagnant sales in his district and loss of a client to the competition. It wasn't exactly a threat of being fired—other reps also received these chats—but Jim felt nervous about his work and began having sleepless nights. He began making more calls to potential clients but was able to find this time only by completing administrative paperwork in the evenings. The evening work wasn't helping relations with his family.

To make matters worse, Noram's parent company in Germany announced that it planned to sell the U.S. operations. Jim had heard rumors that a competitor was going to purchase the firm, mainly to expand its operations through Noram's Western U.S. sales force and production facilities. The competitor was well established in the eastern United States where Jim worked, and probably wouldn't need a larger sales force there. Jim's job would be in jeopardy if the acquisition took place. Jim felt another headache coming on as he stared at the endless line of red taillights stretching along the highway ahead.

Even if Jim kept his job, any promotion into management would be a long way off if the competitor acquired Noram. Jim had no particular desire to become a manager, but his wife was eager for him to receive a promotion because it would involve less travel and provide a more stable salary (less dependent on monthly sales). Business travel was a nuisance, particularly for out-of-town appointments, but Jim felt less comfortable with the idea of sitting behind a desk all day.

The loud honk of another car startled Jim as he swerved into the exit lane that he was supposed to take (but almost missed). A few minutes later, he arrived at the client's parking lot. Jim rummaged through his briefcase for some aspirin to relieve the headache. He heaved a deep sigh as he glanced at his watch. Jim was 15 minutes late for the appointment.

Discussion Questions

1. What stress symptoms is Jim experiencing?
2. What stressors can you identify in this case?
3. What should Jim do to minimize his stress?

MELTDOWN: ARE YOU LOSING IT?

BusinessWeek In our society, entrepreneurs play the hero's role in business stories. We may revile some for ruthless actions and praise others for generous deeds, but either way, we admire entrepreneurs for creating something out of nothing but their drive and imagination. Playing the heroic role of entrepreneur comes at a price, however. Starting a business is demanding and often isolating—in a word, stressful.

This *Business Week* case study describes the stress facing entrepreneurs and their responses to it. The article includes several examples of entrepreneurs who have struggled with job-related stress, including their accounts of what helped them. Read through this *Business Week* case study at www.mhhe.com/mcshane2e and prepare for the discussion questions below.

Discussion Questions

1. According to the author's descriptions, what stressors affected Scott Corlett, Carol Frank, and Jon Brandt? What were some of the consequences of their stress?

2. How did these entrepreneurs learn to manage their stress? What other ways might they use?

3. According to the article, some people assume that stress and unhappiness are necessary aspects of an entrepreneur's life. Expressing a contrasting viewpoint, mental health consultant Jeffrey P. Kahn says, "I've worked with many successful entrepreneurs. I can't think of one who has been less successful as a result of becoming happier." How do the principles in this chapter support (or not support) these points of view?

Source: W. Smith, "Meltdown: Are You Losing It?" *Business Week*, April 23, 2001.

STRESSED OUT OR NO PROBLEM?

Purpose This exercise is designed to help students understand how people will have different stress reactions to the same stressors.

Instructions

- *Step 1*—Students individually indicate their response to each incident on the scoring sheet.
- *Step 2*—The instructor places students into groups (typically four or five people) to compare their results. For each incident, group members should discuss why each person feels more or less stress. They should pay particular attention to the reasons some students would feel little stress. Specifically, they should examine the extent that each person (a) perceives the situation differently, (b) has more or less tolerance to stressors due to health or need to cope with other problems, and (c) would use different coping strategies to deal with any stress related to the incident.
- *Step 3*—After group members have diagnosed these results, the instructor will bring the class together to compare results and discuss why people react differently to stressors.

Circle the number on the right that best describes the extent to which you would feel stressed in each situation	Very little ▼		Moderately ▼				Very much ▼
1. Your final exam for Economics 200 is in 48 hours, and a bad flu and other assignments have prevented you from studying for it. You know that the instructor will not accept your illness and other assignments as an excuse to have the examination at another time. . . .	1	2	3	4	5	6	7
2. You started work last month as a salesclerk in a small clothing store (men's or women's) and have been asked to mind the store while the other two clerks take their lunch break elsewhere in the shopping mall. During this usually slow time, four customers walk in, each one of them wanting your immediate attention.	1	2	3	4	5	6	7
3. You and two friends are driving in an older van with snow tires to a ski resort in the Canadian Rockies. You took over driving duty at 8 P.M., two hours ago. Your friends are asleep in the backseat while you approach a steep pass. It has been snowing so heavily that you must drive at a crawl to see where you are going and avoid sliding off the road. You passed the last community 30 miles back and the resort is 40 miles ahead (nearly two hours at your current speed).	1	2	3	4	5	6	7
4. You work as an accountant in a large insurance company and for the past month have received unwanted attention several times each week from your supervisor, a married person of the opposite sex. The supervisor regularly touches your shoulder and comments on your looks. You are sure that this behavior constitutes advances rather than just friendly gestures.	1	2	3	4	5	6	7
5. You and your spouse purchased your first home one year ago, a detached house with mortgage payments that your spouse barely covers with his or her take-home pay. The economy has since entered a deep recession, and the company informed you today that you will be laid off in two months.	1	2	3	4	5	6	7

TIME STRESS SCALE

Purpose   This self-assessment is designed to help you to identify your level of time-related stress.

Instructions   Read each statement below and circle "Yes" or "No." Then use the scoring key in Appendix B to calculate your results. This exercise is completed alone so that students assess themselves honestly without concerns of social comparison. However, class discussion will focus on the time stress scale.

1. Yes No   Do you plan to slow down in the coming year?

2. Yes No   Do you consider yourself a workaholic?

3. Yes No   When you need more time, do you tend to cut back on your sleep?

4. Yes No   At the end of the day, do you often feel that you have not accomplished what you had set out to do?

5. Yes No   Do you worry that you don't spend enough time with your family or friends?

6. Yes No   Do you feel that you're constantly under stress trying to accomplish more than you can handle?

7. Yes No   Do you feel trapped in a daily routine?

8. Yes No   Do you feel that you just don't have time for fun anymore?

9. Yes No   Do you often feel under stress when you don't have enough time?

10. Yes No   Would you like to spend more time alone?

Source: Statistics Canada's 1998 General Social Survey. Cited in P. DeMont, "Too Much Stress, Too Little Time," *Ottawa Citizen*, November 12, 1999.

After studying the preceding material, be sure to check out our website at

www.mhhe.com/mcshane2e

for more in-depth information and interactivities that correspond to this chapter.

Team Processes

8

Foundations of Team Dynamics

AFTER READING THIS CHAPTER, YOU SHOULD BE ABLE TO:

- Define *teams*.

- Distinguish departmental teams from team-based organizations.

- Explain why virtual teams are becoming more common.

- Outline the model of team effectiveness.

- Identify six organizational and team environmental elements that influence team effectiveness.

- Explain the influence of the team's task, size, and composition on team effectiveness.

- Describe the five stages of team development.

- Identify four factors that shape team norms.

- List six factors that influence team cohesiveness.

- Discuss the limitations of teams.

- Explain how companies minimize social loafing.

- Summarize the four types of team building.

The Chrysler Division of DaimlerChrysler has discovered how to get new products to market faster, more efficiently, and more in line with customer needs. Their secret weapon? Teams, lot of teams. Chrysler has created 3 types of executive and professional teams, including a senior-level product strategy team; 6 product innovation teams; and 50 component parts teams.

The product strategy team—led by Chrysler Group president Dieter Zetsche—is responsible for the discovery phase of a new vehicle. This group analyzes customer trends, new design ideas, technological innovation, and the economic environment to determine which new vehicle line to develop and build.

Of the six product innovation teams, five represent vehicle groups (small vehicles, trucks, etc.) and a sixth oversees engines and transmissions. These are similar to the platform teams that Chrysler has used for the past decade in product development. However, platform teams focused on design and engineering, whereas product innovation teams will bring marketing and manufacturing people into the product development process earlier.

"We want to ensure a balance between creativity and marketing,"

DaimlerChrysler relies on teams to design and manufacture new vehicles faster, more efficiently, and more in line with customer needs. (© Alan Levenson/Getty Images)

says Chrysler Group president and chief executive Dieter Zetsche. Zetsche also expects these teams to reduce product development time from the current average of 24 to 36 months to just 18 months.

Chrysler has also introduced 50 component parts teams that will reduce costs by ensuring that vehicle groups share components. For example, Chrysler now uses about 27 different batteries. The company hopes one of the component teams will cut that number down to about 5 types of batteries.[1]

eams are replacing individuals as the basic building blocks of organizations. DaimlerChrysler has organized employees from engineering, marketing, purchasing, and other departments into product innovation teams to design and manufacture new vehicles faster and more efficiently. At SEI Investments near Philadelphia, employees work in an open space with desks on wheels so that they can form on-the-fly teams for specific investment projects. AES Corporation, the Virginia-based global power company, relies on teams to operate entire power stations. Flexible Steel Lacing Company in Downers Grove, Illinois, has reorganized its employees into autonomous teams that have almost total control over manufacturing a complete product group.[2]

Teams are groups of two or more people who interact and influence each other, are mutually accountable for achieving common objectives, and perceive

teams

Groups of two or more people who interact and influence each other, are mutually accountable for achieving common objectives, and perceive themselves as a social entity within an organization.

Nortel Networks values teamwork. That's what Phuong Truong discovered when she joined the engineering group at the Internet and telecommunications gear company. Truong (shown here at Nortel's fitness center) is part of a project team of 12 engineers who call themselves the Raptors. No particular reason for the name, except maybe that it sounds ferocious. She recruits new employees for the group and determines who would be an effective team member. Truong also volunteers as a member of the employee satisfaction team that communicates with senior management and employees about job concerns. "We have a big departmental discussion every month to tell us how the team is doing, find out where the team is going, what we are we doing next," explains Truong.[3] Why would Nortel Networks rely on teams rather than individuals to perform these tasks? (© D. Chan/Ottawa Citizen)

themselves as a social entity within an organization.[4] All teams exist to fulfill some purpose, such as assembling a product, providing a service, operating a submarine, or making an important decision. Team members are held together by their interdependence and need for collaboration to achieve common goals. All teams require some form of communication so that members can coordinate and share common objectives. Team members also influence each other, although some members are more influential than others regarding the team's goals and activities.

groups

People with a unifying relationship.

All teams are **groups** because they consist of people with a unifying relationship. But not all groups are teams; some groups are just people assembled together.[5] For example, employees who meet for lunch are rarely called teams because they have little or no task interdependence (each person could just as easily eat lunch alone) and no purpose beyond their social interaction. Although the terms *group* and *team* are used interchangeably in this book, our main focus is on teams. This is partly because most of the discussion is about task-oriented teams rather than other types of groups, and partly because the term *teams* has largely replaced *groups* in the business language.[6]

team-based organization

A type of departmentalization with a flat span of control and relatively little formalization, consisting of self-directed work teams responsible for various work processes.

As teams become more popular, corporate leaders run the risk of failing to leverage the potential of these groups. For example, research suggests that DaimlerChrysler's cross-functional product innovation teams often fall short of the desired results because corporate leaders ignore the complex conditions that must be in place to make these teams work effectively.[7] This chapter looks at the complex conditions that make teams more or less effective in organizational settings. After introducing the different types of teams in organizational settings, we present a model of team effectiveness. Most of the chapter examines each part of this model, including team and organizational environment, team design, and the team processes of development, norms, roles, and cohesiveness. The chapter concludes by surveying the strategies for building more effective work teams.

TYPES OF TEAMS AND OTHER GROUPS IN ORGANIZATIONS

There are many types of teams and other groups in organizations. Permanent work teams are responsible for a specific set of tasks in the organization. For instance, most departments are considered permanent teams because employees interact directly and coordinate work activities with each other, as depicted in Exhibit 8.1(a).[8] Increasingly, employees with different skills work together on work processes. Some hospitals have moved in this direction by forming surgical teams made up of nurses, radiologists, anesthetists, pharmacologists, and others. These people previously worked in departments based on their specialty. Now they work together on a specific work process.

self-directed work teams (SDWTs)

Cross-functional work groups that are organized around work processes, that complete an entire piece of work requiring several interdependent tasks, and that have substantial autonomy over the execution of these tasks.

Some companies take this team focus much further by forming a **team-based organization.** Team-based organizations rely extensively on **self-directed work teams (SDWTs)** organized around work processes rather than specialized departments as core work units.[9] These teams complete an entire piece of work requiring several interdependent tasks. They also are fairly autonomous, as indicated by the dashed lines in Exhibit 8.1(b), so there is less need for direct supervision or someone to report continually to the executive team. They are also *cross-functional*. This means that unlike traditional departments where employees have similar competencies (e.g., marketing,

EXHIBIT 8.1   Departments as work teams

(a) Team-oriented department

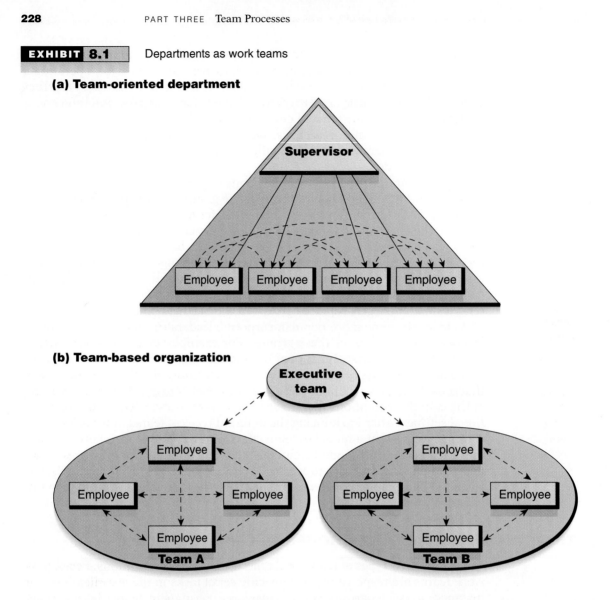

(b) Team-based organization

engineering), SDWTs rely on people with diverse and complementary skills, knowledge, and experience. SDWTs are described more fully in the next chapter because they represent the highest level of employee involvement.

Employees often belong to secondary teams that parallel their more permanent positions in the organization. **Quality circles** fall into this category.[10] Quality circles are small teams of employees who meet for a few hours each week to identify quality and productivity problems, propose solutions to management, and monitor the implementation and consequences of these solutions in their work area. Quality circles are usually permanent and typically include co-workers in the same work unit.

Along with permanent teams, organizations rely on temporary teams to make decisions or complete short-term projects. Companies bring together employees from various departments to design a product, solve a client's problem, or search for new opportunities.[11] *Task forces* (also called *ad hoc* teams) are temporary teams that investigate a particular problem and disband when the decision is made. For instance, Royal Dutch/Shell Group formed a cross-functional team to improve revenues for its service stations along major highways in Malaysia. This team, which included a service station dealer, a union truck driver, and four or five marketing executives, disbanded after it had reviewed the Malaysian service stations and submitted a business plan.[12]

Skunkworks

Skunkworks are usually (but not always) temporary teams formed spontaneously to develop products or solve complex problems. They are initiated by an innovative employee (a *champion*) who borrows people and resources (called *bootlegging*) to help the organization.[13] Some skunkworks are isolated from the rest of the organization and thus are able to ignore the more bureaucratic rules governing other organizational units. The earliest corporate intranets started as skunkworks, championed by employees with a UNIX computer and free software from universities to create a web server. Skunkworks are responsible for several innovations at 3M Corporation. One example is a special micro-surface mouse pad that has become a commercial success. "Management had no idea the project was being worked on, until it was ready to be launched," explains a 3M executive. "Some lab, some manufacturing, and some marketing people got together as an informal team to do it."[14]

Virtual Teams

When Roger Rodriguez goes to work each day at BakBone Software in San Diego, the client service senior engineer typically picks up customer support problems passed on from colleagues in Lanham, Maryland, and Poole, England. At the end of his workday, Rodriguez passes some of his projects on to BakBone co-workers in Tokyo. Rodriguez must be sure the instructions he sends on to Tokyo are clear because overseas co-workers can't ask him questions in the middle of San Diego's night. Rodriguez also admits that working with distance team members has its challenges. "You don't have the time for open-ended conversation," he says.

New Balance Athletic Shoe Inc. is competing against low-wage factories in Asia through technology and a team-based organization. Well-trained employees at New Balance's five factories in Massachusetts and Maine operate computerized equipment running up to 20 sewing-machine heads at once. These employees work in teams of five or six people, performing a half-dozen jobs, switching tasks every few minutes, and picking up the slack for one another. New employees receive 22 hours of classroom instruction on teamwork and other techniques and get continual training on the factory floor. This combination of teams and technology allows New Balance to produce a pair of shoes in 24 minutes, compared with nearly three hours in Asian factories.[15] What other advantages would New Balance Athletic Shoe experience with its team-based organization? (© Mark Garfinkel/ Boston Herald)

skunkworks
Temporary teams formed spontaneously to develop products or solve complex problems.

"You can't informally brainstorm with someone."[16] Roger Rodriguez and his dozen colleagues at BakBone Software are part of the growing trend toward virtual teams. **Virtual teams** are cross-functional groups that operate across space, time, and organizational boundaries with members who communicate mainly through electronic technologies.[17] Some groups become virtual teams when employees telecommute or communicate with team members while

virtual teams
Cross-functional groups that operate across space, time, and organizational boundaries with members who communicate mainly through electronic technologies.

law of telecosm
States that as the web of computer networks expands, distances will shrink and eventually become irrelevant.

informal groups
Two or more people who interact primarily to meet their personal (rather than organizational) needs.

coalition
An informal group that attempts to influence people outside the goup by pooling the resources and power of its members.

visiting clients. BakBone Software created a virtual client support team to benefit from the best possible talent around the world. "Virtual team . . . allow you to draw from a more diverse talent pool because you're hiring in different geographic locations," explains Tim Miller, director of client services at BakBone Software.

Why are virtual teams becoming more common? Emerging information technology has certainly facilitated their development. Recent evidence suggests that effective virtual teams creatively combine e-mail, videoconferencing, intranets, and other traditional electronic communication channels to suit their needs.[18] Virtual teams benefit from the **law of telecosm,** which states that as the web of computer networks expands, distances will shrink and eventually become irrelevant.[19] While distance isn't yet irrelevant, computer connectivity has strengthened bonds among team members in different cities and on different continents. The shift toward knowledge-based rather than production-based work has also made virtual teamwork feasible. Roger Rodriguez's team is able to complete knowledge-based tasks from a distance through information technology, whereas production-based work activities usually require co-location of team members.[20]

Technology and knowledge-based work make virtual teams *possible*, but globalization and the benefits of knowledge sharing and teamwork make them *necessary*. As we described in Chapter 1, globalization has become the new reality in many organizations. As companies open businesses overseas or form tight alliances with companies located elsewhere in the world, there is increasing pressure to form virtual teams that coordinate these operations. For instance, the European Union is providing tens of millions of dollars to fund research into electronic methods of working. The idea is to create virtual teams that leverage their knowledge across the region as well as create more efficient use of transportation systems and office space.[21]

Virtual teams also leverage the benefits of team dynamics. They enable employees in diverse locations to collaborate and make potentially better decisions on complex issues.[22] Virtual teams represent a natural extension of knowledge management because they minimize the "silos of knowledge" problem that tends to develop when employees are geographically scattered. In other words, virtual teams encourage employees to share and use knowledge where geography limits more direct forms of collaboration.

Informal Groups

Along with formal work teams, organizations consist of **informal groups** that exist primarily for the benefit of their members. Informal groups are not specifically formed by organizational decision makers, although their structure may be influenced by the existence of work teams. They shape communication patterns and often create their own set of values that support or oppose the organization's values. Some informal groups, such as the group you meet for lunch, might overlap with the work team. These groups form out of convenience and the need for affiliation. Other groups are bound together for reasons other than social needs. For instance, you might belong to an informal group that shares a car pool and another group that plays together on the company's sports team.

A **coalition** is an informal group that attempts to influence people outside the group by pooling the resources and power of its members. By banding together, coalition members have more power than if each person worked alone to influence others. They also reinforce each other and further mobilize support for their position.[23] The coalition's mere existence can be a source of power by symbolizing the importance or level of support for the issue.

communities of practice
Informal groups bound together by shared expertise and passion for a particular activity or interest.

Communities of practice are informal groups bound together by shared expertise and passion for a particular activity or interest.[24] For instance, Schlumberger Ltd. has communities of practice on deepwater drilling, horizontal drilling, deviated wells, and other topics. Employees are connected to the oil-field services firm's web portal where they share knowledge on their daily experiences.[25] In most organizations, communities of practice are informal groups that congregate in person or in cyberspace to share knowledge. People who have a common passion for environmental concerns, for example, might meet twice each month over lunch to share their knowledge. Other communities interact entirely through list servers and websites where participants exchange information on specific technical issues. Many communities of practice extend beyond organizational boundaries, so they represent a source of knowledge acquisition.

Why Informal Groups Exist   One reason people join informal groups is to fulfill their relatedness needs (see Chapter 5). We meet co-workers for lunch or stop by their work areas for brief chats because this activity satisfies our need for social interaction. Similarly, social identity theory (see Chapter 3) explains that we define ourselves by our group affiliations. If we belong to work teams or informal groups that are viewed favorably by others, then we tend to view ourselves more favorably. We are motivated to become members of groups that are similar to ourselves because this affiliation reinforces our social identity.[26]

Some groups form because they accomplish tasks that cannot be achieved by individuals working alone. Coalitions and other task-oriented informal groups remain intact because members know they cannot achieve the same results alone. When groups are successful, it is easier to attract new members in the future. Informal groups also tend to congregate in stressful situations because we are comforted by the physical presence of other people and are therefore motivated to be near them.[27] This phenomenon explains why soldiers huddle together in battle, even though they are taught to disperse under fire. It also explains why employees tend to congregate when hearing that the company has been sold or that some people may be laid off.

A MODEL OF TEAM EFFECTIVENESS

Why are some teams more effective than others? This question has challenged organizational researchers for some time and, as you might expect, numerous models of team effectiveness have been proposed over the years.[28] **Team effectiveness** refers to how the team affects the organization, individual team members, and the team's existence.[29] First, most teams exist to serve some purpose relating to the organization or other system in which the group operates. Product innovation teams at DaimlerChrysler have been formed to improve the efficiency, speed, and customer delight of new vehicle design. Some informal groups also have task-oriented goals, such as a coalition that wants to persuade senior management to change a corporate policy.

Second, team effectiveness considers the satisfaction and well-being of its members. People join groups to fulfill their personal needs, so it makes sense that effectiveness is measured partly by this need fulfillment. Finally, team

team effectiveness
The extent to which a team achieves its objectives, achieves the needs and objectives of its members, and sustains itself over time.

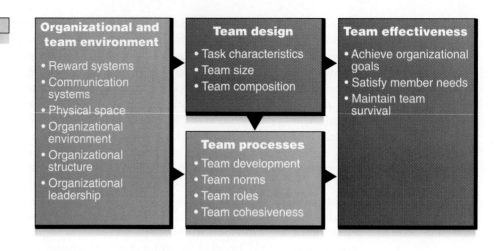

EXHIBIT 8.2

A model of team effectiveness

effectiveness includes the team's viability—its ability to survive. It must be able to maintain the commitment of its members, particularly during the turbulence of the team's development. Without this commitment, people leave and the team will fall apart. It must also secure sufficient resources and find a benevolent environment in which to operate.

Exhibit 8.2 presents the model of team effectiveness that we will describe over the next several pages. We begin by looking at elements of the team's and organization's environment that influence team design, processes, and outcomes.

ORGANIZATIONAL AND TEAM ENVIRONMENT

Our discussion of team effectiveness logically begins with the contextual factors that influence the team's design, processes, and outcomes. There are many elements in the organizational and team environment that influence team effectiveness. Six of the most important elements are reward systems, communication systems, physical space, organizational environment, organizational structure, and organizational leadership.

■ *Reward systems*—Research indicates that team members tend to work together more effectively when they are at least partly rewarded for team performance. Employees at Jostens, Inc., a manufacturer of school rings and other products, developed a stronger team orientation after the company shifted from individual incentives to a team-based gainsharing plan.[30] This strategy doesn't mean that everyone on the team should receive the same amount of pay based on the team's performance. On the contrary, rewards tend to work better in the United States and other Western societies when individual pay is determined by a combination of individual and team performance.[31]

■ *Communication systems*—A poorly designed communication system can starve a team of valuable information and feedback, or it may swamp it with information overload.[32] Virtual teams in particular require the right combination of communication technologies. For example, virtual team members at BakBone Software stay in touch with others via telephone, e-mail, and a companywide database that tracks specific customer problems.[33] Communication systems are also important when team members are located together. Physical space might be arranged to encourage more face-to-face dialogue. In each of these cases, the team's communication systems are aligned with its task and structure.

■ *Physical space*—The layout of an office or factory does more than improve communications among team members. It also influences the team's ability to accomplish tasks and shapes employee perceptions about being together as a team. That's why multinational engineering firm Arup moved its Hong Kong headquarters from an aging city high-rise to a suburban site where offices were replaced by low-rise cubicles. The result has been a significant improvement in interaction among team members as well as between teams.[34]

■ *Organizational environment*—Team success depends on the company's external environment. If the organization cannot secure resources, for instance, the team cannot fulfill its performance targets. Similarly, high demand for the team's output creates feelings of success, which motivates team members to stay with the team. A competitive environment can motivate employees to work together more closely.

■ *Organizational structure*– Many teams fail because the organizational structure does not support them. Teams work better when there are few layers of management and teams are given autonomy and responsibility for their work. This structure encourages interaction with team members rather than with supervisors. Teams also flourish when employees are organized around work processes rather than specialized skills. This structure increases interaction among team members.[35]

■ *Organizational leadership*—Teams require ongoing support from senior executives to align rewards, organizational structure, communication systems, and other elements of team context. They also require team leaders or facilitators who provide coaching and support. Team leaders are enablers, meaning that they ensure that teams have the authority to solve their own problems and the resources to accomplish their tasks.[36] Leaders also maintain a value system that supports team performance more than individual success.

TEAM DESIGN FEATURES

Putting together a team is rather like designing a mini-organization. There are several elements to consider, and the wrong combination will undermine team effectiveness. Three of the main structural elements to consider when designing teams are task characteristics, team size, and team composition. As we saw earlier in the team effectiveness model (Exhibit 8.2), these design features affect team effectiveness directly as well as indirectly through team processes. For example, the skills and diversity of team members affect team cohesiveness, but they also have a direct effect on how well the team performs its task. Similarly, the type of work performed by the team (task characteristics) may influence the types of roles that emerge, but it also has a direct effect on the satisfaction and well-being of team members.

Task Characteristics

Teams are generally more effective when tasks are clear and easy to implement, because team members can learn their roles more quickly.[37] In contrast, teams with ill-defined tasks require more time to agree on the best division of labor and the correct way to accomplish the goal. More complex tasks requiring diverse skills and backgrounds further strain the team's ability to develop and form a cohesive unit.

Another important task characteristic is **task interdependence.** High task interdependence exists when team members must share common inputs to their individual tasks, need to interact in the process of executing their work, or receive outcomes (such as rewards) that are determined partly by the performance of others. Teams are well suited to highly interdependent tasks because people coordinate better when working together than separately. Moreover, recent evidence indicates that task interdependence creates an additional sense of responsibility among team members, which motivates them to work together rather than alone.[38] This is why companies organize employees around work processes. Each team is responsible for highly interdependent tasks, so they coordinate the work more efficiently than individuals working in specialized departments.

task interdependence

The degree to which a task requires employees to share common inputs or outcomes, or to interact in the process of executing their work.

Team Size

St. Luke's is a highly successful British advertising agency that relies on self-directed work teams to serve clients. The London-based firm is so team-oriented that it refuses to participate in industry awards that recognize individual achievement. One way that St. Luke's supports team dynamics is through the "35 rule," which states that no team shall have more than 35 members. "When any one group becomes larger than 35 people, it has to split apart, as an amoeba would," explains Andy Law, St. Luke's CEO and co-founder.[39]

Team size is an important concern at St. Luke's. Some writers claim that team size should be limited to 10 or fewer people, making St. Luke's limit of 35 team members far too high. However, the optimal team size depends on several factors, such as the number of people required to complete the work and the amount of coordination needed to work together. The general rule is that teams should be large enough to provide the necessary competencies and perspectives to perform the work, yet small enough to maintain efficient coordination and meaningful involvement of each member.[40]

Larger teams are typically less effective because members consume more time and effort coordinating their roles and resolving differences. Individuals have less opportunity to participate and, consequently, are less likely to feel that they are contributing to the team's success. Larger work units tend to break into informal subgroups around common interests and work activities, leading members to form stronger commitments to their subgroup than to the larger team. Pharmaceutical giant Pfizer Inc. tries to avoid these problems with large teams at its new research facility in Groton, Connecticut, by organizing five to seven scientists into "families" and grouping about 10 families into a "tribe" of 70 people.[41]

Team Composition

Effective teams require individual team members with the motivation and ability to work in a team environment. With respect to motivation, every member must have sufficient drive to perform the task in a team environment. Specifically, team members must be motivated to agree on the goal, work together

Houston's new H-E-B Central Market is a 75,000-square-foot cornucopia of food delights. To support this customer experience, the San Antonio–based grocery retailer carefully hires job applicants (such as Jesus Guevara, shown in photo) who are outgoing and enjoy working in teams.
Applicants begin by completing an application form and writing detailed examples of when they
used teamwork and communication skills to solve problems on the job. After making the cut,
prospective employees are invited back in groups of about eight people and presented with
samples of store products. Interviewers observe their willingness to try unusual foods and interact with others. "We want to see who can work together as a team, who's creative and who
shows leadership, who's assertive and who's not," says an H-E-B executive. Successful applicants proceed to the third stage where their team, communication, and leadership skills are
further assessed through individual interviews.[42] Along with the selection process, how else
can companies ensure that employees have the ability and motivation to work in teams?
(© E. Joseph Deering/ Houston Chronicle*)*

rather than alone, and abide by the team's rules of conduct. Employees with a
collectivist orientation—those who value group goals more than their own personal goals (see Chapter 4)—tend to perform better in work teams, whereas
those with a strong individualist orientation tend to perform better alone.[43]

Employees must possess the skills and knowledge necessary to accomplish
the team's objectives.[44] Each person needs only some of the necessary skills,
but the entire group must have the full set of competencies. Moreover, each
team member's competencies need to be known to other team members. Team
members also need to be able to work effectively with others. They must have
sufficient emotional intelligence (see Chapter 4) to manage emotions, as well
as conflict management skills to effectively resolve interpersonal differences.
Researchers also emphasize the importance of training employees in ways to
communicate and coordinate with each other in a team environment.[45]

How do companies ensure that employees have the ability and motivation
to work in teams? Team-based reward systems can motivate employees to

work with the team rather than focus on individual effort. However, it is often easiest to hire people at the outset who possess team-oriented competencies and values. Anchor Hocking, the glass and plastic kitchenware manufacturer, requires applicants to complete a project in teams while evaluators identify those who work best in a team environment. Candidates also write an essay on what a team environment means to them.[46]

homogeneous teams

Teams that include members with common technical expertise, demographics (age, gender), ethnicity, experiences, or values.

heterogeneous teams

Teams that include members with diverse personal characteristics and backgrounds.

Team Diversity   Another important dimension of team composition is the diversity of team members.[47] **Homogeneous teams** include members with common technical expertise, demographics (age, gender), ethnicity, experiences, or values, whereas **heterogeneous teams** have members with diverse personal characteristics and backgrounds. Should teams be homogeneous or heterogeneous? Both types of teams have advantages and disadvantages, and their relative effectiveness depends on the situation. Heterogeneous teams experience more conflict and take longer to develop. They are susceptible to fault lines—hypothetical dividing lines that may split a team into subgroups along gender, ethnic, professional, or other dimensions. In some situations, these fault lines may eventually split the team apart.[48] In contrast, members of homogeneous teams experience higher satisfaction, less conflict, and better interpersonal relations. Consequently, homogeneous teams tend to be more effective on tasks requiring a high degree of cooperation and coordination, such as the tasks of emergency response teams or string quartets.

Although heterogeneous teams are more difficult to develop, they are generally more effective than homogeneous teams at solving complex problems requiring innovative solutions because people from different backgrounds see a problem or opportunity from different perspectives.[49] Heterogeneous team members also solve complex problems more easily because they usually have a broader knowledge base. A senior executive at Monsanto Corporation sums up this view: "Every time I have put together a diverse group of people, that team has always come up with a more breakthrough solution than any homogeneous group working on the same problem."[50] Finally, a team's diversity may give it more legitimacy or allow its members to obtain a wide network of cooperation and support in the organization.

Team composition, team size, and task characteristics affect team effectiveness directly as well as indirectly through team processes. The four team processes, identified earlier in the team effectiveness model (Exhibit 8.2), are team development, team norms, team roles, and team cohesiveness.

TEAM PROCESSES

Our discussion so far has presented two sets of elements in the team effectiveness model: (1) organizational and team environment and (2) team design. In this section, we introduce the third set of team effectiveness elements, collectively known as team processes. These processes—team development, norms, roles, and cohesiveness—are influenced by both team design and organizational and team environment factors.

Team Development

Team members must resolve several issues and pass through several stages of development before emerging as an effective work unit. They must get to know

EXHIBIT 8.3

Stages of team development

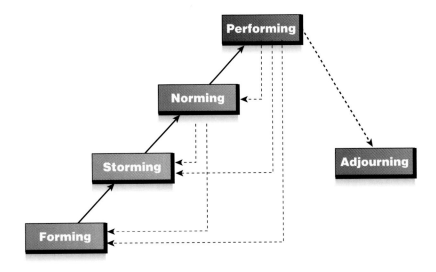

each other, understand their respective roles, discover appropriate and inappropriate behaviors, and learn how to coordinate their work or social activities. This process is ongoing because teams change as new members join and old members leave. The five-stage model of team development, shown in Exhibit 8.3, provides a general outline of how teams evolve by forming, storming, norming, performing, and eventually adjourning.[51] The model shows teams progressing from one stage to the next in an orderly fashion, but the dotted lines illustrate that they might also fall back to an earlier stage of development as new members join or other conditions disrupt the team's maturity.

1. *Forming*—The first stage of team development is a period of testing and orientation in which members learn about each other and evaluate the benefits and costs of continued membership. People tend to be polite during this stage and will defer to the existing authority of a formal or informal leader who must provide an initial set of rules and structures for interaction. Members experience a form of socialization (described in Chapter 18) as they try to find out what is expected of them and how they will fit into the team.

2. *Storming*—The storming stage is marked by interpersonal conflict as members become more proactive and compete for various team roles. Coalitions may form to influence the team's goals and means of goal attainment. Members try to establish norms of appropriate behavior and performance standards. This is a tenuous stage in the team's development, particularly when the leader is autocratic and lacks the necessary conflict management skills.

3. *Norming*—During the norming stage, the team develops its first real sense of cohesion as roles are established and a consensus forms around group objectives. Members have developed relatively similar mental models, so they have common expectations and assumptions about how the team's goals should be accomplished. They have developed a common team-based mental model that allows them to interact more efficiently so that they can move into the next stage, performing.[52]

4. *Performing*—The team becomes more task-oriented in the performing stage. Team members have learned to coordinate and resolve conflicts

more efficiently. Further coordination improvements must occasionally be addressed, but the greater emphasis is on task accomplishment. In high-performance teams, members are highly cooperative, have a high level of trust in each other, are committed to group objectives, and identify with the team. There is a climate of mutual support in which team members feel comfortable about taking risks, making errors, or asking for help.[53]

5. *Adjourning*—Most work teams and informal groups eventually end. Task forces disband when their project is completed. Informal work groups may reach this stage when several members leave the organization or are reassigned elsewhere. Some teams adjourn as a result of layoffs or plant shutdowns. Whatever the cause of team adjournment, members shift their attention away from task orientation to a socioemotional focus as they realize that their relationship is ending.

The team development model is a useful framework for thinking about how teams develop. At the same time, we must keep in mind that it is not a perfect representation of the dynamics of team development.[54] The model does not explicitly show that some teams remain in a particular stage longer than others and that team development is an ongoing process. As membership changes and new conditions emerge, teams cycle back to earlier stages in the developmental process to regain the equilibrium or balance lost by the change (as shown by the dotted lines in Exhibit 8.3).

Team Norms

Have you ever noticed how employees in some departments almost run for the exit door the minute the workday ends, whereas people in the same jobs elsewhere seem to be competing for who can stay at work the longest? These differences are partly due to **norms**—the informal rules and expectations that groups establish to regulate the behavior of their members. Norms apply only to behavior, not to private thoughts or feelings. Moreover, norms exist only for behaviors that are important to the team.[55]

Norms guide the way team members deal with clients, how they share resources, whether they are willing to work long hours, and many other behaviors in organizational life. Some norms ensure that employees support organizational goals, whereas other norms might conflict with organizational objectives. For example, the level of employee absence from work is influenced partly by absence norms in the workplace. In other words, employees are more likely to take off work if they work in teams that support this behavior.[56]

Conformity to Team Norms Everyone has experienced peer pressure at one time or another. Co-workers grimace if we are late for a meeting or make sarcastic comments if we don't have our part of the project completed on time. In more extreme situations, team members may try to enforce their norms by temporarily ostracizing deviant co-workers or threatening to terminate their membership. This heavy-handed peer pressure isn't as rare as you might think. One survey revealed that 20 percent of employees have been pressured by their colleagues to slack off at work. Half of the time, the peer pressure occurred because colleagues didn't want to look like poor performers against their more productive co-workers.[57]

norms
The informal rules and expectations that groups establish to regulate the behavior of their members.

Elite New Zealand Prison Team's "Culture of Obedience"

Members of a special emergency response team congregated at dawn for a covert mission. The 16 hand-picked and specially trained members based at Paparua Prison, New Zealand, were supposed to reduce prison violence, prevent drugs from entering prisons, and improve prisoner compliance. But the mission on this day was different. The response team was hunting for an escapee—a rooster belonging to a member of the response team that had escaped to a neighboring farm.

This is just one of the bizarre incidents involving the special unit, dubbed the "Goon Squad" by adversaries. The team worked independently of the prison officers and had its own distinctive black uniforms. Unfortunately, a government report also concluded that the team developed a distinctive set of norms, some of which violated corrections department policies.

A government investigation heard claims that the team falsified time sheets, juggled the work roster for personal gain, used department vehicles for personal use, used unnecessary intimidation on inmates, disciplined staff inappropriately, and hunted wayward roosters on company time. The special unit also conducted missions in the outside community even though its mandate was restricted to the prison. "Our focus moved to a policeman's role, which we should not have been doing," admits one former member.

None of the members complained during the unit's existence because of "a culture of obedience." For example, when one member refused to go to a party, others in the unit allegedly went to his home, restrained him, hit him over the head with an axe handle, handcuffed him, and dragged him along to the party.

"The most chilling thing about the team was an apparent fear of authority among members, leading to a culture of obedience and silence," says an executive member of the Howard League for Penal Reform. "In effect, they became a law unto themselves."

Sources: Y. Martin, "Goon Squad," *The Press (Christchurch, New Zealand)*, June 9, 2001, p. 2; "'Goon Squad' Prison Staff Disciplined," *New Zealand Press Association*, May 23, 2001; Y. Martin, "Crack Prison Team Members Guilty of Serious Misconduct," *The Press (Christchurch, New Zealand)*, May 24, 2001, p. 1.

Norms are also directly reinforced through praise from high-status members, more access to valued resources, or other rewards available to the team.[58] But team members often conform to prevailing norms without direct reinforcement or punishment because they identify with the group and want to align their behavior with the team's values. This effect is particularly strong in new members because they are uncertain of their status and want to demonstrate their commitment to membership in the team. Global Connections 8.1 provides an extreme example of the consequences of team norms and conformity in organizational settings.

How Team Norms Develop Norms develop as team members learn that certain behaviors help them function more effectively.[59] Some norms develop when team members or outsiders make explicit statements that seem to aid the team's success or survival. For example, the team leader might frequently express the importance of treating customers with respect and courtesy. A second factor triggering the development of a new norm is a critical event in the team's history. A team might develop a strong norm to keep the work area clean after a co-worker slips on metal scraps and seriously injures herself.

Team norms are most strongly influenced by events soon after the team is formed.[60] Future behaviors are influenced by the way members of a newly formed team initially greet each other, where they locate themselves in a meeting, and so on. A fourth influence on team norms is the beliefs and values that members bring to the team. For example, bargaining groups develop norms about appropriate bargaining behavior that are based on each member's previous bargaining experience.[61]

Troubleshooting Dysfunctional Team Norms   Although many team norms are deeply anchored, there are ways to change them or make them less influential on employee behavior. One approach is to introduce performance-oriented norms as soon as the team is created. Another strategy is to select members who will bring desirable norms to the group. If the organization wants to emphasize safety, then it should select team members who already value safety.

Selecting people with positive norms may be effective in new teams, but not when adding new members to existing teams with counterproductive norms. A better strategy for existing teams is to explicitly discuss the counterproductive norm with team members using persuasive communication tactics (see Chapter 12).[62] For example, the surgical team at one hospital had developed a norm of arriving late for operations. Patients and other hospital staff often waited 30 minutes or more for the team to arrive. The hospital CEO eventually spoke to the surgical team about their lateness and, through moral suasion, convinced team members to arrive for operating room procedures no more than 5 minutes late for their appointments.[63]

Team-based reward systems can sometimes weaken counterproductive norms. Unfortunately, the pressure to conform to the counterproductive norm may be stronger than the financial incentive.[64] For instance, employees working in a pajama factory were paid under a piece-rate system. Some individuals in the group were able to process up to 100 units per hour and thereby earn more money, but they all chose to abide by the group norm of 50 units per hour.[65]

Finally, a dysfunctional norm may be so deeply ingrained that the best strategy is to disband the group and replace it with people having more favorable norms. Companies should seize the opportunity to introduce performance-oriented norms when the new team is formed, and to select members who will bring desirable norms to the group.

Team Roles

role
The set of behaviors that people are expected to perform because they hold certain positions in a team and organization.

Every work team and informal group has two sets of roles that help it survive and be more productive. A **role** is the set of behaviors that people are expected to perform because they hold certain positions in a team and organization.[66] One set of roles helps focus the team on its objectives, such as giving and seeking information, elaborating ideas, coordinating activities, and summarizing the discussion or past events (see Exhibit 8.4). The other set of roles tries to maintain good working relations among team members. These relationship-oriented roles include resolving conflicts among team members, keeping communication channels open, reinforcing positive behaviors of other team members, and making team members aware of group process problems when they emerge.

Some team roles are formally assigned to specific people. For example, team leaders are usually expected to initiate discussion, ensure that everyone has an opportunity to present his or her views, and help the team reach agreement on the issues discussed. But team members often take on various roles

EXHIBIT 8.4	Roles for team effectiveness

Role activities	Description	Example
Task-oriented roles		
Initiator	Identifies goals for the meeting, including ways to work on those goals	"The main purpose of this meeting is to solve the problem our client is having with this product."
Information seeker	Asks for clarification of ideas or further information to support an opinion	"Jang, why do you think the client is using the product incorrectly?"
Information giver	Shares information and opinions about the team's task and goals	"Let me tell you what some of my clients did to overcome this problem."
Coordinator	Coordinates subgroups and pulls together ideas	"Susan, will you be meeting with Shaheem's group this week to review common issues with the client?"
Evaluator	Assesses the team's functioning against a standard	"So far, we have resolved three of the client's concerns, but we still have a tough one to wrestle with."
Summarizer	Acts as the team's memory	Person takes notes of meeting and summarizes the discussion when requested.
Orienter	Keeps the team focused on its goals	"We seem to be getting off on a tangent; let's focus on why the product isn't operating properly for our client."
Relationship-oriented roles		
Harmonizer	Mediates intragroup conflicts and reduces tension	"Courtney, you and Brad may want to look at your positions on this; they aren't as different as they seem."
Gatekeeper	Encourages and facilitates participation of all team members	"James, what do you think about this issue?"
Encourager	Praises and supports the ideas of other team members, thereby showing warmth and solidarity to the group	"Tracy, that's a wonderful suggestion. I think we will solve the client's problem sooner than we expected."

Sources: Adapted from information in K. D. Benne and P. Sheats, "Functional Roles of Group Members," *Journal of Social Issues* 4 (1948), pp. 41–49.

informally. Some people like to encourage colleagues to participate more actively. Others prefer to mediate conflicts that may arise among team members. As noted earlier, these preferences are usually worked out during the storming stage of team development. The critical point is that team members need to ensure that these roles are fulfilled so that the team can function effectively.

Team Cohesiveness

team cohesiveness
The degree of attraction people feel toward the team and their motivation to remain members.

Team cohesiveness—the degree of attraction people feel toward the team and their motivation to remain members—is usually an important factor in a team's success.[67] Employees feel cohesiveness when they believe the team will help them achieve their personal goals, fulfill their need for affiliation or status, or provide social support during times of crisis or trouble. Cohesiveness is an emotional experience, not just a calculation of whether to stay with or leave the team. It exists when team members make the team part of their social

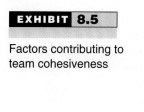

EXHIBIT 8.5

Factors contributing to
team cohesiveness

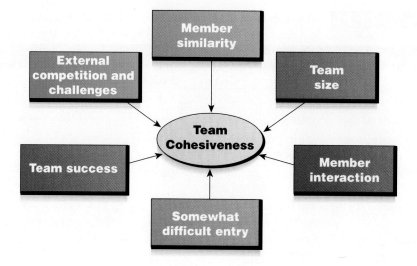

identity (see Chapter 3). Cohesiveness is the glue or *esprit de corps* that holds
the group together and ensures that its members fulfill their obligations.[68]

Causes of Team Cohesiveness   The main factors influencing team cohesiveness are identified in Exhibit 8.5. For the most part, these factors reflect
the individual's identity with the group and beliefs about how team membership will fulfill personal needs.[69] Several of these factors are related to our earlier discussion about why people join informal groups and how teams develop.
Specifically, teams become more cohesive as they reach higher stages of development and are more attractive to potential members.

Member similarity   Homogeneous teams become cohesive more easily than
heterogeneous teams. People in homogeneous teams have similar backgrounds
and values, so they find it easier to agree on team objectives, the means to fulfill those objectives, and the rules applied to maintain group behavior. This
agreement, in turn, leads to greater trust and less dysfunctional conflict within
the group.[70] In contrast, diverse teams are susceptible to the previously described fault lines that psychologically impede cohesiveness, particularly during the early stages of development. The dilemma here is that heterogeneous
teams are usually better than homogeneous teams at completing complex tasks
or solving problems requiring creative solutions.

Team size   Smaller teams tend to be more cohesive than larger teams because it is easier for a few people to agree on goals and coordinate work activities. Nevertheless, the smallest teams are not necessarily the most cohesive,
because not having enough members prevents the team from accomplishing
its objectives. Continued failure may undermine the cohesiveness as members
begin to question the team's ability to satisfy their needs. Thus, team cohesiveness is potentially greatest when teams are as small as possible, yet large
enough to accomplish the required tasks.

Member interaction   Teams tend to be more cohesive when team members
interact with each other fairly regularly. Such interaction occurs when team
members perform highly interdependent tasks and work in the same physical
area.[71] For example, Washington, D.C.–based Chatelain Architects encourages

team interaction with an open office space consisting of low partitions and no special acoustical barriers. Although some might find this arrangement noisy or stressful because of the lack of privacy, it seems to work at this team-oriented architectural firm. "We are always moving around, teaming up and working at other people's desks," says Jill Miernicki, Chatelain Architects' director of business development and environmental initiatives. "It's a very dynamic environment."[72]

The effect of physical proximity on team cohesiveness raises questions about how to maximize cohesiveness in virtual teams.[73] The lack of face-to-face interaction makes it difficult for team members to feel a common bond, even when they work effectively over the Internet. Research suggests that members of virtual teams establish a greater social connection when they have some opportunity to meet face-to-face. The ability to put a face to remote colleagues seems to strengthen the individual's emotional bond to the team. This problem may be worse for telecommuting employees who belong to a team that works in the same physical space. In the long run, these distant workers may feel left out of an otherwise cohesive team.

When Siemens, the German high-technology company, launched a mandatory telecommuting program for its Enterprise Networks group in the United States, productivity dropped and turnover increased. The company's solution was to introduce an annual four-day work-and-play gathering. The annual session provides a much-needed social connection among the 100 people in the work unit; this connection has contributed to lower turnover and higher team cohesiveness. "We feel [the annual meeting is] essential," explains a Siemens executive. "This keeps a touchstone back to other human beings. Cliques can form and people bond, even over the miles."[74]

Somewhat difficult entry   Teams tend to be more cohesive when entry to the team is restricted. The more elite the team, the more prestige it confers on its members and the more its members tend to value their membership in the unit. Existing team members are also more willing to welcome and support new members after they have "passed the test," possibly because they have shared the same entry experience.

One issue is how difficult the initiation should be for entry into the team. Research suggests that severe initiations can potentially lead to humiliation and psychological distance from the group, even for those who successfully endure the initiation.[75] However, as Connections 8.2 describes, the extreme endurance program for Air Force pararescue specialists (PJs) seems to have a strong positive effect on cohesiveness. The explanation here is that this Pipeline training program does not humiliate individuals; rather, it tests the stamina of those who attempt it. Those who endure the two-year program, which has a 90 percent failure rate, feel a special bond with fellow PJs.

Team success   Cohesiveness increases with the team's level of success.[76] Individuals are more likely to attach their social identity to successful teams than to those with a string of failures. Moreover, team members are more likely to believe the group will continue to be successful, thereby fulfilling their personal goals (continued employment, pay bonus, etc.). Team leaders can increase cohesiveness by regularly communicating and celebrating the team's successes. Notice that this can create a spiral effect. Successful teams are more cohesive and, under certain conditions, increased cohesiveness increases the team's success.

Air Force Pararescue Training Creates Cohesiveness

Jason Cunningham's body begged for air. His lungs felt like they would burst, and his brain screamed to swim to the surface for fresh air. But Cunningham ignored these warnings and stayed under until he faded to black. When Cunningham regained consciousness, colleagues were reviving him with an oxygen mask and words of encouragement. "Once you pass out the first time, you get used to it," Cunningham says casually. "It's really not that bad, no big deal."

For most people, drowning ranks pretty high in the "big deal" department. But at the Air Force Pararescue School at Kirtland Air Force Base, New Mexico, it's all part of the learning experience. Air Force pararescue specialists (known as PJs) are extreme emergency medical technicians who locate downed aircrews behind enemy lines, patch them up, and spirit them away to safety.

PJs are also a highly cohesive group of 300 people because they have endured a two-year initiation ritual called the Pipeline, which begins with a two-month-long ordeal of training, including weight-belt swimming, water treading, buddy breathing, and drown-proofing. The underwater school includes such memorable activities as bobbing for precious breaths in the water with your feet bound and your hands tied behind your back. In another segment, trainees are buckled in a mock aircraft that is then dunked and flipped upside down in the water. PJs also get plenty of practice at parachuting, living on meager rations on an island, and handling medical emergencies under difficult conditions.

Air Force pararescue specialists are a highly cohesive group because of their tough initiation into this elite unit. *(Courtesy of Airman)*

It's no wonder that only 10 percent of applicants make it through the Pipeline. Staff Sergeant Doug Isaacks is one of the few who graduated. "All I heard were the statistics, the high washout rates, like only one in a hundred makes it. Nobody gave me much of chance," says Isaacks, who looks as strong as a Clydesdale. "But I did it, and it's one of the greatest moments of my life. It feels great to be part of something special—a brotherhood."

Sources: "Simulated Crash Helps Pararescue People Train," *FDCH Federal Department and Agency Documents*, May 3, 2001; P. McKenna, "Superman School," *Airman*, February 2000, pp. 2–11.

External competition and challenges Team cohesiveness increases when members face external competition or a valued objective that is challenging, such as the threat from an external competitor or friendly competition from other teams. These conditions tend to increase cohesiveness because employees value the team's ability to overcome a threat or competition that they couldn't handle individually. They also value their membership as a form of social support. We need to be careful about the degree of external threat, however. Evidence suggests that teams seem to be less effective when external threats are severe.[77] Although cohesiveness tends to increase, external threats are stressful and cause teams to make less effective decisions under these conditions.

Consequences of Team Cohesiveness Every team must have some minimal level of cohesiveness to maintain its existence.[78] People who belong to high cohesion teams are motivated to maintain their membership and to help the team work effectively. They are generally more sensitive to each other's

Trevor Pound was looking forward to lying on a Mexican beach for his thirtieth birthday. But the Mitel software engineer's crucial role in a major project put those February vacation plans on hold. Pound barely mentioned his disappointment, but fellow team members at the communications systems firm wanted to make up for his loss. Nearly a dozen co-workers spent a weekend transforming Pound's drab gray cubicle into a colorful oasis. They brought in a 5-foot-wide beach umbrella, a beach chair, a heat lamp, a ukulele, some beach toys, a dozen tropical plants, and over 200 pounds of sand. The culprits even supplied colorful shorts and a Hawaiian-style shirt. The result: Pound celebrated his birthday in an almost tropical setting on that cold winter day. More important, the practical joke expressed the team's support for his loss of personal time.[84] How else do cohesive team members support each other? (© *John Major*/Ottawa Citizen)

needs and develop better interpersonal relationships, thereby reducing dysfunctional conflict. When conflict does arise, members of high cohesion teams seem to resolve the differences swiftly and effectively. Compared with members of low cohesion teams, high cohesion team members spend more time together, share information more frequently, and are more satisfied with each other. They provide each other with better social support in stressful situations.[79]

Cohesiveness and team performance   With better cooperation and more conformity to norms, high cohesion teams usually perform better than low cohesion teams.[80] However, the relationship is complex. Exhibit 8.6 illustrates how the effect of cohesiveness on team performance depends on the extent to which team norms are consistent with organizational goals. Cohesive teams will likely have lower task performance when norms conflict with organizational objectives, because cohesiveness motivates employees to perform at a level more consistent with group norms.[81]

THE TROUBLE WITH TEAMS

Scholars and business leaders have long recognized that teams can be a competitive advantage. Yet it is easy to lose sight of the fact that teams aren't always needed.[82] Sometimes, a quick and decisive action by one person is more appropriate. Some tasks are also performed just as easily by one person as by a group. "Teams are overused," admits Philip Condit, CEO of Boeing, Inc. The aircraft manufacturer makes extensive use of teams but knows that they aren't necessary for everything that goes on in organizations. Management guru Peter Drucker agrees. "The now-fashionable team in which everybody works with everybody on everything from the beginning rapidly is becoming a disappointment," he says.[83]

A second problem is that teams take time to develop and maintain. Scholars refer to these hidden costs as **process losses**—resources (including time and energy) expended toward team development and maintenance rather than the task.[85] It is much more efficient for an individual to work out an issue alone than to resolve differences of opinion with other people. The process loss problem becomes apparent when adding new people to the team. The group has to recycle through the team development process to bring

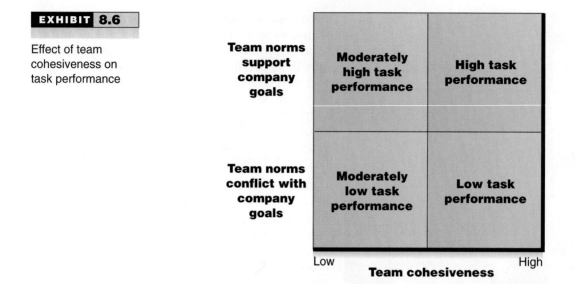

EXHIBIT 8.6

Effect of team
cohesiveness on
task performance

process losses
Resources (including
time and energy)
expended toward
team development
and maintenance
rather than the task.

social loafing
A situation in which
people exert less
effort (and usually
perform at a lower
level) when working
in groups than when
working alone.

everyone up to speed. The software industry even has a name for this problem: Brooks's Law says that adding more people to a late software project only makes it later. Researchers point out that the cost of process losses may be off-set by the benefits of teams. Unfortunately, few companies conduct a cost-benefit analysis of their team activities.[86]

A third problem is that teams require the right environment to flourish. Many companies forget this point by putting people in teams without changing anything else. As we noted earlier, teams require appropriate rewards, communication systems, team leadership, and other conditions. Without these, the shift to a team structure could be a waste of time. At the same time, critics suggest that changing these environmental conditions to improve team-work could result in higher costs than benefits for the overall organization.[87]

Social Loafing

Perhaps the best-known limitation of teams is the risk of productivity loss due to **social loafing.** Social loafing occurs when people exert less effort (and usu-ally perform at a lower level) when working in groups than when working alone.[88] A few scholars question whether social loafing is very common, but students can certainly report many instances of this problem in their team projects!

Social loafing is most likely to occur in large teams where individual output is difficult to identify, particularly in situations in which team members work alone toward a common output pool (i.e., they have low task interdepen-dence). Under these conditions, employees aren't as worried that their perfor-mance will be noticed. Social loafing is less likely to occur when the task is interesting, because individuals have a higher intrinsic motivation to perform their duties. It is also less common when the group's objective is important, possibly because individuals experience more pressure from other team mem-bers to perform well. Finally, social loafing is less common among members with a strong collectivist value, because they value group membership and be-lieve in working toward group objectives (see Chapter 4).[89]

How to Minimize Social Loafing   By understanding the causes of social loafing, we can identify ways to minimize this problem. Some of the strategies listed below reduce social loafing by making each member's performance more visible. Others increase each member's motivation to perform his or her tasks within the group.[90]

▪ *Form smaller teams*—Splitting the team into several smaller groups reduces social loafing because each person's performance becomes more noticeable and important for team performance. A smaller group also potentially increases cohesiveness, so would-be shirkers feel a greater obligation to perform fully for their team.

▪ *Specialize tasks*—It is easier to see everyone's contribution when each team member performs a different work activity. For example, rather than pooling their efforts for all incoming customer inquiries, customer service representatives might each be responsible for handling a particular type of client.

▪ *Measure individual performance*—Social loafing is minimized when each member's contribution is measured. Of course, individual performance is difficult to measure in some team activities, such as problem-solving projects in which the team's performance depends on one person's discovering the best answer.

▪ *Increase job enrichment*—Social loafing is minimized when team members are assigned more motivating jobs, such as jobs requiring more skill variety or having direct contact with clients. However, this strategy minimizes social loafing only if members have a strong growth need strength (see Chapter 6). In general, however, social loafing is less common among employees with high job satisfaction.

▪ *Select motivated employees*—Social loafing can be minimized by carefully selecting job applicants who are motivated by the task and have a collectivist value orientation. Those with a collectivist value are motivated to work harder for the team because they value their membership in the group.

TEAM BUILDING

team building
Any formal activity intended to improve the development and functioning of a work team.

Team building is any formal activity intended to improve the development and functioning of a work team. Most team building accelerates the team development process, which, in turn, might reshape team norms or strengthen cohesiveness. Team building is sometimes applied to newly established teams, but it is more common among existing teams that have regressed to earlier stages of team development. Team building is therefore most appropriate when the team experiences high membership turnover or when members have lost sight of their respective roles and team objectives.[91]

Types of Team Building

There are four main types of team building: role definition, goal setting, problem solving, and interpersonal processes.[92] Role definition team building encourages team members to describe perceptions of their own role as well as the role expectations they have of other team members. After discussing these perceptions, team members revise their roles and work toward a common mental model of their respective responsibilities.[93]

Some team-building interventions clarify the team's performance goals, increase the team's motivation to accomplish those goals, and establish a mechanism for systematic feedback on the team's goal performance. This type of intervention is very similar to individual goal setting, described in Chapter 5, except that the goals are applied to teams. Research suggests that goal setting is an important dimension of team building.[94]

A third type of team building examines the team's task-related decision-making process and identifies ways to make it more effective.[95] Each stage of decision making is examined, such as how the team identifies problems and searches for alternatives (see Chapter 9). To improve their problem-solving skills, some teams participate in simulation games that require team decisions in hypothetical situations.[96] As well as helping team members make better decisions, these team-building activities tend to improve interpersonal processes.

The fourth type of team building is interpersonal processes that try to build trust and open communications among team members by resolving hidden agendas and misperceptions. Such activities include **dialogue** sessions, where team members engage in conversations to develop a common mental model of

dialogue

A process of conversation among team members in which they learn about each other's mental models and assumptions, and eventually form a common model for thinking within the team.

Perched on a narrow beam 25 feet above the ground, Wu Xi never stopped thinking about the possibility of falling. The 30-year-old engineer at Ericsson Cyberlab in Singapore was roped together with five colleagues as they scaled their way up a 75-foot pyramid. "I was so scared, but I couldn't give up," says Wu. "My team members held onto me very firmly and they kept encouraging me." Wu Xi and her co-workers climbed over rock walls, inched across planks, scaled cargo nets, and performed other daunting tasks to improve team dynamics at the Swedish telecommunication firm's Asian research unit. "We all made it to the top with lots of difficulties," explains Ericsson Cyberlab director Andreas Fasbender. "But the best part was that you could really achieve more as a team."[97] Which types of team-building processes would this exercise include?
(© Straits Times)

the ideal team process. As they gain awareness of each other's models and assumptions, members eventually begin to form a common model for thinking within the team.[98] Although dialogue is potentially effective, most organizations tend to rely on wilderness team building, paintball wars, and obstacle course challenges to improve interpersonal processes.

Is Team Building Effective?

Team-building activities have become more popular as companies rely increasingly on teams to get the work done. Some organizations are even experimenting with offbeat team-building activities in the hope that these sessions will improve team dynamics. Coca-Cola executives in China participated in a team-building program that included fire-walking. Deloitte Consulting sent some of its California employees on a three-day extreme adventure race. Among other things, the experience included sleeping in trash bags on the dew-soaked ground and huddling together in "puppy piles" to stay warm. Staffordshire County Council in the United Kingdom sent a team of employees to the fire department for the day, where they learned to navigate through a smoke-filled room and battle a controlled towering inferno. "Faced with danger, people have to work together," explains a Staffordshire employee. "They have no other choice."[99]

Are these and more traditional team-building programs effective? Is the money well spent? So far, the answer is an equivocal maybe. Studies suggest that some team-building activities are successful, but just as many fail to improve team effectiveness.[100] One problem is that corporate leaders assume team-building activities are general solutions to general team problems. No one bothers to diagnose the team's specific needs (e.g., problem solving, interpersonal processes) because the team-building intervention is assumed to be a broad-brush solution. In reality, as we just learned, there are different types of team-building activities for different team needs. A mismatch can potentially lead to ineffective team building.[101]

Another problem is that corporate leaders tend to view team building as a one-shot inoculation that every team should receive when it is formed. In truth, team building is an ongoing process, not a three-day jump start. Some experts suggest, for example, that wilderness experiences often fail because they rarely include follow-up consultation to ensure that team learning is transferred back to the workplace.[102]

Finally, we must remember that team building occurs on the job, not just on an obstacle course or in a national park. Organizations should encourage team members to reflect on their work experiences and to experiment with just-in-time learning for team development.

"Let's agree to blame this on Filmore in accounting."

(FARCUS® is reprinted with permission LaughingStock Licensing Inc., Ottawa, Canada. All rights reserved.)

CHAPTER SUMMARY

Teams are groups of two or more people who interact and influence each other, are mutually accountable for achieving common objectives, and perceive themselves as a social entity within an organization. All teams are groups because they consist of people with a unifying relationship. However, not all groups are teams; some groups do not have purposive interaction.

A team-based organization relies on self-directed work teams rather than functional departments as the core work units. Traditional departments may be teams when employees are encouraged to interact directly and to coordinate work activities with each other. However, unlike traditional departments, team-based organizations tend to rely on cross-functional, autonomous teams with less need for supervisors in a communication or coordination role.

Virtual teams operate across space, time, and organizational boundaries with members who communicate mainly through information technologies. They are becoming more common as a result of advances in computer networks, the shift from physical labor to knowledge-based work, corporate globalization, and the need for greater knowledge sharing.

Team effectiveness includes the group's ability to survive, achieve its system-based objectives, and fulfill the needs of its members. The model of team effectiveness considers the team and organizational environment, team design, and team processes. The team or organizational environment influences team effectiveness directly, as well as through team design and team processes. Six elements in the organizational and team environment that influence team effectiveness are reward systems, communication systems, physical space, organizational environment, organizational structure, and organizational leadership.

Three team design elements are task characteristics, team size, and team composition. Teams work best when tasks are clear and easy to implement, and require a high degree of interdependence. Teams should be large enough to perform the work, yet small enough for efficient coordination and meaningful involvement. Effective teams are composed of people with the competencies and motivation to per-

form tasks in a team environment. Heterogeneous teams operate best on complex projects and problems requiring innovative solutions.

The four team processes are team development, norms, roles, and cohesiveness. Teams develop through the stages of forming, storming, norming, performing, and, eventually, adjourning. Some teams remain in a particular stage longer than others, and team development is an ongoing process. Teams develop norms to regulate and guide member behavior. These norms may be influenced by critical events, explicit statements, initial experiences, and members' pregroup experiences. Team members also have roles—a set of behaviors they are expected to perform because they hold certain positions in a team and organization.

Cohesiveness is the degree of attraction people feel toward the team and their motivation to remain members. Cohesiveness increases with member similarity, smaller team size, higher degree of interaction, somewhat difficult entry, team success, and external challenges. Teams need some level of cohesiveness to survive, but high cohesive units have higher task performance only when their norms do not conflict with organizational objectives.

Teams are not always beneficial or necessary. Moreover, they have hidden costs, known as process losses, and require particular environments to flourish. Teams often fail because they are not set up in supportive environments. Social loafing, another potential problem with teams, is the tendency for individuals to perform at a lower level when working in groups than when working alone. Social loafing can be minimized by making each member's performance more visible and increasing each member's motivation to perform his or her tasks within the group.

Team building is any formal activity intended to improve the development and functioning of a work team. Four team-building strategies are role definition, goal setting, problem solving, and interpersonal processes. Some team-building events succeed, but companies often fail to consider the contingencies of team building.

KEY TERMS

coalition, p. 230

communities of practice, p. 231

dialogue, p. 248

groups, p. 227

heterogeneous teams, p. 236

homogeneous teams, p. 236

informal groups, p. 230

law of telecosm, p. 230

norms, p. 238

process losses, p. 246

quality circles, p. 228

role, p. 240

self-directed work
teams (SDWTs), p. 227

skunkworks, p. 229

social loafing, p. 246

task interdependence, p. 234

team-based organization, p. 227

DISCUSSION QUESTIONS

1. Suppose the instructor for this course assigned you to a project team consisting of three other students who are currently taking similar courses in France, Japan, and Brazil. All students speak English and have similar knowledge of the topic. Use your knowledge of virtual teams to discuss the problems that your team might face compared with a team of local students who can meet face-to-face.

2. Informal groups exist in almost every form of social organization. What types of informal groups exist in your classroom? Why are students motivated to belong to these informal groups?

3. You have been put in charge of a cross-functional task force that will develop Internet banking services for retail customers. The team includes representatives from marketing, information services, customer service, and accounting, all of whom will move to the same location at headquarters for three months. Describe the evidence or behaviors that you might observe during each stage of the team's development.

4. You have just been transferred from the Kansas office to the Denver office of your company, a national sales organization of electrical products for developers and contractors. In Kansas, team members regularly called customers after a sale to ask whether the products arrived on time and whether they were satisfied. But in the Denver office, no one seems to make these follow-up calls. A recently hired co-worker explains that other co-workers discouraged her from making those calls.

Later, another co-worker suggests that your follow-up calls are making everyone else look lazy. Give three possible reasons the norms in Denver might be different from those in the Kansas office, even though the customers, products, sales commissions, and other characteristics of the workplace are almost identical.

5. You have been asked to lead a complex software project over the next year that requires the full-time involvement of approximately 100 people with diverse skills and backgrounds. Using your knowledge of team size, how can you develop an effective team under these conditions?

6. You have been assigned to a class project with five other students, none of whom you have met before. To what extent would team cohesiveness improve your team's performance on this project? What actions would you recommend to build team cohesiveness among student team members in this situation?

7. The CEO of Muluwa Railway Corporation wants employees throughout the organization to perform their work in teams. According to the CEO, "teams are our solution to increasing competition and customer demands." Discuss three problems with teams that Muluwa Railway's CEO may not be aware of.

8. The Johari Window, described in Chapter 3, is sometimes used as the foundation for team building. What type of team building would occur through Johari Window activities?

CASE STUDY 8.1

TREETOP FOREST PRODUCTS

Treetop Forest Products Inc. is a sawmill operation in Oregon that is owned by a major forest products company but operates independently of headquarters. It was built 30 years ago and completely updated with new machinery 5 years ago. Treetop receives raw logs from the area for cutting and planing into building-grade lumber, mostly 2-by-4 and 2-by-6 pieces of standard lengths. Higher-grade logs leave Treetop's sawmill department in finished form and are sent directly to the packaging department. The remaining 40 percent of sawmill output consists of cuts from lower-grade logs, requiring further work by the planing department.

Treetop has one general manager, 16 supervisors and support staff, and 180 unionized employees. The unionized employees are paid an hourly rate specified in the collective agreement, whereas management and support staff are paid a monthly salary. The mill is divided into six operating departments: boom, sawmill, planer, packaging, shipping, and maintenance. The sawmill, boom, and packaging departments operate a morning shift starting at 6 A.M. and an afternoon shift starting at 2 P.M. Employees in these departments rotate shifts every two weeks. The planer and shipping departments operate only morning shifts. Maintenance employees work the night shift (starting at 10 P.M.).

Each department, except for packaging, has a supervisor on every work shift. The planer supervisor is responsible for the packaging department on the morning shift, and the sawmill supervisor is responsible for the packaging department on the afternoon shift. However, the packaging operation is housed in a building separate from the other departments, so supervisors seldom visit the packaging department. This is particularly true for the afternoon shift, because the sawmill supervisor is the farthest distance from the packaging building.

Packaging Quality

Ninety percent of Treetop's product is sold on the international market through Westboard Company, a large marketing agency. Westboard represents all forest products mills owned by Treetop's parent company as well as several other clients in the region. The market for building-grade lumber is very price competitive, because there are numerous mills selling a relatively undifferentiated product. However, some differentiation does occur in product packaging and presentation. Buyers will look closely at the packaging when deciding whether to buy from Treetop or another mill.

To encourage its clients to package their products better, Westboard sponsors a monthly package quality award. The marketing agency samples and rates its clients' packages daily, and the sawmill with the highest score at the end of the month is awarded a plaque. Package quality is a combination of how the lumber is piled (e.g., defects turned in), where the bands and dunnage are placed, how neatly the stencil and seal are applied, how accurate the stencil is, and how neatly and tightly the plastic wrap is attached.

Treetop Forest Products won Westboard's packaging quality award several times over the past five years, and received high ratings in the months that it didn't win. However, the mill's ratings have started to decline over the past year or two, and several clients have complained about the appearance of the finished product. A few large customers switched to competitors' lumber, saying that the decision was based on the substandard appearance of Treetop's packaging when it arrived in their lumberyard.

Bottleneck in Packaging

The planing and sawmill departments have increased productivity significantly over the past couple of years. The sawmill operation recently set a new productivity record on a single day. The planer operation has increased productivity to the point that last year it reduced operations to just one (rather than two) shifts per day. These productivity improvements are due to better operator training, fewer machine breakdowns, and better selection of raw logs. (Sawmill cuts from high-quality logs usually do not require planing work.)

Productivity levels in the boom, shipping, and maintenance departments have remained constant. However, the packaging department has recorded decreasing productivity over the past couple of years, with the result that a large backlog of finished product is typically stockpiled outside the packaging building. The morning shift of the packaging department is unable to keep up with the combined production of the sawmill and planer departments, so the unpackaged output is left for the afternoon shift. Unfortunately, the afternoon shift packages even less product than the morning shift, so the backlog continues to build. The backlog adds to Treetop's inventory costs and increases the risk of damaged stock.

Treetop has added Saturday overtime shifts as well as extra hours before and after the regular shifts for the packaging department employees to process this backlog. Last month, the packaging department employed 10 percent of the workforce but accounted for 85 percent of the overtime. This situation is frustrating to Treetop's management, because time-and-motion studies recently confirmed that the packaging department is capable of processing all the daily sawmill and planer production without overtime. Moreover, with employees earning one and a half or two times their regular pay on overtime, Treetop's cost competitiveness suffers.

Employees and supervisors at Treetop are aware that people in the packaging department tend to extend lunch by 10 minutes and coffee breaks by 5 minutes. They also typically leave work a few minutes before the end of their shift. This abuse has worsened recently, particularly on the afternoon shift. Employees who are temporarily assigned to the packaging department also seem to participate in this time loss pattern after a few days. Although they are punctual and productive in other departments, these temporary employees soon adopt the packaging crew's informal schedule when assigned to that department.

Discussion Questions

1. On the basis of your knowledge of team dynamics, explain why the packaging department is less productive than other departments at Treetop.

2. How should Treetop change the nonproductive norms that exist in the packaging group?

3. What structural and other changes would you recommend that could improve this situation in the long term?

CASE STUDY 8.2

DETROIT IS CRUISING FOR QUALITY

BusinessWeek In the 1980s, Detroit automakers were widely criticized for lagging behind the Japanese in most measures of quality. Since then, Ford, General Motors, and DaimlerChrysler have all made strides in quality improvement, often borrowing methods from Japanese manufacturing. Those methods include team-based approaches such as quality circles and cross-functional teams. At the beginning of the twenty-first century, defect rates in U.S. cars are much lower, but the companies still have far to go, and they continue to rely on teams to solve—and prevent—quality problems.

This *Business Week* case study describes efforts by U.S. carmakers to improve quality. It identifies the kinds of problems that are most prevalent and gives examples of team-based solutions. Read through this *Business Week* case study at www.mhhe.com/mcshane2e and prepare for the discussion questions at right.

Discussion Questions

1. What kinds of teams does the author mention in this article? How effective have they been?

2. What are some of the norms that exist at U.S. automakers and in their teams that may have limited their success in improving quality?

3. The article says Chrysler is forming teams for vehicle development. How might participation of employees from the design, engineering, marketing, manufacturing, and purchasing departments prevent "last-minute design changes that lead to errors later on"? What are some advantages and disadvantages of this team approach, compared with letting designers handle this process on their own?

Source: J. Muller, "Detroit Is Cruising for Quality," *Business Week*, September 3, 2001.

TEAM EXERCISE 8.3

TEAM-TRUST EXERCISE

Purpose This exercise is designed to help you understand the role of interpersonal trust in the development and maintenance of effective teams.

Materials   The instructor will provide the same 15 objects for each team as well as for the model.

Instructions

- *Step 1*—The instructor will divide the class into teams of approximately 10 people.
- *Step 2*—Each team receives 15 objects from the instructor. The same 15 objects are arranged in a specific way on a table at the front of the room (or elsewhere, as designated by the instructor). The table is behind a screened area so that the arrangements cannot be seen by participants from their work areas. The goal of each team is to duplicate the *exact* arrangement (e.g., location, overlap, spacing) of the objects on the table, using its own matching set of objects, within 20 minutes (or other time limit given by the instructor). Participants are allowed one 30-second opportunity at the beginning of the exercise to view the screened table. They

may not write, draw, or talk while viewing the screened table. However, each team has *up to two saboteurs*. These are people who have been selected by the instructor (either before the exercise or through notes distributed to all participants). Saboteurs will use any reasonable method to prevent the team from producing an accurate configuration of objects in their work area. They are forbidden to reveal their identities.

- *Step 3*—At the end of the time limit, the instructor will evaluate each team's configuration and decide which one is the most accurate. The class members will then evaluate their experience in the exercise in terms of team development and other aspects of team dynamics.

Source: This exercise is based on ideas discussed in G. Thompson and P. Pearce, "The Team-Trust Game," *Training and Development*, May 1992, pp. 42–43.

TEAM EXERCISE   8.4

TEAM TOWER POWER

Purpose   This exercise is designed to help you understand team roles, team development, and other issues in the development and maintenance of effective teams.

Materials   The instructor will provide enough Lego pieces or similar materials for each team to complete the assigned task. All teams should have identical (or very similar) amounts and types of pieces. The instructor will need a measuring tape and stopwatch. Students may use writing materials during the design stage (Step 2 below). The instructor will distribute a Team Objectives Sheet and Tower Specifications Effectiveness Sheet to all teams.

Instructions

- *Step 1*—The instructor will divide the class into teams. Depending on class size and space available, teams may have between four and seven members, but all teams should be approximately equal in size.
- *Step 2*—Each team is given 20 minutes to design a tower that uses only the materials

provided, is freestanding, and provides an optimal return on investment. Team members may wish to draw their tower on paper or on a flip chart to assist in the tower's design. Teams are free to practice building their tower during this stage. Preferably, teams are assigned to their own rooms so that the design can be created privately. During this stage, each team will complete the Team Objectives Sheet distributed by the instructor. This sheet requires the Tower Specifications Effectiveness Sheet, also distributed by the instructor.

- *Step 3*—Each team will show the instructor that it has completed its Team Objectives Sheet. Then, with all teams in the same room, the instructor will announce the start of the construction phase. The time elapsed for construction will be closely monitored, and the instructor will occasionally call out time elapsed (particularly if there is no clock in the room).
- *Step 4*—Each team will advise the instructor as soon as it has completed its tower and

will write down the time elapsed that the instructor has determined. The team may be asked to assist the instructor by counting the number of blocks used and the height of the tower. This information is also written on the Team Objectives Sheet. Then the team calculates its profit.

- *Step 5*—After presenting the results, the class will discuss the team dynamics elements that contribute to team effectiveness. Team members will discuss their strategy, division of labor (team roles), expertise within the team, and other elements of team dynamics.

Source: Several published and online sources describe variations of this exercise, but there is no known origin for this activity.

S E L F - A S S E S S M E N T   E X E R C I S E   8.5

TEAM ROLES PREFERENCES SCALE

Purpose This self-assessment exercise is designed to help you identify your preferred roles in meetings and similar team activities.

Instructions Read each statement below and circle the response that you believe best reflects your position regarding that statement. Then use the scoring key in Appendix B to calculate your results for each team role. This exercise is completed alone so that students assess themselves honestly without concerns of social comparison. However, class discussion will focus on the roles that people assume in team settings. This scale assesses only a few team roles.

Team roles preferences scale					
Circle the number that best reflects your position regarding each statement.	Does not describe me at all ▼	Does not describe me very well ▼	Describes me somewhat ▼	Describes me well ▼	Describes me very well ▼
1. I usually take responsibility for getting the team to agree on what the meeting should accomplish. . . .	1	2	3	4	5
2. I tend to summarize to other team members what the team has accomplished so far.	1	2	3	4	5
3. I'm usually the person who helps other team members overcome their disagreements.	1	2	3	4	5
4. I try to ensure that everyone gets heard on issues. . . .	1	2	3	4	5
5. I'm usually the person who helps the team determine how to organize the discussion.	1	2	3	4	5
6. I praise other team members for their ideas more than do others in the meetings.	1	2	3	4	5
7. People tend to rely on me to keep track of what has been said in meetings.	1	2	3	4	5
8. The team typically counts on me to prevent debates from getting out of hand.	1	2	3	4	5
9. I tend to say things that make the group feel optimistic about its accomplishments.	1	2	3	4	5
10. Team members usually count on me to give everyone a chance to speak.	1	2	3	4	5
11. In most meetings, I am less likely than others to put down the ideas of teammates.	1	2	3	4	5

(continued)

Circle the number that best reflects your position regarding each statement.	Does not describe me at all ▼	Does not describe me very well ▼	Describes me somewhat ▼	Describes me well ▼	Describes me very well ▼
Team roles preferences scale (cont.)					
12. I actively help teammates resolve their differences in meetings.	1	2	3	4	5
13. I actively encourage quiet team members to describe their ideas on each issue.	1	2	3	4	5
14. People tend to rely on me to clarify the purpose of the meeting.	1	2	3	4	5
15. I like to be the person who takes notes or minutes of the meeting.	1	2	3	4	5

After studying the preceding material, be sure to check out our website at
www.mhhe.com/mcshane2e
for more in-depth information and interactivities that correspond to this chapter.

9

Decision Making and Employee Involvement

AFTER READING THIS CHAPTER, YOU SHOULD BE ABLE TO:

- Diagram the general model of decision making.

- Explain why people have difficulty identifying problems and opportunities.

- Identify three factors that challenge our ability to choose the best alternative.

- Outline the causes of escalation of commitment to a poor decision.

- Outline the forms and levels of employee involvement.

- Describe sociotechnical systems theory recommendations for more successful self-directed work teams.

- Identify the four contingencies in the Vroom–Jago model that determine the optimal level of employee involvement.

- Discuss the challenges that prevent employee involvement.

Less than two years after its launch, JetBlue has become the buzz of the airline industry. David Neeleman founded the New York–based discount airline using his previous experience launching Morris Air (sold to Southwest Airlines in 1993), then developing WestJet into the most successful discount carrier in Canadian history.

JetBlue's successful start-up is attributed largely to several well-executed decisions. One of the first was to base the business at John F. Kennedy Airport in New York City. New York was one of the few large cities not served by a discount airline, and JFK is less congested than La Guardia. Next, Neeleman and his executive team selected secondary airports near large cities—such as Fort Lauderdale rather than Miami, and Oakland rather than San Francisco—as destinations because they offered lower costs and yet were reasonably convenient for passengers.

Neeleman also decided that JetBlue should use only new aircraft—A320s from Airbus Industrie. His philosophy is that new planes give an airline instant credibility with travelers. Another calculated decision was having luxurious interiors for the all-coach configuration, including wider leather seats, more space between rows, and 24-channel satellite television at every seat. Although JetBlue is a discount carrier, it wants to lure business travelers to its economy service. The plan seems to be working. "We were starved for an airline like this," says one business passenger. "It's hard to compare flying JetBlue to [flying] other airlines."

David Neeleman made numerous decisions leading up to the launch of JetBlue, the New York–based discount airline that has taken the industry by storm. *(© AP/Wide World)*

Not all the decisions about JetBlue were so carefully calculated. For example, JetBlue executives frankly say that some of Neeleman's rejected ideas were a bit wild, such as having separate men's and women's lavatories and serving pizza on planes. "That's why I make sure there are people around me who push back," says Neeleman. One crazy idea that worked was offering naturally blue potato chips free to passengers. The color-coordinated snack was a hit.[1]

David Neeleman and his executive team made thousands of decisions in launching the hottest airline on the continent. **Decision making** is a conscious process of making choices among one or more alternatives with the intention of moving toward some desired state of affairs.[2] Some of Neeleman's decisions, such as in which city and airport to base the business, followed a careful process of searching for alternatives and weighing the advantages. Other decisions, such as whether to offer blue potato chips or pizza on flights, required the creative exploration of previously untested ideas.

Decisions occur in response to problems or opportunities. A *problem* is a deviation between the current and desired situation.[3] It is the gap between what is and what ought to be. An *opportunity* is a deviation between current expectations and the recognition of a potentially better situation that is neither planned nor expected. In other words, decision makers realize that certain decisions may produce results beyond current goals or expectations. For example, Neeleman saw New York City as an opportunity to launch JetBlue because it was poorly serviced with high-priced airlines.

This chapter begins with an overview of the decision-making process. The model is then examined more critically by identifying the human conditions that impede effective decision making. In today's complex environment, executives can rarely afford to make decisions without some level of employee involvement. The latter part of this chapter explores the forms and levels of employee involvement, including a detailed discussion of self-directed work teams and sociotechnical systems theory. Finally, we discuss the potential benefits and the limitations of employee involvement.

A GENERAL MODEL OF DECISION MAKING

How do people make decisions? The best place to start to answer that question is the general model of decision making shown in Exhibit 9.1.[4] Throughout

EXHIBIT 9.1

General model of decision making

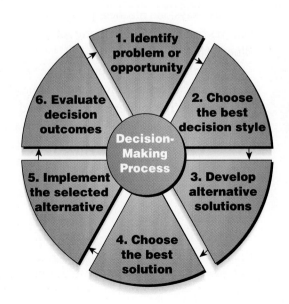

1. Identify problem or opportunity
2. Choose the best decision style
3. Develop alternative solutions
4. Choose the best solution
5. Implement the selected alternative
6. Evaluate decision outcomes

Decision-Making Process

Klugey Communication at Microsoft

"Hi Jack, I've worked out a klugey solution to the UI issue," an employee e-mails to a colleague in the next cubicle. "We need to get granular on this. Unfortunately, I'm OOF next week, so you'll have to burn up a few cycles on it. I'm worried that the blue-badges on this project will go totally nonlinear when they realize the RTM date is slipping."*

Welcome to the world of Microspeak—the unofficial language of Microsoft. Employees at the world's largest software company have acquired a lexicon that would baffle researchers at any dictionary publishing company. Microsoft staffers eat their own dog food, dislike weasel users, and avoid getting caught in reality distortion fields. This all makes sense to insiders, but not to people raised in the English language!

Most of this dialogue occurs in cyber media rather than fiber media (paper) or face mail (face-to-face).

That's not to say that Microsoft employees never meet. They do, in small groups around whiteboards in someone's office to share insights, resolve problems, and confirm deadlines. In fact, Microsoft makes sure that employees work at the same location so that they can communicate and solve problems quickly in face-to-face meetings.

*Translation: "Hi Jack, I've worked out a rough solution to the user interface problem. We need to examine the finer details. Unfortunately, I'm away next week, so you need to devote time and energy to this problem. I'm worried that the permanent Microsoft employees on this project will get really angry when they realize that we are getting behind on the released-to-manufacturing date."

Sources: K. Barnes, "The Microsoft Lexicon" (www.cinepad.com/mslex.htm); S. Greenhouse, "Braindump on the Blue Badge: A Guide to Microspeak," New York Times, August 13, 1998, p. G1; M. A. Cusumano, "How Microsoft Makes Large Teams Work Like Small Teams," Sloan Management Review 39 (Fall 1997), pp. 9–20.

Filtering

Some messages are filtered or stopped altogether on their way up or down the organizational hierarchy. Filtering may involve deleting or delaying negative information, or using less harsh words so that events sound more favorable. Employees and supervisors usually filter communication to create a good impression of themselves to superiors. Filtering is most common where the organization rewards employees who communicate mainly positive information and among employees with strong career mobility aspirations.[14]

Language

Words and gestures carry no inherent meaning, so the sender must ensure the receiver understands these symbols and signs. In reality, lack of mutual understanding is a common reason messages are distorted. Two potential language barriers are jargon and ambiguity.

jargon
The technical language and acronyms as well as recognized words with specialized meaning in specific organizations or groups.

Jargon **Jargon** includes technical language and acronyms as well as recognized words with specialized meaning in specific organizations or social groups. Connections 11.1 illustrates how "Microspeak"—the strange jargon heard at Microsoft and other high-technology firms—potentially increases communication efficiency when both sender and receiver understand this specialized language. Jargon also shapes and maintains an organization's cultural values as well as symbolizes an employee's self-identity in a group (see Chapter 3).[15]

However, jargon can also be a barrier to effective communication. One example is an incident at Sea Launch, the Long Beach, California–based multinational venture that launches satellites. During a test of a countdown protocol devised by the American staff, the Russian scientists involved with

© 2001 Ted Goff

"That's my commendation for deciphering all the sales talk when we needed to upgrade the computer."

(Copyright © 2001 Ted Goff. www.tedgoff.com)

the project fell into a mysterious funk. When Sea Launch's mission control director Steve Thelin eventually asked why they were acting so moody and distant, the Russians complained that no one told them who Roger was. Everyone had a good laugh when Thelin explained that "roger" is jargon used by the Americans to indicate that they understand what the other person in a transmission is saying.[16]

Ambiguity   We usually think of ambiguous language as a communication problem because the sender and receiver interpret the same word or phrase differently. If a co-worker says, "Would you like to check the figures again?" the employee may be politely *telling* you to double-check the figures. But this message is sufficiently ambiguous that you may think the co-worker is merely *asking* if you want to do this. The result is a failure to communicate.

Ambiguous language is sometimes used deliberately in work settings to avoid conveying undesirable emotions. "Sell" is a word often avoided in the brokerage industry because the overvalued company may be a current or future client. Thus, brokers use more ambiguous language. " 'Hold' means 'sell,' " admits one veteran of the brokerage industry. "It's a kind of 'meta' language where you have to look into the meaning behind the word."[17]

Ambiguous language may be a communication barrier, but it is sometimes necessary.[18] Corporate leaders often use metaphors to describe complex organizational values so that they are interpreted broadly enough to apply to diverse situations. Scholars also rely on metaphors because they convey rich meaning about complex ideas. For example, some organizational behavior scholars describe organizations as jazz ensembles or machines to reflect variations of their complex nature.[19]

Information Overload

A year ago, Sean Lapp averaged about 20 e-mails a day. Now, the CEO of the Chicago-based technology company I-Works gets closer to 200 messages daily on his computer. Lapp is also bombarded with dozens of phone calls, voice mails, faxes, paper documents, and other messages every day.[20]

Sean Lapp is not alone. Every day, the average office worker sends and receives more than 150 messages through various media. One survey reports that 49 percent of managers in the United States and several other countries feel they are fairly often or regularly incapable of processing this infoglut. More than 40 percent of them say that receiving so much information weakens their decision-making ability, delays important decisions, and makes it difficult to concentrate on their main tasks. Some medical experts also warn that the bombardment of electronic information is causing memory loss in young people.[21]

Communications guru Marshall McLuhan predicted more than 30 years ago that employees would become overloaded with messages. "One of the effects of living with electric information is that we live in a state of information overload," said McLuhan. "There's always more than you can cope with."[22] **Information overload** occurs when the volume of information received exceeds the person's capacity to process it. Employees have a certain *information-processing capacity,* that is, the amount of information that they are able to process in a fixed unit of time. At the same time, jobs have a varying *information load,* that is, the amount of information to be processed per unit of time.[23]

As Exhibit 11.2 illustrates, information overload occurs when the job's information load exceeds the individual's information-processing capacity. Information overload creates noise in the communication system because information gets overlooked or misinterpreted when people can't process it fast enough. It has also become a common cause of workplace stress.

Information overload is minimized in two ways: by increasing our information-processing capacity and by reducing the job's information load.[24] We can increase information-processing capacity by learning to read faster, scanning documents more efficiently, and removing distractions that slow information-processing speed. Time management also increases information-processing capacity. When information overload is temporary, information-processing capacity can be increased by working longer hours.

We can reduce information load by buffering, summarizing, or omitting the information. Buffering occurs when assistants screen the person's messages and forward only those considered essential reading. Summarizing condenses information into fewer words, such as by providing abstracts and executive summaries rather than the entire document. Omitting is the practice of ignoring less important information. For example, some e-mail software programs have a filtering algorithm that screens out unwanted junk mail (called spam).

information overload
A condition in which the volume of information received exceeds the person's capacity to process it.

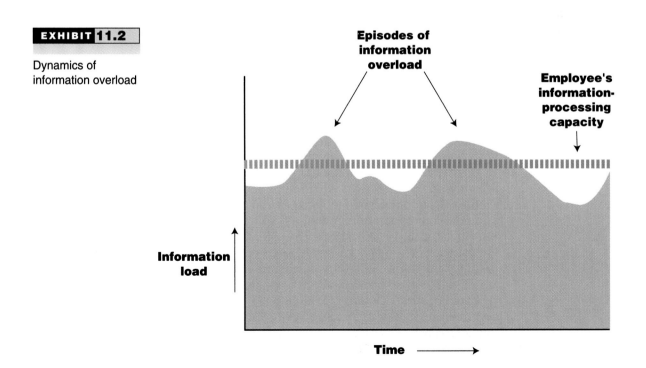

EXHIBIT 11.2

Dynamics of information overload

Perceptions, filtering, language, and information overload are not the only sources of noise in the communication process, but they are probably the most common. Noise also occurs when we choose an inappropriate channel through which to send the message. The next section takes a closer look at communication channels.

COMMUNICATION CHANNELS

A critical part of the communication model is the channel through which information is transmitted. There are two main types of channels: verbal and nonverbal. *Verbal communication* includes any oral or written means of transmitting meaning through words. *Nonverbal communication*, which we discuss later, is any part of communication that does not use words.

Verbal Communication

Different forms of verbal communication should be used in different situations. Face-to-face interaction is usually better than written methods for transmitting emotions and persuading the receiver, because nonverbal cues, such as voice intonations and use of silence, accompany oral communications. Moreover, in face-to-face settings, the sender receives immediate feedback from the receiver and can adjust the emotional tone of the message accordingly.

Written communication is more appropriate for recording and presenting technical details, because ideas are easier to follow when written down than when communicated verbally. Traditionally, written communication has been slow to develop and transmit, but electronic mail and other computer-mediated communication channels have significantly improved written communication efficiency.[25]

Electronic Mail

Electronic mail (e-mail) is revolutionizing the way we communicate in organizational settings. According to various estimates, somewhere between 1 trillion and 3 trillion e-mail messages are transmitted each year.[26] It's easy to understand the popularity of e-mail. Messages are quickly formed, edited, and stored. Information can be appended and transmitted to many people with a simple click of a mouse. E-mail is asynchronous (messages are sent and received at different times), so there is no need to coordinate a communication session. This technology also allows fairly random access of information; you can select any message in any order and skip to different parts of a message.

E-mail tends to be the preferred medium for coordinating work (e.g., confirming a co-worker's production schedule) and for sending well-defined information for decision making. The use of e-mail tends to increase the volume of communication and significantly alter the flow of that information throughout the organization.[27] Specifically, it reduces some face-to-face and telephone communication but increases the flow of information to higher levels in the organization. Some social and organizational status differences still exist with e-mail, but they are less apparent than in face-to-face or telephone communication. E-mail also reduces many selective attention biases because it hides age, race, weight, and other features that are observable in face-to-face meetings.

Problems with E-mail   Anyone who has used e-mail knows that it has several problems and limitations. Perhaps the most obvious of these is that e-mail contributes to information overload. Many e-mail users are overwhelmed by hundreds of messages each week, many of which are either unnecessary or irrelevant to the receiver. This excess occurs because e-mails can be easily created and copied to thousands of people through group mailbox systems.

A second problem is that e-mail is an ineffective medium for communicating emotions. For example, the emotion of sarcasm is difficult to convey through e-mail because the verbal message requires contrasting nonverbal cues. One scholar quipped that the result "of new information technologies within organizations has not been better communication, only faster misunderstandings." This problem is certainly true at Disney, where e-mail is the source of many conflicts. "Every fight that goes on [at Disney] seems to start with a misunderstanding over an e-mail," says Disney CEO Michael Eisner.[28] E-mail aficionados try to clarify the emotional tone of their messages by combining ASCII characters to form graphic faces called emoticons or "smileys." An entire lexicon of emoticons has developed, including those illustrated in Exhibit 11.3. However, some experts warn that smileys do not always solve the difficult task of communicating emotions through e-mail.[29]

A third problem is that e-mail seems to reduce our politeness and respect for others. This aspect is mostly evident through the increased frequency of **flaming**—the act of sending an emotionally charged message to others. Over half of the people questioned in one survey said they receive abusive flame mail and that men are both the most frequent victims and perpetrators.[30] The main cause of flaming is that people can post e-mail messages before their emotions subside, whereas the sender of a traditional memo or letter would have time for sober second thoughts.

Presumably, flaming and other e-mail problems will become less common as employees receive training on how to use this communication medium. For example, all new staff at the New Jersey Hospital Association (NJHA) attend a session where they learn how to create efficient and flame-proof e-mails.[31] The NJHA training also introduces employees to the largely unwritten and evolving

flaming

The act of sending an emotionally charged message to others.

EXHIBIT 11.3

Icons of emotion (emoticons) in e-mail messages

Icon	Meaning
:-)	Happy
:-}	Smirk
:-(	Unhappy
<:-)	Dumb question
0:-)	Angel (I'm being good)
:-p	Tongue sticking out
:-x	Oops!
{}	Hug
12x—<—@	A dozen roses

Source: Based on R. Peck, "Learning to Speak Computer Lingo," *(New Orleans) Times-Picayune*, June 5, 1997, p. E1; R. Weiland, "The Message Is the Medium," *Incentive*, September 1995, p. 37.

EXHIBIT 11.4

Some basic
e-mail netiquette

▨ DO fill in the subject line of the e-mail header with an informative description of the message.

▨ DO keep e-mail messages to fewer than 25 lines—the length of a typical computer screen.

▨ DO quote the relevant parts (but not necessarily all) of the receiver's previous message when replying to ideas in that message. (The automatic ">" indicates the original message.)

▨ DO respond to someone's e-mail (where a reply is expected) within one day for most business correspondence.

▨ DO switch from e-mail to telephone or face-to-face communication when the discussion gets too heated (flaming), the parties experience ongoing misunderstanding, or the issue becomes too complex.

▨ DON'T forward private messages without the permission of the original sender.

▨ DON'T send mass e-mails (using group lists) unless authorized to do so and the message definitely calls for this action.

▨ DON'T send large attachments if the receiver likely has a narrow bandwidth (computer data are transmitted slowly).

▨ DON'T use e-mail to communicate sensitive issues, such as disciplining someone, or to convey urgent information, such as rescheduling a meeting within the next hour.

▨ DON'T write messages in ALL CAPITALS because this conveys anger or shouting. (This rule also applies to **boldface** text as e-mail software develops this feature.)

▨ DON'T use emoticons excessively, and avoid them in formal business e-mails and when there is some chance that the receiver won't know their meaning.

Sources: Based on M. M. Extejt, "Teaching Students to Correspond Effectively Electronically; Tips for Using Electronic Mail Properly," *Business Communication Quarterly* 61 (June 1998), pp. 57+; K. Wasch, "Netiquette: Do's and Don'ts of E-mail Use," *Association Management* 49 (May 1997), pp. 76, 115.

code of conduct for communicating on the Internet, called *netiquette*. Exhibit 11.4 lists a few netiquette rules for e-mail.

Training may reduce some concerns with e-mail, but it cannot correct a fourth problem, namely, that e-mail lacks the warmth of human interaction.[32] As employees increasingly cocoon themselves through information technology, they lose the social support of human contact that potentially keeps their stress in check. Realizing this and other limitations of e-mail, some British companies are banning e-mail one day each week. As Global Connections 11.2 describes, these firms believe that some things are better discussed in person than in cyberspace.

Other Computer-Mediated Communication

IBM executives weren't surprised when a recent survey indicated that IBM employees rated co-workers as one of the two most credible or useful sources of information. What *did* surprise IBM executives was that the other equally credible and important source of information was IBM's intranet.[33] Intranets, extranets, instant messaging, and other forms of computer-mediated communication have fueled the hyperfast world of corporate information sharing.[34] Geographically dispersed work teams can coordinate their work more efficiently through instant messaging software and intranets. Suppliers are networked so tightly through computer-mediated technology that customers see them as one organization (see Chapter 17).

British Firms Encourage Live Conversation with E-mail–Free Fridays

The revolution started on a Friday. A maverick executive at the offices of Camelot, the national lottery operator, issued a startling edict: no more e-mails on the last day of the working week unless totally, absolutely necessary. Staff, it seemed, were forgetting how to talk to each other.

"We needed to make staff more aware of other forms of communication," explains Camelot spokeswoman Jenny Dowden. "If there were elements of the business where you could talk face-to-face instead of sending an e-mail, we wanted to encourage people to do that."

Nestlé Rowntree also decided it was time to discourage e-mail in favor of more personal conversations. By introducing "fewer–e-mail Fridays," the British confectioner hopes its employees will think more carefully about whether they need to copy messages to so many people and whether there are better ways of getting the message across.

"A no–e-mail Friday does two things," explains Andrew Harrison, the marketing director for Nestlé Rowntree. "It removes needless information flow across the organization and it forces people to talk face-to-face and agree on plans mutually. An e-mail ban begins to build a culture of designing and delivering ideas together."

How effective are these edicts to ban or minimize e-mail on Fridays? Camelot restricted its e-mail ban to four Fridays and is "still in the process of reviewing the results." But Jenny Dowden says the 50 e-mails she typically receives dropped to 3 or 4 on Fridays. Nestlé Rowntree executives also say they are noticing changing communication patterns. "People have started to think about how and what they are communicating and are refinding their voices," says one Nestlé manager.

Sources: J. Arlidge, "Office Staff Log Off for E-mail–Free Fridays," *The Observer (London),* August 12, 2001; N. Muktarsingh, "Companies Rediscover the Power of Speech," *Mail on Sunday (London),* July 22, 2001, p. 8; O. Burkeman, "Post Modern," *The Guardian (London),* June 20, 2001.

Instant Messaging *Instant messaging* appears to be the "next great thing" in technology-based communication. Instant messaging software connects two or more specific people and lets them push messages at each other. If you send an instant message to a co-worker who is connected, your message will instantly pop up on the co-worker's computer monitor (or other communications device). Instant messages are much briefer than e-mail, often relying on acronyms (such as R U THR for "Are you there?"). This efficiency and real-time communication explain why Ernst & Young, State Street Bank, Paine Webber, and other companies have implemented instant messaging. In fact, the number of corporate instant messaging users is expected to skyrocket from the 5.5 million in 2000 to more than 180 million in 2004.[35]

Consider the following example: if you require information for a client, you might log into the instant message service that connects to dozens of other employees in your area. Your message would pop up on their computers instantly, and the information you require could be available within minutes. "No other communications technology operates in situations like that in a time-efficient manner," says Andy Konchan, an executive at the financial planning firm UBS Warburg. "Clients are often taken aback by the speed with which we can now respond to specialized or unusual queries." UBS Warburg has thousands of instant messaging channels representing different knowledge or client interests. The company's 13,000 employees connect to the channels most closely aligned with their area of work.[36]

Instant messaging, e-mail, intranet sites, and other forms of computer-mediated communication each have their own advantages and disadvantages. However, they all have one clear benefit: They seem to reduce time and dissolve

Like most other executives, Adamee Itorcheak carries a laptop computer and cellular telephone almost everywhere he goes. The difference is that Itorcheak lives in Iqaluit, the capital city of Nunavut Territory in northern Canada, and his travels include traditional Inuit hunting trips in the Arctic wilderness. As president of Nunavut's largest Internet service provider and a partner in a high-speed wireless service, Itorcheak is probably the most wired person in the region. He is also wiring together most people in Nunavut, from a fish plant in Pangnirtung to a fishing guide in Clyde River. Through online forums and chat rooms, the people of Nunavut are becoming a more closely knit community. "Here in this huge territory, 20,000 people live in scattered groups," explains Itorcheak. "The Internet is the only way to bring us all together."[37] What are the limitations of Internet-based communication for people who rarely communicate face-to-face? *(Nick Didlick, Vancouver Sun)*

law of telecosm
States that as the web of computer networks expands, distances will shrink and eventually become irrelevant.

distances. This capability relates to the **law of telecosm,** which says that as the web of computer networks expands, distances will shrink and eventually become irrelevant.[38]

You might think that emerging computer-mediated technologies further increase information overload. Although this result is true for some forms of technology, preliminary evidence suggests that Internet-based communication actually *reduces* overload because it offers greater control over the amount of information flow. We decide how much information to receive from the Internet and intranet, whereas there is almost no control over the number of voice mails, faxes, and paper-based memos we receive. This conclusion is supported by a survey of executives in 11 countries. Half of them indicated that the Internet is reducing information overload; only 19 percent claim that it is making matters worse.[39]

Nonverbal Communication

Computer-mediated communication is changing the face of organizations, but it hasn't yet replaced nonverbal communication. Nonverbal communication includes facial expressions, voice intonation, physical distance, and even silence. This communication channel is necessary where physical distance or noise prevents effective verbal exchanges and the need for immediate feedback precludes written communication. But even in close face-to-face meetings, most information is communicated nonverbally.[40] Nonverbal communication is also important in emotional labor—the effort, planning, and control needed to express organizationally desired emotions (see Chapter 4). Employees make extensive use of nonverbal cues to transmit prescribed feelings to customers, co-workers, and others.

Nonverbal communication differs from verbal communication in several ways. First, verbal communication is typically conscious, whereas nonverbal communication is more automatic and unconscious. We normally plan the words we say or write, but rarely plan every blink, smile, or gesture during a conversation. Second, nonverbal communication is less rule-bound than verbal communication. We receive a lot of formal training on how to understand spoken words, but very little on understanding the nonverbal signals that accompany those words. Consequently, nonverbal cues are more ambiguous and more susceptible to misinterpretation.

Nonverbal communication is ambiguous, sometimes with dangerous consequences. Such a situation may have occurred on a Qantas flight as it tried to land on a rainy night at Bangkok International Airport. Less than 10 feet above the rain-soaked runway, the captain told the first officer to abort the landing. As the first officer reached for the thrust lever to pull the Boeing 747 out of its descent, the wheels touched the runway. A few seconds later, the captain decided to land rather than fly around, so he slid his right hand over the top of the first officer's left hand and moved the thrust levers to idle. Unfortunately, the captain didn't say anything as he took this action, which left the first officer unsure about who was in control. During the resulting confusion, no one noticed when the auto-brake system disarmed. The jet slid and shook its way down the runway, eventually stopping on its belly 200 yards past the end of the runway.[42] In your opinion, why didn't the captain use verbal communication when he changed his decision about landing the plane? *(P. Kittiwongsakul/AAP Photo)*

Emotional Contagion What happens when you see a co-worker accidentally bang his or her head against a filing cabinet? Chances are you wince and put your hand on your own head as if *you* had hit the cabinet. This automatic and unconscious tendency to mimic and synchronize our nonverbal behaviors with those of other people is called **emotional contagion**.[41] Emotional contagion is not a disease. It refers to the notion that we tend to "catch" other people's emotions by continually mimicking the facial expressions and nonverbal cues of others. For instance, listeners smile more and exhibit other emotional displays of happiness while hearing someone describe a positive event. Similarly, listeners will wince when the speaker describes an event in which she or he was hurt.

Emotional contagion serves three purposes. First, mimicry provides continual feedback, communicating that we understand and empathize with the sender. To consider the significance of this aspect, imagine if employees remained expressionless after watching a co-worker bang his or her head. The lack of parallel behavior conveys a lack of understanding or caring. Second, mimicking the nonverbal behaviors of other people seems to be a way of receiving emotional meaning from those people. If a co-worker is angry with a client, your tendency to frown and show anger while listening helps you share that emotion more fully. In

emotional contagion
The automatic and subconscious tendency to mimic and synchronize our nonverbal behaviors with other people.

other words, we receive meaning by expressing the sender's emotions as well as by listening to the sender's words.

Lastly, emotional contagion is a type of social glue that bonds people together. Social solidarity is built out of each member's awareness of a collective sentiment. Through nonverbal expressions of emotional contagion, people see others share the same emotions that they feel. This common or mutual expression of emotions strengthens team cohesiveness by providing evidence of member similarity.

CHOOSING THE BEST COMMUNICATION CHANNELS

Employees perform better if they can quickly determine the best communication channels for the situation and are flexible enough to use different methods, as the occasion requires.[43] But which communication channels are most appropriate? We partly answered this question in our evaluation of the different communication channels. However, two additional contingencies worth noting are media richness and symbolic meaning.

Media Richness

Soon after Ernst & Young encouraged its employees around the globe to form virtual teams, the accounting firm realized that e-mail and voice mail weren't sufficient for these groups. "Try coming to an agreement on the verbiage of a legal contract with a team of lawyers and engineers representing multiple interests using only the telephone and e-mail," quips John Whyte, Ernst & Young's chief information officer. "You can spend weeks sorting through fragmented e-mail conversations or individual phone calls and voice mails." Now employees discuss complex issues through special software that provides a virtual whiteboard on the computer screen and allows real-time chat (instant messaging). It's not quite as good as face-to-face meetings, but it is much better than the previous patchwork of e-mail and telephone calls.[44]

media richness
The data-carrying capacity of a communication medium, including the volume and variety of information it can transmit.

Ernst & Young discovered that some issues require more **media richness** than e-mail and telephone messages can offer. Media richness refers to the medium's *data-carrying capacity*—the volume and variety of information that can be transmitted.[45] Face-to-face meetings have the highest data-carrying capacity because the sender simultaneously uses multiple communication channels (verbal and nonverbal), the receiver can provide immediate feedback, and the information exchange can be customized to suit the situation. Instant messaging would be somewhat lower in the hierarchy, and e-mail is below instant messaging software. Financial reports and other impersonal documents represent the leanest media because they allow only one form of data transmission (written), the sender does not receive timely feedback from the receiver, and the information exchange is standardized for everyone.

Exhibit 11.5 shows that rich media are better than lean media when the communication situation is nonroutine or ambiguous. Nonroutine situations require rich media because the sender and receiver have little common experience and therefore need to transmit a large volume of information with immediate feedback. During emergencies, for instance, you should use face-to-face meetings to coordinate work efforts quickly and minimize the risk of misunderstanding and confusion. Lean media may be used in routine situations because the sender and receiver have common expectations through

| EXHIBIT 11.5 | A hierarchy of media richness |

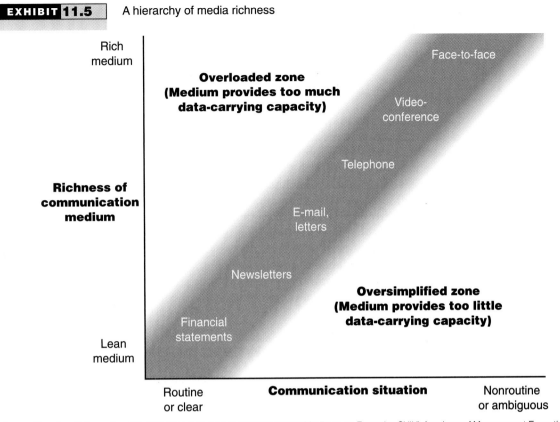

shared mental models.[46] Ambiguous issues, such as Ernst & Young's contract work, also require rich media because the parties must share large amounts of information with immediate feedback to resolve multiple and conflicting interpretations of their observations and experiences. For instance, research indicates that product development presents several ill-defined issues, so team members work better with face-to-face communication than with leaner media.[47]

What happens when we choose the wrong level of media richness for the situation? When the situation is routine or clear, using a rich medium—such as holding a special meeting—would seem like a waste of time. On the other hand, if a unique and ambiguous issue is handled through lean media—such as e-mail—issues take longer to resolve and misunderstandings are more likely to occur. This is the problem that employees at Ernst & Young experienced.

One last point about media richness is that we need to consider previous experience with both the media and the other person in the information exchange. People who have plenty of experience with a particular communication medium can "push" the amount of media richness normally possible through that information channel. Such efficient use of a medium seems to allow more information flow than the channel would allow for people who are new to the medium. Similarly, we can sometimes rely on leaner media when communicating with people who are familiar to us. This familiarity means that the sender and receiver often share common mental models, which reduces the volume of information transmitted.[48]

Symbolic Meaning of the Medium

"The medium is the message."[49] This famous phrase by Marshall McLuhan means that the sender's choice of communication channel transmits meaning beyond the message content. For example, a personal meeting with an employee may indicate that the issue is important, whereas a brief handwritten note may suggest less importance.

The difficulty we face when choosing a communication medium is that its symbolic meaning may vary from one person to the next. Some people view e-mail as a symbol of professionalism, whereas others see it as evidence of the sender's efficiency. Still others might view an e-mail message as a low-status clerical activity because it involves typing.[50] Overall, we must be sensitive to the symbolic meaning of the selected communication medium to ensure that it amplifies rather than contradicts the meaning found in the message content.

COMMUNICATING IN ORGANIZATIONAL HIERARCHIES

In this era when knowledge is competitive advantage, corporate leaders need to maintain an open flow of communication up, down, and across the organization. In this section, we discuss four communication strategies: newsletters and e-zines, work space design, employee surveys, and management by walking around.

Newsletters and E-zines

A decade ago, Hughes Software Systems (HSS) in India had 50 employees and mainly gathered them into a meeting to share company news. Today, HSS employs 1,300 people, so it depends on various electronic and paper media to keep everyone informed. Employees receive hard-copy newsletters about company developments, but they also receive timely information through HSS's intranet. If that's not enough, HSS has an electronic message board called "Junk," where employees share their views on everything from the quality of cafeteria food to ways to get around the electronic blockades HSS has placed on sports websites.[51]

Hughes Software Systems and other large organizations are increasingly applying a multipronged communication strategy to share information with employees. This strategy typically includes both print-based newsletters and web-based electronic newsletters, called e-zines. For example, Hewlett-Packard (HP) posts late-breaking company news every day in its intranet-based publication called *hpNow*. Several times each year, HP employees also receive a print magazine called *Invent*, which features longer, more in-depth articles. HP and other firms have discovered that one communication medium is not enough. Online sources offer instant communication, but many employees still have difficulty reading long articles on a computer screen. Print articles are slower and more costly, but they currently offer more portability than online publications.[52]

Work Space Design

There's nothing like a wall to prevent employees from talking to each other. That's why Phonak, a hearing aid manufacturer in Warrenville, Illinois, has very few walls to block communication. "We're in the communications business," says Phonak CEO Michael R. Jones. "We have no offices and a very open floor plan to foster communication." Other companies have kept the walls up but have rearranged the hallways to support spontaneous, horizontal communication. Seagate Software's offices in Vancouver, Canada, include extrawide hallways so that employees can chat without blocking others. Pearl Assurance, the British financial services group, installed "pit stop" areas along the hallways where people can spontaneously meet and share information.[53]

SEI Investments breaks anyone's stereotype of an investment firm. SEI employees are housed in five colorful buildings in the countryside of Oaks, Pennsylvania. Approximately 150 employees congregate in large, open rooms with windows all around. No walls or cubicle dividers separate work spaces. Each person has a desk on wheels, which is easily moved around to form spontaneous teams. Cables spiral down from the ceilings so that each desk is quickly reconnected to telephone, electricity, and an intranet port in the new location. "It's much, much easier to get things done when everyone is right there working together," says an SEI employee.[56] What are the potential problems of SEI's open office design? *(Tim Hursley/The Arkansas Office)*

Do these open-space offices actually improve communication? Anecdotal evidence lends support to the thesis that people communicate more often with fewer walls between them. However, scientific research also suggests that open office design potentially increases employee stress because of the loss of privacy and personal space.[54] Some employees at the offices of TBWA Chiat/Day resorted to making telephone calls in bathroom stalls and under their desks after the Los Angeles advertising firm moved to open offices. The firm has since reverted to a "nesting" model that consists of some private individual space as well as open space for collaboration. According to an analysis of 13,000 employee surveys in 40 major organizations, work space primarily contributes to individual performance by providing a place to concentrate on work without distraction. The second most important influence of work space on performance is how it facilitates informal communication with co-workers. Thus, work space must encourage social interaction, but it also must support a person's need for some privacy.[55]

Employee Surveys

Many large companies regularly survey employees on a variety of issues. Some surveys measure job satisfaction and loyalty to identify potential morale and employee turnover problems. Companies depend on these job satisfaction surveys for 360-degree feedback for managers, which can influence their performance bonus.

Other organizations use surveys to involve employees in decisions on everything from dress codes to pension plans.[57] For example, Eli Lilly & Company conducted a census of its 14,500 U.S. employees to find out what hours they prefer working. The pharmaceutical company learned that the hours it had mandated for decades were out of date and out of favor. Eli Lilly now offers more flexible hours and optional compressed workweeks.[58]

Management by Walking Around

Cisco Systems is the world's largest manufacturer of routers and other products that run the Internet. Yet John Chambers, Cisco's CEO, doesn't communicate

The uncertain future of Mitsubishi Motors Australia Ltd. (MMAL) has kept CEO Tom Phillips busy as a corporate communicator. When rumors circulated that Mitsubishi headquarters in Japan would shut down the Adelaide-based automaker, Phillips met employees on the assembly line to dispel those myths. When MMAL received a large capital injection, Phillips invited every employee and supplier representative to a meeting (shown in photo) to announce the deal. As the plant thumped to rock music, Phillips led MMAL's 3,200 employees in a human wave, such as the ones seen at sporting events, then told them their future looked stronger than ever. A few months later, when Mitsubishi officially ruled out closing the Adelaide plant, Phillips was quick to communicate the good news to everyone. "I'm going down the (assembly) line tomorrow to shake hands and slap backs," said Phillips when he received the good news.[61] Why should corporate leaders personally meet with employees rather than send a memo under these circumstances? *(Russell Millard/*The Advertiser*)*

just through e-mail or websites. He believes that executives need to regularly meet face-to-face with employees. In other words, corporate leaders need to practice **management by walking around (MBWA).** Coined several years ago at Hewlett-Packard, MBWA means that executives should get out of their offices and learn from others in the organization through face-to-face dialogue.[59] MBWA minimizes filtering because executives listen directly to employees. It also helps executives acquire a deeper meaning and quicker understanding of internal organizational problems.

MBWA can take many forms. Jonathan Hakim, managing director of Hong Kong start-up incubator tp Labs (a subsidary of techpacific.com), likes to break the ice with employees by breaking out the cue sticks for a game of pool in the company's expansive lounge. Richard Zuschlag, CEO of Acadian Ambulance & Air Med Services Inc. in Louisiana, takes the old-fashioned route by wandering around the company's offices and chatting with employees. "I'm a very curious person," explains Zuschlag. "Just walking around and asking a lot of my dumb questions is how I find out what's going on." John Chambers and other Cisco executives attend monthly "birthday breakfasts" with several dozen employees with birthdays in that month. "The birthday breakfast is the most effective vehicle for getting candid feedback from employees and for discovering potential problems," says Chambers.[60]

management by walking around (MBWA)

A communication practice in which executives get out of their offices and learn from others in the organization through face-to-face dialogue.

COMMUNICATING THROUGH THE GRAPEVINE

Whether or not executives get out of their offices, employees will always rely on the oldest communication channel: the corporate **grapevine.** The grapevine is an unstructured and informal network founded on social relationships rather than organizational charts or job descriptions. According to some estimates, 75 percent of employees typically receive news from the grapevine before they hear about it through formal channels.[62]

grapevine

An unstructured and informal communication network founded on social relationships rather than organizational charts or job descriptions.

Grapevine Characteristics

Early research identified several unique features of the grapevine.[63] It transmits information very rapidly in all directions throughout the organization. The typical pattern is a cluster chain, whereby a few people actively transmit rumors to many others. The grapevine works through informal social networks, so it is more active where employees have similar backgrounds and are able to communicate easily. Many rumors seem to have at least a kernel of truth, possibly because rumors are transmitted through media-rich communication channels (e.g., face-to-face) and employees are motivated to communicate effectively. Nevertheless, the grapevine distorts information by deleting fine details and exaggerating key points of the message.

The problem with some of these earlier findings is that they might not be representative of the grapevine in this era of information technology. E-mail and instant messaging have replaced the traditional watercooler as the main place where people share gossip. Social networks have expanded as employees communicate with each other around the globe, not just around the next cubicle. Vault.com and other public websites have become virtual watercoolers by posting anonymous comments about specific companies for all to view. This technology extends gossip to anyone, not just employees connected to social networks.

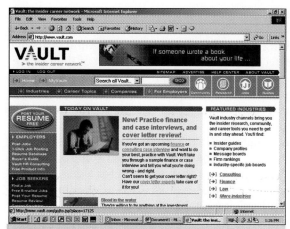

For many employees, the corporate grapevine is now connected to the Internet through Vault.com and other websites. The corporate grapevine is "no longer just four staffers huddling around a dusty watercooler," says Vault co-founder Mark Oldman. "Now there are thousands of people around the world comparing notes." Vault.com has message boards for hundreds of companies. Post some hearsay or an opinion about a particular firm and the world will know about it in seconds. "[W]ith the power of the Internet, there is more of a global and real-time flow to rumors and gossip," says Oldman. Vault.com estimates that up to 9 percent of Goldman Sachs employees check in with Vault's Goldman board during any given week.[66] In your opinion, how does the Internet potentially change the pattern of grapevine information and the accuracy of that information? (*Reprinted with permission of Vault.com—The Insider Career Network, www.vault.com*)

Grapevine Advantages and Disadvantages

Should the grapevine be encouraged, tolerated, or quashed? The difficulty in answering this question is that the grapevine has both advantages and disadvantages. One benefit is that the grapevine helps employees make sense of their workplace when the information is not available through formal channels.[64] It is also the main conduit through which organizational stories and other symbols of the organization's culture are communicated (see Chapter 15).

A third advantage of the grapevine is that this social interaction relieves anxiety and fulfills the need for affiliation.[65] This point explains why rumor mills are most active during times of uncertainty. Finally, because the grapevine is most active when employees are anxious, it is a valuable signal for corporate leaders to take appropriate action. Such action may include resolving the problems behind the rumors or communicating more fully through formal networks.

The grapevine is not always beneficial. Morale tumbles when management is slower than the grapevine in communicating information, because the lag suggests a lack of sincerity and concern for employees. Moreover, grapevine information may become sufficiently distorted that it escalates rather than reduces employee anxieties. This result is most likely when the original information is transmitted through several people rather than by one or two people.

Companies have tried to learn the identities of people who post anonymous rumors on websites, but their quest usually fails. City officials in Cascavel, Brazil, have banned employees from engaging in spreading office gossip, but the grapevine will always exist. A better strategy, as mentioned earlier, is to listen to the grapevine as a signal of employee anxiety and then correct the cause of that anxiety. Some companies also listen to the grapevine and step in to correct blatant errors and fabrications. Shaw's Supermarkets Inc. took this approach after a false rumor quickly spread that the West Bridgewater, Massachusetts, grocery store chain was about to be sold. An online newsletter—appropriately called *The Rumor Buster*—was set up to correct this and subsequent errors.[67]

CROSS-CULTURAL AND GENDER COMMUNICATION

In a world of increasing globalization and cultural diversity, organizations face opportunities as well as communication challenges. Employees must become more sensitive and competent in cross-cultural communication. They must also overcome their reluctance to communicate with co-workers from another cultural group. These communication competencies are also gaining importance as companies increasingly work with clients, suppliers, and joint venture partners from other countries.

Language is the most obvious cross-cultural barrier.[68] Words are easily misunderstood in verbal communication, either because the receiver has a limited vocabulary or the sender's accent makes it difficult for the receiver to understand the sound. The issue is further complicated in global organizations where employees from non-English countries often rely on English as the common business language. On top of other communication problems, English words have different meanings across cultures. For example, a French executive might call an event a "catastrophe" as a casual exaggeration, but the term is often taken to mean an earth-shaking event by someone in Germany.[69]

Mastering the same language improves one dimension of cross-cultural communication, but problems may still occur when interpreting voice intonation.[70] A deep voice symbolizes masculinity in North America, but African men often express their emotions using a high-pitched voice. Middle Easterners sometimes speak loudly to show sincerity and interest in the discussion, whereas Japanese people tend to speak softly to communicate politeness or humility. These different cultural norms regarding voice volume may cause one person to misinterpret the other.

Nonverbal Differences

Nonverbal communication is more important in some cultures than in others. For example, people in Japan interpret much of a message's meaning from nonverbal cues. "A lot of Japanese is either unspoken or communicated through body language," explains Henry Wallace, the Scottish-born CEO of Mazda Corporation in Japan.[71] To avoid offending or embarrassing the receiver (particularly outsiders), Japanese people will often say what the other person wants to hear (called *tatemae*) but send more subtle nonverbal cues indicating the sender's true feelings (called *honne*).[72] A Japanese colleague might politely reject your business proposal by saying "I will think about that," while sending nonverbal signals that he or she is not really interested. This difference explains why Japanese employees may prefer direct conversation to e-mail and other media that lack nonverbal cues.

Most nonverbal cues are specific to a particular culture and may have a completely different meaning to people raised in other cultures. For example, most of us shake our head from side to side to say "no," but a variation of head shaking means "I understand" to some people from India. Filipinos raise their eyebrows to give an affirmative answer, yet Arabs interpret this expression (along with clicking one's tongue) as a negative response. Most Americans are taught to maintain eye contact with the speaker to show interest and respect, yet Native Americans, Australian Aborigines, and others learn at an early age to show respect by looking down when an older or more senior person is talking to them.[73]

Even the common handshake communicates different meaning across cultures. Westerners tend to appreciate a firm handshake as a sign of strength and warmth in a friendship or business relationship. In contrast, many Asians and Middle Easterners favor a loose grip and regard a firm clench as aggressive. Germans prefer one good handshake stroke, whereas anything less than five or six strokes may symbolize a lack of trust in Spain. If this isn't confusing enough, people from some cultures view any touching in public—including handshakes—as a sign of rudeness.

Silence and Conversational Overlaps   Communication includes the silence between our words and gestures. However, the meaning of silence varies from one culture to another. In Japan, people tend to show respect for the speaker by remaining silent for a few seconds after the person has spoken to contemplate what has just been said.[74] To them, silence is an important part of communication (called *haragei*) because it preserves harmony and is more reliable than talk. Silence is shared by everyone and belongs to no one, so it becomes the ultimate form of interdependence. Moreover, Japanese value empathy, which can only be demonstrated by understanding others without using words.

In contrast, most people in the United States and Canada view silence as a *lack* of communication and often interpret long breaks as a sign of disagreement. For example, after presenting their proposal to a potential Japanese client, a group of American consultants expected to be bombarded with questions. Instead, their proposal was greeted with a long silence. As the silence continued, most of the consultants concluded that the Japanese client disapproved, so they prepared to pack and leave. But the lead consultant gestured them to stop, because the client's face and posture seemed to indicate interest rather than rejection. He was right: When the client finally spoke, it was to give the consulting firm the job.[75]

Conversational overlaps also send different messages in different cultures. Japanese usually stop talking when they are interrupted, whereas talking over the other person's speech is more common in Brazil and some other countries. Talking while someone is speaking to you is considered quite rude in Japan, whereas Brazilians are more likely to interpret this conversational overlap as the person's interest and involvement in the conversation.

Gender Differences in Communication

Soon after Susan Herring joined her first Internet discussion group, she noticed that men were much more likely than women to engage in cantankerous debates with their own combative and condescending e-mail messages. To pique her curiosity, the linguistics professor asked list-group subscribers to tell her what they thought of these e-mail "flame wars." The anonymous, informal poll revealed that men generally accepted this communication style and usually found the barbs entertaining. Most women, on the other hand, were offended or cautious when these debates erupted.[76]

Herring and other scholars have observed that men and women often differ in their communication styles. Whether in a corporate meeting or a virtual chat room, men are more likely than women to view conversations as negotiations of relative status and power.[77] They assert their power by directly giving advice to others (e.g., "You should do the following") and using combative language.

There is also evidence that men interrupt women far more often than vice versa and that they dominate the talk time in conversations with women.

Men tend to engage in "report talk," in which the primary function of the conversation is impersonal and efficient information exchange. This behavior may explain why men tend to quantify information (e.g., "It took us six weeks"). Women also engage in report talk, particularly when conversing with men. But conversations among women tend to have a higher incidence of relationship building through "rapport talk." Thus, women use more intensive adverbs ("I was *so happy* that he completed the report") and hedge their statements ("It seems to be . . ."). Rather than asserting status, women use indirect requests ("Have you considered . . .?"). Similarly, women apologize more often and seek advice from others more quickly than do men. Finally, research supports the belief that women are more sensitive than men to nonverbal cues in face-to-face meetings.[78]

After reading some popular-press books, you would think that men and women come from different planets (Mars and Venus) and require United Nations translators![79] This is not so. Although we have identified several differences, men and women mostly overlap in their verbal communication styles. Some men are very passive conversationalists, and some women are aggressive. Moreover, we know that women (and, to a lesser extent, men) vary their communication styles with the situation.

Both men and women usually understand each other, but there are irritants. For instance, Susan Herring and other women feel uncomfortable with aggressive male communication styles on the Internet. Female scientists have similarly complained that adversarial interaction among male scientists makes it difficult for women to participate in meaningful dialogue.[80]

Another irritant occurs when women seek empathy but receive male dominance in response. Specifically, women sometimes discuss their personal experiences and problems to develop closeness with the receiver. They look for expressions of understanding, such as "That's the way I felt when it happened to me." But when men hear problems, they quickly suggest solutions because this response asserts their control over the situation. As well as frustrating a woman's need for common understanding, the advice actually says, "You and I are different; you have the problem and I have the answer." Meanwhile, men become frustrated because they can't understand why women don't appreciate their advice.

IMPROVING INTERPERSONAL COMMUNICATION

Effective interpersonal communication depends on the sender's ability to get the message across and the receiver's performance as an active listener. In this section, we outline these two essential features of effective interpersonal communication.

Getting Your Message Across

This chapter began with the statement that effective communication occurs when the other person receives and understands the message. To accomplish this difficult task, the sender must learn to empathize with the receiver, repeat the message, choose an appropriate time for the conversation, and be descriptive rather than evaluative.

▪ *Empathize*—Recall from Chapter 3 that empathy is a person's ability to understand and be sensitive to the feelings, thoughts, and situation of others. In conversations, empathy involves putting yourself in the receiver's shoes when encoding the message. For instance, be sensitive to words that may be ambiguous or trigger the wrong emotional response.

▪ *Repeat the message*—Rephrase the key points a couple of times. The saying "Tell them what you're going to tell them; tell them; then tell them what you've told them" reflects this need for redundancy.

▪ *Use timing effectively*—Your message competes with other messages and noise, so find a time when the receiver is less likely to be distracted by these other matters.

▪ *Be descriptive*— Focus on the problem, not the person, if you have negative information to convey. People stop listening when the information attacks their self-esteem. Also, suggest things the listener can do to improve, rather than pointing to him or her as the problem.

Active Listening

Darryl Heustis admits that he isn't always good at listening to other people. "I've had the unique ability to start formulating my response before the person is through with the question," says Heustis sheepishly. Fortunately, Heustis, who is the vice president for medical affairs at the Jerry L. Pettis Memorial VA Medical Center in Loma Linda, California, and his colleagues have completed training that helps them listen more actively to what others are saying. "Now, I've learned to practice my listening skills and observation skills. I've improved at watching people carefully, looking for body language and other signals of what they're feeling."[81]

Darryl Heustis and other executives are discovering that listening is at least as important as talking. As one sage wisely wrote: "Nature gave people two ears but only one tongue, which is a gentle hint that they should listen more than they talk."[82] But listening is more than just hearing the other person making sounds; it is a process of actively sensing the sender's signals, evaluating them accurately, and responding appropriately.

These three components of listening—sensing, evaluating, and responding—reflect the listener's side of the communication model described at the beginning of this chapter.[83] Listeners receive the sender's signals, decode them as intended, and provide appropriate and timely feedback to the sender. Active listeners constantly cycle through sensing, evaluating, and responding during the conversation and engage in various activities to improve these processes (see Exhibit 11.6).

Sensing   Sensing is the process of receiving signals from the sender and paying attention to them. These signals include the words spoken, the nature of the sounds (speed of speech, tone of voice, etc.), and nonverbal cues. Active listeners improve sensing by postponing evaluation, avoiding interruptions, and maintaining interest.

EXHIBIT 11.6

Components of
active listening

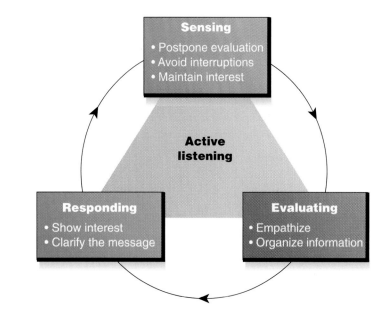

Sensing
• Postpone evaluation
• Avoid interruptions
• Maintain interest

**Active
listening**

Responding
• Show interest
• Clarify the message

Evaluating
• Empathize
• Organize information

> *Postpone evaluation*—Many listeners become victims of first impressions (see Chapter 3). They quickly form an opinion of the speaker's message and subsequently screen out important information. Active listeners, on the other hand, try to stay as open-minded as possible by delaying evaluation of the message until the speaker has finished.
>
> *Avoid interruptions*—Interrupting the speaker's conversation has two adverse effects on the sensing process. First, it disrupts the speaker's idea, so the listener does not receive the entire message. Second, interruptions tend to second-guess what the speaker is trying to say, which contributes to the problem of evaluating the speaker's ideas too early.
>
> *Maintain interest*—As with any other behavior, active listening requires motivation. Too often, we close our minds soon after a conversation begins because the subject is boring. Instead, active listeners maintain interest by taking the view—probably an accurate one—that there is always something of value in a conversation; it's just a matter of actively looking for it.

Evaluating This component of listening includes understanding the message meaning, evaluating the message, and remembering the message. To improve their evaluation of the conversation, active listeners empathize with the speaker and organize information received during the conversation.

> *Empathize*—Active listeners try to understand and be sensitive to the speaker's feelings, thoughts, and situation. Empathy is a critical skill in active listening because the verbal and nonverbal cues from the conversation are accurately interpreted from the other person's point of view.
>
> *Organize information*—Listeners process information three times faster than the average rate of speech (450 words per minute versus 125 words per minute), so they are easily distracted. Active listeners use this spare time to organize the information into key points. In fact, it's a good idea to

imagine that you must summarize what people have said after they are finished speaking.[84]

Responding Responding, the third component of listening, refers to the listener's development and display of behaviors that support the communication process. Responsiveness is feedback to the sender, which motivates and directs the speaker's communication. Active listeners respond by showing interest and clarifying the message.

- *Show interest*—Active listeners show interest by maintaining sufficient eye contact and sending back-channel signals such as "Oh, really!" and "I see" during appropriate breaks in the conversation.
- *Clarify the message*—Active listeners provide feedback by rephrasing the speaker's ideas at appropriate breaks ("So you're saying that . . . ?"). This response further demonstrates interest in the conversation and helps the speaker determine whether you understand the message.

Communication is a complex process of transmitting and understanding information between two or more people. We communicate to make better decisions, distribute valued knowledge, coordinate work, and fulfill social needs. Communication is also an integral part of most processes to gain power, apply organizational politics, and persuade people to change their beliefs and attitudes. These three processes are the themes of the next chapter.

CHAPTER SUMMARY

Communication supports knowledge management, decision making, work coordination, and the need for affiliation. The communication process involves forming, encoding, and transmitting the intended message to a receiver, who then decodes the message and provides feedback to the sender. Effective communication occurs when the sender's thoughts are transmitted to and understood by the intended receiver.

Several barriers create noise in the communication process. People misinterpret messages because of perceptual biases. Some information is filtered out as it gets passed up the hierarchy. Jargon and ambiguous language are barriers when the sender and receiver have different interpretations of the words and symbols used. People also screen out or misinterpret messages as a result of information overload.

Electronic mail (e-mail) is a powerful way to communicate, and it has changed communication patterns in organizational settings. However, e-mail also contributes to information overload, is an ineffective channel for communicating emotions, tends to reduce politeness and respect in the communication process, and lacks the warmth of human interaction.

Computer-mediated communication gives employees the freedom to communicate effectively from any location. This capability is part of the law of telecosm, which says that distances will shrink and eventually become irrelevant as the web of computer networks expands.

Nonverbal communication includes facial expressions, voice intonation, physical distance, and even silence. Employees make extensive use of nonverbal cues when engaging in emotional labor because these cues help transmit prescribed feelings to customers, co-workers, and others. Emotional contagion refers to the automatic and subconscious tendency to mimic and synchronize our nonverbal behaviors with those of other people.

The most appropriate communication medium depends on its data-carrying capacity (media richness) and its symbolic meaning to the receiver. Nonroutine and ambiguous situations require rich media.

Many organizations rely on a combination of print newsletters and intranet-based e-zines to communicate corporate news. Some companies also try to encourage informal communication through work space design, although open offices run the risk of increasing stress and reducing the ability to concentrate on work. Employee surveys are widely used to measure employee attitudes or involve employees in corporate decisions. Some executives also engage in management by walking around to facilitate communication across the organization.

In any organization, employees rely on the grapevine, particularly during times of uncertainty. The grapevine is an unstructured and informal network founded on social relationships rather than organizational charts or job descriptions. Although early research identified several unique features of the grapevine, some of these features may be changing as the Internet plays an increasing role in grapevine communication.

Globalization and workforce diversity have brought new communication challenges. Words are easily misunderstood in verbal communication, and employees are reluctant to communicate across cultures. Voice intonation, silence, and other nonverbal cues have different meanings and degrees of importance in different cultures. There are also some communication differences between men and women, such as the tendency for men to exert status and engage in report talk in conversations, whereas women use more rapport talk and are more sensitive than are men to nonverbal cues.

To get a message across, the sender must learn to empathize with the receiver, repeat the message, choose an appropriate time for the conversation, and be descriptive rather than evaluative. Listening includes sensing, evaluating, and responding. Active listeners support these processes by postponing evaluation, avoiding interruptions, maintaining interest, empathizing, organizing information, showing interest, and clarifying the message.

KEY TERMS

communication, p. 322

communication competence, p. 322

emotional contagion, p. 334

flaming, p. 329

grapevine, p. 339

information overload, p. 327

jargon, p. 325

law of telecosm, p. 332

management by walking around (MBWA), p. 339

media richness, p. 334

DISCUSSION QUESTIONS

1. A city government intends to introduce electronic mail for office staff at its three buildings located throughout the city. Describe two benefits as well as two potential problems that city government employees will likely experience with this medium.

2. Instant messaging will become an increasingly popular form of information technology over the next few years. What are the advantages and disadvantages of this communication medium compared with e-mail and intranet communication?

3. Marshall McLuhan coined this popular phrase: "The medium is the message." What does the phrase mean, and why should we be aware of it when communicating in organizations?

4. Why is emotional contagion important in organizations, and what effect does the increasing reliance on e-mail have on this phenomenon?

5. An executive recently admitted that she deliberately leaks information through the organizational grapevine before communicating the information through formal channels. The reason, she explains, is to give employees an opportunity to think about the information. "[B]y the time the message is formally announced, everybody has had a chance to think about it and feel like they're on the inside track." Discuss the advantages and limitations of this communication strategy.

6. The Bank of Key Largo (BKL) has just moved into one of the tallest buildings in Miami. Senior management is proud of its decision, because each department is neatly located on its own floor with plenty of closed offices. BKL executives have a breathtaking view from their offices on the top floor. There is even a large BKL branch at street level. Unfortunately, other tenants occupy some floors between those leased by BKL. Discuss the potential effects of this physical structure on communication at BKL.

7. Explain why men and women are sometimes frustrated with each other's communication behaviors.

8. This chapter describes several features of communication in Japan. Discuss three features of communication in Japan that differ from communication where you live.

SEA PINES

The coastal town of Sea Pines, Maine, retained a Boston consulting engineer to study the effect of greatly expanding the town's sewage system and discharging the treated waste into the harbor. At that time, fishermen in the town were experiencing massive lobster kills in the harbor and were concerned that the kills were caused by the effluent from the present Sea Pines sewage treatment plant. They were convinced that any expansion of the plant would further aggravate the problem. The fishermen invited Tom Stone, the engineer, to the monthly meeting of the local fishermen's organization to discuss their concerns. On the night of the meeting, the Legion Hall was filled with men in blue jeans and work jackets, many of whom were drinking beer. An account of this meeting follows, with Fred Mitchell, a local fisherman, speaking first.

Mitchell: Well, as you all know, Mr. Stone has been kind enough to meet with us tonight to explain his recommendations concerning the town's sewage disposal problem. We're all concerned about the lobster kills, like the one last summer, and I for one don't want to see any more sewage dumped into that harbor. [*Murmurs of assent are heard throughout the hall.*] So, Mr. Stone, we'd like to hear from you on what it is you want to do.

Stone: Thank you. I'm glad to get this opportunity to hear your concerns on the lobster situation. Let me say from the outset that we are still studying the problem closely and expect to make our formal recommendation to the town about a month from now. I am not prepared to discuss specific conclusions of our study, but I am prepared to incorporate any relevant comments into our study. As most of you are probably aware, we are attempting to model mathematically, or simulate, conditions in the harbor to help us predict the effects of sewage effluent in the harbor. We . . .

Mitchell: Now wait a minute. I don't know anything about models except the kind I used to make as a kid. [*Laughter.*] I can tell you that we never had lobster kills like we have now until they started dumping that sewage into the

harbor a few years back. I don't need any model to tell me that. It seems to me that common sense tells you that if we've got troubles now in the summer with the lobster, that increasing the amount of sewage by 10 times the present amount is going to cause 10 times the problem.

A Fisherman: Yeah, you don't need to be an engineer to see that.

Stone: Although it's true that we're proposing to extend the sewage system in town, and that the resulting sewage flow will be about 10 times the present flow, the area of the sewage discharge will be moved to a larger area of the harbor, where it will be diluted with much more seawater than in the present area. In addition, if the harbor is selected for the new discharge, we will design a special diffuser to mix the treated sewage effluent quickly with ocean water. As I indicated, we are attempting to use data on currents and water quality that we collected in the harbor and combine that data with some mathematical equations in our computer to help us predict what the quality in the harbor will be.

Mitchell: I don't understand what you need a computer to tell you that for. I've been fishing in this area for over 35 years now, and I don't need any computer to tell me that my lobsters are going to die if that sewage goes into the harbor.

Stone: Let me say before this goes too far that we're not talking about discharging raw sewage into the harbor. The sewage is treated and disinfected before it is discharged.

Mitchell: Isn't the sewage that's being dumped into the harbor right now being treated and disinfected, Mr. Stone?

Stone: Yes, it is, but . . .

Mitchell: The lobsters still die, so it's clear to me that "treated and disinfected" doesn't solve the problem.

Stone: Our model will predict whether the treatment provided will be sufficient to maintain the water quality in the harbor at the state's standard for the harbor.

Mitchell: I don't give a damn about any state standard. I just care about my lobsters and how I'm going to put bread on the table for my kids! You engineers from Boston can come out here spouting all kinds of things about models, data, standards, and your concern for lobsters, but what it really comes down to is that it's just another job. You can collect your fees for your study, go back to your office, and leave us holding the bag.

Stone: Now wait a minute, Mr. Mitchell. My firm is well established in New England, and we didn't get that way by giving our clients that fast shuffle and making a quick exit out of town. We have no intention of leaving you with an unworkable solution to your sewage problems. We also will not solve your sewage problem and leave you with a lobster kill problem. Perhaps I have given you the wrong impression about this modeling. We regard this as one method of analysis that may be helpful in predicting future harbor conditions, but not the only method. We have over 40 years' experience in these harbor studies, and we fully intend to use this experience, *in addition to* whatever the model tells us, to come up with a reasonable solution.

Mitchell: Well, that's all well and good, but I can tell you, and I think I speak for all the lobstermen here, that if you recommend dumping that sewage into the harbor, we'll fight you all the way down the line! [*Shouts of agreement.*] Why can't you pipe the sewage out to the ocean if you're so concerned about dilution? I'm sure that your model will tell you there's enough dilution out there.

Stone: I agree that the ocean would certainly provide sufficient dilution, but the whole purpose of this study is to see if we can avoid a deep ocean outfall.

Mitchell: Why?

Stone: Because the cost of constructing a deep ocean outfall in this area is very expensive—say about $700 per yard. Now, if the length of the outfall is 2,000 yards, don't you think that it makes good sense to spend a few thousand dollars studying the harbor area if we can save you millions?

Mitchell: All that money that you're going to save the town doesn't do much for the lobstermen who'll be put out of business if that sewage goes into the harbor.

Stone: As I said, we wouldn't recommend that if we thought, based on our modeling and our experience in this area, that the quality of water in the harbor would kill any lobster or any other aquatic life.

Mitchell: Well, I'm telling you again, if you try to put that stuff in our harbor, we'll fight you all the way. I think we've made our position clear on this thing, so if there are no further comments, I vote that we adjourn the meeting. [*Seconded.*]

When the meeting ended, the fishermen filed out, talking heatedly among themselves, leaving Mr. Stone standing on the platform.

Discussion Questions

1. What barriers to effective communication exist in this case?

2. How would you overcome or minimize each of these barriers?

Source: This case was written by Terence P. Driscoll. Reprinted from Dalmar Fisher, *Communication in Organizations* (St. Paul, MN: West Publishing, 1981).

CASE STUDY 11.2

ACROSS THE GEEK DIVIDE

BusinessWeek Miscommunications between engineers and salespeople have been part of business life at least since the Industrial Revolution. In the Internet age, the communication divide between technical and marketing experts has taken on a fresh urgency. High technology permeates the business world. Organizations need technical experts who can help their colleagues and customers use technology well. Often this means that high-tech employees must develop their will to communicate, as well as their ability to do so.

This *Business Week* case study describes organizations committed to developing the communication skills of their technology experts. It gives examples of how computer experts are learning to be communication experts—and how the employees and their companies both benefit. Read through this *Business Week* case study at www.mhhe.com/mcshane2e and prepare for the discussion questions below.

Discussion Questions

1. According to the examples provided by the author, what barriers have prevented effective communication by high-tech workers?

2. In what ways do organizations try to improve communication by their technical experts? Can you think of any additional measures organizations might take?

3. Why are communication skills important for an organization's computer experts? Would it be more reasonable for the organization to let these employees specialize in computer knowledge alone?

Source: T. Forsman, "Across the Geek Divide," *Business Week*, June 26, 2001.

TEAM EXERCISE 11.3

TINKER TOY COMMUNICATION

Purpose This exercise is designed to help you understand the importance of media richness and related issues that affect communication effectiveness.

Materials This activity requires one student on each team to have a cellular telephone that he or she is willing to use for this exercise. (Alternatively, in-house landline telephones or walkie-talkies may be used.) The instructor will provide each team with a set of Tinker Toys, Legos, Mega Blocks, straws, or other materials suitable for building. Each pair of teams must have pieces identical in number, shape, size, and color. This activity also requires either two large rooms or one large room and a few smaller rooms.

Instructions

■ *Step 1*—The instructor will divide the class into an even number of teams, each with four or five students. Teams should have the same number of members where possible. Remaining students can serve as observers. Teams are paired (e.g., team 1A and team 1B, team 2A and team 2B, etc.), and each team receives a set of building materials identical to that of the other team in the pair. For example, team 1A would have the same set of materials as team 1B. Teams should check their materials to be sure the paired team has identical pieces. Each team must have a member with a cellular telephone, and each team should have the telephone number of its paired team.

■ *Step 2*—The A teams in each pair are moved to a room near the classroom (or to several small rooms) while the B teams remain in the classroom. Ideally, each team would be assigned to its own small tutorial room, with paired teams located beside each other. If the class has only two rooms, then put one team from each pair in each room.

■ *Step 3*—The A teams build a sculpture using *all* the pieces provided. The instructor will set a time limit for this construction (typically about 10 minutes). The B teams, located in another room, must not observe this construction. Ideally, the A team's structure should be able to be moved into the classroom at the end of the exercise.

■ *Step 4*—When the A team members have completed their structure, the B team members try to replicate the A team's structure without seeing it. The A team telephones the corresponding B team and verbally describes the structure over the telephone. Only one person from each team may communicate with the other team throughout this exercise. However, the B team communicator conveys the message to other B team members, who are building the replicated structure. The instructor will limit the time allowed for the B team to replicate the structure (about 15 minutes).

■ *Step 5*—If the A team structures are sturdy enough, they should be brought into the classroom and placed beside the corresponding B team's replication. The class might want to rate each replication for its similarity to the original structure. The class will then discuss the factors that influence communication in this situation, including the importance of communication media, language, and perceptions.

TEAM EXERCISE 11.4

A NOT-SO-TRIVIAL CROSS-CULTURAL COMMUNICATION GAME

Purpose This exercise is designed to develop and test your knowledge of cross-cultural differences in communication and etiquette.

Materials The instructor will provide one set of question and answer cards to each pair of teams.

Instructions

■ *Step 1*—The class is divided into an even number of teams. Ideally, each team would have three students. (Two- or four-student teams are possible if matched with equal-sized teams.) Each team is then paired with another team, and the paired teams (team A and team B) are assigned a private space away from other paired teams.

■ *Step 2*—The instructor will hand each pair of teams a stack of cards with the multiple-choice questions facedown. These cards have questions and answers about cross-cultural differences in communication and etiquette. No books or other aids are allowed.

■ *Step 3*—The exercise begins with a member of team A picking up one card from the top of the pile and asking the question on that card to the people on team B. The information given to team B includes the question and all alternatives listed on the card. Team B has 30 seconds after the question and alternatives have been read to give an answer. Team B earns one point if the correct answer is given. If team B's answer is incorrect, however, team A earns that point. Correct answers to each question are indicated on the card and, of course, should not be revealed until the question is answered correctly or time is up. Whether or not team B answers correctly, one of its members picks up the next card on the pile and asks the question to members of team A. In other words, cards are read alternately to each team. This procedure is repeated until all the cards have been read or time has elapsed. The team receiving the most points wins.

Important note: The textbook provides very little information pertaining to the questions in this exercise. Rather, you must rely on past learning, logic, and luck to win.

SELF-ASSESSMENT EXERCISE 11.5

ACTIVE LISTENING SKILLS INVENTORY

Purpose This self-assessment exercise is designed to help you estimate your strengths and weaknesses on various dimensions of active listening.

Instructions Think back to face-to-face conversations you have had with a co-worker or client in the office, hallway, factory floor, or other setting. Indicate the extent to which each item below describes your behavior during those conversations. Answer each item as truthfully as possible so that you get an accurate estimate of where your active listening skills need improvement. Then use the scoring key in Appendix B to calculate your results for each scale. This exercise is completed alone so that students assess themselves honestly without concerns of social comparison. However, class discussion will focus on the important elements of active listening.

Active listening skills inventory					
Circle the number to the right that best indicates the extent to which each statement describes your behavior when listening to others.	Not at all	A little	Some-what	Very much	Score
1. I keep an open mind about the speaker's point of view until he or she has finished talking.	0	1	2	3	_____
2. While listening, I mentally sort out the speaker's ideas in a way that makes sense to me.	0	1	2	3	_____
3. I stop the speaker and give my opinion when I disagree with something he or she has said.	0	1	2	3	_____
4. People can often tell when I'm not concentrating on what they are saying.	0	1	2	3	_____
5. I don't evaluate what a person is saying until he or she has finished talking.	0	1	2	3	_____
6. When someone takes a long time to present a simple idea, I let my mind wander to other things.	0	1	2	3	_____
7. I jump into conversations to present my views rather than wait and risk forgetting what I wanted to say.	0	1	2	3	_____
8. I nod my head and make other gestures to show I'm interested in the conversation.	0	1	2	3	_____
9. I can usually keep focused on what people are saying to me even when they don't sound interesting. . . .	0	1	2	3	_____
10. Rather than organizing the speaker's ideas, I usually expect the person to summarize them for me. . . .	0	1	2	3	_____
11. I always say things like "I see" or "uh-huh" so that people know that I'm really listening to them.	0	1	2	3	_____
12. While listening, I concentrate on what is being said and regularly organize the information.	0	1	2	3	_____
13. While the speaker is talking, I quickly determine whether I like or dislike his or her ideas.	0	1	2	3	_____
14. I pay close attention to what people are saying even when they are explaining something I already know.	0	1	2	3	_____
15. I don't give my opinion until I'm sure the other person has finished talking.	0	1	2	3	_____

After studying the preceding material, be sure to check out our website at
www.mhhe.com/mcshane2e
for more in-depth information and interactivities that correspond to this chapter.

Organizational Power, Politics, and Persuasion

Learning Objectives

AFTER READING THIS CHAPTER, YOU SHOULD BE ABLE TO:

- Define *power* and *counterpower*.

- Describe the five bases of power in organizations.

- Explain how information relates to power in organizations.

- Discuss the four contingencies of power.

- Discuss the role of power in sexual harassment.

- Explain how organizational power creates problems in romantic relationships at work.

- Summarize the advantages and disadvantages of organizational politics.

- List six types of political activity found in organizations.

- Describe the conditions that encourage organizational politics.

- Identify ways to control dysfunctional organizational politics.

- Summarize the key features of persuasive communication.

As a corporate road warrior, Jane Buckley knows that she needs to take more than her suitcase and computer on important business trips. The corporate director of strategic solutions for Compass Group, a global food services management provider, also carries one of the most important business tools: her golf clubs. "Our company cares who it does business with and likes to establish long-term relationships with clients," explains Buckley. "Golf is one way of establishing those personal connections."

Networking is an important political activity in the workplace, and many men incidentally or deliberately use golf as a way to build their power base for career advancement. "Men have always used the golf course for networking," says Susan G. Weitzman, a Deerfield, Illinois, business owner who teaches both women and men how to play golf and network successfully on the golf course. "Women need to be there, too."

Carolyn Turknett, executive vice president and co-owner of Turknett Leadership Group in Atlanta, agrees. "Women aren't in on all the informal networks yet," she warns. "A lot goes on on the golf course, but a lot of women still aren't there." Almost 50 percent of women in senior executive positions surveyed in one study say that exclusion from informal networks was a major barrier to the career advancement of women. More startling was that only 15 percent of male CEOs saw this as a problem. In other words, CEOs fail to see that the politics of networking is one of the main reasons women are held back in their careers.

Fortunately, some companies are helping women develop networks inside the organization without learning to play golf. More than one-third of Fortune 500 companies sponsor networks for their female employees. For example, about 3,000 female professionals participate in a women's network at General Electric Corporation.[1] ■

Jane Buckley, an executive with Compass Group, travels with her golf clubs to support the power of networking with colleagues and clients. *(C. Price/ Vancouver Province)*

Golfing isn't usually the first thing that comes to mind when discussing organizational power and politics. Yet playing golf and engaging in other informal networks can make a difference to an individual's career progress and, in some cases, the ability to fulfill job duties. The reality is that no one escapes from organizational power and politics. They exist in every business and, according to some writers, in every decision and action.[2]

We begin this chapter by defining power and presenting a basic model depicting the dynamics of power in organizational settings. We then discuss the five bases of power, as well as information as a power base. Next, we look at the contingencies necessary to translate those sources into meaningful power. Our discussion of power finishes with a look at sexual harassment as an abuse of power, as well as how organizational power complicates office romances. Next, the chapter examines the dynamics of organizational politics, including the various types of political activity, the conditions that encourage organizational politics, and the ways that it can be controlled. The final section of this chapter looks at persuasion as a form of influence. This section introduces a model of persuasion, including characteristics of the communicator, message, medium, and audience.

THE MEANING OF POWER

power
The capacity of a person, team, or organization to influence others.

Power is the capacity of a person, team, or organization to influence others.[3] Power is not the act of changing others' attitudes or behavior; it is only the *potential* to do so. People frequently have power they do not use; they might not even know they have power.

The most basic prerequisite of power is that one party believes he or she is dependent on the other for something of value.[4] This relationship is shown in Exhibit 12.1, where person A has power over person B by controlling something that person B needs to achieve his or her goals. You might have power over others by controlling a desired job assignment, useful information, important resources, or even the privilege of being associated with you! Making matters more complex is the fact that power is ultimately a perception, so people might gain power simply by convincing others that they have something of value. Thus, power exists when others believe that you control resources that they want.[5]

Although power requires dependence, it is really more accurate to say that the parties are *interdependent*. One party may be more dependent than the other, but the relationship exists only when both parties have something of

EXHIBIT 12.1

Dependence in the power relationship

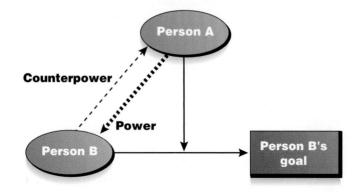

discussion may reveal that the customer would be willing to pay more if the product could be provided earlier than originally arranged. The vendor may actually value that earlier delivery because it saves inventory costs. By looking at the bigger picture, both parties can often discover common ground.

Adopting a win–win or a win–lose orientation influences our conflict management style, that is, our actions toward the other person. Researchers have categorized five interpersonal styles of approaching the other party in a conflict situation. As we see in Exhibit 13.4, each approach can be placed in a two-dimensional grid reflecting the person's motivation to satisfy his or her own interests (called *assertiveness*) and to satisfy the other party's interests (called *cooperativeness*).[33] Collaboration is the only style that represents a purely win–win orientation. The other four styles represent variations of the win–lose approach. For effective conflict management, we should learn to apply different conflict management styles to different situations.[34]

- *Collaborating*—tries to find a mutually beneficial solution for both parties through problem solving. An important feature of collaboration is information sharing so that both parties can identify common ground and potential solutions that satisfy both (or all) of them.
- *Avoiding*—tries to smooth over or avoid conflict situations altogether. For example, some employees will rearrange their work area or tasks to minimize interaction with certain co-workers.[35]

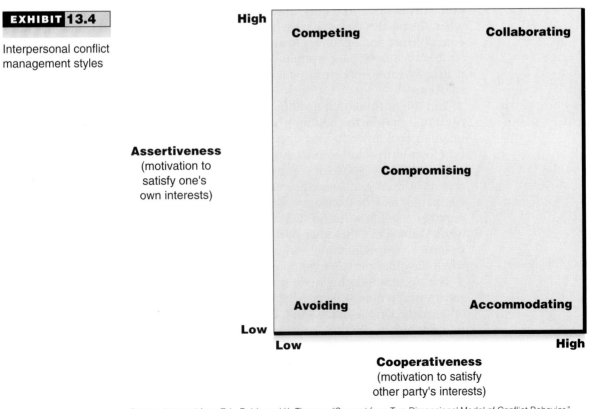

EXHIBIT 13.4

Interpersonal conflict management styles

Source: Adapted from T. L. Ruble and K. Thomas, "Support for a Two-Dimensional Model of Conflict Behavior," *Organizational Behavior and Human Performance* 16 (1976), p. 145.

- *Competing*—tries to win the conflict at the other's expense. This style has the strongest win–lose orientation because it has the highest level of assertiveness and lowest level of cooperativeness.
- *Accommodating*—involves giving in completely to the other side's wishes, or at least cooperating with little or no attention to your own interests.
- *Compromising*—tries to reach a middle ground with the other party. You look for a position in which your losses are offset by equally valued gains.

Choosing the Best Conflict Management Style

Sun Microsystems recently sued memory chip maker Kingston Technology over exclusive rights to a new architecture in memory modules. When the U.S. court threw out Sun's complaint, Kingston co-founder David Sun had another idea; he challenged Sun Microsystems CEO Scott McNealy to a game of golf to settle their differences.[36] A golf game is an unusual way to resolve conflict, but this incident illustrates how people apply different conflict management styles. Ideally, we use different styles under different conditions, but most of us have a preferred conflict management style.

The collaborative style is usually recognized as the preferred approach to conflict resolution. For example, the collaborative conflict management style results in better joint venture performance.[37] The parties discuss concerns more quickly and openly, seek their partner's opinions, and explain their course of action more fully than when a noncollaborative style is used. However, this style works only under certain conditions. Specifically, it is best when the parties do not have perfectly opposing interests and when they have enough trust and openness to share information. Collaborating is usually desirable because organizational conflicts are rarely win–lose situations. There is usually some opportunity for mutual gain if the parties search for creative solutions.[38]

You might think that avoiding is an ineffective conflict management strategy, but it may be the best approach when the issue is trivial or as a temporary tactic to cool down heated disputes. However, conflict avoidance should not be a long-term solution because it increases the other party's frustration.

The competing style of conflict resolution is usually inappropriate because organizational relationships rarely involve complete opposition. However, competing may be necessary when you know you are correct and the dispute requires a quick solution. For example, you might use the competing style when you believe the other party's position is unethical or when it otherwise violates your fundamental values. The competing style may also be necessary when the other party would take advantage of more cooperative strategies.

The accommodating style may be appropriate when the other party has substantially more power or the issue is not as important to you as to the other party. On the other hand, accommodating behaviors may give the other side unrealistically high expectations, thereby motivating that party to seek more from you in the future. In the long run, accommodating may produce more conflict rather than resolve it.

The compromising style may be best when there is little hope for mutual gain through problem solving, both parties have equal power, and both are under time pressure to settle their differences. However, compromise is rarely a final solution and may cause the parties to overlook options for mutual gain.

Cultural and Gender Differences in Conflict Management Styles

Cultural differences are more than just a source of conflict. Cultural background also affects the conflict management style we prefer using, because we are more comfortable with conflict management styles that are consistent with our personal and cultural value system.[39]

Research suggests that people from collectivist cultures—where group goals are valued more than individual goals—are motivated to maintain harmonious relations. Consequently, they tend to rely on avoidance or collaboration to resolve disagreements.[40] In contrast, people from individualistic cultures more frequently apply a compromising or competing style. People from collectivist cultures can be just as competitive as are individualists with people outside their group. However, collectivists are generally more likely to avoid confrontation, where possible.

Some writers suggest that men and women also tend to rely on different conflict management styles.[41] Generally speaking, women pay more attention than do men to the relationship between the parties. Consequently, they tend to adopt a collaborative style in business settings and are more willing to compromise to protect the relationship. Men tend to be more competitive and take a short-term orientation to the relationship. Of course, we must be cautious about these observations because gender has a weak influence on conflict management style.

STRUCTURAL APPROACHES TO CONFLICT MANAGEMENT

Conflict management styles refer to how we approach the other party in a conflict situation. But conflict management also involves altering the underlying structural causes of potential conflict. The main structural approaches are identified in Exhibit 13.5. Although this section discusses ways to reduce conflict,

EXHIBIT 13.5

Structural approaches to conflict management

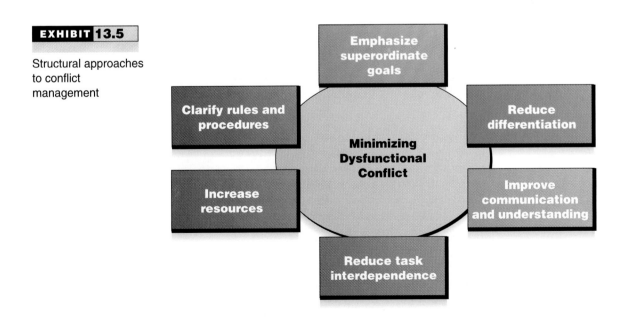

we should keep in mind that conflict management sometimes calls for increasing conflict, mainly by reversing the strategies described over the next few pages.[42]

Emphasizing Superordinate Goals

superordinate goal
A common objective held by conflicting parties that is more important than their conflicting departmental or individual goals.

Carlos Ghosn, described earlier (in Connections 13.1), was able to minimize conflict between French and Japanese executives partly by focusing everyone on the Nissan Revival Plan as a **superordinate goal.** Superordinate goals are common objectives held by conflicting parties that are more important than the departmental or individual goals on which the conflict is based. By increasing commitment to corporatewide goals, employees place less emphasis on and therefore feel less conflict with co-workers regarding competing individual or departmental-level goals.[43] Superordinate goals also potentially reduce the problem of differentiation because they establish a common frame of reference. Heterogeneous team members still perceive different ways to achieve corporate objectives, but superordinate goals ensure they mutually understand and agree on the objectives themselves.

Executives at Tivoli Systems discovered the importance of superordinate goals after participating in an exercise called Paper Airplanes, Inc. Each team at the Austin, Texas, company had 30 minutes to manufacture and sell as many standard-specific planes as possible. The teams initially performed poorly because participants focused on their individual goals. "[T]he biggest problem [was] that you couldn't just focus on your part," explains Tivoli executive Bill Jones (left in photo). Teams eventually won the exercise after their members focused on the organization's success more than their individual tasks. The exercise now represents a reminder that Tivoli employees need to focus on superordinate goals rather than departmental differences. "[W]hen things come up we refer to the exercise to help everyone get on the same page," says Brent Vance (right in photo).[44] In what other ways might the Paper Airplanes exercise reduce dysfunctional conflict? *(Ed Lallo)*

Several research studies indicate that focusing on superordinate goals weakens dysfunctional conflict. One study revealed that marketing managers in Hong Kong, China, Japan, and the United States were more likely to develop a collaborative conflict management style when executives aligned departmental goals with corporate objectives. A U.S. study found that the most effective executive teams consistently apply a superordinate goal strategy. They frame their decisions as collaborations, thereby drawing attention and commitment away from sublevel goals.[45]

Reducing Differentiation

Another way to minimize dysfunctional conflict is to reduce the differences that produce the conflict in the first place.[46] The Manila Diamond Hotel in the Philippines accomplishes this goal by rotating staff across different departments. "In Manila Diamond, there is no turf mentality," explains the hotel's marketing manager. "We all work together. We even share each other's jobs whenever necessary."[47] Similarly, W. L. Gore and Associates reduces differentiation by moving employees around to different teams. The manufacturer of Gore-Tex and other products introduced this team rotation system after it became apparent that employees were becoming too committed to their own team's goals. "You can get a little too focused on your own team and forget the good of the whole company," admits one of Gore's team members.[48]

Improving Communication and Understanding

Communication is critical to effective conflict management. Communication can range from casual gatherings among employees who rarely meet otherwise to formal processes where differences are identified and discussed. Multinational peacekeeping forces work together more effectively when troops eat and socialize together.[49] Given increased opportunity, ability, and motivation to share information, employees develop less extreme perceptions of each other than if they rely on stereotypes and emotions. Direct communication provides a better understanding of the other person's or department's work environment and resource limitations. Ongoing communication is particularly important where the need for functional specialization makes it difficult to reduce differentiation.[50]

Interdepartmental communication includes socializing over a game of Ping-Pong or Foosball. "The more informal communication that happens between various groups in companies, the better they work together as a team," explains Jamey Harvey, CEO of Reston, Virginia–based software maker iKimbo. "Marketing actually understands the intense pressure the development team is under to develop software on time. And the development team understands that the marketing team is spending money that's going to be wasted if the product doesn't come out on time."[51]

Some of the team-building activities described in Chapter 8 help reduce conflict because they help participants understand each other. Siemens AG's nuclear power division in Germany and French nuclear giant Framatome SA took this route when they recently merged. Senior executives at both firms were sent to a retreat an hour outside Paris where they spent a few days in canoe races and blindfolded three-legged races. The consulting firm that operates the

Drumming Out Their Differences

Dozens of businesspeople pour into an auditorium where drums of all types—Latin American congas, African doumbeks, and Brazilian surdos—line the room. The participants anxiously take their seats. Few have played drums before, but they will all play in harmony tonight. They will learn to cooperate and coordinate through the beat of their drums.

Leading the two-hour drumming session is Doug Sole, co-owner of Soul Drums in Toronto, Canada. He starts by pointing randomly to individuals, asking them to play a beat that others will imitate. The rhythm intensifies as others join in, then falls apart into a cacophony. "We're having a communication problem here," Sole interrupts. "If we all start banging our own thing, it's going to be chaos." Sole begins again and repeats the process until the auditorium is filled with the hypnotic beat of strangers working together.

Drum circles represent a metaphor for cooperation, coordination, communication, and teamwork in nontraditional corporate structures. They focus participants on the process of working together, not just on the outcome of achieving a goal. "It forced us to listen to, be dependent on, and have fun with each other," explains Kathleen Ross, an executive at Arbitron, a Maryland-based media research firm whose employees have participated in drum circles.

Onye Onyemaechi, a Nigerian master drummer in California, says that employees often work side by side for years without really getting to know one another. He warns that this lack of unity and understanding hinders the organization's potential, whereas drum circles begin the process of creating harmony among these strangers. "Drum circles bring people together to realize their common base," he advises.

"Drum circles thrive on collaborative creativity, and that is so important in the Internet world," says Christine

Doug Sole and other drum circle facilitators build cooperation and mutual understanding with drumsticks and boomwhackers. *(Gary Diggins, Soul Drums Ltd.; Doug Sole, Mel Bay Productions, Pacific Missouri)*

Stevens, founder of Upbeat Drum Circles in Fort Collins, Colorado. "Drum circles involve creativity and sharing, but they also demonstrate that things need to be coordinated to sound good."

Sources: S. Terry, "Lost in the Rhythm," *Christian Science Monitor,* May 23, 2001, p. 11; R. Segall, "Catch the Beat," *Psychology Today,* July 2000; M. K. Pratt, "A Pound of Cure," *Fast Company,* April 2000; A. Georgiades, "Business Heeds the Beat," *Toronto Star,* August 4, 1999.

---

retreat also spends time with each group to review the cultural differences between French and German executives.[52]

Another team-building activity that can minimize conflict is the dialogue meeting, in which the disputing parties discuss their differences. Dialogue helps participants understand each other's mental models and fundamental assumptions so that they can create a common thinking process and mental models for the team (see Chapter 8).[53] Several companies, including Toyota, Sony, Microsoft, Dell Computer, and Hewlett-Packard, have introduced yet another conflict-busting activity called drum circles. As Connections 13.2 describes, participants in this unique team-building activity use drums and other percussion instruments to learn the process of working together. It teaches harmony, not only in music, but in how employees communicate and understand each other.

Reducing Task Interdependence

Conflict increases with the level of interdependence, so minimizing dysfunctional conflict might involve reducing the level of interdependence between the parties. If cost-effective, this strategy might occur by dividing the shared resource so that each party has exclusive use of part of it. Sequentially or reciprocally interdependent jobs might be combined so that they form a pooled interdependence. For example, rather than having one employee serve customers and another operate the cash register, each employee could handle both customer activities alone. Buffers also help reduce task interdependence between people. Buffers might involve resources, such as the addition of more inventory between people who perform sequential tasks. We also find human buffers in organizations—people who intervene between highly interdependent people or work units.[54]

Increasing Resources

An obvious way to reduce conflict due to resource scarcity is to increase the amount of resources available. Corporate decision makers might dismiss this solution quickly because of the costs involved. However, they need to compare these costs carefully with the costs of dysfunctional conflict arising out of resource scarcity.

Clarifying Rules and Procedures

Some conflicts arise from ambiguous decision rules regarding the allocation of scarce resources. Consequently, these conflicts can be minimized by establishing rules and procedures. Rules clarify the distribution of resources, such as when students can use the laser printer or for how long they can borrow library books. Consider the following situation that occurred when Armstrong World Industries, Inc., brought in consultants to implement a client–server network. Information systems employees at the flooring and building materials company experienced conflict with the consultants over who was in charge. Another conflict occurred when the consultants wanted to work long hours and take Friday off to fly home. Armstrong minimized these conflicts by spelling out as much as possible in the contract about each party's responsibilities and roles. Issues that were unclear or overlooked in the contract were clarified by joint discussion between two senior executives at the companies.[55]

Rules establish changes to the terms of interdependence, such as an employee's hours of work or a supplier's fulfillment of an order. In most cases, the parties affected by these rules are involved in the process of deciding these terms of interdependence. Because it redefines the terms of interdependence, the strategy of clarifying rules is part of the larger process of negotiation.

RESOLVING CONFLICT THROUGH NEGOTIATION

Think back through yesterday's events. Maybe you had to work out an agreement with other students about what tasks to complete for a team project. Chances are that you shared transportation with someone, so you had to clarify

negotiation
Occurs whenever two or more conflicting parties attempt to resolve their divergent goals by redefining the terms of their interdependence.

the timing of the ride. Then perhaps there was the question of who made dinner. Each of these daily events created potential conflict, and they were resolved through negotiation. **Negotiation** occurs whenever two or more conflicting parties attempt to resolve their divergent goals by redefining the terms of their interdependence.[56] In other words, people negotiate when they think that discussion can produce a more satisfactory arrangement (at least for them) in their exchange of goods or services.

As you can see, negotiation is not an obscure practice reserved for labor and management bosses when hammering out a workplace agreement. Everyone negotiates—every day. Most of the time, you often don't even realize that you are in negotiations.[57] Negotiation is particularly evident in the workplace because employees work interdependently. They negotiate with their supervisors over next month's work assignments, with customers over the sale and delivery schedules of their product, and with co-workers over when to have lunch. And yes, they occasionally negotiate with each other in labor disputes and workplace agreements.

Some writers suggest that negotiations are more successful when the parties adopt a collaborative style, whereas others caution that this conflict management style is sometimes costly.[58] We know that any win–lose style (competing, accommodating, etc.) is unlikely to produce the optimal solution, because the parties have not shared information necessary to discover a mutually satisfactory solution. On the other hand, we must be careful about adopting an openly collaborative style until mutual trust has been established.

The concern with collaboration is that information is power, so information sharing gives the other party more power to leverage a better deal if the opportunity occurs. Skilled negotiators often adopt a *cautiously* collaborative style at the outset by sharing information slowly and determining whether the other side will reciprocate. In this respect, they try to establish trust with the other party.[59] They switch to one of the win–lose styles only when it becomes apparent that a win–win solution is not possible or the other party is unwilling to share information with a cooperative orientation.

Bargaining Zone Model of Negotiations

The negotiation process moves each party along a continuum with an area of potential overlap called the *bargaining zone*.[60] Exhibit 13.6 displays one possible bargaining zone situation. This linear diagram illustrates a purely win–lose situation—one side's gain will be the other's loss. However, the bargaining zone model can also be applied to situations in which both sides potentially gain from the negotiations. As this model illustrates, the parties typically establish three main negotiating points. The *initial offer point* is the team's opening offer to the other party. This point may be its best expectation or a pie-in-the-sky starting point. The *target point* is the team's realistic goal or expectation for a final agreement. The *resistance point* is the point beyond which the team will not make further concessions.

The parties begin negotiations by describing their initial offer point for each item on the agenda. In most cases, the participants know that this is only a starting point that will change as both sides offer concessions. In win–lose situations, neither the target nor the resistance points are revealed to the other

| EXHIBIT 13.6 | Bargaining zone model of negotiations |

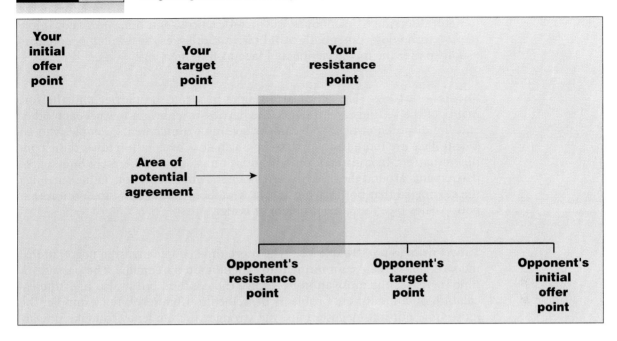

party. However, people try to discover the other side's resistance point because this knowledge helps them determine how much they can gain without breaking off negotiations.

When the parties have a win–win orientation, on the other hand, the objective is to find a creative solution that keeps everyone close to the initial offer points. They hope to find an arrangement by which each side loses relatively little value on some issues and gains significantly more on other issues. For example, a supplier might want to delay delivery dates, whereas delivery times are not important to the business customer. If the parties share this information, they can quickly agree to a delayed delivery schedule, thereby costing the customer very little and gaining the supplier a great deal. On other items (financing, order size, etc.), the supplier might give something with minimal loss even though it is a significant benefit to the business customer.

Situational Influences on Negotiations

The effectiveness of negotiating depends on both the situation and the behaviors of the negotiators. Four of the most important situational factors are location, physical setting, time, and audience.

Location It is easier to negotiate on your own turf because you are familiar with the negotiating environment and are able to maintain comfortable routines.[61] Also, there is no need to cope with travel-related stress or depend on others for resources during the negotiation. Of course, you can't walk out of negotiations as easily when on your own turf, but this is usually a minor issue. Considering these strategic benefits of home turf, many negotiators agree to neutral territory. Telephones, videoconferences, and other forms of information technology potentially avoid territorial issues, but skilled negotiators usually prefer the media richness of face-to-face meetings.

Physical Setting   The physical distance between the parties and the formality of the setting can influence the parties' orientation toward each other and the disputed issues.[62] So can the seating arrangements. People who sit face-to-face are more likely to develop a win–lose orientation toward the conflict situation. In contrast, some negotiation groups deliberately intersperse participants around the table to convey a win–win orientation. Others arrange the seating so that both parties face a whiteboard, reflecting the notion that both parties face the same problem or issue.

Time Passage and Deadlines   The more time people invest in negotiations, the stronger is their commitment to reaching an agreement. The passage of time increases the motivation to resolve the conflict, but it also fuels the escalation of commitment problems described in Chapter 9. For example, the more time put into negotiations, the stronger the tendency to make unwarranted concessions so that the negotiations do not fail.

Time deadlines may be useful to the extent that they motivate the parties to complete negotiations. However, time deadlines may become a liability when exceeding deadlines is costly.[63] Negotiators make concessions and soften their demands more rapidly as the deadline approaches. Moreover, time pressure inhibits a collaborative conflict management style, because the parties have less time to exchange information or present flexible offers.

Audience Characteristics   Most negotiators have audiences—anyone with a vested interest in the negotiation outcomes, such as executives, other team members, or the general public. Negotiators tend to act differently when their audience observes the negotiation or has detailed information about the process, compared with situations in which the audience sees only the end results.[64] When the audience has direct surveillance over the proceedings, negotiators tend to be more competitive, less willing to make concessions, and more likely to engage in political tactics against the other party.[65] This hardline behavior shows the audience that the negotiator is working for their interests. With their audience watching, negotiators also have more interest in saving face. Sometimes audiences are drawn into the negotiations by acting as a source of indirect appeals. The general public often takes on this role when groups negotiate with governments.[66]

Negotiator Behaviors

Negotiator behaviors play an important role in resolving conflict. Four of the most important behaviors are setting goals, gathering information, communicating effectively, and making concessions.

▪ *Planning and setting goals*—Research has consistently reported that people have more favorable negotiation results when they plan and set goals.[67] In particular, negotiators should carefully think through their initial offer, target, and resistance points. They need to check their underlying assumptions, as well as goals and values. Equally important is the need to research what the other party wants from the negotiation.

▪ *Gathering information*—"Seek to understand before you seek to be understood." This popular philosophy from management guru Stephen Covey applies to effective negotiations. It means that we should spend more time listening closely to the other party and asking them for details of their position.[68] One way to improve the information-gathering process is to have a team of people participate in negotiations. Asian companies tend to have large negotiation teams for this purpose.[69] With more information about the opponent's interests and needs, negotiators are better able to discover low-cost concessions or proposals that will satisfy the other side.

▪ *Communicating effectively*—Effective negotiators communicate in a way that maintains effective relationships between the parties.[70] Specifically, they minimize socioemotional conflict by focusing on issues rather than people. Effective negotiators also avoid irritating statements such as "I think you'll agree that this is a generous offer." Effective negotiators are masters of persuasive communication. In particular, negotiators structure the content of their messages so that their goals are accepted by others, not merely understood (see Chapter 12).[71]

▪ *Making concessions*—Concessions are important because they (1) enable the parties to move toward the area of potential agreement, (2) symbolize each party's motivation to bargain in good faith, and (3) tell the other party of the relative importance of the negotiating items.[72] How many concessions should you make? The answer varies with the other party's expectations and the level of trust between you. For instance, many Chinese negotiators are wary of people who change their position during the early stages of negotiations. Similarly, some writers warn that Russian negotiators tend to view concessions as a sign of weakness rather than a sign of trust.[73] Generally, the best strategy is to be moderately tough and give just enough concessions to communicate sincerity and motivation to resolve the conflict.[74] Being too tough can undermine relations between the parties; giving too many concessions implies weakness and encourages the other party to use power and resistance.

THIRD-PARTY CONFLICT RESOLUTION

third-party conflict resolution

Any attempt by a relatively neutral person to help the parties resolve their differences.

Most of this chapter has focused on people directly involved in a conflict, yet many disputes in organizational settings are resolved with the assistance of a third party. **Third-party conflict resolution** is any attempt by a relatively neutral person to help the parties resolve their differences—ranging from formal labor arbitration to informal managerial interventions to resolve disagreements among employees.

There are four main objectives in third-party conflict resolution.[75] One objective is *efficiency*. Those who take the third-party role try to resolve the dispute quickly and with minimum expenditure of organizational resources. Second, conflict resolution should be *effective*, meaning that the process should find the best long-term solution that will correct the underlying causes of the conflict. Third, this process should have outcome fairness. This objective ensures that the parties feel the solution provided by the third-party intervention is fair. Although outcome fairness is similar to effectiveness, they are not the same, because people sometimes think that a solution is fair even though it does not work well in the long term.

Finally, third-party conflict resolution should ensure that the parties feel the dispute resolution process is fair, whether or not the outcome is favorable to them. This objective, known as **procedural fairness,** is particularly important when the third party makes a binding decision to resolve the dispute. In such situations, procedural fairness increases when the third party isn't biased (e.g., doesn't have a vested interest toward one party), is well informed about the facts of the situation, and has listened to all sides of the dispute. It also increases when the decision can be appealed to a higher authority and the third party applies existing policies consistently.[76]

procedural fairness
Perceptions of fairness regarding the dispute resolution process, whether or not the outcome is favorable to the person.

Types of Third-Party Intervention

There are generally three types of third-party dispute resolution activities: arbitration, inquisition, and mediation. These activities can be classified by their level of control over the process and the decision (see Exhibit 13.7).[77]

▪ *Arbitration*—Arbitrators have high control over the final decision, but low control over the process.[78] Executives engage in this strategy by following previously agreed upon rules of due process, listening to arguments from the disputing employees, and making a binding decision. Arbitration is applied as the final stage of grievances by unionized employees, but it is also becoming more common in nonunion conflicts. For instance, some workers' compensation boards rely on a process called alternative dispute resolution (ADR), which typically includes mediation followed by arbitration.

▪ *Inquisition*—Inquisitors control all discussion about the conflict. Like arbitrators, they have high decision control because they choose the form of conflict resolution. However, they also have high process control because they

EXHIBIT 13.7

Types of third-party intervention

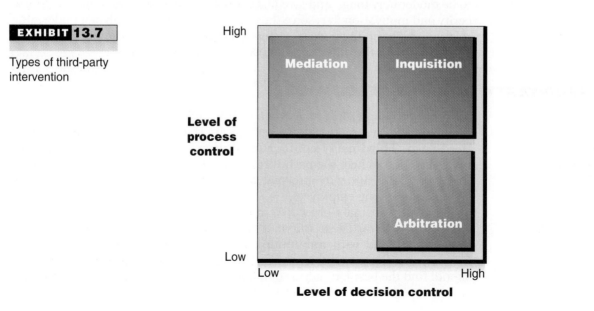

choose which information to examine and how to examine it, and generally decide how the conflict resolution process will be handled.

■ *Mediation*—Mediators have high control over the intervention process. In fact, their main purpose is to manage the process and context of interaction between the disputing parties. However, the parties make the final decision about how to resolve their differences. Thus, mediators have little or no control over the conflict resolution decision.

Choosing the Best Third-Party Intervention Strategy

Team leaders, executives, and co-workers regularly intervene in disputes between employees and departments. Sometimes they adopt a mediator role; other times they serve as arbitrators. However, research suggests that people in positions of authority (e.g., managers) usually adopt an inquisitional approach whereby they dominate the intervention process as well as make a binding decision.[79] Managers like the inquisitional approach because it is consistent with the decision-oriented nature of managerial jobs, gives them control over the conflict process and outcome, and tends to resolve disputes efficiently.

However, the inquisitional approach to third-party conflict resolution is usually the least effective in organizational settings.[80] One problem is that leaders who take an inquisitional role tend to collect limited information about the problem using this approach, so their imposed decision may produce an ineffective solution to the conflict. Moreover, employees tend to think that the procedures and outcomes of inquisitions are unfair because they have little control over this approach.

Which third-party intervention is most appropriate in organizations? The answer depends partly on the situation.[81] For example, arbitration is much less popular in Hong Kong than in North America. But generally speaking, for everyday disputes between two employees, the mediation approach is usually best because it gives employees more responsibility for resolving their own disputes. The third-party representative merely establishes an appropriate context for conflict resolution. Although not as efficient as other strategies, mediation potentially offers the highest level of employee satisfaction with the conflict process and outcomes.[82] When employees cannot resolve their differences, arbitration seems to work best because the predetermined rules of evidence and other processes create a higher sense of procedural fairness. Moreover, arbitration is preferred where the organization's goals should take priority over individual goals.

Alternative Dispute Resolution   Dallas-based energy services company Halliburton Company and Cleveland-based auto parts and aerospace company TRW, Inc., take third-party resolution one step further through a comprehensive **alternative dispute resolution (ADR)** process. ADR combines third-party dispute resolution in an orderly sequence. ADR typically begins with a meeting between the employee and employer to clarify and negotiate their differences. If this fails, a mediator is brought in to help the parties reach a mutually agreeable solution. If mediation fails, the parties submit their case to an arbitrator whose decision may be either binding or voluntarily accepted by the employer. Some firms (such as TRW) allow employees to take the case to court if they lose the arbitration decision.[83]

alternative dispute resolution (ADR)
A third-party dispute resolution process that includes mediation, typically followed by arbitration.

When Buddy's Natural Chickens, Inc., opened its plant in Gonzales, Texas, the poultry farming and processing company experienced a rash of workers' compensation claims and other grievances. Before these conflicts could escalate and undermine morale, Buddy's introduced alternative dispute resolution (ADR). This third-party conflict resolution program begins with informal, face-to-face talks between managers and employees. Almost all disputes have been settled at this stage. However, if unresolved, the dispute then moves on to mediation and, finally, to arbitration.[85] Why doesn't the ADR process include inquisition? *(Bob Daemmrich/The Image Works)*

Within this three-step process, ADR takes various forms. Philadelphia Electric (now part of Chicago-based Exelon Corporation) introduced a process whereby employees meet with trained peer coaches who prepare workers for conversations with their supervisors. This tends to increase the success rate of the first stage in the ADR process. Although most ADR systems rely on professional arbitrators, some firms prefer peer arbitrations, which include a panel of co-workers and managers who are not involved in the dispute.[84]

Whether resolving conflict through third-party dispute resolution or direct negotiation, we need to recognize that many solutions come from the sources of conflict that were identified earlier in this chapter. This conclusion may seem obvious, but in the heat of conflict, people often focus on each other rather than the underlying causes. Recognizing these conflict sources is the role of effective leadership, which is discussed in the next chapter.

CHAPTER SUMMARY

Conflict is the process in which one party perceives that its interests are being opposed or negatively affected by another party. The conflict process begins with the sources of conflict. These sources lead one or both sides to perceive a conflict and to experience conflict emotions. This, in turn, produces manifest conflict, such as behaviors toward the other side.

When conflict is task-related, the parties view the conflict experience as something separate from them. Disputes are much more difficult to resolve when they produce socioemotional conflict, where the parties perceive each other as the problem. The conflict process often escalates through a series of episodes and shifts from task-related to socioemotional.

Conflict management maximizes the benefits and minimizes the dysfunctional consequences of conflict. Conflict is beneficial in the form of constructive controversy because it makes people think more fully about issues. Positive conflict also increases team cohesiveness when conflict is with another group. The main problems with conflict are that it may lead to job stress, dissatisfaction, and turnover. Dysfunctional intergroup conflict may undermine decision making.

Conflict tends to increase when people have incompatible goals, different values and beliefs, interdependent tasks, scarce resources, ambiguous rules, and problems communicating with each other. Conflict is more common in a multicultural workforce because of greater differentiation and communication problems among employees.

People with a win–win orientation believe the parties will find a mutually beneficial solution to their disagreement. Those with a win–lose orientation adopt the belief that the parties are drawing from a fixed pie. The latter orientation tends to escalate conflict. Among the five interpersonal conflict management styles, only collaborating represents a purely win–win orientation. The four other styles—avoiding, competing, accommodating, and compromising—adopt some variation of a win–lose orientation. Women and people with high collectivism tend to use a collaborative or avoidance style more than men and people with high individualism.

Structural approaches to conflict management include emphasizing superordinate goals, reducing differentiation, improving communication and understanding, reducing task interdependence, increasing resources, and clarifying rules and procedures. These elements can also be altered to stimulate conflict.

Negotiation occurs whenever two or more conflicting parties attempt to resolve their divergent goals by redefining the terms of their interdependence. Negotiations are influenced by several situational factors, including location, physical setting, time passage and deadlines, and audience. Important negotiator behaviors include planning and setting goals, gathering information, communicating effectively, and making concessions.

Third-party conflict resolution is any attempt by a relatively neutral person to help the parties resolve their differences. The main objectives are to resolve the dispute efficiently and effectively, and to ensure that the parties feel that the process and outcome of dispute resolution are fair. The three main forms of third-party dispute resolution are mediation, arbitration, and inquisition. Managers tend to use an inquisitional approach, although mediation and arbitration are more appropriate, depending on the situation. Alternative dispute resolution applies mediation, but may also involve negotiation and, eventually, arbitration.

KEY TERMS

alternative dispute resolution (ADR), p. 407

conflict management, p. 388

conflict, p. 386

negotiation, p.402

procedural fairness, p. 406

superordinate goal, p. 398

third-party conflict resolution, p. 405

win–lose orientation, p. 394

win–win orientation, p. 394

DISCUSSION QUESTIONS

1. Distinguish task-related from socioemotional conflict, and explain where these two forms fit into the conflict escalation cycle.
2. The president of Creative Toys, Inc., read about cooperation in Japanese companies and has vowed to bring this same philosophy to the company. The goal is to avoid all conflict so that employees will work cooperatively and be happier at Creative Toys. Discuss the merits and limitations of the president's policy.
3. Conflict among managers emerged soon after a Swedish company was bought by a French company. The Swedes perceived the French management as hierarchical and arrogant, whereas the French thought the Swedes were naive and cautious, and lacked an achievement orientation. Describe ways to reduce dysfunctional conflict in this situation.
4. This chapter describes three levels of task interdependence that exist in interpersonal and intergroup relationships. Identify examples of these three levels in your work or school activities. How do these three levels affect potential conflict for you?
5. Jane has just been appointed purchasing manager of Tacoma Technologies Corporation. The previous purchasing manager, who recently retired, was known for his winner-take-all approach to suppliers. He continually fought for more discounts and was skeptical about any special deals that suppliers would propose. A few suppliers refused to do business with Tacoma Technologies, but senior management was confident that the former purchasing manager's approach minimized the company's costs. Jane wants to try a more collaborative approach to working with suppliers. Will her approach work? How should she adopt a more collaborative approach in future negotiations with suppliers?
6. You are a special assistant to the commander-in-chief of a peacekeeping mission to a war-torn part of the world. The unit consists of a few thousand peacekeeping troops from the United States, France, and four other countries. The troops will work together for approximately one year. What strategies would you recommend to improve mutual understanding and minimize conflict among these troops?
7. Suppose that you head one of five divisions in a multinational organization and are about to begin this year's budget deliberations at headquarters. What are the characteristics of your audience in these negotiations, and what effect might they have on your negotiation behavior?
8. Managers tend to use an inquisitional approach to resolving disputes between employees and departments. Describe the inquisitional approach, and discuss its appropriateness in organizational settings.

CONFLICT IN CLOSE QUARTERS

A team of psychologists at Moscow's Institute for Biomedical Problems (IBMP) wanted to learn more about the dynamics of long-term isolation in space. This knowledge would be applied to the International Space Station, a joint project of several countries that would send people into space for more than six months. It would eventually include a trip to Mars taking up to three years.

IBMP set up a replica of the Mir space station in Moscow. The institute then arranged for three international researchers from Japan, Canada, and Austria to spend 110 days isolated in a chamber the size of a train car. This chamber joined a smaller chamber where four Russian cosmonauts had already completed half of their 240 days of isolation. This was the first time an international crew was involved in the studies. None of the participants spoke English as their first language, yet they communicated throughout their stay in English at varying levels of proficiency.

Judith Lapierre, a French Canadian, was the only female in the experiment. Along with having earned a PhD in public health and social medicine, Lapierre studied space sociology at the International Space University in France and conducted isolation research in the Antarctic. This was her fourth trip to Russia, where she had learned the language. The mission was supposed to have a second female participant from the Japanese space program, but she was not selected by IBMP.

The Japanese and Austrian participants viewed the participation of a woman as a favorable factor, says Lapierre. For example, to make the surroundings more comfortable, they rearranged the furniture, hung posters on the wall, and put a tablecloth on the kitchen table. "We adapted our environment, whereas the Russians just viewed it as something to be endured," she explains. "We decorated for Christmas, because I'm the kind of person who likes to host people."

New Year's Eve Turmoil

Ironically, it was at one of those social events, the New Year's Eve party, that events took a turn for the worse. After drinking vodka (allowed by the Russian space agency), two of the Russian cosmonauts got into a fistfight that left blood splattered on the chamber walls. At one point, a colleague hid the knives in the station's kitchen because of fears that the two Russians were about to stab each other. The two cosmonauts, who generally did not get along, had to be restrained by other men. Soon after that brawl, the Russian commander grabbed Lapierre, dragged her out of view of the television monitoring cameras, and kissed her aggressively—twice. Lapierre fought him off, but the message didn't register. He tried to kiss her again the next morning.

The next day, the international crew complained to IBMP about the behavior of the Russian cosmonauts. The Russian institute apparently took no action against any of the aggressors. Instead, the institute's psychologists replied that the incidents were part of the experiment. They wanted crew members to solve their personal problems with mature discussion, without asking for outside help. "You have to understand that Mir is an autonomous object, far away from anything," Vadim Gushin, the IBMP psychologist in charge of the project, explained after the experiment ended in March. "If the crew can't solve problems among themselves, they can't work together."

Following IBMP's response, the international crew wrote a scathing letter to the Russian institute and the space agencies involved in the experiment. "We had never expected such events to take place in a highly controlled scientific experiment where individuals go through a multistep selection process," they wrote. "If we had known . . . we would not have joined it as subjects." The letter also complained about IBMP's inadequate response to their concerns.

Informed of the New Year's Eve incident, the Japanese space program convened an emergency meeting on January 2 to address the incidents. Soon after, the Japanese team member quit, apparently shocked by IBMP's inaction. He was replaced with a Russian researcher on the international team. Ten days after the fight—a little over a month after the international team began the mission—the doors between the Russian and international crew's chambers were barred at the request of the international research team. Lapierre later emphasized that this action was taken because of concerns about violence, not the incident involving her.

A Stolen Kiss or Sexual Harassment?

By the end of the experiment in March, news of the fistfight between the cosmonauts and the commander's attempts to kiss Lapierre had reached the public. Russian scientists attempted to play down the kissing incident by saying that it involved one fleeting kiss, a clash of cultures, and a female participant who was too emotional.

"In the West, some kinds of kissing are regarded as sexual harassment. In our culture, it's nothing," said Vadim Gushin in one interview. In another interview, he explained: "The problem of sexual harassment is given a lot of attention in North America but less in Europe. In Russia it is even less of an issue, not because we are more or less moral than the rest of the world; we just have different priorities."

Judith Lapierre says the kissing incident was tolerable compared with this reaction from the Russian scientists who conducted the experiment. "They don't get it at all," she complains. "They don't think anything is wrong. I'm more frustrated than ever. The worst thing is that they don't realize it was wrong."

Norbert Kraft, the Austrian scientist on the international team, also disagreed with the Russian interpretation of events. "They're trying to protect themselves," he says. "They're trying to put the fault on others. But this is not a cultural issue. If a woman doesn't want to be kissed, it is not acceptable."

Discussion Questions

1. Identify the different conflict episodes that exist in this case. Who was in conflict with whom?

2. What are the sources or causes of each manifest conflict incident in this case?

3. What conflict management styles did Lapierre, the international team, and Gushin use to resolve these conflicts? What styles would have worked best in these situations?

4. What conflict management interventions were applied here? Did they work? What alternative strategies would work best in this situation and in the future?

Sources: The facts of this case have been pieced together by Steven L. McShane from the following sources: G. Sinclair, Jr., "If You Scream in Space, Does Anyone Hear?" *Winnipeg Free Press,* May 5, 2000, p. A4; S. Martin, "Reining in the Sapce Cowboys," *Globe and Mail (Toronto),* April 19, 2000, p. R1; M. Gray, "A Space Dream Sours," *Maclean's,* April 17, 2000, p. 26; E. Niiler, "In Search of the Perfect Astronaut," *Boston Globe,* April 4, 2000, p. E4; J. Tracy, "110-Day Isolation Ends in Sullen . . . Isolation," *Moscow Times,* March 30, 2000, p. 1; M. Warren, "A Mir Kiss?" *Daily Telegraph (London),* March 30, 2000, p. 22; G. York, "Canadian's Harassment Complaint Scorned," *Globe and Mail (Toronto),* March 25, 2000, p. A2; S. Nolen, "Lust in Space," *Globe and Mail (Toronto),* March 24, 2000, p. A3.

CASE STUDY **13.2**

HOW TO BOOST YOUR BARGAINING POWERS

BusinessWeek When conflicts arise because of differences in goals or a shortage of resources, people in organizations often bargain or negotiate their way to a resolution. This behavior is often behind decisions about which projects to fund, how to resolve labor disputes, and whom to promote to key positions. Individuals with skill at negotiating can advance their group's performance, as well as their own careers. For example, skill in negotiating can help a person win a more favorable compensation package.

This *Business Week* case study describes tactics for effective salary negotiations. The author begins with evidence that women on average have been less successful than men in this regard, then summarizes advice aimed at making women more effective negotiators. Read through the *Business Week* case study at www.mhhe.com/mcshane2e and prepare for the discussion questions on page 412.

Discussion Questions

1. What conflicts in organizations create the need for salary negotiations? According to the background in the article, do women typically face additional or different conflicts than men?

2. Of the five conflict management styles shown in Exhibit 13.4, which do you think is (are) represented in this article's advice for negotiation? Which approaches would be most beneficial to the employee? To the employer?

3. On the basis of the chapter's discussion of negotiation, what additional strategies could improve a person's efforts at negotiating a raise?

Source: T. Gutner, "How to Boost Your Bargaining Powers," *Business Week,* October 16, 2000.

TEAM EXERCISE 13.3

UGLI ORANGE ROLE PLAY

Purpose This exercise is designed to help you understand the dynamics of interpersonal and intergroup conflict as well as the effectiveness of negotiation strategies under specific conditions.

Materials The instructor will distribute roles for Dr. Roland, Dr. Jones, and a few observers. Ideally, each negotiation should occur in a private area away from other negotiations.

Instructions

- *Step 1*—The instructor will divide the class into an even number of teams of three people each. Any students remaining will be given the role of observer. One-half of the teams will take the role of Dr. Roland and the other half will be Dr. Jones. The instructor will distribute roles after the teams have been formed.

- *Step 2*—Members within each team are given 10 minutes (or other time limit stated by the instructor) to learn their roles and decide on their negotiating strategy.

- *Step 3*—After reading their roles and discussing strategy, each Dr. Jones team is matched with a Dr. Roland team to conduct negotiations. Observers will receive observation forms from the instructor, and two observers will be assigned to watch the paired teams during prenegotiations and subsequent negotiations.

- *Step 4*—As soon as Roland and Jones reach agreement or at the end of the time allotted for the negotiation (whichever comes first), the Roland and Jones teams report to the instructor for further instruction.

- *Step 5*—At the end of the exercise, the class will congregate to discuss the negotiations. Observers and negotiators will then discuss their observations and experiences and the implications for conflict management and negotiation.

Source: This exercise was developed by Robert J. House, Wharton Business School, University of Pennsylvania. A similar incident is also attributed to earlier writings by R. R. Blake and J. S. Mouton.

SELF-ASSESSMENT EXERCISE 13.4

CONFLICT MANAGEMENT STYLE ORIENTATION SCALE

Purpose This self-assessment exercise is designed to help you identify your preferred conflict management style.

Instructions Read each statement in the chart on page 413 and circle the response that you believe best reflects your position regarding that statement. Then use the scoring key in Appendix B to calculate your results for each conflict management style. This exercise is completed alone so that students assess themselves honestly without concerns of social comparison. However, class discussion will focus on the different conflict management styles and the situations in which each is most appropriate.

Conflict management style scale				
Circle the number that best indicates how well each statement describes you.	Rarely ▼			Always ▼
1. If someone disagrees with me, I vigorously defend my side of the issue.	1	2	3	4	5
2. I go along with suggestions from co-workers even if I don't agree with them.	1	2	3	4	5
3. I give and take so that a compromise can be reached.	1	2	3	4	5
4. I keep my opinions to myself rather than openly disagree with people.	1	2	3	4	5
5. In disagreements or negotiations, I try to find the best possible solution for both sides by sharing information.	1	2	3	4	5
6. I try to reach a middle ground in disputes with other people.	1	2	3	4	5
7. I accommodate the wishes of people who have points of view different from my own.	1	2	3	4	5
8. I avoid openly debating issues where there is disagreement.	1	2	3	4	5
9. In negotiations, I hold on to my position rather than give in.	1	2	3	4	5
10. I try to solve conflicts by finding solutions that benefit both me and the other person.	1	2	3	4	5
11. I let co-workers have their way rather than jeopardize our relationship.	1	2	3	4	5
12. I try to win my position in a discussion.	1	2	3	4	5
13. I like to investigate conflicts with co-workers so that we can discover solutions that benefit both of us.	1	2	3	4	5
14. I believe that it is not worth the time and trouble discussing my differences of opinion with other people.	1	2	3	4	5
15. To reach an agreement, I give up some things in exchange for others.	1	2	3	4	5

Sources: Adapted from items in M. A. Rahim, "A Measure of Styles of Handling Interpersonal Conflict," *Academy of Management Journal* 26 (June 1983), pp. 368–76; K. W. Thomas and R. H. Kilmann, *Thomas-Kilmann Conflict Mode Instrument* (Sterling Forst, NY: Xicom, 1977).

After studying the preceding material, be sure to check out our website at
www.mhhe.com/mcshane2e
for more in-depth information and interactivties that correspond to this chapter.

Organizational Leadership

The world has changed, and so has our concept of effective leadership. That's what consultants Booz Allen & Hamilton and the World Economic Forum's Strategic Leadership Project recently reported. On the basis of interviews with 6,000 executives and employees in several countries, they found that effective leaders subordinate their own egos and, instead, nurture leadership in others throughout an organization.

This new image is a far cry from the command-and-control leaders of yesteryear who took center stage and pretended to have all the answers. "I don't think that dictatorial leaders will survive," warns United Airlines executive Anne Keating. "It's an old-fashioned way of leading people." Wal King, CEO of Leighton Group, agrees: "Leadership style has gone from an autocratic style to encouraging participation to achieve a common outcome."

To achieve a common outcome, leaders must have a sense of direction, the passion to move forward, and the ability to motivate others to lead with them. "A great leader is one who has vision, perseverance, and the capacity to inspire others," says Cynthia Trudell, president of Brunswick Corporation's Sea Ray Group and former CEO of Saturn Corporation. "Above all, I believe the ability to listen is as fundamental as any other skill in the ability to lead," she says.

Personal values also enter most discussions about the emerging definition of leadership. "In my mind, trust, ethics and honesty [constitute] the new 'leadership currency,'" says Gary Irvin, CEO of FORUM Credit Union in Indianapolis. Rich Teerlink, the recently retired CEO of Harley-Davidson, offers a more detailed list of leadership values: "Tell the truth. Be fair. Keep your promises. Respect individuality. If leaders live by those, they can be successful."[1]

"A great leader is one who has vision, perseverance, and the capacity to inspire others," says Cynthia Trudell, president of Brunswick Corporation's Sea Ray Group and former CEO of Saturn Corporation. *(Mike Hungerford)*

What is leadership? The opening vignette illustrates that our concept of leadership is changing, but it remains a complex issue that stirs up plenty of interest and discussion. Reviews of the leadership literature note that scholars do not sufficiently agree on the definition of leadership.[2] Most writers do agree, however, that leaders do not occupy specific positions. Anyone can be a leader throughout the organization. Indeed, the emerging definition is that effective leaders teach and empower their employees to take leadership roles.

leadership
The process of influencing people and providing an environment for them to achieve team or organizational objectives.

We will cautiously define **leadership** as the process of influencing people and providing an environment for them to achieve team or organizational objectives. Effective leaders help groups of people define their goals and find ways to achieve them.[3] They use power and persuasion to ensure that followers have the motivation and role clarity to achieve specified goals. Leaders also arrange the work environment—such as allocating resources and altering communication patterns—so that employees can achieve corporate objectives more easily. No matter how leadership is defined, however, only 8 percent of executives in large firms think their organizations have enough of it.[4] Most are concerned about a lack of leadership talent.

But leadership isn't restricted to the executive suite. Anyone in the organization can be a leader. "We're quite serious when we talk about leadership even to a bench worker on the assembly line," says an executive at General Semiconductor, the New York–based global high-technology company. "Lots of people will say, 'Oh, I'm not a leader,' but when we point out the essence of leadership is influence, they realize everyone has leadership qualities and responsibilities."[5]

Effective self-directed work teams, for example, consist of members who share leadership responsibilities or otherwise allocate this role to a responsible coordinator. Similarly, research indicates that technology champions—employees who overcome technical and organizational obstacles to introduce technological change in their area of the organization—are most successful when they possess the traits and enact the behaviors we associate with effective leadership.[6] Thus, we should not think of leaders only as people at the top of the organization. Anyone can be a leader at an appropriate time and place.

PERSPECTIVES OF LEADERSHIP

Leadership has been contemplated since the days of Greek philosophers, and it is one of the most popular research topics among organizational behavior scholars. This interest in leadership has resulted in an enormous volume of leadership literature, most of which can be split into the five perspectives shown in Exhibit 14.1. Although some of these perspectives are currently more popular than others, each helps us more fully understand this complex issue.

Some scholars have studied the traits or competencies of great leaders, whereas others have looked at their behaviors. More recent studies have looked at leadership from a contingency approach by considering the appropriate leader behaviors in different settings. Currently, the most popular perspective is that leaders transform organizations through their vision, communication, and ability to build commitment. Finally, an emerging perspective suggests that leadership is mainly a perceptual bias. We distort reality and attribute events to leaders because we feel more comfortable believing

EXHIBIT 14.1

Perspectives of leadership

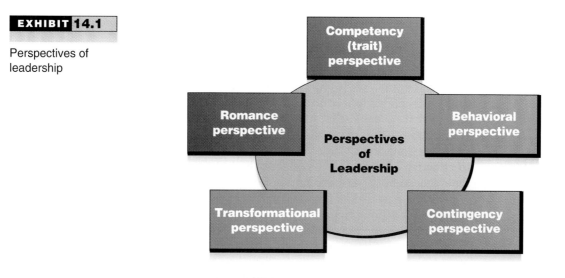

Karenann Terrell is well known for her leadership competencies. The director of e-vehicle product management at DaimlerChrysler is self-confident and possesses the motivation to lead. "I live and breathe the ability to make a difference," she says. Terrell also has an unwavering drive that energizes employees to achieve goals and discover new territory in web-based automobile electronics. "[She leads] with a level of enthusiasm and energy that's breathtaking," says Mark Hogan, president of GM's e-commerce unit, where Terrell worked before being lured to DaimlerChrysler. In your opinion, are people like Karenann Terrell born as great leaders, or can companies develop leaders? *(DaimlerChrysler Media Services)*

that a competent individual is at the organization's helm.[7] This chapter explores each of these five perspectives of leadership. In the final section, we also consider whether men and women lead differently in organizational settings.

COMPETENCY (TRAIT) PERSPECTIVE OF LEADERSHIP

Karenann Terrell is a confident leader with an enthusiastic drive to explore new ideas and achieve results. "This is the very best place to do what I do, which is to be very direct, ask hard questions and give hard answers," says the director of e-vehicle product management at DaimlerChrysler. Mark Hogan, president of General Motors' e-commerce unit, where Terrell worked before being lured to DaimlerChrysler, has no doubts about her competencies as a leader. "[General Motors] wanted a culture that was willing and able to move at Internet speed, as opposed to automotive speed," Hogan explains. "Karenann absolutely had that kind of temperament . . . [She leads] with a level of enthusiasm and energy that's breathtaking."[8]

From these accounts, it seems that Karenann Terrell possesses several leadership competencies. Competencies include the knowledge, natural and learned abilities, values, personality traits, and other characteristics of people that lead to superior performance (see Chapter 2).[9] Since the beginning of recorded civilization, people have been interested in personal characteristics that distinguish great leaders. The ancient Egyptians demanded authority, discrimination, and justice from their leaders. The Greek philosopher Plato called for prudence, courage, temperance, and justice.[10]

For the first half of the twentieth century, organizational behavior scholars used scientific methods to determine whether certain personality traits and physical characteristics (particularly, the person's height and weight) actually distinguished leaders from lesser souls. A major review in the late 1940s concluded that no consistent list of traits could be distilled from the hundreds of studies conducted up to that time. A subsequent review suggested that a few traits are consistently associated with effective leaders, but most are unrelated to effective leadership.[11] These conclusions caused many scholars to give up their search for personal characteristics that distinguish effective leaders.

Over the past decade, management consultants and organizational behavior scholars have popularized competency-based selection and reward practices. Competencies encompass a broader range of personal characteristics—such as knowledge, abilities, and values—that were not considered by earlier studies on leadership traits. This new generation of leadership experts argues that the earlier studies focused too much on abstract personality traits and the physical appearance of leaders. The recent leadership literature identifies seven competencies that are characteristic of effective leaders.[12] These competencies are listed in Exhibit 14.2 and described briefly below.

■ *Drive*—Leaders have a high need for achievement (see Chapter 5). This drive represents the inner motivation that leaders possess to pursue their goals and encourage others to move forward with theirs. Drive inspires an unbridled inquisitiveness and a need for constant learning. You can see this drive in Karenann Terrell through her energy and enthusiasm at both DaimlerChrysler and General Motors.

EXHIBIT 14.2		
Leadership trait	**Description**	
Drive	The leader's inner motivation to pursue goals	
Leadership motivation	The leader's need for socialized power to accomplish team or organizational goals	
Integrity	The leader's truthfulness and tendency to translate words into deeds	
Self-confidence	The leader's belief in his or her own leadership skills and ability to achieve objectives	
Intelligence	The leader's above-average cognitive ability to process enormous amounts of information	
Knowledge of the business	The leader's understanding of the company's environment to make more intuitive decisions	
Emotional intelligence	The leader's ability to monitor his or her own and others' emotions, discriminate among them, and use the information to guide his or her thoughts and actions	

Seven competencies of effective leaders

Sources: Most elements of this list were derived from S. A. Kirkpatrick and E. A. Locke, "Leadership: Do Traits Matter?" *Academy of Management Executive* 5 (May 1991), pp. 48–60. Several of these ideas are also discussed in H. B. Gregersen, A. J. Morrison, and J. S. Black, "Developing Leaders for the Global Frontier," *Sloan Management* 40 (Fall 1998), pp. 21–32; R. J. House and R. N. Aditya, "The Social Scientific Study of Leadership: Quo Vadis?" *Journal of Management* 23 (1997), pp. 409–73.

■ *Leadership motivation*—Leaders have a strong need for power because they want to influence others (see Chapter 5). However, they tend to have a need for "socialized power" because their motivation is constrained by a strong sense of altruism and social responsibility.[13] In other words, effective leaders try to gain power so that they can influence others to accomplish goals that benefit the team or organization.

■ *Integrity*—This competency refers to the leader's truthfulness and tendency to translate words into deeds. Several large-scale studies have reported that integrity is the most important leadership characteristic. Employees want honest leaders whom they can trust.[14]

■ *Self-confidence*—Karenann Terrell and other leaders believe in their leadership skills and ability to achieve objectives. They also use impression management tactics (see Chapter 12) to convince followers of their confidence.

■ *Intelligence*—Leaders have above-average cognitive ability to process enormous amounts of information. Leaders aren't necessarily geniuses; rather, they have superior ability to analyze alternate scenarios and identify potential opportunities.

■ *Knowledge of the business*—Karenann Terrell and other leaders know the business environment in which they operate. This knowledge assists their intuition, enabling them to recognize opportunities and understand their organization's capacity to capture those opportunities.

■ *Emotional intelligence*—Effective leaders have a high level of emotional intelligence. They monitor their own and others' emotions, discriminate among them, and use the information to guide their thoughts and actions (see Chapter 4).[15] Emotional intelligence requires a strong self-monitoring personality (see Chapter 3), because leaders must be sensitive to situational cues and readily adapt their own behavior appropriately.[16] It also requires the ability to empathize with others and the social skills necessary to build rapport as well as network with others. The contingency leadership perspective described later in this chapter assumes that effective leaders are high self-monitors, so they can adjust their behavior to match the situation.

Don't look for Kim Jung-tae in his office. The CEO of Kookmin Bank is busy traveling throughout the company's hundreds of branches and offices, instilling a new way of thinking about banking. "Our bank has to survive doing retail business," explains Kim. "That means customer satisfaction." Kim's marketing savvy and years of experience in the financial services industry make him well suited to lead the largest financial institution in South Korea. Kim also has a strong drive and a high level of integrity, enough to earn the respect of a selection panel that chose him as CEO during a recent merger.[17] What competencies seem to make Kim Jung-tae an effective leader? *(Courtesy of Kookmin Bank)*

Competency (Trait) Perspective Limitations and Practical Implications

One concern with the competency perspective is that it assumes great leaders have the same personal characteristics and all of them are equally important in all situations. This is probably a false assumption; leadership is far too complex to have a universal list of traits that apply to every condition. Some competencies might not be important all the time, although researchers have not yet explored this aspect of traits.

A few scholars have also warned that some personal characteristics might only influence our perception that someone is a leader, not indicate whether the individual really makes a difference to the organization's success.[18] People who exhibit integrity, self-confidence, and other traits are called leaders because they fit our stereotype of an effective leader. Or we might see a successful person, call that person a leader, and then attribute self-confidence and other unobservable traits that we consider essential for great leaders. We will discuss this perceptual distortion more fully toward the end of the chapter. At this point, you should be aware that our knowledge of leadership competencies may be partly due to perceptual distortions.

Aside from these limitations, the competency perspective recognizes that some people possess personal characteristics that offer them a higher potential to be great leaders. The most obvious implication of this is that organizations are relying increasingly on competency-based methods to hire people for future leadership positions.[19] Leadership talents are important throughout the organization, so this recommendation should extend to all levels of hiring, not just senior executives. Companies also need to determine which behaviors represent these competencies so that employees with leadership talents are identified early for promotion.

The competency perspective of leadership does not necessarily imply that great leaders are born, not developed. On the contrary, competencies only indicate leadership potential, not leadership performance. People with these characteristics become effective leaders only after they have developed and mastered the necessary leadership behaviors. People with somewhat lower leadership competencies may become very effective leaders because they have leveraged their potential more fully. Thus, companies must do more than hire people with certain competencies. They must also develop these employees' potential through leadership development programs and practical experience in the field.

BEHAVIORAL PERSPECTIVE OF LEADERSHIP

In the 1940s and 1950s, scholars from Ohio State University launched an intensive research investigation to answer this question: What behaviors make leaders effective? Questionnaires were administered to subordinates, asking them to rate their supervisors on a large number of behaviors. These studies, along with similar research at the University of Michigan and Harvard University, distilled two clusters of leadership behaviors from more than 1,800 leadership behavior items.[20]

One cluster represented people-oriented behaviors, such as showing mutual trust and respect for subordinates, demonstrating a genuine concern for their needs, and having a desire to look out for their welfare. Leaders with a strong people-oriented style listen to employee suggestions, do personal favors for employees, support their interests when required, and treat employees as equals.

The other cluster represented a task-oriented leadership style and included behaviors that define and structure work roles. Task-oriented leaders assign employees to specific tasks, clarify their work duties and procedures, ensure

When Tough Taskmasters Become Abusive Bosses

David Gilmore admits that he can be tough on employees. "I am occasionally a tyrant," confesses the head of Washington, D.C.'s public housing authority. But Gilmore believes that his task-oriented leadership pushes employees just enough to achieve higher performance, and no further. "I try to stretch them as far as they will go without breaking," he says. Gilmore's staff agree with their boss's self-assessment, but that doesn't stop them from teasing the taskmaster. They bought Gilmore a poster from *The Caine Mutiny* and superimposed his face over Humphrey Bogart's as Captain Queeg.

Unfortunately, not everyone has a friendly tyrant for a boss. A recent U.S. Postal Service office report revealed that the postmaster and other managers in Fullerton, California, "used threats, harassment, intimidation and retaliation to control employees' behavior." The postmaster was transferred, and other managers are receiving sensitivity training to develop a more supportive leadership style.

The CEO of Cerner Corporation in North Kansas City, Missouri, recently sent an e-mail missive to 400 managers, warning that employees would be laid off and time clocks installed if staff did not put in more than the usual 40-hour work week. "The pizza man should show up at 7:30 P.M. to feed the starving teams working late," the e-mail stated. "The lot should be half-full on Saturday mornings . . . You have two weeks. Tick, tock." Cerner's shareholders apparently dislike bossy leaders. The medical software firm's stock dropped by 22 percent when the abusive e-mail became public.

These are not isolated cases of abusive bosses. According to one survey, a larger percentage of employees think management abusiveness is higher today than 20 years ago. The most popular explanation is the constant pressure on managers to produce. Most employees recommended better leadership training as well as surveying employees more often for incidents of abuse by their bosses.

Sources: J. Hicks, "Besieged Fullerton Postmaster Reassigned," *Los Angeles Times,* August 28, 2001, p. 2-1; J. Hicks, "Post Office Management Faulted," *Los Angeles Times,* August 18, 2001, p. 2-8; D. Hayes and J. A. Karash, "Harsh E-Mail Roils Cerner," *Kansas City Star,* March 24, 2001, p. A1; D. Armstrong, "Got an Abusive Boss?" *Foxmarketwire.com* (online), February 16, 2000; V. Loeb, "Resident Expert," *Washington Post,* May 7,1998, p. B1.

that they follow company rules, and push them to reach their performance capacity. They establish stretch goals and challenge employees to push beyond those high standards. The problem with task-oriented leadership is that today's workforce is less receptive to command-and-control leadership. Employees want to participate in decisions rather than receive directives and follow them without question.[21] The other problem is knowing how far to challenge employees. As Connections 14.1 describes, some bosses are friendly tyrants whereas others cross the line to become bullies.

Choosing Task- versus People-Oriented Leadership

Should leaders be task-oriented or people-oriented? This is a difficult question to answer because each style has its advantages and disadvantages. People-oriented leadership is associated with higher job satisfaction among subordinates, as well as lower absenteeism, grievances, and turnover. However, job performance tends to be lower than for employees with task-oriented leaders.[22] Task-oriented leadership, on the other hand, is associated with lower job satisfaction as well as higher absenteeism and turnover among subordinates. But this leadership style also seems to increase productivity and team unity. University students apparently value task-oriented instructors because they want clear objectives and well-prepared lectures that abide by the unit's objectives.[23]

Behavioral leadership scholars reported that these two styles are independent of each other. Some people are high or low on both styles, others are high on one style and low on the other, and most are somewhere in between. The hypothesis that emerged was that the most effective leaders exhibit high levels of both task-oriented and people-oriented behaviors.[24] Out of this hypothesis developed a popular leadership development program, called the **Leadership Grid®** (formerly known as the *Managerial Grid*).[25] Participants assess their current levels of task-oriented and people-oriented leadership; then they work with trainers to achieve maximum levels of concern for both people and production (task).

The problem with the behavioral leadership perspective, as subsequent research has discovered, is it implies that high levels of both styles are best in all situations. In reality, the best leadership style depends on the situation.[26] On a positive note, the behavioral perspective laid the foundation for two of the main leadership styles—people-oriented and task-oriented—found in many contemporary leadership theories. These contemporary theories adopt a contingency perspective, which we describe next.

Leadership Grid®
A model of leadership developed by Blake and Mouton that assesses an individual's leadership effectiveness in terms of his or her concern for people and production.

CONTINGENCY PERSPECTIVE OF LEADERSHIP

The contingency perspective of leadership is based on the idea that the most appropriate leadership style depends on the situation. Most (although not all) contingency leadership theories assume that effective leaders must be both insightful and flexible.[27] They must be able to adapt their behaviors and styles to the immediate situation. This isn't easy to do, however. Leaders typically have a preferred style. It takes considerable effort for leaders to learn when and how to alter their styles to match the situation. As we noted earlier, leaders must have a high emotional intelligence, particularly a self-monitoring personality, so that they can diagnose the circumstances and match their behaviors accordingly.[28]

Path–Goal Theory of Leadership

path–goal leadership theory
A contingency theory of leadership based on expectancy theory of motivation that relates several leadership styles to specific employee and situational contingencies.

Several contingency theories have been proposed over the years, but **path–goal leadership theory** has withstood scientific critique better than the others. The theory has its roots in the expectancy theory of motivation (see Chapter 5). Early research by Martin Evans incorporated expectancy theory into the study of how leader behaviors influence employee perceptions of expectancies (paths) between employee effort and performance (goals). On the basis of this perspective, Robert House and other scholars developed and refined path–goal theory as a contingency leadership model.[29]

Path–goal theory states that effective leaders influence employee satisfaction and performance by making their need satisfaction contingent on effective job performance. Leaders strengthen the performance-to-outcome expectancy and valences of those outcomes by ensuring that employees who perform their jobs well have a higher degree of need fulfillment than employees who perform poorly.

Effective leaders strengthen the effort-to-performance expectancy by providing the information, support, and other resources necessary to help employees complete their tasks.[30] Royal Dutch/Shell's leadership development program emphasizes that effective leaders create conditions that enable others to realize their potential in the workplace. The best-performing self-directed work teams at Xerox had leaders who gave first priority to arranging organizational support for the team.[31] In other words, path–goal theory advocates **servant leadership.**[32] Servant leaders do not view leadership as a position of power; rather, they are coaches, stewards, and facilitators. Leadership is an obligation to understand employee needs and to facilitate employee work performance. Servant leaders ask, "How can I help you?" rather than expect employees to serve them.

servant leadership

The belief that leaders serve followers by understanding their needs and facilitating their work performance.

Leadership Styles   Exhibit 14.3 illustrates the path–goal theory of leadership. This model specifically highlights four leadership styles and several contingency factors leading to three indicators of leader effectiveness. The four leadership styles are:[33]

■ *Directive*—These are clarifying behaviors that provide a psychological structure for subordinates. The leader clarifies performance goals, the means to reach those goals, and the standards against which performance will be judged. This style also includes judicious use of rewards and disciplinary actions. Directive leadership is the same as task-oriented leadership, described earlier, and echoes our discussion in Chapter 2 on the importance of clear role perceptions in employee performance.

■ *Supportive*—These behaviors provide psychological support for subordinates. The leader is friendly and approachable, makes the work more pleasant, treats employees with equal respect, and shows concern for the status, needs, and well-being of employees. Supportive leadership is the same as people-oriented leadership, described earlier, and reflects the benefits of social support to help employees cope with stressful situations (see Chapter 7).

■ *Participative*—These behaviors encourage and facilitate subordinate involvement in decisions beyond their normal work activities. The leader consults with employees, asks for their suggestions, and takes these ideas into serious consideration before making a decision. Participative leadership relates to the employee involvement concepts and issues described in Chapter 9.

EXHIBIT 14.3

Path–goal leadership theory

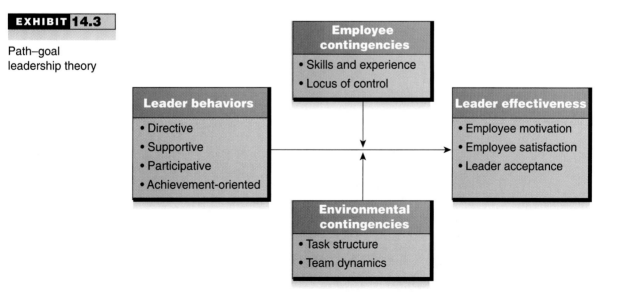

■ *Achievement-oriented*—These behaviors encourage employees to reach their peak performance. The leader sets challenging goals, expects employees to perform at their highest level, continually seeks improvement in employee performance, and shows a high degree of confidence that employees will assume responsibility and accomplish challenging goals. Achievement-oriented leadership applies goal-setting theory (Chapter 5) as well as positive expectations in self-fulfilling prophecy (Chapter 3).

The path–goal model contends that effective leaders are capable of selecting the most appropriate behavioral style (or styles) for a particular situation. Leaders might use more than one style at a time. For example, they might be both supportive and participative in a specific situation.

Contingencies of Path–Goal Theory

As a contingency theory, path–goal theory states that each of these four leadership styles will be effective in some situations but not in others. The path–goal leadership model specifies two sets of situational variables that moderate the relationship between a leader's style and effectiveness: (1) employee characteristics and (2) characteristics of the employee's work environment. Several contingencies have already been studied within the path–goal framework, and the model is open for more variables in the future.[34] However, we will examine only four contingencies here (see Exhibit 14.4).

Skill and Experience   A combination of directive and supportive leadership is best for employees who are (or perceive themselves to be) inexperienced and unskilled. Directive leadership gives subordinates information about how to accomplish the task, whereas supportive leadership helps them cope with the uncertainties of unfamiliar work situations. Directive leadership is detrimental when employees are skilled and experienced because it introduces too much supervisory control.

Locus of Control   Recall from Chapter 3 that people with an internal locus of control believe that they have control over their work environment. Conse-

---

EXHIBIT 14.4   Selected contingencies of path–goal theory

	Directive	Supportive	Particpative	Achievement-oriented
Employee contingencies				
Skill and experience	Low	Low	High	High
Locus of control	External	External	Internal	Internal
Environmental contingencies				
Task structure	Nonroutine	Routine	Nonroutine	?
Team dynamics	Negative norms	Low cohesion	Positive norms	?

quently, these employees prefer participative and achievement-oriented leadership styles and may become frustrated with a directive style. In contrast, people with an external locus of control believe that their performance is due more to luck and fate, so they tend to be more satisfied with directive and supportive leadership.

Task Structure Leaders should adopt the directive style when the task is nonroutine, because this style minimizes role ambiguity that tends to occur in these complex work situations (particularly for inexperienced employees).[35] The directive style is ineffective when employees have routine and simple tasks because the manager's guidance serves no purpose and may be viewed as unnecessarily close control. Employees in highly routine and simple jobs may require supportive leadership to help them cope with the tedious nature of the work and lack of control over the pace of work. Participative leadership is preferred for employees performing nonroutine tasks because the lack of rules and procedures gives them more discretion to achieve challenging goals. The participative style is ineffective for employees in routine tasks because they lack discretion over their work.

Team Dynamics Cohesive teams with performance-oriented norms act as a substitute for most leader interventions. High team cohesiveness substitutes for supportive leadership, whereas performance-oriented team norms substitute for directive and possibly achievement-oriented leadership. Thus, when team cohesiveness is low, leaders should use the supportive style. Leaders should apply a directive style to counteract team norms that oppose the team's formal objectives. For example, the team leader may need to use legitimate power if team members have developed a norm to take it easy rather than get a project completed on time.

Recent Extensions of Path–Goal Theory

The original path–goal theory primarily relates to dyadic relations between a supervisor and an employee.[36] Yet leadership also applies to the work unit and organization. Recognizing this gap, Robert House (who, as mentioned, was a developer of the original path–goal theory) recently extended the model by adding leader styles that apply more to work units and organizations than to individual relations.[37] One of these styles is *networking*, which recognizes that leaders play an important political role. They represent the work unit and engage in political networking activities (see Chapter 12) to legitimize the work unit and maintain positive influences on other areas of the organization. Another style is *value-based leadership*, which includes articulating a vision of the future, displaying passion for this vision, demonstrating self-confidence in the attainment of the vision, communicating the vision, and acting in ways consistent with the vision. This style is the same as the transformational leadership perspective that we describe later in this chapter.

Practical Implications and Limitations of Path–Goal Theory

Path–goal theory reinforces the idea that effective leaders vary their style with the situation. There are times to give directions, times to empathize, times to use stretch goals, and times to involve subordinates in decision making. Path–goal theory also offers a fairly precise set of contingency factors that provide practical advice on when to use various leadership styles.

Path–goal theory has received considerable research support, certainly more than other contingency leadership models.[38] However, one or two contingencies (e.g., task structure) have found limited research support. Other contingencies and leadership styles in the path–goal leadership model haven't received scholarly investigation at all.[39] For example, some cells in Exhibit 14.4 have question marks because we do not yet know how those leadership styles apply to those contingencies. The recently expanded model adds new leadership styles and contingencies, but they have not yet been tested. Until further study comes along, it is unclear whether certain contingencies should be considered when choosing the best leadership style.

Another concern is that as path–goal theory expands, the model may become too complex for practical use. Although the expanded model provides a closer representation of the complexity of leadership, it may become too cumbersome for training people in leadership styles. Few people would be able to remember all the contingencies and appropriate leadership styles for those contingencies. In spite of these limitations, path–goal theory remains a relatively complete and robust contingency leadership theory.

Other Contingency Theories

At the beginning of this chapter, we noted that numerous leadership theories have developed over the years. Most of them are found in the contingency perspective of leadership. Some overlap with the path–goal model in terms of leadership styles, but most use simpler and more abstract contingencies. We will briefly mention two here because of their popularity and historical significance to the field.

situational leadership model

Developed by Hersey and Blanchard, suggests that effective leaders vary their style with the "readiness" of followers.

Situational Leadership Model   One of the most popular contingency theories among trainers is the **situational leadership model,** developed by Paul Hersey and Ken Blanchard.[40] The model suggests that effective leaders vary their style with the readiness of followers. (An earlier version of the model called this concept maturity.) Readiness refers to the employee's or work team's ability and willingness to accomplish a specific task. Ability refers to the extent that the follower has the skills and knowledge to perform the task without the leader's guidance. Willingness refers to the follower's self-motivation and commitment to perform the assigned task. The model compresses these distinct concepts into a single situational condition.

The situational leadership model also identifies four leadership styles—telling, selling, participating, and delegating—that Hersey and Blanchard distinguish in terms of the amount of directive and supportive behavior provided. For example, telling has high task behavior and low supportive behavior. The situational leadership model has four quadrants, with each quadrant showing the leadership style that is most appropriate under certain circumstances.

In spite of its popularity, at least three reviews have concluded that the situational leadership model lacks empirical support.[41] Apparently, only one part of the model works, namely, that leaders should use telling (i.e., a directive style) when employees lack motivation and ability. (That conclusion is also documented in path–goal theory.) The model's elegant simplicity is attractive and entertaining, but other parts don't represent reality very well. The most recent review also concluded that the theory has logical and internal inconsistencies.

Fiedler's Contingency Model The earliest contingency theory of leadership, called **Fiedler's contingency model,** was developed by Fred Fiedler and his associates.[42] According to this model, leader effectiveness depends on whether the person's natural leadership style is appropriately matched to the situation. The theory examines two leadership styles that essentially correspond to the previously described people-oriented and task-oriented styles. Unfortunately, Fiedler's model relies on a questionnaire that does not measure either leadership style very well.

Fiedler's model suggests that the best leadership style depends on the level of *situational control,* that is, the degree of power and influence that the leader possesses in a particular situation. Situational control is affected by three factors, in the following order of importance: leader–member relations, task structure, and position power.[43] Leader–member relations is the degree to which employees trust and respect the leader and are willing to follow his or her guidance. Task structure refers to the clarity or ambiguity of operating procedures. Position power is the extent to which the leader possesses legitimate, reward, and coercive power over subordinates. These three contingencies form the eight possible combinations of *situation favorableness* from the leader's viewpoint. Good leader–member relations, high task structure, and strong position power create the most favorable situation for the leader because he or she has the most power and influence under those conditions.

Fiedler has gained considerable respect for pioneering the first contingency theory of leadership. His theory, however, has fared less well. As mentioned, the leadership style scale used by Fiedler has been widely criticized. There is also no scientific justification for placing the three situational control factors in a hierarchy. Moreover, it seems that leader–member relations is actually an indicator of leader effectiveness (as in path–goal theory) rather than a situational factor. Finally, the theory considers only two leadership styles, whereas other models present a more complex and realistic array of behavior options. These concerns explain why the theory has limited empirical support.[44]

Changing the Situation to Match the Leader's Natural Style Fiedler's contingency model may have become a historical footnote, but it does make an important and lasting contribution by suggesting that leadership style is related to the individual's personality and, consequently, is relatively stable over time. Leaders might be able to alter their style temporarily, but they tend to use a preferred style in the long term. More recent scholars have also proposed that leadership styles are "hardwired" more than most other contingency leadership theories assume.[45]

If leadership style is influenced by a person's personality, then organizations should engineer the situation to fit the leader's dominant style, rather than expect leaders to change their style with the situation. A directive leader might be assigned inexperienced employees who need direction rather than seasoned people who work less effectively under a directive style. Alternatively, companies might transfer supervisors to workplaces where the dominant style fits best. For

---

Fiedler's contingency model

Developed by Fred Fiedler, suggests that leader effectiveness depends on whether the person's natural leadership style is appropriately matched to the situation.

instance, directive leaders might be parachuted into work teams with counter-productive norms, whereas leaders who prefer a supportive style should be sent to departments in which employees face work pressures and other stressors.

Leadership Substitutes So far, we have looked at theories that recommend using different leadership styles in various situations. But one theory, called **leadership substitutes,** identifies contingencies that either limit the leader's ability to influence subordinates or make that particular leadership style unnecessary. When substitute conditions are present, employees are effective without a formal leader who applies a particular style. Although the leadership substitute model requires further refinement, there is general support for the overall notion that some conditions neutralize or substitute for leadership styles.[46]

Several conditions have been identified in the literature that possibly substitute for task-oriented or people-oriented leadership. For example, performance-based reward systems keep employees directed toward organizational goals, so they probably replace or reduce the need for task-oriented leadership. Task-oriented leadership is also less important when employees are skilled and experienced. Notice how these propositions are similar to path–goal leadership theory, namely, in saying that directive leadership is unnecessary—and may be detrimental—when employees are skilled or experienced.[47]

leadership substitutes

A theory that identifies contingencies that either limit the leader's ability to influence subordinates or make that particular leadership style unnecessary.

With no traditional bosses, employees at W. L. Gore & Associates rely on leadership substitutes to get their work done. These substitutes include guidance from co-workers, formal training and socialization, and performance-based rewards. The maker of Gore–Tex and other advanced materials also spends a lot of time hiring people with self-leadership skills.[48] What other leadership substitutes might help teams lead themselves without direct supervision? *(AP/Wide World)*

Leadership substitutes have become more important as organizations remove supervisors and shift toward team-based structures. In fact, an emerging concept is that effective leaders help team members learn to lead themselves through leadership substitutes.[49] Some writers suggest that co-workers are powerful leader substitutes in these organizational structures. Co-workers instruct new employees, thereby providing directive leadership. They also provide social support, which reduces stress among fellow employees (see Chapter 7). Teams with norms that support organizational goals may substitute for achievement-oriented leadership, because employees encourage (or pressure) co-workers to stretch their performance levels.

Self-leadership has also been discussed as a potentially valuable leadership substitute in self-directed work teams.[50] Recall from Chapter 6 that self-leadership is the process of influencing oneself to establish the self-direction and self-motivation needed to perform a task.[51] It includes self-set goals, self-reinforcement, constructive thought processes, and other activities that influence the person's own motivation and behavior. As employees become more proficient in self-leadership, they presumably require less supervision to keep them focused and energized toward organizational objectives.

TRANSFORMATIONAL PERSPECTIVE OF LEADERSHIP

transformational leadership
A leadership perspective that explains how leaders change teams or organizations by creating, communicating, and modeling a vision for the organization or work unit, and inspiring employees to strive for that vision.

As an executive with IBM Global Services, Colleen Arnold saw a unique opportunity to launch an e-business innovation center for the Asia-Pacific region. IBM had contracted 800 information technology (IT) workers to bring together the world's biggest Internet project—the 2000 Sydney Olympics. This valuable pool of talent fit nicely with IBM's need to expand its e-business capability in the region at a time when the industry faced a global IT skills shortage.

Arnold explained her vision to IBM Worldwide, convincing them to leverage this uniquely available talent for an e-business hub. She then convinced her local board of directors to fund the new innovation center, making it the launching pad for an internal corporate culture change that values flexibility, mobility, and customer service. The new e-business center would be free-form and wireless, and would operate around the clock to deliver e-business solutions to customers. Less than two years later, the innovation center became a reality, linking IBM's R&D labs worldwide.[52]

transactional leadership
Leadership that helps organizations achieve their current objectives more efficiently, such as linking job performance to valued rewards and ensuring that employees have the resources needed to get the job done.

Colleen Arnold deomonstrates **transformational leadership.** Through her vision and actions, she created a unique business entity that will eventually spread a new culture and way of working throughout IBM's worldwide operations. Transformational leaders, such as Carly Fiorina (Hewlett-Packard), Herb Kelleher (Southwest Airlines), Carlos Ghosn (Renault–Nissan), and Richard Branson (Virgin), dot the corporate landscape.[53] These people are agents of change. They develop a vision for the organization or work unit, inspire and collectively bond employees to that vision, and give them a can-do attitude that makes the vision achievable.[54]

Transformational versus Transactional Leadership

Transformational leadership is different from **transactional leadership.** Transactional leadership involves managing—helping organizations achieve

Dennis W. Bakke, CEO and co-founder of the global power company AES Corporation, is continually looking for leaders who are both transformational and transactional "We need people who can both lead and manage," says Bakke. "The traditional idea is that a manager takes what is there and makes certain it works well, while a leader takes a visionary look at what is already known to discover something new. But the world changes so much that you can no longer just manage 'what is there.' Leadership that doesn't consider practical execution is ridiculous. It's not either/or. It is much better to think about those two abilities together."[59] How can AES and other organizations ensure that people maintain a balance between transformational and transactional leadership? Or do you think that these roles should occur in different people? *(Courtesy of AES Corporation)*

their current objectives more efficiently, such as by linking job performance to valued rewards and ensuring that employees have the resources needed to get the job done.[55] The contingency and behavioral theories described earlier adopt the transactional perspective because they focus on leader behaviors that improve employee performance and satisfaction.

In contrast, transformational leadership is about leading—changing the organization's strategies and culture so that they have a better fit with the surrounding environment.[56] Transformational leaders are change agents who energize employees and direct them to a new set of corporate values and behaviors. Colleen Arnold is one such leader. The opening story to this section described how she saw a unique opportunity and was able to build commitment from her board and from the Sydney Olympics IT staff to form a new center that would itself further transform IBM worldwide.

Organizations require both transactional and transformational leadership. Transactional leadership improves organizational efficiency, whereas transformational leadership steers companies onto a better course of action. Transformational leadership is particularly important in organizations that require significant alignment with the external environment. Research suggests that organizations that drive societal change—such as environmental organizations—are highly receptive contexts for transformational leadership.[57] Unfortunately, too many leaders get trapped in the daily managerial activities that represent transactional leadership.[58] They lose touch with the transformational aspect of effective leadership. Without transformational leaders, organizations stagnate and eventually become seriously misaligned with their environments.

Transformational versus Charismatic Leadership

One topic that has generated some confusion and controversy is the distinction between transformational and charismatic leadership.[60] A few writers use the terms *charismatic* and *transformational leadership* interchangeably. However, charismatic leadership differs from transformational leadership. As we learned in Chapter 12, *charisma* is a form of interpersonal attraction whereby followers develop a respect for and trust in the charismatic individual. Charismatic leadership, therefore, extends beyond behaviors to personal traits that

Changing organizational culture requires the change management tool kit that we will learn about in the next chapter (Chapter 16). Corporate leaders need to make employees aware of the urgency for change. Then they need to "unfreeze" the existing culture by removing artifacts that represent that culture and "refreeze" the new culture by introducing artifacts that communicate and reinforce the new values.

Strengthening Organizational Culture

Artifacts communicate and reinforce the new corporate culture, but we also need to consider ways to further strengthen that culture. Five approaches that are commonly cited in the literature are the actions of founders and leaders, introducing culturally consistent rewards, maintaining a stable workforce, managing the cultural network, and selecting and socializing new employees (see Exhibit 15.4).

Actions of Founders and Leaders   Founders establish an organization's culture.[59] You can see this at Southwest Airlines, where founder Herb Kelleher has established a culture that is both fun and efficient. Founders develop the systems and structures that support their personal values. They are also typically the visionaries whose energetic style provides a powerful role model for others to follow.

In spite of the founder's effect, subsequent leaders can break the organization away from the founder's values if they apply the transformational leadership concepts that were described in Chapter 14. Transformational leaders alter and strengthen organizational culture by communicating and enacting their vision of the future.[60] The opening vignette in this chapter described how Carly Fiorina is trying to change Hewlett-Packard's culture because she believes H-P employees hide behind their corporate culture to avoid tough decisions. "The phrase 'The H-P Way' became a way of resisting change and resisting radical ideas," argues Fiorina. "One of the things I've been able to do as an outsider is challenge it."[61]

EXHIBIT 15.4

Strategies for strengthening organizational culture

Ray Anderson (shown in photo) admits that he didn't pay much attention to environmentalism when he launched Atlanta-based Interface Inc. in the 1970s. But after reading *The Ecology of Commerce* in 1994, Anderson's newfound environmental values have reshaped the culture of the world's largest floor covering company. "[W]e've got a company full of people who've really bought in to that vision," Anderson says. Today, Interface has solar- powered looms in California, a weaving plant in Maine that uses recycled plastics, and an R&D department that experiments with hemp, sugar cane, and other renewable resources. Most of the company's 8,000 employees on four continents have received environmental training, and many of them have created environmental organizations in their communities. Anderson even replaced his Bentley and Jaguar with a fuel-efficient Toyota that runs on batteries and gas.[65] In what ways do founders and leaders influence their organization's culture? *(Pierre Roussel/The Ottawa Citizen)*

Introducing Culturally Consistent Rewards Reward systems strengthen corporate culture when they are consistent with cultural values.[62] For example, paternalistic cultures would emphasize employee assistance programs, medical insurance, and other benefits that support employee well-being. Home Depot has stock options to support an ownership culture. "We've always wanted this to be part of our culture," explains Home Depot CEO and co-founder Arthur Blank, "that associates feel that they own the stores, that they own the merchandise, that they have total responsibility for the customers in their aisles, and that they create the value."[63]

Maintaining a Stable Workforce An organization's culture is embedded in the minds of its employees. Organizational stories are rarely written down; rituals and ceremonies do not usually exist in procedure manuals; organizational metaphors are not found in corporate directories. Thus, organizations depend on a stable workforce to communicate and reinforce the dominant beliefs and values. The organization's culture can literally disintegrate during periods of high turnover and precipitous downsizing because the corporate memory leaves with those employees.[64]

Conversely, corporate leaders who want to change the corporate culture have accelerated the turnover of senior executives and older employees, those who held the cultural values in place. For instance, the two executives who revived Continental Airlines claim that they introduced a more customer-focused culture partly by replacing most of the 60 executives with people who had more compatible values. Hoechst, the German chemical company, also seems to be applying this tactic through early retirement of its older employees. "The company is trying to lower the average age of the workforce," says a Hoechst spokesperson. "Perhaps the main reason for replacing older workers is that it makes it easier to 'defrost' the corporate culture."[66]

Managing the Cultural Network Organizational culture is learned, so an effective network of cultural transmission is necessary to strengthen the company's underlying assumptions, values, and beliefs. According to Max DePree, former CEO of furniture manufacturer Herman Miller Inc., every organization needs "tribal storytellers" to keep the organization's history and culture alive.[67] The cultural network exists through the organizational grapevine. It is also supported through frequent opportunities for interaction so that employees can share stories and reenact rituals. Senior executives must tap into the cultural network, sharing their own stories and creating new ceremonies and other opportunities to demonstrate shared meaning. Company magazines and other media can also strengthen organizational culture by communicating cultural values and beliefs more efficiently.

Selecting and Socializing Employees   People at Bristol-Myers recently noticed that executives hired from the outside weren't as successful as those promoted from within. Within a year, many quit or were fired. Ben Dowell, who runs Bristol-Myers's Center for Leadership Development, looked closely at the problem and arrived at the following conclusion: "What came through was, those who left were uncomfortable in our culture or violated some core area of our value system." From this discovery, Bristol-Myers assessed its culture—it's team-oriented, consistent with the firm's research and development roots. Now applicants are carefully screened to ensure they have compatible values.[68]

Bristol-Myers and a flock of other organizations strengthen their corporate cultures by hiring people with beliefs, values, and assumptions similar to those cultures. They realize that a good fit of personal and organizational values makes it easier for employees to adopt the corporate culture. A good person–organization fit also improves job satisfaction and organizational loyalty because new hires with values compatible with the corporate culture adjust more quickly to the organization.[69]

Job applicants are also paying more attention to corporate culture during the hiring process. According to one survey, job applicants ask corporate culture questions more than any other topic, aside from pay and benefits.[70] They realize that employees must feel comfortable with the company's values, not just the job duties and hours of work.

Kathy Wheeler learned this important point the hard way. A few years ago, the Hewlett-Packard engineer accepted a career opportunity at Apple Computer. Apple's headquarters is just two miles away from H-P's, but its corporate culture is on another planet. H-P's culture emphasizes collaboration, consensus, and advanced engineering technology, whereas Apple's culture applauds marketers rather than engineers and slick user interfaces rather than advanced technology. Fourteen months later, Wheeler was back at H-P. "I admire Apple to a large extent," says Wheeler. "But I wouldn't work there again because of the cultural issues."[71] The point here is that applicants need to look at corporate culture artifacts when deciding whether to join a particular organization. By diagnosing the company's dominant culture, they are more likely to determine whether its values are compatible with their own.

Along with selecting people with compatible values, companies maintain strong cultures through the effective socialization of new employees. **Organizational socialization** refers to the process by which individuals learn the values, expected behaviors, and social knowledge necessary to assume their roles in the organization.[72] By communicating the company's dominant values, organizations can ensure that new hires are more likely to internalize these values quickly and deeply.

We will learn more about the organizational socialization process in Chapter 18, on employment relations and career dynamics. At this point, you

organizational socialization

The process by which individuals learn the values, expected behaviors, and social knowledge necessary to assume their roles in the organization.

should know that socialization includes the process of learning about the company's culture and adopting its set of values. For example, Carolyn Arnott has lived and breathed the IKEA culture almost all her working life. She started as a cashier and soon got her first lessons about the Scandinavian home furnishing company's values through its mandatory Culture Days. Today, as an IKEA manager, Arnott easily recites the cultural values that make the company unique: thrift, hard work, fair play, and inventiveness.[73]

Throughout this chapter, we have learned that organizational culture is pervasive and powerful. For corporate leaders, it is either a force for change or an insurmountable barrier to it. For employees, it is either the glue that bonds people together or a force that drives them away from the organization. So many artifacts communicate and reinforce the existing culture that it requires monumental effort to replace the current values. Transformational leadership can assist this process, as can the effective management of change, which we explore in the next chapter.

CHAPTER SUMMARY

Organizational culture is the basic pattern of shared assumptions, values, and beliefs that govern behavior within a particular organization. Assumptions are the shared mental models or theories in use that people rely on to guide their perceptions and behaviors. *Beliefs* represent the individual's perceptions of reality. Values are more stable, long-lasting beliefs about what is important. They help us define what is right or wrong, or good or bad, in the world. Cultural content refers to the relative ordering of beliefs, values, and assumptions.

Organizations have subcultures as well as the dominant culture. Some subcultures enhance the dominant culture, whereas others, called countercultures, have values that oppose the organization's core values. Subcultures maintain the organization's standards of performance and ethical behavior. They are also the source of emerging values that replace aging core values.

Artifacts are the observable symbols and signs of an organization's culture. Four broad categories of artifacts are organizational stories and legends, rituals and ceremonies, organizational language, and physical structures and symbols. Understanding an organization's culture requires painstaking assessment of many artifacts, because they are subtle and often ambiguous.

Organizational culture has three main functions. First, it is a deeply embedded form of social control. Second, it is the social glue that bonds people together and makes them feel part of the organizational experience. Third, corporate culture helps employees make sense of the workplace.

Companies with strong cultures generally perform better than those with weak cultures, but only when the cultural content is appropriate for the organization's environment. Also, the culture should not be so strong that it drives out dissenting values, which may form emerging values for the future. Organizations should have adaptive cultures so that employees focus on the need for change and support initiatives and leadership that keep pace with these changes.

Organizational culture relates to business ethics in two ways. First, corporate cultures can support the ethical values of society, thereby reinforcing ethical conduct. Second, some cultures are so strong that they rob a person's individualism and discourage constructive controversy.

Mergers should include a bicultural audit to diagnose the compatibility of the organizational cultures. The four main strategies for merging different corporate cultures are integration, deculturation, assimilation, and separation.

Organizational culture is very difficult to change. However, change may be possible by creating an urgency for change and replacing artifacts that support the old culture with artifacts aligned more with the desired future culture. Organizational culture may be strengthened through the actions of founders and leaders, introducing culturally consistent rewards, maintaining a stable workforce, managing the cultural network, and selecting and socializing employees.

KEY TERMS

adaptive culture, p. 457

artifacts, p. 451

bicultural audit, p. 460

ceremonies, p. 453

organizational culture, p. 448

organizational socialization, p. 465

rituals, p. 453

DISCUSSION QUESTIONS

1. Superb Consultants has submitted a proposal to analyze the cultural values of your organization. The proposal states that Superb has developed a revolutionary new survey to tap the company's true culture. The survey takes just 10 minutes to complete, and the consultants say results can be based on a small sample of employees. Discuss the merits and limitations of this proposal.

2. Some people suggest that the most effective organizations have the strongest cultures. What do we mean by the strength of organizational culture, and what possible problems are there with a strong organizational culture?

3. The chief executive of a midsized food products company wants everyone to support the organization's dominant culture of lean efficiency and hard work. The CEO introduced a new reward system to reinforce this culture and personally interviews all professional and managerial applicants to ensure that they bring similar values to the organization. Some employees who criticized these values have had their careers sidelined, leading to their leaving the company. Two mid-level managers were fired for supporting contrary values, such as work–life balance. On the basis of your knowledge of organizational subcultures, what potential problems is the CEO of this company creating?

4. Identify four types of artifacts used to communicate organizational culture. Why are artifacts used for this purpose?

5. Acme Corporation is planning to acquire Beta Corporation, which operates in a different industry. Acme's culture is entrepreneurial and fast-paced, whereas Beta employees value slow, deliberate decision making by consensus. Which merger strategy would you recommend to minimize culture shock when Acme acquires Beta? Explain your answer.

6. Under what conditions is assimilation likely to occur when two companies merge? Your answer should clearly describe the assimilation strategy.

7. Explain how transformational leadership strengthens corporate culture.

8. Suppose that you are asked by senior executives of a large city government to identify ways to reinforce a new culture of teamwork and collaboration. The senior executive group clearly supports these values, and it wants everyone in the organization to embrace them. Identify four types of activities that would strengthen these cultural values.

CASE STUDY 15.1

ASSETONE BANK

AssetOne Bank is one of Asia's largest financial institutions, but it had difficulty entering the personal investment business, where several other companies dominate the market. To gain entry to this market, AssetOne decided to acquire TaurusBank, a much smaller financial institution that had aggressively developed investment funds (mutual funds) and online banking in the region. Taurus was owned by a European conglomerate that wanted to exit the financial sector, so the company was quietly put up for sale. The opportunity to acquire Taurus seemed like a perfect fit to AssetOne's executives, who saw the purchase as an opportunity to finally gain a competitive position in the personal investment market. In particular, the acquisition would give

AssetOne valuable talent in online banking and investment fund businesses.

Negotiations between AssetOne and TaurusBank occurred secretly, except for communication with government regulatory agencies, and took several months as AssetOne's executive team deliberated over the purchase. When AssetOne finally decided in favor of the acquisition, employees of both companies were notified only a few minutes before the merger was announced publicly. During the public statement, AssetOne's CEO boldly announced that TaurusBank would become a "seamless extension of AssetOne." He explained that, like AssetOne, Taurus employees would learn the value of detailed analysis and cautious decision making.

The comments by AssetOne's CEO shocked many employees at Taurus, which was an aggressive and entrepreneurial competitor in online banking and personal investments. Taurus was well known for its edgy marketing, innovative products, and tendency to involve employees to generate creative ideas. The company didn't hesitate to hire people from other industries who would bring different ideas to the investment and online banking business. AssetOne, on the other hand, almost completely promoted its executives from within the ranks. Everyone on the senior executive team had started at AssetOne. The company also emphasized decision making at the top to maintain better control and consistency.

Frustration was apparent within a few months after the merger. Several Taurus executives quit after repeated failure of AssetOne's executive team to decide quickly on critical online banking initiatives. For example, at the time of the acquisition, Taurus was in the process of forming affinity alliances with several companies. Yet, six months later, AssetOne's executive team still had not decided whether to proceed with these partnerships.

The biggest concerns occurred in the investment fund business, where 20 of TaurusBank's 60 fund managers were lured away by competitors within the first year. Some left for better opportunities. Six fund managers left with the Taurus executive in charge of the investment fund business, who joined an investment firm that specialized in investment funds. Several employees left Taurus after AssetOne executives insisted that all new investment funds must be approved by AssetOne's executive group. Previously, Taurus had given the investment fund division enough freedom to launch new products without approval of the entire executive team.

Two years later, AssetOne's CEO admitted that the acquisition of TaurusBank did not provide the opportunities that the company had originally hoped for. AssetOne had more business in investment funds and online banking, but many of the more talented people in these areas had left the firm. Overall, the merged company had not kept pace with other innovative financial institutions in the market.

Discussion Questions

1. On the basis of your understanding of mergers and organizational culture, discuss the problems that occurred in this case.

2. What strategies would you recommend to AssetOne's executives to avoid these corporate culture clashes in future mergers and acquisitions?

Copyright © 2002. Steven L. McShane.

CASE STUDY 15.2

AVON'S NEW CALLING

BusinessWeek Avon Products pioneered direct selling when Mrs. P. F. E. Albee became the first "Avon lady" in 1886. Since then, Avon representatives have helped the company grow into a multibillion-dollar beauty products business and enter international markets. Those same direct salespeople are at the heart of Avon's organizational culture. As the company struggles to adapt to the Internet age and the busy lives of its customers (today, rarely is anyone home when the Avon lady comes calling), business changes incorporate respect for the central role of Avon representatives.

This *Business Week* case study describes Avon's business plans and organizational culture. It details the role of Avon's CEO, Andrea Jung, in identifying, managing, and embodying that culture. Read through this *Business Week* case study at www.mhhe.com/mcshane2e and prepare for the discussion questions at right.

Discussion Questions

1. What elements of Avon's organizational culture does the author describe?

2. What evidence can you find that Avon's culture is strong? That it is adaptive? Does it seem to be a good fit with its environment?

3. How can Andrea Jung change or strengthen Avon's culture to make it a better fit with the modern environment?

Source: N. Byrnes, "Avon's New Calling," *Business Week*, September 18, 2000.

T E A M   E X E R C I S E   15.3

ORGANIZATIONAL CULTURE METAPHORS

By David L. Luechauer, Butler University, and Gary M. Shulman, Miami University

Purpose Both parts of this exercise are designed to help you understand, assess, and interpret organizational culture using metaphors.

Part A: Assessing Your School's Culture

Instructions A metaphor is a figure of speech that contains an implied comparison between a word or phrase that is ordinarily used for one thing but can be applied to another. Metaphors also carry a great deal of hidden meaning—they say a lot about what we think and feel about that object. This activity asks you to use several metaphors to define the organizational culture of your university, college, or institute. (Alternatively, the instructor might ask students to assess another organization that most students know about.)

- *Step 1*—The class will be divided into teams of four to six members.
- *Step 2*—Each team will reach consensus on which words or phrases should be inserted in the blanks of the statements presented below. This information should be recorded on a flip chart or overhead acetate for class presentation. The instructor will provide 15 to 20 minutes for teams to determine which words best describe the college's culture.

  If our school were an animal, it would be _____ because _____.

  If our school were a food, it would be _____ because _____.

  If our school were a place, it would be _____ because _____.

  If our school were a season, it would be _____ because _____.

  If our school were a TV show or movie, it would be _____ because _____.

- *Step 3*—The class will listen to each team present the metaphors that it believes symbolize the school's culture. For example, a team that picks winter for a season might mean they are feeling cold or distant about the school and its people.
- *Step 4*—The class will discuss the questions below.

Discussion Questions (Part A)

1. How easy was it for your group to reach consensus regarding these metaphors? What does that imply about the culture of your school?

2. How do you see these metaphors in action? In other words, what are some critical school behaviors or other artifacts that reveal the presence of the school's culture?

3. Think of another organization to which you belong (e.g., work, religious congregation). What are its dominant cultural values, how do you see them in action, and how do they affect the effectiveness of that organization?

Part B: Analyzing and Interpreting Cultural Metaphors

Instructions Previously, you completed a metaphor exercise to describe the organizational culture of your school. That exercise gave you a taste of how to administer such a diagnostic tool and draw inferences from the results generated. This activity builds on that experience and is designed to help refine your ability to analyze such data and make suggestions for improvement. Five work teams (four to seven members of mixed gender in all groups) of an organization located in Cincinnati completed a metaphor exercise similar to the exercise you completed in class (see Part A above). Their responses are shown in the table below. Working in teams, analyze the information in this table and answer the questions below.

Discussion Questions (Part B)

1. In your opinion, what are the dominant cultural values in this organization? Explain your answer.

2. What are the positive aspects of this type of culture?

3. What are the negative aspect of this type of culture?

4. What do you think this organization's main business is? Explain your answer.

5. These groups all reported to one manager. What advice would you give to her about this unit?

Metaphor results of five teams in a Cincinnati organization					
Team	Animal	Food	Place	TV show or movie	Season
1	Rabbit	Big Mac	Casino	*48 Hours* (movie)	Spring
2	Horse	Taco	Racetrack	*Miami Vice*	Spring
3	Elephant	Ribs	Circus	*Roseanne*	Summer
4	Eagle	Big Mac	Las Vegas	CNN	Spring
5	Panther	Chinese	New York	*LA Law*	Racing

Source: Adapted from D. L. Luechauer and G. M. Shulman, "Using a Metaphor Exercise to Explore the Principles of Organizational Culture," *Journal of Management Education* 22 (December 1998), pp. 736–44.

SELF-ASSESSMENT EXERCISE 15.4

CORPORATE CULTURE PREFERENCE SCALE

Purpose This self-assessment exercise is designed to help you identify a corporate culture that fits most closely with your personal values and assumptions.

Instructions Read each pair of statements in the corporate culture preference scale, and circle the statement that describes the organization you would prefer to work in. Then use the scoring key in Appendix B to calculate your results for each subscale. This exercise is completed alone so that students assess themselves honestly without concerns of social comparison. However, class discussion will focus on the importance of matching job applicants to the organization's dominant values.

Corporate culture preference scale

I would prefer to work in an organization . . .

1a.	Where employees work well together in teams.	**OR**	1b. That produces highly respected products or services.
2a.	Where top management maintains a sense of order in the workplace.	**OR**	2b. Where the organization listens to customers and responds quickly to their needs.
3a.	Where employees are treated fairly.	**OR**	3b. Where employees continually search for ways to work more efficiently.
4a.	Where employees adapt quickly to new work requirements.	**OR**	4b. Where corporate leaders work hard to keep employees happy.
5a.	Where senior executives receive special benefits not available to other employees.	**OR**	5b. Where employees are proud when the organization achieves its performance goals.
6a.	Where employees who perform the best get paid the most.	**OR**	6b. Where senior executives are respected.
7a.	Where everyone gets his or her job done like clockwork.	**OR**	7b. That is on top of innovations in the industry.
8a.	Where employees receive assistance to overcome any personal problems.	**OR**	8b. Where employees abide by company rules.
9a.	That is always experimenting with new ideas in the marketplace.	**OR**	9b. That expects everyone to put in 110 percent for peak performance.
10a.	That quickly benefits from market opportunities.	**OR**	10b. Where employees are always kept informed of what's happening in the organization.
11a.	That can respond quickly to competitive threats.	**OR**	11b. Where most decisions are made by the top executives.
12a.	Where management keeps everything under control.	**OR**	12b. Where employees care for each other.

Copyright © 2000. Steven L. McShane.

After studying the preceding material, be sure to check out our website at
www.mhhe.com/mcshane2e
for more in-depth information and interactivities that correspond to this chapter.

16

Organizational Change and Development

AFTER READING THIS CHAPTER, YOU SHOULD BE ABLE TO:

■ Identify four forces for change in the business environment.

■ Describe the elements of Lewin's force field analysis model.

■ Outline six reasons people resist organizational change.

■ Discuss six strategies to minimize resistance to change.

■ Outline the conditions for effectively diffusing change from a pilot project.

■ Define *organization development*.

■ Discuss three things consultants need to determine in a client relationship.

■ Explain how appreciative inquiry differs from the more traditional approach to OD.

■ Discuss four ethical issues in organization development.

When Richard H. "Dick" Brown was hired as CEO of Electronic Data Systems (EDS) Corporation, the board of directors gave him an additional title: change agent. The Plano, Texas–based computer services giant was floundering in the industry it created 40 years ago. IBM's Global Services division had steamrolled over EDS to become the market leader, while nimble start-ups ate away at other parts of EDS's market share.

Brown wasted no time transforming EDS into a more responsive, customer-focused company. Within weeks, he was visiting the company's largest clients, hearing their complaints, and replacing account teams to correct the problems. Brown had a "service excellence dashboard" installed on executive computers to monitor the status of major clients. A special task force took just six weeks to create four new client-centered organizational units to replace EDS's previous structure of 48 inward-looking fiefdoms.

Brown replaced most of the executive team he had inherited. "We had too many leaders who didn't believe we could grow," says Brown. "Those people either had to change their beliefs or leave." Brown introduced several challenging financial goals for his new executive team and introduced monthly conference calls in which 125 top worldwide EDS executives reviewed their financial accomplishments.

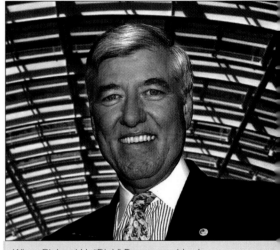

When Richard H. "Dick" Brown was hired as CEO of Electronic Data Systems (EDS) Corporation, the board of directors gave him an additional title: change agent. (AP/Wide World)

But Brown emphasizes that "you can't change a business with numbers. Numbers are the end result. You change a business by changing the behavior of its people." To change the people and culture, Brown holds quarterly "Straight Talk" sessions via satellite to discuss the change process and answer employee questions. He also sends e-mail messages every two weeks to all 128,000 EDS employees, telling them where EDS is going, how it will get there, and what challenges lie ahead.

EDS employees are now embracing Brown's urgency for continual change. "Change is a constant," says Steve Smith, an EDS client delivery executive in Colorado Springs. "In our business, it's the only way we remain competitive because our technology changes every half hour. Our customers look to us to stay on the forefront."[1] ▦

Change is difficult enough in small firms. At EDS and other large organizations, it requires monumental effort and persistence. Organizational change is also very messy. The change process that Dick Brown launched at EDS looks like a well-executed strategy, but all organizational transformations are buffeted by uncertain consequences, organizational politics, and various forms of employee resistance.

This chapter examines ways to bring about meaningful change in organizations. After considering some of the more significant forces for organizational change, we introduce Lewin's model of change and its component parts: identifying sources of resistance to change, minimizing this resistance, and stabilizing desired behaviors. The latter part of this chapter introduces the field of organization development (OD). In particular, we review the OD process, introduce recent OD trends, and identify issues relating to OD effectiveness.

EXTERNAL FORCES FOR CHANGE

Today's business environment is changing so rapidly that it leaves almost everyone breathless. "We're really aggressive at moving at the notion of speed—not only because it's important for internal purposes, but it's also important to our clients," says Joe Forehand, managing partner and chief executive of global consulting firm Accenture. In other words, Accenture's clients are facing rapid change in the marketplace, and they expect Accenture to keep pace with that change.[2]

To illustrate how fast organizations are changing, consider this: American companies that were on the S&P 500 list in the 1920s stayed on the list an average of 67 years. Today, the average company life cycle on the S&P 500 is about 12 years. In other words, your grandparents could work for the same organization all their lives, whereas you will likely outlive two or three companies.[3] Similarly, the most valued companies today—such as Microsoft, Cisco Systems, Capital One Financial, and EMC—were either junior start-ups or nonexistent 20 years ago.[4] And unless these firms anticipate and adapt to continual change, few of them will be around 20 years from now. As open systems (see Chapter 1), successful organizations monitor their environments and take appropriate steps to maintain a compatible fit with the new external conditions. This adaptability requires continual change. It is an ongoing process because environmental change does not end.[5]

There are many forces for change in the external environment, but the prominent forces are information technology, globalization, competition, and demographics. Not surprisingly, most of these are emerging organizational behavior issues that we discussed in the opening chapter of this book.

Information Technology

The network of computers linked around the world has become a major driver of rapid environmental change.[6] Amazon.com, Yahoo!, and other firms are leveraging the power of the Internet to offer a variety of electronic commerce experiences. Intranets have also made it easy and inexpensive to transfer information throughout the organization.[7] Suppliers are hooked up to computer-based networks (called *extranets*) to accelerate just-in-time management deliveries. Major clients are also hooked up to the organization's product database for direct ordering and deliver.[8]

Nokia is a classic example of how companies survive and remain competitive by adapting to environmental changes. The Finnish conglomerate started in 1865 as a pulp and paper company in a mill town near Helsinki (see photo, taken around 1890). The company bought into the rubber business 30 years later and into cable wiring in the 1920s. Many Finns still associate Nokia with the rubber snow boots they wore as children. In the 1960s, Nokia invested in electronics and was soon making televisions and computer monitors. In the 1980s, Nokia executives sensed an emerging market for mobile telecommunications and took enormous risks by investing in that environmental shift. Today, people around the world know of Nokia for its sleek cellular telephones.[9] What factors do you think helped Nokia executives anticipate opportunities and change the organization to realize those opportunities? *(Courtesy of Nokia and the National Museum of Finland)*

Information technology does more than open up business opportunities. It forces corporate leaders to rethink how their organizations are configured, as well as which competencies and expectations employees must have in these emerging organizational forms.[10] Information technology creates new structures that allow companies to compete globally through network alliances (see Chapter 17). It facilitates telecommuting and opens up new employment relationships with employees. It places emphasis on knowledge management rather than physical presence and manufacturing capacity as a driver of competitive advantage.

Global and Local Competition

Betty Coulter is a typical 21-year-old college grad from Illinois. She wears the lastest jeans and is a faithful fan of the TV shows "Friends" and "Buffy the Vampire Slayer." At least, that's what Betty will say, if asked, when Americans call her about a broken appliance or an incorrect sweater ordered from a store catalog. In reality, Betty is Savitha Balasubramanyam, an employee at a call center in Bangalore, India. "It doesn't matter if I'm really Betty or Savitha," says Balasubramanyam with a well-practiced American accent. "What matters is that at the end of the day I've helped the customer."[11]

Welcome to the world of globalization! Whether they are software giants in Europe or call centers in India, competitors are just as likely to be located in a distant part of the world than within your country. SAP, the German software giant, is the leader in enterprise software. Wipro Technologies, India's leading software company, routinely wins multimillion-dollar contracts from the likes of General Electric, Home Depot, and Nokia. CustomerAsset, where Savitha Balasubramanyam works, provides seamless customer service—complete with American accent!—from India's technology hub.

Global and domestic competition often leads to corporate restructuring. To increase their competitiveness, companies reduce layers of management, sell entire divisions of employees, and reduce payroll through downsizing. Global competition has also fueled an unprecedented number of mergers and acquisitions in recent years. Liquor dynasty Seagram Company acquired Universal Studios and other entertainment companies, and then was acquired by Vivendi, based in France. Germany's Daimler-Benz merged with Chrysler, which then increased its stake in Japan's Mitsubishi Motors. These and other mergers potentially improve a firm's competitive advantage through greater efficiency and global reach, but they also result in significant disruptions and changes in employment relationships and the way people work.

Demography

While firms adjust to global competition, they are also adapting to changes in the workforce. Employees are more educated and, consequently, expect more involvement and interesting work. Generation-X and Generation-Y employees are less intimidated by management directives, and they work to live more than live to work. In Japan and other Asian countries, corporate leaders must adjust to a younger workforce that is more individualistic and less patient with cumbersome hierarchies. Meanwhile, in many parts of the world, companies employ a far more diverse workforce than a few decades ago (see Chapter 1). These changes have put pressure on organizational leaders to alter work practices, develop more compatible structures and rewards, and discover new ways to lead.

LEWIN'S FORCE FIELD ANALYSIS MODEL

It is easy to see that these environmental forces push companies to change the way they operate. What is more difficult to see is the complex interplay of these forces against other organizational dynamics. Psychologist Kurt Lewin developed the **force field analysis** model to help us understand how the change process works (see Exhibit 16.1).[12] Although developed over 50 years ago, Lewin's force field analysis model remains the prominent way of viewing this process.

force field analysis
Lewin's model of systemwide change that helps change agents diagnose the forces that drive and restrain proposed organizational change.

One side of the force field model represents the *driving forces*, which push organizations toward a new state of affairs. We began this chapter by describing some of the driving forces in the external environment: information technology, globalization, competition, and demographics. Along with these external forces are driving forces that originate from within the organization, such as competition across divisions of the company and the leader's need to make his or her mark on the company.

EXHIBIT 16.1

Lewin's force field analysis model

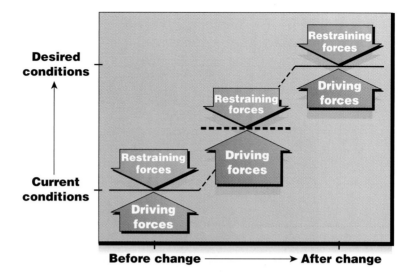

The other side of Lewin's model represents the *restraining forces,* which maintain the status quo. These restraining forces are commonly called "resistance to change" because they appear as employee behaviors that block the change process. Stability occurs when the driving and restraining forces are roughly in equilibrium, that is, when they are of approximately equal strength in opposite directions.

Lewin's force field model emphasizes that effective change occurs by **unfreezing** the current situation, moving to a desired condition, and then **refreezing** the system so that it remains in this desired state. Unfreezing involves producing a disequilibrium between the driving and restraining forces. As we will describe later, this change may occur by increasing the driving forces, reducing the restraining forces, or having a combination of both. Refreezing occurs when the organization's systems and structures are aligned with the desired behaviors. They must support and reinforce the new role patterns and prevent the organization from slipping back into the old way of doing things. This stabilization does not occur automatically; rather, organizational leaders must continually stabilize the desired behaviors. Over the next few pages, we use Lewin's model to understand why change is blocked and how the process can evolve more smoothly.

unfreezing
The first part of the change process whereby the change agent produces disequilibrium between the driving and restraining forces.

refreezing
The latter part of the change process in which systems and conditions are introduced that reinforce and maintain the desired behaviors.

Restraining Forces

BP Norge, the Norwegian subsidiary of British Petroleum, faced more resistance from employees than from the infamous North Sea weather when it introduced self-directed work teams (SDWTs) on its drilling rigs. Many skeptical employees claimed that previous attempts to create SDWTs didn't work. Others were convinced that they already had SDWTs, so why change anything? Several people complained that SDWTs required more responsibility, so they wanted more status and pay. Still others were worried that they lacked the skills to operate in SDWTs. Some BP Norge supervisors were slow to embrace SDWTs because they didn't want to give away their cherished power.[13]

In his two tumultuous years as CEO, Jacques Nasser (left in photo) heaped a lot of change on employees at Ford Motor Company. He tried to shift the automaker from engineering prowess to cyber savvy, from quality to efficiency, and from an old-boys' club to a performance-focused competitor. In one year, Nasser rammed through a performance review system that took General Electric nearly a decade to implement. The changes were too much for many Ford employees. Some engineers grumbled that quality declined; employees stung by the performance system launched age discrimination lawsuits. "When you induce change, you get a reaction," explains a senior Ford executive. "I have letters from employees congratulating us. I have letters from employees doing the opposite." In the latter group was the Ford family, who replaced Nasser with William Clay Ford (right in photo) as CEO.[14] How can corporate leaders change their organizations quickly without experiencing the level of resistance experienced at Ford? *(AP/Wide World)*

BP Norge isn't the only company where employees block organizational change. In one survey, 43 percent of U.S. executives identified employee resistance as the main reason their organization is not more productive.[15] This resistance takes many forms, including passive noncompliance, complaints, absenteeism, turnover, and collective action (e.g., strikes, walkouts). In extreme cases, such as at Ford, Xerox, and Kodak, the chief change agent eventually leaves or is pushed out.[16]

Some organizational behavior scholars suggest that employee resistance represents symptoms of underlying restraining forces that need to be removed.[17] Employees may be worried about the *consequences* of change, such as how the new conditions will take away their power and status. Some are concerned about the *process* of change itself, such as the effort required to break old habits and learn new skills. The main reasons people create obstacles to change are shown in Exhibit 16.2 and are described below. They are direct

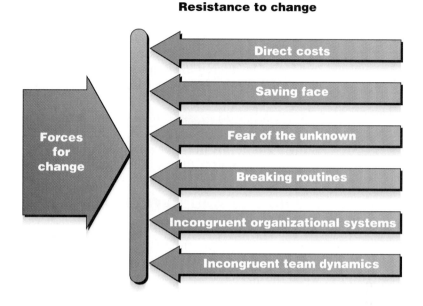

EXHIBIT 16.2

Forces resisting
organizational change

Resistance to change

Forces for change

Direct costs

Saving face

Fear of the unknown

Breaking routines

Incongruent organizational systems

Incongruent team dynamics

costs, saving face, fear of the unknown, breaking routines, incongruent organizational systems, and incongruent team dynamics:[18]

■ *Direct costs*—People tend to block actions that result in higher direct costs or lower benefits than the existing situation. For instance, Ford employees who received low performance ratings resisted change because it threatened their job security and career development.

■ *Saving face*—Some people resist change as a political strategy to "prove" that the decision is wrong or that the person encouraging change is incompetent. For example, senior executives in a manufacturing firm bought a computer other than the system recommended by the information systems department. Soon after the system was in place, several information systems employees let minor implementation problems escalate to demonstrate that senior management had made a poor decision.

■ *Fear of the unknown*—People resist change because they are worried that they cannot adopt the new behaviors. This fear of the unknown increases the *risk* of personal loss. This situation happened at a company where the owner wanted sales staff to telephone rather than personally visit prospective customers. With no experience in telephone sales, the sales staff complained about the changes. Some even avoided the training program that taught them how to make telephone sales. "The salespeople were afraid of failing," explained the owner. "Each of them was very successful in the field, but they had never been exposed to a formalized telephone lead development program."[19]

■ *Breaking routines*—Chapter 1 described how organizations need to unlearn, not just learn.[20] Employees need to abandon the behavioral routines that are no longer appropriate. Unfortunately, people are creatures of habit. They like to stay within their comfort zones by continuing routine role patterns that make life predictable.[21] Consequently, many employees resist organizational changes that force them out of their comfort zones and require investing time and energy learning new role patterns.

■ *Incongruent organizational systems*—Rewards, selection, training, and other control systems ensure that employees maintain desired role patterns. Yet the organizational systems that maintain stability also discourage employees from adopting new ways.[22] The implication, of course, is that organizational systems must be altered to fit the desired change. Unfortunately, control systems can be difficult to change, particularly when they have supported role patterns that worked well in the past.[23]

■ *Incongruent team dynamics*—Teams develop and enforce conformity to a set of norms that guide behavior (see Chapter 8). However, conformity to existing team norms may discourage employees from accepting organizational change. Team norms that conflict with the desired changes need to be altered.

UNFREEZING, CHANGING, AND REFREEZING

According to Lewin's force field analysis model, effective change occurs by unfreezing the current situation, moving to a desired condition, and then refreezing the system so that it remains in this desired state. Unfreezing occurs when the driving forces are stronger than the restraining forces. This process involves making the driving forces stronger, weakening or removing the restraining forces, or having a combination of both.

Certainly, driving forces must be strong enough to motivate employees to change their current ways. However, change rarely occurs by increasing driving forces alone, because the restraining forces often adjust to counterbalance the driving forces. The harder corporate leaders push for change, the stronger the restraining forces push back. This antagonism threatens the change effort by producing tension and conflict within the organization.

The preferred option is to both increase the driving forces and reduce or remove the restraining forces. Increasing the driving forces creates an urgency for change, whereas reducing the restraining forces minimizes resistance to change. "The only way to have people change is because they choose to," explains Carly Fiorina, chief executive of Hewlett-Packard. "You cannot force change onto people—not lasting change, not real change."[24]

Creating an Urgency for Change

Driving forces represent the booster rockets that push employees out of their comfort zones. They energize people to face the risks that change presents to them. Driving forces must be real, not contrived; otherwise, employees will doubt the change agent's integrity. Some threats are well known to employees. PepsiCo employees never forget about their archrivals at Coca-Cola. EDS staff members are always aware of the competitive pressures from IBM Global Services in the computer services business.

However, many driving forces are unknown to anyone below the top ranks of the organization. Thus, the change process must begin by informing employees about competitors, changing consumer trends, impending government regulations, and other driving forces.[25] For instance, James Donald had to communicate the urgency for change when he took over Pathmark Stores. The New Jersey–based supermarket chain was in financial trouble, but few of the company's 28,000 employees knew about these problems. To get employees ready for change and avoid bankruptcy, Donald prepared a video that told everyone about Pathmark's tremendous financial debt. Some employees quit, fearing that the company wasn't going to make it. But the remaining 99 percent quickly developed a commitment to get the company back to health.[26]

Customer Driven Change   Another powerful driver of change is customer expectations.[27] Dissatisfied customers represent a compelling force for change because of the adverse consequences for the organization's survival and success. Customers also provide a human element that further energizes employees to change current behavior patterns. The opening vignette in this chapter described how Dick Brown met with major clients soon after he arrived as CEO of Electronic Data Systems. The purpose of these visits wasn't just to learn about the problems; it was also to let employees know that the problems were real and required urgent change. Al Galdi, CEO of the New Jersey architectural design firm ARCNET, also relied on customer-driven change by having employees listen to a voice mail message from an angry customer. "I played it to the entire staff. It's not something for me to fix, it's something for all of us to fix," he says. [28]

Joel Kocher, CEO of Micron Electronics, also engaged in customer-driven change in his previous job as an executive with Texas-based Power Computing. At a large employee meeting, Kocher read an angry customer letter. Some employees responded defensively by suggesting the customer installed or used the equipment incorrectly, or that the problem is never as serious as customers say. Then, to everyone's surprise, Kocher brought the customer who wrote the letter into the meeting. "We actually brought the customer to the meeting, to personalize it for every single person in the room," says Kocher. "And it was very, very interesting to see the metamorphosis that occurred within the context of these several hundred people when you actually had a customer talking about how their foul-up had hurt this person and hurt their business."[29]

Reducing the Restraining Forces

Effective change involves more than making employees aware of the driving forces. It also involves reducing or removing the restraining forces. Exhibit 16.3 identifies six ways to overcome employee resistance. Communication, training, employee involvement, and stress management try to reduce the restraining forces and, if feasible, should be attempted first.[30] However, negotiation and coercion are necessary for people who will clearly lose something from the change and when the speed of change is critical.

Communication   Communication is the highest priority and the first strategy required for any organizational change. It reduces the restraining forces by keeping employees informed about what to expect from the change effort. Although time-consuming and costly, communication can potentially reduce fear of the unknown and develop team norms that are more consistent with the change effort.

DuPont recognized the importance of communication when it decided to outsource most of its 3,100 information systems (IS) employees to information systems service providers. The chemical giant informed everyone of this decision six months before the change, and it continually communicated with employees throughout the process using e-mail, videos, and face-to-face meetings. By the time the transition took place, employees knew thoroughly what was happening and how it would affect them personally. The result was that

EXHIBIT 16.3 Methods for dealing with resistance to change

Strategy	Example	When used	Problems
Communication	Customer complaint letters are shown to employees.	When employees don't feel an urgency for change or don't know how the change will affect them.	Time-consuming and potentially costly.
Training	Employees learn how to work in teams as the company adopts a team-based structure.	When employees need to break old routines and adopt new role patterns.	Time-consuming and potentially costly.
Employee involvement	Company forms a task force to recommend new customer service practices.	When the change effort needs more employee commitment, some employees need to save face, and/or employee ideas would improve decisions about the change strategy.	Very time-consuming. May also lead to conflict and poor decisions if employees' interests are incompatible with organizational needs.
Stress management	Employees attend sessions to discuss their worries about the change.	When communication, training, and involvement do not sufficiently ease employee worries.	Time-consuming and potentially expensive. Some methods may not reduce stress for all employees.
Negotiation	Employees agree to replace strict job categories with multiskilling in return for increased job security.	When employees will clearly lose something of value from the change and would not otherwise support the new conditions. Also necessary when the company must change quickly.	May be expensive, particularly if other employees want to negotiate their support. Also tends to produce compliance, but not commitment to the change.
Coercion	Company president tells managers to get on board and accept the change or leave.	When other strategies are ineffective and the company needs to change quickly.	Can lead to more subtle forms of resistance, as well as long-term antagonism with the change agent.

Sources: Adapted from J. P. Kotter and L. A. Schlesinger, "Choosing Strategies for Change," *Harvard Business Review* 57 (1979), pp. 106–14; P. R. Lawrence, "How to Deal with Resistance to Change," *Harvard Business Review* (May–June 1954), pp. 49–57.

97 percent of DuPont's IS staff went along with the change. "The communication was so thorough that, by the time we got the offer letter, it was an absolute nonevent," says an outsourced DuPont employee.[31]

Training   Training is an important process in most change initiatives because employees need to learn new knowledge and skills. When a company introduces a new sales database, for instance, representatives need to learn how to adapt their previous behavior patterns to benefit from the new system. Coaching is a variation of training that provides more personalized feedback and direction during the learning process. Global Connections 16.1 describes how an executive at Unilever's Elida Fabergé factory in Seacroft, United Kingdom, brought about significant change by hiring team coaches to train employees. Coaching and other forms of training are time-consuming, but they help employees break routines by learning new role patterns.

Coaching for Change at Unilever's Elida Fabergé Factory in Seacroft

Gary Calveley announced a bold vision soon after he arrived as works director at Unilever's Elida Fabergé factory in Seacroft, United Kingdom. Calveley wanted the facility to apply European quality practices, win the Best Factory award, and become the safest Unilever site in Europe. What's surprising isn't that Calveley set such audacious goals; the surprise is that the plant actually achieved them in three years.

One of the key strategies in Elida Fabergé's success was the introduction of team coaches to guide the change process. Calveley recruited Gene Toner as an independent change agent, who then recruited 10 people with coaching skills from sports, police, teaching, and psychology. Two people were appointed from within the factory.

The coaching process began with "lots of tension and questioning" as employees openly wondered why they needed coaches when experts already worked on the production line. To address these doubts, Calveley worked with a theater company to produce a play portraying current and past work in the factory, and how it could be improved using European quality management practices. After watching the play, coaches guided employees through the process of finding ways to turn this vision of a quality-focused factory into a reality.

The theatrical production helped employees realize that the coaches were there to guide employees toward their goals, just like sports coaches. Another contributing factor to the coaches' role was the variable pay system Calveley negotiated with the union. The new reward system tied pay increases to measurable goals in each employee's personal development plan (PDP). The coaches worked with employees to develop these PDPs

Change consultant Gene Toner (left) and plant manager Gary Calveley (right) introduced coaching to make Unilever's Elida Fabergé factory the best in Europe. *(Dean Smith/The Camera Crew)*

and provided feedback so that they could reach them. This made the coaches valuable allies to both employees and management in the change process.

"[O]nce the targets had been set and people were committed to them, they started coming to the coaches," recalls one coach. "[T]hey came in early, stayed late, or came over during stoppages—it was a bit of a turnaround from being seen as a nuisance factor before." Only 3 employees out of the workforce of 600 didn't get a pay increase in the first year. And by the third year, the entire plant had achieved Calveley's audacious goals.

Source: Adapted from P. Baker, "Change Catalysts," *Works Management* 54 (July 2001), pp. 18–21.

Some training programs, such as action learning projects (see Chapter 2), can also minimize employee resistance caused by saving face, because employees are actively involved in the change process through this type of learning process. In Ford Motor Company's Capstone action learning program, for instance, global teams of six mid-level Ford executives are formed and given six months to tackle a strategic challenge. At the end of six months, team members present their findings and receive feedback from senior Ford executives as well as fellow participants.[32]

Employee Involvement Employee involvement can be an effective way to reduce the restraining forces because it creates a psychological ownership of the decision (see Chapter 9). Rather than viewing themselves as agents of someone else's decision, staff members feel personally responsible for the success of the decision. Employee involvement also minimizes resistance to change by reducing problems of saving face and fear of the unknown. "It is important to have employees take ownership of this," says Colleen Arnold, an executive at IBM Global Services. "It won't work if it's just coming from the top 10 people in the company."[33]

Employee involvement is fairly easy in small organizations, but how do you involve everyone in large firms? One solution is to have representative employees directly involved in the change process. Celestica, Inc., followed this change strategy when it was spun off from IBM a few years ago. Nearly two dozen design teams targeted specific change initiatives by diagnosing Celestica's work processes against the company's critical success factors. Numerous study teams then developed recommendations and implementation strategies in the areas that required change.[34]

search conferences

Systemwide group sessions, usually lasting a few days, in which participants identify the environmental trends and establish strategic solutions for those conditions.

Search conferences represent another way to involve a large number of employees and other stakeholders in the change process. Search conferences are large group sessions, usually lasting a few days, in which participants identify the environmental trends and establish strategic solutions for those conditions.[35] Experts on various topics are sometimes brought in to speak during lunch or dinner. Search conferences "put the entire system in the room," meaning that they try to involve as many employees and other stakeholders associated with the organizational system as possible. For instance, Eicher Motors, a large manufacturer of light commercial vehicles in central India, holds an annual three-day search conference that includes a representation of suppliers, buyers, and shareholders, as well as all employees.[36]

Various organizations, such as Microsoft, the U.S. Forest Service, and Peco Energy, have used search conferences to assist the change process.[37] Of course, search conferences and other forms of employee involvement require follow-up action by decision makers. If employees do not see meaningful decisions and actions resulting from these meetings, they begin to question the credibility of the process and are more cynical of similar change strategies in the future.

Stress Management   For most people, organizational change is a stressful experience.[38] It threatens self-esteem and creates uncertainty about the future. Communication, training, and employee involvement can reduce some of these stressors, but companies also need to introduce stress management practices to help employees cope with the changes. Stress management minimizes resistance by removing some of the direct costs and fear of the unknown associated with the change process. Stress also saps energy, so minimizing stress potentially increases employee motivation to support the change process.

Negotiation   Organizational change is, in large measure, a political activity.[39] People have vested interests and apply their power to ensure that the emerging conditions are consistent with their personal values and needs. Consequently, negotiation may be necessary for employees who will clearly lose out from the change activity. This negotiation offers certain benefits to offset some of the cost of the change.

Coercion   By any account, EDS is one of the most dramatic corporate turnarounds in the computer services industry. As we read in the opening vignette in this chapter, Dick Brown relied on various change management strategies

Executives at Wachovia Corporation knew that its merger with First Union would be stressful for employees, and that stress can make the change process more difficult. To ease the stress, the Winston-Salem–based financial institution set up a toll-free number that employees and other stakeholders could call for updates on the merger process. It also dispatched 400 middle and upper-level managers, called ambassadors, to keep everyone informed. Wachovia offered special sessions to help employees deal with change and stress. Shortly after the merger was announced, the company sent out a memo reminding people about the company's employee assistance counseling service. "I've encouraged people to take care of themselves," says L. M. "Bud" Baker, Wachovia's chairman and chief executive officer (front in photo). "This is a physically and emotionally demanding time."[40] Use Lewin's force field model to explain why stress management strategies improve the change management process. *(AP/Wide World)*

to transform EDS into a more responsive, customer-focused company. Although his change process included communication, training, and employee involvement, it also involved some tough decisions about removing senior executives who didn't fit the new culture.

EDS is not an isolated example. One survey reported that two-thirds of senior management in large U.S. firms were replaced by the time the businesses were revived.[41] Replacing people is the least desirable way to change organizations. However, dismissals and other forms of coercion are sometimes necessary when speed is essential and other tactics are ineffective. For example, it may be necessary to remove several members of an executive team who are unwilling or unable to change their existing mental models of the ideal organization.

Dismissal is also a radical form of organizational "unlearning" (see Chapter 1) because when executives leave, they take knowledge of the organization's past routines, potentially opening up opportunities for new practices to take hold.[42] At the same time, we should keep in mind that coercion is a risky strategy because survivors (employees who are not fired) may have less trust in corporate leaders and engage in more political tactics to protect their own job security. In general, various forms of coercion may change behavior through compliance, but they won't develop commitment to the change effort (see Chapter 12).

Changing to the Desired Future State

Organizational change takes many forms. Dick Brown changed EDS's culture to become more customer-focused, requiring changes in behavior as well as in attitudes and values. Change was more dramatic at Celestica, the IBM spin-off that manufactures high-technology products. Task forces identified specific changes, which resulted in new tasks and roles in the organization. Overall, change results in new behaviors that employees must learn and internalize.

Refreezing the Desired Conditions

After unfreezing and changing behavior patterns, we need to refreeze desired behaviors so that people do not slip back into their old work practices.[43] Refreezing occurs when organizational systems and team dynamics are realigned with the desired changes. The desired patterns of behavior can be nailed down by changing the physical structure and situational conditions. Organizational rewards are also powerful systems that refreeze behaviors.[44] If the change process is supposed to encourage efficiency, then rewards should be realigned to motivate and reinforce efficient behavior. Information systems play a complementary role in the change process, particularly as conduits for feedback.[45]

Feedback mechanisms help employees learn how well they are moving toward the desired objectives, and they provide a permanent architecture to support the new behavior patterns in the long term. Alberto-Culver Company North America transformed into a performance-oriented firm by measuring employees' attitudes toward the top executive team and change agents, called growth development leaders. "I'm a firm believer that you change what you measure," says Carol Lavin Bernick, North American president of the personal care products company.[46]

STRATEGIC VISIONS, CHANGE AGENTS, AND DIFFUSION OF CHANGE

Kurt Lewin's force field analysis model provides a rich understanding of the dynamics of organizational change. But it overlooks three other ingredients in effective change processes: strategic visions, change agents, and diffusion of change.

Strategic Visions

Every successful change requires a clear, well-articulated vision of the desired future state. This vision provides a sense of direction and establishes the critical success factors against which the real changes are evaluated. It also minimizes employee fear of the unknown and provides a better understanding of which behaviors employees must learn for the future state.[47] Although some executives say that strategic visions are too "fluffy," most executives in large U.S. organizations believe a clear vision of the proposed change is the most important feature of successful change initiatives.[48]

You can see the importance of a strategic vision in the change process at EDS. Dick Brown began the turnaround at EDS with a clear vision of a more responsive, customer-focused organization. "[Dick Brown] is the finest communicator I have ever worked with" says Don Uzzi, EDS senior vice president of global marketing, communications, and government affairs. "He has a vision and a mission and employees well know it."[49]

Change Agents

change agent
Anyone who possesses enough knowledge and power to guide and facilitate the change effort.

Organizational change also requires change agents to help form, communicate, and build commitment toward the desired future state. A **change agent** is anyone who possesses enough knowledge and power to guide and facilitate the change effort. Some organizations rely on external consultants to serve as change agents. However, change agents are typically people within the organization who possess the leadership competencies necessary to bring about meaningful change. Corporate executives certainly need to be change agents. However, as companies rely increasingly on self-directed work teams, most employees will become change agents from time to time.

Effective change agents such as Dick Brown are transformational leaders (see Chapter 14).[50] They form a vision of the desired future state, communicate that vision in ways that are meaningful to others, behave in ways that are consistent with the vision, and build commitment to the vision.

Diffusion of Change

organization development (OD)
A planned system-wide effort, managed from the top with the assistance of a change agent, that uses behavioral science knowledge to improve organizational effectiveness.

Change agents often test the transformation process with a pilot project, then diffuse what has been learned from this experience to other parts of the organization. Pilot projects are more flexible and less risky than centralized, organizationwide programs.[51] Scholars have identified several conditions that effectively diffuse change from the pilot project to the rest of the organization.[52] Diffusion is more likely to occur when the pilot project is successful within one or two years and receives visibility (e.g., favorable news media coverage). These conditions tend to increase top management support for the change program and persuade other managers to introduce the change effort in their operations. Successful diffusion also depends on labor union support and active involvement in the diffusion process.

Another important condition is that the diffusion strategy isn't described too abstractly. If the strategy is too abstract, the instructions may be too vague to allow introduction of the change elsewhere. Neither should the strategy be stated too precisely, because it might not seem relevant to other areas of the organization. Finally, without producing excessive turnover in the pilot group, people who have worked under the new system should be moved to other areas of the organization. These employees transfer their knowledge and commitment of the change effort to work units that have not yet experienced it.

ORGANIZATION DEVELOPMENT

So far, we have discussed the dynamics of change that occur every day in organizations. However, an entire field of study, called **organization development (OD),** tries to understand how to manage planned change in organizations. OD is a planned systemwide effort, managed from the top with the

FedEx Custom Critical (formerly Roberts Express) introduced self-directed work teams through a pilot project. Seven employees from operations, customer service, and safety/recruiting at the Akron, Ohio–based expedited delivery service firm agreed to form a pilot team, representing the first cross-functional customer service unit. As problems were ironed out, the company transferred what it learned about forming SDWTs in the pilot group to form other teams. Today, the entire work process is operated by self-directed teams.[53] What conditions would help FedEx Custom Critical diffuse the pilot project to other parts of the organization? *(Courtesy of FedEx Custom Critical)*

assistance of a change agent, that uses behavioral science knowledge to improve organizational effectiveness.[54]

OD relies on many of the organizational behavior concepts described in this book, such as team dynamics, perceptions, job design, and conflict management. OD also takes an open systems perspective, because it recognizes that organizations have many interdependent parts and must adapt to their environments. Thus, OD experts try to ensure that all parts of the organization are compatible with the change effort, and that the change activities help the company fit its environment.[55]

Most OD activities rely on **action research** as the primary blueprint for planned change. As depicted in Exhibit 16.4, action research is a data-based, problem-oriented process that diagnoses the need for change, introduces the OD activity, and then evaluates and stabilizes the desired changes.[56]

Action research is a highly participative process, involving the client throughout the various stages.[57] It typically includes an action research team consisting of people both affected by the organizational change and having the power to facilitate it. This participation, a fundamental philosophy of OD, also increases commitment to the change process and provides valuable

action research

A data-based, problem-orientated process that diagnoses the need for change, introduces the OD intervention, and then evaluates and stabilizes the desired changes.

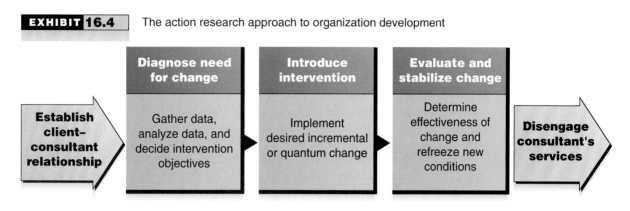

EXHIBIT 16.4   The action research approach to organization development

information for conducting organizational diagnosis and evaluation. Let's look at the main elements of the action research process.

Establish the Client–Consultant Relationship

The organization development process begins by forming a relationship between the client and the consultant. External consultants might become change agents, but they are usually retained as facilitators to assist an internal change agent (usually a senior executive or team leader). Consultants need to determine three things when forming a client relationship in organization development: the client's readiness for change, the consultant's power base, and the consultant's role in the relationship.

First, consultants need to determine the client's readiness for change, including whether people are motivated to participate in the process, are open to meaningful change, and possess the abilities to complete the process. They watch out for people who enter the process with preconceived ideas before the situation is fully diagnosed, or who intend to use the change effort to their personal advantage (e.g., closing down a department or firing a particular employee).

Second, consultants need to establish their power base in the client relationship.[58] Effective consultants rely on expertise and perhaps referent power to have any influence on the participants (see Chapter 12). However, they *should not* use reward, legitimate, or coercive power, because these bases may weaken trust and neutrality in the client–consultant relationship.

Third, consultants need to agree with their clients on the most appropriate role in the relationship.[59] A consultant's role might range from providing technical expertise on a specific change activity to facilitating the change process. Many OD experts prefer the latter role, commonly known as **process consultation**.[60] Process consultation involves helping the organization solve its own problems by making it aware of organizational processes, the consequences of those processes, and the means by which they can be changed. Rather than providing expertise about the content of the change—such as how to introduce continuous improvement teams—process consultants help participants learn how to solve their own problems by guiding them through the change process.[61]

process consultation
Involves helping the organization solve its own problems by making it aware of organizational processes, the consequences of those processes, and the means by which they can be changed.

Diagnose the Need for Change

Action research is a problem-oriented activity that carefully diagnoses the problem (or opportunity) through systematic analysis of the situation. *Organizational diagnosis* involves gathering and analyzing data about an ongoing system. Organizational diagnosis is important because it establishes the appropriate direction for the change effort.[62] Data collection may occur through interviews, survey questionnaires, direct observation, analysis of documents, or any combination of these.

Along with gathering and analyzing data, the diagnostic process involves agreeing on specific prescriptions for action, including the appropriate change method and the schedule for these actions. This process, known as *joint action planning,* ensures that everyone knows what is expected of him or her and that standards are established to properly evaluate the process after the transition.[63]

Introduce Change

An important issue in any change process is whether to implement incremental or quantum change.[64] **Incremental change** is an evolutionary strategy whereby the organization fine-tunes the existing organization and takes small steps toward the change effort's objectives. Incremental change is generally less threatening and stressful to employees because they have time to adapt to the new conditions. Moreover, any problems in the process can be corrected while the change process is occurring, rather than afterward. However, incremental change may be inadequate where companies face extreme environmental turbulence. Instead, they may require **quantum change** (also called *episodic change*) in which the organization breaks out of its existing ways and moves toward a totally different configuration of systems and structures.[65] Organizational restructuring and reengineering are common forms of quantum change.

Executives at Nestlé, the Swiss food giant, prefer continuous improvement because quantum change potentially creates more problems within organizations.[66] Quantum change can be costly as organizational systems and structures and torn apart and replaced. Employees typically need to learn completely new roles, which are not known until the change process has begun. Quantum change is usually traumatic and rapid, so change agents rely more on coercion and negotiation than on employee involvement to build support for the change effort.

Evaluate and Stabilize Change

OD activities can be very expensive, so it makes sense that we should measure their effectiveness. To evaluate an OD process, we need to recall its objectives, which were developed during the organizational diagnosis and action planning stages. But even when these goals are clearly stated, the effectiveness of an OD activity might not be apparent for several years. It is also difficult to separate the effects of the activity from external factors (e.g., improving economy, introduction of new technology).

If the activity has the desired effect, then the change agent and participants need to stabilize the new conditions. This element refers to the refreezing process that we described earlier. Rewards, information systems, team norms, and other conditions are redesigned so that they support the new values and

---

incremental change
An evolutionary strategy whereby the organization fine-tunes the existing organization and takes small steps toward the change effort's objectives.

quantum change
A revolutionary approach to change in which the organization breaks out of its existing ways and moves toward a totally different configuration of systems and structures.

behaviors. Even with stabilizing systems and structures in place, the desired conditions may erode without the ongoing support of a change champion.

For example, Alcoa's magnesium plant in Addy, Washington, became a model of efficiency under the guidance of its plant manager and human resource manager. Then Alcoa transferred both of them to other turnaround projects and cut back on the number of department heads at the plant. These actions unintentionally had the effect of removing the change champions and undermining the previous four years of change effort. "[Alcoa] stripped away the leadership that could have supported the change efforts afterwards," says one of the original change agents.[67]

TRENDS IN ORGANIZATION DEVELOPMENT

Organization development includes any planned change intended to make a firm more effective. In theory, this means that OD covers almost every area of organizational behavior, as well as many aspects of strategic and human resource management. In practice, OD consultants have favored one perspective and level of process more than others at various periods in OD's history.

When the field of organization development emerged in the 1940s and 1950s, OD practitioners focused almost exclusively on interpersonal and small group dynamics. The field was equated with T-groups, encounter groups, and other forms of sensitivity training. **Sensitivity training** is an unstructured and agendaless session in which a small group of people meet face-to-face, often for a few days, to learn more about themselves and their relations with others.[68] Learning occurs as participants disclose information about themselves and receive feedback from others during the session. Few OD activities were involved with macro-level, organizationwide changes.

Today, the reverse is true.[69] OD processes now are aimed mostly at improvements in service quality, corporate restructuring, and organizational learning. They are typically organizationwide, affecting organizational systems and structures, with less emphasis on individual emotions and values. OD practitioners are paying more attention to productivity, customer service, product or service quality, and related business outcomes.[70] Although surveys suggest that OD consultants still value their humanistic roots, there is also increasing awareness that the field's values have shifted to a more bottom-line focus.

There are numerous OD activities. Some are discussed elsewhere in this book, such as job design (Chapter 6), team building (Chapter 8), dialogue meetings (Chapter 13), and changes in organizational culture (Chapter 15). In this section, we briefly discuss two increasingly popular OD activities: parallel learning structures and appreciative inquiry.

Parallel Learning Structures

Parallel learning structures are highly participative arrangements, composed of people from most levels of the organization who follow the action research model to produce meaningful organizational change. They are social structures developed alongside the formal hierarchy with the purpose of increasing the organization's learning.[71] Ideally, parallel learning structure participants are sufficiently free from the constraints of the larger organization so that they can more effectively solve organizational issues.

---

sensitivity training

An unstructured and agendaless session in which a small group of people meet face to face, often for a few days, to learn more about themselves and their relations with others.

parallel learning structures

Highly participative groups constructed alongside (i.e., parallel to) the formal organization with the purpose of increasing the organization's learning and producing meaningful organizational change.

Royal Dutch/Shell Changes through Parallel Learning Structures

A few years ago, competitors were threatening Royal Dutch/Shell's market share. The oil company's executives in London and The Hague spent two years reorganizing, downsizing, and educating several layers of management, but this top-down approach had minimal effect. Managers in charge of Shell's operations for a particular country resisted changes that threatened their autonomy, and headquarters managers couldn't break out of the routines that worked for them in the past.

So Steve Miller, head of Shell's worldwide oil products business, decided to apply a parallel learning structure and change the company from the bottom up. He and his executive team held several five-day workshops, each attended by six-country teams of frontline people (e.g., gas station managers, truck drivers, marketing professionals). Participants at these "retailing boot camps" learned about worrisome competitive trends in their regions and were taught powerful marketing tools to identify opportunities. The teams then returned home to study their markets and develop proposals for improvement. For example, a team in South Africa proposed ways to increase liquid gas market share. The Malaysian team developed plans to increase gasoline sales in that country.

Four months later, the teams returned for a second workshop, where each proposal was critiqued by Miller's executive team in "fishbowl" sessions with the other teams watching. Videotapes from these sessions became socialization tools for other employees back in the home country. Each team had 60 days to put its ideas into action. The team returned for a third workshop to analyze what worked and what didn't.

These workshops, along with field tours and several other grassroots activities, had a tremendous effect.

Royal Dutch/Shell relied on a parallel learning structure to change the company from the bottom up. *(John Thoeming)*

Frontline employees developed an infectious enthusiasm and a stronger business approach to challenging the competition. "I can't overstate how infectious the optimism and energy of these committed employees was on the many managers above them," says Miller. The change process also resulted in solid improvements in profitability and market share in most regions where employees had attended the sessions.

Sources: R. Pascale, M. Millemann, and L. Gioja, *Surfing on the Edge of Chaos* (London: Texere, 2000); R. T. Pascale, "Leading from a Different Place," in J. A. Conger, G. M. Spreitzer, and E. E. Lawler III, eds., *The Leader's Change Handbook* (San Francisco: Jossey-Bass, 1999), pp. 301–20; D. J. Knight, "Strategy in Practice: Making It Happen," *Strategy and Leadership* 26 (July–August 1998), pp. 29–33; R. T. Pascale, "Grassroots Leadership—Royal Dutch/Shell," *Fast Company* 14 (April–May 1998), pp. 110–20.

The change process at EDS relied on a parallel learning structure. CEO Dick Brown formed Project Breakaway—a team of seven people from different units, each with different industry expertise—to develop a customer-focused organizational structure that would increase productivity, promote accountability, and drive a collaborative culture across the entire enterprise. The team was given six weeks to resolve their differences and draft the new structure that would break away from the old ways of doing business.[72] Project Breakaway became a microcosm of the larger organization, complete with internal rivalries that had to be resolved before the new structure took shape.

Connections 16.2 describes how Royal Dutch/Shell's retail boot camp teams represent a form of parallel structure because they work outside the normal structure. These teams represent various countries and establish a more entrepreneurial approach to getting things done at Shell. The retail teams are separated from the traditional hierarchy so that it is easier to instill new attitudes, role patterns, and work behaviors.

Appreciative Inquiry

The action research process described earlier in this chapter is based on the traditional problem-solving model. OD participants focus on problems with the existing organizational system and identify ways to correct those problems. Unfortunately, this deficiency model of the world—in which something is wrong that must be fixed—focuses on the negative dynamics of the group or system rather than its positive opportunities.

appreciative inquiry

An organization development intervention that directs the group's attention away from its own problems and focuses participants on the group's potential and positive elements.

Appreciative inquiry tries to break out of the problem-solving mentality by reframing relationships around the positive and the possible.[73] It takes the view that organizations are creative entities in which people are capable of building synergy beyond their individual capabilities. To avoid dwelling on the group's own shortcomings, the process usually directs its inquiry toward successful events and successful organizations. This external focus becomes a form of behavioral modeling, but it also increases open dialogue by redirecting the group's attention away from its own problems. Appreciative inquiry is especially useful when participants are aware of their "problems" or already suffer from enough negativity in their relationships. The positive orientation of appreciative inquiry enables groups to overcome these negative tensions and build a more hopeful perspective of their future by focusing on what is possible.

Exhibit 16.5 outlines the Four-D model of appreciative inquiry, which was developed in Harare, Zimbabwe, by a group working with the U.S. Agency for International Development and the Save the Children Fund.[74] The process begins with *discovery*—identifying the positive elements of the observed events or organization. This stage might involve documenting positive customer experiences elsewhere in the organization. Or it might include interviewing members of another organization to discover its fundamental strengths. As

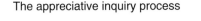

EXHIBIT 16.5   The appreciative inquiry process

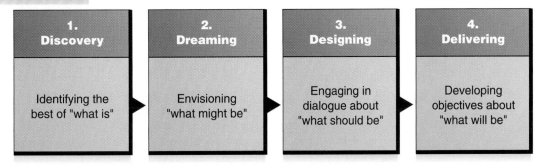

1. Discovery	2. Dreaming	3. Designing	4. Delivering
Identifying the best of "what is"	Envisioning "what might be"	Engaging in dialogue about "what should be"	Developing objectives about "what will be"

Sources: Based on J. M. Watkins and B. J. Mohr, *Appreciative Inquiry: Change at the Speed of Imagination* (San Francisco: Jossey-Bass, 2001), pp. 25, 42–45; D. Whitney and C. Schau, "Appreciative Inquiry: An Innovative Process for Organization Change," *Employment Relations Today* 25 (Spring 1998), pp. 11–21; F. J. Barrett and D. L. Cooperrider, "Generative Metaphor Intervention: A New Approach for Working with Systems Divided by Conflict and Caught in Defensive Perception," *Journal of Applied Behavioral Science* 26 (1990), p. 229.

participants discuss their findings, they shift into the *dreaming* stage by envisioning what might be possible in an ideal organization. By directing their attention to a theoretically ideal organization or situation, participants feel safer revealing their hopes and aspirations than if they were discussing their own organization or predicament.

As participants make their private thoughts public to the group, the process shifts into the third stage, called *designing*. Designing involves the process of dialogue (see Chapter 8), in which participants listen with selfless receptivity to each other's models and assumptions and eventually form a collective model for thinking within the team.[75] In effect, they create a common image of what should be. As this model takes shape, group members shift the focus back to their own situation. In the final stage of appreciative inquiry, called

The HunterDouglas Window Fashions Division (WFD) relied on appreciative inquiry to create a collective vision, reinstill a sense of community among employees, and build leadership within the organization. The Broomfield, Colorado–based business unit sent an advisory team to a weeklong training program where they learned about the Four-D process. The WFD advisory team then described appreciative inquiry and its rationale to employees through a series of town meetings. The discovery phase consisted of over 500 interviews with employees, customers, suppliers, and community members. These results were reviewed at an Appreciative Summit, where WFD employees worked through the dream, design, and deliver stages. A second wave of interviews became background data for a subsequent search conference–type of strategic planning summit. WFD executives say that appreciative inquiry improved productivity and cross-departmental collaboration, and created a can-do attitude toward the company's quality management initiative.[76] What problems might occur if HunterDouglas relied on action research rather than appreciative inquiry to facilitate this change process? *(Courtesy of Amanda Trosten-Bloom)*

delivering, participants establish specific objectives and direction for their own organization based on their model of what will be.

Appreciative inquiry is a relatively new approach to organization development, but several organizations have already applied its basic principles. One of these is AVON Mexico, which conducted sessions to develop employment opportunities for women in the top ranks. A team of employees and consultants interviewed people for their stories illustrating best practices in gender equality at AVON Mexico. These stories were presented at two-day sessions, and participants built on these best practices to discover how AVON could extend these experiences. Over the next few years, the company won the Catalyst award for gender equality, its profit increased dramatically (attributed partly to the appreciative inquiry process), and women found their way into more senior positions at AVON Mexico.[77]

EFFECTIVENESS OF ORGANIZATION DEVELOPMENT

Is organization development effective? Considering the incredible range of organization development activities, answering this question is not easy. Nevertheless, a few studies have generally reported that some OD processes have a moderately positive effect on employee productivity and attitudes. According to some reviews, team building and interpersonal dialogue produce the most favorable results when a single activity is applied.[78] One of the most consistent findings is that OD is most effective when it includes two or more change processes.

Cross-Cultural Concerns with OD

One significant concern with OD techniques originating from North America is that they conflict with cultural values in other countries.[79] Some scholars argue that OD practices in North America assume a linear model of change, as shown earlier in the force field analysis, that is punctuated by tension and overt conflict. Indeed, sensitivity training and other OD practices encourage open display of conflict. But these assumptions are incompatible with cultures that view change as a natural, cyclical process with harmony and equilibrium as the objectives.[80] For instance, people in many Asian countries try to minimize conflict in order to respect others and save face.[81] These concerns do not mean that OD is ineffective elsewhere. Rather, it suggests that the field needs to develop a more contingency-oriented perspective with respect to the cultural values of its participants.

Ethical Concerns with OD

The field of organization development also faces ethical concerns with respect to some processes.[82] One ethical concern is that OD activities may threaten the individual's privacy rights. The action research model is built on the idea of collecting information from organizational members, yet this activity requires employees to provide personal information and emotions that they may not want to divulge. The scientific nature of the data collection exercise may mislead employees into believing that their information is confidential when, in reality, executives can sometimes identify opinions of individual employees.[83]

A second ethical concern is that OD activities potentially increase management's power by inducing compliance and conformity in organizational members. This power shift occurs because OD initiatives create uncertainty and reestablish management's position in directing the organization. Moreover, because OD is a systemwide activity, it *requires* employees to participate rather than allowing individuals to get involved voluntarily. Indeed, one of the challenges of OD consultants is to bring on board those who are reluctant to engage in the process.

A third concern is that some OD activities undermine the individual's self-esteem. The unfreezing process requires participants to disconfirm their existing beliefs, sometimes including their own competence at certain tasks or interpersonal relations. Sensitivity training may involve direct exposure to personal critique by co-workers as well as public disclosure of personal limitations and faults.

A fourth ethical dilemma facing OD consultants is their role in the client relationship. Generally, they should occupy marginal positions with the clients they are serving. That is, they must be sufficiently detached from the organization to maintain objectivity and avoid having the client become too dependent on them.[84] However, this can be a difficult objective to satisfy because of the politics of organizational change. OD consultants and clients have their own agendas, and these are not easily resolved without moving beyond the marginal positions that change agents should ideally attain.

The organization development practices described in this section facilitate the change process, and Lewin's force field analysis model provides a valuable template for understanding how the change process works. Still, you can tell from reading this chapter that organizational change is easier said than done. Many corporate leaders have promised more change than they were able to deliver because they underestimated the time and challenges involved with the process. This is certainly true of corporate restructuring, where leaders typically have difficulty redesigning the organization's departments, reporting relationships, and distribution of formal power. The next chapter looks closely at organizational structure and design.

CHAPTER SUMMARY

Organizations face numerous forces for change, because they are open systems that need to adapt to changing environments. Some current environmental dynamics include computer technology, globalization, competition, and demographics.

Lewin's force field analysis model states that all systems have driving and restraining forces. Change occurs through the process of unfreezing, changing, and refreezing. Unfreezing produces disequilibrium between the driving and restraining forces. Refreezing realigns the organization's systems and structures with the desired behaviors.

Almost all organizational change efforts face one or more forms of employee resistance. The main reasons people resist change are direct costs, saving face, fear of the unknown, breaking routines, incongruent organizational systems, and incongruent team dynamics.

Resistance to change may be minimized by keeping employees informed about what to expect from the change effort (communicating); by teaching employees valuable skills for the desired future (training); by involving them in the change process; by helping employees cope with the stress of change; by negotiating trade-offs with those who will clearly lose from the change effort; and by using coercion (sparingly and as a last resort).

A change agent is anyone who possesses enough knowledge and power to guide and facilitate the change effort. Change agents rely on transformational leadership to develop a vision, communicate that vision, and build commitment to the vision of a desirable future state.

Organization development (OD) is a planned systemwide effort, managed from the top with the assistance of a change agent, that uses behavioral science knowledge to improve organizational effectiveness.

When forming a client relationship, OD consultants need to determine the readiness for change, establish their power base in the client relationship, and understand their appropriate role in the change process. An important issue is whether change should be evolutionary (incremental change) or revolutionary (quantum change).

Parallel learning structures are social structures developed alongside the formal hierarchy with the purpose of increasing the organization's learning. They are highly participative arrangements, composed of people from most levels of the organization who follow the action research model to produce meaningful organizational change. Appreciative inquiry focuses participants on the positive and possible. It tries to break out of the problem-solving mentality that dominates OD through the action research model. The four stages of appreciative inquiry are discovery, dreaming, designing, and delivering.

OD activities, particularly those with multiple components, have a moderately positive effect on employee productivity and attitudes. However, there are some cross-cultural concerns with OD processes. Moreover, there are ethical concerns with some OD activities, including increasing management's power over employees, threatening individual privacy rights, undermining individual self-esteem, and making clients dependent on the OD consultant.

KEY TERMS

action research, p. 488

appreciative inquiry, p. 493

change agent, p. 487

force field analysis, p. 476

incremental change, p. 490

organization development (OD), p. 487

parallel learning structures, p. 491

process consultation, p. 489

quantum change, p. 490

refreezing, p. 477

search conferences, p. 484

sensitivity training, p. 491

unfreezing, p. 477

DISCUSSION QUESTIONS

1. Chances are that the school you are attending is currently undergoing some sort of change to adapt more closely to its environment. Discuss the external forces that are driving these changes. What internal drivers for change also exist?

2. Use Lewin's force field analysis to describe the dynamics of organizational change at Unilever's Elida Fabergé factory, described in Global Connections 16.1.

3. Senior management of a large multinational corporation is planning to restructure the organization. Currently, the organization is decentralized around geographical areas so that the executive responsible for each area has considerable autonomy over manufacturing and sales. The new structure will transfer power to the executives responsible for different product groups; the executives responsible for each geographic area will no longer be responsible for manufacturing in their area but will retain control over sales activities. Describe two types of resistance senior management might encounter from this organizational change.

4. Review the organizational change process at EDS (opening vignette in this chapter); then explain how this process reduced resistance to change.

5. Web Circuits, Inc., is a Singapore-based manufacturer of computer circuit boards for high-technology companies. Senior management wants to introduce value-added management practices to reduce production costs and remain competitive. A consultant has recommended that the company start with a pilot project in one department and, when successful, diffuse those practices to other areas of the organization. Discuss the advantages of this recommendation, and identify three conditions (other than the pilot project's success) that would make diffusion of the change effort more successful.

6. You are an organization development consultant who has been asked by the president of Seattle Photonics Inc. to explore the issues that may account for the slow hardware and software development of three teams under the direction of a particular project manager. Before accepting this role, what three things should you consider when forming the client relationship? How would you determine whether the client is well suited to organizational development?

7. Suppose that you are vice president of branch services at the Bank of East Lansing. You notice that several branches have consistently low customer

service ratings even though there are no apparent differences among branches in resources or staff characteristics. Describe an appreciative inquiry process in one of these branches that might help overcome these problems.

8. This chapter suggests that some organization development activities face ethical concerns. Yet several OD consultants actively use these processes because they believe they benefit the organization and do less damage to employees than it seems on the surface. For example, some OD activities try to open up the employee's hidden area (see Johari Window in Chapter 3) so that there is better mutual understanding with co-workers. Discuss the merits of this argument, and identify where you think OD should limit this process.

CASE STUDY 16.1

TRANSACT INSURANCE CORPORATION

TransAct Insurance Corporation (TIC) provides automobile insurance throughout the Southeastern United States. Last year, a new president was brought in by TIC's board of directors to improve the company's competitiveness and customer service. After spending several months assessing the situation, the new president introduced a strategic plan to improve TIC's competitive position. He also replaced three vice presidents. Jim Leon was hired as vice president of claims, TIC's largest division, with 1,500 employees, 50 claims center managers, and five regional directors.

Jim immediately met with all claims managers and directors, and visited employees at TIC's 50 claims centers. Because he was an outsider, this was a formidable task, but his strong interpersonal skills and uncanny ability to remember names and ideas helped him through the process. Through these visits and discussions, Jim discovered that the claims division had been managed in a relatively authoritarian, top-down manner. He could also see that morale was very low and employee–management relations were guarded. High workloads and isolation (adjusters work in tiny cubicles) were two other common complaints. Several managers acknowledged that the high turnover among claims adjusters was partly due to these conditions.

Following discussions with TIC's president, Jim decided to make morale and supervisory leadership his top priority. He initiated a divisional newsletter with a tear-off feedback form for employees to register their comments. He announced an open-door policy in which any claims division employee could speak to him directly and confidentially without first going to the immediate supervisor. Jim also fought organizational barriers to initiate a flex-time program so that employees could design work schedules around their needs. This program later became a model for other areas of TIC.

One of Jim's most pronounced symbols of change was the "Claims Management Credo" outlining the philosophy that every claims manager would follow. At his first meeting with the complete claims management team, Jim presented a list of what he thought were important philosophies and actions of effective managers. The management group was asked to select and prioritize items from this list. They were told that the resulting list would be the division's management philosophy and all managers would be held accountable for abiding by its principles. Most claims managers were uneasy about this process, but they also understood that the organization was under competitive pressure and that Jim was using this exercise to demonstrate his leadership.

The claims managers developed a list of 10 items, such as encouraging teamwork, fostering a trusting work environment, setting clear and reasonable goals, and so on. The list was circulated to senior management in the organization for their comment and approval, and sent back to all claims managers for their endorsement. Once this was done, a copy of the final document was sent to every claims division employee. Jim also announced plans to follow up with an annual survey to evaluate each claims manager's performance. This plan concerned the managers, but most of them believed that the credo exercise was a result of Jim's initial enthusiasm and that he would be too busy to introduce a survey after settling into the job.

One year after the credo had been distributed, Jim announced that the first annual survey would be conducted. All claims employees would complete the survey and return it confidentially to the human resources department, where the survey results would be compiled for each claims center manager. The survey asked the extent to which the manager had lived up to each of the 10 items in the credo. Each form also provided space for comments.

Claims center managers were surprised that a survey would be conducted, but they were even more worried about Jim's statement that the results would be shared with employees. What "results" would employees see? Who would distribute these results? What would happen if a manager got poor ratings from his or her subordinates? "We'll work out the details later," said Jim in response to these questions. "Even if the survey results aren't great, the information will give us a good baseline for next year's survey."

The claims division survey had a high response rate. In some centers, every employee completed and returned a form. Each report showed the claim center manager's average score for each of the 10 items as well as how many employees rated the manager at each level of the 5-point scale. The reports also included every comment made by employees at that center.

No one was prepared for the results of the first survey. Most managers received moderate or poor ratings on the 10 items. Very few managers averaged above 3.0 (out of a possible 5.0) on more than a couple of items. These results suggested that, at best, employees were ambivalent about whether their claims center manager had abided by the 10 management philosophy items. The comments were even more devastating than the ratings. Comments ranged from mildly disappointed in to extremely critical of their claims manager. Employees also described their long-standing frustration with TIC, high workloads, and isolated working conditions. Several people bluntly stated that they were skeptical about the changes that Jim had promised. "We've heard the promises before, but now we've lost faith," wrote one claims adjuster.

The survey results were sent to each claims manager, the regional director, and employees at the claims center. Jim instructed managers to discuss the survey data and comments with their regional manager and directly with employees. The claims center managers, who thought employees received only the average scores, went into shock when they realized that the reports included individual comments. Some managers went to their regional director, complaining that revealing the personal comments would ruin their careers. Many directors sympathized, but the results were already available to employees.

When Jim heard about these concerns, he agreed that the results were lower than expected and that the comments should not have been shown to employees. After discussing the situation with his directors, he decided that the discussion meetings between claims managers and their employees should proceed as planned. To delay or withdraw the reports would undermine the credibility and trust that Jim was trying to develop with employees. However, the regional director attended the meeting in each claims center to minimize direct conflict between the claims center manager and employees.

Although many of these meetings went smoothly, a few created harsh feelings between managers and their employees. The sources of some comments were easily identified by their content, creating a few delicate moments in several sessions. A few months after these meetings, two claims center managers quit and three others asked for transfers back to nonmanagement positions in TIC. Meanwhile, Jim wondered how to manage this process more effectively, particularly since employees expected another survey the following year.

Discussion Questions

1. Identify the forces pushing for change and the forces restraining the change effort in this case.

2. Was Jim Leon successful at bringing about change? Why or why not?

3. What should Jim Leon do now?

EMC DISHES OUT A LITTLE MORE TLC

BusinessWeek At a big company, data storage used to involve rooms in which paper files were carefully packed into boxes and organized on shelves. Today, data storage is a computer-driven business for safely maintaining electronic files. A major player in the data storage business is EMC Corporation, which originally won customers solely on the basis of the company's leadership in storage technology. After competitors such as IBM and Hitachi Data Systems caught up in terms of technology, EMC had to rethink the way it treats customers.

This *Business Week* case study describes how EMC is making the move from a technology-driven company to a customer-focused company. It discusses how EMC lost customers to rivals offering better service along with better prices and how it is changing in an attempt to win them back. Read through this *Business Week* case study at www.mhhe.com/mcshane2e and prepare for the discussion questions below.

Discussion Questions

1. What driving forces for change at EMC does the author identify?

2. How are managers at EMC enabling change?

3. What resistance to this change would you expect to see at EMC? What strategies for dealing with the resistance would be appropriate?

Source: F. Keenan, "EMC Dishes Out a Little More TLC," *Business Week*, September 10, 2001.

STRATEGIC CHANGE MANAGEMENT

Purpose This exercise is designed to help you identify strategies to facilitate organizational change in various situations.

Instructions

■ *Step 1*—The instructor will place students into teams, and each team will be assigned one of the scenarios presented below.

■ *Step 2*—Each team will diagnose its assigned scenario to determine the most appropriate set of change management practices. Where appropriate, these practices should (a) create an urgency to change, (b) minimize resistance to change, and (c) refreeze the situation to support the change initiative. Each scenario is based on real events that occurred in the United States and Canada.

■ *Step 3*—Each team will present and defend its change management strategy. Class discussion regarding the appropriateness and feasibility of each strategy will occur after all teams assigned the same scenario have presented their proposals. The instructor will then describe what the organizations actually did in these situations.

Scenario 1: Greener Telco The board of directors at a large telephone company wants its executives to make the organization more environmentally friendly by encouraging employees to reduce waste in the workplace. There are also expectations by government and other stakeholders for the company to take this action and be publicly successful. Consequently, the company president wants to significantly reduce the use of paper, refuse, and other waste throughout the company's many widespread offices. Unfortunately, a survey indicates that employees do not value environmental objectives and do not know how to "reduce, reuse, recycle." As the executive responsible for this change, you have been asked to develop a strategy that might bring about meaningful behavioral change toward these environmental goals. What would you do?

Scenario 2: Go Forward Airline   A major airline had experienced a decade of turbulence, including two bouts of bankruptcy protection, 10 executive officers, and morale so low that employees had ripped off company logos from their uniforms out of embarrassment. Service was terrible, and the airplanes rarely arrived or left the terminal on time. Poor performance was costing the airline significant amounts of money in passenger layovers. Managers were paralyzed by anxiety, and many had been with the firm so long that they didn't know how to set strategic goals that worked. One-fifth of all flights were losing money, and the company overall was near financial collapse (just three months from defaulting on payroll obligations). The newly hired CEO and you must get employees to quickly improve operational efficiency and customer service. What actions would you take to bring about these changes?

TEAM EXERCISE 16.4

APPLYING LEWIN'S FORCE FIELD ANALYSIS

Purpose   This exercise is designed to help you understand how to diagnose situations using force field analysis, and to identify strategies to facilitate organizational change.

Instructions   This exercise involves diagnosing the situation described below, identifying the forces for and against change, and recommending strategies to reduce resistance to change. Although the exercise is described as a team activity, the instructor may choose to have it completed individually. Also, the instructor may choose a situation other than the one presented here.

■   *Step 1*—Students will form teams of four or five people, and everyone will read the following situation. (*Note:* If your school currently has a full trimester or a quarter system, then imagine the situation below as though your school currently has a two-semester system.)

> Your college has two semesters (beginning in September and January) as well as a six-week summer session from early May to mid-June. Instructors typically teach their regular load of courses during the two semesters. The summer session is taught mainly by part-time contract faculty, although some full-time faculty teach for extra pay. After carefully reviewing costs, student demand, and competition from other institutions, senior administration has decided that your college should switch to a trimester curriculum. In a trimester system, courses are taught in three equal semesters—September to December, January to April, and May to early August. Faculty with research obligations must teach any two semesters in which their courses are offered; teaching-only faculty teach courses in all three semesters. Senior administration has determined that this change will make more efficient use of college resources, particularly because it will allow the institution to admit more students without building additional classrooms or other facilities. Moreover, market surveys indicate that over 50 percent of current students would continue their studies in the revised summer semester (i.e., the second trimester) and the institution would attract more full-fee students from other countries. The faculty association has not yet had time to state its position on this proposed change.

■   *Step 2*—Using Lewin's force field analysis model (see Exhibit 16.6 on next page), identify the forces that seem to support the

EXHIBIT 16.6 | Force Field Analysis Model

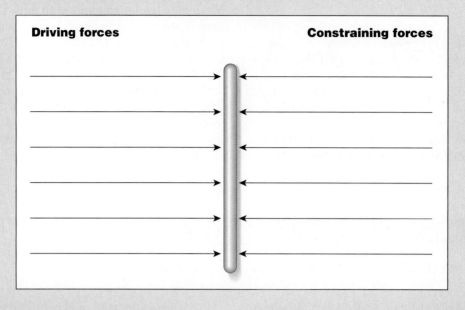

Driving forces   **Constraining forces**

change and the forces that likely oppose the change to a trimester system. Team members should consider all possible sources of support and resistance, not just those stated in the situation on the previous page.

■ *Step 3*—For each source of resistance, identify one or more strategies that would most effectively manage change. Recall from the textbook that the change management strategies include communication, training, employee involvement, stress management, negotiation, and coercion.

■ *Step 4*—The class will discuss each team's results.

S E L F - A S S E S S M E N T   E X E R C I S E   16.5

TOLERANCE OF CHANGE SCALE

Purpose This self-assessment exercise is designed to help you understand how people differ in their tolerance of change.

Instructions Read each statement in the table on the next page and circle the response that best fits your personal belief. Then use the scoring key in Appendix B of this book to calculate your results. This self-assessment exercise is completed alone so that students rate themselves honestly without concerns of social comparison. However, class discussion will focus on the meaning of the concept measured by this scale and its implications for managing change in organizational settings.

Tolerance of change scale

For each statement, indicate your level of agreement by marking the appropriate response on the right.	Strongly agree ▼	Moderately agree ▼	Slightly agree ▼	Neutral ▼	Slightly disagree ▼	Moderately disagree ▼	Strongly disagree ▼
1. An expert who doesn't come up with a definite answer probably doesn't know too much.	☐	☐	☐	☐	☐	☐	☐
2. I would like to live in a foreign country for a while. . . .	☐	☐	☐	☐	☐	☐	☐
3. There is really no such thing as a problem that can't be solved.	☐	☐	☐	☐	☐	☐	☐
4. People who fit their lives into a schedule probably miss most of the joy of living.	☐	☐	☐	☐	☐	☐	☐
5. A good job is one where it is always clear what is to be done and how it is to be done.	☐	☐	☐	☐	☐	☐	☐
6. It is more fun to tackle a complicated problem than to solve a simple one.	☐	☐	☐	☐	☐	☐	☐
7. In the long run, it is possible to get more done by tackling small, simple problems rather than large, complicated ones.	☐	☐	☐	☐	☐	☐	☐
8. Often the most interesting and stimulating people are those who don't mind being different and original.	☐	☐	☐	☐	☐	☐	☐
9. What we are used to is always preferable to what is unfamiliar.	☐	☐	☐	☐	☐	☐	☐
10. People who insist on a yes or no answer just don't know how complicated things really are.	☐	☐	☐	☐	☐	☐	☐
11. A person who leads a life in which few surprises or unexpected happenings arise really has a lot to be grateful for.	☐	☐	☐	☐	☐	☐	☐
12. Many of our most important decisions are based on insufficient information.	☐	☐	☐	☐	☐	☐	☐
13. I like parties where I know most of the people more than ones where all or most of the people are complete strangers.	☐	☐	☐	☐	☐	☐	☐
14. Teachers or supervisors who hand out vague assignments give you a chance to show initiative and originality.	☐	☐	☐	☐	☐	☐	☐
15. The sooner everyone acquires similar values and ideals, the better.	☐	☐	☐	☐	☐	☐	☐
16. A good teacher is one who makes you wonder about your way of looking at things.	☐	☐	☐	☐	☐	☐	☐

Source: Adapted from S. Budner, "Intolerance of Ambiguity as a Personality Variable," *Journal of Personality* 30 (1962), pp. 29–50.

 After studying the preceding material, be sure to check out our website at

www.mhhe.com/mcshane2e

for more in-depth information and interactivities that correspond to this chapter.

17

Organizational Structure and Design

AFTER READING THIS CHAPTER, YOU SHOULD BE ABLE TO:

- Describe the two fundamental requirements of organizational structures.

- Explain why firms can have flatter structures than previously believed.

- Discuss the dynamics of centralization and formalization as organizations get larger and older.

- Contrast functional structures with divisional structures.

- Outline the features and advantages of the matrix structure.

- Describe four features of team-based organizational structures.

- Discuss the merits of the network structure.

- Summarize three contingencies of organizational design.

- Explain how organizational strategy relates to organizational structure.

One of Douglas Daft's first actions as Coca-Cola's latest CEO was to cut half of the staff at the soft drink maker's Atlanta headquarters and move the regional chieftains closer to their local markets. Daft spent most of his career working at Coke's far-flung operations, so he knows how centralized decision making has hampered Coke's ability to serve local needs. For example, Coke was several months behind its rivals in launching a new carbonated tea in northeast China: "We had the formula, we had the flavor, we had done all the taste-testing," complains Daft, "but Atlanta kept saying 'are you sure?'"

Coke executives previously made decisions from Atlanta because they thought Coke had global appeal. But Daft argues that Coke isn't "it" in all cultures. "People don't buy drinks globally," Daft explains. "You can't pander to similarities between people: you have to find the differences." Daft believes it will be easier for Coke executives to anticipate and respond to those differences through a more decentralized organizational structure.

Coca-Cola India CEO Alexander Von Behr has taken Daft's strategy further by radically decentralizing decisions down to six regions representing the country's diverse tastes. Marketing and brand building, which were previously decided nationally, are now controlled by the regional heads. Coke India's 36 bottling operations have also been

Coca-Cola decentralized its worldwide operations so that regional executives would be closer to their customers. *(© AFP/CORBIS)*

organized around these six regions. An area general manager who reports to the regional head has complete profit center responsibility for bottling activities in the region.

"In effect, we have built companies at regional levels and created profit centers with mini-CEOs at area levels," explains Nalin Miglani, Coca-Cola India's vice president of human resources.[1]

omething of a revolution is occurring in how organizations are structured. Driven by global competition and facilitated by information technology, Coca-Cola and many other companies are throwing out the old organizational charts and trying out new designs that they hope will achieve organizational objectives more effectively. **Organizational structure** refers to the division of labor as well as the patterns of coordination, communication, work flow, and formal power that direct organizational activities. An organizational structure reflects the organization's culture and power relationships.[2] Our knowledge of this subject provides the tools to engage in **organizational design,** that is, to create and modify organizational structures.

Organizational structures are frequently used as tools for change. Structures support or inhibit communication and relationships across the organization.[3] They also serve either as sources of resistance to change or supportive mechanisms that refreeze the desired state. They establish new communication patterns and refreeze the change initiatives. For example, Ford Motor Company restructured its many business units so that employees are closer to specific types of customers, such as luxury car buyers (Jaguar, Volvo), services (Hertz, e-commerce), and Ford's mainstream car buyers.[4]

We begin this chapter by considering the two fundamental processes in organizational structure: division of labor and coordination. This discussion is followed by a detailed investigation of the four main elements of organizational structure: span of control, centralization, formalization, and departmentalization. The latter part of this chapter examines the contingencies of organizational design, including organizational size, technology, external environment, and organizational strategy.

organizational structure
The division of labor as well as the patterns of coordination, communication, work flow, and formal power that direct organizational activities.

organizational design
The process of creating and modifying organizational structures.

DIVISION OF LABOR AND COORDINATION

All organizational structures include two fundamental requirements: the division of labor into distinct tasks and the coordination of that labor so that employees are able to accomplish common goals.[5] Organizations are groups of people who work interdependently toward some purpose (see Chapter 1). To accomplish their goals efficiently, these groups typically divide the work into manageable chunks, particularly when there are many different tasks to perform. They also introduce various coordinating mechanisms to ensure that everyone is working effectively toward the same objectives.

Division of Labor

Division of labor refers to the subdivision of work into separate jobs assigned to different people. Subdivided work leads to job specialization, because each job now includes a narrow subset of the tasks necessary to complete the product or service (see Chapter 6). Launching a space shuttle at NASA, for example, requires tens of thousands of specific tasks that are divided among thousands of people. Tasks are also divided vertically, such as having supervisors coordinate work while employees perform the work.

Work is divided into specialized jobs because doing so potentially increases work efficiency.[6] Job incumbents can master their tasks quickly because work cycles are shorter. Less time is wasted changing from one task to another. Training costs are reduced because employees require fewer physical and mental skills to accomplish the assigned work. Finally, job specialization makes it easier to match people with specific aptitudes or skills to the jobs for which they are best suited.

Coordinating Work Activities

As soon as people divide work among themselves, coordinating mechanisms are needed to ensure that everyone works in concert.[7] Every organization—from the two-person corner convenience store to the largest corporate entity—uses one or more of the following coordinating mechanisms: informal communication, formal hierarchy, and standardization (see Exhibit 17.1).

Coordination through Informal Communication   Informal communication is a coordinating mechanism in all organizations.[8] It includes sharing information on mutual tasks as well as forming common mental models so that employees synchronize work activities using the same mental road map.[9] Informal communication permits considerable flexibility because employees transmit a large volume of information through face-to-face communication and other media-rich channels (see Chapter 11). Consequently, informal communication is a vital coordinating mechanism in nonroutine and ambiguous situations.

Coordination through informal communication is easiest in small firms and work units where employees face few communication barriers. Emerging information technologies have further leveraged this coordinating mechanism in large organizations, even where employees are scattered around the globe. Larger organizations can also support informal communication by forming temporary cross-functional teams and moving team members into a common physical area (called *co-locating*). For example, **concurrent engineering** (also called *platform teams*) involves assigning product development to a cross-functional project team consisting of people from marketing, design, manufacturing, customer service, and other areas.[10] These employees are typically

concurrent engineering
Involves assigning product development to a cross-functional project team consisting of people from marketing, design, manufacturing, customer service, and other areas.

EXHIBIT 17.1	Coordinating mechanisms in organizations

Form of coordination	Description	Subtypes
Informal communication	Sharing information on mutual tasks; forming common mental models to synchronize work activities	• Direct communication • Liaison roles • Integrator roles
Formal hierarchy	Assigning legitimate power to individuals, who then use this power to direct work processes and allocate resources	• Direct supervision • Corporate structure
Standardization	Creating routine patterns of behavior or output	• Standardized skills • Standardized processes • Standardized output

Sources: Based on information in D. A. Nadler and M. L. Tushman, *Competing by Design: The Power of Organizational Architecture* (New York: Oxford University Press, 1997), chap. 6; H. Mintzberg, *The Structuring of Organizations* (Englewood Cliffs, NJ: Prentice Hall, 1979), chap. 1; J. Galbraith, *Designing Complex Organizations* (Reading, MA: Addison-Wesley, 1973), pp. 8–19.

W. L. Gore & Associates Inc. avoids hierarchies and formal supervision. Instead, the maker of Gore-Tex fabric and other high-tech products encourages informal communication to coordinate most work activities among its nearly 6,000 employees in 45 locations. It does this by limiting the size of each facility to about 200 people and ensuring that each unit is self-sufficient. "People sometimes get concerned and worried that there is no structure and no organization, and I don't think that is true at all," says a senior Gore associate. Project leaders serve as integrators by coordinating the work of various individuals and work units.[12] Could the coordinating mechanism used at Gore work at a General Motors assembly plant? (*W. L. Gore & Associates, Inc.*)

co-located to improve cross-functional coordination, whereas more formal and less flexible coordinating mechanisms are used when product development occurs through several departments.

Larger organizations also encourage coordination through informal communication by creating *integrator roles.* These people are responsible for coordinating a work process by encouraging employees in each work unit to share information and informally coordinate work activities. Integrators do not have authority over the people involved in that process, so they must rely on persuasion and commitment.[11] Brand managers at Procter & Gamble coordinate work among marketing, production, and design groups. Project leaders at W. L. Gore & Associates and other companies also serve as integrators by encouraging people from various work units to work together on a project.

Coordination through Formal Hierarchy   Informal communication is the most flexible form of coordination, but it can be time-consuming. Consequently, as organizations grow, they develop a second coordinating mechanism in the shape of a formal hierarchy. Hierarchy assigns legitimate power to individuals, who then use this power to direct work processes and allocate resources (see Chapter 12). In other words, work is coordinated through direct supervision.

Any organization with a formal structure coordinates work to some extent through the formal hierarchy. For instance, team leaders at Microsoft coordinate work by ensuring that employees in their group remain on schedule and that their respective tasks are compatible with tasks completed by others in the group. The team leader has direct authority to reassign people to different work activities and to resolve conflicts by dictating solutions. The formal hierarchy also coordinates work among executives through the division of organizational activities. If the organization is divided into geographic areas, the structure gives the heads of those regional groups legitimate power over executives responsible for production, customer service, and other activities in those areas. If the organization is divided into product groups, then the heads of those groups have the right to coordinate work across regions.

The formal hierarchy has traditionally been applauded as the optimal coordinating mechanism for large organizations. Henri Fayol, an early scholar on the subject, argued that organizations are most effective when managers exercise their authority and employees receive orders from only one supervisor. Coordination should occur through the chain of command, that is, up the hierarchy and across to the other work unit.[13] This approach to coordination is practiced at the British conglomerate Rentokil Initial. Rentokil operates like a military organization, with eight levels of management and a strict chain of command. "I don't encourage people to pick up the phone directly to me because that is attempting to bypass their boss," warns Rentokil CEO Sir Clive Thompson.[14]

Coordination through formal hierarchy may have been popular with classic organizational theorists, but it is often a very inefficient coordinating mechanism. Later in this chapter, we will learn that there are limits to how many employees a supervisor can coordinate. Furthermore, the chain of command is rarely as fast or accurate as direct communication between employees. And, as recent scholars have warned, today's educated and individualistic workforce is less tolerant of rigid structures and legitimate power.[15]

Coordination through Standardization   Standardization—creating routine patterns of behavior or output—is the third means of coordination. Many organizations try to improve the quality and consistency of a product or service by standardizing work activities through job descriptions and procedures.[16] Standardization coordinates work requiring routine and simple tasks, but is not effective in complex and ambiguous situations. In these situations,

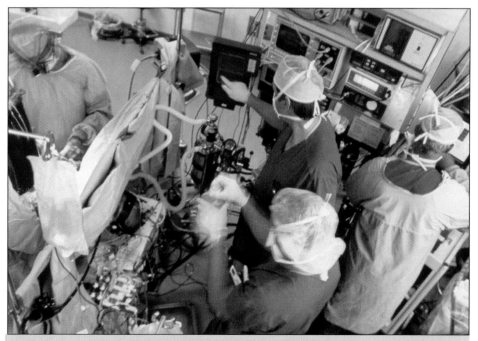

Each member of this medical team at Duke University Medical Center performs specialized jobs requiring special knowledge and skills. To some extent, operating room staff coordinate through informal communication. However, much of the work activity can occur without discussion because team members also coordinate through standardization of skills. Through extensive training, each medical professional has learned precise role behaviors so that his or her task activities are coordinated with the activities of others on the surgical team. What other types of organizations make extensive use of standardization of skills to coordinate work? *(Charles Ledford/Black Star/TimePix)*

companies might coordinate work by standardizing the individual's or team's goals and product or service output (e.g., customer satisfaction, production efficiency). For instance, to coordinate the work of salespeople, companies assign sales targets rather than specific behaviors.

When work activities are too complex to standardize through procedures or goals, companies often coordinate work effort by extensively training employees or hiring people who have learned precise role behaviors from educational programs. This form of coordination is used in hospital operating rooms. Surgeons, nurses, and other operating room professionals coordinate their work more through training than goals or company rules.

Division of labor and coordination of work represent the two fundamental ingredients of all organizations. How work is divided, who makes decisions, which coordinating mechanisms are emphasized, and other issues are related to the four elements of organizational structure.

ELEMENTS OF ORGANIZATIONAL STRUCTURE

Every company is configured in terms of four basic elements of organizational structure. This section introduces three of them: span of control, centralization, and formalization. The fourth element—departmentalization—is presented in the next section.

Span of Control

span of control
The number of people directly reporting to the next level in the hierarchy.

Span of control refers to the number of people reporting directly to the next level in the hierarchy. As we mentioned earlier, Henri Fayol strongly recommended the formal hierarchy as the primary coordinating mechanism. Consequently, he and other theorists of that time prescribed a relatively narrow span of control, typically no more than 20 employees per supervisor and six supervisors per manager. These prescriptions were based on the assumption that managers simply cannot monitor and control closely enough any more subordinates.

Today, we know better. The best-performing manufacturing facilities currently have an average of 31 employees per supervisor—a much wider span of control than past scholars had recommended. Yet these operations plan to stretch this span to an average of 75 employees per supervisor over the next few years.[17]

What's the secret here? Did Fayol and others miscalculate the optimal span of control? The answer is that early scholars thought in terms of Frederick Taylor's scientific management model (see Chapter 6). They believed that employees should do the work, whereas supervisors and other management personnel should monitor employee behavior and make most of the decisions. This division of labor limited the span of control. It is very difficult to directly supervise 75 people. It is much easier to *oversee* 75 subordinates who are grouped into several self-directed work teams. Employees manage themselves, thereby releasing supervisors from the time-consuming tasks of monitoring behavior and making everyone else's decisions.[18]

Vancom Zuid-Limburg, a joint venture that operates a public bus company in The Netherlands, illustrates this point. Vancom has about 40 bus drivers for each manager, whereas other bus companies have 8 drivers per manager. Vancom is able to operate with a much wider span of control because bus drivers

EXHIBIT 18.6

Holland's
hexagon model

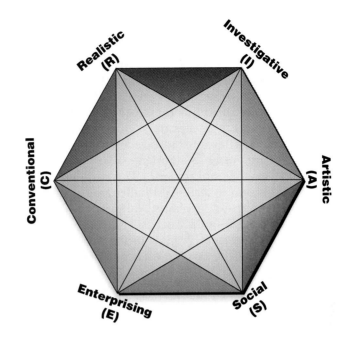

Source: J. L. Holland, *Making Vocational Choices: A Theory of Vocational Personalities and Work Environments,*
2nd ed. (Englewood Cliffs, NJ: Prentice Hall, 1985).

of the Big Five personality dimensions—openness and extroversion (see Chapter 3). This aspect of his theory raises the question of whether Holland's types are incomplete because the three other personality dimensions are not represented. In addition, research has reported that Holland's model should look more like a skewed polygon than a hexagon. In other words, some opposing categories are less opposite than others. Aside from these concerns, research using Holland's concepts has found that job stress is related to a lack of congruence between personality and work environment.[78]

Holland's model of occupational choice has laid the foundation for many career development activities in use today. If you take a vocational interest test, there is a good chance that the results are presented around Holland's six dimensions.[79] The idea that an individual's personality should be congruent with the work environment is now well established in research and practice. Holland's hexagonal model (Exhibit 18.6) helps identify the degree of congruence between an individual's dominant personality type and his or her work environment. Someone who fits mostly in the realistic category would, of course, be most congruent with a realistic environment. The adjacent environments (conventional and investigative) would offer the next best degree of congruence. The lowest congruence occurs for realistic people working in a social environment. Overall, Holland's theory emphasizes the point that effective career development involves finding a good fit between the individual's personality and the work environment. This notion of fit is increasingly important as companies replace the traditional career ladder with more diverse work experiences through lateral career development, which we will discuss next.

Lateral Career Development

lateral career development
The view that career success occurs when employees fulfill their personal needs in different jobs across the organization rather than by moving through the organizational hierarchy.

The traditional career path up the corporate ladder is not as common as it once was. Instead, many firms now define career success in terms of **lateral career development** rather than how many steps employees have taken up the corporate hierarchy. The idea behind lateral career development is that people can fulfill their personal needs in different jobs across the organization. Employees must think about their careers as a lattice rather than a ladder. They must also redefine career success in terms of the variety of challenging work assignments a person completes across the few organizational levels that still remain. "The emphasis would be on discontinuous activity, a continuous series of challenging projects that excites employees and helps them grow," explains Nalin Miglani, vice president (human resources) of Coca-Cola India.[80]

One reason organizations encourage lateral career development is that much of the existing career ladder is still filled with baby boomers who aren't going anywhere.[81] Lateral career development helps employees fulfill their personal needs in different jobs across the organization when promotional opportunities are limited. A second reason for lateral career development is that many organizations have transformed their tall hierarchies into flattened team-based structures. In these structures, employees tend to move to different projects across the organization rather than to higher management levels.

Consider Debbie McNamara's first five years at Lend Lease Corporation, the global real estate development and financial services company. The 26-year-old's first job was working with financial advisors who sell Lend Lease products. A year later, she became project manager to simplify business processes in the fund management division's call center group. When that project was near completion, McNamara was transferred to the United Kingdom, where she helped retailers open their businesses at Lend Lease's Bluewater development. McNamara's career path across the organization is typical at Lend Lease, because the company wants "careening careers" where employees continually acquire new competencies.[82]

A third reason for the increasing emphasis on lateral career development is that it is consistent with the shifting emphasis from job status to competencies. Promotions through the traditional corporate ladder tend to reinforce job status, whereas lateral career development helps people learn new competencies and remain competitive in the labor market. This emphasis on competencies is also aligned with the trend toward employability rather than job security. Employees must anticipate future demand for skills and knowledge, and manage their careers accordingly by seeking out work opportunities that develop those competencies.

Consider IBM in the United States, Glaxo Wellcome in the United Kingdom, Volkswagen in Germany, and Michelin in France. Each of these firms has developed fewer and wider pay grades to reflect the fewer promotional opportunities in the organization (see Chapter 6).[83] Instead, these companies advise employees to broaden their knowledge and experience through lateral career paths. The result is a more flexible workforce with multiple skills.

Encouraging Lateral Career Development   Many people have difficulty adjusting to lateral career development. Baby boomers, in particular, have learned to praise the linear career concept in which career success is defined in terms of how high you go up the corporate hierarchy. Employees are also reluctant to engage in lateral career development because it involves the risk of leaving their longtime jobs and departments. Moreover, they may face interference from supervisors who don't want to see their prized staff move elsewhere.

To encourage lateral career development, companies need to regularly communicate new job openings and help employees with career self-assessments. For example, Starbucks Coffee Company posts all job openings every week. Many firms also have virtual career centers where employees can assess their skills online, determine how those skills fit in the organization, and learn how they can gain the skills needed to meet their career goals. Raychem offers career seminars that encourage employees to think of themselves as self-employed and to explore many career options. The Menlo Park, California, electronics company also has a career development center where employees explore their potential through self-assessments, career workshops, and referrals to career resources. Employees compare their current competencies with current and future market demands.[84]

Boundaryless Careers

Nearly 50 years ago, in his best-selling book *Organization Man,* William H. Whyte painted a satirical picture of American white-collar career success in terms of secure employment with slow, steady promotions through several professional and management layers. These people devoted their entire lives to the same company, slowly working their way up the corporate ladder.[85]

boundaryless career

The idea that careers operate across company and industry boundaries rather than just within a single organizational hierarchy.

Some people still follow this structured model of career development, but most do not. Instead, there is a growing trend toward the **boundaryless career**—the idea that careers operate across company and industry boundaries rather than just within a single organizational hierarchy.[86] It is the view that careers unfold throughout one's life, not necessarily throughout one company. Dan Schmitt, described in the opening vignette in this chapter, developed his competencies in the entertainment events services business by job-hopping rather than waiting for the next great challenge within one organization. In fact, the average employee has 12 to 15 jobs over the course of a career, including between 5 and 7 jobs by age 30.[87]

At the same time, career experts warn that too much job-hopping could undermine the individual's career. The challenge is to find the right balance between career development within and between organizations. "Employers don't want to employ job-hoppers, but if they can see that you're increasing your repertoire of skills each time then it's not so bad," says career coach Paula Stenberg. "But you do have to be careful not to be too ruthless or brash about it."[88]

Reasons Why People Adopt Boundaryless Careers   Boundaryless careers are more common today than 10 years ago, but this trend does not imply that employees enjoy changing jobs. On the contrary, by a two-to-one margin, high-tech job-hoppers would rather stay with one employer for 20 years than have five jobs for 4 years each.[89] This behavior suggests that the boundaryless career is more a function of necessity than motivation. The trend toward boundaryless careers accelerated with massive corporate downsizing over the past decade.[90] These layoffs and early retirements forced people to realign their careers with other organizations. From this painful experience, many people developed the attitude that it is better to accept career opportunities as they come along rather than remain loyal to one employer.

A related explanation for the rise in boundaryless careers is that many psychological contracts have shifted from job security to employability. As we mentioned earlier in this chapter, the new deal rewards people who take control of their own career development.[91] But moving away from a loyalty-based contract also weakens the internal labor market. Thus, employees are more likely to seek career development opportunities outside the organization.

What can organizations do about boundaryless careers and the trend toward job-hopping? One obvious solution is to provide enough career opportunities within the organization to make external job-hopping unnecessary. Although this approach may seem impossible in smaller firms, we must remember that career opportunities can be created through new projects and challenges, not just existing positions elsewhere in the company.

In general, corporate leaders need to reexamine the drivers of organizational loyalty that were identified in Chapter 4. Employees are more likely to keep their careers in-house when they have positive and equitable work experiences, a reasonable level of job security, continual understanding of organizational activities, involvement in organizational decisions, and a high level of trust in corporate leaders and co-workers.

Finally, we need to recognize that it is natural and desirable for some employees to leave for better career opportunities elsewhere. Connections 18.3 describes how many employers are adapting to the emerging reality of boundaryless careers by welcoming back "boomerangers" who have left for opportunities elsewhere. In this wired world, where employees quickly gain information about career opportunities through Monster.com and other websites, organizations need to recognize the benefits of rehiring former employees versus losing them forever.

CAREER DEVELOPMENT: RULES FOR THE ROAD AHEAD

Whether you are just starting your career or are already well along the road, the following ideas should help you improve both your prospects and long-term career satisfaction. These points do not cover everything you need to remember about developing your career. Instead, they highlight some of the key strategies that will help you along the road ahead.

Understand Your Needs and Values

Career development begins with understanding your personal needs and values.[92] "If you're in the wrong career, it doesn't matter if the economy is good or bad, you're still unhappy," advises Atlanta career consultant Deborah R. Brown.[93]

How do you know what type of career is most fulfilling for you? To answer this question, you need to complete self-assessments of your vocational interests and recount experiences that you enjoyed. Holland's occupational choice model, presented earlier in this chapter, helps align your personality and interests with the work environment. It may also be useful to get feedback from others regarding activities that they notice you like or dislike. This approach

Boundaryless Careers Boomerang Back

Lured by the dot-com excitement and potential fortunes, Michael Czyz quit his job at DiamondCluster International and joined TheSauce.com, an Internet marketplace for restaurant vendors. But when TheSauce.com ran out of money less than a year later, Czyz was looking for another job. Fortunately, he found a good employment opportunity—back at DiamondCluster International.

DiamondCluster International and many other companies are opening their doors to boomerangers—former employees who want to come back. "It used to be you couldn't really go home again—you betrayed your company . . . [by] leaving for a better opportunity," says John Challenger, CEO of Chicago placement firm Challenger, Gray and Christmas. "Many companies are [now] welcoming people back with open arms, or they are at least willing to talk to them."

One survey reported that 90 percent of employers in Fortune 1000 companies would consider rehiring a former employee who left their firm in good standing. Corporate leaders reason that boomerangers have lower hiring costs than other job applicants because they adjust more easily to their former work environment and their track record is already known. Moreover, former employees bring additional knowledge to the organization from their experience.

Some employers are bending over backward to bring their wayward staff back into the fold. When discount stockbroker Charles Schwab reluctantly laid off 2,100 staff, it offered a $7,500 rehiring bonus to anyone who returned within 18 months. Consulting firms Accenture and PricewaterhouseCoopers have established alumni lists and actively keep track of former employees. "We are very aggressively seeking them out," says

Michael Czyz tried out a boundaryless career that boomeranged him back to his former employer, Diamond-Cluster International. *(Ellyn Domke. Reprinted with special permission from the Chicago Sun-Times, Inc. © 2001)*

a PricewaterhouseCoopers partner. Accenture has rehired at least 200 boomerangers, particularly the entrepreneurial types who left for dot-com start-ups. "It's a rich source of talent for us," says Steve Colbourn, an industry recruiting director for Accenture. "We would certainly welcome them back."

Sources: K. Clark, "You're Laid Off! Kind Of," *U.S. News & World Report,* July 2, 2001; M. Duvall, "You Look Like You Need a Rest," *Interactive Week,* June 21, 2001; D. Newbart, "Dot-Boomerang Time," *Chicago Sun-Times,* March 5, 2001, p. 46; "Welcome Back!" *PR Newswire,* June 13, 2000.

applies the Johari Window model described in Chapter 3, whereby you learn more about yourself through information presented by close associates.

Understand Your Competencies

Knowing yourself also involves knowing what you are capable of doing.[94] In Chapter 2, we learned that each of us has a set of aptitudes—natural talents that help us learn specific tasks quickly and perform them well. Although we might visualize our future as an engineering wizard or president of the United States, we need to take our abilities into account. The more careers are aligned with our personal competencies, the more we develop a strong sense of self-efficacy—the can-do attitude that further empowers our career.

The recent economic downturn put a damper on job prospects for many business graduates, but Andrew Wang is philosophical. "It's not fun, but at least it forces you to figure out what it is you really want to do," says the graduating MBA student at UCLA's Anderson School of Management. So, rather than jumping into a dot-com start-up, Wang is thinking about joining a company more aligned with his personal interests. "I've had this lifelong interest in cycling, so I'm now looking at the recreational industry for product-management positions," he says. "I've learned [they] don't pay as well, but you're doing something that you like."[96] How can you tell when a particular career path fulfills your personal needs? *(Robert Harbison,* © The Christian Science Monitor*)*

Self-assessments, performance results, and constructive feedback from friends can help us identify our capabilities. Also, keep in mind that employers look beyond technical skills to generic competencies, such as communication, problem solving, and interpersonal relations. Indeed, some recruiters say they pay more attention to these foundations and assume employees will develop job-specific skills at work.

Set Career Goals

Soon after Mary Morse joined Autodesk as a software engineer, the manager above her immediate supervisor asked Morse to draw up a list of short-term and long-term career goals. Then the manager at the California software firm provided Morse with a list of training courses, both inside and outside the company, that would help her meet those career objectives. The manager also spoke to Morse's immediate supervisor to ensure she would have time to complete those courses.[95]

Mary Morse was lucky. She joined an organization that helps employees identify and achieve their career goals. But we usually can't count on others to guide our career development. We need to set our own goals to realize our potential and ultimately fulfill our needs. Goal setting is a powerful way to motivate and achieve results, and this applies as much to careers as to any other activity. Career goals are benchmarks against which we evaluate our progress and identify strategies to develop our competencies.

Career consultant Barbara Moses emphasizes that career goal setting is a fundamental element in becoming a "career activist." It involves writing your own script rather than waiting for someone to write it for you, being vigilant by identifying and preparing for opportunities, and becoming an independent agent by separating your self-identity from your job title, your organization, or what other people think you should be.[97]

Maintain Networks

As people develop boundaryless careers, their career opportunities depend more on trusting relationships than documented information about their performance. For example, a survey by Drake Beam Morin revealed that 64 percent of the 7,435 people in the placement firm's executive career transition programs found new employment through networking. As one successful job hunter advises: "Be prepared, know your story, and network, network, network."[98]

Several research studies have confirmed that networking is an increasingly important feature of career development. In particular, people with large, nonredundant networks tend to be more successful job seekers and receive greater organizational rewards. One important piece of advice is to network in areas beyond your current sphere of work. Careers change much more than in the past, so you need to establish connections to other fields where you may someday find yourself.[99]

Get a Mentor

So far, our discussion has emphasized self-leadership in career development (see Chapter 6). We need to set our own goals, motivate ourselves for career advancement, and visualize where we want to go. But career development also benefits from the help of others. Mentoring involves learning the ropes of organizational life from a senior person within the company (see Chapter 12.) Mentors give protégés more visible and meaningful work opportunities, but they also provide career guidance. You might think of them as career coaches because they provide ongoing advice and feedback.[100]

Mentoring is so important at McKinsey & Company that several offices of the management consulting firm regularly ask all associates to identify which partners they view as mentors. The first of these surveys was a shock because each partner was identified by fewer than five associates as a mentor. In other words, McKinsey partners provided less mentoring than they had assumed. This survey was a wake-up call for McKinsey's partners, who now spend significantly more time and effort mentoring junior staff at the consulting firm.[101]

CAREERS AND ORGANIZATIONAL BEHAVIOR

Wherever your career leads, you will invariably remain inside or close to those abstract constructs called organizations. As a result, the topics discussed throughout this book will continually relate to your career success and personal fulfillment. You will discover how organizational behavior topics are interrelated. It is difficult to discuss motivation without referring to personality. We can't understand communication without noting power and politics. Leadership embraces change. Change embraces knowledge management. And as you apply organizational behavior throughout your career, remember that organizations are the people in them. They are human entities—full of life, sometimes fragile, always exciting.

CHAPTER SUMMARY

The psychological contract is a set of perceived mutual obligations about the employer's and employee's exchange relationship. Some contracts are transactional, whereas others are more relational. Trust is an important factor in the employment relationship. Three levels of trust are calculus-based, knowledge-based, and identification-based. Knowledge-based and identification-based trust are stronger and more flexible than calculus-based trust.

One trend in employment relationships is the shift from job security to employability. This "new deal" psychological contract says that employees must take responsibility for their own careers by continually developing new competencies for future work opportunities within and beyond the organization. The other trend is the increase in contingent work—any job in which the individual does not have an explicit or implicit contract for long-term employment or in which the minimum hours of work can vary in a nonsystematic way. Contingent work is growing because companies want more flexibility and lower payroll costs, and many are outsourcing noncore work activities.

Organizational socialization is the process by which individuals learn the values, expected behaviors, and social knowledge necessary to assume their roles in the organization. It is a learning process because newcomers need to acquire information about performance proficiency, people, politics, language, organizational goals and values, and history. Socialization is also a process of change as newcomers develop new work roles, adopt new team norms, and practice new behaviors.

Employees typically pass through three socialization stages. Preemployment socialization occurs before the first day of work and includes conflicts between the organization's and applicant's needs to collect information and attract the other party. Encounter begins on the first day and typically involves adjusting to reality shock. Role management involves resolving work–nonwork conflicts and settling in to the workplace. To manage the socialization process, organizations should introduce realistic job previews (RJPs) and recognize the value of socialization agents in the process. RJPs give job applicants a realistic balance of positive and negative information about the job and work context. Socialization agents provide information and social support during the socialization process.

A career is a sequence of work-related experiences in which people participate over the span of their working lives. Holland's theory of occupational choice states that the degree of congruence between an individual's personality traits and the work environment affects career performance, satisfaction, and longevity. The theory includes six personality types and work environments: realistic, investigative, artistic, social, enterprising, and conventional. Individuals are differentiated if they fit mainly in one of these categories, and they are consistent if they relate to adjacent rather than opposite types.

Companies are encouraging lateral career development rather than the climb up the traditional corporate ladder, because there are fewer steps on the corporate ladder, baby boomers block upward mobility of employees farther down the hierarchy, and lateral career development is consistent with the shifting emphasis from job status to competencies.

Boundaryless careers operate across company and industry boundaries. They are becoming more common as a result of corporate downsizing and the shift from job security to employability. Five strategies that assist personal career development are the following: Understand your needs and values, understand your competencies, set career goals, maintain networks, and get a mentor.

KEY TERMS

boundaryless career, p. 561

career, p. 556

contingent work, p. 546

lateral career development, p. 560

organizational socialization, p. 549

psychological contract, p. 540

realistic job preview (RJP), p. 554

reality shock, p. 552

DISCUSSION QUESTIONS

1. Jack Santoni works on the field production crew at Gusher Drilling Company. When he joined the company five years ago, the supervisor who hired him said Jack could use the company's old pickup truck on weekends. Now the company plans to sell the truck and won't replace it, leaving Jack without a vehicle on the weekends. Discuss the implications of this action on Jack's psychological contract with Gusher Drilling Company.

2. Many organizations are moving toward a psychological contract based on employability. What does this trend mean, and how does a contract based on employability differ from the psychological contract that most employees believed in a few decades ago? Do you think this employability-based contract will continue, or will it revert to a security-based contract in the future?

3. WestFoods, a major food company, has just decided that its core competency is in food processing, so it will outsource most of its support services (human resources, information systems). This decision will result in a large contingent workforce in these functions. What issues should WestFoods consider before moving to a contingent workforce?

4. The textbook states that organizational socialization is a process of learning and of change. What does this mean, and how do organizations facilitate both learning and change for new employees?

5. After three months on the job, you feel that the company has violated the psychological contract. The job is not as exciting as you originally expected, and your current boss is no better than the supervisor in your previous job. The people

who interviewed you are concerned about your feelings, but say that they didn't misrepresent either the job or the fact that some supervisors are not as good as others. Explain how your perceived psychological contract may have been distorted during preemployment socialization.

6. Progressive, Inc., ExtendMedia, and other organizations rely on current employees to socialize new recruits. What are the advantages of relying on this type of socialization agent? What problems can you foresee (or you have personally experienced) with co-worker socialization practices?

7. You have just completed a vocational test which concludes that you have an enterprising personality, along with fairly high levels of the artistic and investigative types in Holland's model. Assuming that this vocational test is accurate, what are its implications for your career?

8. Although companies encourage lateral career development, many baby boom–generation employees still prefer the opportunity to climb the corporate ladder. Do you think that these employees are correct in thinking that "real" career development occurs only when you are promoted? Will Generation-X and Generation-Y employees develop a similar attachment to promotions later in their careers?

CASE STUDY 18.1

QUANTOR CORPORATION'S CONTINGENT WORKFORCE POLICY

Three years ago, Quantor Corporation, a large manufacturer of computer printers and other peripherals, established a task force to determine the most appropriate use of contingent workers throughout the company. The company had started to rely on contract, part-time, and temporary help agency people to fill temporary jobs. At the time, these workers represented less than 1 percent of Quantor's workforce, and the company wanted to review these practices to ensure consistency and effectiveness.

After reviewing current ad hoc practices, the task force concluded that Quantor needed contingent workers when demand for the company's products expanded rapidly or a new product was launched. Quantor needed this workforce flexibility because of uncertain production demand beyond the short term. At the same time, the task force warned that treating contingent workers the same as permanent employees would undermine the benefits of flexibility, create false hopes of permanent employment among contingent workers, and possibly create feelings of inequity between the two groups. Thus, policies were introduced that treated contingent workers differently from permanent employees.

Quantor's task force established two contingent worker categories: on-call and on-contract. On-call people are employed by Quantor as part-time staff. They work a full day, but only up to two-thirds of the hours of a full-time permanent employee. Their managers can alter their work schedules at will to suit production demands. On-contract people are employed full-time by Quantor for a fixed period, usually six months. Their contract may be renewed up to three times for a maximum employment of two years.

On-call and on-contract employees receive no employee benefits other than the government-mandated minimum vacation and holiday pay. Benefits therefore represent approximately 10 percent of their total pay, compared with nearly 40 percent for permanent employees. However, contingent workers earn the midpoint of the pay grade for their job group, which represents 15 percent above the entry rate. This rate is paid even when the contingent worker lacks experience in the job.

Quantor's Contingent Workforce Problems

Three years after the initiation of Quantor's task force recommendations, the contingent workforce policy was in trouble. Current practices succeeded in creating a more flexible workforce, and there was some evidence that using contingent workers increased profitability. However, these practices created unanticipated problems that became apparent as the percentage of contingent workers increased.

One problem was that few people wanted only contract employment. Most were seeking full-time permanent work and were using their contingent position as a stepping-stone to those jobs at Quantor. The result was that many contract workers remained for the entire two-year maximum period and beyond. The company was reluctant to apply the task force's recommendation of not renewing contracts beyond two years because of the perceived arbitrariness of this action as well as loss of knowledge to the organization. Several contract staff members asked the company for an employee-paid benefit package (benefits are mainly employer-paid for permanent employees). However, Quantor rejected this request because it would add further permanence to their employment relationship.

Quantor's managers also began to complain about the company policy that contingent workers could not be offered permanent employment. They appreciated the opportunity to select permanent employees based on observations of their performance in on-contract or on-call positions. Quantor's task force had warned against this practice because it might create inequities and raise false expectations about the likelihood of permanent employment. Managers acknowledged this risk, but the inability to permanently hire good contract staff was frustrating to them.

The third problem was that Quantor's treatment of contingent workers was incompatible with its organizational culture. Quantor had a strong culture based on the philosophy of employee well-being. The company had a generous benefits package, supportive leadership, and a belief system that made employees a top priority in corporate decisions. The company did not treat contingent workers in a way that was consistent with this philosophy. Yet if Quantor treated contingent workers the same as permanent staff members, then flexibility would be lost. For example, managers would continue renewing contract workers even when their employment was not essential and would be reluctant to schedule on-call people at awkward times.

Quantor's team orientation was also incompatible with its use of contingent workers. Permanent staff members frequently gathered to discuss organizational and group decisions. Contingent workers were not invited to these team activities because they might be working at Quantor for only a few more months. This barrier created some awkward moments for managers as contingent workers continued working while permanent employees went to meetings and team sessions.

As these problems intensified, senior management formed another task force to reexamine Quantor's contingent workforce policy. The company needed contingent workers, but it was increasingly apparent that the current practices were not working.

Discussion Questions

1. Identify the problems that Quantor experienced with its contingent workforce practices. Also identify other possible contingent workforce problems that have not been explicitly mentioned in this case.

2. Discuss the problems with contingent workers at Quantor in terms of the psychological contract and organizational commitment.

3. What alternative strategies might allow Quantor to include a contingent workforce with fewer problems?

Source: This case was prepared by Steven L. McShane based on information about an actual experience. The company name and some details have been altered.

C A S E   S T U D Y   **18.2**

ANNE MULCAHY: SHE'S HERE TO FIX THE XEROX

BusinessWeek Anne M. Mulcahy may not know how to repair a copier, but Xerox Corporation's board of directors evidently thinks she knows how to fix the company. After Xerox reported its first quarterly loss in a decade and a half, the board appointed Mulcahy to the post of chief executive. That job marks the peak of a very successful career at Xerox. After earning a degree in English and journalism, Mulcahy joined Xerox as a sales representative, then worked her way up through the company's retail division, and held a job as vice president for human resources. The directors considered Mulcahy a decisive leader and charged her with restoring the company's profitability.

This *Business Week* case study describes Mulcahy's career at Xerox and her objectives as the company's CEO. Those objectives will require changes in Xerox's relationships with its employees. Read through this *Business Week* case study at www.mhhe.com/mcshane2e and prepare for the discussion questions below.

1. How do Anne Mulcahy's objectives to eliminate unprofitable operations and focus more on business solutions change the psychological contract at Xerox?

2. Assuming Xerox succeeds in shifting from a focus on selling "boxes" to selling "solutions," how does this new focus change the work environment characteristics at Xerox and the career types needed? Refer to the categories in Exhibit 18.5, detailing John Holland's theory of occupational choice.

Source: P. L. Moore, "Anne Mulcahy: She's Here to Fix the Xerox," *Business Week,* August 6, 2001.

TEAM EXERCISE 18.3

ORGANIZATIONAL SOCIALIZATION DIAGNOSTIC EXERCISE

Purpose This exercise is designed to help students understand the socialization strategies that organizations should use for new employees, and learn about the impediments to forming an accurate psychological contract.

Instructions The instructor will form teams (typically of four or five people). Each team will follow these steps:

■ *Step 1*—Each team member will describe one particularly memorable positive or negative experience encountered when entering an organization. (Students with limited organizational experience may describe entry to school.) Entry to the organization would include any interaction with the company up to, including, and a short while after the first day of work. The incident might describe how the individual was greeted during the first day of work, how the company kept him or her informed before the first day of work, how the company did (or didn't) tell the person about negative aspects of the work or job context, and so forth. The team will consider all these experiences, but will pick the most interesting one for description in class.

■ *Step 2*—On the basis of these experiences, the team will develop a list of strategies that companies should use to improve the organizational entry process. Some experiences will reflect effective management of this process. Other experiences will indicate what companies have done ineffectively, so the team must identify strategies to avoid those problems.

■ *Step 3*—In class, one person from each team will describe his or her organizational entry experience. (This person is chosen in Step 1.) The team will explain what the company did well or poorly with respect to that incident. After each team has presented one anecdote, the class will discuss other ideas from the team discussion.

TEAM EXERCISE 18.4

TRUTH IN ADVERTISING

Purpose This team exercise is designed to help you diagnose the degree to which recruitment advertisements and brochures provide realistic previews of the job and/or organization.

Materials The instructor will bring to class either recruiting brochures or newspaper advertisements.

Instructions The instructor will place students into teams and give them copies of recruiting brochures and/or advertisements. The instructor might assign one lengthy brochure; alternatively, several newspaper advertisements may be assigned. All teams should receive the same materials so that everyone is familiar with the items and results can be compared. Teams will evaluate the recruiting material(s) and answer the questions at right for each item:

1. What information in the text of this brochure/advertisement identifies conditions or activities in this organization or job that some applicants may not like?
2. If there are photographs or images of people at work, do they show only positive conditions, or do any show conditions or events that some applicants may not like?
3. After reading this item, would you say that it provides a realistic preview of the job and/or organization?

SELF-ASSESSMENT EXERCISE 18.5

MATCHING HOLLAND'S CAREER TYPES

Purpose This self-assessment exercise is designed to help you understand Holland's career types.

Instructions Holland's theory identifies six types of work environments. A brief description of each type appears below. Although few jobs fit purely into a single category, all have a dominant work environment type. In the table below, for each occupation, circle the letter representing the Holland type that you believe *best* fits that occupation's work environment.

Descriptions of Holland's six work environments

R Realistic—Work involves using hands, machines, or tools; focus on tangible results

I Investigative—Work involves discovering, collecting, and analyzing; focus on solving problems

A Artistic—Work involves creation of new products or ideas, typically in an unstructured setting

S Social—Work involves serving or helping others; focus on working in teams

E Enterprising—Work involves leading others; focus on achieving goals through others in a results-oriented setting

C Conventional —Work involves systematic manipulation of data or information

Occupation	Holland category						Occupation	Holland category					
Actuary	R	I	A	S	E	C	Mathematics teacher	R	I	A	S	E	C
Archeologist	R	I	A	S	E	C	Medical illustrator	R	I	A	S	E	C
Buyer	R	I	A	S	E	C	Minister/priest/rabbi	R	I	A	S	E	C
Computer operator	R	I	A	S	E	C	Pediatrician	R	I	A	S	E	C
Corporate executive	R	I	A	S	E	C	Pharmacist	R	I	A	S	E	C
Corporate trainer	R	I	A	S	E	C	Pilot	R	I	A	S	E	C
Dietitian	R	I	A	S	E	C	Production manager	R	I	A	S	E	C
Economist	R	I	A	S	E	C	Professional athlete	R	I	A	S	E	C
Elementary school teacher	R	I	A	S	E	C	Public relations director	R	I	A	S	E	C
Fashion model	R	I	A	S	E	C	Recreation leader	R	I	A	S	E	C
Firefighter	R	I	A	S	E	C	School administrator	R	I	A	S	E	C
Foreign exchange trader	R	I	A	S	E	C	Sculptor	R	I	A	S	E	C
Jeweler	R	I	A	S	E	C	Tax auditor	R	I	A	S	E	C
Life insurance agent	R	I	A	S	E	C	Veterinarian	R	I	A	S	E	C
Lobbyist	R	I	A	S	E	C	Wine maker	R	I	A	S	E	C

Interpreting Your Score When everyone is finished, the instructor will provide the correct answers. Add up the number of occupations that you matched correctly to determine your score. Then use your score to find out how well you understand Holland's career types.

Number Correct	Interpretation
26–30	Excellent understanding of Holland's career types
21–25	Good understanding of Holland's career types
16–20	Fair understanding of Holland's career types
11–15	Need to look more closely at Holland's descriptions
<11	Career counseling might not be your calling!

After studying the preceding material, be sure to check out our website at

www.mhhe.com/mcshane2e

for more in-depth information and interactivities that correspond to this chapter.

CASE 1   Arctic Mining Consultants

Tom Parker enjoyed working outdoors. At various times in the past, he worked as a ranch hand, high steel rigger, headstone installer, prospector, and geological field technician. Now 43, Parker is a geological field technician and field coordinator with Arctic Mining Consultants. He has specialized knowledge and experience in all nontechnical aspects of mineral exploration, including claim staking, line cutting and grid installation, soil sampling, prospecting, and trenching. He is responsible for hiring, training, and supervising field assistants for all of Arctic Mining Consultants' programs. Field assistants are paid a fairly low daily wage (no matter how long they work, which may be up to 12 hours or more) and are provided meals and accommodations. Many of the programs are operated by a project manager who reports to Parker.

Parker sometimes acts as a project manager, as he did on a job that involved staking 15 claims near Eagle Lake, Alaska. He selected John Talbot, Greg Boyce, and Brian Millar, all of whom had previously worked with Parker, as the field assistants. To stake a claim, the project team

marks a line with flagging tape and blazes along the perimeter of the claim, cutting a claim post every 500 yards (called a length). The 15 claims would require almost 60 miles of line. Parker had budgeted seven days (plus mobilization and demobilization) to complete the job. This schedule meant that each of the four stakers (Parker, Talbot, Boyce, and Millar) would have to complete a little over seven lengths each day. The following is a chronology of the project.

Day 1

The Arctic Mining Consultants crew assembled in the morning and drove to Eagle Lake, from where they were flown by helicopter to the claim site. On arrival, they set up tents at the edge of the area to be staked and agreed on a schedule for cooking duties. After supper, they pulled out the maps and discussed the job—how long it would take, the order in which the areas were to be staked, possible helicopter landing spots, and areas that might be more difficult to stake.

Parker pointed out that with only a week to complete the job, everyone would have to average seven and a half lengths per day. "I know that is a lot," he said, "but you've all staked claims before and I'm confident that each of you is capable of it. And it's only for a week. If we get the job done in time, there's a $300 bonus for each man." Two hours later, Parker and his crew members had developed what seemed to be a workable plan.

Day 2

Millar completed six lengths; Boyce, six lengths; Talbot, eight; and Parker, eight. Parker was not pleased with Millar's or Boyce's production. However, he didn't make an issue of it, thinking that they would develop their rhythm quickly.

Day 3

Millar completed five and a half lengths; Boyce, four; and Talbot, seven. Parker, who was nearly twice as old as the other three, completed eight lengths. He also had enough time remaining to walk over and check the quality of stakes that Millar and Boyce had completed, then walk back to his own area for helicopter pickup back to the tent site.

That night Parker exploded with anger. "I thought I told you that I wanted seven and a half lengths a day!" he shouted at Boyce and Millar. Boyce said that he was slowed down by unusually thick underbrush in his assigned area. Millar said that he had done his best and would try to pick up the pace. Parker did not mention that he had inspected their work. He explained that, as far as he was concerned, the field assistants were supposed to finish their assigned area for the day, no matter what.

Talbot, who was sharing a tent with Parker, talked to him later. "I think that you're being a bit hard on them, you know. I know that it has been more by luck than anything else that I've been able to do my quota. Yesterday I had only five lengths done after the first seven hours, and there was only an hour before I was supposed to be picked up. Then I hit a patch of really open bush and was able to do three lengths in 70 minutes. Why don't I take Millar's area tomorrow and he can have mine? Maybe that will help."

"Conditions are the same in all the areas," replied Parker, rejecting Talbot's suggestion. "Millar just has to try harder."

Day 4

Millar did seven lengths, and Boyce completed six and a half. When they reported their production that evening, Parker grunted uncommunicatively. Parker and Talbot did eight lengths each.

Day 5

Millar completed six lengths; Boyce, six; Talbot, seven and a half; and Parker, eight. Once again Parker blew up, but he concentrated his diatribe on Millar. "Why don't you do what you say you are going to do? You know that you have to do seven and a half lengths a day. We went over that when we first got here, so why don't you do it? If you aren't willing to do the job, then you never should have taken it in the first place!"

Millar replied by saying that he was doing his best, that he hadn't even stopped for lunch, and that he didn't know how he could possibly do any better. Parker launched into him again: "You have to work harder! If you put enough effort into it, you will get the area done!"

Later Millar commented to Boyce, "I hate getting dumped on all the time! I'd quit if it didn't mean that I'd have to walk 50 miles to the highway. And besides, I need the bonus money. Why doesn't he pick on you? You don't get any more done than I do; in fact, you usually do less. Maybe if you did a bit more he wouldn't be so bothered about me."

"I work only as hard as I have to," Boyce replied.

Day 6

Millar raced through breakfast, was the first one to be dropped off by the helicopter, and arranged to be the last one picked up. That evening the production figures were Millar, eight and a quarter lengths; Boyce, seven; and Talbot and Parker, eight each. Parker remained silent when the field assistants reported their performance for the day.

Day 7

Millar was again the first out and last in. That night, he collapsed in an exhausted heap at the table, too tired to eat. After a few moments, he announced in an abject tone, "Six lengths. I worked like a dog all day and I got only a lousy six lengths!" Boyce completed five lengths; Talbot, seven; and Parker, seven and a quarter.

Parker was furious. "That means we have to do a total of 34 lengths tomorrow if we are to finish this job on time!" With his eyes directed at Millar, he added: "Why is it that you never finish the job? Don't you realize that you are part of a team, and that you are letting the rest of the team down? I've been checking your lines, and you're doing too much blazing and wasting too much time making picture-perfect claim posts! If you worked smarter, you'd get a lot more done!"

Day 8

Parker cooked breakfast in the dark. The helicopter drop-offs began as soon as morning light appeared on the horizon. Parker instructed each assistant to complete eight lengths and, if they finished early, to help the others. Parker said that he would finish the other 10 lengths. Helicopter pickups were arranged for one hour before dark.

By noon, after working as hard as he could, Millar had completed only three lengths. "Why bother," he thought to himself, "I'll never be able to do another five lengths before the helicopter comes, and I'll catch the same amount of abuse from Parker for doing six lengths as for seven and a half." So he sat down and had lunch and a rest. "Boyce won't finish his eight lengths either, so even if I did finish mine, I still wouldn't get the bonus. At least I'll get one more day's pay this way."

That night, Parker was livid when Millar reported that he had completed five and a half lengths. Parker had done ten and a quarter lengths, and Talbot had completed eight. Boyce proudly announced that he finished seven and a half lengths, but sheepishly added that Talbot had helped him with some of it. All that remained were the two and a half lengths that Millar had not completed.

The job was finished the next morning, and the crew was demobilized. Millar has never worked for Arctic Mining Consultants again, despite being offered work several times by Parker. Boyce sometimes does staking for Arctic, and Talbot works full-time with the company.

CASE 2   A Window on Life

For Gilbert LaCrosse, there is nothing quite as beautiful as a handcrafted wood-framed window. LaCrosse's passion for windows goes back to his youth in Eau Claire, Wisconsin, where he learned how to make residential windows from an elderly carpenter. He learned about the characteristics of good wood, the best tools to use, and how to choose the best glass from local suppliers. LaCrosse apprenticed with the carpenter in his small workshop and, when the carpenter retired, was given the opportunity to operate the business himself.

LaCrosse hired his own apprentice as he built up business in the local area. His small operation soon expanded as the quality of windows built by LaCrosse Industries Ltd. became better known. Within eight years, the company employed nearly 25 people, and the business had moved to larger facilities to accommodate the increased demand throughout Wisconsin. In these early years, LaCrosse spent most of his time in the production shop, teaching new apprentices the unique skills that he had mastered and applauding the journeymen for their accomplishments. He would constantly repeat the point that LaCrosse products had to be of the highest quality because they gave families a "window on life."

After 15 years, LaCrosse Industries employed over 200 people. A profit-sharing program was introduced to give employees a financial reward for their contribution to the organization's success. As a result of the company's expansion, headquarters had to be moved to another area of the city, but the founder never lost touch with the workforce. Although new apprentices were now taught entirely by the master carpenters and other craftspeople, LaCrosse would still chat with plant and office employees several times each week.

When a second work shift was added, LaCrosse would show up during the evening break with coffee and boxes of donuts and discuss how the business was doing and how it became so successful through quality workmanship. Production employees enjoyed the times when he would gather them together to announce new contracts with developers from Chicago and New York. After each announcement, LaCrosse would thank everyone for making the business a success. They knew that LaCrosse quality had become a standard of excellence in window manufacturing across the eastern part of the country.

It seemed that almost every time he visited, LaCrosse would repeat the now well-known phrase that LaCrosse products had to be of the highest quality because they provided a window on life to so many families. Employees never grew tired of hearing this phrase from the company founder. However, it gained extra meaning when LaCrosse began posting photos of families looking through LaCrosse windows. At first, LaCrosse would personally visit developers and homeowners with a camera in hand. Later, as the "window on life" photos became known by developers and customers, people would send in photos of their own families looking through elegant front windows made by LaCrosse Industries. The company's marketing staff began using this idea, as well as LaCrosse's famous phrase, in their advertising. After one such marketing campaign, hundreds of photos were sent in by satisfied customers. Production and office employees took time after work to write personal letters of thanks to those who had submitted photos.

As the company's age reached the quarter-century mark, LaCrosse, now in his mid-fifties, realized that the organization's success and survival depended on expansion to other parts of the United States. After consulting with employees, LaCrosse made the difficult decision to sell a majority share to Build-All Products, Inc., a conglomerate with international marketing expertise in building products. As part of the agreement, Build-All brought in a vice president to oversee production operations while LaCrosse spent more time meeting with developers. LaCrosse would return to the plant and office at every opportunity, but often this would be only once a month.

Rather than visiting the production plant, Jan Vlodoski, the new production vice president, would rarely leave his office in the company's downtown headquarters. Instead, production orders were sent to supervisors by memorandum. Although product quality had been a priority throughout the company's history, less attention had been paid to inventory controls. Vlodoski introduced strict inventory guidelines and outlined procedures on using supplies for each shift. Goals were established for supervisors to meet specific inventory targets. Whereas employees previously tossed out several pieces of warped wood, they would now have to justify this action, usually in writing.

Vlodoski also announced new procedures for purchasing production supplies. LaCrosse Industries had highly trained purchasing staff who worked closely with senior craftspeople when selecting suppliers, but Vlodoski wanted to bring in Build-All's procedures. The new purchasing methods removed production leaders from the decision process and, in some cases, resulted in trade-offs that LaCrosse's employees would not have made earlier. A few employees quit during this time, saying that they did not feel comfortable about producing a window that would not stand the test of time. However, there were few jobs for carpenters at the time, so most staff members remained with the company.

After one year, inventory expenses decreased by approximately 10 percent, but the number of defective windows returned by developers and wholesalers had increased markedly. Plant employees knew that the number of defective windows would increase as they used somewhat lower-quality materials to reduce inventory costs. However, they heard almost no news about the seriousness of the problem until Vlodoski sent a memo to all production staff saying that quality must be maintained. During the latter part of the first year under Vlodoski, a few employees had the opportunity to personally ask LaCrosse about the changes and express their concerns. LaCrosse apologized, saying that as a result of his travels to new regions, he had not heard about the problems, and that he would look into the matter.

Exactly 18 months after Build-All had become majority shareholder of LaCrosse Industries, LaCrosse called together five of the original staff in the plant. The company founder looked pale and shaken as he said that Build-All's actions were inconsistent with his vision of the company, and, for the first time in his career, he did not know what to do. Build-All was not pleased with the arrangement either. Although LaCrosse windows still enjoyed a healthy market share and were competitive for the value, the company did not quite provide the minimum 18 percent return on equity that the conglomerate expected. LaCrosse asked his long-time companions for advice.

CASE 3   Maelstrom Communications

Sales manager Roger Todd was fuming. Thanks to, as he put it, "those nearsighted addleheads in service," he had nearly lost one of his top accounts. When told of Todd's complaint, senior serviceperson Ned Rosen retorted, "That figures. Anytime Mr. Todd senses even the remotest possibility of a sale, he immediately promises the customer the world on a golden platter. We can't possibly provide the service they request under the time constraints they give us and do an acceptable job."

Feelings of this sort were common in the departments both Roger and Ned worked for in Maelstrom Communications. Sales and service, the two dominant functions in the company, never saw eye to eye on anything, it seemed. The problems dated well back in the history of the company, even before Roger and Ned were hired some years ago.

Maelstrom Communications is a franchised distributorship belonging to a nationwide network of communications companies that sell products such as intercom, paging, sound, and interconnect telephone systems. Maelstrom competes directly with companies in the telephone hardware market. Equipment installation and maintenance service are an integral part of the total package Maelstrom offers.

Modern telephone system hardware is highly sophisticated, and few, if any, system users have the technological know-how to do their own equipment servicing. An excellent service record is crucial to the success of any company in the field. After the direct sale of a Maelstrom system, the sales force maintains contacts with customers. There is nothing the salespeople dislike so much as hearing that a customer hasn't received the type of service promised at the time of sale. On the other hand, service technicians complain of being hounded by the salespeople whenever a preferred customer needs a wire spliced. As Ned Rosen put it, "I can't remember the last time a service request came through that *wasn't* an emergency from a preferred customer."

Maelstrom's owner and president, Al Whitfield, has a strong sales background and views sales as the bread-and-butter department of the company. He is in on all major decisions and has final say on any matter brought to his attention. He spends most of his time working with sales and marketing personnel, and rarely concerns himself with the day-to-day activities of the service department unless a major problem of some sort crops up.

Next in line in Maelstrom's corporate hierarchy is the vice president in charge of production, Lawrence Henderson. Henderson is responsible for the acquisition and distribution of all job-related equipment and materials and for the scheduling of all service department activities. His sympathies lie primarily with the service department.

Each week Whitfield, Henderson, and all members of the sales force hold a meeting in Maelstrom's conference room. The sales personnel present their needs to Henderson so that equipment can be ordered and jobs scheduled. Service requests reported to salespeople from customers are also relayed to Henderson at this point. Once orders for service have been placed with production, sales personnel receive no feedback on the disposition of them (unless a customer complains to them directly) other than at these weekly meetings. It is common for a salesperson to think all is well with his or her accounts when, in fact, they are receiving delayed service or none at all. When an irate customer phones the sales representative to complain, it sets in motion the machinery that leads to disputes such as the one between Roger Todd and Ned Rosen.

It has become an increasingly common occurrence at Maelstrom for sales personnel to go to Henderson to complain when their requests are not met by the service department. Henderson has exhibited an increasing tendency to side with the service department and to tell the salespeople that existing service department priorities must be adhered to and that any sales requests will have to wait for rescheduling. At this point, a salesperson's only recourse is to go to Whitfield, who invariably agrees with the salesperson and instructs Henderson to take appropriate action. All of this is time-consuming and only serves to produce friction between the president and the vice president in charge of production.

Source: Written by Daniel Robey, Georgia State University, in collaboration with Todd Anthony. Used with permission.

CASE 4 Perfect Pizzeria

Perfect Pizzeria in Southville, deep in southern Illinois, is the chain's second-largest franchise. The headquarters is located in Phoenix, Arizona. Although the business is prospering, it has employee and managerial problems.

Each operation has one manager, an assistant manager, and from two to five night managers. The managers of each pizzeria work under an area supervisor. There are no systematic criteria for being a manager or becoming a manager trainee. The franchise has no formalized training period for the manager. No college education is required. The managers for whom the case observer worked during a four-year period were relatively young (ages 24 to 27), and only one had completed college. They came from the ranks of night managers, assistant managers, or both. The night managers were chosen for their ability to perform the duties of the regular employees. The assistant managers worked a two-hour shift during the luncheon period five days a week to gain knowledge about bookkeeping and management. Those becoming managers remained at that level unless they expressed interest in investing in the business.

The employees were mostly college students, with a few high school students performing the less challenging jobs. Because Perfect Pizzeria was located in an area with few job opportunities, it had a relatively easy task of filling its employee quotas. All the employees, with the exception of the manager, were employed part-time. Consequently, they earned only the minimum wage.

The Perfect Pizzeria system is devised so that food and beverage costs and profits are set up according to a percentage. If the percentage of food unsold or damaged in any way is very low, the manager gets a bonus. If the percentage is high, the manager does not receive a bonus; rather, he or she receives only his or her normal salary.

There are many ways in which the percentage can fluctuate. Because the manager cannot be in the store 24 hours a day, some employees make up for their paychecks by helping themselves to the food. When a friend comes in to order a pizza, extra ingredients are put on the friend's pizza. Occasional nibbles by 18 to 20 employees throughout the day at the meal table also raise the percentage figure. An occasional bucket of sauce may be spilled or a pizza accidentally burned. Sometimes the wrong size of pizza may be made.

In the event of an employee mistake or a burned pizza by the oven person, the expense is supposed to come from the individual. Because of peer pressure, the night manager seldom writes up a bill for the erring employee. Instead, the establishment takes the loss and the error goes unnoticed until the end of the month when the inventory is taken. That's when the manager finds out that the percentage is high and that there will be no bonus.

In the present instance, the manager took retaliatory measures. Previously, each employee was entitled to a free pizza, salad, and all the soft drinks he or she could drink for every 6 hours of work. The manager raised this figure from 6 to 12 hours of work. However, the employees had received these 6-hour benefits for a long time. Therefore, they simply took advantage of the situation whenever the manager or the assistant was not in the building. Although the night managers theoretically had complete control of the operation in the evenings, they did not command the respect that the manager or assistant manager did. That was because night managers received the same pay as the regular employees, could not reprimand other employees, and were basically the same age or sometimes even younger than the other employees.

Thus, apathy grew within the pizzeria. There seemed to be a further separation between the manager and his workers, who started out to be a closely knit group. The manager made no attempt to alleviate the problem, because he felt it would iron itself out. Either the employees who were dissatisfied would quit or they would be content to put up with the new regulations. As it turned out, there was a rash of employee dismissals. The manager had no problem in filling the vacancies with new workers, but the loss of key personnel was costly to the business.

With the large turnover, the manager found he had to spend more time in the building, supervising and sometimes taking the place of inexperienced workers. This was in direct violation of the franchise regulation, which stated that a manager would act as a supervisor and at no time take part in the actual food preparation. Employees were not placed under strict supervision with the manager working alongside them. The operation no longer worked smoothly because of differences between the remaining experienced workers and the manager concerning the way in which a particular function should be performed.

Within a two-month period, the manager was again free to go back to his office and leave his subordinates in charge of the entire operation. During this two-month period, in spite of the differences between experienced workers and the manager, the unsold/damaged food percentage had returned to the previous low level and the manager received a bonus each month. The manager felt that his problems had been resolved and that conditions would remain the same, since the new personnel had been properly trained.

It didn't take long for the new employees to become influenced by the other employees. Immediately after the manager had returned to his supervisory role, the unsold/damaged food percentage began to rise. This time the manager took a bolder step. He cut out any benefits that the employees had—no free pizzas, salads, or drinks. With the job market at an even lower ebb than usual, most employees were forced to stay. The appointment of a new area supervisor made it impossible for the manager to "work behind the counter," because the supervisor was centrally located in Southville.

The manager tried still another approach to alleviate the rising unsold/damaged food percentage problem and maintain his bonus. He placed a notice on the bulletin board, stating that if the percentage remained at a high level, a lie detector test would be given to all employees. All those found guilty of taking or purposefully wasting food or drinks would be immediately terminated. This did not have the desired effect on the employees, because they knew if they were all subjected to the test, all would be found guilty and the manager would have to dismiss all of them. This would leave him in a worse situation than ever.

Even before the following month's percentage was calculated, the manager knew it would be high. He had evidently received information from one of the night managers about the employees' feelings toward the notice. What he did not expect was that the percentage would reach an all-time high. That is the state of affairs at the present time.

Source: J. E. Dittrich and R. A. Zawacki, *People and Organizations* (Plano, TX: Business Publications, 1981), pp. 126–28. Used by permission of Irwin/McGraw-Hill.

CASE 5   TriVac Industries Inc.

TriVac Industries Inc., an Akron, Ohio–based manufacturer of centralized vacuum systems, was facing severe cash flow problems due to increasing demand for its products and rapid expansion of production facilities. Steve Heinrich, TriVac's founder and majority shareholder, flew to Germany to meet with management of Rohrtech Gmb to discuss the German company's willingness to become majority shareholder of TriVac Industries in exchange for an infusion of much-needed cash. A deal was struck whereby Rohrtech would become majority shareholder while Heinrich would remain as TriVac's president. One of Rohrtech's senior executives would become the chairperson of TriVac's board of directors and Rohrtech would appoint two other board members.

This relationship worked well until Rohrtech was acquired by a European conglomerate two years later. Rohrtech's new owner wanted more precise financial information and controls placed on its holdings, including TriVac Industries, but Heinrich resented this imposition and refused to provide the necessary information. Relations between Rohrtech and TriVac Industries quickly soured to the point where Heinrich refused to let Rohrtech representatives into the TriVac Industries plant. He also instituted legal proceedings to regain control of the company.

According to the original agreement between TriVac and Rohrtech, any party who possessed over two-thirds of a company's shares could force the others to sell their shares to the majority shareholder. Heinrich owned 29 percent of TriVac's shares, whereas Rohrtech owned 56 percent. The remaining 15 percent of TriVac Industries shares were held by Tex Weston, TriVac's vice president of sales and marketing. Weston was one of TriVac's original investors and a longtime executive at TriVac Industries, but he had remained quiet throughout most of the battle between Rohrtech and Heinrich. However, Weston finally agreed to sell his shares to Rohrtech, thereby forcing Heinrich to give up his shares. When Heinrich's bid for control failed, Rohrtech purchased all remaining shares and TriVac's board of directors (now dominated by Rohrtech) fired Heinrich as president. The board immediately appointed Weston as TriVac Industries' new president.

Searching for a New COO

Several months before Heinrich was fired as president, the chairman of TriVac's board of directors privately received instructions from Rohrtech to hire an executive search firm in New York to identify possible outside candidates for the new position of chief operating officer

(COO) at TriVac Industries. The successful candidate would be hired after the conflict with Heinrich had ended (presumably with Heinrich's departure). The COO would report to the president (the person eventually replacing Heinrich) and would be responsible for day-to-day management of the company. Rohrtech's management correctly believed that most of TriVac's current managers were loyal to Heinrich, and, by hiring an outsider, the German firm would gain more inside control over its American subsidiary (TriVac).

The executive search firm identified several qualified executives interested in the COO position, and three candidates were interviewed by TriVac's chairman and another Rohrtech representative. One of these candidates, Kurt Devine, was vice president of sales at an industrial packaging firm in Albany, New York, and, at 52 years of age, was looking for one more career challenge before retirement. The Rohrtech representatives explained the current situation and said that they were offering stable employment after the problem with Heinrich was resolved so that the COO could help settle TriVac's problems. When Devine expressed his concern about rivalry with internal candidates, the senior Rohrtech manager stated: "We have a bookkeeper, but he is not our choice. The sales manager is capable, but he is located in California and doesn't want to move to Ohio."

One week after Heinrich was fired and Weston was appointed president, TriVac's chairman invited Devine to a meeting at a posh hotel attended by the chairman, another Rohrtech manager on TriVac's board of directors, and Weston. The chairman explained the recent events at TriVac Industries and formally invited Devine to accept the position of chief operating officer. After discussing salary and details about job duties, Devine asked the others whether he had their support as well as the support of TriVac's employees. The two Rohrtech representatives said yes while Weston remained silent. When the chairman left the room to get a bottle of wine to toast the new COO, Devine asked Weston how long he had known about the decision to hire him. Weston replied: "Just last week when I became president. I was surprised . . . I don't think I would have hired you."

Confrontation with Tom O'Grady

Devine began work at TriVac Industries in early October and, within a few weeks, noticed that the president and two other TriVac Industries managers were not giving him the support he needed to accomplish his work. For example, Weston would call the salespeople almost daily yet spoke to Devine only when Devine approached him first. The vice president of sales acted cautiously toward Devine, whereas Tom O'Grady, the vice president of finance and administration, seemed to resent his presence the most. O'Grady had been promoted from the position of controller in October and now held the highest rank at TriVac Industries below Devine. After Heinrich's departure, TriVac's board of directors had placed O'Grady in charge of day-to-day operations until Devine took over.

Devine depended on O'Grady for general operations information because he had more knowledge than anyone else about many aspects of the business. However, O'Grady provided incomplete information on many occasions and would completely refuse to educate the COO on some matters. O'Grady was also quick to criticize many of Devine's decisions and made indirect statements to Devine about his appropriateness as a COO. He also mentioned how he and other TriVac managers didn't want the German company (Rohrtech) to interfere with their company.

Devine would later learn about other things O'Grady had said and done to undermine his position. For example, O'Grady actively spoke to office staff and other managers about the problems with Devine and encouraged them to tell the president about their concerns. Devine overheard O'Grady telling another manager that Devine's memoranda were a "complete joke" and that "Devine didn't know what he was talking about most of the time." On one occasion, O'Grady let Devine present incorrect information to resellers (companies that sold TriVac products to customers) even though O'Grady knew that it was incorrect "just to prove what an idiot Rohrtech had hired."

Just six weeks after joining TriVac Industries, Devine confronted O'Grady with his concerns. O'Grady was quite candid with the COO, saying everyone felt that Devine was a "plant" by Rohrtech and was trying to turn TriVac Industries into a branch office of the German company. He said that some employees would quit if Devine did not leave because they wanted TriVac Industries to maintain its independence from Rohrtech. In a later meeting with Devine and Weston, O'Grady repeated these points and added that Devine's management style was not appropriate for TriVac Industries. Devine responded that he had not received any support from TriVac Industries since the day he had arrived even though Rohrtech had sent explicit directions to Weston and other TriVac Industries managers that he was to have complete support in managing the company's daily operations. Weston told the two men that they should work together and that, of course, Devine was the more senior person.

Decision by TriVac's Board of Directors

As a member of TriVac's board of directors, Weston included Devine's performance on the January meeting's agenda and invited O'Grady to provide comments at that meeting. On the basis of this this testimony, the board decided to remove Devine from the COO job and give him a special project instead. O'Grady was immediately named acting COO. The chairman and other Rohrtech representatives on TriVac's board were disappointed that events did not unfold as they had hoped, but they agreed to remove Devine rather than face the mass exodus of TriVac managers that Weston and O'Grady had warned about.

In late April, Devine attended a morning meeting of TriVac's board of directors to present his interim report on the special project. The board agreed to give Devine until mid-June to complete the project. However, the board recalled Devine into the boardroom in the afternoon and Weston bluntly asked Devine why he didn't turn in his resignation. Devine replied: "I can't think of a single reason why I should. I will not resign. I joined your company six months ago as a challenge. I have not been allowed to do my job. My decision to come here was based on support from Rohrtech and upon a great product." The next day, Weston came to Devine's office with a letter of termination signed by the chairman of TriVac's board of directors.

Theory Building and Scientific Research Methods

People need to make sense of their world, so they form theories about the way the world operates. A **theory** is a general set of propositions that describes interrelationships among several concepts. We form theories for the purpose of predicting and explaining the world around us.[1] What does a good theory look like? First, it should be stated as clearly and simply as possible so that the concepts can be measured and no ambiguity exists regarding the theory's propositions. Second, the elements of the theory must be logically consistent with each other, because we cannot test anything that doesn't make sense. Finally, a good theory provides value to society; it helps people understand their world better than they could without the theory.[2]

The Process of Theory Building

Theory building is a continuous process that typically includes the inductive and deductive stages shown in Exhibit A.1.[3] The inductive stage draws on personal experience to form a preliminary theory, whereas the deductive stage uses the scientific method to test the theory.

The inductive stage of theory building involves observing the world around us, identifying a pattern of relationships, and then forming a theory from these personal observations. For example, you might casually notice that new employees want their supervisor to give direction, whereas this leadership style irritates long-service employees. From these observations, you form a theory about the effectiveness of directive leadership. (See Chapter 14 for a discussion of this leadership style.)

Positivism versus Interpretivism Research requires an interpretation of reality, and researchers tend to perceive reality in one of two ways. A common view, called **positivism,** is that reality exists independent of people. It is "out there" to be discovered and tested. Positivism is the foundation for most quantitative research (statistical analysis). It assumes that we can measure variables and that those variables have fixed relationships with other variables. For example, the positivist perspective says that we could study whether a supportive style of leadership reduces stress. If we find evidence of this connection, then someone else studying leadership and stress would "discover" the same relationship.

Interpretivism takes a different view of reality. It suggests that reality comes from shared

EXHIBIT A.1

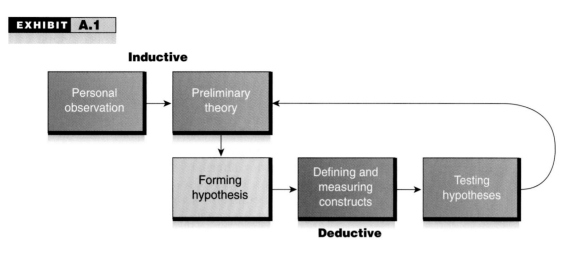

meaning among people in that environment. For example, supportive leadership is a personal interpretation of reality, not something that can be measured across time and people. Interpretivists rely mainly on qualitative data, such as observation and nondirective interviews. They particularly listen to the language people use to understand the common meaning that people have toward various events or phenomena. For example, they might argue that you need to experience and observe supportive leadership to study it effectively. Moreover, you can't really predict relationships because the specific situation shapes reality.[4]

Most OB scholars identify themselves somewhere in between the extreme views of positivism and interpretivism. Many believe that inductive research should begin with an interpretivist angle. We should enter a new topic with an open mind and search for shared meaning of people in that situation. In other words, researchers should let the participants define reality rather than let the researcher's preconceived notions shape that reality. This process involves gathering qualitative information and letting this information shape the theory.[5] After the theory emerges, researchers shift to a positivist perspective by quantitatively testing relationships in that theory.

Theory Testing: The Deductive Process   Once a theory has been formed, we shift into the deductive stage of theory building. This process includes forming hypotheses, defining and measuring constructs, and testing hypotheses (see Exhibit A.1). **Hypotheses** make empirically testable declarations that certain variables and their corresponding measures are related in a specific way proposed by the theory. For instance, to find support for the directive leadership theory described earlier, we need to form and then test a specific hypothesis from that theory. One such hypothesis might be: "New employees are more satisfied with supervisors who exhibit a directive rather than a nondirective leadership style." Hypotheses are indispensable tools of scientific research, because they provide the vital link between the theory and empirical verification.

Defining and measuring constructs   Hypotheses are testable only if we can define and then form measurable indicators of the concepts stated in those hypotheses. Consider the hypothesis in the previous paragraph about new employees and directive leadership. To test this hypothesis, we first need to define the concepts, such as "new employees," "directive leadership," and "supervisor." These concepts are known as **constructs,** because they are abstract ideas constructed by the researcher that can be linked to observable information. Organizational behavior scholars developed the construct called *directive leadership* to help them understand the different effects that leaders have over followers. We can't directly see, taste, or smell directive leadership; instead, we rely on indirect indicators that it exists, such as observing someone giving directions, maintaining clear performance standards, and ensuring that procedures and practices are followed.

As you can see, defining constructs well is very important, because these definitions become the foundation for finding or developing acceptable measures of those constructs. We can't measure directive leadership if we have only a vague idea about what this concept means. The better the definition is, the better our chances are of applying a measure that adequately represents that construct. However, even with a good definition, constructs can be difficult to measure, because the empirical representation must capture several elements in the definition. A measure of directive leadership must be able to identify not only people who give directions but also those who maintain performance standards and ensure that procedures are followed.

Testing hypotheses   The third step in the deductive process is to collect data for the empirical measures of the variables. Following our directive leadership example, we might conduct a formal survey in which new employees indicate the behavior of their supervisors and their attitudes toward their supervisor. Alternatively, we might design an experiment in which people work with someone who applies either a directive or nondirective leadership style. When the data have been collected, we can use various procedures to test our hypotheses statistically.

A major concern in theory building is that some researchers might inadvertently find support for their theory simply because they use the same information used to form the theory during the inductive stage. Consequently, the deductive stage must collect new data that are completely independent of the data used during the inductive stage. For instance, you might decide to test your theory of directive leadership by studying employees in another organization. Moreover, the inductive process may have relied mainly on personal observation, whereas the deductive process might use survey questionnaires. By studying different samples and using different measurement tools, we minimize the risk of conducting circular research.

Using the Scientific Method   Earlier, we said that the deductive stage of theory building follows the scientific method. The **scientific method** is a systematic, controlled, empirical, and critical investigation of hypothetical propositions about the presumed relationships among natural phenomena.[6] There are several elements to this definition, so let's look at each one. First, scientific research is systematic and controlled, because researchers want to rule out all but one explanation for a set of interrelated events. To rule out alternative explanations, we need to control them in some way, such as by keeping them constant or removing them entirely from the environment.

Second, we say that scientific research is empirical because researchers need to use objective reality—or as close as they can get to it—to test a theory. Researchers measure observable elements of the environment, such as what a person says or does, rather than rely on their own subjective opinion to draw conclusions. Moreover, scientific research analyzes these data using acceptable principles of mathematics and logic.

Finally, scientific research involves critical investigation. This aspect means that the study's hypotheses, data, methods, and results are openly described so that other experts in the field can properly evaluate this research. It also means that scholars are encouraged to critique and build on previous research. The scientific method encourages the refinement and, eventually, the replacement of a particular theory with one that better suits our understanding of the world.

Selected Issues in Organizational Behavior Research

There are many issues to consider in theory building, particularly when we use the deductive process to test hypotheses. Some of the more important issues are sampling, causation, and ethical practices in organizational research.

Sampling in Organizational Research   When finding out why things happen in organizations, we typically gather information from a few sources and then draw conclusions about the larger population. If we survey several employees and determine that older employees are more loyal to their company, then we would like to generalize this statement to all older employees in our population, not just those whom we surveyed. Scientific inquiry generally requires researchers to engage in **representative sampling**—that is, sampling a population in such a way that we can extrapolate the results of that sample to the larger population.

One factor that influences representativeness is whether the sample is selected in an unbiased way from the larger population. Let's suppose that you want to study organizational commitment among employees in your organization. A casual procedure might result in sampling too few employees from the head office and too many located elsewhere in the country. If head office employees actually have higher loyalty than employees located elsewhere, then the biased sampling would cause the results to underestimate the true level of loyalty among employees in the company. If you repeat the process again next year but somehow overweight employees from the head office, the results might wrongly suggest that employees have increased their organizational commitment over the past year. In reality, the only change may be the direction of sampling bias.

How do we minimize sampling bias? The answer is to randomly select the sample. A randomly drawn sample gives each member of the population an equal probability of being chosen, so there is less likelihood that a subgroup within that population dominates the study's results.

The same principle applies to random assignment of subjects to groups in experimental designs. If we want to test the effects of a team development training program, we need to randomly place some employees in the training group and randomly place others in a group that does not receive training. Without this random selection, each group might have different types of employees, so we wouldn't know whether the training explains the differences between the two groups. Moreover, if employees respond differently to the training program, we couldn't be sure that the training program results are representative of the larger population. Of course, random sampling does not necessarily produce a perfectly representative sample, but we do know that this is the best approach to ensure unbiased selection.

The other factor that influences representativeness is sample size. Whenever we select a portion of the population, there will be some error in our estimate of the population values. The larger the sample, the less error will occur in our estimate. Let's suppose that you want to find out how employees in a 500-person firm feel about smoking in the workplace. If you ask 400 of those employees, the information would provide a very good estimate of how the entire workforce in that organization feels. If you survey only 100 employees, the estimate might deviate more from the true population. If you ask only 10 people, the estimate could be quite different from what all 500 employees feel.

Notice that sample size goes hand in hand with random selection. You must have a sufficiently large sample size for the principle of randomization to work effectively. In our example of attitudes toward smoking, we would do a poor job of random selection if our sample consisted of only 10 employees from the 500-person organization. These 10 people probably wouldn't capture the diversity of employees throughout the organization. In fact, the more diverse the population, the larger the sample size should be, to provide adequate representation through random selection.

Causation in Organizational Research   Theories present notions about relationships among constructs. Often, these propositions suggest a causal relationship, namely, that one variable has an effect on another variable. When discussing causation, we refer to variables as being independent or dependent. Independent variables are the presumed causes of dependent variables, which are the presumed effects. In our earlier example of directive leadership, the main independent variable (although there might be others) would be the supervisor's directive or nondirective leadership style, because we presume that it causes the dependent variable (satisfaction with supervision).

In laboratory experiments (described later), the independent variable is always manipulated by the experimenter. In our research on directive leadership, we might have subjects (new employees) work with supervisors who exhibit directive or nondirective leadership behaviors.

If subjects are more satisfied under the directive leaders, then we would be able to infer an association between the independent and dependent variables.

Researchers must satisfy three conditions to provide sufficient evidence of causality between two variables.[7] The first condition of causality is that the variables are empirically associated with each other. An association exists whenever one measure of a variable changes systematically with a measure of another variable. This condition of causality is the easiest to satisfy, because there are several well-known statistical measures of association. A research study might find, for instance, that heterogeneous groups (in which members come from diverse backgrounds) produce more creative solutions to problems. This association would be observed when the measure of creativity (such as number of creative solutions produced within a fixed time) is higher for teams that have a high score on the measure of group heterogeneity. They are statistically associated or correlated with each other.

The second condition of causality is that the independent variable precedes the dependent variable in time. Sometimes, this condition is satisfied through simple logic. In our group heterogeneity example, it doesn't make sense to say that the number of creative solutions caused the group's heterogeneity, because the group's heterogeneity existed before it produced the creative solutions. In other situations, however, the temporal relationship among variables is less clear. One example is the ongoing debate about job satisfaction and organizational commitment. Do companies develop more loyal employees by increasing their job satisfaction, or do changes in organizational loyalty cause changes in job satisfaction? Simple logic does not answer these questions; instead, researchers must use sophisticated longitudinal studies to build up evidence of a temporal relationship between these two variables.

The third requirement for evidence of a causal relationship is that the statistical association between two variables cannot be explained by a third variable. There are many associations that we quickly dismiss as being causally related. For example, there is a statistical association between the number of storks in an area and the birthrate in that area. We know that storks don't bring babies, so something else must cause the association between these two variables. The real explanation is that both storks and birthrates have a higher incidence in rural areas.

In other studies, the third variable effect is less apparent. Many years ago, before polio vaccines were available, a study in the United States reported a surprisingly strong association between consumption of a certain soft drink and the incidence of polio. Was polio caused by drinking this soft drink, or did people with polio have a unusual craving for this beverage? Neither. Both polio and consumption of the soft drink were caused by a third variable: climate. There was a higher incidence of polio in the summer months and in warmer climates, and people drink more liquids in these climates.[8] As you can see from this example, researchers have a difficult time supporting causal inferences, because third variable effects are sometimes difficult to detect.

Ethics in Organizational Research   Organizational behavior researchers need to abide by the ethical standards of the society in which the research is conducted. One of the most important ethical considerations is the individual subject's freedom to participate in the study. For example, it is inappropriate to force employees to fill out a questionnaire or attend an experimental intervention for research purposes only. Moreover, researchers have an obligation to tell potential subjects about any potential risks inherent in the study so that participants can make an informed choice about whether or not to be involved.

Finally, researchers must be careful to protect the privacy of those who participate in the study. Researchers should let people know when they are being studied as well as guaranteeing that their individual information will remain confidential (unless publication of identities is otherwise granted). Researchers maintain anonymity through careful security of data. The research results usually aggregate data in numbers large enough that they do not reveal the opinions or characteristics of any specific individual. For example, we would report the average absenteeism of employees in a department rather than state the absence rates of each person. When data are shared with other researchers, it is usually necessary to specially code each case so that individual identities are not known.

Research Design Strategies

So far, we have described how to build a theory, including the specific elements of empirically testing that theory within the standards of scientific inquiry. But what are the different ways to design a research study so that we get the data necessary to achieve our research objectives? There are many strategies, but they fall mainly under three headings: laboratory experiments, field surveys, and observational research.

Laboratory Experiments   A **laboratory experiment** is any research study in which independent variables and variables outside the researcher's main focus of inquiry can be controlled to some extent. Laboratory experiments are usually located outside the everyday work environment, such as a classroom, simulation lab, or any other artificial setting in which the researcher can manipulate the environment. Organizational behavior researchers sometimes conduct experiments in the workplace (called *field experiments*) in which the independent variable is manipulated. However, the researcher has less control over the effects of extraneous factors in field experiments than in laboratory situations.

Advantages of laboratory experiments   There are many advantages of laboratory experiments. By definition, this research method offers a high degree of control over extraneous variables that would otherwise confound the relationships being studied. Suppose we want to test the effects of directive leadership on the satisfaction of new employees. One concern might be that employees are influenced by how much leadership is provided, not just the type of leadership style. An experimental design would allow us to control how often the supervisor exhibited this style so that this extraneous variable does not confound the results.

A second advantage of lab studies is that the independent and dependent variables can be developed more precisely than in field settings.

For example, the researcher can ensure that supervisors in a lab study apply specific directive or nondirective behaviors, whereas real-life supervisors would use a more complex mixture of leadership behaviors. By using more precise measures, we are more certain that we are measuring the intended construct. Thus, if new employees are more satisfied with supervisors in the directive leadership condition, we are more confident that the independent variable was directive leadership rather than some other leadership style.

A third benefit of laboratory experiments is that the independent variable can be distributed more evenly among participants. In our directive leadership study, we can ensure that approximately half of the subjects have a directive supervisor, whereas the other half have a nondirective supervisor. In natural settings, we might have trouble finding people who have worked with a nondirective leader and, consequently, we couldn't determine the effects of this condition.

Disadvantages of laboratory experiments   With these powerful advantages, you might wonder why laboratory experiments are the least appreciated form of organizational behavior research.[9] One obvious limitation of this research method is that it lacks realism and, consequently, the results might be different in the real world. One argument is that laboratory experiment subjects are less involved than their counterparts in an actual work situation. This argument is sometimes true, although many lab studies have highly motivated participants. Another criticism is that the extraneous variables controlled in the lab setting might produce a different effect of the independent variable on the dependent variables. This might also be true, but remember that the experimental design controls variables in accordance with the theory and its hypotheses. Consequently, this concern is really a critique of the theory, not the lab study.

Finally, there is the well-known problem that participants are aware they are being studied and this awareness causes them to act differently than they normally would. Some participants try to figure out how the researcher wants them to behave and then deliberately try to act that way. Other participants try to upset the experiment by doing just the opposite of what they believe the researcher expects. Still others might act unnaturally simply because they know they are being observed. Fortunately, experimenters are well aware of these potential problems and are usually (although not always) successful at disguising the study's true intent.

Field Surveys   **Field surveys** collect and analyze information in a natural environment—an office, factory, or other existing location. The researcher takes a snapshot of reality and tries to determine whether elements of that situation (including the attitudes and behaviors of people in that situation) are associated with each other as hypothesized. Everyone does some sort of field research. You might think that people from some states are better drivers than others, so you "test" your theory by looking at the way people with out-of-state license plates drive. Although your methods of data collection might not satisfy scientific standards, this is a form of field research because it takes information from a naturally occurring situation.

Advantages and disadvantages of field surveys
One advantage of field surveys is that the variables often have a more powerful effect than they would in a laboratory experiment. Consider the effect of peer pressure on the behavior of members within the team. In a natural environment, team members would form very strong cohesive bonds over time, whereas a researcher would have difficulty replicating this level of cohesiveness and corresponding peer pressure in a lab setting.

Another advantage of field surveys is that the researcher can study many variables simultaneously, thereby permitting a fuller test of more complex theories. Ironically, this is also a disadvantage of field surveys, because it is difficult for the researcher to contain his or her scientific inquiry. There is a tendency to shift from deductive hypothesis testing to more inductive exploratory browsing through the data. If these two activities become mixed, the researcher can lose sight of the strict covenants of scientific inquiry.

The main weakness of field surveys is that it is very difficult to satisfy the conditions for causal conclusions. One reason is that the data are usually collected at one point in time, so the researcher must rely on logic to decide whether the independent variable really preceded the dependent variable. Contrast this situation with the lab study, in which the researcher can usually be confident that the independent variable was applied before the dependent variable occurred. Increasingly, organizational behavior studies use longitudinal research to provide a better indicator of temporal relations among variables, but this is still not as precise as the lab setting. Another reason causal analysis is difficult in field surveys is that extraneous variables are not controlled as they are in lab studies. Without this control, there is a higher chance that a third variable might explain the relationship between the hypothesized independent and dependent variables.

Observational Research   In their study of brainstorming and creativity, Robert Sutton and Andrew Hargadon observed 24 brainstorming sessions at IDEO, a product design firm in Palo Alto, California. They also attended a dozen "Monday morning meetings," conducted 60 semistructured interviews with IDEO executives and designers, held hundreds of informal discussions with these people, and read through several dozen magazine articles about the company.[10]

Sutton and Hargadon's use of observational research and other qualitative methods was quite appropriate for their research objectives, which were to reexamine the effectiveness of brainstorming beyond the number of ideas generated. Observational research generates a wealth of descriptive accounts about the drama of human existence in organizations. It is a useful vehicle for learning about the complex dynamics of people and their activities, such as brainstorming. (The results of Sutton and Hargadon's study are discussed in Chapter 10.)

Participant observation takes the observation method one step further by having the observer take part in the organization's activities. This experience gives the researcher a fuller understanding of the activities compared with just watching others participate in those activities.

Disadvantages of observational research   In spite of its intuitive appeal, observational research has a number of weaknesses. The main problem is that the observer is subject to the perceptual screening and organizing biases that we discuss in Chapter 6 of this textbook. There is a tendency to overlook the routine aspects of organizational life, even though they may prove to be the most important data for research purposes. Instead, observers tend to focus on unusual information, such as activities that deviate from what the observer expects. Because observational research usually records only what the observer notices, valuable information is often lost.

Another concern with the observation method is that the researcher's presence and involvement may influence the people whom he or she is studying. This factor can be a problem in short-term observations, but in the long term people tend to return to their usual behavior patterns. With ongoing observations, such as Sutton and Hargadon's study of brainstorming sessions at IDEO, employees eventually forget that they are being studied.

Finally, observation is usually a qualitative process, so it is more difficult to empirically test hypotheses with the data. Instead, observational research provides rich information for the inductive stages of theory building. It helps us form ideas about the way things work in organizations. We begin to see relationships that lay the foundation for new perspectives and theory. We must not confuse this inductive process of theory building with the deductive process of theory testing.

B

Scoring Keys for Self-Assessment Exercises

CHAPTER 2

Scoring Key for Assessing Your General Self-Efficacy To calculate your score on the general self-efficacy scale, use the table below to assign the appropriate number to each statement. For example, if you indicated "Disagree" for statement 1, assign a 2 to that statement. Then add the numbers for all statements. Higher scores indicate that you have a higher level of self-efficacy; that is, you have a stronger can-do attitude toward new tasks and other challenges in life.

For statement items 1, 3, 8, 9, 13, 15	For statement items 2, 4, 5, 6, 7, 10, 11, 12, 14, 16, 17
Strongly agree = 5	Strongly agree = 1
Agree = 4	Agree = 2
Neutral = 3	Neutral = 3
Disagree = 2	Disagree = 4
Strongly disagree = 1	Strongly disagree = 5

CHAPTER 4

Scoring Key for Individualism–Collectivism Scale

Individualism: Add your circled numbers for the odd-numbered items (i.e., items 1, 3, 5, 7, 9, 11, 13, and 15). The maximum score is 40. Higher scores indicate more individualism.

Collectivism: Add your circled numbers for the even-numbered items (i.e., items 2, 4, 6, 8, 10, 12, 14, and 16). The maximum score is 40. Higher scores indicate more collectivism.

CHAPTER 5

Scoring Key for Growth Need Strength Scale

Step 1: The growth need strength scale yields a number from 1 ("Strongly prefer A") to 5 ("Strongly prefer B"). Write your circled numbers for the items indicated below, and add them to determine subtotal A.

$$\underline{\quad} + \underline{\quad} + \underline{\quad} + \underline{\quad} + \underline{\quad} + \underline{\quad} = \underline{\qquad}$$
(1)   (5)   (7)   (10)   (11)   (12)   Subtotal A

Step 2: The remaining items in the growth need strength scale need to be reverse-scored. To calculate a reverse score, subtract the direct score from 6. For example, if you circled 4 in one of these items, the reverse score would be 2 (i.e., $6 - 4 = 2$). If you circled 1, the reverse score would be 5 (i.e., $6 - 1 = 5$). Calculate the *reverse score* for the items indicated below and write them in the spaces provided. Then calculate subtotal B by adding these reverse scores.

$$\underline{\quad} + \underline{\quad} + \underline{\quad} + \underline{\quad} + \underline{\quad} + \underline{\quad} = \underline{\qquad}$$
(2)   (3)   (4)   (6)   (8)   (9)   Subtotal B

Step 3: Calculate the total scores by summing subtotal A and subtotal B. A total score below 30 indicates relatively low growth need strength, whereas a score above 42 indicates a relatively high growth need strength. Growth need strength indicates the strength of your growth needs, including self-esteem, personal achievement, and self-actualization.

$$\underset{\text{Subtotal A}}{\underline{\qquad}} + \underset{\text{Subtotal B}}{\underline{\qquad}} = \underset{\text{Total}}{\underline{\qquad}}$$

CHAPTER 5

Scoring Key for Equity Sensitivity   To score this equity scale, called the Equity Preference Questionnaire (EPQ), complete the three steps below.

Step 1: Write your circled numbers for the items indicated below, and add them to determine subtotal A.

$$\underset{(1)}{\underline{\quad}} + \underset{(2)}{\underline{\quad}} + \underset{(3)}{\underline{\quad}} + \underset{(4)}{\underline{\quad}} + \underset{(5)}{\underline{\quad}} + \underset{(6)}{\underline{\quad}} + \underset{(7)}{\underline{\quad}} + \underset{(10)}{\underline{\quad}} = \underset{\text{Subtotal A}}{\underline{\qquad}}$$

Step 2: The remaining items in the Equity Preference Questionnaire need to be reverse-scored. To calculate a reverse score, subtract the direct score from 6. For example, if you circled 4 in one of these items, the reverse score would be 2 (i.e., $6 - 4 = 2$). If you circled 1, the reverse score would be 5 (i.e., $6 - 1 = 5$). Calculate the *reverse score* for the items indicated below and write them in the spaces provided. Then calculate subtotal B by adding these reverse scores.

$$\underset{(8)}{\underline{\quad}} + \underset{(9)}{\underline{\quad}} + \underset{(11)}{\underline{\quad}} + \underset{(12)}{\underline{\quad}} + \underset{(13)}{\underline{\quad}} + \underset{(14)}{\underline{\quad}} + \underset{(15)}{\underline{\quad}} + \underset{(16)}{\underline{\quad}} = \underset{\text{Subtotal B}}{\underline{\qquad}}$$

Step 3: Calculate the total score by summing subtotal A and subtotal B.

$$\underset{\text{Subtotal A}}{\underline{\qquad}} + \underset{\text{Subtotal B}}{\underline{\qquad}} = \underset{\text{Total}}{\underline{\qquad}}$$

The Equity Preference Questionnaire measures the extent to which you are a "benevolent," an "equity sensitive," or an "entitled." Use the table below to determine your category as indicated by your total score.

EPQ score	Equity preference category
16–37	Entitleds—want to receive proportionately more than others (i.e., like to be overrewarded)
38–58	Equity Sensitives—want an outcome/input ratio equal to the ratio of the comparison other
59–80	Benevolents—are tolerant of situations where they are underrewarded

CHAPTER 6

Scoring Key for Money Attitude Scale   This instrument presents three dimensions with a smaller set of items than the original five-dimension, 62-item money attitude scale. However, this scale will provide some estimate of your money attitude on these three dimensions.

To calculate your score on each dimension, write the number that you circled in the scale to the corresponding item number in the scoring key below. For example, write the number you circled in the scale's first statement ("I sometimes purchase things . . .") on the line above "Item 1." Then add up the numbers for that dimension. The money attitude total score is calculated by adding up all scores for all dimensions.

Money attitude dimension	Calculation				Your score
Money as power/prestige	$\underline{\quad}$ Item 1	$+\ \underline{\quad}$ Item 4	$+\ \underline{\quad}$ Item 7	$+\ \underline{\quad}$ Item 10	$=\ \underline{\quad}$
Retention time	$\underline{\quad}$ Item 2	$+\ \underline{\quad}$ Item 5	$+\ \underline{\quad}$ Item 8	$+\ \underline{\quad}$ Item 11	$=\ \underline{\quad}$
Money anxiety	$\underline{\quad}$ Item 3	$+\ \underline{\quad}$ Item 6	$+\ \underline{\quad}$ Item 9	$+\ \underline{\quad}$ Item 12	$=\ \underline{\quad}$
Money Attitude Total	Add up all dimension scores =				$\underline{\quad}$

The three money attitude scale dimensions measured here, as well as the total score, are defined as follows:

Money as power/prestige: People with higher scores (between 13 and 20 points) on this dimension tend to use money to influence and impress others.

Retention time: People with higher scores (between 13 and 20 points) on this dimension tend to be careful financial planners.

Money anxiety: People with higher scores (between 13 and 20 points) on this dimension tend to view money as a source of anxiety.

Money attitude total: This is a general estimate of how much respect and attention you give to money.

CHAPTER 6

Scoring Key for Self-Leadership Questionnaire   To calculate your score on the self-leadership questionnaire, write the number that you circled in the scale to the corresponding item number in the scoring key on the next page. For example, write the number you circled in the scale's third statement ("I like to work toward specific goals . . .") on the line above "Item 3." Then add the numbers for each dimension. Calculate the self-leadership total score by adding up all scores for all dimensions.

Self-leadership dimension	Calculation	Your score
Personal goal setting	$\underline{\quad}_{\text{Item 3}} + \underline{\quad}_{\text{Item 9}} + \underline{\quad}_{\text{Item 15}} =$	$\underline{\quad}$
Mental practice	$\underline{\quad}_{\text{Item 6}} + \underline{\quad}_{\text{Item 12}} + \underline{\quad}_{\text{Item 18}} =$	$\underline{\quad}$
Designing natural rewards	$\underline{\quad}_{\text{Item 5}} + \underline{\quad}_{\text{Item 11}} + \underline{\quad}_{\text{Item 17}} =$	$\underline{\quad}$
Self-monitoring	$\underline{\quad}_{\text{Item 1}} + \underline{\quad}_{\text{Item 7}} + \underline{\quad}_{\text{Item 13}} =$	$\underline{\quad}$
Self-reinforcement	$\underline{\quad}_{\text{Item 4}} + \underline{\quad}_{\text{Item 10}} + \underline{\quad}_{\text{Item 16}} =$	$\underline{\quad}$
Cueing strategies	$\underline{\quad}_{\text{Item 2}} + \underline{\quad}_{\text{Item 8}} + \underline{\quad}_{\text{Item 14}} =$	$\underline{\quad}$
Self-Leadership Total	Add up all dimension scores =	$\underline{\quad}$

The six self-leadership dimensions measured here, as well as the total score, are defined as follows:

Personal goal setting: People with higher scores (10 or more points) have a strong tendency to set their own performance-oriented goals.

Mental practice: Mental practice is similar to constructive thought patterns. People with higher scores (10 or more points) have a strong tendency to rehearse future events and practice behaviors in their mind.

Designing natural rewards: People with higher scores (10 or more points) have a strong tendency to organize their work and seek out work activities that maximize their need fulfillment.

Self-monitoring: People with higher scores (10 or more points) have a strong tendency to keep track of how well they are performing a task.

Self-reinforcement: People with higher scores (10 or more points) have a strong tendency to reward themselves after successfully completing a task.

Cueing Strategies: People with higher scores (10 or more points) have a strong tendency to create symbols or indicators that remind them of their task or keep them focused on the task. Although not explicitly described in Chapter 6, cueing strategies are similar to "antecedents" in the A-B-C model of organizational behavior modification described in Chapter 2. The only difference is that these antecedents are self-developed or self-controlled rather than introduced and controlled by others.

Self-leadership (total): Self-leadership is the process of influencing oneself to establish the self-direction and self-motivation needed to perform a task. People with higher scores (60 or more points) have a high incidence of self-leadership.

CHAPTER 7

Scoring Key for Time Stress Scale To estimate how time-stressed you are, add the number of items for which you circled "Yes." You are considered time-stressed if you answered "Yes" to seven or more of these items. Low time-stress is indicated by fewer than four "yes" answers.

CHAPTER 8

Scoring Key for Team Roles Preferences Scale Write your circled score for each statement on the appropriate line below (statement numbers are in parentheses), and add the numbers for each role category. These roles are described in Chapter 8.

Encourager	$\underline{\quad}_{(6)} + \underline{\quad}_{(9)} + \underline{\quad}_{(11)} =$		$\underline{\quad}$
Gatekeeper	$\underline{\quad}_{(4)} + \underline{\quad}_{(10)} + \underline{\quad}_{(13)} =$		$\underline{\quad}$
Harmonizer	$\underline{\quad}_{(3)} + \underline{\quad}_{(8)} + \underline{\quad}_{(12)} =$		$\underline{\quad}$
Initiator	$\underline{\quad}_{(1)} + \underline{\quad}_{(5)} + \underline{\quad}_{(14)} =$		$\underline{\quad}$
Summarizer	$\underline{\quad}_{(2)} + \underline{\quad}_{(7)} + \underline{\quad}_{(15)} =$		$\underline{\quad}$

The five team roles dimensions measured here are defined as follows:

Encourager: People who score higher (10 points or above) in this dimension have a strong tendency to praise and support the ideas of other team members, thereby showing warmth and solidarity to the group.

Gatekeeper: People who score higher (10 points or above) in this dimension have a strong tendency to encourage all team members to participate in discussions.

Harmonizer: People who score higher (10 points or above) in this dimension have a strong tendency to mediate intragroup conflicts and reduce tension.

Initiator: People who score higher (10 points or above) in this dimension have a strong tendency to identify goals for meetings, including ways to work on goals.

Summarizer: People who score higher (10 points or above) in this dimension have a strong tendency to keep track of what was said in meetings (i.e., act as the team's memory).

CHAPTER 9

Scoring Key for Decision Making Style Inventory Write your circled score for each statement on the appropriate line (statement numbers are in parentheses), and add the numbers for each decision style.

Rational
decision style   ___ + ___ + ___ + ___ = ___
               (1)   (2)   (6)   (8)

Intuitive
decision style   ___ + ___ + ___ + ___ = ___
               (3)   (4)   (5)   (7)

CHAPTER 10

Scoring Key for Assessing Your Creative Disposition

Assign +1 to the following words if you marked them: capable, clever, confident, egotistical, humorous, individualistic, informal, insightful, intelligent, inventive, original, reflective, resourceful, self-confident, sexy, snobbish, unconventional, wide interests.

Assign −1 to the following words if you marked them: affected, cautious, commonplace, conservative, conventional, dissatisfied, honest, mannerly, narrow interests, sincere, submissive, suspicious.

Add the numbers to determine the total score, which will range from −12 to +18. Generally, people who score above +5 on this scale have more creative personalities than typical college students or people working in most professional occupations.

CHAPTER 11

Scoring Key for Active Listening Skills Inventory

Step 1: Using the table below, assign the appropriate number to each statement. For example, if you indicated "Very much" for statement 1, assign a 3 to that statement.

For statement items 3, 4, 6, 7, 10, 13	For statement items 1, 2, 5, 8, 9, 11, 12, 14, 15
Not at all = 3	Not at all = 0
A little = 2	A little = 1
Somewhat = 1	Somewhat = 2
Very much = 0	Very much = 3

Step 2: Write the score for each statement on the appropriate line below (statement numbers are in parentheses), and add the scores for each dimension.

Then calculate the overall score by summing the scores for all dimensions.

Avoiding
interruption (AI)   ___ + ___ + ___ = ___
               (3) (7) (15) (AI)

Maintaining
interest (MI)   ___ + ___ + ___ = ___
             (6) (9) (14) (MI)

Postponing
evaluation (PE)   ___ + ___ + ___ = ___
              (1) (5) (13) (PE)

Organizing
information (OI)   ___ + ___ + ___ = ___
              (2) (10) (12) (OI)

Showing
interest (SI)   ___ + ___ + ___ = ___
             (4) (8) (11) (SI)

Total score   ___ + ___ + ___ + ___ + ___ = ___
         (AI) (MI) (PE) (OI) (SI) Total

The five active listening dimensions and the overall active listening scale measured here are defined as follows:

Avoiding interruption: People who score higher (10 points or above) in this dimension have a strong tendency to let the speaker finish his or her statements before responding.

Maintaining interest: People who score higher (10 points or above) in this dimension have a strong tendency to remain focused and concentrate on what the speaker is saying even when the conversation is boring or the information is well known.

Postponing evaluation: People who score higher (10 points or above) in this dimension have a strong tendency to keep an open mind and avoid evaluating what the speaker is saying until the speaker has finished.

Organizing information: People who score higher (10 points or above) in this dimension have a strong tendency to actively organize the speaker's ideas into meaningful categories.

Showing interest: People who score higher (10 points or above) in this dimension have a strong tendency to use nonverbal gestures or brief verbal acknowledgments to demonstrate that they are paying attention to the speaker.

Active listening (total): People who score higher (50 points or above) in this dimension have a strong tendency to actively sense the sender's signals, evaluate them accurately, and respond appropriately.

Note: This scale does not explicitly measure two other dimensions of active listening, namely, empathizing and providing feedback. Empathizing is difficult to measure, and providing feedback involves behaviors similar to those for showing interest.

CHAPTER 12
Scoring Key for Perceptions of Politics Scale (POPS)

Step 1: To calculate your score on the Perceptions of Politics Scale, use the table below to assign the appropriate number to each statement.

People who score 7 or above on the "General political behavior" dimension believe that their school has a politicized culture. People who score 25 or higher on the "Go along to get ahead" dimension believe that employees at this school get ahead by avoiding disagreements.

For statement items 1, 4, 5, 6, 7, 8, 9	For statement items 2, 3
Strongly agree = 5	Strongly agree = 1
Agree = 4	Agree = 2
Neutral = 3	Neutral = 3
Disagree = 2	Disagree = 4
Strongly disagree = 1	Strongly disagree = 5

Step 2: Write the score for each statement on the appropriate line below (statement numbers are in parentheses), and add the scores to determine subtotals A and B. Then calculate the total score by summing subtotals A and B.

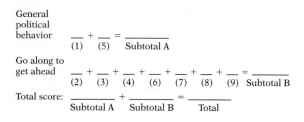

CHAPTER 13
Scoring Key for Conflict Management Style Orientation Scale

Write your circled score for each statement on the appropriate line (statement numbers are in parentheses), and add the numbers for each style category. Higher scores indicate that you are stronger in that conflict management style.

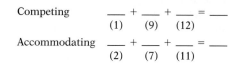

Compromising $\underline{\quad} + \underline{\quad} + \underline{\quad} = \underline{\quad}$
         (3)   (6)   (15)

Avoiding $\underline{\quad} + \underline{\quad} + \underline{\quad} = \underline{\quad}$
         (4)   (8)   (14)

Collaborating $\underline{\quad} + \underline{\quad} + \underline{\quad} = \underline{\quad}$
         (5)   (10)   (13)

CHAPTER 14
Scoring Key for Leadership Dimensions Instrument

Transactional leadership: Add your circled numbers for the odd-numbered items (i.e., items 1, 3, 5, 7, 9, 11, 13, and 15). The maximum score is 40. High scores indicate that your supervisor has a strong inclination toward transactional leadership.

Transformational leadership: Add your circled numbers scores for the even-numbered items (i.e., items 2, 4, 6, 8, 10, 12, 14, and 16). The maximum score is 40. High scores indicate that your supervisor has a strong inclination toward transformational leadership.

CHAPTER 15
Scoring Key for Corporate Culture Preference Scale

All item numbers are listed in parentheses in the equations below. For each item, in the space provided, write a 1 if you circled that item and a 0 if you did not. Then add the numbers for each subscale. The maximum score for each subscale is 6, and the minimum is 0. The higher the score, the more that you would likely feel comfortable in that type of culture.

Control culture $\underline{\quad} + \underline{\quad} + \underline{\quad} + \underline{\quad} + \underline{\quad} + \underline{\quad} = \underline{\quad}$
    (2a) (5a) (6b) (8b) (11b) (12a)

Performance culture $\underline{\quad} + \underline{\quad} + \underline{\quad} + \underline{\quad} + \underline{\quad} + \underline{\quad} = \underline{\quad}$
    (1b) (3b) (5b) (6a) (7a) (9b)

Relationship culture $\underline{\quad} + \underline{\quad} + \underline{\quad} + \underline{\quad} + \underline{\quad} + \underline{\quad} = \underline{\quad}$
    (1a) (3a) (4b) (8a) (10b) (12b)

Responsive culture $\underline{\quad} + \underline{\quad} + \underline{\quad} + \underline{\quad} + \underline{\quad} + \underline{\quad} = \underline{\quad}$
    (2b) (4a) (7b) (9a) (10a) (11a)

These subscales, which be found in many organizations, represent only four of the many possible organizational culture values. Keep in mind that none of these subscales is inherently good or bad. Each is effective in different situations.

Control culture: This culture values the role of senior executives to lead the organization. Its goal is to keep everyone aligned and under control.

Performance culture: This culture values individual and organizational performance and strives for effectiveness and efficiency.

Relationship culture: This culture values nurturing and well-being. It considers open communication, fairness, teamwork, and sharing vital parts of organizational life.

Responsive culture: This culture values its ability to keep in tune with the external environment, including being competitive and realizing opportunities.

CHAPTER 16
Scoring Key for Tolerance of Change Scale

This measurement instrument is formally known as the Tolerance of Ambiguity Scale. Although it was developed 40 years ago, the instrument is still used today in research. People with a high tolerance of ambiguity are comfortable with uncertainty, sudden change, and new situations. These are characteristics of the hyperfast changes occurring in many organizations today.

To calculate your tolerance of change score, use the table below to assign the appropriate number to each statement. For example, if you indicated "Strongly agree" for statement 2, assign a 7 to that statement. Then add the numbers for all statements. Higher scores indicate that you have a higher tolerance of ambiguity.

For statement items 2, 4, 6, 8, 10, 12, 14, 16	For statement items 1, 3, 5, 7, 9, 11, 13, 15
Strongly agree = 7	Strongly agree = 1
Moderately agree = 6	Moderately agree = 2
Slightly agree = 5	Slightly agree = 3
Neutral = 4	Neutral = 4
Slightly disagree = 3	Slightly disagree = 5
Moderately disagree = 2	Moderately disagree = 6
Strongly disagree = 1	Strongly disagree = /

CHAPTER 17
Scoring Key for Organizational Structure Preference Scale

Step 1: Using the table below, assign the appropriate number to each statement. For example, if you indicated "Very much" for statement 1, assign a 3 to that statement.

For statement items 2, 3, 8, 10, 11, 12, 14, 15	For statement items 1, 4, 5, 6, 7, 9, 13
Not at all = 3	Not at all = 0
A little = 2	A little = 1
Somewhat = 1	Somewhat = 2
Very much = 0	Very much = 3

Step 2: Write the score for each statement on the appropriate line below (statement numbers are in parentheses), and add the scores for each scale. Then calculate the overall score by summing the scores for all scales.

Tall hierarchy (H) $\underline{\quad}$ + $\underline{\quad}$ + $\underline{\quad}$ + $\underline{\quad}$ + $\underline{\quad}$ = $\underline{\quad}$
                      (1)   (4)   (10)   (12)   (15)   (H)

Formalization (F) $\underline{\quad}$ + $\underline{\quad}$ + $\underline{\quad}$ + $\underline{\quad}$ + $\underline{\quad}$ = $\underline{\quad}$
                      (2)   (6)   (8)   (11)   (13)   (F)

Centralization (C) $\underline{\quad}$ + $\underline{\quad}$ + $\underline{\quad}$ + $\underline{\quad}$ + $\underline{\quad}$ = $\underline{\quad}$
                      (3)   (5)   (7)   (9)   (14)   (C)

Total score $\underline{\quad}$ + $\underline{\quad}$ + $\underline{\quad}$ = $\underline{\quad}$
                      (H)   (F)   (C)   Total

A higher total score indicates a preference for mechanistic organizations, whereas a lower score indicates a preference for more organic organizations.

The number following each definition indicates the chapter in which the term receives the fullest description.

A

ability The natural aptitudes and learned capabilities required to successfully complete a task. (2)

action learning A variety of experiential learning activities in which employees are involved in a real, complex, and stressful problem, usually in teams, with immediate relevance to the company. (2)

action research A data-based, problem-oriented process that diagnoses the need for change, introduces the organization development (OD) intervention, and then evaluates and stabilizes the desired changes. (16)

adaptive culture An organizational culture in which employees focus on the changing needs of customers and other stakeholders, and support initiatives to keep pace with those changes. (15)

affiliate networks Network organizations in which the satellite companies have a special affiliation with the core firm, such as investment or start-up support. (17)

alternative dispute resolution (ADR) A third-party dispute resolution process that includes mediation, typically followed by arbitration. (13)

appreciative inquiry An organization development intervention that directs the group's attention away from its own problems and focuses participants on the group's potential and positive elements. (16)

artifacts The observable symbols and signs of an organization's culture. (15)

attitudes The cluster of beliefs, assessed feelings, and behavioral intentions toward an object. (4)

attribution process The perceptual process of deciding whether an observed behavior or event is caused largely by internal or by external factors. (3)

autonomy The degree to which a job gives employees the freedom, independence, and discretion to schedule their work and determine the procedures used in completing it. (6)

B

behavior modification A theory that explains learning in terms of the antecedents and consequences of behavior. (2)

bicultural audit A process used to diagnose cultural relations between the companies in a potential merger and determine the extent to which cultural clashes are likely to occur. (15)

Big Five personality dimensions The five abstract dimensions representing most personality traits: conscientiousness, emotional stability, openness to experience, agreeableness, and extroversion. (3)

boundaryless career A career that operates across company and industry boundaries rather than just within a single organizational hierarchy. (18)

brainstorming A team decision-making process in which team members, in a freewheeling, face-to-face meeting, generate as many ideas as possible, piggyback on the ideas of others, and avoid evaluating anyone's ideas during the idea-generation stage. (10)

C

career A sequence of work-related experiences that people participate in over the span of their working lives. (18)

centrality The degree and nature of interdependence between the power holder and others. (12)

centralization The degree to which formal decision authority is held by a small group of people, typically those at the top of the organizational hierarchy. (17)

ceremonies Planned and usually dramatic displays of organizational culture, conducted specifically for the benefit of an audience. (15)

change agent Anyone who possesses enough knowledge and power to guide and facilitate the organizational change effort. (16)

coalition An informal group that attempts to influence people outside the group by pooling the resources and power of its members. (8)

codetermination A form of employee involvement required by some governments that typically operates at the work site as works councils and at the corporate level as supervisory boards. (9)

coercive power The ability to apply punishment. (12)

cognitive dissonance The conflict that occurs when people perceive an inconsistency between their beliefs and feelings and their behavior. (4)

communication The process by which information is transmitted and understood between two or more people. (11)

communication competence A person's ability to identify appropriate communication patterns in a given situation and to achieve goals by applying that knowledge. (11)

communities of practice Informal groups bound by shared expertise and a passion for a particular activity or interest. (1, 8)

competencies The abilities, values, personality traits, and other characteristics of people that lead to superior performance. (2)

concurrent engineering The cross-functional integration and concurrent development of a product or service and its associated processes, usually guided by a cross-functional project team consisting of people from marketing, design, manufacturing, customer service, and other areas. (17)

conflict The process in which one party perceives that its interests are being opposed or negatively affected by another party. (13)

conflict management Interventions that alter the level and form of conflict in ways that maximize its benefits and minimize its dysfunctional consequences. (13)

conscientiousness A Big Five personality dimension that characterizes people who are careful, dependable, and self-disciplined. (3)

constructive controversy Any situation in which people debate their differing opinions about an issue in a way that keeps the conflict focused on the task rather than the people. (10)

constructs Abstract ideas constructed by researchers that can be linked to observable information. (Appendix A)

content theories of motivation Theories that explain the dynamics of employee needs, such as why people have different needs at different times. (5)

contingency approach The idea that a particular action may have different consequences in different situations. (1)

contingent work Any job in which the individual does not have an explicit or implicit contract for long-term employment, or one in which the minimum hours of work can vary in a nonsystematic way. (1, 18)

continuous reinforcement A behavior modification schedule that reinforces every occurrence of a desired behavior. (2)

counterpower The capacity of a person, team, or organization to keep a more powerful person or group in the exchange relationship. (12)

creativity The capacity to develop an original product, service, or idea that makes a socially recognized contribution. (10)

D

decision making A conscious process of making choices among one or more alternatives with the intention of moving toward some desired state of affairs. (9)

Delphi technique A structured team decision-making process of systematically pooling the collective knowledge of experts on a particular subject to make decisions, predict the future, or identify opposing views. (10)

dialogue A process of conversation among team members in which they

learn about each other's mental models and assumptions, and eventually form a common model for thinking within the team. (8, 13)

divergent thinking The creative ability to reframe a problem in a unique way and generate different approaches to the issue. (10)

divisional structure An organizational structure that groups employees around geographic areas, clients, or outputs. (17)

E

effort-to-outcome (E→P) expectancy The individual's perceived probability that his or her effort will result in a particular level of performance. (5)

electronic brainstorming A team decision-making process whereby participants individually generate ideas by using special computer software that posts each participant's ideas or opinions anonymously, thereby minimizing the team dynamics problems inherent in traditional brainstorming sessions. (10)

emotional contagion The automatic and subconscious tendency to mimic and synchronize one's own nonverbal behaviors with those of other people. (11)

emotional dissonance The conflict between required and true emotions. (4)

emotional intelligence (EQ) The ability to monitor one's own and others' feelings and emotions, to discriminate among them, and to use this information to guide one's thinking and actions. (4)

emotional labor The effort, planning, and control needed to express organizationally desired emotions during interpersonal transactions. (4)

emotions The feelings experienced toward an object, person, or event that create a state of readiness. (4)

empathy A person's ability to understand and be sensitive to the feelings, thoughts, and situations of others. (3)

employability An employment relationship in which employees are expected to continually develop their skills to remain employed. (1)

employee assistance programs (EAPs) Counseling services that help

employees overcome personal or organizational stressors and adopt more effective coping mechanisms. (7)

employee involvement The degree to which employees share information, knowledge, rewards, and power throughout the organization. (9)

employee stock ownership plans (ESOPs) Reward systems that encourage employees to buy shares of the company. (6)

empowerment A feeling of control and self-efficacy that emerges when people are given power in a previously powerless situation. (6)

equity sensitivity One's outcome–input preferences and reaction to various outcome–input ratios. (5)

equity theory A process motivation theory that explains how people develop perceptions of fairness in the distribution and exchange of resources. (5)

ERG theory Alderfer's content motivation theory of three instinctive needs arranged in a hierarchy, in which people progress to the next higher need when a lower one is fulfilled, and regress to a lower need if unable to fulfill a higher one. (5)

escalation of commitment The tendency to repeat an apparently bad decision or allocate more resources to a failing course of action. (9)

ethical sensitivity A personal characteristic that enables people to recognize the presence and determine the relative importance of an ethical issue. (4)

ethics The study of moral principles or values that determine whether actions are right or wrong and outcomes are good or bad. (1)

evaluation apprehension An individual's reluctance to mention ideas that seem silly because the individual believes (often correctly) that other team members are silently evaluating him or her. (10)

existence needs A person's physiological and physically related safety needs, such as the needs for food, shelter, and safe working conditions. (5)

expectancy theory The process motivation theory based on the idea that work effort is directed toward behaviors that people believe will lead to desired outcomes. (5)

expert power Power that originates from within the person and is the individual's or work unit's capacity to influence others by possessing knowledge or skills that others want. (12)

extinction The contingency of reinforcement in which the target behavior decreases because no consequence follows it. (2)

extroversion A Big Five personality dimension that characterizes people who are outgoing, talkative, sociable, and assertive. (3)

F

feedback Any information that people receive about the consequences of their behavior. (2)

Fiedler's contingency model A contingency theory of leadership developed by Fred Fiedler, which states that leader effectiveness depends on whether the person's natural leadership style is appropriately matched to the situation. (14)

field surveys A research design strategy that involves collecting and analyzing information in a natural environment, an office, a factory, or other existing location. (Appendix A)

fixed interval schedule A behavior modification schedule that reinforces a behavior after a fixed time. (2)

fixed ratio schedule A behavior modification schedule that reinforces a behavior after a fixed number of times. (2)

flaming The act of sending an emotionally charged electronic mail message to others. (11)

force field analysis Lewin's model of systemwide change that helps change agents diagnose the forces that drive and restrain proposed organizational change. (16)

formalization The degree to which organizations standardize behavior through rules, procedures, formal training, and related mechanisms. (17)

frustration-regression process In ERG theory, a process whereby a person who is unable to satisfy a higher need becomes frustrated and regresses to the next lower need level. (5)

functional structure An organizational structure that organizes employees around specific knowledge or other resources. (17)

fundamental attribution error The tendency to attribute the behavior of other people more to internal than to external factors. (3)

G

gainsharing plan A system that rewards team members with a bonus for reducing costs and increasing labor efficiency in their work process. (6)

general adaptation syndrome A model of the stress experience, consisting of three stages: alarm reaction, resistance, and exhaustion. (7)

globalization The trend in organizations toward extending activities to other parts of the world, actively participating in other markets, and competing against organizations located in other countries. (1)

goal setting The process of motivating employees and clarifying their role perceptions by establishing performance objectives. (5)

goals The immediate or ultimate objectives that employees are trying to accomplish from their work effort. (5)

grafting The process of acquiring knowledge by hiring individuals or buying entire companies. (1)

grapevine An unstructured and informal communication network founded on social relationships rather than organizational charts or job descriptions. (11)

group polarization The tendency of teams to make more extreme decisions than individuals working alone. (10)

groups People with a unifying relationship. (8)

groupthink The tendency of highly cohesive groups to value consensus at the price of decision quality. (10)

growth needs A person's needs for self-esteem through personal achievement as well as for self-actualization. (5)

H

halo error A perceptual error whereby one's general impression of a person, usually based on one prominent characteristic, colors the perception of other characteristics of that person. (3)

heterogeneous teams Teams that include members with diverse personal characteristics and backgrounds. (8)

homogeneous teams Teams that include members with common technical expertise, demographics (age, gender), ethnicity, experiences, or values. (8)

hypotheses Statements making empirically testable declarations that certain variables and their corresponding measures are related in a specific way proposed by theory. (Appendix A)

I

impression management The practice of actively shaping one's public image. (12)

incremental change An evolutionary strategy whereby the organization fine-tunes the existing organization and takes small steps toward the change effort's objectives. (16)

individualism versus collectivism The degree to which people value their individual versus their group goals. (4)

informal groups Two or more people who interact primarily to meet their personal (rather than organizational) needs. (8)

information overload A condition in which the volume of information received exceeds the person's capacity to process it. (11)

inoculation effect A persuasive communication strategy of warning listeners that others will try to influence them in the future and that they should be wary about the opponents' arguments. (12)

intellectual capital The sum of an organization's human capital, structural capital, and relationship capital. (1)

interpretivism The view held in many qualitative studies that reality comes from shared meaning among people in that environment. (Appendix A)

introversion A Big Five personality dimension that characterizes people who are quiet, shy, and cautious. (3)

intuition The ability to know when a problem or opportunity exists and select the best course of action without conscious reasoning. (9)

J

jargon The technical language and acronyms as well as recognized words with specialized meanings in specific organizations or groups. (11)

job burnout The emotional exhaustion, depersonalization, and reduced personal accomplishment resulting from prolonged exposure to stress. (7)

job characteristics model A job design model that relates the motivational properties of jobs to specific personal and organizational consequences of those properties. (6)

job design The process of assigning tasks to a job, including the interdependency of those tasks with other jobs. (6)

job enlargement The process of increasing the number of tasks employees perform within their job. (6)

job enrichment The process of giving employees more responsibility for scheduling, coordinating, and planning their own work. (6)

job evaluation The process of systematically evaluating the worth of jobs within an organization by measuring their required skill, effort, responsibility, and working conditions. Job evaluation results create a hierarchy of job worth. (6)

job feedback Direct sensory information from the job itself, which allows employees to tell how well they are doing. (6)

job rotation The practice of moving employees from one job to another. (6)

job satisfaction A person's attitude regarding his or her job and work content. (2)

job specialization The result of division of labor in which each job includes a subset of the tasks required to complete the product or service. (6, 17)

Johari Window The model of personal and interpersonal understanding that encourages disclosure and feedback to increase the open area and reduce the blind, hidden, and unknown areas of oneself. (3)

K

knowledge management Any structured activity that improves an organization's capacity to acquire, share, and use knowledge in ways that improve its survival and success. (1)

L

laboratory experiment Any research study in which independent variables and variables outside the researcher's main focus of inquiry can be controlled to some extent. (Appendix A)

lateral career development Career success that occurs when employees fulfill their personal needs in different jobs across the organization rather than by moving through the organizational hierarchy. (18)

law of effect A principle stating that the likelihood that an operant behavior will be repeated depends on its consequences. (2)

law of telecosm A principle stating that as the web of computer networks expands, distances will shrink and eventually become irrelevant. (8, 11)

leadership The process of influencing people and providing an environment for them to achieve team or organizational objectives. (14)

Leadership Grid® A model of leadership that assesses an individual's leadership effectiveness in terms of his or her concern for people and production. (14)

leadership substitutes Contingencies that either limit the leader's ability to influence subordinates or make that particular leadership style unnecessary. (14)

learning A relatively permanent change in behavior that occurs as a result of a person's interaction with the environment. (2)

learning orientation The extent that an organization or individual supports knowledge management, particularly opportunities to acquire knowledge through experience and experimentation. (2)

legitimate power The capacity to influence others through formal authority. (12)

locus of control A personality trait referring to the extent to which people believe that events are within their control. (3)

M

Machiavellian values The belief that deceit is a natural and acceptable way to influence others. (12)

management by objectives (MBO) A participative goal-setting process in which organizational objectives are cascaded down to work units and individual employees. (5)

management by walking around (MBWA) A communication practice in which executives get out of their offices and learn from others in the organization through face-to-face dialogue. (11)

matrix structure A type of departmentalization that overlays a divisionalized structure (typically a project team) with a functional structure. (17)

mechanistic structure An organizational structure with a narrow span of control and high degrees of formalization and centralization. (17)

media richness The data-carrying capacity of a communication medium, including the volume and variety of information it can transmit. (11)

mental imagery The process of mentally practicing a task and visualizing its successful completion. (6)

mental models The broad worldviews or theories in use that people rely on to guide their perceptions and behaviors. (3, 9)

mentoring The process of learning the ropes of organizational life from a senior person within the company. (12)

moral intensity The degree to which an issue demands the application of ethical principles. (4)

motivation The forces within a person that affect his or her direction, intensity, and persistence of voluntary behavior. (2, 5)

motivator–hygiene theory Herzberg's theory stating that employees are motivated primarily by growth and esteem needs, not by lower-level needs. (5)

Myers-Briggs Type Indicator (MBTI) A personality test that measures each of the traits in Jung's personality theory. (3)

N

need for achievement (nAch) A learned need in which people want to accomplish reasonably challenging goals through their own efforts, like to be successful in competitive situations, and desire unambiguous feedback regarding their success. (5)

need for affiliation (nAff) A learned need in which people seek approval from others, conform to their wishes and expectations, and avoid conflict and confrontation. (5)

need for power (nPow) A learned need in which people want to control their environment, including people and material resources, to benefit either themselves (personalized power) or others (socialized power). (5)

needs Deficiencies that energize or trigger behaviors to satisfy those needs. (5)

needs hierarchy theory Maslow's content motivation theory of five instinctive needs arranged in a hierarchy, whereby people are motivated to fulfill a higher need as a lower one becomes gratified. (5)

negative affectivity (NA) The tendency to experience negative emotions. (4)

negative reinforcement The contingency of reinforcement in which the removal or avoidance of a consequence increases or maintains the frequency or future probability of a behavior. (2)

negotiation An attempt by two or more conflicting parties to resolve their divergent goals by redefining the terms of their interdependence. (13)

network structure An alliance of several organizations for the purpose of creating a product or serving a client. (1, 17)

networking Cultivating social relationships with others to accomplish one's goals. (12)

nominal group technique A structured team decision-making process whereby team members independently write down ideas, describe and clarify them to the group, and then independently rank or vote on them. (10)

nonprogrammed decision The process applied to unique, complex, or ill-defined situations whereby decision makers follow the full decision-making process, including a careful search for and/or development of unique solutions. (9)

norms The informal rules and expectations that groups establish to regulate the behavior of their members. (8)

O

open book management An employee involvement approach that involves sharing financial information with employees and encouraging them to recommend ideas that improve those financial results. (9)

open systems Organizations that take their sustenance from the environment and, in turn, affect that environment through their output. (1)

organic structure An organizational structure with a wide span of control, little formalization, and decentralized decision making. (17)

organization development (OD) A planned systemwide effort, managed from the top with the assistance of a change agent, that uses behavioral science knowledge to improve organizational effectiveness. (16)

organizational behavior (OB) The study of what people think, feel, and do in and around organizations. (1)

organizational citizenship Organizational membership characterized by behaviors that extend beyond the employee's normal job duties. (2)

organizational commitment The employee's emotional attachment to, identification with, and involvement in a particular organization. (4)

organizational culture The basic pattern of shared assumptions, values, and beliefs governing the way employees within an organization think about and act on problems and opportunities. (1, 15)

organizational design The process of creating and modifying organizational structures. (17)

organizational memory The storage and preservation of intellectual capital. (1)

organizational politics The attempts to influence others using discretionary behaviors to promote personal objectives. (12)

organizational socialization The process by which individuals learn the values, expected behaviors, and social knowledge necessary to assume their roles in the organization. (15, 18)

organizational strategy The way an organization positions itself in its setting in relation to its stakeholders, given the organization's resources, capabilities, and mission. (17)

organizational structure The division of labor and the patterns of coordination, communication, work flow, and formal power that direct organizational activities. (17)

organizations Groups of people who work interdependently toward some purpose. (1)

P

parallel learning structures Highly participative groups constructed alongside (i.e., parallel to) the formal organization with the purpose of increasing the organization's learning and producing meaningful organizational change. (16)

path–goal leadership theory A contingency theory of leadership based on expectancy theory of motivation that relates several leadership styles to specific employee and situational contingencies. (14)

perception The process of selecting, organizing, and interpreting information to make sense of the world around us. (3)

perceptual defense A psychological process in which emotions screen out large blocks of information that threaten one's beliefs and values. (3)

perceptual grouping The perceptual organization process of placing people and objects into recognizable and manageable patterns or categories. (3)

performance-to-outcome (P→O) expectancy The perceived probability that a specific behavior or performance level will lead to specific outcomes. (5)

personality The relatively stable pattern of behaviors and consistent internal states that explain a person's behavioral tendencies. (3)

persuasive communication The process of having listeners accept rather than just understand a sender's message. (12)

positive affectivity (PA) The tendency to experience positive emotional states. (4)

positive reinforcement The contingency of reinforcement in which the introduction of a consequence increases or maintains the frequency or future probability of a behavior. (2)

positivism A view held in quantitative research in which reality exists independent of the perceptions and interpretations of people. (Appendix A)

postdecisional justification The tendency to justify choices by unconsciously inflating the quality of the selected option and deflating the quality of the discarded options. (9)

power The capacity of a person, team, or organization to influence others. (12)

power distance The extent to which people accept unequal distribution of power in a society. (4)

prejudice The unfounded negative emotions toward people belonging to a particular stereotyped group. (3)

primacy effect A perceptual error in which one quickly forms an opinion of people based on the first information received about them. (3)

procedural fairness Perceptions of fairness regarding the dispute resolution process, whether or not the outcome is favorable to the person. (13)

process consultation A method of helping the organization solve its own problems by making it aware of organizational processes, the consequences of those processes, and the means by which they can be changed. (16)

process losses Resources (including time and energy) expended toward team development and maintenance rather than the task. (8)

process theories of motivation Theories that describe the processes through which needs are translated into behavior. (5)

production blocking A time constraint in team decision making due to the procedural requirement that only one person may speak at a time. (10)

profit-sharing plan A reward system that pays bonuses to employees based on the previous year's level of corporate profits. (6)

programmed decision The process whereby decision makers follow standard operating procedures to select the preferred solution without the need to identify or evaluate alternative choices. (9)

projection bias A perceptual error in which an individual believes that other people have the same beliefs and behaviors that he or she has. (3)

psychological contract The individual's beliefs about the terms and conditions of a reciprocal exchange agreement between that person and another party. (18)

punishment The contingency of reinforcement in which a consequence decreases the frequency or future probability of a behavior. (2)

Q

quality circles Small teams of employees who meet for a few hours each week to identify quality and productivity problems, propose solutions to management, and monitor the implementation and consequences of those solutions in their work area. (8)

quantum change A revolutionary approach to change in which the organization breaks out of its existing ways and moves toward a totally different configuration of systems and structures. (16)

R

realistic job preview (RJP) A recruiting strategy that involves giving job applicants a balance of positive and negative information about the job and the work context. (18)

reality shock The reaction of newcomers to perceived discrepancies between their preemployment expectations and on-the-job reality. (18)

recency effect A perceptual error in which the most recent information dominates one's perception of others. (3)

referent power The capacity to influence others based on the identification and respect they have for the power holder. (12)

refreezing The latter part of the change process in which systems and conditions are introduced that reinforce and maintain the desired behaviors. (16)

relatedness needs A person's needs to interact with other people, receive public recognition, and feel secure around other people. (5)

representative sampling The process of sampling a population in such a way that one can extrapolate the results of that sample to the larger population. (Appendix A)

reward power The capacity to influence others by controlling the allocation of rewards valued by others them and removing negative sanctions. (12)

rituals The programmed routines of daily organizational life that dramatize the organization's culture. (15)

role The set of behaviors that people are expected to perform because they hold certain positions in a team and organization. (8)

role ambiguity Uncertainty about job duties, performance expectations, level of authority, and other job conditions. (7)

role conflict A situation in which an individual faces competing demands. (7)

role perceptions A person's beliefs about the behaviors that are appropriate or necessary in a particular situation, including the specific tasks that make up the job, their relative importance, and the preferred behaviors to accomplish those tasks. (2)

S

satisfaction-progression process A process whereby people become increasingly motivated to fulfill a higher need as a lower need is gratified. (5)

satisficing Selecting a solution that is satisfactory, or "good enough," rather than optimal, or "the best." (9)

scenario planning A systematic process of thinking about alternative futures and determining what the organization should do to anticipate and react to those environments. (9)

scientific management The process of systematically partitioning work into its smallest elements and standardizing tasks to achieve maximum efficiency. (6)

scientific method A systematic, controlled, empirical, and critical investigation of hypothetical propositions about the presumed relationships among natural phenomena. (Appendix A)

search conference A systemwide group session, usually lasting a few days, in which participants identify the environmental trends and establish strategic solutions for those conditions. (16)

selective attention The process of filtering information received by the senses. (3)

self-directed work teams (SDWTs) Cross-functional work groups that are organized around work processes, that complete an entire piece of work requiring several interdependent tasks, and that have substantial autonomy over the execution of those tasks. (8, 9)

self-efficacy A person's belief that he or she has the ability, motivation, and resources to complete a task successfully. (2)

self-fulfilling prophecy The perceptual process in which one's expectations about another person cause that person to act in a way that is consistent with those expectations. (3)

self-leadership The process of influencing oneself to establish the self-direction and self-motivation needed to perform a task. (6)

self-monitoring A personality trait referring to an individual's level of sensitivity and ability to adapt to situational cues. (3)

self-serving bias A perceptual error whereby people tend to attribute our their favorable outcomes to internal factors and our their failures to external factors. (3)

self-talk Talking to oneself about one's own thoughts or actions for the purpose of increasing self-efficacy and navigating through decisions in a future event. (6)

sensitivity training An unstructured and agendaless session in which a small group of people need meet face-to-face, often for a few days, to learn more about themselves and their relations with others. (16)

servant leadership The belief that leaders serve followers by understanding their needs and facilitating their work performance. (14)

sexual harassment Unwelcome conduct of a sexual nature that detrimentally affects the work environment or leads to adverse job-related consequences for its victims. (7)

situational leadership model A leadership model developed by Hersey and Blanchard suggesting that effective leaders vary their style according to the readiness of followers. (14)

skill variety The extent to which employees must use different skills and talents to perform tasks within their job. (6)

skill-based pay Pay structures in which employees earn higher pay rates according to the number of skill modules they have mastered. (6)

skunkworks Temporary teams formed spontaneously to develop products or solve complex problems. (8)

social identity theory A model that explains self-perception and social perception in terms of the person's unique characteristics (personal identity) and membership in various social groups (social identity.) (3)

social learning theory A theory stating that much learning occurs by observing others and then modeling the behaviors that lead to favorable outcomes and avoiding the behaviors that lead to punishing consequences. (2)

social loafing A phenomenon in which people exert less effort (and usually perform at a lower level) when working in groups than when working alone. (8)

social responsibility A person's or an organization's moral obligation toward others who are affected by that person's or organization's actions. (2)

sociotechnical systems (STS) theory A theory stating that effective work sites have joint optimization of their social and technological systems, and that teams should have sufficient autonomy to control key variances in the work process. (9)

span of control The number of people directly reporting to the next level in the organizational hierarchy. (17)

splatter vision The process of perceiving everything in as a whole rather than focusing on specific elements of the perceptual field. (3)

stakeholders Shareholders, customers, suppliers, governments, and any other groups with a vested interest in the organization. (1)

stereotyping The process of assigning traits to people based on their membership in a social category. (3)

stock options The right given to employees to purchase company stock at a future date at a predetermined price. (6)

strategic choice The idea that an organization interacts with its environment rather than being totally determined by it. (17)

stress An individual's adaptive response to a situation that is perceived as challenging or threatening to the person's well-being. (7)

stressors The causes of stress, including any environmental conditions that place a physical or emotional demand on the person. (7)

substitutability The extent to which people dependent on a resource have alternatives. (12)

superordinate goal A common objectives held by conflicting parties that is more important than their conflicting departmental or individual goals. (13)

synergy A phenomenon in which people generate more and better solutions by working together and sharing ideas than if they worked alone. (9)

T

tacit knowledge Knowledge embedded in actions and ways of thinking, and transmitted only through observation and experience. (2)

task identity The degree to which a job requires completion of a whole or an identifiable piece of work. (6)

task interdependence The degree to which a task requires employees to share common inputs or outcomes, or to interact in the process of executing their work. (8)

task performance An individual's level of performance with regard to goal-directed activities that are under that individual's control. (2)

task significance The degree to which the job has a substantial impact on the organization and/or larger society. (6)

team-based organization A type of departmentalization with a flat span of control and relatively little formalization, consisting of self-directed work teams responsible for various work processes. (8)

team building Any formal activity intended to improve the development and functioning of a work team. (8)

team cohesiveness The degree of attraction people feel toward the team and their motivation to remain members of that team. (8)

team effectiveness The extent to which a team achieves its objectives, fulfills the needs and objectives of its members, and sustains itself over time. (8)

teams Groups of two or more people who interact and influence each other, are mutually accountable for achieving common objectives, and perceive themselves as a social entity within an organization. (8)

telecommuting Working from home, usually with a computer connection to the office; also called *teleworking*. (1)

theory A general set of propositions that describes interrelationships among several concepts. (Appendix A)

third-party conflict resolution Any attempt by a relatively neutral person to help the parties resolve their differences. (13)

360-degree feedback Performance feedback received from a full circle of people around an employee. (2)

transactional leadership Leadership that helps organizations achieve their current objectives more efficiently, such as linking job performance to valued rewards and ensuring that employees have the resources needed to get the job done. (14)

transformational leadership A leadership perspective that explains how leaders change teams or organizations by creating, communicating, and modeling a vision for the organization or work unit, and inspiring employees to strive for that vision. (14)

trust Positive expectations about another party's intentions and actions in risky situations. (4)

type A behavior pattern A behavior pattern associated with people having premature coronary heart disease; type A's tend to be impatient, lose their temper, talk rapidly, and interrupt others. (7)

type B behavior pattern A behavior pattern associated with people having a low risk of coronary heart disease; type B's tend to work steadily, take a relaxed approach to life, and be even-tempered. (7)

U

uncertainty avoidance The degree to which people tolerate ambiguity or feel threatened by ambiguity and uncertainty. (4)

unfreezing The first part of the change process whereby the change agent produces disequilibrium between the driving and restraining forces. (16)

utilitarianism A moral principle stating that decision makers should seek the greatest good for the greatest number of people when choosing among alternatives. (4)

V

valence The anticipated satisfaction or dissatisfaction that an individual feels toward an outcome. (5)

values Stable, long-lasting beliefs about what is important in a variety of situations. (1)

variable interval schedule A behavior modification schedule that reinforces behavior after it has occurred for a varying length of time around some average. (2)

variable ratio schedule A behavior modification schedule that reinforces behavior after it has occurred a varying number of times around some average. (2)

virtual corporations Network structures that represent several independent companies that form unique partnership teams to provide customized products or services, usually to specific clients, for a limited time. (17)

virtual teams Cross-functional groups that operate across space, time, and organizational boundaries with members who communicate mainly through electronic technologies. (1, 8)

W

win–lose orientation The belief that conflicting parties are drawing from a fixed pie, so the more one party receives, the less the other party will receive. (13)

win–win orientation The belief that conflicting perception that parties will find a mutually beneficial solution to their disagreement. (13)

workplace bullying Offensive, intimidating, or humiliating behavior that degrades, ridicules, or insults another person at work. (7)

NOTES

CHAPTER ONE

1. B. Broadway, "Good for the Soul—and for the Bottom Line," *Washington Post*, August 19, 2001, p. A1; L. Kline, "The Secret of Their Success," *D Magazine–Dallas/Fort Worth* 28 (July 2001), p. 32; "Container Store to Open in Walnut Creek," *East Bay (CA) Business Times*, May 4, 2001, p. 5; J. Laabs, "Thinking Outside the Box at The Container Store," *Workforce* 80 (March 2001), pp. 34–38; M. Mazzetti, "Managing, Texas-Style," *Texas Monthly*, December 2000, p. 64; M. Forseter, "Associates Keep Score at The Container Store," *Chain Store Age* 76 (May 2000), p. 18; K. M. Kroll, "Container Store a Hit with Customers, Employees," *Shopping Centers Today*, May 2000; Daniel Roth, "My Job at The Container Store," *Fortune*, January 10, 2000, pp. 74–78.

2. M. Warner, "Organizational Behavior Revisited," *Human Relations* 47 (October 1994), pp. 1151–66. The various historical sources are described in T. Takala, "Plato on Leadership," *Journal of Business Ethics* 17 (May 1998), pp. 785–98; R. Kanigel, *The One Best Way: Frederick Winslow Taylor and the Enigma of Efficiency* (New York: Viking, 1997); M. Weber, *The Theory of Social and Economic Organization*, A. M. Henderson and T. Parsons, trans., (New York: Oxford University Press, 1947); N. Machiavelli, *The Prince and the Discourses* (New York: Modern Library, 1940); F. J. Roethlisberger and W. J. Dickson, *Management and the Worker* (Cambridge, MA: Harvard University Press, 1939); A. Smith, *The Wealth of Nations* (London: Dent, 1910).

3. R. Harley, "The Man in the Hot Seat for the Games," *Australian Financial Review*, September 16, 2000, p. 14; T. Harris, "The Men Whose Reputations Rise and Fall with the Olympics," *Australian Financial Review*, September 16, 2000, p. 22; E. Wilson, "Big Blue in the Balance," *Sydney Morning Herald*, September 12, 2000, p. 38; T. Condon, "Exit the Circus, Enter the Games," *Business Review Weekly*, September 1, 2000, p. 66; S. A. Teicher, "It's Not Just Games at 'Olympics U.,'" *Christian Science Monitor*, June 20, 2000, p. 15.

4. L. E. Greiner, "A Recent History of Organizational Behavior," in S. Kerr, ed., *Organizational Behavior* (Columbus, OH: Grid, 1979), pp. 3–14.

5. B. Schlender, "The Three Faces of Steve," *Fortune*, November 9, 1998.

6. R. N. Stern and S. R. Barley, "Organizations as Social Systems: Organization Theory's Neglected Mandate," *Administrative Science Quarterly* 41 (1996), pp. 146–62; D. Katz and R. L. Kahn, *The Social Psychology of Organizations* (New York: Wiley, 1966), chap. 2.

7. J. Pfeffer, *New Directions for Organization Theory* (New York: Oxford University Press, 1997), pp. 7–9.

8. A. Etzioni, *Modern Organizations* (Englewood Cliffs, NJ: Prentice Hall, 1964), p. 1.

9. P. R. Lawrence, "Historical Development of Organizational Behavior," in L. W. Lorsch, ed., *Handbook of Organizational Behavior* (Englewood Cliffs, NJ: Prentice Hall, 1987), pp. 1–9; D. S. Pugh, "Modern Organizational Theory: A Psychological and Sociological Study," *Psychological Bulletin* 66 (1966), pp. 235–51. For a contrary view, see A. P. Brief and J. M. Dukerich, "Theory in Organizational Behavior: Can It Be Useful?" *Research in Organizational Behavior* 13 (1991), pp. 327–52.

10. M. S. Myers, *Every Employee a Manager* (New York: McGraw-Hill, 1970). The phrase "adult supervision" as a derogatory term for managers is mentioned in T. A. Stewart, "Just Think: No Permission Needed," *Fortune*, January 8, 2001, p. 190.

11. A. Edgecliffe-Johnson, "Two Brains May Be Better Than One Big Cheese," *Financial Times (London)*, September 3, 2001, p. 9; P. Brabeck, "The Business Case against Revolution: An Interview with Nestlés Peter Brabeck," *Harvard Business Review* 79 (February 2001), p. 112; P. Stevenson, "Cheers End Dairy Merger Pain," *New Zealand Herald*, December 23, 2000.

12. H. Schachter, "The 21st Century CEO," *Profit* 18 (April 1999), pp. 25–35; M. A. Hitt, B. W. Keats, and S. M. DeMarie, "Navigating in the New Competitive Landscape: Building Strategic Flexibility and Competitive Advantage in the 21st Century," *Academy of Management Executive* 12 (November 1998), pp. 22–42.

13. J. Garten, *The Mind of the CEO* (New York: Perseus, 2001), chap. 3.

14. E. Van Bronhorst, "On Eve of Turning 30, Starbucks Exports Seattle 'Coffee Culture' to the Globe," *Associated Press Newswire*, September 9, 2001.

15. A. Teo, "Creating a Global Real Estate Player," *Business Times (Singapore)*, October 18, 2000.

16. T. H. Wagar, "Consequences of Work Force Reduction: Some Employer and Union Evidence," *Journal of Labor Research* 22 (Fall 2001), pp. 851–62; T. D. Allen et al., "Survivor Reactions to Organizational Downsizing: Does Time Ease the Pain?" *Journal of Occupational and Organizational Psychology* 74 (June 2001), pp. 145–64; M. L. Marks and P. H. Mirvis, "Making Mergers and Acquisitions Work: Strategic and Psychological Preparation," *Academy of Management Executive* 15 (May 2001), pp. 80–94; J. Vahtera, M. Kivimaki, and J. Pentti, "Effect of Organizational Downsizing on Health of Employees," *Lancet* 350 (1997), pp. 1124–28.

17. C. Kleiman, "Work Issues the Same the Whole World Over," *Seattle Times*, September 2, 2001.

18. K. L. Newman and S. D. Nollen, "Culture and Congruence: The Fit

between Management Practices and National Culture," *Journal of International Business Studies* 27 (1996), pp. 753–78. Early warnings came from A. R. Negandhi and B. D. Estafen, "A Research Model to Determine the Applicability of American Management Knowhow in Different Cultures and/or Environment," *Academy of Management Journal* 8 (1965), pp. 309–18.

19. P. R. Sparrow, "Reappraising Psychological Contracting: Lessons for the Field of Human-Resource Development from Cross-Cultural and Occupational Psychology Research," *International Studies of Management and Organization* 28 (March 1998), pp. 30–63; R. Schuler and N. Rogovsky, "Understanding Compensation Practice Variations across Firms: The Impact of National Culture," *Journal of International Business Studies* 29 (1998), pp. 159–77.

20. F. Swoboda, "Trust in Employers Is Eroding, Survey Finds," *Washington Post*, August 31, 2001, p. E2.

21. "Managing a Multicultural Workforce," *Black Enterprise*, July 2001, p. 121; M. F. Riche, "America's Diversity and Growth: Signposts for the 21st Century," *Population Bulletin*, June 2000, pp. 3–43; C. Bowman, "BLS Projections to 2006: A Summary," *Monthly Labor Review*, November 1997, pp. 3–5.

22. N. Glazer, "American Diversity and the 2000 Census," *The Public Interest*, Summer 2001, pp. 3–18.

23. J. Milicia, "Companies Change to Fit Muslim Employees' Needs," *Detroit News*, May 16, 2001.

24. D. Mangan, "Remember When . . . a Women Doctor Was a Rarity?" *Medical Economics* 75 (May 11, 1998), pp. 225–26; P. M. Flynn, J. D. Leeth, and E. S. Levy, "The Accounting Profession in Transition," *CPA Journal* 67 (May 1997), pp. 42–45.

25. Most writers define Generation X as people born immediately after the baby boom generation ended (1964) through around 1977. See B. Losyk, "Generation X: What They Think and What They Plan to Do," *The Futurist* 31 (March–April 1997), pp. 29–44.

26. N. Mui, "Here Come the Kids," *New York Times*, February 4, 2001, p. 1; R. Zemke and B. Filipczak, *Genera-*

tions at Work: Managing the Clash of Veterans, Boomers, Xers, and Nexters in Your Workplace (New York: AMACOM, 2000); B. R. Kupperschmidt, "Multigeneration Employees: Strategies for Effective Management," *Health Care Manager*, September 2000, pp. 65–76; S. Hays, "Generation X and the Art of the Reward," *Workforce* 78 (November 1999), pp. 44–48; Losyk, "Generation X: What They Think and What They Plan to Do."

27. D. C. Lau and J. K. Murnighan, "Demographic Diversity and Faultlines: The Compositional Dynamics of Organizational Groups," *Academy of Management Review* 23 (April 1998), pp. 325–40; G. Robinson and K. Dechant, "Building a Business Case for Diversity," *Academy of Management Executive* 11 (August 1997), pp. 21–31; J. R. W. Joplin and C. S. Daus, "Challenges of Leading a Diverse Workforce," *Academy of Management Executive* 11 (August 1997), pp. 32–47.

28. "Mixing Nationalities in the Workplace," *Guardian (London)*, November 11, 1999, p. 23.

29. D. L. Nelson and R. J. Burke, "Women Executives: Health, Stress, and Success," *Academy of Management Executive* 14, May 2000, pp. 107–21; "What Blacks Think of Corporate America," *Fortune*, July 6, 1998, pp. 140–43.

30. D. Woodruff, "Crossing Culture Divide Early Clears Merger Paths," *Asian Wall Street Journal*, May 28, 2001, p. 9; S. J. A. Talvi, "Stars of All Stripes," *Christian Science Monitor*, November 13, 2000, p. 11; Hays, "Generation X and the Art of the Reward."

31. J. Dionne-Proulx, J.-C. Bernatchez, and R. Boulard, "Attitudes and Satisfaction Levels Associated with Precarious Employment," *International Journal of Employment Studies* 6 (1998), pp. 91–114; P. Cappelli et al., *Change at Work* (New York: Oxford University Press, 1997). Employability is also extending into parts of Asia. For example, see R. Ong, "Skills and Lifelong Employability," *Business Times (Singapore)*, March 20, 2001.

32. A. E. Polivka, "Contingent and Alternative Work Arrangements, Defined," *Monthly Labor Review* 119 (October 1996), pp. 3–10; S. Nollen

and H. Axel, *Managing Contingent Workers* (New York: AMACOM, 1996), pp. 4–9.

33. M. Saville, "The Future is e-Me," *Sydney Morning Herald*, February 26, 2000.

34. D. H. Pink, "Land of the Free," *Fast Company* 46 (May 2001), pp. 125–33; D. H. Pink, "Free Agent Nation," *Fast Company* 12 (December–January 1998), pp. 131–47; S. B. Gould, K. J. Weiner, and B. R. Levin, *Free Agents: People and Organizations Creating a New Working Community*, (San Francisco: Jossey-Bass, 1997).

35. K. Voigt, "Virtual Work: Some Telecommuters Take Remote Work to the Extreme," *Wall Street Journal Europe*, February 1, 2001, p. 1.

36. D. Stafford, "Workplace Policies about Snow- and Ice-Related Absences Vary Widely," *Kansas City Star*, December 21, 2000.

37. N. B. Kurland and D. E. Bailey, "Telework: The Advantages and Challenges of Working Here, There, Anywhere, and Anytime," *Organizational Dynamics* 28 (Autumn 1999), pp. 53–68; A. Dunkin, "Saying Adios to the Office," *Business Week*, October 12, 1998; J. A. Challenger, "There Is No Future for the Workplace," *Futurist* 32 (October 1998), pp. 16–20; A. Mahlon, "The Alternative Workplace: Changing Where and How People Work," *Harvard Business Review* 76 (May–June 1998), pp. 121–30.

38. J. Lipnack and J. Stamps, *Virtual Teams: People Working across Boundaries with Technology*, (New York: Wiley, 2001); D. J. Armstrong and P. Cole, "Managing Distances and Differences in Geographically Distributed Work Groups," in S. E. Jackson and M. N. Ruderman, eds., *Diversity in Work Teams: Research Paradigms for a Changing Workplace* (Washington, DC: American Psychological Association, 1995), pp. 187–215.

39. R. D. Foster, "Internet Takes Ancient Craft Global," *Christian Science Monitor*, September 7, 2001, p. 7.

40. J. A. Byrne, "The Corporation of the Future," *Business Week*, August 31, 1998, pp. 102–4.

41. A. Sagie and D. Elizur, "Work Values: A Theoretical Overview and a Model of Their Effects," *Journal of*

Organizational Behavior 17 (1996), pp. 503–14; W. H. Schmidt and B. Z. Posner, *Managerial Values in Perspective* (New York: American Management Association, 1983).

42. Cited in T. Schubert, "Stop Bad Vibes Rising," *New Zealand Management* 47 (September 2000), pp. 32–35.

43. For early writing on values in the context of organizations, see E. H. Schein, *Organizational Culture and Leadership* (San Francisco: Jossey-Bass, 1985); G. Hofstede, *Culture's Consequences: International Differences in Work-Related Values* (Beverly Hills, CA: Sage, 1980); A. M. Pettigrew, "On Studying Organizational Cultures," *Administrative Science Quarterly* 24 (1979), pp. 570–81; G. W. England, "Personal Value Systems of American Managers," *Academy of Management Journal* 10 (1967), pp. 53–68; W. D. Guth and R. Tagiuri, "Personal Values and Corporate Strategy," *Harvard Business Review* 43 (1965), pp. 123–32.

44. B. R. Agle and C. B. Caldwell, "Understanding Research on Values in Business," *Business and Society* 38 (September 1999), pp. 326–87; B. M. Meglino and E. C. Ravlin, "Individual Values in Organizations: Concepts, Controversies, and Research," *Journal of Management* 24 (May 1998), pp. 351–89.

45. C. Pearson and L. Entrekin, "Structural Properties, Work Practices, and Control in Asian Businesses: Some Evidence from Singapore and Malaysia," *Human Relations* 51 (October 1998), pp. 1285–1306.

46. S. R. Chatterjee and C. A. L. Pearson, "Indian Managers in Transition: Orientations, Work Goals, Values and Ethics," *Management International Review*, January 2000, pp. 81–95.

47. M. N. Zald, "More Fragmentation? Unfinished Business in Linking the Social Sciences and the Humanities," *Administrative Science Quarterly* 41 (1996), pp. 251–61.

48. J. Barbian, "The Charit Able Worker," *Training*, July 2001, p. 50.

49. T. S. Kuhn, *The Structure of Scientific Revolutions* (Chicago: University of Chicago Press, 1970).

50. For an excellent critique of the "one best way" approach by past scholars, see P. F. Drucker, "Management's

New Paradigms," *Forbes*, October 5, 1998, pp. 152–77.

51. H. L. Tosi and J. W. Slocum, Jr., "Contingency Theory: Some Suggested Directions," *Journal of Management* 10 (1984), pp. 9–26.

52. D. M. Rousseau and R. J. House, "Meso Organizational Behavior: Avoiding Three Fundamental Biases," in C. J. Cooper and D. M. Rousseau, eds., *Trends in Organizational Behavior*, vol. 1 (Chichester, UK: Wiley, 1994), pp. 13–30.

53. H. Trinca, "Her Way," *Australian Financial Review (Boss Supplement)*, October 9, 2000.

54. R. T. Pascale, M. Millemann, and L. Gioja, *Surfing the Edge of Chaos* (New York: Crown, 2000); P. Senge et al., *The Dance of Change* (New York: Currency Doubleday, 1999), pp. 137–48; A. De Geus, *The Living Company* (Boston: Harvard Business School Press, 1997); A. Waring, *Practical Systems Thinking*, (Boston : International Thomson Business Press, 1997); P. M. Senge, *The Fifth Discipline: The Art and Practice of the Learning Organization* (New York: Doubleday, 1990), chap. 4; F. E. Kast and J. E. Rosenweig, "General Systems Theory: Applications for Organization and Management," *Academy of Management Journal* 00 (1972), pp. 447–65.

55. S. G. Scott and V. R. Lane, "A Stakeholder Approach to Organizational Identity," *Academy of Management Review* 25 (January 2000), pp. 43–62; A. A. Atkinson, J. H. Waterhouse, and R. B. Wells, "A Stakeholder Approach to Strategic Performance Measurement," *Sloan Management Review* 38 (Spring 1997), pp. 25–37; G. T. Savage, T. W. Nix, C. J. Whitehead, and J. D. Blair, "Strategies for Assessing and Managing Organizational Stakeholders," *Academy of Management Executive* 5 (May 1991), pp. 61–75; R. E. Freeman, *Strategic Management: A Stakeholder Approach* (Marshfield, MA: Pitman, 1984).

56. H. Mintzberg, *The Rise and Fall of Strategic Planning* (New York: Free Press, 1994).

57. M. L. Tushman, M. B. Nadler, and D. A. Nadler, *Competing by Design: The Power of Organizational Architecture* (New York: Oxford University Press, 1997).

58. E. P. Lima, "Pioneering in People," *Air Transport World*, April 1995, pp. 51–54; "British Airways Encourages Employees to Be Conceited," *Travel Weekly*, October 8, 1992, pp. 41, 42; K. Macher, "Creating Commitment," *Training and Development Journal* (April 1991), pp. 45–52; J. Aspery, "British Companies Meet the Challenge of Change," *IABC Communication World* 7 (December 1990), pp. 39–41.

59. G. F. B. Probst, "Practical Knowledge Management: A Model That Works," *Prism* (Second Quarter 1998), pp. 17–23; G. Miles, R. E. Miles, V. Perrone, and L. Edvinsson, "Some Conceptual and Research Barriers to the Utilization of Knowledge," *California Management Review* 40 (Spring 1998), pp. 281–88; E. C. Nevis, A. J. DiBella, and J. M. Gould, "Understanding Organizations as Learning Systems," *Sloan Management Review* 36 (Winter 1995), pp. 73–85; G. Huber, "Organizational Learning: The Contributing Processes and Literature," *Organizational Science* 2 (1991), pp. 88–115.

60. F. Belaire, "IC: The Ultimate Renewable Resource," *Silicon Valley North* 2 (December 1998), p. 16; T. A. Stewart, *Intellectual Capital: The New Wealth of Organizations* (New York: Doubleday, 1997); H. Saint-Onge, "Tacit Knowledge: The Key to the Strategic Alignment of Intellectual Capital," *Strategy and Leadership* 24 (March/April 1996), pp. 10–14; G. Petrash, "Dow's Journey to a Knowledge Value Management Culture," *European Management Journal* 14 (August 1996), pp. 365–73.

61. Relationship capital was initially called customer capital in the knowledge management literature. However, the concept is evolving to include relationships among external stakeholders. For example, see D. Halloran, "Putting Knowledge Management Initiatives into Action at Motorola," Presentation by Motorola Vice President and Director of Human Resources Dan Halloran at the Future of Business in the New Knowledge Economy Conference, March 22–23, 2000, Pan Pacific Hotel, Singapore.

62. P. N. Bukh, H. T. Larsen, and J. Mouritsen, "Constructing Intellectual Capital Statements," *Scandinavian*

Journal of Management 17 (March 2001), pp. 87–108.

63. There is no complete agreement on the meaning of organizational learning, and the relationship between organizational learning and knowledge management is still somewhat ambiguous. For writing on organizational learning, see Huber, "Organizational Learning"; Senge, *The Fifth Discipline*, pp. 3–5.

64. Huber, "Organizational Learning."

65. A. L. Brown, "In Economic Slowdown, Wal-Mart Counts on Its Cultural Roots," *Detroit News*, June 9, 2001; L. Wah, "Behind the Buzz," *Management Review* 88 (April 1999), pp. 16–19; C. W. Wick and L. S. Leon, "From Ideas to Actions: Creating a Learning Organization," *Human Resource Management* 34 (Summer 1995), pp. 299–311; D. Ulrich, T. Jick, and M. Von Glinow, "High Impact Learning: Building and Diffusing Learning Capability," *Organizational Dynamics* 22 (Autumn 1993), pp. 52–66. Experimentation is similar to synthetic learning described in D. Miller, "A Preliminary Typology of Organizational Learning: Synthesizing the Literature," *Journal of Management* 22 (1996), pp. 485–505.

66. C. O'Dell and C. J. Grayson, "If Only We Knew What We Know: Identification and Transfer of Internal Best Practices," *California Management Review* 40 (Spring 1998), pp. 154–74; R. Ruggles, "The State of the Notion: Knowledge Management in Practice," *California Management Review* 40 (Spring 1998), pp. 80–89; G. S. Richards and S. C. Goh, "Implementing Organizational Learning: Toward a Systematic Approach," *The Journal of Public Sector Management* (Autumn 1995), pp. 25–31.

67. E. C. Wenger and W. M. Snyder, "Communities of Practice: The Organizational Frontier," *Harvard Business Review* 78 (January–February 2000), pp. 139–45; O'Dell and Grayson, "If Only We Knew What We Know."

68. M. Hopkins, "Zen and the Art of the Self-Managing Company," *Inc.*, November 2000, p. 55.

69. G. Barker, "High Priest of the PC," *The Age*, April 4, 2001; N. Way, "Talent War," *Business Review Weekly*, August 18, 2000, p. 64.

70. J. McKay, "The Smell of Success," *Pittsburgh (PA) Post-Gazette*, October 28, 1999.

71. Stewart, *Intellectual Capital*, chap. 7.

72. B. P. Sunoo, "The Sydney Challenge," *Workforce*, September 2000, pp. 70–76.

73. D. Lei, J. W. Slocum, and R. A. Pitts, "Designing Organizations for Competitive Advantage: The Power of Unlearning and Learning," *Organizational Dynamics* 27 (Winter 1999), pp. 24–38; M. E. McGill and J. W. Slocum, Jr., "Unlearn the Organization," *Organizational Dynamics* 22 (2) (1993), pp. 67–79.

CHAPTER TWO

1. S. Silver, "Behind Many Successful Business Leaders Is an Executive Coach," *AP Worldstream*, June 5, 2001; D. C. Feldman, "Career Coaching: What HR Professionals and Managers Need to Know," *Human Resource Planning* 24 (June 2001), p. 26; K. Kicklighter, "Put Me In, Coach," *Atlanta Journal and Constitution*, January 12, 2001, p. E1; D. E. Lewis, "Companies Are Hiring Coaches to Teach Executives How to Sharpen Management Skills and Communicate Effectively Leading the Corporate League," *Boston Globe*, November 26, 2000, p. G1; J. Laabs, "Need Peak HR Performance? Consider a Coach," *Workforce* 79 (October 2000), pp. 132–35.

2. C. C. Pinder, *Work Motivation in Organizational Behavior* (Upper Saddle River, NJ: Prentice Hall, 1998); E. E. Lawler III, *Motivation in Work Organizations* (Monterey, CA: Brooks/Cole, 1973), pp. 2–5.

3. J. Kochanski, "Competency-Based Management," *Training and Development*, October 1997, pp. 40–44; Hay Group et al., *Raising the Bar: Using Competencies to Enhance Employee Performance* (Scottsdale, AZ: American Compensation Association, 1996); L. M. Spencer and S. M. Spencer, *Competence at Work: Models for Superior Performance* (New York: Wiley, 1993).

4. T. Hellström, "Knowledge and Competence Management at Ericsson: Decentralization and Organizational Fit," *Journal of Knowledge Management* 4 (2000).

5. J. R. Edwards, "Person-Job Fit: A Conceptual Integration, Literature Review, and Methodological Critique," *International Review of Industrial and Organizational Psychology* 6 (1991), pp. 283–357; J. E. Hunter and R. F. Hunter, "Validity and Utility of Alternative Predictors of Job Performance," *Psychological Bulletin* 96 (1984), pp. 72–98.

6. S. Pearlstein, "Canadian Stores Take On U.S. Rivals," *Plain Dealer (Cleveland)*, January 24, 1999, p. H1. For research on customer service and training, see J. W. Johnson, "Linking Employee Perceptions of Service Climate to Customer Satisfaction," *Personnel Psychology* 49 (1996), pp. 831–51; A. Sharma and D. Sarel, "The Impact of Customer Satisfaction Based Incentive Systems on Salespeople's Customer Service Response: An Empirical Study," *Journal of Personal Selling and Sales Management* 15 (Summer 1995), pp. 17–29; R. A. Guzzo, R. D. Jette, and R. A. Katzell, "The Effects of Psychologically Based Intervention Programs on Worker Productivity: A Meta-Analysis," *Personnel Psychology* 38 (1985), pp. 275–91.

7. B. Riggs and M. E. Thyfault, "The Modern Call Center—Customer Relationships and Loyalty Take Center Stage," *Information Week*, October 4, 1999.

8. L. Welch, "Watch Out for That Ice!" *Capital Times (Madison, WI)*, February 27, 2001, p. A1.

9. S. P. Brown and R. A. Peterson, "The Effect of Effort on Sales Performance and Job Satisfaction," *Journal of Marketing* 58 (April 1994), pp. 70–80.

10. Gary Johns discusses situational factors in terms of constraints both on behavior and on the complexities of organizational research. G. Johns, "Commentary: In Praise of Context," *Journal of Organizational Behavior* 22 (2001), pp. 31–42; Also see S. B. Bacharach and P. Bamberger, "Beyond Situational Constraints: Job Resources Inadequacy and Individual Performance at Work," *Human Resource Management Review* 5 (1995), pp. 79–102; K. F. Kane, ed., "Special Issue: Situational Constraints and Work Performance," *Human Resource Management Review* 3 (Summer 1993), pp. 83–175.

11. J. H. Sheridan, "Lockheed Martin Corp.," *Industry Week* 247 (October 19, 1998), pp. 54–56.

12. D. Yankelovich, "Got to Give to Get," *Mother Jones* 22 (July 1997), pp. 60–63.

13. B. Clements, "Skilled-Labor Shortage Compels Tacoma, Wash.–Area Photo Lab to Close for Good," *News Tribune (Tacoma, WA)*, October 21, 2000.

14. "War for Talent II: Seven Ways to Win," *Fast Company* 42 (January 2001).

15. S. M. Jacoby, "Most Workers Find a Sense of Security in Corporate Life," *Los Angeles Times*, September 7, 1998, p. B5.

16. S. Patrick, "D–FW Hospitals in 'Quicksand' over Worsening Nurse Shortage," *Dallas Business Journal*, May 25, 2001; N. M. Moore, "Outside Agencies Offer Nursing Relief, but at What Cost?" *Cleveland Sun*, May 3, 2001; S. A. Webster, "Area Short of Nurses; Care Suffers," *Detroit News*, January 11, 2001.

17. T. Romita, "The Talent Search," *Business 2.0*, June 12, 2001; K. Dobbs, "Knowing How to Keep Your Best and Brightest," *Workforce* 80 (April 2001), pp. 56–60.

18. S. K. Witcher, "Asian Companies Grasp at Ways to Keep Staff," *Asian Wall Street Journal*, August 22, 2000, p. 8. Also see R. W. Griffeth and P. W. Hom, "The Employee Turnover Process," *Research in Personnel and Human Resource Management* 13 (1995), pp. 245–93.

19. P. Eaton-Robb, "For Employees, Solutions That Work," *Providence (RI) Journal*, January 10, 2001, p. E1; D. Stafford, "Workplace Policies about Snow- and Ice-Related Absences Vary Widely," *Kansas City Star*, December 21, 2000. For details about the causes of absenteeism, see S. R. Rhodes and R. M. Steers, *Managing Employee Absenteeism* (Reading, MA: Addison-Wesley, 1990).

20. D. A. Harrison and J. J. Martocchio, "Time for Absenteeism: A 20-Year Review of Origins, Offshoots, and Outcomes," *Journal of Management* 24 (Spring 1998), pp. 305–50; R. D. Hackett and P. Bycio, "An Evaluation of Employee Absenteeism as a Coping Mechanism among Hospital Nurses," *Journal of Occupational and Organizational Psychology* 69 (December 1996) pp. 327–38; R. G. Ehrenberg, R. A. Ehrenberg, D. I. Rees, and E. L. Ehrenberg, "School District Leave Policies, Teacher Absenteeism, and Student Achievement," *Journal of Human Resources* 26 (Winter 1991), pp. 72–105.

21. J. P. Campbell, R. A. McCloy, S. H. Oppler, and C. E. Sager, "A Theory of Performance," in N. Schmitt, W. C. Borman, and Associates, eds., *Personnel Selection in Organizations* (San Francisco: Jossey-Bass, 1993), pp. 35–70.

22. S. T. Hunt, "Generic Work Behavior: An Investigation into the Dimensions of Entry-Level, Hourly Job Performance," *Personnel Psychology* 49 (1996), pp. 51–83.

23. A. Czarnecki, "Customer Service Training: More Than an 'Event,'" *Learning for the Workplace (Canadian HR Reporter,* Supplement), May 20, 1996, pp. L4–L7.

24. C. I. Barnard, *The Functions of the Executive* (Cambridge, MA: Harvard University Press, 1938), pp. 83–84; D. Katz and R. L. Kahn, *The Social Psychology of Organizations* (New York: Wiley, 1966), pp. 337–40.

25. P. M. Podsakoff, M. Ahearne, and S. B. MacKenzie, "Organizational Citizenship Behavior and the Quantity and Quality of Work Group Performance," *Journal of Applied Psychology* 82 (1997), pp. 262–70; D. W. Organ, "The Motivational Basis of Organizational Citizenship Behavior," *Research in Organizational Behavior* 12 (1990), pp. 43–72. The discussion of altruism is also based on R. N. Kanungo and J. A. Conger, "Promoting Altruism as a Corporate Goal," *Academy of Management Executive* 7, no. 3 (1993), pp. 37–48.

26. G. Fauntleroy, "Top Education Employee Runs Office with Celestial Precision," *Santa Fe New Mexican*, July 22, 2001, p. E5.

27. P. Cappelli and N. Rogovsky, "Employee Involvement and Organizational Citizenship: Implications for Labor Law Reform and 'Lean Production,'" *Industrial and Labor Relations Review* 51 (July 1998), pp. 633–53; R. H. Moorman, G. L. Blakely, and B. P. Niehoff, "Does Perceived Organizational Support Mediate the Relationship between Procedural Justice and Organizational Citizenship Behavior?" *Academy of Management Journal* 41 (1998), pp. 351–57; Organ, "The Motivational Basis of Organizational Citizenship Behavior," pp. 60–63.

28. Kanungo and Conger, "Promoting Altruism as a Corporate Goal," p. 42.

29. K. Hanson, "Perks Help Keep Four Seasons Staff Pampering Guests," *National Post*, January 13, 2001, p. D8.

30. T. A. Stewart, "Gray Flannel Suit? Moi?" *Fortune*, March 16, 1998, pp. 76–82.

31. D. M. Harris and R. L. DeSimone, *Human Resource Development* (Fort Worth, TX: Harcourt Brace, 1994), p. 54; B. Bass and J. Vaughn, *Training in Industry: The Management of Learning* (Belmont, CA: Wadsworth, 1966), p. 8; W. McGehee and P. W. Thayer, *Training in Business and Industry* (New York: Wiley, 1961), pp. 131–34.

32. G. F. B. Probst, "Practical Knowledge Management: A Model That Works," *Prism* (Second Quarter 1998), pp. 17–23; G. Miles, R. E. Miles, V. Perrone, and L. Edvinsson, "Some Conceptual and Research Barriers to the Utilization of Knowledge," *California Management Review* 40 (Spring 1998), pp. 281–88; E. C. Nevis, A. J. DiBella, and J. M. Gould, "Understanding Organizations as Learning Systems," *Sloan Management Review* 36 (Winter 1995), pp. 73–85; D. Ulrich, T. Jick, and M. Von Glinow, "High Impact Learning: Building and Diffusing Learning Capability," *Organizational Dynamics* 22 (Autumn 1993), pp. 52–66; G. Huber, "Organizational Learning: The Contributing Processes and Literature," *Organizational Science* 2 (1991), pp. 88–115.

33. W. L. P. Wong and D. F. Radcliffe, "The Tacit Nature of Design Knowledge," *Technology Analysis and Strategic Management*, December 2000, pp. 493–512; R. Madhavan and R. Grover, "From Embedded Knowledge to Embodied Knowledge: New Product Development as Knowledge Management," *Journal of Marketing* 62 (October 1998), pp. 1–12; D. Leonard and S. Sensiper, "The Role of Tacit Knowledge in Group Innovation," *California Management Review* 40 (Spring 1998), pp. 112–32;

I. Nonaka and H. Takeuchi, *The Knowledge-Creating Company* (New York: Oxford University Press, 1995); R. K. Wagner and R. J. Sternberg, "Practical Intelligence in Real-World Pursuits: The Role of Tacit Knowledge," *Journal of Personality and Social Psychology* 49 (1985), pp. 436–58.

34. A. Lam, "Tacit Knowledge, Organizational Learning and Societal Institutions: An Integrated Framework," *Organization Studies,* May 2000.

35. M. J. Kerr, "Tacit Knowledge as a Predictor of Managerial Success: A Field Study," *Canadian Journal of Behavioral Science* 27 (1995), pp. 36–51.

36. W. F. Dowling, "Conversation with B. F. Skinner," *Organizational Dynamics,* Winter 1973, pp. 31–40.

37. R. G. Miltenberger, *Behavior Modification: Principles and Procedures* (Pacific Grove, CA: Brooks/Cole, 1997); J. Komaki, T. Coombs, and S. Schepman, "Motivational Implications of Reinforcement Theory," in R. M. Steers, L. W. Porter, and G. A. Bigley, eds., *Motivation and Leadership at Work* (New York: McGraw-Hill, 1996), pp. 34–52; H. P. Sims and P. Lorenzi, *The New Leadership Paradigm: Social Learning and Cognition in Organizations* (Newbury Park, CA: Sage, 1992), part II.

38. B. F. Skinner, *The Behavior of Organisms* (New York: Appleton-Century-Crofts, 1938).

39. F. Luthans and R. Kreitner, *Organizational Behavior Modification and Beyond* (Glenview, IL: Scott, Foresman, 1985); pp. 85–88; T. K. Connellan, *How to Improve Human Performance* (New York: Harper & Row, 1978), pp. 48–57.

40. Miltenberger, *Behavior Modification,* chaps. 4–6.

41. T. C. Mawhinney and R. R. Mawhinney, "Operant Terms and Concepts Applied to Industry," in R. M. O'Brien, A. M. Dickinson, and M. P. Rosow, eds., *Industrial Behavior Modification: A Management Handbook* (New York: Pergamon Press, 1982), p. 117; R. Kreitner, "Controversy in OBM: History, Misconceptions, and Ethics," in L. W. Frederiksen, ed., *Handbook of Organizational Behavior Management* (New York: Wiley, 1982), pp. 76–79.

42. Luthans and Kreitner, *Organizational Behavior Modification and Beyond,* pp. 53–54.

43. K. D. Butterfield, L. K. Trevino, and G. A. Ball, "Punishment from the Manager's Perspective: A Grounded Investigation and Inductive Model," *Academy of Management Journal* 39 (1996), pp. 1479–1512; L. K. Trevino, "The Social Effects of Punishment in Organizations: A Justice Perspective," *Academy of Management Review* 17 (1992), pp. 647–76.

44. B. S. Klaas and H. N. Wheeler, "Managerial Decision Making about Employee Discipline: A Policy-Capturing Approach," *Personnel Psychology* 43 (1990), pp. 117–34.

45. Butterfield et al., "Punishment from the Manager's Perspective"; Luthans and Kreitner, *Organizational Behavior Modification and Beyond,* pp. 139–44; J. M. Beyer and H. M. Trice, "A Field Study of the Use and Perceived Effects of Discipline in Controlling Work Performance," *Academy of Management Journal* 27 (1984), pp. 743–64.

46. G. P. Latham and V. L. Huber, "Schedules of Reinforcement: Lessons from the Past and Issues for the Future," *Journal of Organizational Behavior Management* 13 (1992), pp. 125–49.

47. A. Zipkin, "Kinder, Gentler Workplace Replaces Era of Tough Boss," *New York Times,* June 26, 2000.

48. F. Luthans and A. D. Stajkovic, "Reinforce for Performance: The Need to Go Beyond Pay and Even Rewards," *Academy of Management Executive* 13 (May 1999), pp. 49–57; A. D. Stajkovic and F. Luthans, "A Meta-Analysis of the Effects of Organizational Behavior Modification on Task Performance, 1975–95," *Academy of Management Journal* 40 (1997), pp. 1122–49.

49. P. Eaton-Robb, "For Employees, Solutions That Work," *Providence Journal,* January 10, 2001, p. E1; D. Behar, "Firm Launches Lottery to Beat 'Sickies' Plague," *Daily Mail (UK),* January 8, 2001, p. 27; G. Masek, "Dana Corp.," *Industry Week,* October 19, 1998, p. 48.

50. G. A. Merwin, J. A. Thomason, and E. E. Sanford, "A Methodological and Content Review of Organizational Behavior Management in the Private Sector: 1978–1986," *Journal of Organizational Behavior Management* 10 (1989), pp. 39–57.

51. P. Drucker, *Management: Tasks, Responsibilities, Practices* (New York: Harper & Row, 1974).

52. R. Curren, "Lottery Helps Solve Absenteeism," *Winnipeg Free Press,* November 6, 1999. Further information about NOVA Chemicals was provided by Ms. Roxann Good, NOVA Chemicals Ltd., July 2000. All amounts are in U.S. dollars.

53. Latham and Huber, "Schedules of Reinforcement," pp. 132–33.

54. T. C. Mawhinney, "Philosophical and Ethical Aspects of Organizational Behavior Management: Some Evaluative Feedback," *Journal of Organizational Behavior Management* 6 (Spring 1984), pp. 5–31; F. L. Fry, "Operant Conditioning in Organizational Settings: Of Mice or Men?" *Personnel* 51 (July–August 1974), pp. 17–24.

55. A. N. Kluger and A. DeNisi, "The Effects of Feedback Interventions on Performance: A Historical Review, A Meta-Analysis, and a Preliminary Feedback Intervention Theory," *Psychological Bulletin* 119 (March 1996), pp. 254–84; A. A. Shikdar and B. Das, "A Field Study of Worker Productivity Improvements," *Applied Ergonomics* 26 (1995), pp. 21–27; L. M. Sama and R. E. Kopelman, "In Search of a Ceiling Effect on Work Motivation: Can Kaizen Keep Performance 'Risin'?" *Journal of Social Behavior and Personality* 9 (1994), pp. 231–37.

56. R. Waldersee and F. Luthans, "The Impact of Positive and Corrective Feedback on Customer Service Performance," *Journal of Organizational Behavior* 15 (1994), pp. 83–95; P. K. Duncan and L. R. Bruwelheide, "Feedback: Use and Possible Behavioral Functions," *Journal of Organizational Behavior Management* 7 (Fall 1985), pp. 91–114; J. Annett, *Feedback and Human Behavior* (Baltimore: Penguin, 1969).

57. M. C. Andrews and K. M. Kacmar, "Confirmation and Extension of the Sources of Feedback Scale in Service-Based Organizations," *Journal of Business Communication* 38 (April 2001), pp. 206–26.

58. For discussion of multisource feedback, see W. W. Tornow and M. London, *Maximizing the Value of 360-degree Feedback: A Process for Successful Individual and Organizational Development* (San

Francisco: Jossey-Bass, 1998); D. A. Waldman and L. E. Atwater, *The Power of 360 Feedback: How to Leverage Performance Evaluations for Top Productivity* (Houston: Gulf, 1998); M. Edwards and A. Ewan, *360 Feedback: The Powerful New Model for Employee Assessment and Performance Improvement* (New York: AMACOM, 1996).

59. P. G. Dominick, R. R. Reilly, and J. W. McGourty, "The Effects of Peer Feedback on Team Member Behavior," *Group and Organization Management* 22 (December 1997), pp. 508–20. Employee concerns with 360-degree feedback are reported in B. Usher and J. Morley, "Overcoming the Obstacles to a Successful 360-Degree Feedback Program," *Canadian HR Reporter*, February 8, 1999, p. 17.

60. The problems with 360-degree feedback are discussed in M. A. Peiperl, "Getting 360 Degree Feedback Right," *Harvard Business Review* 79 (January 2001), pp. 142–47; A. S. DeNisi and A. N. Kluger, "Feedback Effectiveness: Can 360-Degree Appraisals Be Improved?" *Academy of Management Executive* 14 (February 2000), pp. 129–39; J. Ghorpade, "Managing Five Paradoxes of 360-Degree Feedback," *Academy of Management Executive* 14 (February 2000), pp. 140–50.

61. D. M. Herold, R. C. Linden, and M. L. Leatherwood, "Using Multiple Attributes to Assess Sources of Performance Feedback," *Academy of Management Journal* 30 (December 1987), pp. 826–35.

62. M. London, "Giving Feedback: Source-Centered Antecedents and Consequences of Constructive and Destructive Feedback," *Human Resource Management Review* 5 (1995), pp. 159–88; D. Antonioni, "The Effects of Feedback Accountability on 360-Degree Appraisal Ratings," *Personnel Psychology* 47 (1994), pp. 375–90; S. J. Ashford and G. B. Northcraft, "Conveying More (or Less) Than We Realize: The Role of Impression Management in Feedback Seeking," *Organizational Behavior and Human Decision Processes* 53 (1992), pp. 310–34; E. W. Morrison and R. J. Bies, "Impression Management in the Feedback-Seeking Process: A Literature Review and Research Agenda," *Academy of Management Review* 16 (1991), pp. 522–41.

63. J. R. Williams, C. E. Miller, L. A. Steelman, and P. E. Levy, "Increasing Feedback Seeking in Public Contexts: It Takes Two (or More) to Tango," *Journal of Applied Psychology* 84 (December 1999), pp. 969–76; G. B. Northcraft and S. J. Ashford, "The Preservation of Self in Everyday Life: The Effects of Performance Expectations and Feedback Context on Feedback Inquiry," *Organizational Behavior and Human Decision Processes* 47 (1990), pp. 42–64.

64. R. D. Pritchard, P. L. Roth, S. D. Jones, and P. G. Roth, "Implementing Feedback Systems to Enhance Productivity: A Practical Guide," *National Productivity Review* 10 (Winter 1990–1991), pp. 57–67.

65. P. M. Posakoff and J. Fahr, "Effects of Feedback Sign and Credibility on Goal Setting and Task Performance," *Organizational Behavior and Human Decision Processes* 44 (1989), pp. 45–67.

66. R. D. Guzzo and B. A. Gannett, "The Nature of Facilitators and Inhibitors of Effective Task Performance," in F. D. Schoorman and B. Schneider, eds., *Facilitating Work Effectiveness* (Lexington, MA.: Lexington Books, 1988), p. 23; R. C. Linden and T. R. Mitchell, "Reactions to Feedback: The Role of Attributions," *Academy of Management Journal* 28 (June 1985), pp. 291–308.

67. S. Robinson and E. Weldon, "Feedback Seeking in Groups: A Theoretical Perspective," *British Journal of Social Psychology* 32 (1993), pp. 71–86; S. J. Ashford and L. L. Cummings, "Feedback as an Individual Resource: Personal Strategies of Creating Information," *Organizational Behavior and Human Performance* 32 (1983), pp. 370–98; S. J. Ashford, "Feedback Seeking in Individual Adaptation: A Resource Perspective," *Academy of Management Journal* 29 (1986), pp. 465–87.

68. J. M. Mishra and S. M. Crampton, "Employee Monitoring: Privacy in the Workplace?" *SAM Advanced Management Journal* 63 (June 1998), pp. 4–14.

69. A. Miller, "Being Sued? Roll Video," *Broward Daily Business Review*, August 15, 2001, p. A9; T. Joyner, "Work Hard, Step Straight: Big Boss Is Watching," *Chattanooga (TN) Times*, July 29, 2001, p. G1; G. T. Pakulski, "The Boss Is Watching," *Toledo (OH) Blade*, May 27, 2001; "CT Employees Sue Airline over Hidden Camera," *Amarillo (TX) Globe*, May 20, 2001.

70. K. D. Grimsley, "35% of Firms Found to Monitor Workers Electronically," *Washington Post*, May 24, 1997, p. F1. For discussion of the ethical issues of monitoring, see N. B. Fairweather, "Surveillance in Employment: The Case of Teleworking," *Journal of Business Ethics* 22 (October 1999), pp. 39–49; B. E. Bohling, "Workplace Video Surveillance," *Monthly Labor Review* 120 (July 1997), p. 41.

71. J. M. Stanton and E. M. Weiss, "Electronic Monitoring in Their Own Words: An Exploratory Study of Employees' Experiences with New Types of Surveillance," *Computers in Human Behavior* 16 (July 2000), pp. 423–40; D. Lyon, *The Electronic Eye: The Rise of the Surveillance Society* (Minneapolis: University of Minnesota Press, 1994); B. P. Niehoff and R. H. Moorman, "Justice as a Mediator of the Relationship between Methods of Monitoring and Organizational Citizenship Behavior," *Academy of Management Journal* 36 (1993), pp. 527–56; J. Chalykoff and T. A. Kochan, "Computer-Aided Monitoring: Its Influence on Employee Job Satisfaction and Turnover," *Personnel Psychology* 42 (1989), pp. 807–34.

72. A. Bandura, *Social Foundations of Thought and Action: A Social Cognitive Theory* (Englewood Cliffs, NJ: Prentice Hall, 1986).

73. A. Pescuric and W. C. Byham, "The New Look of Behavior Modeling," *Training and Development* 50 (July 1996), pp. 24–30; H. P. Sims, Jr., and C. C. Manz, "Modeling Influences on Employee Behavior," *Personnel Journal*, January 1982, pp. 58–65.

74. A. D. Stajkovic and F. Luthans, "Social Cognitive Theory and Self-Efficacy: Going Beyond Traditional Motivational and Behavioral Approaches," *Organizational Dynamics* 26 (Spring 1998), pp. 62–74; A. Bandura, *Self-Efficacy: The Exercise of Control* (New York: Freeman, 1996); M. E. Gist and T. R. Mitchell, "Self-Efficacy: A Theoretical Analysis of Its Determinants and Malleability," *Academy of Management Review* 17 (1992), pp. 183–211; R. F. Mager, "No Self-Efficacy, No Performance," *Training* 29 (April 1992), pp. 32–36.

75. L. K. Trevino, "The Social Effects of Punishment in Organizations: A Justice Perspective," *Academy of Management Review* 17 (1992), pp. 647–76; M. E. Schnake, "Vicarious Punishment in a Work Setting," *Journal of Applied Psychology* 71 (1986), pp. 343–45.

76. M. Foucault, *Discipline and Punish: The Birth of the Prison* (Harmondsworth, UK: Penguin, 1977).

77. L. K. Trevino, "The Social Effects of Punishment in Organizations: A Justice Perspective," *Academy of Management Review* 17 (1992), pp. 647–76; M. E. Schnake, "Vicarious Punishment in a Work Setting," *Journal of Applied Psychology* 71 (1986), pp. 343–45.

78. A. W. Logue, *Self-Control: Waiting until Tomorrow for What You Want Today.* (Englewood Cliffs, NJ: Prentice Hall, 1995); A. Bandura, "Self-Reinforcement: Theoretical and Methodological Considerations," *Behaviorism* 4 (1976), pp. 135–55.

79. C. A. Frayne, "Improving Employee Performance through Self-Management Training," *Business Quarterly* 54 (Summer 1989), pp. 46–50.

80. D. Woodruff, "Putting Talent to the Test," *Wall Street Journal Europe*, November 14, 2000, p. 25. The simulation events described here were experienced by the author of this article, but we reasonably assume that Mandy Chooi, who also completed the simulation, went through similar events in her simulation.

81. S. Gherardi, D. Nicolini, and F. Odella, "Toward a Social Understanding of How People Learn in Organizations," *Management Learning* 29 (September 1998), pp. 273–97; Ulrich, Jick, and Von Glinow, "High Impact Learning."

82. D. A. Kolb, *Experiential Learning* (Englewood Cliffs, NJ: Prentice Hall, 1984).

83. The learning orientation concept is the focus of current attention in marketing. See M. A. Farrell, "Developing a Market-Oriented Learning Organization," *Australian Journal of Management* 25 (September 2000); W. E. Baker and J. M. Sinkula, "The Synergistic Effect of Market Orientation and Learning Orientation," *Journal of the Academy of Marketing Science* 27 (1999), pp. 411–27.

84. A. Lee, "Mock City Rises in Mich.," *Detroit News*, May 4, 2001, p. 1.

85. J. Jusko, "Always Lessons to Learn," *Industry Week*, February 15, 1999, p. 23; A. C. Edmondson, "Learning from Mistakes Is Easier Said Than Done: Group and Organizational Influences on the Detection and Correction of Human Error," *Journal of Applied Behavioral Science* 32 (1996), pp. 5–28.

86. R. W. Revans, *The Origin and Growth of Action Learning* (London: Chartwell Bratt, 1982), pp. 626–27.

87. V. J. Marsick, "The Many Faces of Action Learning," *Management Learning* 30 (June 1999), pp. 159–76.

88. R. M. Fulmer, P. Gibbs, and J. B. Keys, "The Second Generation Learning Organizations: New Tools for Sustaining Competitive Advantage," *Organizational Dynamics* 27 (Autumn 1998), pp. 6–20; A. L. Stern "Where the Action Is," *Across the Board* 34 (September 1997), pp. 43–47; R. W. Revans, "What Is Action Learning?" *Journal of Management Development* 15 (1982), pp. 64–75.

89. R. M. Fulmer, P. A. Gibbs and M. Goldsmith, "Developing Leaders: How Winning Companies Keep On Winning," *Sloan Management Review*, October 2000, pp. 49–59; J. A. Conger and K. Xin, "Executive Education in the 21st Century," *Journal of Management Education* (February 2000), pp. 73ff.

90. T. T. Baldwin, C. Danielson, and W. Wiggenhorn, "The Evolution of Learning Strategies in Organizations: From Employee Development to Business Redefinition," *Academy of Management Executive* 11 (November 1997), pp. 47–58.

CHAPTER THREE

1. N. Bendavid, "Report Criticizes Work in Lee Case," *Chicago Tribune*, August 14, 2001, p. N1; E. Lichtblau, "Report Assails Botched Probe of Lee Spy Case," *Los Angeles Times*, August 14, 2001, p. A1; F. Davila, "Prejudice Stings 'Model Minority,'" *Baltimore Sun*, July 29, 2001, p. C5; S. Hepinstall, "Chinese-Americans Face Stereotyping—Survey," *Reuters English News Service*, April 25, 2001; O. Barker, "The Asianization of America," *USA Today*, March 22, 2001, p. A1; J. Glanz, "Amid Race Profiling Claims, Asian-Americans Avoid Labs," *New York Times*, July 16, 2000, p. 1. Dr. Wen Ho Lee was detained for nine months and eventually pleaded guilty to one count of downloading classified information on his computer. The other 58 counts of mishandling classified information were dropped.

2. Plato, *The Republic*, trans. D. Lee (Harmondsworth, UK: Penguin, 1955), part VII, sec. 7.

3. S. F. Cronshaw and R. G. Lord, "Effects of Categorization, Attribution, and Encoding Processes on Leadership Perceptions," *Journal of Applied Psychology* 72 (1987), pp. 97–106.

4. R. H. Fazio, D. R. Roskos-Ewoldsen, and M. C. Powell, "Attitudes, Perception, and Attention," in P. M. Niedenthal and S. Kitayama, eds., *The Heart's Eye: Emotional Influences in Perception and Attention* (San Diego, CA: Academic Press, 1994), pp. 197–216.

5. D. Goleman, *Vital Lies, Simple Truths: The Psychology of Deception* (New York: Touchstone, 1985); M. Haire and W. F. Grunes, "Perceptual Defenses: Processes Protecting an Organized Perception of Another Personality," *Human Relations* 3 (1950), pp. 403–12.

6. C. N. Macrae, G. V. Bodenhausen, A. M. Schloerscheidt, and A. B. Milne, "Tales of the Unexpected: Executive Function and Person Perception," *Journal of Personality and Social Psychology* 76 (1999), pp. 200–13; J. M. Beyer et al., "The Selective Perception of Managers Revisited," *Academy of Management Journal* 40 (June 1997), pp. 716–37; C. N. Macrae and G. V. Bodenhausen, "The Dissection of Selection in Person Perception: Inhibitory Processes in Social Stereotyping," *Journal of Personality and Social Psychology* 69 (1995), pp. 397–407; J. P. Walsh, "Selectivity and Selective Perception: An Investigation of Managers' Belief Structures and Information Processing," *Academy of Management Journal* 31 (1988), pp. 873–96; D. C. Dearborn and H. A. Simon, "Selective Perception: A Note on the Departmental Identification of Executives," *Sociometry* 21 (1958), pp. 140–44.

7. J. Rupert, "We Haven't Forgotten about Her," *Ottawa Citizen*, December 6, 1999; W. Burkan, "Developing Your Wide-Angle Vision; Skills for Anticipating the Future," *Futurist* 32 (March

1998), pp. 35–38. For splatter vision applied to professional bird watchers, see E. Nickens, "Window on the Wild," *Backpacker* 25 (April 1997), pp. 28–32.

8. D. Gurteen, "Knowledge, Creativity and Innovation," *Journal of Knowledge Management* 2 (September 1998), p. 5; C. Argyris and D. A. Schön, *Organizational Learning II* (Reading, MA: Addison-Wesley, 1996); P. M. Senge, *The Fifth Discipline: The Art and Practice of the Learning Organization* (New York: Doubleday Currency, 1990), chap. 10; P. N. Johnson-Laird, *Mental Models* (Cambridge, UK: Cambridge University Press, 1984). Mental models are widely discussed in the philosophy of logic. For example, see J. L. Aronson, "Mental Models and Deduction," *American Behavioral Scientist* 40 (May 1997), pp. 782–97.

9. Burkan, "Developing Your Wide-Angle Vision."

10. "What Are Mental Models?" *Sloan Management Review* 38 (Spring 1997), p. 13; P. Nystrom and W. Starbuck, "To Avoid Organizational Crises, Unlearn," *Organizational Dynamics* 12 (Winter 1984), pp. 53–65.

11. T. Abate, "Meet Bill Gates, Stand-up Comic," *San Francisco Examiner*, March 13, 1996, p. D1; P. J. H. Schoemaker, "Scenario Planning: A Tool for Strategic Thinking," *Sloan Management Review* 36 (Winter 1995), pp. 25–40.

12. P. Roberts, "Sony Changes the Game," *Fast Company* 10 (1997), p. 116.

13. M. A. Hogg and D. J. Terry, "Social Identity and Self-Categorization Processes in Organizational Contexts," *Academy of Management Review* 25 (January 2000), pp. 121–40; B. E. Ashforth and F. Mael, "Social Identity Theory and the Organization," *Academy of Management Review* 14 (1989), pp. 20–39; H. Tajfel, *Social Identity and Intergroup Relations* (Cambridge, UK: Cambridge University Press, 1982).

14. The interaction between personal and social identity is quite complex, as researchers are now discovering. See J. A. Howard, "Social Psychology of Identities," *Annual Review of Sociology* 26 (2000), pp. 367–93.

15. J. E. Dutton, J. M. Dukerich, and C. V. Harquail, "Organizational Images and Member Identification," *Adminis-trative Science Quarterly* 39 (June 1994), pp. 239–63. For recent research on the selection of identity groups, see B. Simon and C. Hastedt, "Self-Aspects as Social Categories: The Role of Personal Importance and Valence," *European Journal of Social Psychology* 29 (1999), pp. 479–87.

16. J. W. Jackson and E. R. Smith, "Conceptualizing Social Identity: A New Framework and Evidence for the Impact of Different Dimensions," *Personality and Social Psychology Bulletin* 25 (January 1999), pp. 120–35.

17. G. Brenneman, "Right Away and All at Once: How We Saved Continental," *Harvard Business Review* 76 (September–October 1998), pp. 162–79; T. Kennedy, "Confidence Returns with Continental's Strong Comeback," *Minneapolis Star Tribune*, February 1, 1998, p. 1A.

18. C. N. Macrae and G. V. Bodenhausen, "Social Cognition: Thinking Categorically about Others," *Annual Review of Psychology* 51 (2000), pp. 93–120; W. G. Stephan and C. W. Stephan, *Intergroup Relations* (Boulder, CO: Westview, 1996), chap. 1; L. Falkenberg, "Improving the Accuracy of Stereotypes within the Workplace," *Journal of Management* 16 (1990), pp. 107–18; D. L. Hamilton, S. J. Sherman, and C. M. Ruvolo, "Stereotype-Based Expectancies: Effects on Information Processing and Social Behavior," *Journal of Social Issues* 46 (1990), pp. 35–60.

19. F. T. McAndrew et al., "A Multicultural Study of Stereotyping in English-Speaking Countries," *Journal of Social Psychology* 740 (August 2000), pp. 487–502; S. Madon et al., "The Accuracy and Power of Sex, Social Class, and Ethnic Stereotypes: A Naturalistic Study in Person Perception," *Personality and Social Psychology Bulletin* 24 (December 1998), pp. 1304–18; Y. Lee, L. J. Jussim, and C. R. McCauley, eds., *Stereotype Accuracy: Toward Appreciating Group Differences* (Washington, DC: American Psychological Association, 1996). For an early discussion of stereotypes, see W. Lippmann, *Public Opinion* (New York: Macmillan, 1922).

20. D. L. Stone and A. Colella, "A Model of Factors Affecting the Treatment of Disabled Individuals in Organizations," *Academy of Management Review* 21 (1996), pp. 352–401.

21. C. Stangor and D. McMillan, "Memory for Expectancy-Congruent and Expectancy-Incongruent Information: A Review of the Social and Social Development Literatures," *Psychological Bulletin* 111 (1992), pp. 42–61; C. Stangor, L. Lynch, C. Duan, and B. Glass, "Categorization of Individuals on the Basis of Multiple Social Features," *Journal of Personality and Social Psychology* 62 (1992), pp. 207–18.

22. P. J. Oaks, S. A. Haslam, and J. C. Turner, *Stereotyping and Social Reality* (Cambridge, MA: Blackwell, 1994).

23. J. W. Sherman, A. Y. Lee, G. R. Bessenoff, and L. A. Frost, "Stereotype Efficiency Reconsidered: Encoding Flexibility under Cognitive Load," *Journal of Personality and Social Psychology* 75 (1998), pp. 589–606; C. N. Macrae, A. B. Milne, and G. V. Bodenhausen, "Stereotypes as Energy-Saving Devices: A Peek Inside the Cognitive Toolbox," *Journal of Personality and Social Psychology* 66 (1994), pp. 37–47; S. T. Fiske, "Social Cognition and Social Perception," *Annual Review of Psychology* 44 (1993), pp. 155–94.

24. Z. Kunda and P. Thagard, "Forming Impressions from Stereotypes, Traits, and Behaviors: A Parallel-Constraint Satisfaction Theory," *Psychological Review* 103 (1996), pp. 284–308.

25. S. O. Gaines and E. S. Reed, "Prejudice: From Allport to DuBois," *American Psychologist* 50 (February 1995), pp. 96–103; L. Jussim and T. E. Nelson, "Prejudice, Stereotypes, and Labeling Effects: Sources of Bias in Person Perception," *Journal of Personality and Social Psychology* 68 (February 1995), pp. 228–46.

26. P. Porco, "Intolerance Claims Mount," *Anchorage Daily News*, July 19, 2001, p. A1; K. Sinclair, "New Laws Unlikely to Stamp Out Racial Prejudice," *South China Morning Post*, April 25, 2001, p. 17; M. C. Quinn, "Southern's Big Day," *Atlanta Journal–Constitution*, April 1, 2001, p. G1; L. Hunt, "Racism in Hong Kong Seen Tarnishing Territory's Reputation," *Agence France Presse*, January 29, 2001.

27. A. P. Brief et al., "Beyond Good Intentions: The Next Steps toward Racial Equality in the American Workplace," *Academy of Management Executive* 11 (November 1997), pp. 59–72; M. J.

Monteith, "Self-Regulation of Prejudiced Responses: Implications for Progress in Prejudice-Reduction Efforts," *Journal of Personality and Social Psychology* 65 (1993), pp. 469–85.

28. P. M. Buzzanell, "Reframing the Glass Ceiling as a Socially Constructed Process: Implications for Understanding and Change," *Communication Monographs* 62 (December 1995), pp. 327–54; M. E. Heilman, "Sex Stereotypes and Their Effects in the Workplace: What We Know and What We Don't Know," *Journal of Social Behavior and Personality* 10 (1995), pp. 3–26.

29. Age bias is also making headlines in the United States. See M. Ortiz, "Age-Bias Claims Jolt Ford Culture Change," *Detroit News*, April 29, 2001; L. B. Song, "Technology Workers Say Age Bias Becoming More Noticeable," *Chicago Tribune*, April 13, 2001; R. Pogrebin, "At 40, They're Finished, Television Writers Say," *New York Times*, January 30, 2001, p. 9.

30. S. T. Fiske and P. Glick, "Ambivalence and Stereotypes Cause Sexual Harassment: A Theory with Implications for Organizational Change," *Journal of Social Issues* 51 (1995), pp. 97–115; K. Deaux, "How Basic Can You Be? The Evolution of Research on Gender Stereotypes," *Journal of Social Issues* 51 (1995), pp. 11–20.

31. E. Rosell and K. Miller, "Firefighting Women and Sexual Harassment," *Public Personnel Management* 24 (Fall 1995), pp. 339–50.

32. H. H. Kelley, *Attribution in Social Interaction* (Morristown, NJ: General Learning Press, 1971).

33. H. H. Kelley, "The Processes of Causal Attribution," *American Psychologist* 28 (1973), pp. 107–28; J. M. Feldman, "Beyond Attribution Theory: Cognitive Processes in Performance Appraisal," *Journal of Applied Psychology* 66 (1981), pp. 127–48.

34. J. D. Ford, "The Effects of Causal Attributions on Decision Makers' Responses to Performance Downturns," *Academy of Management Review* 10 (1985), pp. 770–86; M. J. Martinko and W. L. Gardner, "The Leader/Member Attribution Process," *Academy of Management Review* 12 (1987), pp. 235–49.

35. J. Martocchio and J. Dulebohn, "Performance Feedback Effects in Training: The Role of Perceived Controllability," *Personnel Psychology* 47 (1994), pp. 357–73; J. M. Crant and T. S. Bateman, "Assignment of Credit and Blame for Performance Outcomes," *Academy of Management Journal* 36 (1993), pp. 7–27; D. R. Norris and R. E. Niebuhr, "Attributional Influences on the Job Performance–Job Satisfaction Relationship," *Academy of Management Journal* 27 (1984), pp. 424–31.

36. H. J. Bernardin and P. Villanova, "Performance Appraisal," in E. A. Locke, ed., *Generalising from Laboratory to Field Settings* (Lexington, MA: Lexington Books, 1986), pp. 43–62; S. G. Green and T. R. Mitchell, "Attributional Processes of Leader-Member Interactions," *Organizational Behavior and Human Performance* 23 (1979), pp. 429–58.

37. P. J. Taylor and J. L. Pierce, "Effects of Introducing a Performance Management System on Employees' Subsequent Attitudes and Effort," *Public Personnel Management* 28 (Fall 1999), pp. 423–52.

38. J. R. Bettman and B. A. Weitz, "Attributions in the Board Room: Causal Reasoning in Corporate Annual Reports," *Administrative Science Quarterly* 28 (1983), pp. 165–83.

39. P. Rosenthal and D. Guest, "Gender Difference in Managers' Causal Explanations for Their Work Performance: A Study in Two Organizations," *Journal of Occupational and Organizational Psychology* 69 (1996), pp. 145–51.

40. B. McElhinny, "Printing Plant Makes Its Mark," *Charleston (WV) Daily Mail*, May 6, 1997, p. D1.

41. J. M. Darley and K. C. Oleson, "Introduction to Research on Interpersonal Expectations," in P. D. Blanck, ed., *Interpersonal Expectations: Theory, Research, and Applications* (Cambridge, UK: Cambridge University Press, 1993), pp. 45–63; D. Eden, *Pygmalion in Management* (Lexington, MA: Lexington, 1990); L. Jussim, "Self-Fulfilling Prophecies: A Theoretical and Integrative Review," *Psychological Review* 93 (1986), pp. 429–45.

42. D. Eden and A. B. Shani, "Pygmalion Goes to Boot Camp: Expectancy, Leadership, and Trainee Performance," *Journal of Applied Psychology* 67 (1982), pp. 194–99.

43. Similar models are presented in R. H. G. Field and D. A. Van Seters, "Management by Expectations (MBE): The Power of Positive Prophecy," *Journal of General Management* 14 (Winter 1988), pp. 19–33; D. Eden, "Self-Fulfilling Prophecy as a Management Tool: Harnessing Pygmalion," *Academy of Management Review* 9 (1984), pp. 64–73.

44. M. J. Harris and R. Rosenthal, "Mediation of Interpersonal Expectancy Effects: 31 Meta-Analyses," *Psychological Bulletin* 97 (1985), pp. 363–86.

45. D. Eden, "Interpersonal Expectations in Organizations," in , ed., *Interpersonal Expectations: Theory, Research, and Applications* (Cambridge, UK: Cambridge University Press, 1993), pp. 154–78.

46. A. Bandura, *Self-Efficacy: The Exercise of Control* (New York: Freeman, 1996); M. E. Gist and T. R. Mitchell, "Self-Efficacy: A Theoretical Analysis of Its Determinants and Malleability," *Academy of Management Review* 17 (1992), pp. 183–211.

47. J-F. Manzoni, "The Set-Up-to-Fail Syndrome," *Harvard Business Review* 76 (March–April 1998), pp. 101–13; J. S. Livingston, "Retrospective Commentary," *Harvard Business Review* 66 (September–October 1988), p. 125.

48. The earlier advice on positive expectations is found in S. Oz and D. Eden, "Restraining the Golem: Boosting Performance by Changing the Interpretation of Low Scores," *Journal of Applied Psychology* 79 (1994), pp. 744–54; D. Eden, "OD and Self-Fulfilling Prophecy: Boosting Productivity by Raising Expectations," *Journal of Applied Behavioral Science* 22 (1986), pp. 1–13.

49. S. S. White and E. A. Locke, "Problems with the Pygmalion Effect and Some Proposed Solutions," *Leadership Quarterly* 11 (Autumn 2000), pp. 389–415. This source also cites recent studies on the failure of traditional Pygmalion training. For an early application of self-efficacy in self-fulfilling prophecy, see K. S. Crawford, E. D. Thomas, and J. J. Fink, "Pygmalion at Sea: Improving the Work Effectiveness of Low Performers," *Journal of Applied Behavioral Science* 16 (1980), pp. 482–505.

50. T. Hill, P. Lewicki, M. Czyzewska, and A. Boss, "Self-Perpetuating

Development of Encoding Biases in Person Perception," *Journal of Personality and Social Psychology* 57 (1989), pp. 373–87; C. L. Kleinke, *First Impressions: The Psychology of Encountering Others* (Englewood Cliffs, NJ: Prentice Hall, 1975).

51. R. Wright, "Great X-pectations," *Canadian Banker* 106 (January–February 1999), pp. 11–15.

52. D. D. Steiner and J. S. Rain, "Immediate and Delayed Primacy and Recency Effects in Performance Evaluation," *Journal of Applied Psychology* 74 (1989), pp. 136–42; R. L. Heneman and K. N. Wexley, "The Effects of Time Delay in Rating and Amount of Information Observed in Performance Rating Accuracy," *Academy of Management Journal* 26 (1983), pp. 677–86.

53. W. H. Cooper, "Ubiquitous Halo," *Psychological Bulletin* 90 (1981), pp. 218–44; K. R. Murphy, R. A. Jako, and R. L. Anhalt, "Nature and Consequences of Halo Error: A Critical Analysis," *Journal of Applied Psychology* 78 (1993), pp. 218–25.

54. S. Kozlowski, M. Kirsch, and G. Chao, "Job Knowledge, Ratee Familiarity, Conceptual Similarity, and Halo Error: An Exploration," *Journal of Applied Psychology* 71 (1986), pp. 45–49; H. C. Min, "Country Image: Halo or Summary Construct?" *Journal of Marketing Research* 26 (1989), pp. 222–29.

55. W. K. Balzer and L. M. Sulsky, "Halo and Performance Appraisal Research: A Critical Examination," *Journal of Applied Psychology* 77 (1992), pp. 975–85; H. J. Bernardin and R. W. Beatty, *Performance Appraisal: Assessing Human Behavior at Work* (Boston: Kent, 1984).

56. R. L Gross and S. E. Brodt, "How Assumptions of Consensus Undermine Decision Making," *Sloan Management Review* 42 (January 2001), pp. 86–94; G. G. Sherwood, "Self-Serving Biases in Person Perception: A Re-examination of Projection as a Mechanism of Defense," *Psychological Bulletin* 90 (1981), pp. 445–59.

57. "Women Flourish in Schwab's Climate," *San Francisco Business Times*, April 27, 2001, p. S10.

58. "Diversity Initiatives Help Keep a Competitive Edge," *PR Newswire*, June 4, 2001; R. M. Wentling and N. Palma-Rivas, "Current Status of Diversity Initiatives in Selected Multinational Corporations," *Human Resource Development Quarterly* 11 (Spring 2000), pp. 35–60; J. A. Gilbert, B. A. Stead, and J. M. Ivancevich, "Diversity Management: A New Organizational Paradigm," *Journal of Business Ethics* 21 (August 1999), pp. 61–76; G. Robinson and K. Dechant, "Building a Business Case for Diversity," *Academy of Management Executive* 11 (August 1997), pp. 21–31.

59. J. Neff, "Johnson Layers Diversity," *Advertising Age*, February 19, 2001, pp. S1–S2.

60. R. Hudson, "Employers Find a More Diverse Work Force Brings a Variety of Religious Beliefs," *St. Louis Post-Dispatch*, August 6, 2001, p. 10.

61. D. E. Owens, "Walt Disney Resort: Winner—Cutting Edge Award," *Orlando Sentinel*, August 5, 2001, p. 35; L. Eckelbecker, "Raytheon Celebrates Diversity," *Telegram and Gazette* (Worcester, MA), June 8, 2001, p. E1.

62. H. Hemphill and R. Haines, *Discrimination, Harassment, and the Failure of Diversity Training: What to Do Now* (Westport, CT: Quorum Books, 1997); J. R. W. Joplin and C. S. Daus, "Challenges of Leading a Diverse Workforce," *Academy of Management Executive* 11 (August 1997), pp. 32–47.

63. B. Parks, "Club Swinging a Sticky Situation in NHL," *Star-Ledger (Newark, NJ)*, March 28, 2000, p. 61; L. Hornby, "Racism Meeting Hits Home with Leafs Players," *Toronto Sun*, September 27, 1999, p. 81; K. C. Johnson, "When Words Collide," *Chicago Tribune*, May 2, 1999, p. 7.

64. B. Whitaker, "United Parcel's School for Hard Hearts, Sort Of," *New York Times*, July 26, 2000; M. J. Reid, "Profit Motivates Corporate Diversity," *San Francisco Examiner*, March 15, 1998, p. W42.

65. W. G. Stephen and K. A. Finlay, "The Role of Empathy in Improving Intergroup Relations," *Journal of Social Issues* 55 (Winter 1999), pp. 729–43; D. B. Fedor and K. M. Rowland, "Investigating Supervisor Attributions of Subordinate Performance," *Journal of Management* 15 (1989), pp. 405–16; G. Egan, *The Skilled Helper: A Model for Systematic Helping and Interpersonal Relating* (Belmont, CA: Brooks/Cole, 1975).

66. D. Goleman, "What Makes a Leader?" *Harvard Business Review* 76 (November–December 1998), pp. 92–102.

67. C. Tsai, "Molly Maid President Calls It an Honor to Serve," *Associated Press Newswire*, October 6, 1999.

68. L. Beamer, "Learning Intercultural Communication Competence," *Journal of Business Communication* 29 (1992), pp. 285–303; D. Landis and R. W. Brislin, eds., *Handbook of Intercultural Training* (New York: Pergamon, 1983).

69. T. W. Costello and S. S. Zalkind, *Psychology in Administration: A Research Orientation* (Englewood Cliffs, NJ: Prentice Hall, 1963), pp. 45–46.

70. J. Luft, *Group Processes* (Palo Alto, CA: Mayfield, 1984). For a variation of this model, see J. Hall, "Communication Revisited," *California Management Review* 15 (Spring 1973), pp. 56–67.

71. L. C. Miller and D. A. Kenny, "Reciprocity of Self-Disclosure at the Individual and Dyadic Levels: A Social Relations Analysis," *Journal of Personality and Social Psychology* 50 (1986), pp. 713–19.

72. L. Himelstein, "The General Says 'Charge!'" *Business Week*, February 19, 2001, p. 34.

73. R. T. Hogan, "Personality and Personality Measurement," in M. D. Dunnette and L. M. Hough, eds., *Handbook of Industrial and Organizational Psychology*, 2nd ed., vol. 2 (Palo Alto, CA: Consulting Psychologists Press, 1991), pp. 873–919. Also see W. Mischel, *Introduction to Personality* (New York: Holt, Rinehart & Winston, 1986).

74. H. M. Weiss and S. Adler, "Personality and Organizational Behavior," *Research in Organizational Behavior* 6 (1984), pp. 1–50.

75. W. Revelle, "Personality Processes," *Annual Review of Psychology* 46 (1995), pp. 295–328.

76. R. M. Guion and R. F. Gottier, "Validity of Personality Measures in Personnel Selection," *Personnel Psychology* 18 (1965), pp. 135–64. Also see N. Schmitt, R. Z. Gooding, R. D. Noe, and M. Kirsch, "Meta-Analyses of Validity Studies Published between 1964 and 1982 and the Investigation of

Study Characteristics," *Personnel Psychology* 37 (1984), pp. 407–22.

77. P. G. Irving, "On the Use of Personality Measures in Personnel Selection," *Canadian Psychology* 34 (April 1993), pp. 208–14.

78. K. M. DeNeve and H. Cooper, "The Happy Personality: A Meta-Analysis of 137 Personality Traits and Subjective Well-Being," *Psychological Bulletin* 124 (September 1998), pp. 197–229; M. K. Mount and M. R. Barrick, "The Big Five Personality Dimensions: Implications for Research and Practice in Human Resources Management," *Research in Personnel and Human Resources Management* 13 (1995), pp. 153–200; B. M. Bass, *Stogdill's Handbook of Leadership: A Survey of Theory and Research,* 3rd ed. (New York: Free Press, 1990); J. L. Holland, *Making Vocation Choices: A Theory of Careers* (Englewood Cliffs, NJ: Prentice Hall, 1973).

79. C. Daniels, "Does This Man Need a Shrink?" *Fortune*, February 5, 2001, p. 205.

80. This historical review and the trait descriptions in this section are discussed in R. J. Schneider and L. M. Hough, "Personality and Industrial/Organizational Psychology," *International Review of Industrial and Organizational Psychology* 10 (1995), pp. 75–129; Mount and Barrick, "The Big Five Personality Dimensions"; J. M. Digman, "Personality Structure: Emergence of the Five-Factor Model," *Annual Review of Psychology* 41 (1990), pp. 417–40.

81. G. M. Hurtz and J. J. Donovan, "Personality and Job Performance: The Big Five Revisited," *Journal of Applied Psychology* 85 (December 2000), pp. 869–79; M. K. Mount, M. R. Barrick, and J. P. Strauss, "Validity of Observer Ratings of the Big Five Personality Factors," *Journal of Applied Psychology* 79 (1994), pp. 272–80; R. P. Tett, D. N. Jackson, and M. Rothstein, "Personality Measures as Predictors of Job Performance: A Meta-Analytic Review," *Personnel Psychology* 44 (1991), pp. 703–42.

82. J. M. Howell and C. A. Higgins, "Champions of Change: Identifying, Understanding, and Supporting Champions of Technological Innovations," *Organizational Dynamics* 19 (Summer 1990), pp. 40–55.

83. M. Dalton and M. Wilson, "The Relationship of the Five-Factor Model of Personality to Job Performance for a Group of Middle Eastern Expatriate Managers," *Journal of Cross-Cultural Psychology* 31 (March 2000), pp. 250–58; K. P. Carson and G. L. Stewart, "Job Analysis and the Sociotechnical Approach to Quality: A Critical Examination," *Journal of Quality Management* 1 (1996), pp. 49–64; Mount and Barrick, "The Big Five Personality Dimensions," pp. 177–78.

84. I. B. Myers, *The Myers-Briggs Type Indicator* (Palo Alto, CA: Consulting Psychologists Press, 1987); C. G. Jung, *Psychological Types*, trans. H. G. Baynes, rev. R. F. C. Hull (Princeton, NJ: Princeton University Press, 1971) (Original work published 1921).

85. L. R. Offermann and R. K. Spiros, "The Science and Practice of Team Development: Improving the Link," *Academy of Management Journal* 44 (April 2001), pp. 376–92.

86. G. Potts, "Oklahoma City Employers Use Personality Tests to Improve Placement," *Daily Oklahoman*, February 26, 2001.

87. D. W. Salter and N. J. Evans, "Test-Retest of the Myers-Briggs Type Indicator: An Examination of Dominant Functioning," *Educational and Psychological Measurement* 57 (August 1997), pp. 590–97; W. L. Gardner and M. J. Martinko, "Using the Myers-Briggs Type Indicator to Study Managers: A Literature Review and Research Agenda," *Journal of Management* 22 (1996), pp. 45–83; R. Zemke, "Second Thoughts about the MBTI," *Training*, April 1992, pp. 42–47; M. H. McCaulley, "The Myers-Briggs Type Indicator: A Measure for Individuals and Groups," *Measurement and Evaluation in Counseling and Development* 22 (1990), pp. 181–95.

88. C. Caggiano, "Psycho Path," *Inc.* 20 (July 1998), pp. 76–85.

89. Gardner and Martinko, "Using the Myers-Briggs Type Indicator to Study Managers."

90. S. S. K. Lam and J. Schaubroeck, "The Role of Locus of Control in Reactions to Being Promoted and to Being Passed Over: A Quasi Experiment," *Academy of Management Journal* 43 (February 2000), pp. 66–78; J. M. Howell and B. J. Avolio, "Transformational Leadership, Transactional Leadership, Locus of Control, and Support for Innovation: Key Predictors of Consolidated-Business-Unit Performance," *Journal of Applied Psychology* 78 (1993), pp. 891–902; D. Miller and J-M. Toulouse, "Chief Executive Personality and Corporate Strategy and Structure in Small Firms," *Management Science* 32 (1986), pp. 1389–1409; P. E. Spector, "Behavior in Organizations as a Function of Employee's Locus of Control," *Psychological Bulletin* 91 (1982), pp. 482–97.

91. M. Snyder, *Public Appearances/Private Realities: The Psychology of Self-Monitoring* (New York: Freeman, 1987).

92. M. A. Warech, J. W. Smither, R. R. Reilly, R. E. Millsap, and S. P. Reilly, "Self-Monitoring and 360-Degree Ratings," *Leadership Quarterly* 9 (Winter 1998), pp. 449–73; M. Kilduff and D. V. Day, "Do Chameleons Get Ahead? The Effects of Self-Monitoring on Managerial Careers," *Academy of Management Journal* 37 (1994), pp. 1047–60; R. J. Ellis and S. E. Cronshaw, Self-Monitoring and Leader Emergence: A Test of Moderator Effects," *Small Group Research* 23 (1992), pp. 113–29; S. J. Zaccaro, R. J. Foti, and D. A. Kenny, "Self-Monitoring and Trait-Based Variance in Leadership: An Investigation of Leader Flexibility across Multiple Group Situations," *Journal of Applied Psychology* 76 (1991), pp. 308–15.

93. H. A. Simon, *Administrative Behavior* (New York: Free Press, 1957), p. xv.

CHAPTER FOUR

1. J. Doebele, "Kiwi Category Killer," *Forbes*, August 20, 2001; S. Fea, "Tindall Pushes Zero Waste," *Southland Times (Chistchurch, NZ)*, May 11, 2001, p. 3; A. Miriyana, "A Southern Man," *Sunday Star-Times (Auckland, NZ)*, March 4, 2001, p. A3; "Warehouse Grasps the Bigger Picture," *New Zealand Herald*, January 4, 2001; M. Alexander, "Warehouse Boss Just Loves Seeing Red," *Sunday Star-Times (Auckland, NZ)*, December 31, 2000; J. E. Hilsenrath, "Value Creators: In the Company of Asia's Superheroes," *Asian Wall Street Journal*, December 8, 2000, p. P3; S. Hendery, "Warehouse Plans to Give Us All a Foot in the Store," *New Zealand Herald*, November 25, 2000; S. Hendery, "Expansion Hits

Warehouse Sales," *New Zealand Herald*, November 8, 2000.

2. A. Sagie and D. Elizur, "Work Values: A Theoretical Overview and a Model of Their Effects," *Journal of Organizational Behavior* 17 (1996), pp. 503–14; S. H. Schwartz, "Are There Universal Aspects in the Structure and Contents of Human Values?" *Journal of Social Issues* 50 (1994), pp. 19–45; W. H. Schmidt and B. Z. Posner, *Managerial Values in Perspective* (New York: American Management Association, 1983); M. Rokeach, *The Nature of Human Values* (New York: Free Press, 1973); F. Kluckhorn and F. L. Strodtbeck, *Variations in Value Orientations* (Evanston, IL: Row, Peterson, 1961).

3. C. Kleiman, "Self-Assessment Essential Aspect of Balanced Life," *Chicago Tribune*, May 1, 2001.

4. M. Rokeach, *Understanding Human Values* (New York: Free Press, 1979).

5. B. M. Meglino and E. C. Ravlin, "Individual Values in Organizations: Concepts, Controversies, and Research," *Journal of Management* 24 (May 1998), pp. 351–89.

6. Meglino and Ravlin, "Individual Values in Organizations"; C. Argyris and D. A. Schön, *Organizational Learning: A Theory of Action Perspective* (Reading, MA: Addison-Wesley, 1978).

7. B. R. Agle and C. B. Caldwell, "Understanding Research on Values in Business," *Business and Society* 38 (September 1999), pp. 326–87; P. McDonald and J. Gandz, "Getting Value from Values," *Organizational Dynamics*, Winter 1992, pp. 64–77.

8. S. R. Chatterjee and C. A. L. Pearson, "Indian Managers in Transition: Orientations, Work Goals, Values and Ethics," *Management International Review* 40 (January 2000), pp. 81–95.

9. The role of values as a control system is discussed in T. M. Begley, "Articulating Corporate Values through Human Resource Policies," *Business Horizons*, July 2000; J. C. McCune, "Exporting Corporate Culture," *Management Review* 88 (December 1999), pp. 52–56; M. S. Fenwick, H. L. DeCieri, and D. E. Welch, "Cultural and Bureaucratic Control in MNEs: The Role of Expatriate Performance Management," *Management International Review* 39 (1999), Special Issue no. 3.

10. P. Pruzan, "The Question of Organizational Consciousness: Can Organizations Have Values, Virtues and Visions?" *Journal of Business Ethics* 29 (February 2001), pp. 271–84.

11. Chatterjee and Pearson, "Indian Managers in Transition"; K. F. Alam, "Business Ethics in New Zealand Organizations: Views from the Middle and Lower Level Managers," *Journal of Business Ethics* 22 (November 1999), pp. 145–53.

12. C. Salter, "This Is One Fast Factory," *Fast Company* 49 (August 2001), pp. 32–33; M. Howard, "All About Attitude," *Richmond (VA) Times-Dispatch*, May 7, 2001, p. D16.

13. B. Pheasant, "Business Searches for a Soul," *Australian Financial Review*, April 21, 2001, p. 28; H. Trinca, "The McKinsey Rapport," *Boss Magazine*, March 9, 2001, p. 34.

14. C. Fox, "Firms Go Warm and Fuzzy to Lure Staff," *Australian Financial Review*, May 15, 2001, p. 58.

15. A. Gove, "Culture Club," *Red Herring*, November 1998.

16. K. L. Newman and S. D. Nolan, "Culture and Congruence: The Fit between Management Practices and National Culture," *Journal of International Business Studies* 27 (1996), pp. 753–79; G. Hofstede, "Cultural Constraints in Management Theories," *Academy of Management Executive* 7 (1993), pp. 81–94; G. Hofstede, *Culture's Consequences: International Differences in Work-Related Values* (Beverly Hills, CA: Sage, 1980).

17. F. S. Niles, "Individualism-Collectivism Revisited," *Cross-Cultural Research* 32 (November 1998), pp. 315–41; C. P. Earley and C. B. Gibson, "Taking Stock in Our Progress on Individualism-Collectivism: 100 Years of Solidarity and Community," *Journal of Management* 24 (May 1998), pp. 265–304; J. A. Wagner III, "Studies of Individualism-Collectivism: Effects of Cooperation in Groups," *Academy of Management Journal* 38 (1995), pp. 152–72; H. C. Triandis, *Individualism and Collectivism* (Boulder, CO: Westview, 1995). Some research suggests that individualism and collectivism are two separate values, not polar opposites of one value. At the risk of being too traditional, we have kept these as

one value until research leads to more definitive conclusions. See D. A. Ralston, V. T. Nguyen, and N. K. Napier, "A Comparative Study of the Work Values of North and South Vietnamese Managers," *Journal of International Business Studies* 30 (October 1999), pp. 655–72.

18. M. Erez and P. Christopher Earley, *Culture, Self-Identity, and Work* (New York: Oxford University Press, 1993), pp. 126–27.

19. G. Hofstede, *Cultures and Organizations: Software of the Mind* (New York: McGraw-Hill, 1991), p. 124. Hofstede used the terms *masculinity* and *femininity* for achievement and nurturing orientation, respectively. We have adopted the latter terminology to minimize the sexist perspective of these concepts. The achievement and nurturing orientation labels are also used in G. R. Jones, J. M. George, and C. W. L. Hill, *Contemporary Management* (Burr Ridge, IL: Irwin/McGraw-Hill, 1998), pp. 112–13.

20. For counterarguments to these criticisms, see G. Hofstede, "Attitudes, Values and Organizational Culture: Disentangling the Concepts," *Organization Studies* 19 (June 1998), pp. 477–92.

21. C. W. Stephan, W. G. Stephan, I. Saito, and S. M. Barnett, "Emotional Expression in Japan and the United States: The Nonmonolithic Nature of Individualism and Collectivism," *Journal of Cross-Cultural Psychology* 29 (November 1998), pp. 728–48; D. Matsumoto, T. Kudoh, and S. Takeuchi, "Changing Patterns of Individualism and Collectivism in the United States and Japan," *Culture and Psychology* 2 (1996), pp. 77–107. For a discussion of Americanization, see C. McGregor, "It's the United States of Australia, and Let Us All Rejoice," *The Age*, April 11, 2001.

22. S. S. Sarwono and R. W. Armstrong, "Microcultural Differences and Perceived Ethical Problems: An International Business Perspective," *Journal of Business Ethics* 30 (March 2001), pp. 41–56; C. J. Robertson, "The Global Dispersion of Chinese Values: A Three-Country Study of Confucian Dynamism," *Management International Review* 40 (Third Quarter 2000), pp. 253–68; J. S. Osland, A. Bird, J. Delano, and M. Jacob, "Beyond Sophisticated

Stereotyping: Cultural Sensemaking in Context," *Academy of Management Executive* 14 (February 2000), pp. 65–79.

23. C. Hess and K. Hey, " 'Good' Doesn't Always Mean 'Right,' " *Across the Board* 38 (July–August 2001), pp. 61–64.

24. For a discussion of the relationship between work values and ethics, see J. J. Dose, "Work Values: An Integrative Framework and Illustrative Application to Organizational Socialization," *Journal of Occupational and Organizational Psychology* 70 (September 1997), pp. 219–40.

25. C. Savoye, "Workers Say Honesty Is Best Company Policy," *Christian Science Monitor*, June 15, 2000.

26. L. Koss-Feder, "The Good Works Perk," *Time*, January 22, 2001, p. B1.

27. W. H. Shaw and V. Barry, *Moral Issues in Business*, 5th ed. (Belmont, CA: Wadsworth, 1992), chaps. 1–3; M. G. Velasquez, *Business Ethics*, 2nd ed. (Englewood Cliffs, NJ: Prentice Hall, 1988), chap. 2.

28. R. Berenbeim, "The Search for Global Ethics," *Vital Speeches of the Day* 65 (January 1999), pp. 177–78.

29. B. H. Frey, "The Impact of Moral Intensity on Decision Making in a Business Context," *Journal of Business Ethics* 26 (August 2000), pp. 181–95; J. M. Dukerich, M. J. Waller, E. George, and G. P. Huber, "Moral Intensity and Managerial Problem Solving," *Journal of Business Ethics* 24 (March 2000), pp. 29–38; T. J. Jones, "Ethical Decision Making by Individuals in Organizations: An Issue Contingent Model," *Academy of Management Review* 16 (1991), pp. 366–95.

30. J. R. Sparks and S. D. Hunt, "Marketing Researcher Ethical Sensitivity: Conceptualization, Measurement, and Exploratory Investigation," *Journal of Marketing* 62 (April 1998), pp. 92–109.

31. B. Stoneman and K. K. Holliday, "Pressure Cooker," *Banking Strategies*, January–February 2001, p. 13; Alam, "Business Ethics in New Zealand Organizations"; K. Blotnicky, "Is Business in Moral Decay?" *Halifax (Nova Scotia) Chronicle-Herald*, June 11, 2000; D. McDougall and B. Orsini, "Fraudbusting Ethics," *CMA Management* 73 (June 1999), pp. 18–21; J. Evensen, "Ethical Behavior in Business and Life Is Its Own Reward," *Desert News (Salt Lake City, UT)*, October 19, 1997. For a discussion of the situational effects on ethical conduct, see C. J. Thompson, "A Contextualist Proposal for the Conceptualization and Study of Marketing Ethics," *Journal of Public Policy and Marketing* 14 (1995), pp. 177–91.

32. P. Haapaniemi and W. R. Hill, "Not Just for the Big Guys!" *Chief Executive*, September 1998, pp. 62–73.

33. M. Milliet-Einbinder, "Writing Off Tax Deductibility," *OECD Observer*, April 2000, pp. 38–40; F. Rotherham, "NZ Moves to Curb Corruption by Ending Tax Deductible Bribes," *Independent Business Weekly*, June 30, 1999, p. 27.

34. T. H. Stevenson and C. D. Bodkin, "A Cross-National Comparison of University Students' Perceptions Regarding the Ethics and Acceptability of Sales Practices," *Journal of Business Ethics* 17 (January 1998), pp. 45–55; T. Jackson and M. C. Artola, "Ethical Beliefs and Management Behavior: A Cross-Cultural Comparison," *Journal of Business Ethics* 16 (August 1997), pp. 1163–73; M.-K. Nyaw and I. Ignace, "A Comparative Analysis of Ethical Beliefs: A Four Country Study," *Journal of Business Ethics* 13 (1994), pp. 543–55; W. R. Swinyard, H. Rinne, and A. K. Kau, "The Morality of Software Piracy: A Cross-Cultural Analysis," *Journal of Business Ethics* 9 (1990), pp. 655–64.

35. P. F. Buller, J. J. Kohls, and K. S. Anderson, "A Model for Addressing Cross-Cultural Ethical Conflicts," *Business and Society* 36 (June 1997), pp. 169–93.

36. F. T. McCarthy, "Doing Well by Doing Good," *The Economist*, April 22, 2000; Institute of Business Ethics, *Report on Business Ethics Codes 1998* (from www.ibe.org.uk). J. Alexander, "On the Right Side," *Worldbusiness* 3 (January–February 1997), pp. 38–41.

37. M. S. Schwartz, "The Nature of the Relationship between Corporate Codes of Ethics and Behavior," *Journal of Business Ethics* 32 (August 2001), pp. 247–62; M. A. Clark and S. L. Leonard, "Can Corporate Codes of Ethics Influence Behavior?" *Journal of Business Ethics* 17 (April 1998), pp. 619–30.

38. K. Hirani, "B'lore Firms Keen on Ethics Code for Employees," *Times of India*, April 28, 2001.

39. For a discussion of additional ethical practices, see McCarthy, "Doing Well by Doing Good"; E. Van Zyl and K. Lazenby, "Ethical Behavior in the South African Organizational Context: Essential and Workable," *Journal of Business Ethics* 21 (August 1999), pp. 15–22.

40. N. M. Ashkanasy, C. E. Haertel, and W. J. Zerbe, eds., *Emotions in the Workplace: Research, Theory, and Practice* (Westport, CT: Quorum, 2000); B. E. Ashforth and R. H. Humphrey, "Emotion in the Workplace: A Reappraisal," *Human Relations* 48 (1995), pp. 97–125.

41. This definition is based on material in H. M. Weiss and R. Cropanzano, "Affective Events Theory: A Theoretical Discussion of the Structure, Causes, and Consequences of Affective Experiences at Work," *Research in Organizational Behavior* 18 (1996), pp. 1–74; S. Kitayama and P. M. Niedenthal, "Introduction," in P. M. Niedenthal and S. Kitayama, eds., *The Heart's Eye: Emotional Influences in Perception and Attention* (San Diego, CA: Academic Press, 1994), pp. 6–7.

42. R. B. Zajonc, "Emotions," in D. T. Gilbert, S. T. Fiske, and L. Gardner, eds., *Handbook of Social Psychology* (New York: Oxford University Press, 1998), pp. 591–634; K. Oatley and J. M. Jenkins, "Human Emotions: Function and Dysfunction," *Annual Review of Psychology* 43 (1992), pp. 55–85.

43. For a fuller discussion of specific emotions, see R. Pekrun and M. Frese, "Emotions in Work and Achievement," *International Review of Industrial and Organizational Psychology* 7 (1992), pp. 153–200.

44. J. M. George and A. P. Brief, "Motivational Agendas in the Workplace: The Effects of Feelings on Focus of Attention and Work Motivation," *Research in Organizational Behavior* 18 (1996), pp. 75–109; J. M. George, "Mood and Absence," *Journal of Applied Psychology* 74 (1989), pp. 317–24.

45. J. M. George and G. R. Jones, "Experiencing Work: Values, Attitudes, and Moods," *Human Relations* 50 (April 1997), pp. 393–416; J. M. Olson and M. P. Zama, "Attitudes and Attitude Change," *Annual Review of Psychology* 44 (1993), pp. 117–54; M. Fishbein and I. Ajzen, *Belief, Attitude, Intention,*

and Behavior (Reading, MA: Addison-Wesley, 1975).

46. M. D. Zalesny and J. K. Ford, "Extending the Social Information Processing Perspective: New Links to Attitudes, Behaviors, and Perceptions," *Organizational Behavior and Human Decision Processes* 52 (1992), pp. 205–46; G. Salancik and J. Pfeffer, "A Social Information Processing Approach to Job Attitudes and Task Design," *Administrative Science Quarterly* 23 (1978), pp. 224–53.

47. Weiss and Cropanzano, "Affective Events Theory."

48. For a full discussion of several theories on this topic, see K. T. Strongman, *The Psychology of Emotion: Theories of Emotion in Perspective*, 4th ed. (Chichester, UK: Wiley, 1996), chap. 6.

49. D. M. Irvine and M. G. Evans, "Job Satisfaction and Turnover among Nurses: Integrating Research Findings across Studies," *Nursing Research* 44 (1995), pp. 246–53.

50. Weiss and Cropanzano, "Affective Events Theory," pp. 52–57.

51. L. Festinger, *A Theory of Cognitive Dissonance* (Evanston, IL: Row, Peterson, 1957); G. R. Salancik, "Commitment and the Control of Organizational Behavior and Belief," in B. M. Staw and G. R. Salancik, eds., *New Directions in Organizational Behavior* (Chicago: St. Clair, 1977), pp. 1–54.

52. T. A. Judge, E. A. Locke, and C. C. Durham, "The Dispositional Causes of Job Satisfaction: A Core Evaluations Approach," *Research in Organizational Behavior* 19 (1997), pp. 151–88; A. P. Brief, A. H. Butcher, and L. Roberson, "Cookies, Disposition, and Job Attitudes: The Effects of Positive Mood-Inducing Events and Negative Affectivity on Job Satisfaction in a Field Experiment," *Organizational Behavior and Human Decision Processes* 62 (1995), pp. 55–62.

53. J. Schaubroeck, D. C. Ganster, and B. Kemmerer, "Does Trait Affect Promote Job Attitude Stability?" *Journal of Organizational Behavior* 17 (1996), pp. 191–96; R. D. Arvey, B. P. McCall, T. L. Bouchard, and P. Taubman, "Genetic Differences on Job Satisfaction and Work Values," *Personality and Individual Differences* 17 (1994), pp. 21–33; B. M. Staw and J. Ross, "Stabil-

ity in the Midst of Change: A Dispositional Approach to Job Attitudes," *Journal of Applied Psychology* 70 (1985), pp. 469–80.

54. D. Matheson, "A Vancouver Cafe Where Rudeness Is Welcomed," *CTV Television*, "Canada AM," January 11, 2000; R. Corelli, "Dishing Out Rudeness," *Maclean's*, January 11, 1999, p. 44.

55. J. A. Morris and D. C. Feldman, "The Dimensions, Antecedents, and Consequences of Emotional Labor," *Academy of Management Review* 21 (1996), pp. 986–1010; B. E. Ashforth and R. H. Humphrey, "Emotional Labor in Service Roles: The Influence of Identity," *Academy of Management Review* 18 (1993), pp. 88–115.

56. J. A. Morris and D. C. Feldman, "Managing Emotions in the Workplace," *Journal of Managerial Issues* 9 (Fall 1997), pp. 257–74.

57. J. S. Sass, "Emotional Labor as Cultural Performance: The Communication of Caregiving in a Nonprofit Nursing Home," *Western Journal of Communication* 64 (Summer 2000), pp. 330–58; R. I. Sutton, "Maintaining Norms about Expressed Emotions: The Case of Bill Collectors," *Administrative Science Quarterly* 36 (1991), pp. 245–68.

58. J. Strasburg, "The Making of a Grand Hotel," *San Francisco Chronicle*, March 25, 2001, p. B1.

59. E. Forman, "'Diversity Concerns Grow as Companies Head Overseas,' Consultant Says," *Fort Lauderdale (FL) Sun-Sentinel*, June 26, 1995.

60. J. Schaubroeck and J. R. Jones, "Antecedents of Workplace Emotional Labor Dimensions and Moderators of Their Effects on Physical Symptoms," *Journal of Organizational Behavior* 21 (2000), 163–83; R. Buck, "The Spontaneous Communication of Interpersonal Expectations," in P. D. Blanck, ed., *Interpersonal Expectations: Theory, Research, and Applications* (Cambridge, UK: Cambridge University Press, 1993), pp. 227–41. The quotation from George Burns comes from the Buck source. However, this line has also been attributed to Groucho Marx.

61. K. Pugliesi, "The Consequences of Emotional Labor: Effects on Work Stress, Job Satisfaction, and Well-

Being," *Motivation and Emotion* 23 (June 1999), pp. 125–54; A. S. Wharton, "The Psychosocial Consequences of Emotional Labor," *Annals of the American Academy of Political and Social Science* 561 (January 1999), pp. 158–76; J. A. Morris and D. C. Feldman, "Managing Emotions in the Workplace," *Journal of Managerial Issues* 9 (Fall 1997), pp. 257–74; P. K. Adelmann "Emotional Labor as a Potential Source of Job Stress," in S. Sauter and L. R. Murphy, eds., *Organizational Risk Factors for Job Stress* (Washington, DC: American Psychological Association, 1995), chap. 24.

62. M. Savidge, "Retailers Focus on Quality Workers," *The Morning Call (Allentown, PA)*, December 10, 2000, p. D1. The "hire for attitude, train for skills" phrase is also widely recognized as the policy of Southwest Airlines. See M. Brelis, "Herb's Way," *Boston Globe*, November 5, 2000, p. F1.

63. T. Schwartz, "'How Do You Feel?'" *Fast Company*, June 2000, p. 296; J. Stuller, "Unconventional Smarts," *Across the Board* 35 (January 1998), pp. 22–23.

64. D. Goleman, "What Makes a Leader?" *Harvard Business Review* 76 (November–December 1998), pp. 92–102. The definition of *emotional intelligence* appears in J. D. Mayer and P. Salovey, "The Intelligence of Emotional Intelligence," *Intelligence* 17 (1993), pp. 433–42. The levels of emotional intelligence are discussed in J. D. Mayer and P. Salovey, "What Is Emotional Intelligence," in P. Salovey and D. Sluyter, eds., *Emotional Development and Emotional Intelligence: Educational Implications* (New York: Basic Books, 1997), pp. 3–34.

65. A brief history of emotional intelligence is presented in S. Newsome, A. L. Day, and V. M. Catano, "Assessing the Predictive Validity of Emotional Intelligence," *Personality and Individual Differences* 29 (December 2000), pp. 1005–16.

66. R. J. Grossman, "Emotions at Work," *Health Forum Journal* 43 (September–October 2000), pp. 18–22; D. Swift, "Do Doctors Have an Emotional Handicap?" *Medical Post*, March 9, 1999, p. 30.

67. J. V. Ciarrochi, A. Y. C. Chan, and P. Caputi, "A Critical Evaluation of the

Emotional Intelligence Construct," *Personality and Individual Differences* 28 (2000) 539–61; S. Fox and P. E. Spector, "Relations of Emotional Intelligence, Practical Intelligence, General Intelligence, and Trait Affectivity with Interview Outcomes: It's Not All Just G," *Journal of Organizational Behavior* 21 (2000), pp. 203–20; R. Bar-On, J. M. Brown, B. D. Kirkcaldy, and E. P. Thomé, "Emotional Expression and Implications for Occupational Stress: An Application of the Emotional Quotient Inventory," *Personality and Individual Differences* 28 (2000) 1107–18.

68. D. Dawda and S. D. Hart, "Assessing Emotional Intelligence: Reliability and Validity of the Bar-On Emotional Quotient Inventory (EQ-i) in University Students," *Personality and Individual Differences* 28 (2000), pp. 797–812.

69. J. Brown, "School Board, Employment Centers Test Emotional Intelligence," *Technology in Government* 8 (April 2001), p. 9; Grossman, "Emotions at Work."

70. "Emotional Intelligence (EQ) Gets Better with Age," EQi News Release, March 3, 1997.

71. Weiss and Cropanzano, "Affective Events Theory." The *job satisfaction* definition is still being debated. This definition captures the most popular view that job satisfaction is an evaluation and represents both beliefs and feelings. For details, see A. P. Brief, *Attitudes In and Around Organizations* (Thousand Oaks, CA: Sage, 1998), chaps. 2 and 4.

72. E. A. Locke, "The Nature and Causes of Job Satisfaction," in M. Dunnette, ed., *Handbook of Industrial and Organizational Psychology* (Chicago: Rand McNally, 1976), pp. 1297–1350.

73. D. W. Moore, "Most American Workers Satisfied with Their Job," *Gallup News Service*, August 31, 2001. Also see T. Lemke, "Poll Data Show Americans' Long-Term Positive Attitude toward Jobs," *Washington Times*, August 28, 2001, p. B8.

74. S. MacDonald, "Do You Really Enjoy Your Work?" *Times of London*, January 15, 1998.

75. See G. Law, "If You're Happy and You Know It, Tick the Box," *Management-Auckland* 45 (March 1998), pp. 34–37. The problems with measuring

work attitudes across cultures are also discussed in K. Bae and C. Chung, "Cultural Values and Work Attitudes of Korean Industrial Workers in Comparison with Those of the United States and Japan," *Work and Occupations* 24 (February 1997), pp. 80–96.

76. A. J. Rucci, S. P. Kirn, and R. T. Quinn, "The Employee-Customer-Profit Chain at Sears," *Harvard Business Review* 76 (January–February 1998), pp. 83–97; W. Bole, "Workers Getting Say in CEOs' Pay," *Orlando (FL) Sentinel*, September 14, 1997, p. H1; M. Kerr, "Developing a Corporate Culture for the Maximum Balance between the Utilization of Human Resources and Employee Fulfillment in Canada," *Canada–United States Law Journal* 22 (1996), pp. 169–76.

77. R. D. Hackett and P. Bycio, "An Evaluation of Employee Absenteeism as a Coping Mechanism among Hospital Nurses," *Journal of Occupational and Organizational Psychology* 69 (December 1996), pp. 327–38; J. Barling, "The Prediction, Psychological Experience, and Consequences of Workplace Violence," in G. R. VandenBos and E. Q. Bulatao, eds., *Violence on the Job* (Washington, DC: American Psychological Association, 1996), pp. 29–49. S. D. Bluen, "The Psychology of Strikes," *International Review of Industrial and Organizational Psychology* 9 (1994), pp. 113–45; P. Y. Chen and P. E. Spector, "Relationships of Work Stressors with Aggression, Withdrawal, Theft and Substance Use: An Exploratory Study," *Journal of Occupational and Organizational Psychology* 65 (1992), pp. 177–84.

78. B. M. Staw and S. G. Barsade, "Affect and Managerial Performance: A Test of the Sadder-but-Wiser vs. Happier-and-Smarter Hypotheses," *Administrative Science Quarterly* 38 (1993), pp. 304–31; M. T. Iaffaldano and P. M. Muchinsky, "Job Satisfaction and Job Performance: A Meta-Analysis," *Psychological Bulletin* 97 (1985), pp. 251–73; D. P. Schwab and L. L. Cummings, "Theories of Performance and Satisfaction: A Review," *Industrial Relations* 9 (1970), pp. 408–30.

79. E. E. Lawler III and L. W. Porter, "The Effect of Performance on Job Satisfaction," *Industrial Relations* 7 (1967), pp. 20–28.

80. J. I. Heskett, W. E. Sasser, and L. A. Schlesinger, *The Service Profit Chain*, (New York: Free Press, 1997). For recent support of this model, see D. J. Koys, "The Effects of Employee Satisfaction, Organizational Citizenship Behavior, and Turnover on Organizational Effectiveness: A Unit-Level, Longitudinal Study," *Personnel Psychology* 54 (April 2001), pp. 101–14.

81. "Happy, Passionate Employees Key to Good Business, Top Executives Say," *Ascribe News*, April 16, 2001; S. Chandler, "Sears' System of Rewards Has Ups and Downs," *Chicago Tribune*, February 15, 1998, p. C1; Rucci, Kirn, and Quinn, "The Employee-Customer-Profit Chain at Sears."

82. T. Kirchofer, "Firm Takes Boat of Confidence," *Boston Herald*, March 20, 2001, p. 27.

83. K. Gwinner, D. Gremier, and M. Bitner, "Relational Benefits in Services Industries: The Customer's Perspective," *Journal of the Academy of Marketing Science* 26 (1998), pp. 101–14.

84. R. T. Mowday, L. W. Porter, and R. M. Steers, *Employee Organization Linkages: The Psychology of Commitment, Absenteeism, and Turnover* (New York: Academic Press, 1982).

85. C. W. Mueller and E. J. Lawler, "Commitment to Nested Organizational Units: Some Basic Principles and Preliminary Findings," *Social Psychology Quarterly* (December 1999), pp. 325–46; T. E. Becker, R. S. Billings, D. M. Eveleth, and N. L. Gilbert, "Foci and Bases of Employee Commitment: Implications for Job Performance," *Academy of Management Journal* 39 (1996), pp. 464–82.

86. J. P. Meyer, "Organizational Commitment," *International Review of Industrial and Organizational Psychology* 12 (1997), pp. 175–228. Along with affective and continuance commitment, Meyer identifies normative commitment, which refers to employee feelings of obligation to remain with the organization. This commitment has been excluded so that students focus on the two most common perspectives of commitment.

87. R. D. Hackett, P. Bycio, and P. A. Hausdorf, "Further Assessments of Meyer and Allen's (1991) Three-Component Model of Organizational

Commitment," *Journal of Applied Psychology* 79 (1994), pp. 15–23.

88. K. Phillips, "The Loyalty Trap," *Boss Magazine*, May 8, 2000, pp. 33–37; Watson Wyatt, "Survey Says Employee Commitment Declining," News Release, March 14, 2000; C. W. Mueller and E. J. Lawler, "Commitment to Nested Organizational Units: Some Basic Principles and Preliminary Findings," *Social Psychology Quarterly* 62 (December 1999), pp. 325–46; "Employees' Morale Plummets," *Management Services* 41 (February 1997), p. 6. In contrast, the Gallup Organization has reported consistently high loyalty ratings for the past decade. See Moore, "Most American Workers Satisfied with Their Job."

89. F. F. Reichheld, "Lead for Loyalty," *Harvard Business Review* 79 (July–August 2001), p. 76; D. S. Bolon, "Organizational Citizenship Behavior among Hospital Employees: A Multidimensional Analysis Involving Job Satisfaction and Organizational Commitment," *Hospital and Health Services Administration* 42 (Summer 1997), pp. 221–41; Meyer, "Organizational Commitment," pp. 203–15; F. F. Reichheld, *The Loyalty Effect* (Boston: Harvard Business School Press, 1996), chap. 4.

90. Phillips, "The Loyalty Trap."

91. J. P. Meyer and N. J. Allen, *Commitment in the Workplace: Theory, Research, and Application* (Thousand Oaks, CA: Sage, 1997), chap. 4.

92. E. W. Morrison and S. L. Robinson, "When Employees Feel Betrayed: A Model of How Psychological Contract Violation Develops," *Academy of Management Review* 22 (1997), pp. 226–56.

93. C. Hendry and R. Jenkins, "Psychological Contracts and New Deals," *Human Resource Management Journal* 7 (1997), pp. 38–44; D. M. Noer, *Healing the Wounds* (San Francisco: Jossey-Bass, 1993); S. Ashford, C. Lee, and P. Bobko, "Content, Causes, and Consequences of Job Insecurity: A Theory-Based Measure and Substantive Test," *Academy of Management Journal* 32 (1989), pp. 803–29.

94. R. J. Lewicki and B. B. Bunker, "Developing and Maintaining Trust in Work Relationships," in R. M. Kramer and T. R. Tyler, eds., *Trust in Organizations: Frontiers of Theory and Research*, (Thousand Oaks, CA: Sage, 1996), pp. 114–39; S. L. Robinson, "Trust and Breach of the Psychological Contract," *Administrative Science Quarterly* 41 (1996), pp. 574–99; J. M. Kouzes and B. Z. Posner, *The Leadership Challenge* (San Francisco: Jossey-Bass, 1987), pp. 146–52.

95. P. Mackey, "Old Ireland Tries New Hooks," *Computerworld*. April 23, 2001, p. 46.

96. A. A. Luchak and I. R. Gellatly, "Employer-Sponsored Pensions and Employee Commitment," *Proceedings of the Annual ASAC Conference, Human Resource Management Division* 17 (9) (1996), pp. 64–71; H. L. Angle and M. B. Lawson, Organizational Commitment and Employees' Performance Ratings: Both Type of Commitment and Type of Performance Count," *Psychological Reports* 75 (1994), pp. 1539–51; L. M. Shore and S. J. Wayne, "Commitment and Employee Behavior: Comparison of Affective Commitment and Continuance Commitment with Perceived Organizational Support," *Journal of Applied Psychology* 78 (1993), pp. 774–80; J. P. Meyer, S. V. Paunonen, I. R. Gellatly, R. D. Goffin, and D. N. Jackson, "Organizational Commitment and Job Performance: It's the Nature of the Commitment That Counts," *Journal of Applied Psychology* 74 (1989), pp. 152–56.

CHAPTER FIVE

1. M. Leuchter, "Capital One: Fanaticism That Works," *US Banker* 111 (August 2001), pp. 24–29; N. Pandya, "Cool Companies: No 60: Capital One," *The Guardian (London)*, July 14, 2001, p. 5; P. Knight, "Capital One Shows How to Keep Its Staff," *Computer Weekly*, June 7, 2001; M. Zelsman, "Most Likely to Succeed," *InfoWorld*, May 7, 2001, p. 45.

2. C. C. Pinder, *Work Motivation in Organizational Behavior* (Upper Saddle River, NJ: Prentice Hall, 1998); E. E. Lawler III, *Motivation in Work Organizations* (Monterey, CA: Brooks/Cole, 1973), pp. 2–5.

3. "Towers Perrin Study Finds, Despite Layoffs and Slow Economy, a New, More Complex Power Game Is Emerging between Employers and Employees," *Business Wire*, August 30, 2001.

4. T. D. Allen et al., "Survivor Reactions to Organizational Downsizing: Does Time Ease the Pain?" *Journal of Occupational and Organizational Psychology* 74 (June 2001), pp. 145–64; R. Burke, "Downsizing and Restructuring in Organizations: Research Findings and Lessons Learned—Introduction," *Canadian Journal of Administrative Sciences* 15 (December 1998), pp. 297–99.

5. R. Zemke and B. Filipczak, *Generations at Work: Managing the Clash of Veterans, Boomers, Xers, and Nexters in Your Workplace* (New York: AMACOM, 2000); B. Losyk, "Generation X: What They Think and What They Plan to Do," *The Futurist* 31 (March–April 1997), pp. 29–44; B. Tulgan, *Managing Generation X: How to Bring Out the Best in Young Talent* (Oxford, UK: Capstone, 1996).

6. S. H. Schwartz, "Are There Universal Aspects in the Structure and Contents of Human Values?" *Journal of Social Issues* 50 (1994), pp. 19–45; W. H. Schmidt and B. Z. Posner, *Managerial Values in Perspective* (New York: American Management Association, 1983); M. Rokeach, *The Nature of Human Values* (New York: Free Press, 1973); F. Kluckhorn and F. L. Strodtbeck, *Variations in Value Orientations* (Evanston, IL: Row, Peterson, 1961).

7. Pinder, *Work Motivation in Organizational Behavior*, chap. 3.

8. A. H. Maslow, "A Theory of Human Motivation," *Psychological Review* 50 (1943), pp. 370–96; A. H. Maslow, *Motivation and Personality* (New York: Harper & Row, 1954).

9. J. Sidener, "Easter Eggs Turning Up in Software for DVDs," *Arizona Republic*, April 10, 2001, p. F4; L. Kahney, "Taking the Fun Out of Win2000," *Wired News*, February 16, 2000; "Cracking Open the Eggs," *The Economist*, December 18, 1999; D. Claymon, "Apple Tradition Dies As Named Credits End," *Arizona Republic*, December 6, 1999, p. E5; L. Gornstein, "Software Harbors Treasures," *Arizona Republic*, March 9, 1998, p. E1; T. Standage "Easter Eggs beyond a Joke," *Daily Telegraph (London)*, February 19, 1998, p. 4. Some information was also collected from the website http://www.eeggs.com.

10. M. A. Wahba and L. G. Bridwell, "Maslow Reconsidered: A Review of

Research on the Need Hierarchy Theory," *Organizational Behavior and Human Performance* 15 (1976), pp. 212–40.

11. C. P. Alderfer, *Existence, Relatedness, and Growth* (New York: Free Press, 1972).

12. J. P. Wanous and A. A. Zwany, "A Cross-Sectional Test of Need Hierarchy Theory," *Organizational Behavior and Human Performance* 18 (1977), pp. 78–97.

13. H. M. Weiss and R. Cropanzano, "Affective Events Theory: A Theoretical Discussion of the Structure, Causes, and Consequences of Affective Experiences at Work," *Research in Organizational Behavior* 18 (1996), pp. 1–74.

14. F. Herzberg, B. Mausner, and B. B. Snyderman, *The Motivation to Work* (New York: Wiley, 1959).

15. The motivational value of money is effectively argued in T. Kinni, "Why We Work," *Training* 35 (August 1998), pp. 34–39. For critiques of Herzberg's theory, see A. K. Korman, *Industrial and Organizational Psychology* (Englewood Cliffs, NJ: Prentice Hall, 1971), p. 149; N. King, "Clarification and Evaluation of the Two Factor Theory of Job Satisfaction," *Psychological Bulletin* 74 (1970), pp. 18–31.

16. R. Beck, "Pop Go Those Pricey Perks," *Toronto Star*, August 7, 2001, p. E7; S. Caudron, "Be Cool!" *Workforce* 77 (April 1998), pp. 50–61.

17. J. Jacobs, "Helping 'Small Guys' Compete with Big Firms," *Business Times (Malaysia)*, April 6, 2001.

18. R. M. Steers and L. W. Porter, *Motivation and Work Behavior*, 5th ed. (New York: McGraw-Hill, 1991), p. 413.

19. D. C. McClelland, *The Achieving Society* (New York: Van Nostrand Reinhold, 1961); M. Patchen, *Participation, Achievement, and Involvement on the Job* (Englewood Cliffs, NJ: Prentice Hall, 1970).

20. For example, see J. Langan-Fox and S. Roth, "Achievement Motivation and Female Entrepreneurs," *Journal of Occupational and Organizational Psychology* 68 (1995), pp. 209–18; H. A. Wainer and I. M. Rubin, "Motivation of Research and Development Entrepreneurs: Determinants of Company Success, Part I," *Journal of Applied Psychology* 53 (June 1969), pp. 178–84.

21. D. C. McClelland, "Retrospective Commentary," *Harvard Business Review* 73 (January–February 1995), pp. 138–39; D. McClelland and R. Boyatzis, "Leadership Motive Pattern and Long-Term Success in Management," *Journal of Applied Psychology* 67 (1982), pp. 737–43.

22. G. Scotton, "Pamela Grof's InterVisual on the Fast Lane to Success," *Calgary Herald*, January 10, 2000.

23. McClelland, *The Achieving Society*; R. deCharms and G. H. Moeller, "Values Expressed in American Children's Readers: 1800–1950," *Journal of Abnormal and Social Psychology* 64 (1962), pp. 136–42.

24. R. J. House and R. N. Aditya, "The Social Scientific Study of Leadership: Quo Vadis?" *Journal of Management* 23 (1997), pp. 409–73; D. C. McClelland and D. H. Burnham, "Power Is the Great Motivator," *Harvard Business Review* 73 (January–February 1995), pp. 126–39 (Reprinted from *Harvard Business Review,* 1976).

25. D. Vredenburgh and Y. Brender, "The Hierarchical Abuse of Power in Work Organizations," *Journal of Business Ethics* 17 (September 1998), pp. 1337–47; McClelland and Burnham, "Power Is the Great Motivator."

26. D. G. Winter, "A Motivational Model of Leadership: Predicting Long-Term Management Success from TAT Measures of Power Motivation and Responsibility," *Leadership Quarterly* 2 (1991), pp. 67–80.

27. House and Aditya, "The Social Scientific Study of Leadership."

28. D. C. McClelland and D. G. Winter, *Motivating Economic Achievement* (New York: Free Press, 1969); D. Miron and D. McClelland, "The Impact of Achievement Motivation Training on Small Business," *California Management Review* 21 (1979), pp. 13–28.

29. A. Kohn, *Punished by Rewards* (New York: Houghton Mifflin, 1993).

30. D. S. Elenkov, "Can American Management Concepts Work in Russia? A Cross-Cultural Comparative Study," *California Management Review* 40 (Summer 1998), pp. 133–56; N. J. Adler, *International Dimensions of Organizational Behavior*, 3rd ed. (Cincinnati, OH: South-Western, 1997), chap. 6; G. Hofstede, "Motivation, Leadership, and Organization: Do American Theories Apply Abroad?" *Organizational Dynamics*, Summer 1980, pp. 42–63.

31. A. Sagie, D. Elizur, and H. Yamauchi, "The Structure and Strength of Achievement Motivation: A Cross-Cultural Comparison," *Journal of Organizational Behavior* 17 (September 1996), pp. 431–44; D. Elizur, I. Borg, R. Hunt, and I. M. Beck, "The Structure of Work Values: A Cross Cultural Comparison," *Journal of Organizational Behavior* 12 (1991), pp. 21–38.

32. Expectancy theory of motivation in work settings originated in V. H. Vroom, *Work and Motivation* (New York: Wiley, 1964). The version of expectancy theory presented here was developed by Edward Lawler. Lawler's model provides a clearer presentation of the model's three components. P→O expectancy is similar to instrumentality in Vroom's original expectancy theory model. The difference is that instrumentality is a correlation whereas P→O expectancy is a probability. See D. A. Nadler and E. E. Lawler, "Motivation: A Diagnostic Approach," in J. R. Hackman, E. E. Lawler III, and L. W. Porter, eds., *Perspectives on Behavior in Organizations*, 2nd ed. (New York: McGraw-Hill, 1983), pp. 67–78; J. P. Campbell, M. D. Dunnette, E. E. Lawler, and K. E. Weick, *Managerial Behavior, Performance, and Effectiveness* (New York: McGraw-Hill, 1970), pp. 343–48; E. E. Lawler, *Motivation in Work Organizations* (Monterey, CA: Brooks/Cole, 1973), chap. 3.

33. Nadler and Lawler, "Motivation."

34. K. A. Karl, A. M. O'Leary-Kelly, and J. J. Martoccio, "The Impact of Feedback and Self-Efficacy on Performance in Training," *Journal of Organizational Behavior* 14 (1993), pp. 379–94; T. Janz, "Manipulating Subjective Expectancy through Feedback: A Laboratory Study of the Expectancy-Performance Relationship," *Journal of Applied Psychology* 67 (1982), pp. 480–85.

35. D. Jones, "Firms Spend Billions to Fire Up Workers—with Little Luck," *USA Today*, May 10, 2001, p. A1.

36. J. B. Fox, K. D. Scott, and J. M. Donohoe, "An Investigation into Pay Valence and Performance in a Pay-for-

Performance Field Setting," *Journal of Organizational Behavior* 14 (1993), pp. 687–93.

37. J.-I. Lee, "Recent Exodus of Core Human Resources Disturbing Trend for Domestic Companies," *Korea Herald*, May 14, 2001; Y. Ghahremani, "In the Company of Millionaires," *Asia Week*, March 17, 2000; B. McKenna, "Restructuring Fever Sweeps Japan," *Globe and Mail*, May 29, 1999; M. Tanikawa, "The Corporate Samurai Are Getting Less Loyal," *Business Week*, March 16, 1998; R. M. Hodgetts, "Discussing Incentive Compensation with Donald Hastings of Lincoln Electric," *Compensation and Benefits Review* 29 (September 1997), pp. 60–66.

38. W. Van Eerde and H. Thierry, "Vroom's Expectancy Models and Work-Related Criteria: A Meta-Analysis," *Journal of Applied Psychology* 81 (1996), pp. 575–86; T. R. Mitchell, "Expectancy Models of Job Satisfaction, Occupational Preference and Effort: A Theoretical, Methodological, and Empirical Appraisal," *Psychological Bulletin* 81 (1974), pp. 1053–77.

39. Elenkov, "Can American Management Concepts Work in Russia?"; N. A. Boyacigiller and N. J. Adler, "The Parochial Dinosaur: Organizational Science in a Global Context," *Academy of Management Review* 16 (1991), pp. 262–90; N. J. Adler, *International Dimensions of Organizational Behavior*, 3rd ed. (Cincinnati, OH: South-Western, 1997), chap. 6.

40. D. H. B. Welsh, F. Luthans, and S. M. Sommer, "Managing Russian Factory Workers: The Impact of U.S.–Based Behavioral and Participative Techniques," *Academy of Management Journal* 36 (1993), pp. 58–79; T. Matsui and I. Terai, "A Cross-Cultural Study of the Validity of the Expectancy Theory of Motivation," *Journal of Applied Psychology* 60 (1979), pp. 263–65.

41. M. L. Ambrose and C. T. Kulik, "Old Friends, New Faces: Motivation Research in the 1990s," *Journal of Management* 25 (May 1999), pp. 231–92; K. C. Snead and A. M. Harrell, "An Application of Expectancy Theory to Explain a Manager's Intention to Use a Decision Support System," *Decision Sciences* 25 (1994), pp. 499–513.

42. J. S. Adams, "Toward an Understanding of Inequity," *Journal of Abnormal and Social Psychology* 67 (1963), pp. 422–36; R. T. Mowday, "Equity Theory Predictions of Behavior in Organizations," in R. M. Steers and L. W. Porter, eds., *Motivation and Work Behavior*, 5th ed. (New York: McGraw-Hill, 1991), pp. 111–31. The incident involving Tracy Jones is described in M. W. Walsh, "Workers Challenge Employer Policies on Pay Confidentiality," *New York Times*, July 28, 2000.

43. G. Blau, "Testing the Effect of Level and Importance of Pay Referents on Pay Level Satisfaction," *Human Relations* 47 (1994), pp. 1251–68; C. T. Kulik and M. L. Ambrose, "Personal and Situational Determinants of Referent Choice," *Academy of Management Review* 17 (1992), pp. 212–37; J. Pfeffer, "Incentives in Organizations: The Importance of Social Relations," in O. E. Williamson, ed., *Organization Theory: From Chester Barnard to the Present and Beyond* (New York: Oxford University Press, 1990), pp. 72–97.

44. P. P. Shah, "Who Are Employees' Social Referents? Using a Network Perspective to Determine Referent Others," *Academy of Management Journal* 41 (June 1998), pp. 249–68; K. S. Law and C. S. Wong, "Relative Importance of Referents on Pay Satisfaction: A Review and Test of a New Policy-Capturing Approach," *Journal of Occupational and Organizational Psychology* 71 (March 1998), pp. 47–60.

45. T. P. Summers and A. S. DeNisi, "In Search of Adams' Other: Reexamination of Referents Used in the Evaluation of Pay," *Human Relations* 43 (1990), pp. 497–511.

46. J. S. Adams, "Inequity in Social Exchange," in L. Berkowitz, ed., *Advances in Experimental Psychology* (New York: Academic Press, 1965), pp. 157–89.

47. J. Barling, C. Fullagar, and E. K. Kelloway, *The Union and Its Members: A Psychological Approach* (New York: Oxford University Press, 1992).

48. L. Greenberg and J. Barling, "Employee Theft," in C. L. Cooper and D. M. Rousseau, eds., *Trends in Organizational Behavior* 3 (1996), pp. 49–64.

49. J. Greenberg, "Cognitive Reevaluation of Outcomes in Response to Underpayment Inequity," *Academy of Management Journal* 32 (1989), pp. 174–84; E. Hatfield and S. Sprecher, "Equity Theory and Behavior in Organizations," *Research in the Sociology of Organizations* 3 (1984), pp. 94–124.

50. Cited in *Canadian Business*, February 1997, p. 39.

51. J. Rawls, *A Theory of Justice* (Cambridge, MA: Harvard University Press, 1971). For a recent discussion of justice and ethics, see M. Schminke, M. L. Ambrose, and T. W. Noel, "The Effect of Ethical Frameworks on Perceptions of Organizational Justice," *Academy of Management Journal* 40 (October 1997), pp. 1190–1207.

52. K. Crawford, "Bonus Puts Apple Boss Way above High Flyers," *Sydney Morning Herald*, January 21, 2000, p. 3; J. Fortt, "Apple Gives CEO Steve Jobs a Jet," *San Jose (CA) Mercury*, January 20, 2000.

53. M. Gordon, "CEOs Still Getting Big Pay," *AP Online*, August 28, 2001.

54. T. W. Gerdel, "Paying for the Privilege," *Cleveland (OH) Plain Dealer*, February 15, 1998, p. H1.

55. M. N. Bing and S. M. Burroughs, "The Predictive and Interactive Effects of Equity Sensitivity in Teamwork-Oriented Organizations," *Journal of Organizational Behavior* 22 (2001), pp. 271–90; K. S. Sauleya and A. G. Bedeian, "Equity Sensitivity: Construction of a Measure and Examination of Its Psychometric Properties," *Journal of Management* 26 (September 2000), pp. 885–910; P. E. Mudrack, E. S. Mason, and K. M. Stepanski, "Equity Sensitivity and Business Ethics," *Journal of Occupational and Organizational Psychology* 72 (December 1999), pp. 539–60; R. P. Vecchio, "An Individual-Differences Interpretation of the Conflicting Predictions Generated by Equity Theory and Expectancy Theory," *Journal of Applied Psychology* 66 (1981), pp. 470–81.

56. The meaning of these three groups has evolved over the years. These definitions are based on W. C. King, Jr., and E. W. Miles, "The Measurement of Equity Sensitivity," *Journal of Occupational and Organizational Psychology* 67 (1994), pp. 133–42.

57. L. Y. Fok, S. J. Hartman, M. F. Villere, and R. C. Freibert III, "A Study of the Impact of Cross Cultural Differences on Perceptions of Equity and Organizational Citizenship Behavior," *International Journal of Management* 13 (1996), pp. 3–14.

58. R. Folger and R. A. Baron, "Violence and Hostility at Work: A Model of Reactions to Perceived Injustice," in G. R. VandenBos and E. Q. Bulatao, eds., *Violence on the Job: Identifying Risks and Developing Solutions* (Washington, DC: American Psychological Association, 1996); J. Greenberg, "Stealing in the Name of Justice: Informational and Interpersonal Moderators of Theft Reactions to Underpayment Inequity," *Organizational Behavior and Human Decision Processes* 54 (1993), pp. 81–103; R. D. Bretz, Jr., and S. L. Thomas, "Perceived Equity, Motivation, and Final-Offer Arbitration in Major League Baseball," *Journal of Applied Psychology* 77 (1993), pp. 280–87. For a summary of recent equity theory studies, see M. L. Ambrose and C. T. Kulik, "Old Friends, New Faces: Motivation Research in the 1990s," *Journal of Management* 25 (May 1999), pp. 231–92.

59. Walker Information, *The 1999 U.S. National Employee Relationship Benchmark Report* (Indianapolis, IN: Walker Information, 2000). Similar levels of inequity are reported in Australia, as reported in *The Australian* survey, "Overworked and Underpaid," Morgan and Banks News Release, January 2001.

60. R. P. Vecchio and J. R. Terborg, "Salary Increment Allocation and Individual Differences," *Journal of Organizational Behavior* 8 (1987), pp. 37–43.

61. D. Beardsley, "This Company Doesn't Brake for (Sacred) Cows," *Fast Company* 16 (August 1998), p. 66.

62. For recent research on the effectiveness of goal setting, see L. A. Wilk and W. K. Redmon, "The Effects of Feedback and Goal Setting on the Productivity and Satisfaction of University Admissions Staff," *Journal of Organizational Behavior Management* 18 (1998), pp. 45–68; K. H. Doerr and T. R. Mitchell, "Impact of Material Flow Policies and Goals on Job Outcomes," *Journal of Applied Psychology* 81 (1996), pp. 142–52; A. A. Shikdar and B. Das, "A Field Study of Worker Productivity Improvements," *Applied Ergonomics* 26 (February 1995), pp. 21–27; M. D. Cooper and R. A. Phillips, "Reducing Accidents Using Goal Setting and Feedback: A Field Study," *Journal of Occupational and Organizational Psychology* 67 (1994), pp. 219–40.

63. T. H. Poister and G. Streib, "MBO in Municipal Government: Variations on a Traditional Management Tool," *Public Administration Review* 55 (1995), pp. 48–56.

64. E. A. Locke and G. P. Latham, *A Theory of Goal Setting and Task Performance* (Englewood Cliffs, NJ: Prentice Hall, 1990); A. J. Mento, R. P. Steel, and R. J. Karren, "A Meta-Analytic Study of the Effects of Goal Setting on Task Performance: 1966–1984," *Organizational Behavior and Human Decision Processes* 39 (1987), pp. 52–83; M. E. Tubbs, "Goal-Setting: A Meta-Analytic Examination of the Empirical Evidence," *Journal of Applied Psychology* 71 (1986), pp. 474–83.

65. I. R. Gellatly and J. P. Meyer, "The Effects of Goal Difficulty on Physiological Arousal, Cognition, and Task Performance," *Journal of Applied Psychology* 77 (1992), pp. 694–704; A. Mento, E. A. Locke, and H. Klein, "Relationship of Goal Level to Valence and Instrumentality," *Journal of Applied Psychology* 77 (1992), pp. 395–405.

66. R. Kaiser, "Human Touch Selling Online," *Chicago Tribune*, September 10, 2001, p. CN1; F. Knowles "CDW Chief Gung-Ho," *Chicago Sun-Times*, April 23, 2001, p. 51.

67. J. T. Chambers, "The Future of Business," *Executive Excellence* 17 (February 2000), pp. 3–4; K. R. Thompson, W. A. Hochwarter, and N. J. Mathys, "Stretch Targets: What Makes Them Effective?" *Academy of Management Executive* 11 (August 1997), pp. 48–60; S. Sherman, "Stretch Goals: The Dark Side of Asking for Miracles," *Fortune* 132 (November 13, 1995), pp. 231–32.

68. H. J. Klein, "Further Evidence of the Relationship between Goal Setting and Expectancy Theory," *Organizational Behavior and Human Decision Processes* 49 (1991), pp. 230–57.

69. M. E. Tubbs, "Commitment as a Moderator of the Goal-Performance Relation: A Case for Clearer Construct Definition," *Journal of Applied Psychology* 78 (1993), pp. 86–97.

70. G. P. Latham, D. C. Winters, and E. A. Locke, "Cognitive and Motivational Effects of Participation: A Mediator Study," *Journal of Organizational Behavior* 15 (1994), pp. 49–63.

71. J. Chowdhury, "The Motivational Impact of Sales Quotas on Effort," *Journal of Marketing Research* 30 (1993), pp. 28–41; Locke and Latham, *A Theory of Goal Setting and Task Performance*, chaps. 6 and 7; E. A. Locke, G. P. Latham, and M. Erez, "The Determinants of Goal Commitment," *Academy of Management Review* 13 (1988), pp. 23–39.

72. P. M. Wright, "Goal Setting and Monetary Incentives: Motivational Tools That Can Work Too Well," *Compensation and Benefits Review* 26 (May–June, 1994), pp. 41–49.

73. F. M. Moussa, " Determinants and Process of the Choice of Goal Difficulty," *Group and Organization Management* 21 (1996), pp. 414–38.

CHAPTER SIX

1. J. Mayne, "Bonuses Abound," *Seattle Post-Intelligencer*, December 5, 2000, p. C5; J. Mayne, "IKEA Workers in Renton Looking Like $1 Million," *Seattle Post-Intelligencer*, December 2, 2000, p. C5; K. Richter, "IKEA's Successful One-Day Bonus May Have Been a One-Time Deal," *Wall Street Journal Europe*, October 19, 1999, p. 4; N. R. Brooks, "IKEA Bonus Day Exceeds Expectations," *Los Angeles Times*, October 12, 1999, p. 3; "IKEA Puts $118m into Workers' Pay," *Edmonton (Alberta) Sun*, October 12, 1999, p. 51.

2. M. C. Bloom and G. T. Milkovich, "Issues in Managerial Compensation Research," in C. L. Cooper and D. M. Rousseau, eds., *Trends in Organizational Behavior*, vol. 3 (Chicester, UK: Wiley, 1996), pp. 23–47.

3. T. Kinni, "Why We Work," *Training* 35 (August 1998), pp. 34–39; A. Furnham and M. Argyle, *The Psychology of Money* (London: Routledge, 1998); T. L-P. Tang, "The Meaning of Money Revisited," *Journal of Organizational Behavior* 13 (March 1992), pp. 197–202.

4. Cited in T. R. Mitchell and A. E. Mickel, "The Meaning of Money: An Individual-Difference Perspective," *Academy of Management Review* (July 1999), pp. 568–78.

5. A. Furnham, B. D. Kirkcaldy, and R. Lynn, "National Attitudes to Competitiveness, Money, and Work among Young People: First, Second, and Third

World Differences," *Human Relations* 47 (January 1994), pp. 119–32; R. Lynn, *The Secret of the Miracle Economy* (London: SAE, 1991), cited in A. Furnham and R. Okamura, "Your Money or Your Life: Behavioral and Emotional Predictors of Money Pathology," *Human Relations* 52 (September 1999), pp. 1157–77.

6. M. Leder, "Better Perks Resonate in Boom Times," *New York Times*, November 21, 1999, p. 24; J. Juergens, "Corporate Spotlight: ARCNET," *Incentive* 173 (September 1999), pp. 68–69.

7. Furnham and Okamura, "Your Money or Your Life." For discussion of the money ethic, see T. L-P. Tang, J. K. Kim, and D. S-H. Tang, "Does Attitude toward Money Moderate the Relationship between Intrinsic Job Satisfaction and Voluntary Turnover?" *Human Relations* 53 (February 2000), pp. 213–45; T. L-P. Tang and J. K. Kim, "The Meaning of Money among Mental Health Workers: The Endorsement of Money Ethic as Related to Organizational Citizenship Behavior, Job Satisfaction, and Commitment," *Public Personnel Management* 28 (Spring 1999), pp. 15–26.

8. A. K. Kau, S. J. Tan and J. Wirtz, *Seven Faces of Singaporeans: Their Values, Aspirations, and Lifestyles* (Singapore: Prentice Hall, 1998); Furnham, Kirkcaldy, and Lynn, "National Attitudes to Competitiveness, Money, and Work among Young People." However, one recent study reported that "belief in the wonders of money" was higher among a sample of Canadian university students than students in Singapore, Hong Kong, or Hawaii. See S. H. Ang, "The Power of Money: A Cross-Cultural Analysis of Business-Related Beliefs," *Journal of World Business* 35 (March 2000), pp. 43–60.

9. C. Fox, "Never Fear, Aussies Are Here," *Australian Financial Review*, June 29, 2000, p. 38.

10. O. Mellan, "Men, Women and Money," *Psychology Today* 32 (February 1999), pp. 46–50.

11. Lynn, *The Secret of the Miracle Economy*, cited in Furnham and Okamura, "Your Money or Your Life."

12. M. Steen, "Study Looks at What Good Employees Want from a Company," *San Jose (CA) Mercury*, December 19, 2000; J. O'Rourke, "Show Boys the Money and Tell Girls You Care," *Sydney Morning Herald*, December 10, 2000.

13. Steen, "Study Looks at What Good Employees Want from a Company"; Mellan, "Men, Women and Money"; V. K. G. Lim and T. S. H. Teo, "Sex, Money and Financial Hardship: An Empirical Study of Attitudes towards Money among Undergraduates in Singapore," *Journal of Economic Psychology* 18 (1997), pp. 369–86; A. Furnham, "Attitudinal Correlates and Demographic Predictors of Monetary Beliefs and Behaviors," *Journal of Organizational Behavior* 17 (1996), 375–88.

14. Y. Park, "A Comparative Analysis of Work Incentives in U.S. and Japanese Firms," *Multinational Business Review* 4 (Fall 1996), pp. 59–70. Longevity pay in some Nevada counties is described in F. Greary, "Salary Incentives: County May Replace Longevity Pay," *Las Vegas Review-Journal*, August 14, 2001, p. B1.

15. J. M. Newman and F. J. Krzystofiak, "Value-Chain Compensation," *Compensation and Benefits Review* 30 (May 1998), pp. 60–66.

16. Q. Chan and C. Wan, "Equal Pay under the Microscope," *South China Morning Post*, May 31, 2001, p. 4.

17. "A Fair Day's Pay," *Economist*, May 8, 1999, p. 12; F. F. Reichheld, *The Loyalty Effect* (Boston, MA: Harvard Business School Press, 1996), p. 137. On the problems with job evaluation, see M. Quaid, *Job Evaluation: The Myth of Equitable Assessment* (Toronto: University of Toronto Press, 1993); S. L. McShane, "Two Tests of Direct Gender Bias in Job Evaluation Ratings," *Journal of Occupational Psychology* 63 (1990), pp. 129–40.

18. J. Kochanski, "Competency-Based Management," *Training and Development*, October 1997, pp. 40–44; Hay Group et al., *Raising the Bar: Using Competencies to Enhance Employee Performance* (Scottsdale, AZ: American Compensation Association, 1996).

19. E. Lawler, *Rewarding Excellence* (San Francisco: Jossey-Bass, 2000); R. Shareef, "A Midterm Case Study Assessment of Skill-Based Pay in the Virginia Department of Transportation," *Review of Public Personnel Administration* 18 (Winter 1998), pp. 5–22; D. Hofrichter, "Broadbanding: A 'Second Generation' Approach," *Compensation and Benefits Review* 25 (September–October 1993), pp. 53–58.

20. B. Murray and B. Gerhart, "Skill-Based Pay and Skill Seeking," *Human Resource Management Review* 10 (Autumn 2000), pp. 271–87; J. R. Thompson and C. W. LeHew, "Skill-Based Pay as an Organizational Innovation," *Review of Public Personnel Administration* 20 (Winter 2000), pp. 20–40; D-O. Kim and K. Mericle, "From Job-Based Pay to Skill-Based Pay in Unionized Establishments: A Three-Plant Comparative Analysis," *Relations Industrielles* 54 (Summer 1999), pp. 549–80; E. E. Lawler III, "From Job-Based to Competency-Based Organizations," *Journal of Organizational Behavior* 15 (1994), pp. 3–15.

21. C. T. Crumpley, "Skill-Based Pay Replaces Traditional Ranking," *Kansas City Star*, June 30, 1997, p. B6.

22. E. E. Lawler III, G. E. Ledford, Jr., and L. Chang, "Who Uses Skill-Based Pay, and Why," *Compensation and Benefits Review* 25 (March–April 1993), pp. 22–26.

23. E. E. Lawler III, "Competencies: A Poor Foundation for the New Pay," *Compensation and Benefits Review*, November–December 1996, pp. 20, 22–26.

24. E. B. Peach and D. A. Wren, "Pay for Performance from Antiquity to the 1950s," *Journal of Organizational Behavior Management*, 1992, pp. 5–26. Bank One's incentive is described in S. Brenowitz, "Bank One Launches Effort to Lure Customers with Bounties, Contests," *Columbus (OH) Dispatch*, June 7, 2001, p. E1.

25. S. Jones, "The Wages of Compression," *News and Observer (Raleigh, NC)*, December 14, 1999, p. D1.

26. F. Russo, "Aggression Loses Some of Its Punch," *Time*, July 30, 2001.

27. J. S. DeMatteo, L. T. Eby, and E. Sundstrom, "Team-Based Rewards: Current Empirical Evidence and Directions for Future Research," in B. M. Staw and L. L. Cummings, eds., *Research in Organizational Behavior* 20 (1998), pp. 141–83; P. Pascarella, "Compensating Teams," *Across the Board* 34 (February 1997), pp. 16–23; D. G. Shaw and C. E. Schneier, "Team Measurement and Rewards: How Some Companies Are Getting It Right," *Human Resource Planning* (1995), pp. 34–49.

28. L. R. Gomez-Mejia, T. M. Welbourne, and R. M. Wiseman, "The Role of Risk Sharing and Risk Taking under Gainsharing," *Academy of Management Review* 25 (July 2000), pp. 492–507.

29. J. Creswell, "America's Elite Factories," *Fortune,* September 3, 2001.

30. A. Miller, "St. Joseph's to Reward Surgeons for Savings," *Atlanta Journal-Constitution,* January 20, 2001, p. F1.

31. D. P. O'Bannon and C. L. Pearce, "An Exploratory Examination of Gainsharing in Service Organizations: Implications for Organizational Citizenship Behavior and Pay Satisfaction," *Journal of Managerial Issues* 11 (Fall 1999), pp. 363–78; C. Cooper and B. Dyck, "Improving the Effectiveness of Gainsharing: The Role of Fairness and Participation," *Administrative Science Quarterly* 37 (1992), pp. 471–90.

32. M. Jarman, "Stock Plans for Workers," *Arizona Republic,* June 14, 1998; D. Bencivenga, "Employee-Owners Help Bolster the Bottom Line," *HRMagazine* 42 (February 1997), pp. 78–83.

33. J. M. Newman and M. Waite, "Do Broad-Based Stock Options Create Value?" *Compensation and Benefits Review* 30 (July 1998), pp. 78–86.

34. H. Hamid, "Tien Wah's Flexi-Wage a Success," *Business Times (Malaysia),* December 7, 2000.

35. S. J. Marks, "Incentives that Really Reward and Motivate," *Workforce* 80 (June 2001), pp. 108–14; "A Fair Day's Pay," *Economist,* May 8, 1999, p. 12; Bencivenga, "Employee-Owners Help Bolster the Bottom Line"; J. Chelius and R. S. Smith, "Profit Sharing and Employment Stability," *Industrial and Labor Relations Review* 43 (1990), pp. 256s–273s.

36. A. Leckey, "Some Are Left Sizing Up Their Options," *Chicago Tribune,* May 9, 2001.

37. A. Kohn, "Challenging Behaviorist Dogma: Myths about Money and Motivation," *Compensation and Benefits Review* 30 (March 1998), pp. 27–33; A. Kohn, *Punished by Rewards* (Boston: Houghton Mifflin, 1993); W. C. Hamner, "How to Ruin Motivation with Pay," *Compensation Review* 7, no. 3 (1975), pp. 17–27.

38. M. O'Donnell and J. O'Brian, "Performance-Based Pay in the Australian Public Service," *Review of Public Personnel Administration* 20 (Spring 2000), pp. 20–34.

39. B. Nelson, *1001 Ways to Reward Employees* (New York: Workman, 1994), p. 148.

40. "Global Survey Finds Common Trends in Ways Top Companies Reward High Performers," *Business Wire,* May 22, 2000; J. Pfeffer, *The Human Equation* (Boston: Harvard Business School Press, 1998). For an early summary of research supporting the motivational value of performance-based rewards, see E. E. Lawler III, *Pay and Organizational Effectiveness: A Psychological View* (New York: McGraw-Hill, 1971).

41. S. Kerr, "Organization Rewards: Practical, Cost-Neutral Alternatives That You May Know, but Don't Practice," *Organizational Dynamics* 28 (Summer 1999), pp. 61–70.

42. "New Survey Finds Variable Pay Has Yet to Deliver on Its Promise," *Pay for Performance Report,* March 2000, p. 1. The politics of pay is discussed in D. Collins, *Gainsharing and Power? Lessons from Six Scanlon Plans* (Ithaca, NY: Cornell University Press, 1998); K. M. Bartol and D. C. Martin, "When Politics Pays: Factors Influencing Managerial Compensation Decisions," *Personnel Psychology* 43 (1990), pp. 599–614.

43. Kerr, "Organization Rewards."

44. "New Survey Finds Variable Pay Has Yet to Deliver on Its Promise."

45. S. Chandler, "Sears' System of Rewards Has Ups and Downs," *Chicago Tribune,* February 15, 1998, p. C1.

46. DeMatteo et al., "Team-Based Rewards."

47. R. Wageman, "Interdependence and Group Effectiveness," *Administrative Science Quarterly* 40 (1995), pp. 145–80.

48. "Dream Teams," *Human Resources Professional,* November 1994, pp. 17–19.

49. S. Kerr, "On the Folly of Rewarding A, While Hoping for B," *Academy of Management Journal* 18 (1975), pp. 769–83.

50. D. R. Spitzer, "Power Rewards: Rewards That Really Motivate," *Management Review,* May 1996, pp. 45–50.

51. P. M. Perry, "Holding Your Top Talent," *Research Technology Management* 44 (May 2001), pp. 26–30; "Strong Leaders Make Great Workplaces," *(Minneapolis–St. Paul) CityBusiness,* August 28, 2000.

52. This definition is more consistent with popular use of the word *job* and with the definition in *Random House Webster's College Dictionary.* However, some scholars have used this definition for *position* and have defined *job* as a group of similar positions. See K. Pearlman, "Job Families: A Review and Discussion of Their Implications for Personnel Selection," *Psychological Bulletin* 87 (January 1980), pp. 1–28.

53. M. Bensaou and M. Earl, "The Right Mind-Set for Managing Information Technology," *Harvard Business Review,* September–October 1998, pp. 118–28; B. B. Arnetz, "Technological Stress: Psychophysiological Aspects of Working with Modern Information Technology," *Scandinavian Journal of Work and Environmental Health* 23, suppl. 3 (1997), pp. 97–103; J. W. Medcof, "The Effect of Extent of Use and Job of the User upon Task Characteristics," *Human Relations* 42 (1989), pp. 23–41, R. J. Long, *New Office Information Technology: Human and Managerial Implications* (London: Crom Helm, 1987).

54. G. L. Dalton, "The Collective Stretch: Workforce Flexibility," *Management Review* 87 (December 1998), pp. 54–59; C. Hendry and R. Jenkins, "Psychological Contracts and New Deals," *Human Resource Management Journal* 7 (1997), pp. 38–44.

55. D. Whitford, "A Human Place to Work," *Fortune,* January 8, 2001, pp. 108–19.

56. A. Smith, *The Wealth of Nations* (London: Dent, 1910). Earlier examples are described in "Scientific Management: Lessons from Ancient History through the Industrial Revolution" (www.accel-team.com).

57. M. A. Campion, "Ability Requirement Implications of Job Design: An Interdisciplinary Perspective," *Personnel Psychology* 42 (1989), pp. 1–24; H. Fayol, *General and Industrial Management,* trans. C. Storrs (London: Pitman, 1949); E. E. Lawler III, *Motivation in Work Organizations* (Monterey, CA: Brooks/Cole, 1973), chap. 7.

58. For a review of Taylor's work and life, see R. Kanigel, *The One Best Way: Frederick Winslow Taylor and the Enigma of Efficiency* (New York:

Viking, 1997). See also C. R. Littler, "Taylorism, Fordism, and Job Design," in D. Knights, H. Willmott, and D. Collinson, eds., *Job Design: Critical Perspectives on the Labor Process* (Aldershot, UK: Gower, 1985), pp. 10–29; F. W. Taylor, *The Principles of Scientific Management* (New York: Harper & Row, 1911).

59. E. E. Lawler III, *High-Involvement Management* (San Francisco: Jossey-Bass, 1986), chap. 6; C. R. Walker and R. H. Guest, *The Man on the Assembly Line* (Cambridge, MA: Harvard University Press, 1952).

60. W. F. Dowling, "Job Redesign on the Assembly Line: Farewell to Blue-Collar Blues?" *Organizational Dynamics*, Autumn 1973, pp. 51–67; Lawler, *Motivation in Work Organizations*, p. 150.

61. M. Keller, *Rude Awakening* (New York: Harper Perennial, 1989), p. 128.

62. C. S. Wong and M. A. Campion, "Development and Test of a Task Level Model of Motivational Job Design," *Journal of Applied Psychology* 76 (1991), pp. 825–37; R. W. Griffin, "Toward an Integrated Theory of Task Design," *Research in Organizational Behavior* 9 (1987), pp. 79–120.

63. F. Herzberg, B. Mausner, and B. B. Snyderman, *The Motivation to Work* (New York: Wiley, 1959).

64. J. R. Hackman and G. Oldham, *Work Redesign* (Reading, MA: Addison-Wesley, 1980).

65. Whitford, "A Human Place to Work."

66. M. C. Andrews and K. M. Kacmar, "Confirmation and Extension of the Sources of Feedback Scale in Service-Based Organizations," *Journal of Business Communication* 38 (April 2001), pp. 206–26.

67. G. Johns, J. L. Xie, and Y. Fang, "Mediating and Moderating Effects in Job Design," *Journal of Management* 18 (1992), pp. 657–76.

68. P. E. Spector, "Higher-Order Need Strength as a Moderator of the Job Scope–Employee Outcome Relationship: A Meta Analysis," *Journal of Occupational Psychology* 58 (1985), pp. 119–27.

69. S. Shepard, "Safety Program at Carrier Plant in Collierville Paying Dividends," *Memphis Business Journal*, May 25, 2001, p. 38.

70. J. L. White, "Police Practice: The Work Itself as a Motivator," *FBI Law Enforcement Bulletin*, February 2001, pp. 7–9.

71. N. G. Dodd and D. C. Ganster, "The Interactive Effects of Variety, Autonomy, and Feedback on Attitudes and Performance," *Journal of Organizational Behavior* 17 (1996), pp. 329–47; M. A. Campion and C. L. McClelland, "Follow-up and Extension of the Interdisciplinary Costs and Benefits of Enlarged Jobs," *Journal of Applied Psychology* 78 (1993), pp. 339–51.

72. This point is emphasized in C. Pinder, *Work Motivation* (Glenview, IL: Scott Foresman, 1984), p. 244; and F. Herzberg, "One More Time: How Do You Motivate Employees?" *Harvard Business Review* 46 (January–February 1968), pp. 53–62. For a full discussion of job enrichment, also see R. W. Griffin, *Task Design: An Integrative Approach* (Glenview, IL: Scott Foresman, 1982); J. R. Hackman, G. Oldham, R. Janson, and K. Purdy, "A New Strategy for Job Enrichment," *California Management Review* 17 (4) (1975), pp. 57–71.

73. S. Ross, "Workers Turn Off Autopilot and Take Charge on Assembly Lines of the 21st Century," *Globe and Mail*, September 3, 2001, p. B12; M. Truby, "Change Becomes Mantra of Ford's New Leaders," *Detroit News*, August 20, 2000.

74. M. Grotticelli, "CNN Moves to Small-Format ENG," *Broadcasting and Cable*, May 14, 2001, p. 46.

75. For a full discussion of empowerment, including its many definitions, see W. A. Randolph, "Re-Thinking Empowerment: Why Is It So Hard to Achieve?" *Organizational Dynamics* 29 (November 2000), pp. 94–107; R. Forrester, "Empowerment: Rejuvenating a Potent Idea," *Academy of Management Executive* 14 (August 2000), pp. 67–80; C. S. Koberg, R. W. Boss, J. C. Senjem, and E. A. Goodman, "Antecedents and Outcomes of Empowerment," *Group and Organization Management* 24 (1999), pp. 71–91; R. C. G. M. Spreitzer, "Psychological Empowerment in the Workplace: Dimensions, Measurement, and Validation," *Academy of Management Journal* 38 (1995), pp. 1442–65; J. A. Conger and R. N. Kanungo, "The Empowerment Process: Integrating

Theory and Practice," *Academy of Management Review* 13 (1988), pp. 471–82.

76. J-C. Chebat and P. Kollias, "The Impact of Empowerment on Customer Contact Employees' Role in Service Organizations," *Journal of Service Research* 3 (August 2000), pp. 66–81.

77. Hackman and Oldham, *Work Redesign*, pp. 137–38.

78. S. L. Paulson, "Training for Change," *American Gas* 79 (December 1997–January 1998), pp. 26–29.

79. R. Saavedra and S. K. Kwun, "Affective States in Job Characteristics Theory," *Journal of Organizational Behavior* 21 (2000), pp. 131–46; P. Osterman, "How Common Is Workplace Transformation and Who Adopts It?" *Industrial and Labor Relations Review* 47 (1994), pp. 173–88; D. E. Bowen and E. E. Lawler III, "The Empowerment of Service Workers: What, Why, How, and When," *Sloan Management Review* Spring 1992, pp. 31–39; P. E. Spector and S. M. Jex, "Relations of Job Characteristics from Multiple Data Sources with Employee Affect, Absence, Turnover Intentions, and Health," *Journal of Applied Psychology* 76 (1991), pp. 46–53; Y. Fried and G. R. Ferris, "The Validity of the Job Characteristics Model: A Review and Meta-analysis," *Personnel Psychology* 40 (1987), pp. 287–322.

80. C-S. Wong, C. Hui, and K. S. Law, "A Longitudinal Study of the Job Perception–Job Satisfaction Relationship: A Test of the Three Alternative Specifications," *Journal of Occupational and Organizational Psychology* 71 (June 1998), pp. 127–46.

81. Forrester, "Empowerment"; D. I. Levine, *Reinventing the Workplace* (Washington, DC: Brookings, 1995), pp. 63–66, 86. However, a more complex curvilinear relationship between employee empowerment and supervisor reactions is reported in M. Fenton-O'Creevy, "Employee Involvement and the Middle Manager: Saboteur or Scapegoat?" *Human Resource Management Journal* 11 (2001), pp. 24–40.

82. R. Hodson, "Dignity in the Workplace under Participative Management: Alienation and Freedom Revisited," *American Sociological Review* 61 (1996), pp. 719–38; J. Rinehart, "Improving the Quality of Working Life through Job Redesign: Work Humanization or Work

Rationalization?" *Canadian Review of Sociology and Anthropology* 23 (1986), pp. 507–30.

83. Campion, "Ability Requirement Implications of Job Design," p. 20; R. B. Dunham, "Relationships of Perceived Job Design Characteristics to Job Ability Requirements and Job Value," *Journal of Applied Psychology* 62 (1977), pp. 760–63.

84. R. Martin and T. D. Wall, "Attentional Demand and Cost Responsibility as Stressors in Shopfloor Jobs," *Academy of Management Journal* 32 (1989), pp. 69–86; D. P. Schwab and L. L. Cummings, "Impact of Task Scope on Employee Productivity: An Evaluation Using Expectancy Theory," *Academy of Management Review* 1 (1976), pp. 23–35.

85. M. Heroux, "CEOs Try Better Ways to Hire, Motivate Employees," *Akron (OH) Beacon Journal*, November 21, 1999.

86. T. Romita, "The Talent Search," *Business 2.0*, June 12, 2001.

87. C. P. Neck and C. C. Manz, "Thought Self-Leadership: The Impact of Mental Strategies Training on Employee Cognition, Behavior, and Affect," *Journal of Organizational Behavior* 17 (1996), pp. 445–67.

88. C. C. Manz and H. P. Sims, Jr., *Superleadership: Leading Others to Lead Themselves* (Englewood Cliffs, NJ: Prentice Hall, 1989); C. C. Manz, "Self-Leadership: Toward an Expanded Theory of Self-Influence Processes in Organizations," *Academy of Management Review* 11 (1986), pp. 585–600.

89. H. P. Sims, Jr., and C. C. Manz, *Company of Heroes: Unleashing the Power of Self-Leadership* (New York: Wiley, 1996); A. M. Saks, R. R. Haccoun, and D. Laxer, "Transfer Training: A Comparison of Self-Management and Relapse Prevention Interventions," *ASAC 1996 Conference Proceedings, Human Resources Division* 17 (9) (1996), pp. 81–91; M. E. Gist, A. G. Bavetta, and C. K. Stevens, "Transfer Training Method: Its Influence on Skill Generalization, Skill Repetition, and Performance Level," *Personnel Psychology* 43 (1990), pp. 501–23.

90. R. M. Duncan and J. A. Cheyne, "Incidence and Functions of Self-Reported Private Speech in Young Adults: A Self-Verbalization Questionnaire," *Canadian Journal of Behavioral Science* 31 (April 1999), pp. 133–36. For an organizational behavior discussion of constructive thought patterns, see C. P. Neck and C. C. Manz, "Thought Self-Leadership: The Influence of Self-Talk and Mental Imagery on Performance," *Journal of Organizational Behavior* 13 (1992), pp. 681–99.

91. G. E. Prussia, J. S. Anderson, and C. C. Manz, "Self-Leadership and Performance Outcomes: The Mediating Influence of Self-Efficacy," *Journal of Organizational Behavior*, September 1998, pp. 523–38; Neck and Manz, "Thought Self-Leadership: The Impact of Mental Strategies Training on Employee Cognition, Behavior, and Affect."

92. Early scholars seem to distinguish mental practice from mental imagery, whereas recent literature combines mental practice with visualizing positive task outcomes within the meaning of mental imagery. For recent discussion of this concept, see C. P. Neck, G. L. Stewart, and C. C. Manz, "Thought Self-Leadership as a Framework for Enhancing the Performance of Performance Appraisers," *Journal of Applied Behavioral Science* 31 (September 1995), pp. 278–302; W. P. Anthony, R. H. Bennett III, E. N. Maddox, and W. J. Wheatley, "Picturing the Future: Using Mental Imagery to Enrich Strategic Environmental Assessment," *Academy of Management Executive* 7 (2) (1993), pp. 43–56.

93. C. Salter, "This Is Brain Surgery," *Fast Company* 13 (February–March 1998), pp. 147–50.

94. J. E. Driscoll, C. Cooper, and A. Moran, "Does Mental Practice Enhance Performance?" *Journal of Applied Psychology* 79 (1994), pp. 481–92.

95. A. Wrzesniewski and J. E. Dutton, "Crafting a Job: Revisioning Employees as Active Crafters of Their Work," *Academy of Management Review* 26 (April 2001), pp. 179–201; Manz, "Self-Leadership."

96. M. I. Bopp, S. J. Glynn, and R. A. Henning, "Self-Management of Performance Feedback during Computer-Based Work by Individuals and Two-Person Work Teams," Paper presented at the APA-NIOSH conference, March 1999.

97. A. W. Logue, *Self-Control: Waiting until Tomorrow for What You Want Today* (Englewood Cliffs, NJ: Prentice Hall, 1995).

98. J. Bauman, "The Gold Medal Mind," *Psychology Today* 33 (May 2000), pp. 62–69; K. E. Thiese and S. Huddleston, "The Use of Psychological Skills by Female Collegiate Swimmers," *Journal of Sport Behavior*, December 1999, pp. 602–10; D. Landin and E. P. Hebert, "The Influence of Self-Talk on the Performance of Skilled Female Tennis Players," *Journal of Applied Sport Psychology* 11 (September 1999), pp. 263–82; C. Defrancesco and K. L. Burke, "Performance Enhancement Strategies Used in a Professional Tennis Tournament," *International Journal of Sport Psychology* 28 (1997), pp. 185–95; S. Ming and G. L. Martin, "Single-Subject Evaluation of a Self-Talk Package for Improving Figure Skating Performance," *Sport Psychologist* 10 (1996), pp. 227–38.

99. A. M. Saks and B. E. Ashforth, "Proactive Socialization and Behavioral Self-Management." *Journal of Vocational Behavior* 48 (1996), pp. 301–23; Neck and Manz, "Thought Self-Leadership: The Impact of Mental Strategies Training on Employee Cognition, Behavior, and Affect."

100. A. L. Kazan, "Exploring the Concept of Self-Leadership: Factors Impacting Self-Leadership of Ohio Americorps Members," *Dissertation Abstracts International* 60 (June 2000); S. Ross, "Corporate Measurements Shift from Punishment to Rewards," *Reuters* February 28, 2000; M. Castaneda, T. A. Kolenko, and R. J. Aldag, "Self-Management Perceptions and Practices: A Structural Equations Analysis," *Journal of Organizational Behavior* 20 (1999), pp. 101–20; G. L. Stewart, K. P. Carson, and R. L. Cardy, "The Joint Effects of Conscientiousness and Self-Leadership Training on Employee Self-Directed Behavior in a Service Setting," *Personnel Psychology* 49 (1996), pp. 143–64.

CHAPTER SEVEN

1. G. Hassell, "Energy Trading Fast, Furious and Lucrative," *Houston Chronicle*, May 20, 2001, p. 25; J. Warren, "Secrecy Cloaks State's Buyers on Their Prowl for Power," *Los Angeles Times*, February 23, 2001, p. A1.

2. "CareerBuilder Survey Finds Growing Worker Disenchantment, Long Hours and Stress," *PR Newswire*, August 30, 2001; D. Stafford, "Nearly One-Third of Workers Often Feel Overworked, Study Says," *Philadelphia Inquirer*, May 21, 2001; E. Galinsky, S. S. Kim, J. T. Bond, *Feeling Overworked: When Work Becomes Too Much* (New York: Families and Work Institute, 2001); American Institute of Stress (www.stress.org).

3. S. Lem, "Snowed Under by Stress," *London Free Press*, February 3, 2000, p. C4; "Good Bosses Are Hard to Find," Morgan & Banks news release, August 2000; S. Efron, "Jobs Take a Deadly Toll on Japanese," *Los Angeles Times*, April 12, 2000, p. A1; N. Chowdhury and S. Menon, "Beating Burnout," *India Today*, June 9, 1997, p. 86; Cross-National Collaborative Group, "The Changing Rate of Major Depression: Cross-National Comparisons," *JAMA: The Journal of the American Medical Association* 268 (December 2, 1992), pp. 3098–3105.

4. R. S. DeFrank and J. M. Ivancevich, "Stress on the Job: An Executive Update," *Academy of Management Executive* 12 (August 1998), pp. 55–66; J. C. Quick and J. D. Quick, *Organizational Stress and Prevention Management* (New York: McGraw-Hill, 1984).

5. J. C. Quick, J. D. Quick, D. L. Nelson, and J. J. Hurrell, Jr., *Preventive Stress Management in Organizations* (Washington, DC: American Psychological Association, 1997).

6. S. Sauter and L. R. Murphy (eds.), *Organizational Risk Factors for Job Stress* (Washington, DC: American Psychological Association, 1995).

7. H. Selye, *Stress without Distress* (Philadelphia: Lippincott, 1974).

8. S. E. Taylor, R. L. Repetti, and T. Seeman, "Health Psychology: What Is an Unhealthy Environment and How Does It Get under the Skin?" *Annual Review of Psychology*, 48 (1997), pp. 411–47.

9. K. Danna and R. W. Griffin, "Health and Well-being in the Workplace: A Review and Synthesis of the Literature," *Journal of Management*, Spring 1999, pp. 357–84; Quick and Quick, *Organizational Stress and Prevention Management*, p. 3.

10. S. Cassidy, "Record Payouts for Assaults and Accidents in Class," *The Independent (London)*, May 12, 2001, p. 13; R. Hancock, "Teachers Top Stress Bill," *Sunday Mail (Adelaide)*, March 25, 2001, p. 19; "Teacher Payouts," *Sunday Telegraph (Sydney)*, March 4, 2001, p. 27; N. Webber, "Teachers Terrorized," *Herald Sun (Melbourne)*, February 26, 2001, p. 11; N. Webber, "Stressed Teachers Win $34m Compo," *Herald Sun (Melbourne)*, February 22, 2001; S. O'Connell, "Too Tense to Teach," *Times of London*, December 7, 2000, p. 22; L. Lightfoot, "Teacher Receives Record £254,000 Payout for Stress," *The Telegraph (London)*, December 5, 2000; J. Judd, "Teacher Awarded £250,000 over Stress Illnesses," *The Independent (London)*, December 5, 2000, p. 5.

11. G. Evans and D. Johnson, "Stress and Open-Office Noise," *Journal of Applied Psychology* 85 (2000), pp. 779–83; S. Melamed and S. Bruhis, "The Effects of Chronic Industrial Noise Exposure on Urinary Cortisol, Fatigue, and Irritability: A Controlled Field Experiment," *Journal of Occupational and Environmental Medicine* 38 (1996), pp. 252–56.

12. M. Siegall and L. L. Cummings, "Stress and Organizational Role Conflict," *Genetic, Social, and General Psychology Monographs* 12 (1995), pp. 65–95; E. K. Kelloway and J. Barling, "Job Characteristics, Role Stress and Mental Health," *Journal of Occupational Psychology* 64 (1991), pp. 291–304; R. L. Kahn, D. M. Wolfe, R. P. Quinn, J. D. Snoek, and R. A. Rosenthal, *Organizational Stress: Studies in Role Conflict and Ambiguity* (New York: Wiley, 1964).

13. B. Stoneman and K. K. Holliday, "Pressure Cooker," *Banking Strategies*, January–February, 2001, p. 13.

14. G. R. Cluskey and A. Vaux, "Vocational Misfit: Source of Occupational Stress among Accountants," *Journal of Applied Business Research* 13 (Summer 1997), pp. 43–54; J. R. Edwards, "An Examination of Competing Versions of the Person–Environment Fit Approach to Stress," *Academy of Management Journal* 39 (1996), pp. 292–339; B. E. Ashforth and R. H. Humphrey, "Emotional Labor in Service Roles: The Influence of Identity," *Academy of Management Review* 18 (1993), pp. 88–115.

15. A. M. Saks and B. E. Ashforth, "Proactive Socialization and Behavioral Self-Management," *Journal of Vocational Behavior* 48 (1996), pp. 301–23; D. L. Nelson and C. Sutton, "Chronic Work Stress and Coping: A Longitudinal Study and Suggested New Directions," *Academy of Management Journal* 33 (1990), pp. 859–69.

16. J. Vahtera, M. Kivimaki, J. Pentti, and T. Theorell, "Effect of Change in the Psychosocial Work Environment on Sickness Absence: A Seven-Year Follow-up of Initially Healthy Employees," *Journal of Epidemiology & Community Health* 54 (July 2000), pp. 482–83; L. D Sargent and D. J. Terry, "The Effects of Work Control and Job Demands on Employee Adjustment and Work Performance," *Journal of Occupational and Organizational Psychology* 71 (September 1998), pp. 219–36; M. G. Marmot, H. Bosma, H. Hemingway, E. Brunner, and S. Stansfeld, "Contribution of Job Control and Other Risk Factors to Social Variations in Coronary Heart Disease Incidence," *Lancet* 350 (July 26, 1997), pp. 235–39; P. M. Elsass and J. F. Veiga, "Job Control and Job Strain: A Test of Three Models," *Journal of Occupational Health Psychology* 2 (July 1997), pp. 195–211; B. B. Arnetz, "Technological Stress: Psychophysiological Aspects of Working with Modern Information Technology," *Scandinavian Journal of Work and Environment Health* 23 (1997, suppl. 3), pp. 97–103; R. Karasek and T. Theorell, *Healthy Work: Stress, Productivity, and the Reconstruction of Working Life* (New York: Basic Books, 1990).

17. B. Lubinger, "Even on Vacation, There's No Getting Away," *Plain Dealer (Cleveland)*, June 10, 2001, p. L1.

18. J. MacFarland, "Many Are Called, But What Are the Choices: Working in New Brunswick's 1-800 Call Centres," *New Maritimes* 14 (July/August 1996), pp. 10–19.

19. D. F. Elloy and A. Randolph, "The Effect of Superleader Behavior on Autonomous Work Groups in a Government Operated Railway Service," *Public Personnel Management* 26 (June 1997), pp. 257+.

20. J. T. Madore, C. Mason-Draffen, and R. Feigenbaum, "When Work Turns Ugly," *Newsday*, April 5, 1998, p. A4.

21. V. Schultz, "Reconceptualizing Sexual Harassment," *Yale Law Journal* 107 (April 1998), pp. 1683–1805. Several U.S. court cases have discussed these two causes for action, including *Lehman v. Toys 'R' Us Inc.* (1993) 132 N.J. 587; 626 A. (2nd) 445; *Meritor Savings Bank* v. *Vinson*, 477 U.S. 57 (1986) (U.S.S.C.).

22. L. J. Munson, C. Hulin, and F. Drasgow, "Longitudinal Analysis of Dispositional Influences and Sexual Harassment: Effects on Job and Psychological Outcomes," *Personnel Psychology* (Spring 2000), pp. 21–46; C. S. Piotrkowski, "Gender Harassment, Job Satisfaction, and Distress among Employed White and Minority Women," *Journal of Occupational Health Psychology* 3 (January 1998), pp. 33–43; L. F. Fitzgerald, F. Drasgow, C. L. Hulin, M. J. Gelfand, and V. Magley, "The Antecedents and Consequences of Sexual Harassment in Organizations: A Test of an Integrated Model," *Journal of Applied Psychology* 82 (1997), pp. 578–89; J. Barling, I. Dekker, C. A. Loughlin, E. K. Kelloway, C. Fullagar, and D. Johnson, "Prediction and Replication of the Organizational and Personal Consequences of Workplace Sexual Harassment," *Journal of Managerial Psychology* 11 (5) (1996), pp. 4–25.

23. H. W. French, "Fighting Sex Harassment, and Stigma, in Japan," *New York Times*, July 15, 2001, p. 1.

24. J. H. Neuman and R. A. Baron, "Workplace Violence and Workplace Aggression: Evidence Concerning Specific Forms, Potential Causes, and Preferred Targets," *Journal of Management* 24 (May 1998), pp. 391–419.

25. D. Reiss-Koncar, "The War against Nurses," *Salon.com*, July 27, 2001.

26. G. Lardner, Jr., "Violence at Work Is Largely Unreported," *Washington Post*, July 27, 1998, p. A2; "ILO Survey Reveals Extent of Violence at Work," *Agence France-Presse*, July 19, 1998.

27. J. Barling, "The Prediction, Experience, and Consequences of Workplace Violence," In G. R. VandenBos and E. Q. Bulatao, eds., *Violence on the Job: Identifying Risks and Developing Solutions* (Washington, DC: American Psychological Association, 1996), pp. 29–49.

28. C. A. Duffy and A. E. McGoldrick, "Stress and the Bus Driver in the UK Transport Industry," *Stress and Work* 4 (1990), pp. 17–27.

29. C. M. Pearson, L. M. Andersson, and C. L. Porath, "Assessing and Attacking Workplace Incivility," *Organizational Dynamics* 29 (November 2000), pp. 123–37. We would like to thank Dr. Michael Sheehan at Griffith University, Queensland, Australia, for assisting the research on this topic.

30. The University of Michigan study of workplace bullying is cited in M. Fletcher Stoeltje, "Jerks at Work," *San Antonio (TX) Express-News*, August 31, 2001, p. F1. M. Kivimaki, M. Elovainio, and J. Vahtera, "Workplace Bullying and Sickness Absence in Hospital Staff," *Occupational and Environmental Medicine* 57 (October 2000), pp. 656–60.

31. Kivimaki et al., "Workplace Bullying and Sickness Absence in Hospital Staff"; P. McCarthy and M. Barker, "Workplace Bullying Risk Audit," *Journal of Occupational Health and Safety, Australia and New Zealand* 16 (2000), pp. 409–18; M. O'Moore, E. Seigne, L. McGuire, and M. Smith, "Victims of Bullying at Work in Ireland," *Journal of Occupational Health and Safety* 14 (1998), pp. 569–74; G. Namie, "Hostile Workplace Survey" (http://www.bullybusters.org/home/twd/bb/res/surv2000.html).

32. S. Einarsen, "Harassment and Bullying at Work: A Review of the Scandinavian Approach," *Aggression and Violent Behavior* 5 (2000), pp. 379–401.

33. Pearson et al., "Assessing and Attacking Workplace Incivility."

34. M. Schorr, "Left in Limbo," *ABC News*, October 26, 2000; M. Kivimaki, J. Vahtera, J. Pentti, and J. E. Ferrie, "Factors Underlying the Effect of Organizational Downsizing on Health of Employees: Longitudinal Cohort Study," *BMJ: British Medical Journal* 320 (April 8, 2000), pp. 971–75.

35. G. A. Adams, L. A. King, and D. W. King, "Relationships of Job and Family Involvement, Family Social Support, and Work–Family Conflict with Job and Life Satisfaction," *Journal of Applied Psychology* 81 (August 1996), pp. 411–20; S. Lewis and C. L. Cooper, "Balancing the Work/Home Interface: A European Perspective," *Human Resource Management Review* 5 (1995), pp. 289–305; K. J. Williams and G. M. Alliger, "Role Stressors, Mood Spillover, and Perceptions of Work–Family Conflict in Employed Parents," *Academy of Management Journal* 37 (1994), pp. 837–68.

36. L. Washburn, "Sleepless in America," *Bergen (NJ) Record*, March 28, 2001, p. A1.

37. D. S. Carlson, "Work–Family Conflict in the Organization: Do Life Role Values Make a Difference?" *Journal of Management*, September 2000; M. Jamal and V. V. Baba, "Shiftwork and Department Type Related to Job Stress, Work Attitudes and Behavioral Intentions: A Study of Nurses," *Journal of Organizational Behavior* 13 (1992), pp. 449–64; C. Higgins, L. Duxbury, and R. Irving, "Determinants and Consequences of Work–Family Conflict," *Organizational Behavior and Human Decision Processes* 51 (February 1992), pp. 51–75.

38. D. L Nelson and R. J Burke, "Women Executives: Health, Stress, and Success," *Academy of Management Executive* 14 (May 2000), pp. 107–21; C. S. Rogers, "The Flexible Workplace: What Have We Learned?" *Human Resource Management* 31 (Fall 1992), pp. 183–99; L. E. Duxbury and C. A. Higgins, "Gender Differences in Work–Family Conflict," *Journal of Applied Psychology* 76 (1991), pp. 60–74; A. Hochschild, *The Second Shift* (New York: Avon, 1989).

39. M. P. Leiter and M. J. Durup, "Work, Home, and In-Between: A Longitudinal Study of Spillover," *Journal of Applied Behavioral Science* 32 (1996), pp. 29–47; W. Stewart and J. Barling, "Fathers' Work Experiences' Effect on Children's Behaviors via Job-Related Affect and Parenting Behaviors," *Journal of Organizational Behavior* 17 (1996), pp. 221–32; C. A. Beatty, "The Stress of Managerial and Professional Women: Is the Price Too High?" *Journal of Organizational Behavior* 17 (1996), pp. 233–51. See also: D. L. Morrison and R. Clements, "The Effect of

One Partner's Job Characteristics on the Other Partner's Distress: A Serendipitous, but Naturalistic, Experiment," *Journal of Occupational and Organizational Psychology* 70 (December 1997), pp. 307–24; Higgins, Duxbury, and Irving, "Determinants and Consequences of Work–Family Conflict."

40. A. S. Wharton and R. J. Erickson, "Managing Emotions on the Job and at Home: Understanding the Consequences of Multiple Emotional Roles," *Academy of Management Review* 18 (1993), pp. 457–86; S. E. Jackson and C. Maslach, "After-Effects of Job-Related Stress: Families as Victims," *Journal of Occupational Behavior* 3 (1982), pp. 66–77.

41. "Office Workers More Stressed Than Nurses," *The Independent (London)*, August 7, 2000, p. 8; B. Keil, "The 10 Most Stressful Jobs in NYC," *New York Post*, April 6, 1999, p. 50; International Labor Office (ILO), *World Labor Report* (Geneva: ILO, 1993), chap. 5; Karasek and Theorell, *Healthy Work*.

42. Quick et al., *Preventive Stress Management in Organizations*, chap. 3.

43. J. A. Roberts, R. S. Lapidus, and L. B. Chonko, "Salespeople and Stress: The Moderating Role of Locus of Control on Work Stressors and Felt Stress," *Journal of Marketing Theory and Practice* 5 (Summer 1997), pp. 93–108; J. Schaubroeck and D. E. Merritt, "Divergent Effects of Job Control on Coping with Work Stressors: The Key Role of Self-Efficacy," *Academy of Management Journal* 40 (June 1997), pp. 738+; A. O'Leary and S. Brown, "Self-Efficacy and the Physiological Stress Response," in J. E. Maddux, ed., *Self-Efficacy, Adaptation, and Adjustment: Theory, Research, and Application* (New York: Plenum, 1995).

44. S. C. Segerstrom, S. E. Taylor, M. E. Kemeny, and J. L. Fahey, "Optimism Is Associated with Mood, Coping, and Immune Change in Response to Stress," *Journal of Personality and Social Psychology* 74 (June 1998), pp. 1646–55.

45. K. R. Parkes, "Personality and Coping as Moderators of Work Stress Processes: Models, Methods and Measures," *Work and Stress* 8 (April 1994), pp. 110–29; S. J. Havlovic and J. P.

Keenen, "Coping with Work Stress: The Influence of Individual Differences," in P. L. Perrewé, ed., "Handbook on Job Stress" [Special Issue], *Journal of Social Behavior and Personality* 6 (1991), pp. 199–212.

46. B. C. Long and S. E. Kahn, eds., *Women, Work, and Coping: A Multidisciplinary Approach to Workplace Stress* (Montreal: McGill-Queen's University Press, 1993); E. R. Greenglass, R. J. Burke, and M. Ondrack, "A Gender-Role Perspective of Coping and Burnout," *Applied Psychology: An International Review* 39 (1990), pp. 5–27; T. D. Jick and L. F. Mitz, "Sex Differences in Work Stress," *Academy of Management Review* 10 (1985), pp. 408–20.

47. B. Bergman, R. Sheppard, and J. DeMont, "Pressure Point," *Maclean's*, February 7, 2000, p. 48.

48. M. Friedman and R. Rosenman, *Type A Behavior and Your Heart* (New York: Knopf, 1974). For a more recent discussion, see P. E. Spector and B. J. O'Connell, "The Contribution of Personality Traits, Negative Affectivity, Locus of Control" and Type A to the Subsequent Reports of Job Stressors and Job Strains," *Journal of Occupational and Organizational Psychology* 67 (1994), pp. 1–11; Parkes, "Personality and Coping as Moderators of Work Stress Processes."

49. M. Jamal, "Type A Behavior and Job Performance: Some Suggestive Findings," *Journal of Human Stress* 11 (Summer 1985), pp. 60–68; C. Lee, P. C. Earley, and L. A. Hanson, "Are Type A's Better Performers?" *Journal of Organizational Behavior* 9 (1988), pp. 263–69.

50. S. Cohen, D. A. Tyrrell, and A. P. Smith, "Psychological Stress and Susceptibility to the Common Cold," *New England Journal of Medicine* 325 (August 29, 1991), pp. 654–56.

51. S. A. Everson et al., "Stress-Induced Blood Pressure Reactivity and Incident Stroke in Middle-Aged Men," *Stroke* 32 (June 2001), pp. 1263–70; R. J. Benschop et al., "Cardiovascular and Immune Responses to Acute Psychological Stress in Young and Old Women: A Meta-Analysis," *Psychosomatic Medicine* 60 (May–June 1998), pp. 290–96; H. Bosma, R. Peter, J. Siegrist, and M. Marmot, "Two Alter-

native Job Stress Models and the Risk of Coronary Heart Disease," *American Journal of Public Health* 88 (January 1998), pp. 68–74.

52. A. Dabrow, "Improving the Odds against Hypertension," *Nursing* 31 (August 2001), p. 36; *National Vital Statistics Reports*, vol. 48, no. 11, July 24, 2000, pp. 26–36. Many of these statistics are also available at the website of the National Center for Health Statistics (www.cdc.gov/nchs/).

53. D. K. Sugg, "Study Shows Link between Minor Stress, Early Signs of Coronary Artery Disease," *Baltimore Sun*, December 16, 1997, p. A3.

54. R. C. Kessler, "The Effects of Stressful Life Events on Depression," *Annual Review of Psychology* 48 (1997), pp. 191–214; H. M. Weiss and R. Cropanzano, "Affective Events Theory: A Theoretical Discussion of the Structure, Causes, and Consequences of Affective Experiences at Work," *Research in Organizational Behavior* 18 (1996), pp. 1–74.

55. R. T. Lee and B. E. Ashforth, "A Meta-Analytic Examination of the Correlates of the Three Dimensions of Job Burnout," *Journal of Applied Psychology*, 81 (1996) pp. 123–33; R. J. Burke, "Toward a Phase Model of Burnout: Some Conceptual and Methodological Concerns," *Group and Organization Studies* 14 (1989), pp. 23–32; and C. Maslach, *Burnout: The Cost of Caring* (Englewood Cliffs, NJ: Prentice Hall, 1982).

56. C. L. Cordes and T. W. Dougherty, "A Review and Integration of Research on Job Burnout," *Academy of Management Review* 18 (1993), pp. 621–56.

57. R. T. Lee and B. E. Ashforth, "A Further Examination of Managerial Burnout: Toward an Integrated Model," *Journal of Organizational Behavior* 14 (1993), pp. 3–20.

58. M. Jamal, "Job Stress and Job Performance Controversy: An Empirical Assessment," *Organizational Behavior and Human Performance* 33 (1984), pp. 1–21; G. Keinan, "Decision Making under Stress: Scanning of Alternatives under Controllable and Uncontrollable Threats," *Journal of Personality and Social Psychology* 52 (1987), pp. 638–44; S. J. Motowidlo, J. S. Packard, and M. R. Manning, "Occupational Stress:

Its Causes and Consequences for Job Performance," *Journal of Applied Psychology* 71 (1986), pp. 618–29.

59. R. D. Hackett and P. Bycio, "An Evaluation of Employee Absenteeism as a Coping Mechanism among Hospital Nurses," *Journal of Occupational and Organizational Psychology* 69 (December 1996) pp. 327–38; V. V. Baba and M. J. Harris, "Stress and Absence: A Cross-Cultural Perspective," *Research in Personnel and Human Resources Management*, suppl. 1 (1989), pp. 317–37.

60. DeFrank and Ivancevich, "Stress on the Job"; Neuman and Baron, "Workplace Violence and Workplace Aggression."

61. L. Greenberg and J. Barling, "Predicting Employee Aggression against Coworkers, Subordinates and Supervisors: The Roles of Person Behaviors and Perceived Workplace Factors," *Journal of Organizational Behavior* 20 (1999), pp. 897–913; M. A. Diamond, "Administrative Assault: A Contemporary Psychoanalytic View of Violence and Aggression in the Workplace," *American Review of Public Administration* 27 (September 1997), pp. 228–47.

62. Neuman and Baron, "Workplace Violence and Workplace Aggression"; L. Berkowitz, *Aggression: Its Causes, Consequences, and Control* (New York: McGraw-Hill, 1993).

63. "Stressed Out: How the Big Shots Get Some Stability," *Wall Street Journal Europe*, January 18, 2001, p. 21.

64. Siegall and Cummings, "Stress and Organizational Role Conflict"; Havlovic and Keenen, "Coping with Work Stress."

65. T. Newton, J. Handy, and S. Fineman, *Managing Stress: Emotion and Power at Work* (Newbury Park, CA: Sage, 1995).

66. N. Elkes, "Hospital Tackles Health of Stressed-Out Staff," *Birmingham (UK) Evening Mail*, August 24, 2001, p. 73.

67. N. Terra, "The Prevention of Job Stress by Redesigning Jobs and Implementing Self-Regulating Teams," in L. R. Murphy, ed., *Job Stress Interventions* (Washington, DC: American Psychological Association, 1995); T. D. Wall and K. Davids, "Shopfloor Work Organization and Advanced Manufac-

turing Technology," *International Review of Industrial and Organizational Psychology* 7 (1992), pp. 363–98; Karasek and Theorell, *Healthy Work*.

68. T. Layman, "Minimizing Travel's Toll Helps Retain Consultants," *Atlanta Business Chronicle*, September 17, 2001.

69. B. S. Watson, "Share and Share Alike," *Management Review*, October 1995, pp. 50–52.

70. E. J. Hill, B. C. Miller, S. P. Weiner, and J. Colihan, "Influences of the Virtual Office on Aspects of Work and Work/Life Balance," *Personnel Psychology* 51 (Autumn 1998), 667–83; A. Mahlon, "The Alternative Workplace: Changing Where and How People Work," *Harvard Business Review* (May–June 1998), pp. 121–30.

71. D. Coates, "Ford Exec Turns Work Day to Fit Children's Life," *Detroit News*, June 17, 2001.

72. Over 100 countries have paid maternity leave. Among the industrialized countries, only the United States, Australia, and New Zealand do not provide this support. See T. Allard and L. Glendinning, "For Now, Aussie Mums Are Still a World Apart," *Sydney Morning Herald*, August 16, 2001; J. Satterfield, "U.S. Lags Behind Other Nations on Family Leave," *Knoxville (TN) News-Sentinel*, May 7, 2001, p. A1. For discussion of the FMLA, see S. Kim, "Toward Understanding Family Leave Policy in Public Organizations: Family Leave Use and Conceptual Framework for the Family Leave Implementation Process," *Public Productivity and Management Review* 22 (September 1998), pp. 71–87.

73. "Work/Life Balance a Key to Productivity," *Employee Benefit Plan Review* 53 (September 1998), pp. 30–31.

74. S. Hale, "Execs Embrace Wide-Open Spaces," *Los Angeles Times*, May 13, 2001; P. DeMont, "Too Much Stress, Too Little Time," *Ottawa Citizen*, November 12, 1999.

75. E. Cowing, "Get Richer by Keeping Your Staff Happy," *Sunday Times (London)*, November 28, 1999, p. 20.

76. R. Levering and M. Moskowitz, "The 100 Best Companies to Work For," *Fortune*, January 8, 2001, p. 148.

77. M. Stobbe, "Charlotte, N.C., Workers Find Ways to Beat Stress, 'Pump

Up Their Own Morale,'" *Charlotte (NC) Observer*, September 21, 2001.

78. A. M. Saks and B. E. Ashforth, "Proactive Socialization and Behavioral Self-Management," *Journal of Vocational Behavior* 48 (1996), pp. 301–23; M. Waung, "The Effects of Self-Regulatory Coping Orientation on Newcomer Adjustment and Job Survival," *Personnel Psychology* 48 (1995), pp. 633–50; J. E. Maddux, ed. *Self-Efficacy, Adaptation, and Adjustment: Theory, Research, and Application* (New York: Plenum, 1995).

79. A. J. Daley and G. Parfitt, "Good Health—Is It Worth It? Mood States, Physical Well-Being, Job Satisfaction and Absenteeism in Members and Non-Members of British Corporate Health and Fitness Clubs," *Journal of Occupational and Organizational Psychology* 69 (1996), pp. 121–34; L. E. Falkenberg, "Employee Fitness Programs: Their Impact on the Employee and the Organization," *Academy of Management Review* 12 (1987), pp. 511–22; R. J. Shephard, M. Cox, and P. Corey, "Fitness Program Participation: Its Effect on Workers' Performance," *Journal of Occupational Medicine* 23 (1981), pp. 359–63.

80. For a more detailed discussion of stress and wellness in organizations, see K. Danna and R. W. Griffin, "Health and Well-Being in the Workplace: A Review and Synthesis of the Literature," *Journal of Management* 25 (May 1999), pp. 357–84

81. A. S. Sethi, "Meditation for Coping with Organizational Stress," in A. S. Sethi and R. S. Schuler, eds., *Handbook of Organizational Stress Coping Strategies* (Cambridge, MA: Ballinger, 1984), pp. 145–65; M. T. Matteson and J. M. Ivancevich, *Managing Job Stress and Health* (New York: Free Press, 1982), pp. 160–66.

82. J. J. L. van der Klink, R. W. B. Blonk, A. H. Schene, and F. J. H. van Dijk, "The Benefits of Interventions for Work-Related Stress," *American Journal of Public Health* 91 (February 2001), pp. 270–76; T. Rotarius, A. Liberman, and J. S. Liberman, "Employee Assistance Programs: A Prevention and Treatment Prescription for Problems in Health Care Organizations," *Health Care Manager* 19 (September 2000), pp. 24–31.

83. P. D. Bliese and T. W. Britt, "Social Support, Group Consensus, and Stressor–Strain Relationships: Social Context Matters," *Journal of Organizational Behavior* 22 (2001), pp. 425–36; B. N. Uchino, J. T. Cacioppo, and J. K. Kiecolt-Glaser, "The Relationship Between Social Support and Physiological Processes: A Review with Emphasis on Underlying Mechanisms and Implications for Health," *Psychological Bulletin* 119 (May 1996), pp. 488–531; M. R. Manning, C. N. Jackson, and M. R. Fusilier, "Occupational Stress, Social Support, and the Costs of Health Care," *Academy of Management Journal* 39 (June 1996), pp. 738–50.

84. J. S. House, *Work Stress and Social Support* (Reading, MA: Addison-Wesley, 1981); S. Cohen and T. A. Wills, "Stress, Social Support, and the Buffering Hypothesis," *Psychological Bulletin* 98 (1985), pp. 310–57.

85. S. Schachter, *The Psychology of Affiliation* (Stanford, CA: Stanford University Press, 1959).

86. L. Tickner, "Miners Take Health Road," *West Australian*, March 17, 2001, pp. 1, 4.

CHAPTER EIGHT

1. S. Carney, "DaimlerChrysler Launches Product Teams," *Detroit News*, July 13, 2001, p. 1; J. Dixon, "Lean, Mean Is Theme for Chrysler," *Detroit Free Press*, July 12, 2001; E. Garsten, "Chrysler Has New Product Process," *AP Online*, July 12, 2001.

2. R. Kulwiec, "Self-Managed Work Teams—Reality or Fad?" *Material Handling Management—Strategies for Top Management Supplement*, April 2001, pp. 15–22; J. Sung, "Designed for Interaction," *Fortune*, January 8, 2001; S. Kirsner, "Every Day, It's a New Place," *Fast Company*, April–May 1998, pp. 130–34.

3. M. Orton, "Enamoured with Creativity," *Ottawa Citizen* [High Tech Supplement], May 30, 1999.

4. S. G. Cohen and D. E. Bailey, "What Makes Teams Work: Group Effectiveness Research from the Shop Floor to the Executive Suite," *Journal of Management* 23 (May 1997), pp. 239–90; M. A. West, "Preface: Introducing Work Group Psychology," in M. A. West, ed., *Handbook of Work Group Psychology* (Chichester, UK: Wiley, 1996), p. xxvi; S. A. Mohrman, S. G. Cohen, and A. M. Mohrman, Jr., *Designing Team-Based Organizations: New Forms for Knowledge Work* (San Francisco: Jossey-Bass, 1995), pp. 39–40; J. R. Katzenbach and K. D. Smith, "The Discipline of Teams," *Harvard Business Review* 71 (March–April 1993), pp. 111–20; M. E. Shaw, *Group Dynamics*, 3rd ed. (New York: McGraw-Hill, 1981), p. 8.

5. L. R. Offermann and R. K. Spiros, "The Science and Practice of Team Development: Improving the Link," *Academy of Management Journal* 44 (April 2001), pp. 376–92. David Nadler similarly distinguishes *crowds* from *groups* and *teams*. See D. A. Nadler, "From Ritual to Real Work: The Board as a Team," *Directors and Boards* 22 (Summer 1998), pp. 28–31.

6. The preference for using the term *team* rather than *group* is also discussed in Cohen and Bailey, "What Makes Teams Work"; R. A. Guzzo and M. W. Dickson, "Teams in Organizations: Recent Research on Performance and Effectiveness," *Annual Review of Psychology* 47 (1996), pp. 307–38.

7. A. R. Jassawalla and G. H. C. Sashittal, "The Role of Senior Management and Team Leaders in Building Collaborative New Product Teams," *Engineering Management Journal* 13 (June 2001), pp. 33–39.

8. G. E. Huszczo, *Tools for Team Excellence* (Palo Alto, CA: Davies-Black, 1996), pp. 9–15; R. Likert, *New Patterns of Management* (New York: McGraw-Hill, 1961), pp. 106–8.

9. D. E. Yeatts and C. Hyten, *High-Performing Self-Managed Work Teams: A Comparison of Theory and Practice* (Thousand Oaks, CA: Sage, 1998); Mohrman, Cohen, and Mohrman, Jr., *Designing Team-Based Organizations*, p. 6; J. H. Shonk, *Team-Based Organizations: Developing a Successful Team Environment* (Homewood, IL: Business Irwin One, 1992).

10. N. S. Bruning and P. R. Liverpool, "Membership in Quality Circles and Participation in Decision Making," *Journal of Applied Behavioral Science* 29 (March 1993), pp. 76–95.

11. Mohrman, Cohen, and Mohrman, Jr., *Designing Team-Based Organizations*, chap. 2; R. S. Wellins, W. C. Byham, and G. R. Dixon, *Inside Teams* (San Francisco: Jossey-Bass, 1994), pp. 9–10.

12. R. Pascale, M. Millemann, and L. Gioja, *Surfing on the Edge of Chaos* (London: Texere, 2000), pp. 181–95, 223–26; R. Pascale, "Change How You Define Leadership, and You Change How You Run a Company," *Fast Company*, April–May 1998, pp. 110–20.

13. T. Peters, *Thriving on Chaos* (New York: Knopf, 1987), pp. 211–18; T. Kidder, *Soul of a New Machine* (Boston: Little, Brown, 1981); T. Peters and N. Austin, *A Passion for Excellence* (New York: Random House, 1985), chaps. 9 and 10.

14. S. Zesiger, "Dial 'M' For Mystique," *Fortune*, January 12, 1998, p. 175; R. Hertzberg, "No Longer a Skunkworks," *Internet World*, November 3, 1997; R. Lim, "Innovation, Innovation, Innovation," *Business Times (Singapore)*, October 27, 1997, p. 18.

15. J. Kurlantzick, "New Balance Stays a Step Ahead," *U.S. News & World Report*, July 2, 2001, p. 34; A. Bernstein, "Low-Skilled Jobs: Do They Have to Move?" *Business Week*, February 26, 2001, p. 92; G. Gatlin, "Firm Boasts of New Balance of Power," *Boston Herald*, January 24, 2001, p. 27.

16. S. Alexander, "Virtual Teams Going Global," *InfoWorld*, November 13, 2000, pp. 55–56.

17. J. Lipnack and J. Stamps, *Virtual Teams: People Working across Boundaries with Technology* (New York: Wiley, 2001); D. J. Armstrong and P. Cole, "Managing Distances and Differences in Geographically Distributed Work Groups," in S. E. Jackson and M. N. Ruderman, eds., *Diversity in Work Teams: Research Paradigms for a Changing Workplace* (Washington, DC: American Psychological Association, 1995), pp. 187–215.

18. D. Robey, H. M. Khoo, and C. Powers, "Situated Learning in Cross-Functional Virtual Teams," *Technical Communication*, February 2000, pp. 51–66.

19. G. Gilder, *Telecosm: How Infinite Bandwidth Will Revolutionize Our*

World (New York: Free Press, 2001); J. S. Brown, "Seeing Differently: A Role for Pioneering Research," *Research Technology Management* 41 (May–June 1998), pp. 24–33.

20. A. M. Townsend, S. M. DeMarie, and A. R. Hendrickson, "Virtual Teams: Technology and the Workplace of the Future," *Academy of Management Executive* 12 (August 1998), pp. 17–29.

21. J. Pollard, "Anyway, Anyhow, Anywhere," *Observer (London)*, September 3, 2000, p. 16.

22. J. A. Wagner III, C. R. Leana, E. A. Locke, and D. M. Schweiger, "Cognitive and Motivational Frameworks in U.S. Research on Participation: A Meta-Analysis of Primary Effects," *Journal of Organizational Behavior* 18 (1997), pp. 49–65.

23. W. B. Stevenson, J. L. Pearce, and L. W. Porter, "The Concept of 'Coalition' in Organization Theory and Research," *Academy of Management Review* 10 (1985), pp. 256–68; Shaw, *Group Dynamics*, pp. 105–10.

24. E. C. Wenger and W. M. Snyder, "Communities of Practice: The Organizational Frontier," *Harvard Business Review* 78 (January–February 2000), pp. 139–45; J. W. Botkin, *Smart Business: How Knowledge Communities Can Revolutionize Your Company* (New York: Free Press, 1999).

25. M. Finlay, "Panning for Gold," *ComputerUser*, July 1, 2001.

26. M. A. Hogg and D. J. Terry, "Social Identity and Self-Categorization Processes in Organizational Contexts," *Academy of Management Review* 25 (January 2000), pp. 121–40; B. E. Ashforth and F. Mael, "Social Identity Theory and the Organization," *Academy of Management Review* 14 (1989), pp. 20–39.

27. A. S. Tannenbaum, *Social Psychology of the Work Organization* (Belmont, CA: Wadsworth, 1966), p. 62; S. Schacter, *The Psychology of Affiliation* (Stanford, CA: Stanford University Press, 1959), pp. 12–19.

28. R. Forrester and A. B. Drexler, "A Model for Team-based Organization Performance," *Academy of Management Executive* 13 (August 1999), pp. 36–49; M. A. West, C. S. Borrill, and K. L. Unsworth, "Team Effectiveness in Organizations," *International Review of Industrial and Organizational Psychology* 13 (1998), pp. 1–48; R. A. Guzzo and M. W. Dickson, "Teams in Organizations: Recent Research on Performance and Effectiveness," *Annual Review of Psychology* 47 (1996), pp. 307–38.

29. West et al., "Team Effectiveness in Organizations"; Mohrman, Cohen, and Mohrman, Jr., *Designing Team-Based Organizations*, pp. 58–65; J. E. McGrath, "Time, Interaction, and Performance (TIP): A Theory of Groups," *Small Group Research* 22 (1991), pp. 147–74; G. P. Shea and R. A. Guzzo, "Group Effectiveness: What Really Matters?" *Sloan Management Review* 27 (1987), pp. 33–46.

30. D. K. Denton, "How a Team Can Grow," *Quality Progress*, June 1999, p. 53.

31. S. Sarin and V. Mahajan, "The Effect of Reward Structures on the Performance of Cross-Functional Product Development Teams," *Journal of Marketing* 65 (April 2001), pp. 35–53; J. S. DeMatteo, L. T. Eby, and E. Sundstrom, "Team-Based Rewards: Current Empirical Evidence and Directions for Future Research," *Research in Organizational Behavior* 20 (1998), pp. 141–83; R. L. Heneman and C. von Hippel, "Balancing Group and Individual Rewards: Rewarding Individual Contributions to the Team," *Compensation and Benefits Review* 27 (July–August 1995), pp. 63–68.

32. P. Bordia, "Face-to-Face versus Computer-Mediated Communication: A Synthesis of the Experimental Literature," *Journal of Business Communication* 34 (January 1997), pp. 99–120; A. D. Shulman, "Putting Group Information Technology in its Place: Communication and Good Work Group Performance," in S. R. Clegg, C. Hardy, and W. R. Nord, eds., *Handbook of Organization Studies* (London: Sage, 1996), pp. 357–74; J. E. McGrath and A. B. Hollingshead, *Groups Interacting with Technology* (Thousand Oaks, CA: Sage, 1994).

33. S. Alexander, "Virtual Teams Going Global," *InfoWorld*, November 13, 2000, pp. 55–56. For further discussion of communication in virtual teams, see W. G. Cascio, "Managing a Virtual Workplace," *Academy of Management Executive*, August 2000, pp. 81–90.

34. J. Hansen, "Wide Open Spaces," *AsiaWeek,* May 25, 2001.

35. R. Wageman, "Case Study: Critical Success Factors for Creating Superb Self-Managing Teams at Xerox," *Compensation and Benefits Review* 29 (September–October 1997), pp. 31–41; D. Dimancescu and K. Dwenger, "Smoothing the Product Development Path," *Management Review* 85 (January 1996), pp. 36–41.

36. E. F. McDonough III, "Investigation of Factors Contributing to the Success of Cross-Functional Teams," *Journal of Product Innovation Management* 17 (May 2000), pp. 221–35; A. Edmondson, "Psychological Safety and Learning Behavior in Work Teams," *Administrative Science Quarterly* 44 (1999), pp. 350–83; D. G. Ancona and D. E. Caldwell, "Demography and Design: Predictors of New Product Team Performance," *Organization Science* 3 (August 1992), pp. 331–41.

37. M. A. Campion, E. M. Papper, and G. J. Medsker, "Relations between Work Team Characteristics and Effectiveness: A Replication and Extension," *Personnel Psychology* 49 (1996), pp. 429–52; S. Worchel and S. L. Shackelford, "Groups Under Stress: The Influence of Group Structure and Environment on Process and Performance," *Personality and Social Psychology Bulletin* 17 (1991), pp. 640–47; E. Sundstrom, K. P. De Meuse, and D. Futrell, "Work Teams: Applications and Effectiveness," *American Psychologist* 45 (1990), pp. 120–33.

38. G. van der Vegt, B. Emans, and E. van de Vliert, "Motivating Effects of Task and Outcome Interdependence in Work Teams," *Group and Organization Management* 23 (June 1998), pp. 124–43; R. C. Liden, S. J. Wayne, and L. K. Bradway, "Task Interdependence as a Moderator of the Relation between Group Control and Performance," *Human Relations* 50 (1997), pp. 169–81; R. Wageman, "Interdependence and Group Effectiveness," *Administrative Science Quarterly* 40 (1995), pp. 145–80; M. A. Campion, G. J. Medsker, and A. C. Higgs, "Relations between Work Group Characteristics and Effectiveness: Implications for Designing Effective Work Groups," *Personnel Psychology* 46 (1993), pp. 823–50; M. N. Kiggundu, "Task Interdependence and the Theory

of Job Design," *Academy of Management Review* 6 (1981), pp. 499–508.

39. A. Muoio, "Growing Smart," *Fast Company* 16 (August 1998); A. R. Sorkin, "Gospel According to St. Luke's," *New York Times*, February 12, 1998, p. D1.

40. G. R. Hickman and A. Creighton-Zollar, "Diverse Self-Directed Work Teams: Developing Strategic Initiatives for 21st-Century Organizations," *Public Personnel Management* 27 (Spring 1998), pp. 187–200; J. R. Katzenbach and D. K. Smith, *The Wisdom of Teams: Creating the High-Performance Organization* (Boston: Harvard University Press, 1993), pp. 45–47; G. Stasser, "Pooling of Unshared Information during Group Discussion," in S. Worchel, W. Wood, and J. A. Simpson, eds., *Group Process and Productivity* (Newbury Park, CA: Sage, 1992), pp. 48–67.

41. T. Willmert, "Smart Workplace Design Should Bring People, and Their Ideas, Together," *Minneapolis Star Tribune*, January 28, 2001, p. D11.

42. D. Huynh, "Central Market Caters to Hungry Shoppers on the Run," *Houston Chronicle*, June 1, 2001, p. 2; "Creative Hiring Replaces Yesterday's Staid Interview," *Houston Business Journal*, March 9, 2001, p. 35.

43. L. T. Eby and G. H. Dobbins, "Collectivist Orientation in Teams: An Individual and Group-Level Analysis," *Journal of Organizational Behavior* 18 (1997), pp. 275–95; P. C. Earley, "East Meets West Meets Mideast: Further Explorations of Collectivistic and Individualistic Work Groups," *Academy of Management Journal* 36 (1993), pp. 319–48.

44. Mohrman, Cohen, and Mohrman, Jr., *Designing Team-Based Organizations*, pp. 248–54; M. J. Stevens and M. A. Campion, "The Knowledge, Skill and Ability Requirements for Teamwork: Implications for Human Resources Management," *Journal of Management* 20 (1994), pp. 503–30; A. P. Hare, *Handbook of Small Group Research*, 2nd ed. (New York: Free Press, 1976), pp. 12–15.

45. B. Buzaglo and S. Wheelan, "Facilitating Work Team Effectiveness: Case Studies from Central America," *Small Group Research* 30 (1999), pp. 108–29; B. Schultz, "Improving Group Com-

munication Performance: An Overview of Diagnosis and Intervention," in L. Frey, D. Gouran, and M. Poole, eds., *Handbook of Group Communication Theory and Research* (Thousand Oaks, CA: Sage, 1999), pp. 371–94.

46. "New Anchor Hocking Plant Incorporates 'Socio-Tech' Work Environment Philosophy," *Business Wire*, October 19, 1995. For a comprehensive discussion of selecting people for team-based work, see R. J. Klimoski and L. B. Zukin, "Selection and Staffing for Team Effectiveness," in E. Sundstrom and Associates, eds., *Supporting Work Team Effectiveness* (San Francisco: Jossey-Bass, 1998), pp. 63–91.

47. D. C. Hambrick, S. C. Davison, S. A. Snell, and C. C. Snow, "When Groups Consist of Multiple Nationalities: Towards a New Understanding of the Implications," *Organization Studies* 19 (1998), pp. 181–205; F. J. Milliken and L. L. Martins, "Searching for Common Threads: Understanding the Multiple Effects of Diversity in Organizational Groups," *Academy of Management Review* 21 (1996), pp. 402–33; J. K. Murnighan and D. Conlon, "The Dynamics of Intense Work Groups: A Study of British String Quartets," *Administrative Science Quarterly* 36 (1991), pp. 165–86.

48. P. C. Earley and E. Mosakowski, "Creating Hybrid Team Cultures: An Empirical Test of Transnational Team Functioning," *Academy of Management Journal* 43 (February 2000), pp. 26–49; D. C. Lau and J. K. Murnighan, "Demographic Diversity and Faultlines: The Compositional Dynamics of Organizational Groups," *Academy of Management Review* 23 (April 1998), pp. 325–40.

49. L. H. Pelled, K. M. Eisenhardt, and K. R. Xin, "Exploring the Black Box: An Analysis of Work Group Diversity, Conflict, and Performance," *Administrative Science Quarterly* 44 (March 1999), pp. 1–28; K. Y. Williams and C. A. O'Reilly III, "Demography and Diversity in Organizations: A Review of 40 Years of Research," *Research in Organizational Behavior* 20 (1998), pp. 70–140; B. Daily, A. Wheatley, S. R. Ash, and R. L. Steiner, "The Effects of a Group Decision Support System on Culturally Diverse and Culturally Homogeneous

Group Decision Making," *Information and Management* 30 (1996), pp. 281–89; W. E. Watson, K. Kumar, and L. K. Michaelson, "Cultural Diversity's Impact on Interaction Process and Performance: Comparing Homogeneous and Diverse Task Groups," *Academy of Management Journal* 36 (1993), pp. 590–602.

50. L. Tucci, "Owens Drake Consulting Fosters Systematic Change," *St. Louis Business Journal*, May 25, 1998.

51. B. W. Tuckman and M. A. C. Jensen, "Stages of Small-Group Development Revisited," *Group and Organization Studies* 2 (1977), pp. 419–42. For a humorous and somewhat cynical discussion of team dynamics through these stages, see H. Robbins and M. Finley, *Why Teams Don't Work* (Princeton, NJ: Peterson's/Pacesetters, 1995), chap. 21.

52. J. E. Mathieu and G. F. Goodwin, "The Influence of Shared Mental Models on Team Process and Performance," *Journal of Applied Psychology* 85 (April 2000), pp. 273–84; J. A. Cannon-Bowers, S. I. Tannenbaum, E. Salas, and C. E. Volpe, "Defining Competencies and Establishing Team Training Requirements," in Guzzo, Salas, and Associates, eds., *Team Effectiveness and Decision Making in Organizations* (San Francisco: Jossey-Bass, 1995), pp. 333–80.

53. A. Edmondson, "Psychological Safety and Learning Behavior in Work Teams," *Administrative Science Quarterly* 44 (1999), pp. 350–83.

54. D. L. Miller, "Synergy in Group Development: A Perspective on Group Performance," *Proceedings of the Annual ASAC Conference, Organizational Behavior Division* 17, pt. 5 (1996), pp. 119–28; S. Worchel, D. Coutant-Sassic, and M. Grossman, "A Developmental Approach to Group Dynamics: A Model and Illustrative Research," in Worchel et al., eds., *Group Process and Productivity*, pp. 181–202; C. J. G. Gersick, "Time and Transition in Work Teams: Toward a New Model of Group Development," *Academy of Management Journal* 31 (1988), pp. 9–41.

55. D. C. Feldman, "The Development and Enforcement of Group Norms," *Academy of Management Review* 9 (1984), pp. 47–53; L. W. Porter, E. E.

Lawler III, and J. R. Hackman, *Behavior in Organizations* (New York: McGraw-Hill, 1975), pp. 391–94.

56. I. R. Gellatly, "Individual and Group Determinants of Employee Absenteeism: Test of a Causal Model," *Journal of Organizational Behavior* 16 (1995), pp. 469–85; G. Johns, "Absenteeism Estimates by Employees and Managers: Divergent Perspectives and Self-Serving Perceptions," *Journal of Applied Psychology* 79 (1994), pp. 229–39.

57. "Employees Terrorized by Peer Pressure in the Workplace," Morgan & Banks news release, September 2000. See also B. Latané, "The Psychology of Social Impact," *American Psychologist* 36 (1981), pp. 343–56; C. A. Kiesler and S. B. Kiesler, *Conformity* (Reading, MA: Addison-Wesley, 1970).

58. Porter, Lawler, and Hackman, *Behavior in Organizations*, pp. 399–401.

59. Feldman, "The Development and Enforcement of Group Norms," pp. 50–52.

60. Katzenbach and Smith, *The Wisdom of Teams*, pp. 121–23.

61. K. L. Bettenhausen and J. K. Murnighan, "The Development of an Intragroup Norm and the Effects of Interpersonal and Structural Challenges," *Administrative Science Quarterly* 36 (1991), pp. 20–35.

62. R. S. Spich and K. Keleman, "Explicit Norm Structuring Process: A Strategy for Increasing Task-Group Effectiveness," *Group and Organization Studies* 10 (March 1985), pp. 37–59.

63. L. Y. Chan and B. E. Lynn, "Operating in Turbulent Times: How Ontario's Hospitals Are Meeting the Current Funding Crisis," *Health Care Management Review* 23 (June 1998), p. 7.

64. D. I. Levine, "Piece Rates, Output Restriction, and Conformism," *Journal of Economic Psychology* 13 (1992), pp. 473–89.

65. L. Coch and J. R. P. French, Jr., "Overcoming Resistance to Change," *Human Relations* 1 (1948), pp. 512–32.

66. D. Katz and R. L. Kahn, *The Social Psychology of Organizations* (New York: Wiley, 1966), chap. 7; J. W. Thibault and H. H. Kelley, *The Social Psychology of Groups* (New York: Wiley, 1959), chap. 8.

67. D. Vinokur-Kaplan, "Treatment Teams That Work (and Those That Don't): An Application of Hackman's Group Effectiveness Model to Interdisciplinary Teams in Psychiatric Hospitals," *Journal of Applied Behavioral Science* 31 (1995), pp. 303–27; Shaw, *Group Dynamics*, pp. 213–26; D. S. Goodman, E. Ravin, and M. Schminke, "Understanding Groups in Organizations," *Research in Organizational Behavior* 9 (1987), pp. 144–46.

68. S. Lembke and M. G. Wilson, "Putting the 'Team' into Teamwork: Alternative Theoretical Contributions for Contemporary Management Practice," *Human Relations* 51 (July 1998), pp. 927–44; B. E. Ashforth and R. H. Humphrey, "Emotion in the Workplace: A Reappraisal," *Human Relations* 48 (1995), pp. 97–125; P. R. Bernthal and C. A. Insko, "Cohesiveness without Groupthink: The Interactive Effects of Social and Task Cohesiveness," *Group and Organization Management* 18 (1993), pp. 66–87.

69. A. Lott and B. Lott, "Group Cohesiveness as Interpersonal Attraction: A Review of Relationships with Antecedent and Consequent Variables," *Psychological Bulletin* 64 (1965), pp. 259–309.

70. S. E. Jackson, "Team Composition in Organizational Settings: Issues in Managing an Increasingly Diverse Work Force," in Worchel et al., eds., *Group Process and Productivity*, pp. 138–73; J. Virk, P. Aggarwal, and R. N. Bhan, "Similarity versus Complementarity in Clique Formation," *Journal of Social Psychology* 120 (1983), pp. 27–34.

71. M. B. Pinto, J. K. Pinto, and J. E. Prescott, "Antecedents and Consequences of Project Team Cross-Functional Cooperation," *Management Science* 39 (1993), pp. 1281–96; W. Piper, M. Marrache, R. Lacroix, A. Richardson, and B. Jones, "Cohesion as a Basic Bond in Groups," *Human Relations* 36 (1983), pp. 93–108.

72. M. Frase-Blunt, "The Cubicles Have Ears. Maybe They Need Earplugs," *Washington Post*, March 6, 2001, p. HE7.

73. F. G. Mangrum, M. S. Fairley, and D. L. Wieder, "Informal Problem Solving in the Technology-Mediated Work Place," *Journal of Business Communication* 38 (July 2001), pp. 315–36; Robey et al., "Situated Learning in Cross-Functional Virtual Teams"; E. J. Hill, B. C. Miller, S. P. Weiner, and J. Colihan, "Influences of the Virtual Office on Aspects of Work and Work/Life Balance," *Personnel Psychology* 51 (Autumn 1998), pp. 667–83; S. B. Gould, K. J. Weiner, and B. R. Levin, *Free Agents: People and Organizations Creating a New Working Community* (San Francisco: Jossey-Bass, 1997), pp. 158–60.

74. J. Zbar, "Home Base," *Network World Fusion*, March 12, 2001.

75. J. E. Hautaluoma and R. S. Enge, "Early Socialization into a Work Group: Severity of Initiations Revisited," *Journal of Social Behavior and Personality* 6 (1991) pp. 725–48; E. Aronson and J. Mills, "The Effects of Severity of Initiation on Liking for a Group," *Journal of Abnormal and Social Psychology* 59 (1959), pp. 177–81.

76. B. Mullen and C. Copper, "The Relation between Group Cohesiveness and Performance: An Integration," *Psychological Bulletin* 115 (1994), pp. 210–27; Shaw, *Group Dynamics*, p. 215.

77. M. Rempel and R. J. Fisher, "Perceived Threat, Cohesion, and Group Problem Solving in Intergroup Conflict," *International Journal of Conflict Management* 8 (1997), pp. 216–34.

78. J. M. McPherson and P. A. Popielarz, "Social Networks and Organizational Dynamics," *American Sociological Review* 57 (1992), pp. 153–70; Piper et al., "Cohesion as a Basic Bond in Groups," pp. 93–108.

79. C. A. O'Reilly III, D. F. Caldwell, and W. P. Barnett, "Work Group Demography, Social Integration, and Turnover," *Administrative Science Quarterly* 34 (1989), pp. 21–37.

80. R. D. Banker, J. M. Field, R. G. Schroeder, and K. K. Sinha, "Impact of Work Teams on Manufacturing Performance: A Longitudinal Study," *Academy of Management Journal* 39 (1996), pp. 867–90; Vinokur-Kaplan, "Treatment Teams That Work (and Those That Don't)"; Mullen and Copper, "The Relation between Group Cohesiveness and Performance"; C. R. Evans and K. L. Dion, "Group Cohesion and Performance: A Meta-Analysis," *Small Group Research*, 22 (1991), pp. 175–86.

81. C. Langfred, "Is Group Cohesiveness a Double-Edged Sword? An Investigation of the Effects of Cohesiveness on Performance," *Small Group Research* 29 (1998), pp. 124–43.

82. Robbins and Finley, *Why Teams Don't Work,* chap. 20; "The Trouble with Teams," *Economist,* January 14, 1995, p. 61; A. Sinclair, "The Tyranny of Team Ideology," *Organization Studies* 13 (1992), pp. 611–26. For discussion of the benefits of teams, see J. Pfeffer, "Seven Practices of Successful Organizations," *California Management Review* 40 (1998), pp. 96–124.

83. P. Panchak, "The Future Manufacturing," *Industry Week* 247 (September 21, 1998), pp. 96–105; B. Dumaine, "The Trouble with Teams," *Fortune,* September 5, 1994, pp. 86–92.

84. J. Pappone, "Sometimes Life's Truly a Beach . . . ," *Ottawa Citizen,* February 3, 2000.

85. I. D. Steiner, *Group Process and Productivity,* (New York: Academic Press, 1972).

86. D. Dunphy and B. Bryant, "Teams: Panaceas or Prescriptions for Improved Performance?" *Human Relations* 49 (1996), pp. 677–99. For discussion of Brooke's Law, see M. A. Cusumano, "How Microsoft Makes Large Teams Work Like Small Teams," *Sloan Management Review* 39 (Fall 1997), pp. 9–20.

87. R. Cross, "Looking before You Leap: Assessing the Jump to Teams in Knowledge-Based Work," *Business Horizons,* September 2000.

88. M. Erez and A. Somech, "Is Group Productivity Loss the Rule or the Exception? Effects of Culture and Group-Based Motivation," *Academy of Management Journal* 39 (1996), pp. 1513–37; S. J. Karau and K. D. Williams, "Social Loafing: A Meta-Analytic Review and Theoretical Integration," *Journal of Personality and Social Psychology* 65 (1993), pp. 681–706; J. M. George, "Extrinsic and Intrinsic Origins of Perceived Social Loafing in Organizations," *Academy of Management Journal* 35 (1992), pp. 191–202; R. Albanese and D. D. Van Fleet, "Rational Behavior in Groups: The Free- Riding Tendency," *Academy of Management Review* 10 (1985), pp. 244–55.

89. Erez and Somech, "Is Group Productivity Loss the Rule or the Exception?"; P. C. Earley, "Social Loafing and Collectivism: A Comparison of the U.S. and the People's Republic of China," *Administrative Science Quarterly* 34 (1989), pp. 565–81.

90. T. A. Judge and T. D. Chandler, "Individual-Level Determinants of Employee Shirking," *Relations Industrielles* 51 (1996), pp. 468–86; J. M. George, "Asymmetrical Effects of Rewards and Punishments: The Case of Social Loafing," *Journal of Occupational and Organizational Psychology* 68 (1995), pp. 327–38; R. E. Kidwell and N. Bennett, "Employee Propensity to Withhold Effort: A Conceptual Model to Intersect Three Avenues of Research," *Academy of Management Review* 19 (1993), pp. 429–56; J. A. Shepperd, "Productivity Loss in Performance Groups: A Motivation Analysis," *Psychological Bulletin* 113 (1993), pp. 67–81.

91. W. G. Dyer, *Team Building: Issues and Alternatives,* 2nd ed. (Reading, MA: Addison-Wesley, 1987); S. J. Liebowitz and K. P. De Meuse, "The Application of Team Building," *Human Relations* 35 (1982), pp. 1–18.

92. Sundstrom et al., "Work Teams," p. 128; M. Beer, *Organizational Change and Development: A Systems View* (Santa Monica, CA: Goodyear, 1980), pp. 143–46.

93. Beer, *Organizational Change and Development,* p. 145.

94. G. Coetzer, *A Study of the Impact of Different Team Building Techniques on Work Team Effectiveness,* Unpublished MBA research project, Simon Fraser University, Burnaby, British Columbia, 1993.

95. T. G. Cummings and C. G. Worley, *Organization Development and Change,* 6th ed. (Cincinnati: South-Western, 1997), pp. 218–19; P. F. Buller and C. H. Bell, Jr., "Effects of Team Building and Goal Setting on Productivity: A Field Experiment," *Academy of Management Journal* 29 (1986), pp. 305–28.

96. C. J. Solomon, "Simulation Training Builds Teams through Experience," *Personnel Journal* 72 (June 1993), pp. 100–1.

97. D. Goh, "Firms Strike Out for Adventure Learning," *Sunday Times (Singapore),* April 8, 2001, pp. 7, 29.

98. M. J. Brown, "Let's Talk About It, Really Talk About It," *Journal for Quality and Participation* 19, no. 6 (1996), pp. 26–33; E. H. Schein, "On Dialogue, Culture, and Organizational Learning," *Organizational Dynamics,* Autumn 1993, pp. 40–51; P. M. Senge, *The Fifth Discipline* (New York: Doubleday Currency, 1990), pp. 238–49.

99. B. Oaff, "Team Games Take Turn for the Verse," *Mail on Sunday (UK),* January 28, 2001, p. 56; K. Cross, "Adventure Capital," *Business 2.0,* July 11, 2000; C. Prystay, "Executive Rearmament: Tempering Asia's Executive Mettle," *Asian Business,* October 1996.

100. R. W. Woodman and J. J. Sherwood, "The Role of Team Development in Organizational Effectiveness: A Critical Review," *Psychological Bulletin* 88 (1980), pp. 166–86; Sundstrom et al., "Work Teams," p. 128.

101. Robbins and Finley, *Why Teams Don't Work,* chap. 17.

102. P. McGraw, "Back from the Mountain: Outdoor Management Development Programs and How to Ensure the Transfer of Skills to the Workplace," *Asia Pacific Journal of Human Resources* 31 (Spring 1993), pp. 52–61; G. E. Huszczo, "Training for Team Building," *Training and Development Journal* 44 (February 1990), pp. 37–43.

CHAPTER NINE

1. R. Beck, "Jet Blue Takes Wing on Low Rates, Hip Jets," *Baton Rouge (LA) Advocate,* August 7, 2001; S. B. Donnelly, "Is JetBlue the Next Great Airline—Or Just a Little Too Good to Be True?" *Time,* July 30, 2001, p. 24; R. Mowbray, "Blue Skies Ahead," *Times-Picayune (New Orleans),* July 27, 2001, p. 1.

2. F. A. Shull, Jr., A. L. Delbecq, and L. L. Cummings, *Organizational Decision Making* (New York: McGraw-Hill, 1970), p. 31. See also J. G. March, "Understanding How Decisions Happen in Organizations," in Z. Shapira, ed., *Organizational Decision Making* (New York: Cambridge University Press, 1997), pp. 9–32.

3. B. M. Bass, *Organizational Decision Making* (Homewood, IL: Irwin, 1983), chap. 3; W. F. Pounds, "The Process of Problem Finding," *Industrial Management Review* 11 (Fall 1969), pp. 1–19; C. Kepner and B. Tregoe, *The Rational*

Manager (New York: McGraw-Hill, 1965).

4. This model is adapted from several sources: H. Mintzberg, D. Raisinghani, and A. Théorét, "The Structure of 'Unstructured' Decision Processes," *Administrative Science Quarterly* 21 (1976), pp. 246–75; H. A. Simon, *The New Science of Management Decision* (New York: Harper & Row, 1960); C. Kepner and B. Tregoe, *The Rational Manager* (New York: McGraw-Hill, 1965); W. C. Wedley and R. H. G. Field, "A Predecision Support System," *Academy of Management Review* 9 (1984), pp. 696–703.

5. J. W. Dean, Jr., and M. P. Sharfman, "Does Decision Process Matter? A Study of Strategic Decision-Making Effectiveness," *Academy of Management Journal* 39 (1996), pp. 368–96.

6. P. F. Drucker, *The Practice of Management* (New York: Harper & Brothers, 1954), pp. 353–57.

7. Wedley and Field, "A Predecision Support System," p. 696; Drucker, *The Practice of Management*, p. 357; L. R. Beach and T. R. Mitchell, "A Contingency Model for the Selection of Decision Strategies," *Academy of Management Review* 3 (1978), pp. 439–49.

8. I. L. Janis, *Crucial Decisions* (New York: Free Press, 1989), pp. 35–37; Simon, *The New Science of Management Decision*, pp. 5–6.

9. I. Nonaka and H. Takeuchi, *The Knowledge-Creating Company* (New York: Oxford University Press, 1995), p. 69.

10. Mintzberg, Raisinghani, and Théorét, "The Structure of 'Unstructured' Decision Processes," pp. 255–56.

11. B. Fischhoff and S. Johnson, "The Possibility of Distributed Decision Making," in Shapira, ed., *Organizational Decision Making*, pp. 216–37.

12. J. E. Dutton, "Strategic Agenda Building in Organizations," in Shapira, ed., *Organizational Decision Making*, pp. 81–107; M. Lyles and H. Thomas, "Strategic Problem Formulation: Biases and Assumptions Embedded in Alternative Decision-Making Models," *Journal of Management Studies* 25 (1988), pp. 131–45; I. I. Mitroff, "On Systematic Problem Solving and the Error of the Third Kind," *Behavioral Science* 9 (1974), pp. 383–93.

13. D. Gurteen, "Knowledge, Creativity and Innovation," *Journal of Knowledge Management* 2 (September 1998), pp. 5–13; P. M. Senge, *The Fifth Discipline: The Art and Practice of the Learning Organization* (New York: Doubleday Currency, 1990), chap. 10.

14. D. Domer, *The Logic of Failure* (Reading, MA: Addison-Wesley, 1996); M. Basadur, "Managing the Creative Process in Organizations," in M. A. Runco, ed., *Problem Finding, Problem Solving, and Creativity* (Norwood, NJ: Ablex, 1994), pp. 237–68.

15. P. C. Nutt, "Preventing Decision Debacles," *Technological Forecasting and Social Change* 38 (1990), pp. 159–74.

16. J. A. Byrne, *Chainsaw* (New York: HarperCollins, 1999).

17. P. C. Nutt, *Making Tough Decisions* (San Francisco: Jossey-Bass, 1989).

18. J. Conlisk, "Why Bounded Rationality?" *Journal of Economic Literature* 34 (1996), pp. 669–700; B. L. Lipman, "Information Processing and Bounded Rationality: A Survey," *Canadian Journal of Economics* 28 (1995), pp. 42–67.

19. L. T. Pinfield, "A Field Evaluation of Perspectives on Organizational Decision Making," *Administrative Science Quarterly* 31 (1986), pp. 365–88. The recent survey, conducted by Kepner-Tregoe, is described in D. Sandahl and C. Hewes, "Decision Making at Digital Speed," *Pharmaceutical Executive* 21 (August 2001), p. 62.

20. H. A. Simon, *Administrative Behavior*, 2nd ed. (New York: Free Press, 1957), pp. xxv, 80–84; and J. G. March and H. A. Simon, *Organizations* (New York: Wiley, 1958), pp. 140–41.

21. P. O. Soelberg, "Unprogrammed Decision Making," *Industrial Management Review* 8 (1967), pp. 19–29; H. A. Simon, "A Behavioral Model of Rational Choice," *Quarterly Journal of Economics* 69 (1955), pp. 99–118.

22. J. E. Russo, V. H. Medvec, and M. G. Meloy, "The Distortion of Information during Decisions," *Organizational Behavior and Human Decision Processes*, 66 (1996), pp. 102–10.

23. H. A. Simon, *Models of Man: Social and Rational* (New York: Wiley, 1957), p. 253.

24. Y. Ganzach, A. H. Kluger, and N. Klayman, "Making Decisions from an Interview: Expert Measurement and Mechanical Combination," *Personnel Psychology* 53 (Spring 2000), pp. 1–20.

25. J. Gregoire, "Leading the Charge for Change," *CIO*, June 1, 2001.

26. A. Rangaswamy and G. L. Lilien, "Software Tools for New Product Development," *Journal of Marketing Research* 34 (1997), pp. 177–84.

27. G. H. Anthes, "Learning How to Share," *Computerworld* 32 (February 23, 1998), pp. 75–77.

28. P. Goodwin and G. Wright, "Enhancing Strategy Evaluation in Scenario Planning: A Role for Decision Analysis," *Journal of Management Studies* 38 (January 2001), pp. 1–16; R. Rosen, P. Digh, M. Singer, and C. Phillips, *Global Literacies* (New York: Simon & Schuster, 2000), pp. 269–70; C. Pratt, "Planning Noranda's Future," *Research Technology Management* 42 (January–February 1999), pp. 15–18; P. J. H. Schoemaker, "Disciplined Imagination: From Scenarios to Strategic Options," *International Studies of Management and Organization* 27 (Summer 1997), pp. 43–70; K. Van Der Heijden, *Scenarios: The Art of Strategic Conversation* (New York: Wiley, 1996).

29. This incident is described in B. Breen, "What's Your Intuition?" *Fast Company* 38 (September 2000), p. 290.

30. L. A. Burke and M. K. Miller, "Taking the Mystery out of Intuitive Decision Making," *Academy of Management Executive* 13 (November 1999), pp. 91–99.

31. O. Behling and N. L. Eckel, "Making Sense out of Intuition," *Academy of Management Executive* 5 (February 1991), pp. 46–54; Nutt, *Making Tough Decisions*, p. 54; H. A. Simon, "Making Management Decisions: The Role of Intuition and Emotion," *Academy of Management Executive* (February 1987), pp. 57–64; W. H. Agor, "The Logic of Intuition," *Organizational Dynamics* (Winter 1986), pp. 5–18.

32. N. Khatri, "The Role of Intuition in Strategic Decision Making," *Human Relations* 53 (January 2000), pp. 57–86; Burke and Miller, "Taking the Mystery out of Intuitive Decision Making."

33. E. N. Brockmann and W. P. Anthony, "The Influence of Tacit

Knowledge and Collective Mind on Strategic Planning," *Journal of Managerial Issues* 10 (Summer 1998), pp. 204–22; D. Leonard and S. Sensiper, "The Role of Tacit Knowledge in Group Innovation," *California Management Review* 40 (Spring 1998), pp. 112–32. For a discussion of the problems with intuition in business start-ups, see L. Broderick and M. Sponer, "The Death of Gut Instinct," *Inc.* 23 (January 2001), pp. 38–42.

34. A. M. Hayashi, "When to Trust Your Gut," *Harvard Business Review* 79 (February 2001), pp. 59–65; E. Gubbins and B. Quinton, "Serial Entrepreneurs: They're Grrreat!" *Upstart*, January 30, 2001.

35. R. N. Taylor, *Behavioral Decision Making* (Glenview, IL: Scott Foresman, 1984), pp. 163–66.

36. D. R. Bobocel and J. P. Meyer, "Escalating Commitment to a Failing Course of Action: Separating the Role of Choice and Justification," *Journal of Applied Psychology* 79 (1994), pp. 360–63; G. Whyte, "Escalating Commitment in Individual and Group Decision Making: A Prospect Theory Approach," *Organizational Behavior and Human Decision Processes* 54 (1993), pp. 430–55; G. Whyte, "Escalating Commitment to a Course of Action: A Reinterpretation," *Academy of Management Review* 11 (1986), pp. 311–21.

37. M. Keil and R. Montealegre, "Cutting Your Losses: Extricating Your Organization When a Big Project Goes Awry," *Sloan Management Review* 41, Spring 2000, pp. 55–68; M. Fackler, "Tokyo's Newest Subway Line a Saga of Hubris, Humiliation," *Associated Press Newswires*, July 20, 1999; P. Ayton and H. Arkes, "Call It Quits," *New Scientist*, June 20, 1998.

38. F. D. Schoorman and P. J. Holahan, "Psychological Antecedents of Escalation Behavior: Effects of Choice, Responsibility, and Decision Consequences," *Journal of Applied Psychology* 81 (1996), pp. 786–93.

39. S. W. Geiger, C. J. Robertson, and J. G. Irwin, "The Impact of Cultural Values on Escalation of Commitment," *International Journal of Organizational Analysis* 6 (April 1998), pp. 165–76; D. K. Tse, K. Lee, I. Vertinsky, and D. A. Wehrung, "Does Culture Matter? A Cross-Cultural Study of Executives' Choice, Decisiveness, and Risk Adjustment in International Marketing," *Journal of Marketing* 52 (1988), pp. 81–95.

40. M. Keil and D. Robey, "Turning around Troubled Software Projects: An Exploratory Study of the Deescalation of Commitment to Failing Courses of Action," *Journal of Management Information Systems* 15 (Spring 1999), pp. 63–87.

41. B. M. Staw, K. W. Koput, and S. G. Barsade, "Escalation at the Credit Window: A Longitudinal Study of Bank Executives' Recognition and Write-Off of Problem Loans," *Journal of Applied Psychology* 82 (1997), pp. 130–42.

42. W. Boulding, R. Morgan, and R. Staelin, "Pulling the Plug to Stop the New Product Drain," *Journal of Marketing Research* 34 (1997), pp. 164–76; I. Simonson and B. M. Staw, "De-escalation Strategies: A Comparison of Techniques for Reducing Commitment to Losing Courses of Action," *Journal of Applied Psychology* 77 (1992), pp. 419–26.

43. D. Ghosh, "De-Escalation Strategies: Some Experimental Evidence," *Behavioral Research in Accounting* 9 (1997), pp. 88–112.

44. W. A. Randolph, "Re-Thinking Empowerment: Why Is It So Hard to Achieve?" *Organizational Dynamics* 29 (November 2000), pp. 94–107; G. C. McMahon and E. E. Lawler III, "Effects of Union Status on Employee Involvement: Diffusion and Effectiveness," *Research in Organizational Change and Development* 8 (1995), pp. 47–76; V. H. Vroom and A. G. Jago, *The New Leadership: Managing Participation in Organizations* (Englewood Cliffs, NJ: Prentice Hall, 1988), p. 15.

45. B. Broadway, "Good for the Soul—and for the Bottom Line," *Washington Post*, August 19, 2001, p. A1; M. Forseter, "Associates Keep Score at The Container Store," *Chain Store Age* 76 (May 2000), p. 18.

46. R. O. Esler and D. A. Nipp, "Worker Designed Culture Change," *Nursing Economics* 19 (July 2001), pp. 161ff. C. Hymowitz, "How to Keep Innovation Alive," *The Wall Street Journal*, May 23, 2001, p. N1; C. Brenner, "Pride in Ownership Is Byword for Bank's Employees," *News-Sun (Waukegan, IL)*, February 11, 1997, p. A3.

47. A. M. Berg, "Participatory Strategies in Quality Improvement Programs," *Public Productivity & Management Review* 21 (September 1997), pp. 30–43; D. I. Levine, *Reinventing the Workplace* (Washington, DC: Brookings, 1995), chap. 3; E. A. Locke and D. M. Schweiger, "Participation in Decision-Making: One More Look," *Research in Organizational Behavior* 1 (1979), pp. 265–339.

48. V. A. Sun, "Great Plains Software Phils. Inc.: Workplace of the 21st Century," *BusinessWorld (Philippines)*, May 15, 2000, p. 30.

49. J. T. Addison, "Nonunion Representation in Germany," *Journal of Labor Research* 20 (Winter 1999), pp. 73–92; G. Strauss, "Collective Bargaining, Unions, and Participation," in F. Heller, E. Pusic, G. Strauss, and B. Wilpert, eds., *Organizational Participation: Myth and Reality* (New York: Oxford University Press, 1998), pp. 97–143; Levine, *Reinventing the Workplace*, pp. 47–48.

50. L. Zuckerman, "Management: Employee–Ownership Experiment Unravels at United," *New York Times*, March 14, 2001; J. Singer and S. Duvall, "High-Performance Partnering by Self-Managed Teams in Manufacturing," *Engineering Management Journal* 12 (December 2000), pp. 9–15.

51. R. C. Liden and S. Arad, "A Power Perspective of Empowerment and Work Groups: Implications for Human Resources Management Research," *Research in Personnel and Human Resources Management* 14 (1996), pp. 205–51; R. C. Ford and M. D. Fottler, "Empowerment: A Matter of Degree," *Academy of Management Executive* 9 (August 1995), pp. 21–31; R. W. Coye and J. A. Belohlav, "An Exploratory Analysis of Employee Participation," *Group and Organization Management* 20 (1995), pp. 4–17; Vroom and Jago, *The New Leadership*.

52. P. E. Rossler and C. P. Koelling, "The Effect of Gainsharing on Business Performance at a Papermill," *National Productivity Review* 12 (Summer 1993), pp. 365–82; C. R. Gowen, III, "Gainsharing Programs: an Overview of History and Research," *Journal of*

Organizational Behavior Management 11 (2) (1990), pp. 77–99; F. G. Lesieur, ed., *The Scanlon Plan: A Frontier in Labor–Management Cooperation.* (Cambridge, MA: MIT Press, 1958).

53. Open book management at The Container Store, American Brass, and Voyant Technologies is described in C. Hymowitz, "How to Keep Innovation Alive," *The Wall Street Journal*, May 23, 2001, p. N1; M. Forseter, "Associates Keep Score at The Container Store," *Chain Store Age* 76 (May 2000), p. 18; W. Royal, "A Factory's Crash Course in Economics Pays Off," *New York Times*, April 25, 2001, p. 9.

54. J. Case, "Opening the Books," *Harvard Business Review* 75 (March–April 1997), pp. 118–27; T. R. V. Davis, "Open-Book Management: Its Promise and Pitfalls," *Organizational Dynamics*, Winter 1997, pp. 7–20; J. Case, *Open Book Management: The Coming Business Revolution* (New York: Harper Business, 1995).

55. D. E. Yeatts and C. Hyten, *High-Performing Self-Managed Work Teams: A Comparison of Theory and Practice* (Thousand Oaks, CA: Sage, 1998); S. A. Mohrman, S. G. Cohen, and A. M. Mohrman, Jr., *Designing Team-Based Organizations: New Forms for Knowledge Work* (San Francisco: Jossey-Bass, 1995); E. E. Lawler III, *High-Involvement Management* (San Francisco: Jossey-Bass, 1986), chaps. 11 and 12; L. C. Plunkett and R. Fournier, *Participative Management: Implementing Empowerment* (New York: Wiley, 1991).

56. Singer and Duvall, "High-Performance Partnering by Self-Managed Teams in Manufacturing"; D. Fields, "Harley Teams Shoot for Better Bike," *Akron (OH) Beacon Journal*, June 15, 1998; M. Savage, "Harley Irons Out an Innovative Way of Working," *Milwaukee Journal Sentinel*, May 25, 1998, p. 12; L. Ziegler, "Labor's Role at New Harley Plant," National Public Radio, "All Things Considered," February 25, 1998, 8:00 P.M., EST; C. Eberting, "The Harley Mystique Comes to Kansas City," *Kansas City Star*, January 6, 1998, p. A1.

57. E. E. Lawler III, *Organizing for High Performance* (San Francisco: Jossey-Bass, 2001).

58. The SDT attributes discussed here are discussed in Yeatts and Hyten, *High-Performing Self-Managed Work Teams*; B. L. Kirkman and D. L. Shapiro, "The Impact of Cultural Values on Employee Resistance to Teams: Toward a Model of Globalized Self-Managing Work Team Effectiveness," *Academy of Management Review* 22 (July 1997), pp. 730–57; Mohrman et al., *Designing Team-Based Organizations.*

59. L. Rittenhouse, "Dennis W. Bakke—Empowering a Workforce with Principles," *Electricity Journal*, January 1998, pp. 48–59.

60. P. S. Goodman, R. Devadas, and T. L. G. Hughson, "Groups and Productivity: Analyzing the Effectiveness of Self-Managing Teams," in J. P. Campbell, R. J. Campbell, and Associates, eds., *Productivity in Organizations*, (San Francisco: Jossey-Bass, 1988), pp. 295–327.

61. D. Tjosvold, *Teamwork for Customers* (San Francisco: Jossey-Bass, 1993); D. E. Bowen and E. E. Lawler III, "The Empowerment of Service Workers: What, Why, How, and When," *Sloan Management Review*, Spring 1992, pp. 31–39.

62. E. L. Trist, G. W. Higgin, H. Murray, and A. B. Pollock, *Organizational Choice* (London: Tavistock, 1963). The origin of SDTs from sociotechnical systems research is also noted in R. Beckham, "Self-Directed Work Teams: The Wave of the Future?" *Hospital Materiel Management Quarterly* 20 (August 1998), pp. 48–60.

63. The main components of socio technical systems are discussed in M. Moldaschl and W. G. Weber, "The 'Three Waves' of Industrial Group Work: Historical Reflections on Current Research on Group Work," *Human Relations* 51 (March 1998), pp. 347–88; W. Niepce and E. Molleman, "Work Design Issues in Lean Production from a Sociotechnical Systems Perspective: Neo-Taylorism or the Next Step in Sociotechnical Design?" *Human Relations* 51 (March 1998), pp. 259–87.

64. E. Ulich and W. G. Weber, "Dimensions, Criteria, and Evaluation of Work Group Autonomy," in M. A. West, ed., *Handbook of Work Group Psychology* (Chichester, UK: Wiley, 1996), pp. 247–82.

65. C. C. Manz and G. L. Stewart, "Attaining Flexible Stability by Integrating Total Quality Management and Socio-Technical Systems Theory," *Organization Science* 8 (1997), pp. 59–70; K. P. Carson and G. L. Stewart, "Job Analysis and the Sociotechnical Approach to Quality: A Critical Examination," *Journal of Quality Management* 1 (1996), pp. 49–65.

66. D. Zell, *Changing by Design: Organizational Innovation at Hewlett-Packard* (Ithaca, NY: ILR Press, 1997); "New Anchor Hocking Plant Incorporates 'Socio-Tech' Work Environment Philosophy," *Business Wire*, October 19, 1995; R. Reese, "Redesigning for Dial Tone: A Socio-Technical Systems Case Study," *Organizational Dynamics* 24 (Autumn 1995), pp. 80+.

67. K. Kane, "L.L. Bean Delivers the Goods," *Fast Company* 10 (August 1997), p. 104.

68. P. S. Adler and R. E. Cole, "Designed for Learning: A Tale of Two Auto Plants," *Sloan Management Review* 34 (Spring 1993), pp. 85–94; O. Hammarström and R. Lansbury, "The Art of Building a Car: The Swedish Experience Re-examined," *New Technology, Work and Employment* 2 (Autumn 1991), pp. 85–90; J. P. Womack, D. T. Jones, and D. Roos, *The Machine That Changed the World* (New York: Macmillan, 1990). For more favorable evaluations of Volvo's plants, see I. Magaziner and M. Patinkin, *The Silent War* (New York: Random House, 1988); P. G. Gyllenhammar, *People at Work* (Reading, MA: Addison-Wesley, 1977).

69. M. Evans, T. Hamilton, L. Surtees, and S. Tuck, "The Road to a Billion," *Globe and Mail*, January 6, 2000; R. Dyck and N. Halpern, "Team-Based Organizations Redesign at Celestica," *Journal for Quality and Participation* 22 (September–October 1999), pp. 36–40.

70. R. Likert, *New Patterns of Management* (New York: McGraw-Hill, 1961); D. McGregor, *The Human Side of Enterprise* (New York: McGraw-Hill, 1960); C. Argyris, *Personality and Organization* (New York: Harper & Row, 1957).

71. J. A. Wagner III, C. R. Leana, E. A. Locke, and D. M. Schweiger, "Cognitive and Motivational Frameworks in U.S. Research on Participation: A Meta-Analysis of Primary Effects," *Journal of Organizational Behavior* 18 (1997), pp. 49–65; G. P. Latham, D. C. Winters, and E. A. Locke, "Cognitive

and Motivational Effects of Participation: A Mediator Study," *Journal of Organizational Behavior* 15 (1994), pp. 49–63; J. L. Cotton, *Employee Involvement: Methods for Improving Performance and Work Attitudes* (Newbury Park, CA: Sage, 1993), chap. 8; S. J. Havlovic, "Quality of Work Life and Human Resource Outcomes," *Industrial Relations*, 1991, pp. 469–79; K. I. Miller and P. R. Monje, "Participation, Satisfaction, and Productivity: A Meta-Analytic Review," *Academy of Management Journal* 29 (1986), pp. 727–53.

72. K. Y. Williams and C. A. O'Reilly III, "Demography and Diversity in Organizations: A Review of 40 Years of Research," *Research in Organizational Behavior* 20 (1998).

73. J. P. Walsh and S-F. Tseng, "The Effects of Job Characteristics on Active Effort at Work," *Work and Occupations* 25 (February 1998), pp. 74–96; K. T. Dirks, L. L. Cummings, and J. L. Pierce, "Psychological Ownership in Organizations: Conditions under Which Individuals Promote and Resist Change," *Research in Organizational Change and Development* 9 (1996), pp. 1–23.

74. C. L. Cooper, B. Dyck, and N. Frohlich, "Improving the Effectiveness of Gainsharing: The Role of Fairness and Participation," *Administrative Science Quarterly* 37 (1992), pp. 471–90.

75. J. P. Guthrie, "High-Involvement Work Practices, Turnover, and Productivity: Evidence from New Zealand," *Academy of Management Journal* 44 (February 2001), pp. 180–90. See also R. Hodson, *Working with Dignity* (Cambridge, UK: Cambridge University Press, 2000); D. J. Glew, A. M. O'Leary-Kelly, R. W. Griffin, and D. D. Van Fleet, "Participation in Organizations: A Preview of the Issues and Proposed Framework for Future Analysis," *Journal of Management* 21 (1995), pp. 395–421. The limits of employee involvement for improving employee satisfaction are discussed in J. A. Wagner III, C. R. Leana, E. A. Locke, and D. Schweiger, "Cognitive and Motivational Frameworks in U.S. Research on Participation: A Meta-Analysis of Primary Effects," *Journal of Organizational Behavior*, 1997, pp. 49–65.

76. Vroom and Jago, *The New Leadership*, pp. 151–52.

77. Vroom and Jago, *The New Leadership*.

78. C. Robert and T. M. Probst, "Empowerment and Continuous Improvement in the United States, Mexico, Poland, and India," *Journal of Applied Psychology* 85 (October 2000), pp. 643–58; B. L. Kirkman and D. L. Shapiro, "The Impact of Cultural Values on Employee Resistance to Teams: Toward a Model of Globalized Self-Managing Work Team Effectiveness," *Academy of Management Review* 22 (July 1997), pp. 730–57; C. Pavett and T. Morris, "Management Styles within a Multinational Corporation: A Five Country Comparative Study," *Human Relations* 48 (1995) pp. 1171–91; M. Erez and P. C. Earley, *Culture, Self-Identity, and Work* (New York: Oxford University Press, 1993), pp. 104–12.

79. X. Chen and W. Barshes, "To Team or Not to Team?" *China Business Review* 27 (March–April 2000), pp. 30–34; C. E. Nicholls, H. W. Lane, and M. B. Brechu, "Taking Self-Managed Teams to Mexico," *Academy of Management Executive* 13 (August 1999), pp. 15–25.

80. "The Changing Workplace," *Business Line (The Hindu)*, February 24, 2001.

81. H. Hamid, "Tien Wah's Flexi-Wage a Success," *Business Times (Malaysia)*, December 7, 2000.

82. This quotation is found at www.quoteland.com

83. J. D. Orsburn and L. Moran, *The New Self-Directed Work Teams: Mastering the Challenge* (New York: McGraw-Hill, 2000), chap. 11; C. C. Manz, D. E. Keating, and A. Donnellon, "Preparing for an Organizational Change to Employee Self-Management: The Managerial Transition," *Organizational Dynamics* 19 (Autumn 1990), pp. 15–26.

84. D. Gerwin, "Team Empowerment in New Product Development," *Business Horizons*, July 1999, p. 29.

85. G. T. Fairhurst, S. Green, and J. Courtright, "Inertial Forces and the Implementation of a Socio-Technical Systems Approach: A Communication Study," *Organization Science* 6 (1995), pp. 168–85; Manz et al., "Preparing for an Organizational Change to Employee Self-Management," pp. 23–25.

86. J. Jusko, "Always Lessons to Learn," *Industry Week*, February 15, 1999,

pp. 23–30. Another manager made a similar comment in R. Cross, "Looking before You Leap: Assessing the Jump to Teams in Knowledge-Based Work," *Business Horizons*, September 2000.

87. M. Fenton-O'Creevy, "Employee Involvement and the Middle Manager: Saboteur or Scapegoat?" *Human Resource Management Journal* 11 (2001), pp. 24–40.

88. R. Yonatan and H. Lam, "Union Responses to Quality Improvement Initiatives: Factors Shaping Support and Resistance," *Journal of Labor Research* 20 (Winter 1999), pp. 111–31; Levine, *Reinventing the Workplace*, pp. 66–69; I. Goll and N. B. Johnson, "The Influence of Environmental Pressures, Diversification Strategy, and Union/Nonunion Setting on Employee Participation," *Employee Responsibilities and Rights Journal* 10 (1997), pp. 141–54; R. Hodson, "Dignity in the Workplace under Participative Management: Alienation and Freedom Revisited," *American Sociological Review* 61 (1996), pp. 719–38.

89. E. C. Rosenthal, "Sociotechnical Systems and Unions: Nicety or Necessity," *Human Relations* 50 (May 1997), pp. 585–604; R. E. Allen and K. L. Van Norman, "Employee Involvement Programs: The Noninvolvement of Unions Revisited," *Journal of Labor Research* 17 (Summer 1996), pp. 479–95; B. Gilbert, "The Impact of Union Involvement on the Design and Introduction of Quality of Working Life," *Human Relations* 42 (1989), pp. 1057–78; T. A. Kochan, H. C. Katz, and R. B. McKersie, *The Transformation of American Industrial Relations* (New York: Basic Books, 1986), pp. 238–45.

CHAPTER TEN

1. T. Kelley, *The Art of Innovation* (New York: Doubleday Currency, 2001); B. Roberts, "Innovation Quotient," *Electronic Business*, December 2000, p. 96; A. Hargadon and R. I. Sutton, "Building an Innovation Factory," *Harvard Business Review* 78 (May–June 2000), pp. 157–66; R. Garner, "Innovation for Fun and Profit," *Upside Magazine*, March 2000; P. Sinton, "Teamwork the Name of the Game for IDEO," *San Francisco Chronicle*, February 23, 2000; E. Brown, "A Day at Innovation U.," *Fortune*, April 12, 1999,

pp. 163–65; R. I. Sutton and A. Hargadon, "Brainstorming Groups in Context: Effectiveness in a Product Design Firm," *Administrative Science Quarterly* 41 (December 1996), pp. 685–718.

2. D. Gurteen, "Knowledge, Creativity and Innovation," *Journal of Knowledge Management* 2 (September 1998), pp. 5–13.

3. A. Cummings and G. R. Oldham, "Enhancing Creativity: Managing Work Contexts for the High Potential Employee," *California Management Review* 40 (Fall 1997), pp. 22–38; T. M. Amabile, *The Social Psychology of Creativity* (New York: Springer-Verlag, 1983), pp. 32–35.

4. P. Swisher, "Soaring Creativity," *Successful Meetings* 50 (August 2001), p. 83; A. Tizon, "Spirit at Work," *Seattle Times*, September 13, 2000.

5. R. Grover, T. Lowry, and L. Armstrong, "Henry Yuen: TV Guy," *Business Week*, March 12, 2001; A. MacKensie, "Innovate or Be Damned," *Asian Business*, January 1995, pp. 30–34.

6. B. Kabanoff and J. R. Rossiter, "Recent Developments in Applied Creativity," *International Review of Industrial and Organizational Psychology* 9 (1994), pp. 283–324.

7. J. R. Hayes, "Cognitive Processes in Creativity," in J. A. Glover, R. R. Ronning, and C. R. Reynolds, eds., *Handbook of Creativity* (New York: Plenum, 1989), pp. 135–45.

8. R. S. Nickerson, "Enhancing Creativity," in R. J. Sternberg, ed., *Handbook of Creativity* (New York: Cambridge University Press, 1999), pp. 392–430; A. Hiam, "9 Obstacles to Creativity—and How You Can Remove Them," *Futurist* 32 (October 1998), pp. 30–34.

9. R. T. Brown, "Creativity: What Are We to Measure?" in Glover, Ronning, and Reynolds, eds., *Handbook of Creativity*, pp. 3–32.

10. Hargadon and Sutton, "Building an Innovation Factory."

11. For a thorough discussion of insight, see R. J. Sternberg and J. E. Davidson, eds., *The Nature of Insight* (Cambridge, MA: MIT Press, 1995).

12. V. Parv, "The Idea Toolbox: Techniques for Being a More Creative Writer," *Writer's Digest* 78 (July 1998), p. 18; J. Ayan, *Aha! 10 Ways to Free Your Creative Spirit and Find Your Great Ideas* (New York: Crown Trade, 1997), pp. 50–56.

13. A. Chandrasekaran, "Bye, Bye Serendipity," *Business Standard*, March 28, 2000, p. 1; K. Cottrill, "Reinventing Innovation," *Journal of Business Strategy*, March–April 1998, pp. 47–51.

14. C. Martindale, "Biological Bases of Creativity," in Sternberg, ed., *Handbook of Creativity*, pp. 137–52. For a critical view of "right-brained thinking," see T. Hines, "Left Brain/Right Brain Mythology and Implications for Management and Training," *Academy of Management Review* 12 (1987), pp. 600–6.

15. R. J. Sternberg and L. A. O'Hara, "Creativity and Intelligence," in Sternberg, ed., *Handbook of Creativity*, pp. 251–72.

16. R. J. Sternberg, L. A. O'Hara, and T. I. Lubart, "Creativity as Investment," *California Management Review* 40 (Fall 1997), pp. 8–21.

17. R. W. Weisberg, "Creativity and Knowledge: A Challenge to Theories," in Sternberg, ed., *Handbook of Creativity*, pp. 226–50.

18. R. J. Sternberg, *Thinking Styles* (New York: Cambridge University Press, 1997).

19. M. Michalko, "Thinking Like a Genius: Eight Strategies Used by the Supercreative, from Aristotle and Leonardo to Einstein and Edison," *The Futurist* 32 (May 1998), pp. 21–25; J. S. Dacey, "Peak Periods of Creative Growth across the Lifespan," *Journal of Creative Behavior* 23 (1989), pp. 224–47; F. Barron and D. M. Harrington, "Creativity, Intelligence, and Personality," *Annual Review of Psychology* 32 (1981), pp. 439–76.

20. P. Roberts, "Sony Changes the Game," *Fast Company* 10 (1997), p. 116.

21. G. J. Feist, "The Influence of Personality on Artistic and Scientific Creativity," in Sternberg, ed., *Handbook of Creativity*, pp. 273–96; M. A. West, *Developing Creativity in Organizations* (Leicester, UK: BPS Books, 1997), pp. 10–19.

22. D. C. McClelland, *The Achieving Society* (New York: Van Nostrand Reinhold, 1961); M. Patchen, *Participation, Achievement, and Involvement on the Job* (Englewood Cliffs, NJ: Prentice Hall, 1970).

23. B. Breen, "Rapid Motion," *Fast Company* 49 (August 2001), p. 49; L. Pratt, "Persistence in Motion," *Profit Magazine* 20 (May 2001), pp. 18–22.

24. D. K. Simonton, "Creativity: Cognitive, Personal, Developmental, and Social Aspects," *American Psychologist* 55 (January 2000), pp. 151–58; Cummings and Oldham, "Enhancing Creativity."

25. S. Long, "They Slaughter Sacred Cows," *Straits Times (Singapore)*, February 28, 1999, p. 3.

26. S. Bharadwaj and A. Menon, "Making Innovation Happen in Organizations: Individual Creativity Mechanisms, Organizational Creativity Mechanisms or Both?" *Journal of Product Innovation Management* 17 (November 2000), pp. 424–34; M. D. Mumford, "Managing Creative People: Strategies and Tactics for Innovation," *Human Resource Management Review* 10 (Autumn 2000), pp. 313–51; T. M. Amabile, R. Conti, H. Coon, J. Lazenby, and M. Herron, "Assessing the Work Environment for Creativity," *Academy of Management Journal* 39 (1996), pp. 1154–84; G. R. Oldham and A. Cummings, "Employee Creativity: Personal and Contextual Factors at Work," *Academy of Management Journal* 39 (1996), pp. 607–34.

27. C. Sams, "The Difference Is Graphic," *Sun Herald (Sydney, Australia)*, November 19, 2000, p. 7; G. Maddox, "Oz Fx in Effect, the Best," *Sydney Morning Herald*, April 1, 2000, p. 39; S. Pipe, "Animal Logic Drives Budding Artists," *The Australian*, November 16, 1999, p. C9; H. Jacobs, "Up from Down Under," *Shoot* 40 (October 1999), pp. 19–22; I. Cuthbertson, "Wizards of Oz," *Weekend Australian*, June 26, 1999, p. 48.

28. D. Maitra, "Livio D. Desimone: We Do Not See Failures As Failure," *Business Today (India)*, June 22, 1998, p. 66.

29. T. M. Amabile, "Changes in the Work Environment for Creativity during Downsizing," *Academy of Management Journal* 42 (December 1999), pp. 630–40.

30. P. Luke, "Business World's a Stage," *Vancouver Province*, September 2, 2001.

31. Cummings and Oldham, "Enhancing Creativity."

32. C. E. Shalley, L. L. Gilson, and T. C. Blum, "Matching Creativity Requirements and the Work Environment: Effects on Satisfaction and Intentions to Leave," *Academy of Management Journal*, April 2000, pp. 215–23; R. Tierney, S. M. Farmer, and G. B. Graen, "An Examination of Leadership and Employee Creativity: The Relevance of Traits and Relationships," *Personnel Psychology* 52 (Autumn 1999), pp. 591–620; Cummings and Oldham, "Enhancing Creativity."

33. Michalko, "Thinking Like a Genius."

34. T. M. Amabile, "Motivating Creativity in Organizations: On Doing What You Love and Loving What You Do," *California Management Review* 40 (Fall 1997), pp. 39–58.

35. M. Csikszentmihalyi, *Creativity—Flow and the Psychology of Discovery and Invention* (New York: HarperCollins, 1996).

36. T. M. Amabile, "A Model of Creativity and Innovation in Organizations," *Research in Organizational Behavior* 10 (1988), pp. 123–67. The survey about time pressure in advertising and marketing is summarized in "No Time for Creativity," *London Free Press*, August 7, 2001, p. D3.

37. S. M. Rostan, "Problem Finding, Problem Solving, and Cognitive Controls: An Empirical Investigation of Critically Acclaimed Productivity," *Creativity Research Journal* 7 (1994), pp. 97–110. See also S. Z. Dudek and R. Côté, "Problem Finding Revisited," in M. A. Runco, ed., *Problem Finding, Problem Solving, and Creativity* (Norwood, NJ: Ablex, 1994), pp. 130–50.

38. Sternberg et al., "Creativity as Investment."

39. J. Kao, *Jamming* (New York: HarperCollins Business, 1996).

40. Hiam, "Obstacles to Creativity—and How You Can Remove Them."

41. West, *Developing Creativity in Organizations*, pp. 33–35.

42. Cathy Olofson, "Monster Board Has Fun," *Fast Company* 16 (August 1998), p. 50.

43. P. Brown, "Across the Table into the Bedroom," *Times of London*, March 1, 2001, p. D4.

44. K. W. Jesse, "A Creative Approach to Doing Business," *Dayton (OH) Daily News*, June 19, 1998, p. C1.

45. W. J. J. Gordon, *Synectics: The Development of Creative Capacity* (New York: Harper & Row, 1961).

46. J. Neff, "At Eureka Ranch, Execs Doff Wing Tips, Fire Up Ideas," *Advertising Age* 69 (March 9, 1998), pp. 28–29.

47. A. G. Robinson and S. Stern, *Corporate Creativity, How Innovation and Improvement Actually Happen* (San Francisco: Berrett-Koehler, 1997).

48. Kelley, *The Art of Innovation*, pp. 158–62; Hargadon and Sutton, "Building an Innovation Factory."

49. D. Beardsley, "This Company Doesn't Brake for (Sacred) Cows," *Fast Company* 16 (August 1998).

50. V. H. Vroom and A. G. Jago, *The New Leadership* (Englewood Cliffs, NJ: Prentice Hall, 1988), pp. 28–29.

51. R. B. Gallupe, W. H. Cooper, M. L. Grisé, and L. M. Bastianutti, "Blocking Electronic Brainstorms," *Journal of Applied Psychology* 79 (1994), pp. 77–86; M. Diehl and W. Stroebe, "Productivity Loss in Idea-Generating Groups: Tracking Down the Blocking Effects," *Journal of Personality and Social Psychology* 61 (1991), pp. 392–403.

52. Kelley, *The Art of Innovation*, p. 70; Hargadon and Sutton, "Building an Innovation Factory."

53. P. W. Mulvey, J. F. Veiga, and P. M. Elsass, "When Teammates Raise a White Flag," *Academy of Management Executive* 10 (February 1996), pp. 40–49.

54. S. Plous, T*he Psychology of Judgment and Decision Making* (Philadelphia: Temple University Press, 1993), pp. 200–2.

55. B. Mullen, T. Anthony, E. Salas, and J. E. Driskell, "Group Cohesiveness and Quality of Decision Making: An Integration of Tests of the Groupthink Hypothesis," *Small Group Research* 25 (1994), pp. 189–204; I. L. Janis, *Crucial Decisions* (New York: Free Press, 1989), pp. 56–63; I. L. Janis, Groupthink: *Psychological Studies of Policy Decisions and Fiascoes*, 2nd ed. (Boston: Houghton Mifflin, 1982).

56. M. E. Turner and A. R. Pratkanis, "Threat, Cohesion, and Group Effectiveness: Testing a Social Identity Maintenance Perspective on Groupthink," *Journal of Personality and Social Psychology* 63 (1992), pp. 781–96.

57. M. Rempel and R. J. Fisher, "Perceived Threat, Cohesion, and Group Problem Solving in Intergroup Conflict," *International Journal of Conflict Management* 8 (1997), pp. 216–34.

58. G. Moorhead, R. Ference, and C. P. Neck, "Group Decision Fiascoes Continue: Space Shuttle *Challenger* and a Revised Groupthink Framework," *Human Relations* 44 (1991), pp. 539–50; Janis, *Crucial Decisions*, pp. 76–77.

59. C. McGarty, J. C. Turner, M. A. Hogg, B. David, and M. S. Wetherell, "Group Polarization as Conformity to the Prototypical Group Member," *British Journal of Social Psychology* 31 (1992), pp. 1–20; D. Isenberg, "Group Polarization: A Critical Review and Meta-analysis," *Journal of Personality and Social Psychology* 50 (1986), pp. 1141–51; D. G. Myers and H. Lamm, "The Group Polarization Phenomenon," *Psychological Bulletin* 83 (1976), pp. 602–27.

60. D. Friedman, "Monty Hall's Three Doors: Construction and Deconstruction of a Choice Anomaly," *American Economic Review* 88 (September 1998), pp. 933–46; D. Kahneman and A. Tversky, "Prospect Theory: An Analysis of Decision under Risk," *Econometrica* 47 (1979), pp. 263–91.

61. Janis, *Crucial Decisions*, pp. 244–49.

62. F. A. Schull, A. L. Delbecq, and L. L. Cummings, *Organizational Decision Making* (New York: McGraw-Hill, 1970), pp. 144–49.

63. A. C. Amason, "Distinguishing the Effects of Functional and Dysfunctional Conflict on Strategic Decision Making: Resolving a Paradox for Top Management Teams," *Academy of Management Journal* 39 (1996), pp. 123–48; G. Katzenstein, "The Debate on Structured Debate: Toward a Unified Theory," *Organizational Behavior and Human Decision Processes* 66 (1996), pp. 316–32; D. Tjosvold, *Team Organization: An Enduring Competitive Edge* (Chichester, UK: Wiley, 1991).

64. K. M. Eisenhardt, J. L. Kahwajy, and L. J. Bourgeois III, "Conflict and Strategic Choice: How Top Management Teams Disagree," *California Management Review* 39 (Winter 1997), pp. 42–62.

65. J. S. Valacich and C. Schwenk, "Structuring Conflict in Individual, Face-to-Face, and Computer-Mediated Group Decision Making: Carping versus Objective Devil's Advocacy," *Decision Sciences* 26 (1995), pp. 369–93; D. M. Schweiger, W. R. Sandberg, and P. L. Rechner, "Experiential Effects of Dialectical Inquiry, Devil's Advocacy, and Consensus Approaches to Strategic Decision Making," *Academy of Management Journal* 32 (1989), pp. 745–72.

66. P. J. H. Schoemaker, "Disciplined Imagination: From Scenarios to Strategic Options," *International Studies of Management and Organization* 27 (Summer 1997), pp. 43–70.

67. A. F. Osborn, *Applied Imagination* (New York: Scribner, 1957).

68. A. Chandrasekaran, "Bye, Bye Serendipity," *Business Standard*, March 28, 2000, p. 1.

69. B. Oaff, "Great Idea, Even if It Can Get You Fired," *Mail on Sunday* (UK), May 6, 2001, p. 43.

70. B. Mullen, C. Johnson, and E. Salas, "Productivity Loss in Brainstorming Groups: A Meta-Analytic Integration," *Basic and Applied Psychology* 12 (1991), pp. 2–23.

71. R. I. Sutton and A. Hargadon, "Brainstorming Groups in Context: Effectiveness in a Product Design Firm," *Administrative Science Quarterly* 41 (1996), pp. 685–718; P. B. Paulus and M. T. Dzindolet, "Social Influence Processes in Group Brainstorming," *Journal of Personality and Social Psychology* 64 (1993), pp. 575–86; B. Mullen, C. Johnson, and E. Salas, "Productivity Loss in Brainstorming Groups: A Meta-Analytic Integration," *Basic and Applied Psychology* 12 (1991), pp. 2–23.

72. Gallupe et al., "Blocking Electronic Brainstorms."

73. P. Bordia, "Face-to-Face versus Computer-Mediated Communication: A Synthesis of the Experimental Literature," *Journal of Business Communication* 34 (1997), pp. 99–120; J. S. Valacich, A. R. Dennis, and T. Connolly, "Idea Generation in Computer-Based Groups: A New Ending to an Old Story," *Organizational Behavior and Human Decision Processes* 57 (1994), pp. 448–67; Gallupe et al., "Blocking Electronic Brainstorms."

74. A. R. Dennis and J. S. Valacich, "Electronic Brainstorming: Illusions and Patterns of Productivity," *Information Systems Research* 10 (1999), pp. 375–77; R. B. Gallupe, A. R. Dennis, W. H. Cooper, J. S. Valacich, L. M. Bastianutti, and J. F. Nunamaker, Jr., "Electronic Brainstorming and Group Size," *Academy of Management Journal* 35 (June 1992), pp. 350–69; R. B. Gallupe, L. M. Bastianutti, and W. H. Cooper, "Unblocking Brainstorms," *Journal of Applied Psychology* 76 (1991), pp. 137–42.

75. A. Pinsoneault, H. Barki, R. B. Gallupe, and N. Hoppen. "Electronic Brainstorming: The Illusion of Productivity," *Information Systems Research* 10 (1999), pp. 110–33; B. Kabanoff and J. R. Rossiter, "Recent Developments in Applied Creativity," *International Review of Industrial and Organizational Psychology* 9 (1994), pp. 283–324.

76. H. A. Linstone and M. Turoff, eds., *The Delphi Method: Techniques and Applications* (Reading, MA: Addison-Wesley, 1975).

77. C. Critcher and B. Gladstone, "Utilizing the Delphi Technique in Policy Discussion: A Case Study of a Privatized Utility in Britain," *Public Administration* 76 (Autumn 1998), pp. 431–49; S. R. Rubin et al., "Research Directions Related to Rehabilitation Practice: A Delphi Study," *Journal of Rehabilitation* 64 (Winter 1998), p. 19.

78. A. L. Delbecq, A. H. Van de Ven, and D. H. Gustafson, *Group Techniques for Program Planning: A Guide to Nominal Group and Delphi Processes* (Middleton, WI: Green Briar Press, 1986).

79. A. B. Hollingshead, "The Rank-Order Effect in Group Decision Making," *Organizational Behavior and Human Decision Processes* 68 (1996), pp. 181–93.

80. S. Frankel, "NGT + MDS: An Adaptation of the Nominal Group Technique for Ill-Structured Problems," *Journal of Applied Behavioral Science* 23 (1987), pp. 543–51; D. M. Hegedus and R. Rasmussen, "Task Effectiveness and Interaction Process of a Modified Nominal Group Technique in Solving an Evaluation Problem," *Journal of Management* 12 (1986), pp. 545–60.

CHAPTER ELEVEN

1. P. Tam, "The Bulldog Unchained," *Ottawa Citizen*, July 24, 2000; K. Goff, "Workers Ponder Their Futures," *Ottawa Citizen*, February 24, 2000; K. Standen, "Just What the Doctor Ordered," *Ottawa Citizen*, November 3, 1999; E. Mulqueen, "The Director's Chair—Pearse Flynn, Vice-President, Newbridge," *Irish Times*, August 27, 1999, p. 64; J. Bagnall, "Shaking Newbridge to the Core," *Ottawa Citizen*, March 17, 1999. Pearse Flynn is now CEO of Damovo, a spin-off from Ericsson that sells and services call center telecommunications systems. See J. Boxell, "Man Who Sold $7bn Newbridge in Fresh Challenge," *Financial Times (London)*, September 10, 2001.

2. N. Sriussadaporn-Charoenngam and F. M. Jablin, "An Exploratory Study of Communication Competence in Thai Organizations," *Journal of Business Communication* 36 (October 1999), pp. 382–418; F. M. Jablin et al., "Communication Competence in Organizations: Conceptualization and Comparison across Multiple Levels of Analysis," in L. Thayer and G. Barnett, eds., *Organization Communication: Emerging Perspectives*, vol. 4 (Norwood, NJ: Ablex, 1994), pp. 114–40.

3. S. L. Pan and H. Scarbrough, "Knowledge Management in Practice: An Exploratory Case Study," *Technology Analysis and Strategic Management* 11 (September 1999), pp. 359–74; S. Greengard, "Will Your Culture Support KM?" *Workforce* 77 (October 1998), pp. 93–94; M. N. Martinez, "The Collective Power of Employee Knowledge," *HRMagazine* 43 (February 1998), pp. 88–94; R. K. Buckman, "Knowledge Sharing at Buckman Labs," *Journal of Business Strategy*, January–February 1998, pp. 11–15.

4. H. Mintzberg, *The Nature of Managerial Work* (New York: Harper & Row, 1973); E. T. Klemmer and F. W. Snyder, "Measurement of Time Spent Communicating," *Journal of Communication* 22 (June 1972), pp. 142–58.

5. R. T. Barker and M. R. Camarata, "The Role of Communication in Creating and Maintaining a Learning Organization: Preconditions, Indicators, and Disciplines," *Journal of Business Communication* 35 (October 1998), pp. 443–67.

6. R. Grenier and G. Metes, "Wake Up and Smell the Syzygy," *Business Communications Review* 28 (August 1998), pp. 57–60; "We Are the World," *CIO* 9 (August 1996), p. 24.

7. G. Calabrese, "Communication and Co-operation in Product Development: A Case Study of a European Car Producer," *R&D Management* 27 (July 1997), pp. 239–52; C. Downs, P. Clampitt, and A. L. Pfeiffer, "Communication and Organizational Outcomes," in G. Goldhaber and G. Barnett, eds., *Handbook of Organizational Communication* (Norwood, NJ: Ablex, 1988), pp. 171–211.

8. V. L. Shalin, and G. V. Prabhu, "A Cognitive Perspective on Manual Assembly," *Ergonomics* 39 (1996), pp. 108–27; I. Nonaka and H. Takeuchi, The *Knowledge-Creating Company* (New York: Oxford University Press, 1995).

9. L. K. Lewis and D. R. Seibold, "Communication during Intraorganizational Innovation Adoption: Predicting User's Behavioral Coping Responses to Innovations in Organizations," *Communication Monographs* 63 (2) (1996), pp. 131–57; R. J. Burke and D. S. Wilcox, "Effects of Different Patterns and Degrees of Openness in Superior— Subordinate Communication on Subordinate Satisfaction," *Academy of Management Journal* 12 (1969), pp. 319–26.

10. C. E. Shannon and W. Weaver, *The Mathematical Theory of Communication* (Urbana: University of Illinois Press, 1949). For a more recent discussion, see K. J. Krone, F. M. Jablin, and L. L. Putnam, "Communication Theory and Organizational Communication: Multiple Perspectives," in F. M. Jablin, L. L. Putnam, K. H. Roberts, and L. W. Porter, eds., *Handbook of Organizational Communication: An Interdisciplinary Perspective* (Newbury Park, CA: Sage, 1987), pp. 18–40.

11. S. Axley, "Managerial and Organizational Communication in Terms of the Conduit Metaphor," *Academy of Management Review* 9 (1984), pp. 428–37.

12. D. Jones, "Corning Chief Says Keep Open Mind, Challenge Strategy," *USA Today*, June 1, 2001, p. B5; The George Bernard Shaw quotation is cited at the website www.synco.com/communct.html.

13. M. Meissner, "The Language of Work," in R. Dubin, ed., *Handbook of Work, Organization, and Society* (Chicago: Rand McNally, 1976), pp. 205–79.

14. M. J. Glauser, "Upward Information Flow in Organizations: Review and Conceptual Analysis," *Human Relations* 37 (1984), pp. 613–43.

15. L. Larwood, "Don't Struggle to Scope Those Metaphors Yet," *Group and Organization Management* 17 (1992), pp. 249–54; L. R. Pondy, P. J. Frost, G. Morgan, and T. C. Dandridge, eds., *Organizational Symbolism* (Greenwich, CT: JAI Press, 1983).

16. L. Sahagun, "Cold War Foes Find Harmony in Satellite Launch Partnership," *Los Angeles Times*, July 25, 2001, p. B1.

17. B. Robins, "Why 'Sell' Is Now a Four-Letter Word," *The Age (Melbourne)*, June 16, 2001.

18. A. Markham, "Designing Discourse: A Critical Analysis of Strategic Ambiguity and Workplace Control," *Management Communication Quarterly* 9 (1996), pp. 389–421; Larwood, "Don't Struggle to Scope Those Metaphors Yet"; R. Mead, *Cross-Cultural Management Communication* (Chichester, UK: Wiley, 1990), pp. 130–37; E. M. Eisenberg, "Ambiguity as a Strategy in Organizational Communication," *Communication Monographs* 51 (1984), pp. 227–42; R. Daft and J. Wiginton, "Language and Organization," *Academy of Management Review* 4 (1979), pp. 179–91.

19. M. J. Hatch, "Exploring the Empty Spaces of Organizing: How Improvisational Jazz Helps Redescribe Organizational Structure," *Organization Studies* 20 (1999), pp. 75–100; G. Morgan, *Images of Organization*, 2nd ed. (Thousand Oaks, CA: Sage, 1997); L. L. Putnam, N. Phillips, and P. Chapman, "Metaphors of Communication and Organization," in S. R. Clegg, C. Hardy, and W. R. Nord, eds., *Handbook of Organization Studies* (London: Sage, 1996), pp. 373–408.

20. B. Beaupre, "You've Got Too Much Mail," *Chicago Sun-Times*, August 7, 2000.

21. J. T. Koski, "Reflections on Information Glut and Other Issues in Knowledge Productivity," *Futures* 33 (August 2001), pp. 483–95; C. Norton

and A. Nathan, "Computer-Mad Generation Has a Memory Crash," *Sunday Times (London)*, February 4, 2001; S. Bury, "Does E-mail Make You More Productive?" *Silicon Valley North*, September 1999.

22. From "The Best of Ideas," CBC Radio, 1967. (Cited at the website www.mcluhan4managers.com).

23. K. Alesandrini, *Survive Information Overload* (Homewood, IL: Business One–Irwin, 1993); A. G. Schick, L. A. Gordon, and S. Haka, "Information Overload: A Temporal Approach," *Accounting, Organizations and Society* 15 (1990), pp. 199–220.

24. Schick et al., "Information Overload," pp. 209–14; C. Stohl and W. C. Redding, "Messages and Message Exchange Processes," in Jablin et al., eds., *Handbook of Organizational Communication*, pp. 451–502.

25. J. H. E. Andriessen, "Mediated Communication and New Organizational Forms," *International Review of Industrial and Organizational Psychology* 6 (1991), pp. 17–70; L. Porter and K. Roberts, "Communication in Organizations," in M. Dunnette, ed., *Handbook of Industrial and Organizational Psychology* (Chicago: Rand McNally, 1976), pp. 1553–89.

26. F. Moore, "Storage Faces Newest Challenge—Coping with Success," *Computer Technology Review* 21 (September 2001), p. 1; S. D. Kennedy, "Finding a Cure for Information Anxiety," *Information Today*, May 1, 2001, p. 40; M. R. Overly, "E-Policy," *Messaging Magazine*, January–February 1999. For a discussion of the merits of e-mail, see J. Hunter and M. Allen, "Adaptation to Electronic Mail," *Journal of Applied Communication Research*, August 1992, pp. 254–74; M. Culnan and M. L. Markus, "Information Technologies," in Jablin et al., eds., *Handbook of Organizational Communication*, pp. 420–43.

27. C. S. Saunders, D. Robey, and K. A. Vaverek, "The Persistence of Status Differentials in Computer Conferencing," *Human Communications Research* 20 (1994), pp. 443–72; D. A. Adams, P. A. Todd, and R. R. Nelson, "A Comparative Evaluation of the Impact of Electronic and Voice Mail on Organizational Communication,"

Information and Management 24 (1993), pp. 9–21.

28. "Eisner: E-mail Is Biggest Threat," *Associated Press*, May 12, 2000; A. D. Shulman, "Putting Group Information Technology in Its Place: Communication and Good Work Group Performance," in Clegg et al., eds., *Handbook of Organization Studies*, pp. 373–408.

29. S. Schafer, "Misunderstandings @ the Office," *Washington Post*, October 31, 2000, p. E1; M. Gibbs, "Don't Say It with Smileys," *Network World*, August 9, 1999, p. 62.

30. A. Gumbel, "How E-mail Puts Us in a Flaming Bad Temper," *The Independent (London)*, January 3, 1999, p. 14; J. Kaye, "The Devil You Know," *Computer Weekly*, March 19, 1998, p. 46; S. Kennedy, "The Burning Issue of Electronic Hate Mail," *Computer Weekly*, June 5, 1997, p. 22

31. A. C. Poe, "Don't Touch That 'Send' Button!" *HRMagazine* 46 (July 2001), pp. 74–80. Problems with e-mail are discussed in M. M. Extejt, "Teaching Students to Correspond Effectively Electronically: Tips for Using Electronic Mail Properly," *Business Communication Quarterly* 61 (June 1998), pp. 57–67; V. Frazee, "Is E-mail Doing More Harm Than Good?" *Personnel Journal* 75 (May 1996), p. 23.

32. J. L. Locke, "Q: Is E-Mail Degrading Public and Private Discourse? Yes: Electronic Mail Is Making Us Rude, Lonely, Insensitive and Dishonest," *Insight on the News*, October 19, 1998, p. 24.

33. S. Stellin, "The Intranet Is Changing Many Firms from Within," *New York Times*, January 30, 2001.

34. Stellin, "The Intranet Is Changing Many Firms from Within"; A. Mahlon, "The Alternative Workplace: Changing Where and How People Work," *Harvard Business Review*, May–June 1998, pp. 121–30; C. Meyer and S. Davis, *Blur: The Speed of Change in the Connected Economy* (Reading, MA: Addison-Wesley, 1998); P. Bordia, "Face-to-Face versus Computer-Mediated Communication: A Synthesis of the Experimental Literature," *Journal of Business Communication* 34 (January 1997), pp. 99–120.

35. M. McCance, "IM: Rapid, Risky," *Richmond (VA) Times-Dispatch*, July 19, 2001, p. A1; C. Hempel, "Instant-Message Gratification Is What People Want," *Ventura County (CA) Star*, April 9, 2001.

36. D. Robb, "Ready or Not . . . Instant Messaging Has Arrived as a Financial Planning Tool," *Journal of Financial Planning*, July 2001, pp. 12–14.

37. W. Boei, "The Most Wired Person in Nunavut," *Ottawa Citizen*, November 13, 1999; S. De Santis, "Across Tundra and Cultures, Entrepreneur Wires Arctic," *The Wall Street Journal*, October 19, 1998, p. B1; T. Saito, "Internet Helps Keep Scattered Inuit in Touch," *Daily Yomiuri (Tokyo)*, June 7, 1997.

38. J. S. Brown, "Seeing Differently: A Role for Pioneering Research," *Research Technology Management* 41 (May–June 1998), pp. 24–33; See G. Gilder, *Telecosm: How Infinite Bandwidth will Revolutionize Our World* (New York: Free Press, 2001).

39. "New Age Heralds End of Information Overload," *Financial News*, December 8, 1998.

40. T. E. Harris, *Applied Organizational Communication: Perspectives, Principles, and Pragmatics* (Hillsdale, NJ: Erlbaum, 1993), chap. 5; R. E. Rice and D. E. Shook, "Relationships of Job Categories and Organizational Levels to Use of Communication Channels, Including Electronic Mail: A Meta-Analysis and Extension," *Journal of Management Studies* 27 (1990), pp. 195–229; S. B. Sitkin, K. M. Sutcliffe, and J. R. Barrios-Choplin, "A Dual-Capacity Model of Communication Media Choice in Organizations," *Human Communication Research* 18 (June 1992), pp. 568–98.

41. B. Parkinson, *Ideas and Realities of Emotion* (London: Routledge, 1995), pp. 182–83; E. Hatfield, J. T. Cacioppo, and R. L. Rapson, *Emotional Contagion* (Cambridge, UK: Cambridge University Press, 1993).

42. D. Goodsire, "Seconds from Disaster, the Captain Aborts," *The Age (Melbourne)*, April 25, 2001.

43. R. L. Daft, R. H. Lengel, and L. K. Tevino, "Message Equivocality, Media Selection, and Manager Performance: Implications for Information Systems," *MIS Quarterly* 11 (1987), pp. 355–66.

44. I. Lamont, "Do Your Far-Flung Users Want to Communicate as if They Share an Office?" *Network World*, November 13, 2000.

45. R. Lengel and R. Daft, "The Selection of Communication Media as an Executive Skill," *Academy of Management Executive* 2 (1988), pp. 225–32; G. Huber and R. Daft, "The Information Environments of Organizations," in Jablin et al., eds., *Handbook of Organizational Communication*, pp. 130–64; R. Daft and R. Lengel, "Information Richness: A New Approach to Managerial Behavior and Organization Design," *Research in Organizational Behavior* 6 (1984), pp. 191–233.

46. R. E. Rice, "Task Analyzability, Use of New Media, and Effectiveness: A Multi-Site Exploration of Media Richness," *Organization Science* 3 (1992), pp. 475–500; J. Fulk, C. W. Steinfield, J. Schmitz, and J. G. Power, "A Social Information Processing Model of Media Use in Organizations," *Communication Research* 14 (1987), pp. 529–52.

47. R. Madhavan and R. Grover, "From Embedded Knowledge to Embodied Knowledge: New Product Development As Knowledge Management," *Journal of Marketing* 62 (October 1998), pp. 1–12; D. Stork and A. Sapienza, "Task and Human Messages over the Project Life Cycle: Matching Media to Messages," *Project Management Journal* 22 (December 1992), pp. 44–49.

48. J. R. Carlson and R. W. Zmud, "Channel Expansion Theory and the Experiential Nature of Media Richness Perceptions," *Academy of Management Journal* 42 (April 1999), pp. 153–70.

49. M. McLuhan, *Understanding Media: The Extensions of Man* (New York: McGraw-Hill, 1964).

50. Sitkin et al., "A Dual-Capacity Model of Communication Media Choice in Organizations"; J. Schmitz and J. Fulk, "Organizational Colleagues, Media Richness, and Electronic Mail: A Test of the Social Influence Model of Technology Use," *Communication Research* 18 (1991), pp. 487–523.

51. M. Misra and P. Misra, "Hughes Software: Fun and Flexibility," *Business Today*, January 7, 2001, p. 182.

52. B. Sosnin, "Digital Newsletters 'E-volutionize' Employee Communications," *HRMagazine* 46 (May 2001), pp. 99–107; G. Grates, "Is the Employee Publication Extinct?" *Communication*

World 17 (December 1999–January 2000), pp. 27–30.

53. R. Hotch, "Put the 'Quality' in Equality," *Success* 48 (April 2001), pp. 28ff.; N. Hulsman, "Farewell, Corner Office," *BC Business*, June 1999, pp. 48ff.; L. Stuart, "Why Space Is the New Frontier," *The Guardian (London)*, October 31, 1998, p. 24.

54. G. Evans and D. Johnson, "Stress and Open-Office Noise," *Journal of Applied Psychology* 85 (2000), pp. 779–83.

55. F. Russo, "My Kingdom for a Door," *Time*, October 23, 2000, p. B1. The TBWA Chiat/Day office design and its problems are described in Hulsman, "Farewell, Corner Office"; "Why Chiat/Day Is Putting Down Its Binoculars," *Creative Review*, April 1998, p. 67; C. Knight, "Gone Virtual," *Canadian HR Reporter*, December 16, 1996, pp. 24, 26.

56. J. Sung, "Designed for Interaction," *Fortune*, January 8, 2001; S. Kirsner, "Every Day, It's a New Place," *Fast Company*, April–May, 1998, pp. 130–34; J. S. Russell, "A Company Headquarters Planned for Flexibility," *New York Times*, September 7, 1997, p. 7.

57. B. Schneider, S. D. Ashworth, A. C. Higgs, and L. Carr, "Design, Validity, and Use of Strategically Focused Employee Attitude Surveys," *Personnel Psychology* 49 (1996), pp. 695–705; T. Geddie, "Surveys Are a Waste of Time . . . Until You Use Them," *Communication World*, April 1996, pp. 24–26; D. M. Saunders and J. D. Leck, "Formal Upward Communication Procedures: Organizational and Employee Perspectives," *Canadian Journal of Administrative Sciences* 10 (1993), pp. 255–68.

58. L. Girion, "Employee Inner Views," *Los Angeles Times*, September 10, 2000, p. G1.

59. The original term is "management by *wandering* around," but "wandering" has been replaced with "walking" over the years. T. Peters and R. Waterman, *In Search of Excellence* (New York: Harper & Row, 1982), p. 122; W. Ouchi, *Theory Z* (New York: Avon, 1981), pp. 176–77.

60. J. Hansen, "Wide Open Spaces," *AsiaWeek*, May 25, 2001; S. Bongiorni, "LSU Students Get Business Tips," *Louisiana State Times/Morning Advocate*, November 11, 2000, p. C1; M. Goldberg,

"Cisco's Most Important Meal of the Day," *Fast Company* 13 (February 1998), p. 56.

61. M. Duffy, "Jobs Cloud Lifts for Staff at Mitsubishi," *The Advertiser (Adelaide, Australia)*, April 3, 2001, p. 12; M. Duffy, "Contract a Lifeline for Mitsubishi," *Herald Sun (Melbourne)*, April 3, 2001; M. Duffy, "Welcome to the Future," *The Advertiser (Adelaide, Australia)*, November 29, 2000, p. 1; M. Duffy, "Japan Backs Mitsubishi," *The Advertiser (Adelaide, Australia)*, November 28, 2000, pp. 1, 6; M. Duffy, "Let Us Get On with It," *The Advertiser (Adelaide, Australia)*, November 18, 2000, p. 1.

62. "Survey Finds Good and Bad Points on Worker Attitudes," *Eastern Pennsylvania Business Journal*, May 5, 1997, p. 13.

63. G. Kreps, *Organizational Communication* (White Plains, NY: Longman, 1986), pp. 202–6; W. L. Davis and J. R. O'Connor, "Serial Transmission of Information: A Study of the Grapevine," *Journal of Applied Communication Research* 5 (1977), pp. 61–72; K. Davis, "Management Communication and the Grapevine," *Harvard Business Review* 31 (September–October 1953), pp. 43–49.

64. D. Krackhardt and J. R. Hanson, "Informal Networks: The Company Behind the Chart," *Harvard Business Review* 71 (July–August 1993), pp. 104–11; H. Mintzberg, *The Structuring of Organizations* (Englewood Cliffs, NJ: Prentice Hall, 1979), pp. 46–53.

65. M. Noon and R. Delbridge, "News from Behind My Hand: Gossip in Organizations," *Organization Studies* 14 (1993), pp. 23–36; R. L. Rosnow, "Inside Rumor: A Personal Journey," *American Psychologist* 46 (May 1991), pp. 484–96; C. J. Walker and C. A. Beckerle, "The Effect of State Anxiety on Rumor Transmission," *Journal of Social Behavior and Personality* 2 (August 1987), pp. 353–60.

66. J. N. Lynem, "Sex, Lies and Message Boards," *San Francisco Chronicle*, July 1, 2001, p. W1; D. E. Lewis, "Firms Try to Cope with Rumors, Gossip on Online Message Boards," *Boston Globe*, May 17, 2001; M. Schrage, "If You Can't Say Anything Nice, Say It Anonymously," *Fortune*, December 6, 1999, p. 352; S. Caudron, "Employeechat.com:

Bashing HR on the Web," *Workforce* 78 (December 1999), pp. 36–42.

67. Lewis, "Firms Try to Cope with Rumors, Gossip on Online Message Boards." The banning of office gossip in Cascavel, Brazil, is described in "Odd Spot," *The Age (Melbourne)*, July 20, 2001, p. 1.

68. G. Dutton, "One Workforce, Many Languages," *Management Review* 87 (December 1998), pp. 42–47.

69. D. Woodruff, "Crossing Culture Divide Early Clears Merger Paths," *Asian Wall Street Journal*, May 28, 2001, p. 9.

70. Mead, *Cross-Cultural Management Communication*, pp. 161–62; J. V. Thill and C. L. Bovée, *Excellence in Business Communication*, 2nd ed. (New York: McGraw-Hill, 1993), chap. 17.

71. F. Cunningham, "A Touch of the Tartan Treatment for Mazda," *The Scotsman*, October 14, 1997, p. 27.

72. R. M. March, *Reading the Japanese Mind* (Tokyo: Kodansha International, 1996), chap. 1; H. Yamada, *American and Japanese Business Discourse: A Comparison of Interaction Styles* (Norwood, NJ: Ablex, 1992), p. 34.

73. One writer explains that Aboriginal people tend to avoid conflict, so differences are discussed over an open campfire, which absorbs some of the potential conflict and allows people to avoid direct eye contact. See H. Blagg, "A Just Measure of Shame?" *British Journal of Criminology* 37 (Autumn 1997), pp. 481–501. For other differences in cross-cultural communication, see R. Axtell, *Gestures: The Do's and Taboos of Body Language around the World* (New York: Wiley, 1991); P. Harris and R. Moran, *Managing Cultural Differences* (Houston: Gulf, 1987); P. Ekman, W. V. Friesen, and J. Bear, "The International Language of Gestures," *Psychology Today*, May 1984, pp. 64–69.

74. H. Yamada, *Different Games, Different Rules* (New York: Oxford University Press, 1997), pp. 76–79; Yamada, *American and Japanese Business Discourse*, chap. 2; D. Tannen, *Talking from 9 to 5* (New York: Avon, 1994), pp. 96–97; D. C. Barnlund, *Communication Styles of Japanese and Americans: Images and Realities* (Belmont, CA: Wadsworth, 1988).

75. D. Goleman, What Makes a Leader?" *Harvard Business Review* 76 (November–December 1998), pp. 92–102.

76. S. Herring, "Gender Differences in Computer-Mediated Communication: Bringing Familiar Baggage to the New Frontier," Paper presented at the American Library Association Annual Conference, Miami, June 27, 1994.

77. M. Crawford, *Talking Difference: On Gender and Language* (Thousand Oaks, CA: Sage, 1995), pp. 41–44; Tannen, *Talking from 9 to 5;* D. Tannen, *You Just Don't Understand: Men and Women in Conversation* (New York: Ballantine, 1990); S. Helgesen, *The Female Advantage: Women's Ways of Leadership* (New York: Doubleday, 1990).

78. A. Mulac et al., "'Uh-Huh. What's That All About?' Differing Interpretations of Conversational Backchannels and Questions as Sources of Miscommunication across Gender Boundaries," *Communication Research* 25 (December 1998), pp. 641–68; G. H. Graham, J. Unruh, and P. Jennings, "The Impact of Nonverbal Communication in Organizations: A Survey of Perceptions," *Journal of Business Communication* 28 (1991), pp. 45–61; J. Hall, "Gender Effects in Decoding Nonverbal Cues," *Psychological Bulletin* 68 (1978), pp. 845–57.

79. This stereotypic notion is prevalent throughout J. Gray, *Men Are from Mars, Women Are from Venus* (New York: HarperCollins, 1992). For a critique of this view, see Crawford, *Talking Difference*, chap. 4; D. J. Canary and T. M. Emmers-Sommer, *Sex and Gender Differences in Personal Relationships* (New York: Guilford 1997), chap. 1.

80. P. Tripp-Knowles, "A Review of the Literature on Barriers Encountered by Women in Science Academia," *Resources for Feminist Research* 24 (Spring–Summer 1995) pp. 28–34.

81. R. J. Grossman, "Emotions at Work," *Health Forum Journal* 43 (September–October 2000), pp. 18–22.

82. Cited in K. Davis and J. W. Newstrom, *Human Behavior at Work: Organizational Behavior*, 7th ed. (New York: McGraw-Hill, 1985), p. 438.

83. The three components of listening discussed here are based on several recent studies in the field of marketing, including K. de Ruyter and M. G. M. Wetzels, "The Impact of Perceived Listening Behavior in Voice-to-Voice Service Encounters," *Journal of Service Research* 2 (February 2000), pp. 276–84; S. B. Castleberry, C. D. Shepherd, and R. Ridnour, "Effective Interpersonal Listening in the Personal Selling Environment: Conceptualization, Measurement, and Nomological Validity," *Journal of Marketing Theory and Practice* 7 (Winter 1999), pp. 30–38; L. B. Comer and T. Drollinger, "Active Empathetic Listening and Selling Success: A Conceptual Framework," *Journal of Personal Selling and Sales Management* 19 (Winter 1999), pp. 15–29.

84. S. Silverstein, "On the Job, but Do They Listen?" *Los Angeles Times*, July 19, 1998.

CHAPTER TWELVE

1. T. Wanless, "Business and Golfing—Par for the Course," *Vancouver Province*, June 10, 2001; S. J. Wells, "Smoothing the Way," *HRMagazine* 46 (June 2001), pp. 52–58; C. Kleiman, "Women's Networks Play Essential Role in Career Advancement," *The Record (Bergen County, NJ)*, October 15, 2000, p. 5; D. L Nelson and R. J. Burke, "Women Executives: Health, Stress, and Success," *Academy of Management Executive* 14 (May 2000), pp. 107–21.

2. C. Hardy and S. Leiba-O'Sullivan, "The Power behind Empowerment: Implications for Research and Practice," *Human Relations* 51 (April 1998), pp. 451–83; R. Farson, *Management of the Absurd* (New York: Simon & Schuster, 1996), chap. 13; R. M. Cyert and J. G. March, *A Behavioral Theory of the Firm* (Englewood Cliffs, NJ: Prentice Hall, 1963).

3. For a discussion of the definition of *power*, see J. Pfeffer, *New Directions in Organizational Theory* (New York: Oxford University Press, 1997), chap. 6; J. Pfeffer, *Managing with Power* (Boston: Harvard Business University Press, 1992), pp. 17, 30; H. Mintzberg, *Power In and Around Organizations* (Englewood Cliffs, NJ: Prentice Hall, 1983), chap. 1.

4. A. M. Pettigrew, *The Politics of Organizational Decision-Making* (London: Tavistock, 1973); R. M. Emerson, "Power-Dependence Relations," *American Sociological Review* 27 (1962), pp. 31–41; R. A. Dahl, "The Concept of Power," *Behavioral Science* 2 (1957), pp. 201–18.

5. D. J. Brass and M. E. Burkhardt, "Potential Power and Power Use: An Investigation of Structure and Behaviour," *Academy of Management Journal* 36 (1993), pp. 441–70; K. M. Bartol and D. C. Martin, "When Politics Pays: Factors Influencing Managerial Compensation Decisions," *Personnel Psychology* 43 (1990), pp. 599–614.

6. P. P. Carson and K. D. Carson, "Social Power Bases: A Meta-Analytic Examination of Interrelationships and Outcomes," *Journal of Applied Social Psychology* 23 (1993), pp. 1150–69; P. Podsakoff and C. Schreisheim, "Field Studies of French and Raven's Bases of Power: Critique, Analysis, and Suggestions for Future Research," *Psychological Bulletin* 97 (1985), pp. 387–411; J. R. P. French and B. Raven, "The Bases of Social Power," in D. Cartwright, ed., *Studies in Social Power* (Ann Arbor: University of Michigan Press, 1959), pp. 150–67.

7. For example, see S. Finkelstein, "Power in Top Management Teams: Dimensions. Measurement, and Validation," *Academy of Management Journal* 35 (1992), pp. 505–38.

8. G. Yukl and C. M. Falbe, "Importance of Different Power Sources in Downward and Lateral Relations," *Journal of Applied Psychology* 76 (1991), pp. 416–23.

9. G. A. Yukl, *Leadership in Organizations*, 3rd ed. (Englewood Cliffs, NJ: Prentice Hall, 1994), p. 13; B. H. Raven, "The Bases of Power: Origins and Recent Developments," *Journal of Social Issues* 49 (1993), pp. 227–51.

10. C. Hardy and S. R. Clegg, "Some Dare Call It Power," in S. R. Clegg, C. Hardy, and W. R. Nord, eds., *Handbook of Organization Studies* (London: Sage, 1996), pp. 622–41; C. Barnard, *The Function of the Executive* (Cambridge, MA: Harvard University Press, 1938).

11. I. Nonaka and H. Takeuchi, *The Knowledge-Creating Company* (New York: Oxford University Press, 1995), pp. 138–39.

12. J. A. Conger, *Winning 'Em Over: A New Model for Managing in the Age of Persuasion* (New York: Simon & Shuster, 1998), Appendix A.

13. "Employees Terrorized by Peer Pressure in the Workplace," Morgan & Banks news release, September 2000. For a discussion of peer pressure at work, see R. Hodson, "Group Relations at Work: Solidarity, Conflict, and Relations with Management," *Work and Occupations* 24 (November 1997), pp. 426–52.

14. G. Sewell, "The Discipline of Teams: The Control of Team-Based Industrial Work through Electronic and Peer Surveillance," *Administrative Science Quarterly* 43 (June 1998), pp. 397–428.

15. "Empowerment Torture to Some," *Tampa (FL) Tribune*, October 5, 1997, p. 6.

16. P. Panchak, "The Future of Manufacturing," *Industry Week* 247 (September 21, 1998), pp. 96–105.

17. J. D. Kudisch and M. L. Poteet, "Expert Power, Referent Power, and Charisma: Toward the Resolution of a Theoretical Debate," *Journal of Business and Psychology* 10 (Winter 1995), pp. 177–95.

18. Information was identified as a form of influence, but not power, in the original French and Raven writing. Information was added as a sixth source of power in subsequent writings by Raven, but this textbook takes the view that information power is derived from the original five sources. See B. H. Raven, "Kurt Lewin Address: Influence, Power, Religion, and the Mechanisms of Social Control," *Journal of Social Issues* 55, Spring 1999, pp. 161–86; Yukl and Falbe, "Importance of Different Power Sources in Downward and Lateral Relations."

19. "Corporate Culture Instilled Online," *The Economist*, November 11, 2000.

20. Pitney Bowes, "Study Finds Growth of Communication Options Is Fundamentally Changing Work," Pitney Bowes news release, April 8, 1997 (www.pitneybowes.com).

21. D. J. Brass, "Being in the Right Place: A Structural Analysis of Individual Influence in an Organization," *Administrative Science Quarterly* 29 (1984), pp. 518–39; N. M. Tichy, M. L. Tuchman, and C. Frombrun, "Social Network Analysis in Organizations," *Academy of Management Review* 4 (1979), pp. 507–19; H. Guetzkow and H. Simon, "The Impact of Certain Communication Nets upon Organization and Performance in Task-Oriented Groups," *Management Science* 1 (1955), pp. 233–50.

22. C. S. Saunders, "The Strategic Contingency Theory of Power: Multiple Perspectives," *Journal of Management Studies* 27 (1990), pp. 1–21; D. J. Hickson, C. R. Hinings, C. A. Lee, R. E. Schneck, and J. M. Pennings, "A Strategic Contingencies Theory of Intraorganizational Power," *Administrative Science Quarterly* 16 (1971), pp. 216–27; J. D. Thompson, *Organizations in Action* (New York: McGraw-Hill, 1967).

23. C. R. Hinings, D. J. Hickson, J. M. Pennings, and R. E. Schneck, "Structural Conditions of Intraorganizational Power," *Administrative Science Quarterly* 19 (1974), pp. 22–44.

24. Hickson et al., "A Strategic Contingencies Theory of Intraorganizational Power"; Hinings et al., "Structural Conditions of Intraorganizational Power"; and R. M. Kanter, "Power Failure in Management Circuits," *Harvard Business Review*, July–August 1979, pp. 65–75.

25. M. Crozier, *The Bureaucratic Phenomenon* (London: Tavistock, 1964).

26. M. F. Masters, *Unions at the Crossroads: Strategic Membership, Financial, and Political Perspectives* (Westport, CT: Quorum Books, 1997).

27. Brass and Burkhardt, "Potential Power and Power Use"; Hickson et al., "A Strategic Contingencies Theory of Intraorganizational Power," pp. 219–21; J. D. Hackman, "Power and Centrality in the Allocation of Resources in Colleges and Universities," *Administrative Science Quarterly* 30 (1985), pp. 61–77.

28. D. Beveridge, "Job Actions Hit World's Airlines during Year's Busiest Flying Season," *Canadian Press*, July 10, 2001; M. O'Dell, "Airlines Grounded by the Rise of Pilot Power," *Financial Times (UK)*, July 3, 2001.

29. L. Holden, "European Managers: HRM and an Evolving Role," *European Business Review* 12 (2000); Kanter, "Power Failure in Management Circuits," p. 68; B. E. Ashforth, "The Experience of Powerlessness in Organizations," *Organizational Behaviour and Human Decision Processes* 43 (1989), pp. 207–42.

30. M. L. A. Hayward and W. Boeker, "Power and Conflicts of Interest in Professional Firms: Evidence from Investment Banking," *Administrative Science Quarterly* 43 (March 1998), pp. 1–22.

31. R. Madell, "Ground Floor," *Pharmaceutical Executive (Women in Pharma Supplement)*, June 2000, pp. 24–31.

32. L. A. Perlow, "The Time Famine: Toward a Sociology of Work Time," *Administrative Science Quarterly* 44 (March 1999), pp. 5–31.

33. Perlow, "The Time Famine."

34. Raven, "The Bases of Power," pp. 237–39.

35. B. R. Ragins, "Diversified Mentoring Relationships in Organizations: A Power Perspective," *Academy of Management Review* 22 (1997), pp. 482–521; G. R. Ferris, D. D. Frink, D. P. S. Bhawuk, J. Zhou, and D. C. Gilmore, "Reactions of Diverse Groups to Politics in the Workplace," *Journal of Management* 22 (1996), pp. 23–44.

36. C. M. Falbe and G. Yukl, "Consequences for Managers of Using Single Influence Tactics and Combinations of Tactics," *Academy of Management Journal* 35 (1992), pp. 638–52.

37. D. Kipnis, *The Powerholders* (Chicago: University of Chicago Press, 1976); G. R. Salancik and J. Pfeffer, "The Bases and Use of Power in Organizational Decision Making: The Case of a University," *Administrative Science Quarterly* 19 (1974), pp. 453–73.

38. K. Voigt, "When Work Is a Beach," *Asian Wall Street Journal*, January 26, 2001, p. W1; J. K. Stewart, "Out-of-Sight Telecommuters Might Be Out of Mind," *Chicago Tribune*, April 5, 1998, p. 7; S. Fea, "Boss Moves Office to Lakeside," *Southland Times (Christchurch, NZ)*, February 26, 1998, p. 1.

39. G. E. G. Catlin, *Systematic Politics* (Toronto: University of Toronto Press, 1962), p. 71.

40. G. Kalogerakis, "Fired Manager Fined over Office Pass," *National Post*, May 9, 2000, p. A5.

41. B. James, "EU Drafts Measure to Outlaw Sexual Harassment," *International Herald Tribune*, June 8, 2000; C. S. Piotrkowski, "Gender Harassment, Job Satisfaction, and Distress among Em-

ployed White and Minority Women," *Journal of Occupational Health Psychology* 3 (January 1998), pp. 33–43.

42. D. E. Terpstra, "The Effects of Diversity on Sexual Harassment: Some Recommendations on Research," *Employee Responsibilities and Rights Journal* 9 (1996), pp. 303–13; J. A. Bargh and P. Raymond, "The Naive Misuse of Power: Nonconscious Sources of Sexual Harassment," *Journal of Social Issues* 51 (1995), pp. 85–96; R. A. Thacker and G. R. Ferris, "Understanding Sexual Harassment in the Workplace: The Influence of Power and Politics with the Dyadic Interaction of Harasser and Target," *Human Resource Management Review* 1 (1991), pp. 23–37.

43. For a discussion of the ethical implications of sexual harassment, see T. I. White, "Sexual Harassment: Trust and the Ethic of Care," *Business and Society Review* (January 1998), pp. 9–20; J. Keyton and S. C. Rhodes, "Sexual Harassment: A Matter of Individual Ethics, Legal Definitions, or Organizational Policy?" *Journal of Business Ethics* 16 (February 1997), pp. 129–46.

44. T. L. Tang and S. L. McCollum, "Sexual Harassment in the Workplace," *Public Personnel Management* 25 (1996), pp. 53–58; Bargh and Raymond, "The Naive Misuse of Power."

45. C. M. Schaefer and T. R. Tudor, "Managing Workplace Romances," *SAM Advanced Management Journal* 66, July 2001, pp. 4–10; S. Ulfelder, "Cupid Hits Cubeland," *Boston Globe*, February 11, 2001, p. H1; R. Dhooma, "Taking Care of Business and Pleasure," *Toronto Sun*, September 20, 1999, p. 38; E. Edmonds, "Love and Work," *Ottawa Sun*, February 14, 1999, p. S10. See also G. N. Powell and S. Foley, "Something to Talk About: Romantic Relationships in Organizational Settings," *Journal of Management* 24 (1998), pp. 421–28.

46. "Work Life," *Arizona Daily Star*, February 18, 2001, p. D1. For a discussion of perceived justice and office romance, see S. Foley and G. N. Powell, "Not All Is Fair in Love and Work: Coworkers' Preferences for and Responses to Managerial Interventions Regarding Workplace Romances," *Journal of Organizational Behavior* 20 (1999), pp. 1043–56.

47. Ulfelder, "Cupid Hits Cubeland."

48. M. Solomon, "The Secret's Out: How to Handle the Truth of Workplace Romance," *Workforce* 7 (July 1998), pp. 42–50. See also C. A. Pierce and H. Aguinis, "A Framework for Investigating the Link between Workplace Romance and Sexual Harassment," *Group and Organization Management* 26 (June 2001), pp. 206–29; N. Nejat-Bina, "Employers as Vigilant Chaperones Armed with Dating Waivers: The Intersection of Unwelcomeness and Employer Liability in Hostile Work Environment Sexual Harassment Law," *Berkeley Journal of Employment and Labor Law*, December 22, 1999, pp. 325ff.

49. T. Petzinger, Jr., *The New Pioneers: The Men and Women Who Are Transforming the Workplace and Marketplace* (New York: Simon & Schuster, 1999), chap. 1.

50. K. M. Kacmar and R. A. Baron, "Organizational Politics: The State of the Field, Links to Related Processes, and an Agenda for Future Research," *Research in Personnel and Human Resources Management* 17 (1999), pp. 1–39; K. M. Kacmar and G. R. Ferris, "Politics at Work: Sharpening the Focus of Political Behaviour in Organizations," *Business Horizons* 36 (July–August 1993), pp. 70–74; A. Drory and T. Romm, "The Definition of Organizational Politics: A Review," *Human Relations* 43 (1990), pp. 1133–54.

51. K. Ohlson, "Leadership in an Age of Mistrust," *Industry Week* 247 (February 2, 1998), pp. 37–46.

52. D. J. Burrough, "Office Politics Mirror Popular TV Program," *Arizona Republic*, February 4, 2001, p. EC1. See also T. H. Davenport, R. G. Eccles, and L. Prusak, "Information Politics," *Sloan Management Review*, Fall 1992, pp. 53–65; Pfeffer, *Managing with Power*, chap. 17.

53. D. Sandahl and C. Hewes, "Decision Making at Digital Speed," *Pharmaceutical Executive* 21 (August 2001), p. 62; "Notes about Where We Work and How We Make Ends Meet," *Arizona Daily Star*, February 18, 2001, p. D1.

54. J. C. Howes, A. A. Grandey, and P. Toth, "The Relationship of Organizational Politics and Support to Work Behaviours, Attitudes, and Stress," *Journal of Organizational Behaviour* 18

(March 1997), pp. 159–80; G. R. Ferris and D. D. Frink, "Reactions of Diverse Groups to Politics in the Workplace," *Journal of Management* 22 (Spring 1996), pp. 23–44; P. Kumar and R. Ghadially, "Organizational Politics and Its Effects on Members of Organizations," *Human Relations* 42 (1989), pp. 305–14.

55. M. Velasquez, D. J. Moberg, and G. F. Cavanaugh, "Organizational Statesmanship and Dirty Politics: Ethical Guidelines for the Organizational Politician," *Organizational Dynamics* 11 (1983), pp. 65–79.

56. R. W. Allen, D. L. Madison, L. W. Porter, P. A. Renwick, and B. T. Mayes, "Organizational Politics: Tactics and Characteristics of Its Actors," *California Management Review* 22 (Fall 1979), pp. 77–83; V. Murray and J. Gandz, "Games Executives Play: Politics at Work," *Business Horizons*, December 1980, pp. 11–23.

57. B. E. Ashforth and R. T. Lee, "Defensive Behaviour in Organizations: A Preliminary Model," *Human Relations* 43 (1990), pp. 621–48.

58. For examples and discussion of these information turf wars, see A. Simmons, *Territorial Games: Understanding and Ending Turf Wars* (New York: AMACOM, 1998).

59. "Be Part of the Team if You Want to Catch the Eye," *Birmingham Post (UK)*, August 31, 2000, p. 14.

60. Y. Gabriel, "An Introduction to the Social Psychology of Insults in Organizations," *Human Relations* 51 (November 1998), pp. 1329–54.

61. M. Warshaw, "The Good Guy's Guide to Office Politics," *Fast Company* 14 (April–May 1998), pp. 157–78.

62. E. A. Mannix, "Organizations as Resource Dilemmas: The Effects of Power Balance on Coalition Formation in Small Groups," *Organizational Behaviour and Human Decision Processes* 55 (1993), pp. 1–22; A. T. Cobb, "Toward the Study of Organizational Coalitions: Participant Concerns and Activities in a Simulated Organizational Setting," *Human Relations* 44 (1991), pp. 1057–79; W. B. Stevenson, J. L. Pearce, and L. W. Porter, "The Concept of 'Coalition' in Organization Theory and Research," *Academy of Management Review* 10 (1985), pp. 256–68.

63. Falbe and Yukl, "Consequences for Managers of Using Single Influence Tactics and Combinations of Tactics."

64. D. Krackhardt and J. R. Hanson, "Informal Networks: The Company behind the Chart," *Harvard Business Review* 71 (July–August 1993), pp. 104–11; R. E. Kaplan, "Trade Routes: The Manager's Network of Relationships," *Organizational Dynamics*, Spring 1984, pp. 37–52.

65. M. Linehan, "Barriers to Women's Participation in International Management," *European Business Review* 13 (2001); R. J. Burke and C. A. McKeen, "Women in Management," *International Review of Industrial and Organizational Psychology* 7 (1992), pp. 245–83; B. R. Ragins and E. Sundstrom, "Gender and Power in Organizations: A Longitudinal Perspective," *Psychological Bulletin* 105 (1989), pp. 51–88.

66. D. M. McCracken, "Winning the Talent War for Women: Sometimes It Takes a Revolution," *Harvard Business Review* 78 (November–December 2000), pp. 159–67.

67. A. R. Cohen and D. L. Bradford, "Influence without Authority: The Use of Alliances, Reciprocity, and Exchange to Accomplish Work," *Organizational Dynamics* 17 (3) (1989), pp. 5–17.

68. A. Rao and S. M. Schmidt, "Upward Impression Management: Goals, Influence Strategies, and Consequences," *Human Relations* 48 (1995), pp. 147–67; R. A. Giacalone and P. Rosenfeld, eds., *Applied Impression Management* (Newbury Park, CA: Sage, 1991); J. T. Tedeschi, ed., *Impression Management Theory and Social Psychological Research* (New York: Academic, 1981).

69. W. L. Gardner III, "Lessons in Organizational Dramaturgy: The Art of Impression Management," *Organizational Dynamics*, Summer 1992, pp. 33–46; R. C. Liden and T. R. Mitchell, "Ingratiatory Behaviours in Organizational Settings," *Academy of Management Review* 13 (1988), pp. 572–87.

70. A. Vuong, "Job Applicants Often Don't Tell Whole Truth," *Denver Post*, May 30, 2001, p. C1. For a discussion of research on false résumés, see S. L. McShane, "Applicant Misrepresentation in Résumés and Interviews," *Labor Law Journal* 45 (January 1994), pp. 15–24.

71. S. Romero and M. Richtel, "Second Chance," *New York Times*, March 5, 2001, p. C1; L. Faught, J. Collins, and R. Srisavasdi, "Senior Center Head Fired in Costa Mesa," *Orange County (CA) Register*, May 18, 2000, p. A1.

72. C. Hardy, *Strategies for Retrenchment and Turnaround: The Politics of Survival* (Berlin: de Gruyter, 1990), chap. 14; J. Gandz and V. V. Murray, "The Experience of Workplace Politics," *Academy of Management Journal* 23 (1980), pp. 237–51.

73. P. Dillon, "Failure Is an Option," *Fast Company* 22 (February–March 1999), pp. 154–71.

74. G. R. Ferris, G. S. Russ, and P. M. Fandt, "Politics in Organizations," in R. A. Giacalone and P. Rosenfeld, eds., *Impression Management in the Organization* (Hillsdale, NJ: Erlbaum, 1989), pp. 143–70; H. Mintzberg, "The Organization as Political Arena," *Journal of Management Studies* 22 (1985), pp. 133–54.

75. R. J. House, "Power and Personality in Complex Organizations," *Research in Organizational Behaviour* 10 (1988), pp. 305–57; L. W. Porter, R. W. Allen, and H. L. Angle, "The Politics of Upward Influence in Organizations," *Research in Organizational Behaviour* 3 (1981), pp. 120–22.

76. K. S. Sauleya and A. G. Bedeian, "Equity Sensitivity: Construction of a Measure and Examination of Its Psychometric Properties," *Journal of Management* 26 (September 2000), pp. 885–910; S. M. Farmer, J. M. Maslyn, D. B. Fedor, and J. S. Goodman, "Putting Upward Influence Strategies in Context," *Journal of Organizational Behaviour* 18 (1997), pp. 17–42; P. E. Mudrack, "An Investigation into the Acceptability of Workplace Behaviours of a Dubious Ethical Nature," *Journal of Business Ethics* 12 (1993), pp. 517–24; R. Christie and F. Geis, *Studies in Machiavellianism* (New York: Academic Press, 1970).

77. D. Tannen, *Talking from 9 to 5* (New York: Avon, 1995), pp. 137–41, 151–52.

78. N. Martin, "Men 'Gossip More than Women to Boost Their Egos,'" *Daily Telegraph (UK)*, June 15, 2001, p. P13; Tannen, *Talking from 9 to 5*, chap. 2; M. Crawford, *Talking Difference: On Gender and Language* (Thousand Oaks, CA: Sage, 1995), pp. 41–44; D. Tannen, *You Just Don't Understand: Men and Women in Conversation* (New York: Ballantine, 1990); S. Helgesen, *The Female Advantage: Women's Ways of Leadership* (New York: Doubleday, 1990).

79. S. Mann, "Politics and Power in Organizations: Why Women Lose Out," *Leadership and Organization Development Journal* 16 (1995), pp. 9–15; L. Larwood and M. M. Wood, "Training Women for Management: Changing Priorities," *Journal of Management Development* 14 (1995), pp. 54–65. A recent popular-press book serves as a guide for women to learn organizational politics; see H. Rubin, *The Princessa: Machiavelli for Women* (New York: Doubleday Currency, 1996).

80. G. R. Ferris et al., "Perceptions of Organizational Politics: Prediction, Stress-Related Implications, and Outcomes," *Human Relations* 49 (1996), pp. 233–63.

81. A. P. Brief, *Attitudes In and Around Organizations* (Thousand Oaks, CA: Sage, 1998), pp. 69–84; K. K. Reardon, *Persuasion in Practice* (Newbury Park, CA: Sage, 1991); P. Zimbardo and E. B. Ebbeson, *Influencing Attitudes and Changing Behavior* (Reading, MA: Addison-Wesley, 1969).

82. J. J. Jiang, G. Klein, and R. G. Vedder, "Persuasive Expert Systems: The Influence of Confidence and Discrepancy," *Computers in Human Behavior* 16 (March 2000), pp. 99–109; J. Cooper and R. T. Coyle, "Attitudes and Attitude Change," *Annual Review of Psychology* 35 (1984), pp. 395–426; N. MacLachlan, "What People Really Think about Fast Talkers," *Psychology Today* 113 (November 1979), pp. 112–17.

83. J. A. Conger, *Winning 'Em Over*.

84. D. B. Freeland, "Turning Communication into Influence," *HRMagazine* 38 (September 1993), pp. 93–96; M. Snyder and M. Rothbart, "Communicator Attractiveness and Opinion Change," *Canadian Journal of Behavioural Science* 3 (1971), pp. 377–87.

85. E. Aronson, *The Social Animal* (San Francisco: Freeman, 1976), pp. 67–68; R. A. Jones and J. W. Brehm, "Persuasiveness of One- and Two-Sided Communications as a Function of Awareness That There Are Two Sides,"

Journal of Experimental Social Psychology 6 (1970), pp. 47–56.

86. D. G. Linz and S. Penrod, "Increasing Attorney Persuasiveness in the Courtroom," *Law and Psychology Review* 8 (1984), pp. 1–47; R. B. Zajonc, "Attitudinal Effects of Mere Exposure," *Journal of Personality and Social Psychology Monograph* 9 (1968), pp. 1–27; R. Petty and J. Cacioppo, *Attitudes and Persuasion: Classic and Contemporary Approaches* (Dubuque, IA: Brown, 1981).

87. Conger, *Winning 'Em Over.*

88. Zimbardo and Ebbeson, *Influencing Attitudes and Changing Behavior.*

89. M. Zellner, "Self-Esteem, Reception, and Influenceability," *Journal of Personality and Social Psychology* 15 (1970), pp. 87–93.

CHAPTER THIRTEEN

1. M. King and S. Stripling, "Blend of Generations," *Seattle Times*, March 12, 2001; T. S. Taylor, "An Age-Old Conflict," *Chicago Tribune*, January 7, 2001, p. C1; T. Aeppel, "Power Generation: Young and Old See Technology Sparking Friction on Shop Floor," *The Wall Street Journal*, April 7, 2000, p. A1; V. Uhland, "Generations at Crossroads," *Denver Rocky Mountain News*, February 6, 2000, p. J1.

2. J. A. Wall and R. R. Callister, "Conflict and Its Management," *Journal of Management* 21 (1995), pp. 515–58; D. Tjosvold, *Working Together to Get Things Done* (Lexington, MA: Lexington, 1986), pp. 114–15.

3. The conflict process is described in K. W. Thomas, "Conflict and Negotiation Processes in Organizations," in M. D. Dunnette and L. M. Hough, eds., *Handbook of Industrial and Organizational Psychology*, 2nd ed., vol. 3 (Palo Alto, CA: Consulting Psychologists Press, 1992), pp. 651–718; L. Pondy, "Organizational Conflict: Concepts and Models," *Administrative Science Quarterly* 2 (1967), pp. 296–320.

4. A. C. Ward, "Another Look at How Toyota Integrates Product Development," *Harvard Business Review*, July–August 1998, pp. 36–49.

5. L. H. Pelled, K. R. Xin, and A. M. Weiss, "No Es Como Mi: Relational Demography and Conflict in a Mexican Production Facility," *Journal of Occupational and Organizational Psychology* 74 (March 2001), pp. 63–84; L. H. Pelled, K. M. Eisenhardt, and K. R. Xin, "Exploring the Black Box: An Analysis of Work Group Diversity, Conflict, and Performance," *Administrative Science Quarterly* 44 (March 1999), pp. 1–28; A. C. Amason, "Distinguishing the Effects of Functional and Dysfunctional Conflict on Strategic Decision Making: Resolving a Paradox for Top Management Teams," *Academy of Management Journal* 39 (1996), pp. 123–48; K. A. Jehn, "A Multimethod Examination of the Benefits and Detriments of Intragroup Conflict," *Administrative Science Quarterly* 40 (1995), pp. 256–82.

6. J. M. Brett, D. L. Shapiro, and A. L. Lytle, "Breaking the Bonds of Reciprocity in Negotiations," *Academy of Management Journal* 41 (August 1998), pp. 410–24; G. E. Martin and T. J. Bergman, "The Dynamics of Behavioral Response to Conflict in the Workplace," *Journal of Occupational and Organizational Psychology* 69 (December 1996), pp. 377–87; G. Wolf, "Conflict Episodes," in M. H. Bazerman and R. J. Lewicki , eds., *Negotiating in Organizations* (Beverly Hills, CA: Sage, 1983), pp. 135–40; L. R. Pondy, "Organizational Conflict: Concepts and Models," *Administrative Science Quarterly* 12 (1967), pp. 296–320.

7. H. Witteman, "Analyzing Interpersonal Conflict: Nature of Awareness, Type of Initiating Event, Situational Perceptions, and Management Styles," *Western Journal of Communications* 56 (1992), pp. 248–80; F. J. Barrett and D. L. Cooperrider, "Generative Metaphor Intervention: A New Approach for Working with Systems Divided by Conflict and Caught in Defensive Perception," *Journal of Applied Behavioral Science* 26 (1990), pp. 219–39.

8. Wall and Callister, "Conflict and Its Management," pp. 526–33.

9. T. Wallace, "Fear and Loathing," *Australian Financial Review (Boss Magazine)*, April 12, 2001, p. 42.

10. R. R. Blake and J. S. Mouton, *Solving Costly Organizational Conflicts* (San Francisco: Jossey-Bass, 1984).

11. F. Rose, "The Eisner School of Business," *Fortune*, July 6, 1998, pp. 29–30. For a more favorable interpretation of conflict at Disney, see S. Wetlaufer, "Common Sense and Conflict: An Interview with Disney's Michael Eisner," *Harvard Business Review* 78 (January–February 2000), pp. 114–24.

12. M. Rempel and R. J. Fisher, "Perceived Threat, Cohesion, and Group Problem Solving in Intergroup Conflict," *International Journal of Conflict Management* 8 (1997), pp. 216–34.

13. Amason, "Distinguishing the Effects of Functional and Dysfunctional Conflict on Strategic Decision Making"; L. L. Putnam, "Productive Conflict: Negotiation as Implicit Coordination," *International Journal of Conflict Management* 5 (1994), pp. 285–99; D. Tjosvold, *The Conflict-Positive Organization* (Reading, MA: Addison-Wesley, 1991); R. A. Baron, "Positive Effects of Conflict: A Cognitive Perspective," *Employee Responsibilities and Rights Journal* 4 (1991), pp. 25–36.

14. K. M. Eisenhardt, J. L. Kahwajy, and L. J. Bourgeois III, "Conflict and Strategic Choice: How Top Management Teams Disagree," *California Management Review* 39 (Winter 1997), pp. 42–62; J. K. Bouwen and R. Fry, "Organizational Innovation and Learning: Four Patterns of Dialog between the Dominant Logic and the New Logic," *International Studies of Management and Organizations* 21 (1991), pp. 37–51.

15. R. Rosen, P. Digh, M. Singer, and C. Phillips, *Global Literacies* (New York: Simon & Schuster, 2000), pp. 285–89; "Face Value: Tractebel the Intractable," *The Economist*, February 27, 1999, p. 66.

16. S. Armour, "Moderate Amounts of Conflict Contribute to Healthy Workplace," *Des Moines (IA) Register*, May 20, 1997, p. 8.

17. R. E. Walton and J. M. Dutton, "The Management of Conflict: A Model and Review," *Administrative Science Quarterly* 14 (1969), pp. 73–84.

18. D. Evans, "Team Players," *Canadian Business*, August 1991, pp. 28–31.

19. D. M. Brock, D. Barry, and D. C. Thomas, "'Your Forward Is Our Reverse, Your Right, Our Wrong': Rethinking Multinational Planning Processes in Light of National Culture," *International Business Review* 9 (December 2000), pp. 687–701.

20. For a fuller discussion of conflict across the generations, see R. Zemke and B. Filipczak, *Generations at Work: Managing the Clash of Veterans, Boomers, Xers, and Nexters in Your Workplace* (New York: AMACOM, 1999).

21. R. C. Liden, S. J. Wayne, and L. K. Bradway, "Task Interdependence as a Moderator of the Relation between Group Control and Performance," *Human Relations* 50 (1997), pp. 169–81; R. Wageman, "Interdependence and Group Effectiveness," *Administrative Science Quarterly* 40 (1995), pp. 145–80; M. A. Campion, G. J. Medsker, and A. C. Higgs, "Relations between Work Group Characteristics and Effectiveness: Implications for Designing Effective Work Groups," *Personnel Psychology* 46 (1993), pp. 823–50; M. N. Kiggundu, "Task Interdependence and the Theory of Job Design," *Academy of Management Review* 6 (1981), pp. 499–508.

22. K. Jelin, "A Multimethod Examination of the Benefits and Detriments of Intragroup Conflict," *Administrative Science Quarterly* 40 (1995), pp. 245–82; P. C. Earley and G. B. Northcraft, "Goal Setting, Resource Interdependence, and Conflict Management," in M. A. Rahim, ed., *Managing Conflict: An Interdisciplinary Approach* (New York: Praeger, 1989), pp. 161–70.

23. J. D. Thompson, *Organizations in Action* (New York: McGraw-Hill, 1967), pp. 54–56.

24. K. H. Doerr, T. R. Mitchell, and T. D. Klastorin, "Impact of Material Flow Policies and Goals on Job Outcomes," *Journal of Applied Psychology* 81 (1996), pp. 142–52.

25. W. W. Notz, F. A. Starke, and J. Atwell, "The Manager as Arbitrator: Conflicts over Scarce Resources," in Bazerman and Lewicki, eds., *Negotiating in Organizations*, pp. 143–64.

26. P. Roberts, "Sony Changes the Game," *Fast Company* 10 (1997), p. 116.

27. A. Risberg, "Employee Experiences of Acquisition Processes," *Journal of World Business* 36 (March 2001), pp. 58–84.

28. Brett et al., "Breaking the Bonds of Reciprocity in Negotiations"; R. A. Baron, "Reducing Organizational Conflict: An Incompatible Response Approach," *Journal of Applied Psychology* 69 (1984), pp. 272–79.

29. K. D. Grimsley, "Slings and Arrows on the Job," *Washington Post*, July 12, 1998, p. H1; "Flame Throwers," *Director* 50 (July 1997), p. 36.

30. T. A. Abma, "Stakeholder Conflict: A Case Study," *Evaluation and Program Planning* 23 (May 2000), pp. 199–210; J. W. Jackson and E. R. Smith, "Conceptualizing Social Identity: A New Framework and Evidence for the Impact of Different Dimensions," *Personality and Social Psychology Bulletin* 25 (January 1999), pp. 120–35.

31. D. C. Dryer and L. M. Horowitz, "When Do Opposites Attract? Interpersonal Complementarity versus Similarity," *Journal of Personality and Social Psychology* 72 (1997), pp. 592–603.

32. S. Vaughn, "Common Ground for Differences," *Los Angeles Times*, July 15, 2001, p. W1.

33. K. W. Thomas, "Conflict and Conflict Management," in M. D. Dunnette, ed., *Handbook of Industrial and Organizational Psychology* (Chicago: Rand McNally, 1976), pp. 889–935; R. R. Blake and J. S. Mouton, *The Managerial Grid* (Houston: Gulf, 1964); M. A. Rahim, "A Measure of Styles of Handling Interpersonal Conflict," *Academy of Management Journal* 26 (1983), pp. 368–76. A more complex variation of eight conflict styles is discussed in E. Van de Vliert and O. Janssen, "Description, Explanation, and Prescription of Intragroup Conflict Behaviors," in M. E. Turner, ed., *Groups at Work: Theory and Research* (Mahwah, NJ: Lawrence Erlbaum, 2001), pp. 267–97.

34. R. J. Lewicki and J. A. Litterer, Negotiation (Homewood, IL: Irwin, 1985), pp. 102–6; K. W. Thomas, "Toward Multi-Dimensional Values in Teaching: The Example of Conflict Behaviors," *Academy of Management Review* 2 (1977), pp. 484–90.

35. Jehn, "A Multimethod Examination of the Benefits and Detriments of Intragroup Conflict," p. 276.

36. M. Lyster et al., "The Changing Guard," *Orange County (CA) Business Journal*, May 7, 2001, p. 31.

37. L. Xiaohua and R. Germain, "Sustaining Satisfactory Joint Venture Relationships: The Role of Conflict Resolution Strategy," *Journal of International Business Studies* 29 (March 1998), pp. 179–96.

38. Tjosvold, *Working Together to Get Things Done*, chap. 2; D. W. Johnson, G. Maruyama, R. T. Johnson, D. Nelson, and S. Skon, "Effects of Cooperative, Competitive, and Individualistic Goal Structures on Achievement: A Meta-Analysis," *Psychological Bulletin* 89 (1981), pp. 47–62; R. J. Burke, "Methods of Resolving Superior–Subordinate Conflict: The Constructive Use of Subordinate Differences and Disagreements," *Organizational Behavior and Human Performance* 5 (1970), pp. 393–441.

39. K. Leung and D. Tjosvold, eds., *Conflict Management in the Asia Pacific* (Singapore: Wiley, 1998); M. A. Rahim and A. A. Blum, eds., *Global Perspectives on Organizational Conflict* (Westport, CT: Praeger, 1995); M. Rabie, *Conflict Resolution and Ethnicity* (Westport, CT: Praeger, 1994).

40. C. C. Chen, X. P. Chen, and J. R. Meindl, "How Can Cooperation Be Fostered? The Cultural Effects of Individualism–Collectivism," *Academy of Management Review* 23 (1998), pp. 285–304; S. M. Elsayed-Ekhouly and R. Buda, "Organizational Conflict: A Comparative Analysis of Conflict Styles across Cultures," *International Journal of Conflict Management* 7 (1996), pp. 71–81; D. K. Tse, J. Francis, and J. Walls, "Cultural Differences in Conducting Intra- and Inter-Cultural Negotiations: A Sino-Canadian Comparison," *Journal of International Business Studies* 25 (1994), pp. 537–55; S. Ting-Toomey et al., "Culture, Face Management, and Conflict Styles of Handling Interpersonal Conflict: A Study in Five Cultures," *International Journal of Conflict Management* 2 (1991), pp. 275–96.

41. L. Karakowsky, "Toward an Understanding of Women and Men at the Bargaining Table: Factors Affecting Negotiator Style and Influence in Multi-Party Negotiations," *Proceedings of the Annual ASAC Conference, Women in Management Division*, 1996, pp. 21–30; W. C. King, Jr., and T. D. Hinson, "The Influence of Sex and Equity Sensitivity on Relationship Preferences, Assessment of Opponent, and Outcomes in a Negotiation Experiment," *Journal of Management* 20 (1994), pp. 605–24; R. Lewicki, J. Litterer, D. Saunders, and J. Minton, eds., *Negotiation: Readings,*

Exercises, and Cases (Homewood, IL: Irwin, 1993).

42. E. Van de Vliert, "Escalative Intervention in Small Group Conflicts," *Journal of Applied Behavioral Science* 21 (Winter 1985), pp. 19–36.

43. M. B. Pinto, J. K. Pinto, and J. E. Prescott, "Antecedents and Consequences of Project Team Cross-Functional Cooperation," *Management Science* 39 (1993), pp. 1281–97; M. Sherif, "Superordinate Goals in the Reduction of Intergroup Conflict," *American Journal of Sociology* 68 (1958), pp. 349–58.

44. L. Mulitz, "Flying Off over Office Politics," *InfoWorld,* November 6, 2000.

45. X. M. Song, J. Xile, B. Dyer, "Antecedents and Consequences of Marketing Managers' Conflict-Handling Behaviors," *Journal of Marketing* 64, January 2000, pp. 50–66; K. M. Eisenhardt, J. L. Kahwajy, and L. J. Bourgeois III, "How Management Teams Can Have a Good Fight," *Harvard Business Review,* July–August 1997, pp. 77–85.

46. Song et al., "Antecedents and Consequences of Marketing Managers' Conflict-Handling Behaviors."

47. "Teamwork Polishes This Diamond," *Philippine Daily Inquirer,* October 4, 2000, p. 10.

48. "American Factories Halt Their Assembly Lines," *Globe and Mail (Toronto),* January 7, 1995, p. D4.

49. This strategy and other conflict management practices in joint military operations are fully discussed in E. Elron, B. Shamir, and E. Ben-Ari, "Why Don't They Fight Each Other? Cultural Diversity and Operational Unity in Multinational Forces," *Armed Forces and Society* 26 (October 1999), pp. 73–97.

50. R. J. Fisher, E. Maltz, and B. J. Jaworski, "Enhancing Communication between Marketing and Engineering: The Moderating Role of Relative Functional Identification," *Journal of Marketing* 61 (1997), pp. 54–70. For a discussion of minimizing conflict through understanding as "other point multiplicity," see T. A. Abma, "Stakeholder Conflict: A Case Study," *Evaluation and Program Planning* 23 (May 2000), pp. 199–210.

51. A. Zurcher, "Techies and Non-Techies Don't Always Interface Well," *Washington Post,* September 3, 2000, p. L5.

52. D. Woodruff, "Crossing Culture Divide Early Clears Merger Paths," *Asian Wall Street Journal,* May 28, 2001, p. 9.

53. L. Ellinor and G. Gerard, *Dialogue: Rediscovering the Transforming Power of Conversation* (New York: Wiley, 1998); W. N. Isaacs, "Taking Flight: Dialog, Collective Thinking, and Organizational Learning," *Organizational Dynamics,* Autumn 1993, pp. 24–39; E. H. Schein, "On Dialog, Culture, and Organizational Learning," *Organizational Dynamics,* Autumn 1993, pp. 40–51; P. M. Senge, *The Fifth Discipline* (New York: Doubleday Currency, 1990), pp. 238–49.

54. P. R. Lawrence and J. W. Lorsch, *Organization and Environment* (Homewood, IL: Irwin, 1969).

55. E. Horwitt, "Knowledge, Knowledge, Who's Got the Knowledge?" *Computerworld,* April 8, 1996, pp. 80, 81, 84.

56. D. G. Pruitt and P. J. Carnevale, *Negotiation in Social Conflict* (Buckingham, UK: Open University Press, 1993), p. 2; J. A. Wall, Jr., *Negotiation: Theory and Practice* (Glenview, IL: Scott Foresman, 1985), p. 4.

57. L. Edson, "The Negotiation Industry," *Across the Board,* April 2000, pp. 14–20.

58. For a critical view of collaboration in negotiation, see J. M. Brett, "Managing Organizational Conflict," *Professional Psychology: Research and Practice* 15 (1984), pp. 664–78.

59. R. E. Fells, "Overcoming the Dilemmas in Walton and McKersie's Mixed Bargaining Strategy," *Industrial Relations* (Laval) 53 (March 1998), pp. 300–25; R. E. Fells, "Developing Trust in Negotiation," *Employee Relations* 15 (1993), pp. 33–45.

60. L. Thompson, *The Mind and Heart of the Negotiator* (Upper Saddle River, NJ: Prentice Hall, 1998), chap. 2; R. Stagner and H. Rosen, *Psychology of Union—Management Relations* (Belmont, CA: Wadsworth, 1965), pp. 95–96, 108–10; R. E. Walton and R. B. McKersie, *A Behavioral Theory of Labor Negotiations: An Analysis of a Social In-*

teraction System (New York: McGraw-Hill, 1965), pp. 41–46.

61. J. Mayfield, M. Mayfield, D. Martin, and P. Herbig, "How Location Impacts International Business Negotiations," *Review of Business* 19 (December 1998), pp. 21–24; J. W. Salacuse and J. Z. Rubin, "Your Place or Mine? Site Location and Negotiation," *Negotiation Journal* 6 (January 1990), pp. 5–10; Lewicki and Litterer, *Negotiation,* pp. 144–46.

62. Lewicki and Litterer, *Negotiation,* pp. 146–51; B. Kniveton, *The Psychology of Bargaining* (Aldershot, UK: Avebury, 1989), pp. 76–79.

63. Pruitt and Carnevale, *Negotiation in Social Conflict,* pp. 59–61; Lewicki and Litterer, *Negotiation,* pp. 151–54.

64. B. M. Downie, "When Negotiations Fail: Causes of Breakdown and Tactics for Breaking the Stalemate," *Negotiation Journal,* April 1991, pp. 175–86.

65. Pruitt and Carnevale, *Negotiation in Social Conflict,* pp. 56–58; Lewicki and Litterer, *Negotiation,* pp. 215–22.

66. V. V. Murray, T. D. Jick, and P. Bradshaw, "To Bargain or Not to Bargain? The Case of Hospital Budget Cuts," in Brazerman and Lewicki, eds., *Negotiating in Organizations,* pp. 272–95.

67. S. Doctoroff, "Reengineering Negotiations," *Sloan Management Review* 39 (March 1998), pp. 63–71; R. L. Lewicki, A. Hiam, and K. Olander, *Think before You Speak: The Complete Guide to Strategic Negotiation* (New York: Wiley, 1996); G. B. Northcraft and M. A. Neale, "Joint Effects of Assigned Goals and Training on Negotiator Performance," *Human Performance* 7 (1994), pp. 257–72.

68. M. A. Neale and M. H. Bazerman, *Cognition and Rationality in Negotiation* (New York: Free Press, 1991), pp. 29–31; L. L. Thompson, "Information Exchange in Negotiation," *Journal of Experimental Social Psychology* 27 (1991), pp. 161–79.

69. Y. Paik and R. L. Tung, "Negotiating with East Asians: How to Attain 'Win-Win' Outcomes," *Management International Review* 39 (1999), pp. 103–22; L. Thompson, E. Peterson, and S. E. Brodt, "Team Negotiation: An Examination of Integrative and Distributive Bargaining," *Journal of Personality and Social Psychology* 70 (1996), pp. 66–78.

70. L. L. Putnam and M. E. Roloff, eds., *Communication and Negotiation* (Newbury Park, CA: Sage, 1992).

71. L. Hall, ed., *Negotiation: Strategies for Mutual Gain* (Newbury Park, CA: Sage, 1993); D. Ertel, "How to Design a Conflict Management Procedure That Fits Your Dispute," *Sloan Management Review* 32 (Summer 1991), pp. 29–42.

72. Lewicki and Litterer, *Negotiation*, pp. 89–93.

73. J. J. Zhao, "The Chinese Approach to International Business Negotiation," *Journal of Business Communication*, July 2000, pp. 209–37; Paik and Tung, "Negotiating with East Asians"; N. J. Adler, *International Dimensions of Organizational Behavior*, 2nd ed., (Belmont, CA: Wadsworth, 1991), pp. 180–81.

74. Kniveton, *The Psychology of Bargaining*, pp. 100–1; J. Z. Rubin and B. R. Brown, *The Social Psychology of Bargaining and Negotiation* (New York: Academic, 1976), chap. 9; Brett, "Managing Organizational Conflict," pp. 670–71.

75. B. H. Sheppard, R. J. Lewicki, and J. W. Monton, *Organizational Justice: The Search for Fairness in the Workplace* (New York: Lexington, 1992).

76. L. B. Bingham, "Mediating Employment Disputes: Perceptions of Redress at the United States Postal Service," *Review of Public Personnel Administration* 17 (Spring 1997), pp. 20–30; R. Folger and J. Greenberg, "Procedural Justice: An Interpretive Analysis of Personnel Systems," *Research in Personnel and Human Resources Management* 3 (1985), pp. 141–83.

77. A. R. Elangovan, "The Manager as the Third Party: Deciding How to Intervene in Employee Disputes," in R. Lewicki, J. Litterer, and D. Saunders, eds., *Negotiation: Readings, Exercises, and Cases*, 3rd ed., (New York: McGraw-Hill, 1999), pp. 458–69; L. L. Putnam, "Beyond Third Party Role: Disputes and Managerial Intervention," *Employee Responsibilities and Rights Journal* 7 (1994), pp. 23–36; Sheppard et al., *Organizational Justice*.

78. M. A. Neale and M. H. Bazerman, *Cognition and Rationality in Negotiation* (New York: Free Press, 1991), pp. 140–42.

79. B. H. Sheppard, "Managers as Inquisitors: Lessons from the Law," in M. Bazerman and R. J. Lewicki, eds., *Bargaining inside Organizations* (Beverly Hills, CA: Sage, 1983), pp. 193–213.

80. R. Cropanzano, H. Aguinis, M. Schminke, and D. L. Denham, "Disputant Reactions to Managerial Conflict Resolution Tactics," *Group and Organization Management* 24 (June 1999), pp. 124–53; R. Karambayya and J. M. Brett, "Managers Handling Disputes: Third Party Roles and Perceptions of Fairness," *Academy of Management Journal* 32 (1989), pp. 687–704.

81. A. R. Elangovan, "Managerial Intervention in Organizational Disputes: Testing a Prescriptive Model of Strategy Selection," *International Journal of Conflict Management* 4 (1998), pp. 301–35.

82. J. P. Meyer, J. M. Gemmell, and P. G. Irving, "Evaluating the Management of Interpersonal Conflict in Organizations: A Factor-Analytic Study of Outcome Criteria," *Canadian Journal of Administrative Sciences* 14 (1997), pp. 1–13.

83. C. Hirschman, "Order in the Hearing!" *HRMagazine* 46 (July 2001), p. 58; S. L. Hayford, "Alternative Dispute Resolution," *Business Horizons* 43 (January–February 2000), pp. 2–4.

84. D. Hechler, "No Longer a Novelty: ADR Winning Corporate Acceptance," *Fulton County (GA) Daily Report*, June 29, 2001.

85. M. Barrier, "A Working Alternative for Settling Disputes," *Nation's Business* 86 (July, 1998) pp. 43–46.

CHAPTER FOURTEEN

1. L. Veit, "Ethical Matters," *Credit Union Management* 24 (June 2001), pp. 18–20; P. Gallagher, "How Can You Be a Great Leader—Drive the Vision," *Success* 48 (April 2001), pp. 28ff.; S-J. Yim, "Behind the Mystique at the Top," *Portland Oregonian*, April 29, 2001, p. L11; C. Fox, "CEOs Slipping into Old Habits," *Australian Financial Review*, February 6, 2001, p. 38; "New Economy, Old Values," *Corporate Report Wisconsin* 16 (October 2000), pp. 12ff.; "Leadership A to Z" (Interview), *Training and Development*, March 2000, p. 58; P. Clark and E. Mychasuk, "The New Leadership," *Boss Magazine*, September 11, 2000, p. 32.

2. R. A. Barker, "How Can We Train Leaders if We Do Not Know What Leadership Is?" *Human Relations* 50 (1997), pp. 343–62; P. C. Drucker, "Foreward," in F. Hesselbein et al., *The Leader of the Future* (San Francisco, CA: Jossey-Bass, 1997).

3. D. Miller, M. F. R. Ket de Vries, and J. M. Toulouse, "Top Executive Locus of Control and Its Relationship to Strategy-Making, Structure, and Environment," *Academy of Management Journal* 25 (1982), pp. 237–53; P. Selznick, *Leadership in Administration* (Evanston, IL: Row, Peterson, 1957), p. 37.

4. M. Groves, "Cream Rises to the Top, but from a Small Crop," *Los Angeles Times*, June 8, 1998. A recent study also reported that only 3 percent of executives in large firms agreed that their companies develop leadership talent quickly and effectively. See H. Handfield-Jones, "How Executives Grow," *McKinsey Quarterly*, January 2000, pp. 116–23.

5. C. L. Cole, "Eight Values Bring Unity to a Worldwide Company," *Workforce* 80 (March 2001), pp. 44–45.

6. C. A. Beatty, "Implementing Advanced Manufacturing Technologies: Rules of the Road," *Sloan Management Review*, Summer 1992, pp. 49–60; J. M. Howell and C. A. Higgins, "Champions of Technological Innovation," *Administrative Science Quarterly* 35 (1990), pp. 317–41.

7. Many of these perspectives are summarized in R. N. Kanungo, "Leadership in Organizations: Looking Ahead to the 21st Century," *Canadian Psychology* 39 (Spring 1998), pp. 71–82.

8. L. Ortiz, "Karenann Terrell Was a GM Loyalist, until DCX Called," *Automotive News*, May 21, 2001, p. 18T-B; S. Carney and D. Howes, "Exodus Reshapes Chrysler," *Detroit News*, March 18, 2001, p. 1; L. Vaas, "Putting Pedal to the Metal," *EWeek*, September 11, 2000, p. 67; C. J. Murray, "Auto Engineer Helps Steer Carmaker to Internet Era," *Electronic Engineering Times*, May 22, 2000, pp. 34–37.

9. J. Kochanski, "Competency-Based Management," *Training and Development*, October 1997, pp. 40–44; Hay Group et al., *Raising the Bar: Using Competencies to Enhance Employee Performance* (Scottsdale, AZ: American Compensation Association, 1996); L. M. Spencer and S. M. Spencer, *Competence*

at Work: Models for Superior Performance (New York: Wiley, 1993).

10. T. Takala, "Plato on Leadership," *Journal of Business Ethics* 17 (May 1998), pp. 785–98.

11. R. M. Stogdill, *Handbook of Leadership* (New York: Free Press, 1974), chap. 5.

12. Most elements of this list were derived from S. A. Kirkpatrick and E. A. Locke, "Leadership: Do Traits Matter?" *Academy of Management Executive* 5 (May 1991), pp. 48–60. Several of these ideas are also discussed in H. B. Gregersen, A. J. Morrison, and J. S. Black, "Developing Leaders for the Global Frontier," *Sloan Management Review* 40 (Fall 1998), pp. 21–32; R. J. House and R. N. Aditya, "The Social Scientific Study of Leadership: Quo Vadis?" *Journal of Management* 23 (1997), pp. 409–73; R. J. House and M. L. Baetz, "Leadership: Some Empirical Generalizations and New Research Directions," *Research in Organizational Behavior* 1 (1979), pp. 341–423.

13. House and Aditya, "The Social Scientific Study of Leadership."

14. C. Savoye, "Workers Say Honesty Is Best Company Policy," *Christian Science Monitor*, June 15, 2000; "Canadian CEOs Give Themselves Top Marks for Leadership!" *Canada NewsWire*, September 9, 1999; J. M. Kouzes and B. Z. Posner, *Credibility: How Leaders Gain and Lose It, Why People Demand It* (San Francisco: Jossey-Bass, 1993).

15. J. George, "Emotions and Leadership: The Role of Emotional Intelligence," *Human Relations* 53 (August 2000), pp. 1027–55; D. Goleman, What Makes a Leader?" *Harvard Business Review* 76 (November–December 1998), pp. 92–102; J. D. Mayer and P. Salovey, "The Intelligence of Emotional Intelligence," *Intelligence* 17 (1993), pp. 433–42.

16. J. A. Kolb, "The Relationship between Self-Monitoring and Leadership in Student Project Groups," *Journal of Business Communication* 35 (April 1998), pp. 264–82; S. J. Zaccaro, R. J. Foti, and D. A. Kenny, "Self-Monitoring and Trait-Based Variance in Leadership: An Investigation of Leader Flexibility across Multiple Group Situations," *Journal of Applied Psychology* 76 (1991), pp. 308–15; S. E. Cronshaw and R. J.

Ellis, "A Process Investigation of Self-Monitoring and Leader Emergence," *Small Group Research* 22 (1991), pp. 403–20; S. J. Zaccaro, R. J. Foti, and D. A. Kenny, "Self-Monitoring and Trait-Based Variance in Leadership: An Investigation of Leader Flexibility across Multiple Group Situations," *Journal of Applied Psychology* 76 (1991); pp. 308–15; G. H. Dobbins, W. S. Long, E. J. Dedrick, and T. C. Clemons, "The Role of Self-Monitoring and Gender on Leader Emergence: A Labouratory and Field Study," *Journal of Management* 16 (1990), pp. 609–18.

17. "S Korea H&CB's Kim Jung-tae Named New Kookmin Bank CEO," *Dow Jones International News*, July 25, 2001; L. Nakarmi, "Here Come the Mavericks," *Asiaweek*, April 9, 1999; "Korea's Kim Jung Tae," *Business Week*, June 29, 1998.

18. R. G. Lord and K. J. Maher, *Leadership and Information Processing: Linking Perceptions and Performance* (Cambridge, MA: Unwin Hyman, 1991).

19. W. C. Byham, "Grooming Next-Millennium Leaders," *HRMagazine* 44 (February 1999), pp. 46–50; R. Zemke and S. Zemke, "Putting Competencies to Work," *Training* 36 (January 1999), pp. 70–76.

20. G. A. Yukl, *Leadership in Organizations*, 3rd ed. (Englewood Cliffs, NJ: Prentice Hall, 1994), pp. 53–75; R. Likert, *New Patterns of Management* (New York: McGraw-Hill, 1961).

21. M. D. Abrashoff, "Retention through Redemption," *Harvard Business Review* 79 (February 2001), pp. 136–41.

22. A. K. Korman, "Consideration, Initiating Structure, and Organizational Criteria—A Review," *Personnel Psychology* 19 (1966), pp 349–62; E. A. Fleishman, "Twenty Years of Consideration and Structure," in E. A. Fleishman and J. C. Hunt, eds., *Current Developments in the Study of Leadership* (Carbondale, IL: Southern Illinois University Press, 1973), pp. 1–40.

23. V. V. Baba, "Serendipity in Leadership: Initiating Structure and Consideration in the Classroom," *Human Relations* 42 (1989), pp. 509–25.

24. P. Weissenberg and M. H. Kavanagh, "The Independence of Initiating Structure and Consideration: A Review

of the Evidence," *Personnel Psychology* 25 (1972), pp. 119–30; Stogdill, *Handbook of Leadership*, chap. 11; R. L. Kahn, "The Prediction of Productivity," *Journal of Social Issues* 12 (2) (1956), pp. 41–49.

25. R. R. Blake and A. A. McCanse, Leadership Dilemmas—Grid Solutions (Houston: Gulf, 1991); R. R. Blake and J. S. Mouton, "Management by Grid Principles or Situationalism: Which?" *Group and Organization Studies* 7 (1982), pp. 207–10.

26. L. L. Larson, J. G. Hunt, and R. N. Osborn, "The Great Hi–Hi Leader Behavior Myth: A Lesson from Occam's Razor," *Academy of Management Journal* 19 (1976), pp. 628–41; S. Kerr, C. A. Schriesheim, C. J. Murphy, and R. M. Stogdill, "Towards a Contingency Theory of Leadership Based upon the Consideration and Initiating Structure Literature," *Organizational Behavior and Human Performance* 12 (1974), pp. 62–82; A. K. Korman, "Consideration, Initiating Structure, and Organizational Criteria—A Review," *Personnel Psychology* 19 (1966), pp. 349–62.

27. R. Tannenbaum and W. H. Schmidt, "How to Choose a Leadership Pattern," *Harvard Business Review*, May–June 1973, pp. 162–80.

28. For a recent discussion of the contingency perspective of leadership and emotional intelligence, see D. Goleman, "Leadership That Gets Results," *Harvard Business Review* 78 (March–April 2000), pp. 78–90.

29. M. G. Evans, "The Effects of Supervisory Behavior on the Path–Goal Relationship," *Organizational Behavior and Human Performance* 5 (1970), pp. 277–98; M. G. Evans, "Extensions of a Path–Goal Theory of Motivation," *Journal of Applied Psychology* 59 (1974), pp. 172–78; R. J. House, "A Path–Goal Theory of Leader Effectiveness," *Administrative Science Quarterly* 16 (1971), pp. 321–38.

30. R. J. House and T. R. Mitchell, "Path–Goal Theory of Leadership," *Journal of Contemporary Business*, Autumn 1974, pp. 81–97.

31. M. Fulmer, "Learning across a Living Company: The Shell Companies' Experiences," *Organizational Dynamics* 27 (Autumn 1998), pp. 61–69; R. Wageman, "Case Study: Critical Success

Factors for Creating Superb Self-Managing Teams at Xerox," *Compensation and Benefits Review* 29 (September–October 1997), pp. 31–41.

32. M. E. McGill and J. W. Slocum, Jr., "A Little Leadership, Please?" *Organizational Dynamics* 39 (Winter 1998), pp. 39–49; R. J. Doyle, "The Case of a Servant Leader: John F. Donnelly, Sr." in R. P. Vecchio, ed., *Leadership: Understanding the Dynamics of Power and Influence in Organizations* (Notre Dame, IN: University of Notre Dame Press, 1997), pp. 439–57.

33. R. J. House, "Path–Goal Theory of Leadership: Lessons, Legacy, and a Reformulated Theory," *Leadership Quarterly* 7 (1996), pp. 323–52.

34. J. C. Wofford and L. Z. Liska, "Path–Goal Theories of Leadership: A Meta-Analysis," *Journal of Management* 19 (1993), pp. 857–76; J. Indvik, "Path–Goal Theory of Leadership: A Meta-Analysis," *Academy of Management Proceedings*, 1986, pp. 189–92.

35. R. T. Keller, "A Test of the Path–Goal Theory of Leadership with Need for Clarity as a Moderator in Research and Development Organizations," *Journal of Applied Psychology* 74 (1989), pp. 208–12.

36. J. M. Jermier, "The Path–Goal Theory of Leadership: A Subtextural Analysis," *Leadership Quarterly* 7 (1996), pp. 311–16.

37. House, "Path–Goal Theory of Leadership."

38. Wofford and Liska, "Path–Goal Theories of Leadership"; Yukl, *Leadership in Organizations*, pp. 102–4; Indvik, "Path–Goal Theory of Leadership."

39. C. A. Schriesheim and L. L. Neider, "Path–Goal Leadership Theory: The Long and Winding Road," *Leadership Quarterly* 7 (1996), pp. 317–21. One of the more prominent studies that found evidence against path–goal theory is H. K. Downey, J. E. Sheridan, and J. W. Slocum, "Analysis of Relationships among Leader Behavior, Subordinate Job Performance and Satisfaction: A Path–Goal Approach," *Academy of Management Journal* 18 (1975), pp. 253–62.

40. P. Hersey and K. H. Blanchard, *Management of Organizational Behavior: Utilizing Human Resources*, 5th ed. (Englewood Cliffs, NJ: Prentice Hall, 1988).

41. C. L. Graeff, "Evolution of Situational Leadership Theory: A Critical Review," *Leadership Quarterly* 8 (1997), pp. 153–70; W. Blank, J. R. Weitzel, and S. G. Green, "A Test of the Situational Leadership Theory," *Personnel Psychology* 43 (1990), pp. 579–97; R. P. Vecchio, "Situational Leadership Theory: An Examination of a Prescriptive Theory," *Journal of Applied Psychology* 72 (1987), pp. 444–51.

42. F. E. Fiedler, *A Theory of Leadership Effectiveness* (New York: McGraw-Hill, 1967); F. E. Fiedler and M. M. Chemers, *Leadership and Effective Management* (Glenview, IL: Scott Foresman, 1974).

43. F .E. Fiedler, "Engineer the Job to Fit the Manager," *Harvard Business Review* 43 (5) (1965), pp. 115–22.

44. For a summary of criticisms, see Yukl, *Leadership in Organizations*, pp. 197–98.

45. N. Nicholson, *Executive Instinct* (New York: Crown, 2000).

46. P. M. Podsakoff and S. B. MacKenzie, "Kerr and Jermier's Substitutes for Leadership Model: Background, Empirical Assessment, and Suggestions for Future Research," *Leadership Quarterly* 8 (1997), pp. 117–32; P. M. Podsakoff, B. P. Niehoff, S. B. MacKenzie, and M. L. Williams, "Do Substitutes Really Substitute for Leadership? An Empirical Examination of Kerr and Jermier's Situational Leadership Model," *Organizational Behavior and Human Decision Processes* 54 (1993), pp. 1–44.

47. This observation has also been made by C. A. Schriesheim, "Substitutes-for-Leadership Theory: Development and Basic Concepts," *Leadership Quarterly* 8 (1997), pp. 103–8.

48. D. Anfuso, "Core Values Shape W. L. Gore's Innovative Culture," *Workforce* 78 (March 1999), pp. 48–53; A. Dominguez, "Employees Flourish at No-Boss Firm," *Deseret News (Salt Lake City, UT)*, July 4, 1998; M. Kaplan, "You Have No Boss," *Fast Company* 11 (November 1997), p. 226.

49. D. F. Elloy and A. Randolph, "The Effect of Superleader Behavior on Autonomous Work Groups in a Government Operated Railway Service," *Public Personnel Management* 26 (Summer 1997), pp. 257–72.

50. C. Manz and H. Sims, *Superleadership; Getting to the Top by Motivating Others* (San Francisco, CA: Berkley, 1990).

51. C. P. Neck and C. C. Manz, "Thought Self-Leadership: The Impact of Mental Strategies Training on Employee Cognition, Behavior, and Affect," *Journal of Organizational Behavior* 17 (1996), pp. 445–67.

52. D. Tarrant, "Boss Aha!" *Australian Financial Review*, December 29, 2000, p. 24.

53. R. Eglin, "Leadership Success: The Key Ingredient," *Sunday Times (London)*, July 22, 2001; A. R. Gold, M. Hirano, and Y. Yokoyama, "An Outsider Takes On Japan: An Interview with Nissan's Carlos Ghosn," *McKinsey Quarterly*, January 2001, p. 95; P. Sellers, "The 50 Most Powerful Women in American Business," *Fortune*, October 12, 1998, pp. 76–98; R. Slater, *Jack Welch and the GE Way: Management Insights and Leadership Secrets of the Legendary CEO* (New York: McGraw-Hill, 1998); K. Freiberg and J. Freiberg, *Nuts! Southwest Airlines' Crazy Recipe for Business and Personal Success* (New York: Bantam Doubleday Dell, 1998).

54. J. M. Howell and B. J. Avolio, "Transformational Leadership, Transactional Leadership, Locus of Control, and Support for Innovation: Key Predictors of Consolidated-Business-Unit Performance," *Journal of Applied Psychology* 78 (1993), pp. 891–902; J. A. Conger and R. N. Kanungo, "Perceived Behavioral Attributes of Charismatic Leadership," *Canadian Journal of Behavioral Science* 24 (1992), pp. 86–102; J. Seltzer and B. M. Bass, "Transformational Leadership: Beyond Initiation and Consideration," *Journal of Management* 16 (1990), pp. 693–703.

55. B. J. Avolio and B. M. Bass, "Transformational Leadership, Charisma, and Beyond," in J. G. Hunt, H. P. Dachler, B. R. Baliga, and C. A. Schriesheim, eds., *Emerging Leadership Vistas* (Lexington, MA: Lexington, 1988), pp. 29–49.

56. J. Kotter, *A Force for Change* (Cambridge, MA: Harvard Business School Press, 1990); W. Bennis and B. Nanus, *Leaders: The Strategies for Taking Charge* (New York: Harper & Row, 1985), p. 21; A. Zaleznik, "Managers and Leaders: Are They Different?" *Harvard Business Review* 55 (5) (1977), pp. 67–78.

57. C. P. Egri and S. Herman, "Leadership in the North American Environmental Sector: Values, Leadership Styles, and Contexts of Environmental Leaders and Their Organizations," *Academy of Management Journal* 43 (August 2000), pp. 571–604.

58. For discussion on the tendency to slide from transformational to transactional leadership, see W. Bennis, *An Invented Life: Reflections on Leadership and Change* (Reading, MA: Addison-Wesley, 1993).

59. L. Rittenhouse, "Dennis W. Bakke— Empowering a Workforce with Principles," *Electricity Journal*, January 1998, pp. 48–59.

60. J. A. Conger and R. N. Kanungo, "Toward a Behavioral Theory of Charismatic Leadership in Organizational Settings," *Academy of Management Review* 12 (1987), pp. 637–47; R. J. House, "A 1976 Theory of Charismatic Leadership," in J. G. Hunt and L. L. Larson, eds., *Leadership: The Cutting Edge* (Carbondale, IL: Southern Illinois University Press, 1977), pp. 189–207.

61. Y. A. Nur, "Charisma and Managerial Leadership: The Gift That Never Was," *Business Horizons* 41 (July 1998), pp. 19–26; J. E. Barbuto, Jr., "Taking the Charisma out of Transformational Leadership," *Journal of Social Behavior and Personality* 12 (September 1997), pp. 689–97.

62. L. Sooklal, "The Leader as a Broker of Dreams," *Organizational Studies,* 1989, pp. 833–55.

63. I. M. Levin, "Vision Revisited," *Journal of Applied Behavioral Science* 36 (March 2000), pp. 91–107; J. M. Stewart, "Future State Visioning—A Powerful Leadership Process," *Long Range Planning* 26 (December 1993), pp. 89–98; Bennis and Nanus, *Leaders,* pp. 27–33, 89.

64. T. J. Peters, "Symbols, Patterns, and Settings: An Optimistic Case for Getting Things Done," *Organizational Dynamics* 7 (Autumn 1978), pp. 2–23.

65. I. R. Baum, E. A. Locke, and S. A. Kirkpatrick, "A Longitudinal Study of the Relation of Vision and Vision Communication to Venture Growth in Entrepreneurial Firms," *Journal of Applied Psychology* 83 (1998), pp. 43–54; S. A. Kirkpatrick and E. A. Locke, "Direct and Indirect Effects of Three Core Charismatic Leadership Components on Performance and Attitudes," *Journal of Applied Psychology* 81 (1996), pp. 36–51.

66. G. T. Fairhurst and R. A. Sarr, *The Art of Framing: Managing the Language of Leadership* (San Francisco: Jossey-Bass, 1996); J. A. Conger, "Inspiring Others: The Language of Leadership," *Academy of Management Executive* 5 (February 1991), pp. 31–45.

67. R. S. Johnson, "Home Depot Renovates," *Fortune*, November 23, 1998, pp. 200–6.

68. Fairhurst and Sarr, *The Art of Framing*, chap. 5; J. Pfeffer, "Management as Symbolic Action: The Creation and Maintenance of Organizational Paradigms," *Research in Organizational Behavior* 3 (1981), pp. 1–52.

69. L. Black, "Hamburger Diplomacy," *Report on Business Magazine* 5 (August 1988), pp. 30–36; S. Franklin, *The Heroes: A Saga of Canadian Inspiration* (Toronto: McClelland and Stewart, 1967), p. 53.

70. McGill and Slocum, Jr., "A Little Leadership, Please?"; N. H. Snyder and M. Graves, "Leadership and Vision," *Business Horizons* 37 (January 1994), pp. 1–7; D. E. Berlew, "Leadership and Organizational Excitement," in D. A. Kolb, I. M. Rubin, and J. M. McIntyre, eds., *Organizational Psychology: A Book of Readings* (Englewood Cliffs, NJ: Prentice Hall, 1974).

71. M. F. R. Kets de Vries "Charisma in Action: The Transformational Abilities of Virgin's Richard Branson and ABB's Percy Barnevik," *Organizational Dynamics* 26 (Winter 1998), pp. 6–21; M. F. R. Kets de Vries, "Creative Leadership: Jazzing Up Business," *Chief Executive*, March 1997, pp. 64–66; F. Basile, "Hotshots in Business Impart Their Wisdom," *Indianapolis Business Journal*, July 21, 1997, p. A40.

72. E. M. Whitener, S. E. Brodt, M. A. Korsgaard, and J. M. Werner, "Managers as Initiators of Trust: An Exchange Relationship Framework for Understanding Managerial Trustworthy Behavior," *Academy of Management Review* 23 (July 1998), pp. 513–30; Bennis and Nanus, *Leaders*, pp. 43–55; Kouzes and Posner, *Credibility*.

73. J. J. Sosik, S. S. Kahai, and B. J. Avolio, "Transformational Leadership and Dimensions of Creativity: Motivating Idea Generation in Computer-Mediated Groups," *Creativity Research Journal* 11 (1998), pp. 111–21; P. Bycio, R. D. Hackett, and J. S. Allen, "Further Assessments of Bass's (1985) Conceptualization of Transactional and Transformational Leadership," *Journal of Applied Psychology* 80 (1995), pp. 468–78; W. L. Koh, R. M. Steers, and J. R. Terborg, "The Effects of Transformational Leadership on Teacher Attitudes and Student Performance in Singapore," *Journal of Organizational Behavior* 16 (1995), pp. 319–33; Howell and Avolio, "Transformational Leadership, Transactional Leadership, Locus of Control, and Support for Innovation."

74. J. Barling, T. Weber, and E. K. Kelloway, "Effects of Transformational Leadership Training on Attitudinal and Financial Outcomes: A Field Experiment," *Journal of Applied Psychology* 81 (1996), pp. 827–32.

75. A. Bryman, "Leadership in Organizations," in S. R. Clegg, C. Hardy, and W. R. Nord, eds., *Handbook of Organization Studies* (Thousand Oaks, CA: Sage, 1996), pp. 276–92.

76. Egri and Herman, "Leadership in the North American Environmental Sector"; B. S. Pawar and K. K. Eastman, "The Nature and Implications of Contextual Influences on Transformational Leadership: A Conceptual Examination," *Academy of Management Review* 22 (1997), pp. 80–109.

77. K. Boehnke, A. C. DiStefano, J. J. DiStefano, and N. Bontis, "Leadership for Extraordinary Performance," *Business Quarterly* 61 (Summer 1997), pp. 56–63.

78. For a review of this research, see House and Aditya, "The Social Scientific Study Of Leadership."

79. R. J. Hall and R. G. Lord, "Multilevel Information Processing Explanations of Followers' Leadership Perceptions," *Leadership Quarterly* 6 (1995), pp. 265–87; R. Ayman, "Leadership Perception: The Role of Gender and Culture," in M. M. Chemers and R. Ayman, eds., *Leadership Theory and Research: Perspectives and Directions* (San Diego: Academic, 1993), pp. 137–66; J. R. Meindl, "On Leadership: An Alternative to the Conventional Wisdom," *Research in Organizational Behavior* 12 (1990), pp. 159–203.

80. G. R. Salancik and J. R. Meindl, "Corporate Attributions as Strategic Illusions of Management Control," *Administrative Science Quarterly* 29 (1984), pp. 238–54; J. M. Tolliver, "Leadership and Attribution of Cause: A Modification and Extension of Current Theory," *Proceedings of the Annual ASAC Conference, Organizational Behavior Division* 4, pt. 5 (1983), pp. 182–91.

81. L. M. Ah Chong and D. C. Thomas, "Leadership Perceptions in Cross-Cultural Context: Pakeha and Pacific Islanders in New Zealand," *Leadership Quarterly* 8 (1997), pp. 275–93; J. L. Nye and D. R. Forsyth, "The Effects of Prototype-Based Biases on Leadership Appraisals: A Test of Leadership Categorization Theory," *Small Group Research* 22 (1991), pp. 360–79; S. F. Cronshaw and R. G. Lord, "Effects of Categorization, Attribution, and Encoding Processes on Leadership Perceptions," *Journal of Applied Psychology* 72 (1987), pp. 97–106.

82. Meindl, "On Leadership," p. 163.

83. J. Pfeffer, "The Ambiguity of Leadership," *Academy of Management Review* 2 (1977), pp. 102–12; Yukl, *Leadership in Organizations*, pp. 265–67.

84. Cronshaw and Lord, "Effects of Categorization, Attribution, and Encoding Processes on Leadership Perceptions," pp. 104–5.

85. D. Barboza, "Teacher, Cheerleader and C.E.O.," *New York Times*, May 28, 2000.

86. The study was conducted by the Conference Board of Canada and was reported in L. Elliott, "Women Switch Jobs to Climb the Power Ladder," *Toronto Star*, June 15, 2000, p. NE1.

87. N. Wood, "Venus Rules," *Incentive* 172 (February 1998), pp. 22–27; S. H. Appelbaum and B. T. Shapiro, "Why Can't Men Lead Like Women?" *Leadership and Organization Development Journal* 14 (1993), pp. 28–34; J. B. Rosener, "Ways Women Lead," *Harvard Business Review* 68 (November–December 1990), pp. 119–25.

88. K. Goff, "The Muscle behind Martha," *Ottawa Citizen*, October 21, 1999.

89. G. N. Powell, "One More Time: Do Female and Male Managers Differ?" *Academy of Management Executive* 4

(August 1990), pp. 68–75; G. H. Dobbins and S. J. Platts, "Sex Differences in Leadership: How Real Are They?" *Academy of Management Review* 11 (1986), pp. 118–27. In contrast to these studies, one review cites an unpublished study reporting that women demonstrate more people-oriented leadership and are rated higher than men on their leadership. See M-T. Claes, "Women, Men and Management Styles," *International Labour Review* 138 (1999), pp. 431–46.

90. A. H. Eagly and B. T. Johnson, "Gender and Leadership Style: A Meta-Analysis," *Psychological Bulletin* 108 (1990), pp. 233–56.

91. J. Eckberg, "When It's Time to Get Tough—It's Tough," *Cincinnati Enquirer*, August 28, 2000, p. B18; A. H. Eagly, S. J. Karau, and M. G. Makhijani, "Gender and the Effectiveness of Leaders: A Meta-Analysis," *Psychological Bulletin* 117 (1995), pp. 125–45; M. E. Heilman and C. J. Block, "Sex Stereotypes: Do They Influence Perceptions of Managers?" *Journal of Social Behavior and Personality* 10 (1995), pp. 237–52; R. L. Kent and S. E. Moss, "Effects of Sex and Gender Role on Leader Emergence," *Academy of Management Journal* 37 (1994), pp. 1335–46; A. H. Eagly, M. G. Makhijani, and B. G. Klonsky, "Gender and the Evaluation of Leaders: A Meta-Analysis," *Psychological Bulletin* 111 (1992), pp. 3–22.

92. M. Sappenfield, "Women, It Seems, Are Better Bosses," *Christian Science Monitor*, January 16, 2001. R. Sharpe, "As Leaders, Women Rule," *Business Week*, November 20, 2000, C. D'Nan Bass, "Women May Outdo Men As Sales Managers, Study Says," *Chicago Tribune*, January 26, 2000.

CHAPTER FIFTEEN

1. B. Pimentel, "The HP–Compaq Deal: Losing Their Way?" *San Francisco Chronicle*, September 6, 2001; J. Swartz, "How Will Compaq, H-P Fit Together?" *USA Today*, September 6, 2001, p. 3B; D. Olive, "Fiorina: A Woman in a Hurry," *National Post*, September 5, 2001; M. Veverka, "Carly's Challenge," *Barron's*, August 13, 2001, pp. 21–27; "H-P's Employee-Friendly Culture in Flux," *Sacramento (CA) Business Journal*, August 3, 2001, p. 3; J. Foley, "Hewlett-Packard Reaches a

Cultural Crossroads," *InformationWeek*, July 23, 2001, p. 40.

2. T. O. Davenport, "The Integration Challenge: Managing Corporate Mergers," *Management Review* 87 (January 1998), pp. 25–28; E. H. Schein, "What Is Culture?" in P. J. Frost, L. F. Moore, M. R. Louis, C. C. Lundberg, and J. Martin, eds., *Reframing Organizational Culture* (Beverly Hills, CA: Sage, 1991), pp. 243–53; A. Williams, P. Dobson, and M. Walters, *Changing Culture: New Organizational Approaches* (London: Institute of Personnel Management, 1989).

3. A. Sagie and D. Elizur, "Work Values: A Theoretical Overview and a Model of Their Effects," *Journal of Organizational Behavior* 17 (1996), pp. 503–14; W. H. Schmidt and B. Z. Posner, *Managerial Values in Perspective* (New York: American Management Association, 1983).

4. M. Fan, "Cary, N.C., Software Firm Posts Steady Growth without IPO," *San Jose (CA) Mercury News*, July 29, 2001; K. S. Hymowitz, "Ecstatic Capitalism's Brave New Work Ethic," *City Journal* 11 (Winter 2001), pp. 33–43.

5. B. M. Meglino and E. C. Ravlin, "Individual Values in Organizations: Concepts, Controversies, and Research," *Journal of Management* 24 (May 1998), pp. 351–89; C. Argyris and D. A. Schön, *Organizational Learning: A Theory of Action Perspective* (Reading, MA: Addison-Wesley, 1978).

6. Fan, "Cary, N.C., Software Firm Posts Steady Growth without IPO"; E. P. Dalesio, "A Quiet Software Company Considers Raising Its Profile," *Philadelphia Inquirer*, May 6, 2001.

7. "Job Satisfaction Means More Than Pay," *Business Day (South Africa)*, December 6, 2000, p. 14; S. Planting, "Mirror, Mirror . . . Here Are the Fairest of Them All," *Financial Mail (South Africa)*, November 24, 2000, p. 48.

8. K. Doler, "Interview: Jeff Bezos, Founder and CEO of Amazon.com Inc.," *Upside* 10 (September 1998), pp. 76–80.

9. S. Sackmann, "Culture and Subcultures: An Analysis of Organizational Knowledge," *Administrative Science Quarterly* 37 (1992), pp. 140–61; J. Martin and C. Siehl, "Organizational Culture and Counterculture: An Un-

easy Symbiosis," *Organizational Dynamics*, Autumn 1983, pp. 52–64; J. S. Ott, *The Organizational Culture Perspective* (Pacific Grove, CA: Brooks/Cole, 1989), pp. 45–47; T. E. Deal and A. A. Kennedy, *Corporate Cultures* (Reading, MA: Addison-Wesley, 1982), pp. 138–39.

10. A. Sinclair, "Approaches to Organizational Culture and Ethics," *Journal of Business Ethics* 12 (1993), pp. 63–73.

11. M. Cooke, "Humiliation as Motivator?" *Meetings and Conventions* 36 (July 2001), p. 26; G. Groeller, "Eat or Be Eaten Ethic Boosts Bottom Line," *Orlando (FL) Sentinel*, April 30, 2001, p. 16.

12. M. O. Jones, *Studying Organizational Symbolism: What, How, Why?* (Thousand Oaks, CA: Sage, 1996); Ott, *The Organizational Culture Perspective*, chap. 2; J. S. Pederson and J. S. Sorensen, *Organizational Cultures in Theory and Practice* (Aldershot, UK: Gower, 1989), pp. 27–29.

13. "Making Work Fun," *Minneapolis Star Tribune*, August 18, 1998, p. E9

14. E. H. Schein, *The Corporate Culture Survival Guide* (San Francisco: Jossey-Bass, 1999), chap. 4; A. Furnham and B. Gunter, "Corporate Culture: Definition, Diagnosis, and Change," *International Review of Industrial and Organizational Psychology* 8 (1993), pp. 233–61; E. H. Schein, "Organizational Culture," *American Psychologist*, February 1990, pp. 109–19; Ott, *The Organizational Culture Perspective*, chap. 2; W. J. Duncan, "Organizational Culture: 'Getting a Fix' on an Elusive Concept," *Academy of Management Executive* 3 (1989), pp. 229–36.

15. J. C. Meyer, "Tell Me a Story: Eliciting Organizational Values from Narratives," *Communication Quarterly* 43 (1995), pp. 210–24.

16. K. Frieberg and J. Frieberg, *Nuts! Southwest Airlines' Crazy Recipe for Business and Personal Success* (New York: Bantam Doubleday Dell, 1998).

17. This story is cited in K. Foss, "Isadore Sharp," *Foodservice and Hospitality*, December 1989, pp. 20–30; J. DeMont, "Sharp's Luxury Empire," *Maclean's*, June 5, 1989, pp. 30–33. See also S. Kemp and L. Dwyer, "An Examination of Organizational Culture—The Regent Hotel, Sydney," *International*

Journal of Hospitality Management 20 (March 2001), pp. 77–93.

18. J. Z. DeLorean, *On a Clear Day You Can See General Motors* (Grosse Pointe, MI: Wright Enterprises, 1979).

19. R. Zemke, "Storytelling: Back to a Basic," *Training* 27 (March 1990), pp. 44–50; A. L. Wilkins, "Organizational Stories as Symbols Which Control the Organization," in L. R. Pondy, P. J. Frost, G. Morgan, and T. C. Dandridge, eds., *Organizational Symbolism* (Greenwich, CT: JAI Press, 1984), pp. 81–92; J. Martin and M. E. Powers, "Truth or Corporate Propaganda: The Value of a Good War Story," in Pondy et al., eds., *Organizational Symbolism*, pp. 93–107.

20. J. Martin et al., "The Uniqueness Paradox in Organizational Stories," *Administrative Science Quarterly* 28 (1983), pp. 438–53.

21. P. S. DeLisi, "A Modern-Day Tragedy: The Digital Equipment Story," *Journal of Management Inquiry* 7 (June 1998), pp. 118–30. Digital's famous shouting matches are also described in E. Schein, "How to Set the Stage for a Change in Organizational Culture," in P. Senge et al., *The Dance of Change* (New York: Doubleday Currency, 1999), pp. 334–44.

22. J. M. Beyer and H. M. Trice, "How an Organization's Rites Reveal Its Culture," *Organizational Dynamics* 15 (4) (1987), pp. 5–24; L. Smirchich, "Organizations as Shared Meanings," in Pondy et al., eds., *Organizational Symbolism*, pp. 55–65.

23. D. Roth, "My Job at The Container Store," *Fortune*, January 10, 2000, pp. 74–78.

24. L. A. Krefting and P. J. Frost, "Untangling Webs, Surfing Waves, and Wildcatting," in P. J. Frost, L. F. Moore, M. R. Louis, C. C. Lundberg, and J. Martin, eds., *Organizational Culture* (Beverly Hills, CA: Sage, 1985), pp. 155–68.

25. J. A. Byrne, "How Jack Welch Runs GE," *Business Week*, June 8, 1998.

26. R. E. Quinn and N. T. Snyder, "Advance Change Theory: Culture Change at Whirlpool Corporation," in J. A. Conger, G. M. Spreitzer, and E. E. Lawler III, eds., *The Leader's Change Handbook* (San Francisco: Jossey-Bass, 1999), pp. 162–93.

27. Adapted from P. Roberts, "The Empire Strikes Back," *Fast Company* 22 (February–March 1999), pp. 122–31.

28. J. Myerson, "Britain's Most Creative Offices," *Management Today*, April 1999, pp. 62–67.

29. J. M. Kouzes and B. Z. Posner, *The Leadership Challenge* (San Francisco: Jossey-Bass, 1995), pp. 230–31.

30. G. Levitch, "Rethinking the Office," *Report on Business Magazine*, September 2001; T. Kelley, *The Art of Innovation* (New York: Doubleday Currency, 2001), chap. 7.

31. C. Siehl and J. Martin, "Organizational Culture: A Key to Financial Performance?" in B. Schneider, ed., *Organizational Climate and Culture* (San Francisco: Jossey-Bass, 1990), pp. 241–81; J. B. Barney, "Organizational Culture: Can It Be a Source of Sustained Competitive Advantage?" *Academy of Management Review* 11 (1986), pp. 656–65; V. Sathe, *Culture and Related Corporate Realities* (Homewood, IL: Irwin, 1985), chap. 2; Deal and Kennedy, *Corporate Cultures*, chap. 1. Information about Viant, Inc., comes from L. Daniel, "Within the Viant Experiment," *WebTechniques*, April 2000 (www.webtechniques.com).

32. C. A. O'Reilly and J. A. Chatman, "Culture as Social Control: Corporations, Cults, and Commitment," *Research in Organizational Behavior* 18 (1996), pp. 157–200. For a discussion of organizational culture as social control at The Regent, Sydney, see S. Kemp and L. Dwyer, "An Examination of Organizational Culture—The Regent Hotel, Sydney," *International Journal of Hospitality Management* 20 (March 2001), pp. 77–93.

33. B. Ashforth and F. Mael, "Social Identity Theory and the Organization," *Academy of Management Review* 14 (1989), pp. 20–39.

34. S. G. Harris, "Organizational Culture and Individual Sensemaking: A Schema-Based Perspective," *Organization Science* 5 (1994), pp. 309–21; M. R. Louis, "Surprise and Sensemaking: What Newcomers Experience in Entering Unfamiliar Organizational Settings," *Administrative Science Quarterly* 25 (1980), pp. 226–51.

35. G. S. Saffold III, "Culture Traits, Strength, and Organizational Perfor-

mance: Moving Beyond 'Strong' Culture," *Academy of Management Review* 13 (1988), pp. 546–58; Williams et al., *Changing Culture*, pp. 24–27.

36. J. P. Kotter and J. L. Heskett, *Corporate Culture and Performance* (New York: Free Press, 1992); G. G. Gordon and N. DiTomasco, "Predicting Corporate Performance from Organizational Culture," *Journal of Management Studies* 29 (1992), pp. 783–98; D. R. Denison, *Corporate Culture and Organizational Effectiveness* (New York: Wiley, 1990).

37. C. Fishman, "Why Can't Lego Click?" *Fast Company* 50 (September 2001), p. 144.

38. E. H. Schein, "On Dialogue, Culture, and Organizational Learning," *Organization Dynamics*, Autumn 1993, pp. 40–51.

39. T. Parker-Pope, "New CEO Preaches Rebellion for P&G's 'Cult,' " *The Wall Street Journal*, December 11, 1998.

40. J. Kotter, "Cultures and Coalitions," *Executive Excellence* 15 (March 1998), pp. 14–15; Kotter and Heskett, *Corporate Culture and Performance*.

41. The features of adaptive cultures are described in W. F. Joyce, *MegaChange: How Today's Leading Companies Have Transformed Their Workforces* (New York: Free Press, 1999), pp. 44–47.

42. S. Peck and J. Larson, "Making Change: Some Major Corporations Are Making Sustainability Their Business," *Alternatives* 27 (Spring 2001), pp. 17–20; S. J. Carroll and M. J. Gannon, *Ethical Dimensions of International Management* (Thousand Oaks, CA: Sage, 1997), chap. 5; A. Sinclair, "Approaches to Organizational Culture and Ethics," *Journal of Business Ethics* 12 (1993), pp. 63–73.

43. J. Mizuo, "Business Ethics and Corporate Governance in Japanese Corporations," *Business and Society Review*, March 1999, p. 65; "Shiseido," *Forbes (Supplement)*, January 11, 1999, p. S6.

44. W. J. Holstein, "Dump the Cookware," *Business 2.0*, May 2001; S. N. Mehta, "Can Corning Find Its Optic Nerve?" *Fortune*, March 19, 2001, pp. 148–50.

45. C. Fox, "Mergers and Desires II," *Business Review Weekly*, May 11, 2001.

46. D. B. Marron, "Is This Marriage Made in Heaven?" *Chief Executive*, May 2001, pp. 50–52; P. Troiano, "Post-Merger Challenges," *Management Review* 88 (January 1999), p. 6. For a discussion of corporate culture issues in mergers, see M. L. Marks, "Mixed Signals," *Across the Board*, May 2000, pp. 21–26; M. L. Marks, "Adding Cultural Fit to Your Diligence Checklist," *Mergers and Acquisitions*, December 1999; E. H. Schein, *The Corporate Culture Survival Guide* (San Francisco: Jossey-Bass, 1999), chap. 8; A. F. Buono and J. L. Bowditch, *The Human Side of Mergers and Acquisitions* (San Francisco: Jossey-Bass, 1989), chap. 6.

47. E. Krell, "Merging Corporate Cultures," *Training* 38 (May 2001), pp. 68–78; J. K. Stewart, "Imperfect Partners," *Chicago Tribune*, March 18, 2001, p. 1.

48. J. K. Stewart, "3COM–Robotics Merger a Lesson in Frustration," *Chicago Tribune*, March 21, 2001, p. N1.

49. Marks, "Adding Cultural Fit to Your Diligence Checklist"; S. Greengard, "Due Diligence: The Devil in the Details," *Workforce*, October 1999, p. 68; Schein, *The Corporate Culture Survival Guide*. A corporate culture audit is also recommended for joint ventures. For details, see K. J. Fedor and W. B. Werther, Jr., "The Fourth Dimension: Creating Culturally Responsive International Alliances," *Organizational Dynamics* 25 (Autumn 1996), pp. 39–53.

50. D. Kramer-Kawakami, "Merging Cultures: The Challenges of Convergence," *LIMRA's MarketFacts* 19 (September–October 2000), pp. 24.

51. T. Evanoff, "Crash of a Titan," *Indianapolis Star*, April 15, 2001, p.E1; J. Mann, J. Flock, and R. Charles, "The Crashing of Chrysler," *CNN International*, January 30, 2001; H. Greimel, "Merger Woes at DaimlerChrysler," *Associated Press*, December 24, 2000; J. Hyde, "Chrysler's New Boss Faces Same Merger Problems as Old Boss," *Associated Press*, November 16, 2000; J. Ball and S. Miller, "DaimlerChrysler Isn't Living Up to Its Promise," *Wall Street Journal Europe*, July 26, 2000; B. Vlasic and B. A. Stertz, "Taken for a Ride," *Business Week*, June 5, 2000, pp. 80–92.

52. D. Buckner, "Nortel versus Cisco," *Venture*, CBC TV, January 4, 2000; R. N. Ashkenas, L. J. DeMonaco, and S. C. Francis, "Making the Deal Real: How GE Capital Integrates Acquisitions," *Harvard Business Review* 76 (January–February 1998), pp. 165–76.

53. K. W. Smith, "A Brand-New Culture for the Merged Firm," *Mergers and Acquisitions* 35 (June 2000), pp. 45–50; A. R. Malekazedeh and A. Nahavandi, "Making Mergers Work by Managing Cultures," *Journal of Business Strategy*, May–June 1990, pp. 55–57.

54. A. Levy, "Mergers Spread Despite Failures," *Plain Dealer (Cleveland, OH)*, August 9, 1998, p. H1.

55. S. F. Walker and J. W. Marr, *Stakeholder Power* (New York: Perseus, 2001); S. Silverstein and D. Vrana, "After Back-Slapping Wanes, Mega-Mergers Often Fail," *Los Angeles Times*, April 19, 1998, p. 1.

56. "Nortel Uses Acquisition to Transform Role," *Wall Street Journal Europe*, July 26, 2000, p. 13.

57. "Split Personality," *Baltimore Business Journal*, July 20, 2001, p. 1.

58. J. P. Kotter, "Leading Change: The Eight Steps of Transformation," in Conger et al., eds., *The Leader's Change Handbook*, pp. 87–99.

59. E. H. Schein, "The Role of the Founder in Creating Organizational Culture," *Organizational Dynamics* 12 (1) (Summer 1983), pp. 13–28.

60. E. H. Schein, *Organizational Culture and Leadership* (San Francisco, CA: Jossey-Bass, 1985), chap. 10; T. J. Peters, "Symbols, Patterns, and Settings: An Optimistic Case for Getting Things Done," *Organizational Dynamics* 7 (2) (Autumn 1978), pp. 2–23.

61. A. Effinger, "With Charm, Poise and Attitude Fiorina Rousting Hewlett-Packard," *Seattle-Post Intelligencer*, January 3, 2000, p. E1.

62. J. Kerr and J. W. Slocum, Jr., "Managing Corporate Culture Through Reward Systems," *Academy of Management Executive* 1 (May 1987), pp. 99–107; Williams et al., *Changing Culture*, pp. 120–24; K. R. Thompson and F. Luthans, "Organizational Culture: A Behavioral Perspective," in Schneider, ed., *Organizational Climate and Culture*, pp. 319–44.

63. "Get Rich? Work at Home Depot," *Baltimore Sun*, July 27, 1998.

64. W. G. Ouchi and A. M. Jaeger, "Type Z Organization: Stability in the Midst of Mobility," *Academy of Management Review* 3 (1978), pp. 305–14; K. Mc-

Neil and J. D. Thompson, "The Regeneration of Social Organizations," *American Sociological Review* 36 (1971), pp. 624–37.

65. B. Broadway, "Good for the Soul—and for the Bottom Line," *Washington Post*, August 19, 2001, p. A1; N. Hoogeveen, "Reinventing Industry," *Business Record*, April 10, 2001, p. 22; M. Haskell, "It's Incredibly Important That Businesses Wake Up Now and Get It Straight," *Maine Times*, October 12, 2000, p. 3.

66. "A Full Life," *The Economist*, September 4, 1999.

67. M. De Pree, *Leadership Is an Art* (East Lansing: Michigan State University Press, 1987).

68. C. Daniels, "Does This Man Need a Shrink?" *Fortune*, February 5, 2001, pp. 205–8.

69. A. E. M. Van Vianen, "Person–Organization Fit: The Match between Newcomers' and Recruiters' Preferences for Organizational Cultures," *Personnel Psychology* 53 (Spring 2000), pp. 113–49; C. A. O'Reilly III, J. Chatman, and D. F. Caldwell, "People and Organizational Culture: A Profile Comparison Approach to Assessing Person–Organization Fit," *Academy of Management Journal* 34 (1991), pp. 487–516.

70. "Corporate Culture Rivals Company Benefits in Importance to Job Applicants," Robert Half International news release, May 1, 1996.

71. M. Siegal, "The Perils of Culture Conflict," *Fortune*, November 9, 1998, pp. 257–62.

72. J. Van Maanen, "Breaking In: Socialization to Work," in R. Dubin, ed., *Handbook of Work, Organization, and Society* (Chicago: Rand McNally, 1976), p. 67.

73. P. Tam, "Frugal Founder Rewards Employees," *Ottawa Citizen*, November 21, 1999.

CHAPTER SIXTEEN

1. B. Breen, "How EDS Got Its Groove Back," *Fast Company* 51 (October 2001), pp. 106–17; L. B. Ward, "EDS Chief Confident in Role as Change Agent," *Dallas Morning News*, August 14, 2001, p. 1D; C. Hymowitz, "Executive Action Drafting a Winning Team," *Asian Wall Street Journal*, March 30, 2001, p. W3; W. Zellner, "Meet the 'Completely Different EDS,'" *Business Week*, December 18, 2000, p. 204; D. Callaghan, "Everything Old Is New Again. Really," *MC Technology Marketing Intelligence* 20 (April 2000), pp. 70–76; J. Bean, "EDS Trying to Shed Buttoned-down Image," *Montreal Gazette*, March 20, 2000, p. IB8.

2. J. P. Donlon, "Built for Speed," *Chief Executive*, October 2000, pp. 58–68.

3. R. Mitchell, "Feeding the Flames," *Business 2.0*, May 1, 2001.

4. These four companies appear on recent *Business Week* "Best Performers" lists. See J. Weber, "The Best Performers," *Business Week*, April 7, 2001, p. 10; A. Barrett, "The 50 Best Performers," *Business Week*, March 27, 2000, p. 124.

5. R. T. Pascale, M. Millemann, and L. Gioja, *Surfing on the Edge of Chaos* (London: Texere, 2000).

6. D. Tapscott, A. Lowy, and D. Ticoll, eds., *Blueprint to the Digital Economy: Creating Wealth in the Era of E-business* (New York: McGraw-Hill, 1998); C. Meyer and S. Davis, *Blur: The Speed of Change in the Connected Economy* (Reading, MA: Addison-Wesley, 1998). For an excellent discussion of how computer networks are changing the world of business, see also K. Kelly, *New Rules for the New Economy* (New York: Viking, 1998).

7. D. Tapscott and A. Laston, *Paradigm Shift* (New York: McGraw-Hill, 1993); W. H. Davidow and M. S. Malone, *The Virtual Corporation* (New York: HarperBusiness, 1992).

8. Tapscott et al., *Blueprint to the Digital Economy.*

9. N. Bannister, "Nokia: From Start to Finnish," *The Age (Melbourne)*, October 26, 1999; K. Lyytinen and S. Goodman, "Finland: The Unknown Soldier on the IT Front," *Communications of the ACM* 42 (March 1999), pp. 13–17; S. Baker, "Can CEO Ollila Keep the Cellular Superstar Flying High?" *Business Week*, August 10, 1998, pp. 54–61; J. Dromberg, "Nokia's Line to the Top Slot," *Independent (London)*, August 9, 1998, p. 5.

10. T. Keller, "Reinventing the Firm," *National Post Business Magazine*, June 1, 2000, p. 68.

11. B. Duff-Brown, "Service Centers Booming in India," *Chicago Tribune*, July 9, 2001, p. 6; M. Landler, "Hi, I'm in Bangalore (but I Can't Say So)," *New York Times*, March 21, 2001, p. A1.

12. K. Lewin, *Field Theory in Social Science* (New York: Harper & Row, 1951).

13. M. Moravec, O. J. Johannessen, and T. A. Hjelmas, "The Well-Managed SMT," *Management Review* 87 (June 1998), pp. 56–58; M. Moravec, O. J. Johannessen, and T. A. Hjelmas, "Thumbs Up for Self-Managed Teams," *Management Review*, July 17, 1997, p. 42.

14. M. Riley, "High-Revving Nasser Undone by a Blind Spot," *Sydney Morning Herald*, November 3, 2001; J. McCracken, "Nasser Out; Ford In," *Detroit Free Press*, October 30, 2001; M. Truby, "Can Ford Chief Ride Out Storm?" *Detroit News*, June 24, 2001; M. Truby, "Ford Revolution Spawns Turmoil," *Detroit News*, April 29, 2001.

15. C. O. Longenecker, D. J. Dwyer, and T. C. Stansfield, "Barriers and Gateways to Workforce Productivity," *Industrial Management* 40 (March–April 1998), pp. 21–28. Several sources discuss resistance to change, including D. A. Nadler, Champions of Change (San Francisco: Jossey-Bass, 1998), chap. 5; P. Strebel, "Why Do Employees Resist Change?" *Harvard Business Review*, May–June 1996, pp. 86–92; R. Maurer, *Beyond the Wall of Resistance: Unconventional Strategies to Build Support for Change* (Austin, TX: Bard Books, 1996); C. Hardy, *Strategies for Retrenchment and Turnaround: The Politics of Survival* (Berlin: de Gruyter, 1990), chap. 13.

16. F. Vogelstein and P. Sloan, "Corporate Dowagers Go for a Makeover," *U.S. News & World Report*, November 6, 2000.

17. E. B. Dent and S. G. Goldberg, "Challenging 'Resistance to Change,'" *Journal of Applied Behavioral Science* 35 (March 1999), pp. 25–41.

18. D. A. Nadler, "The Effective Management of Organizational Change," in J. W. Lorsch, ed., *Handbook of Organizational Behavior* (Englewood Cliffs, NJ: Prentice Hall, 1987), pp. 358–69; D. Katz and R. L. Kahn, *The Social Psychology of Organizations*, 2nd ed. (New York: Wiley, 1978).

19. "Making Change Work for You—Not against You," *Agency Sales Magazine* 28 (June 1998), pp. 24–27.

20. M. E. McGill and J. W. Slocum, Jr., "Unlearn the Organization," *Organizational Dynamics* 22 (2) (1993), pp. 67–79.

21. R. Katz, "Time and Work: Toward an Integrative Perspective," *Research in Organizational Behavior* 2 (1980), pp. 81–127.

22. D. Nicolini and M. B. Meznar, "The Social Construction of Organizational Learning: Conceptual and Practical Issues in the Field," *Human Relations* 48 (1995), pp. 727–46.

23. D. Miller, "What Happens after Success: The Perils of Excellence," *Journal of Management Studies* 31 (1994), pp. 325–58.

24. H. Trinca, "Her Way," *Boss Magazine*, October 9, 2000.

25. T. G. Cummings, "The Role and Limits of Change Leadership," in J. A. Conger, G. M. Spreitzer, and E. E. Lawler III, eds., *The Leader's Change Handbook* (San Francisco: Jossey-Bass, 1999), pp. 301–20.

26. J. P. Donlon et al., "In Search of the New Change Leader," *Chief Executive*, November 1997, pp. 64–75.

27. L. D. Goodstein and H. R. Butz, "Customer Value: The Linchpin of Organizational Change," *Organizational Dynamics* 27 (June 1998), pp. 21–35.

28. J. Juergens, "Corporate Spotlight: ARCNET," *Incentive* 173 (September 1999), pp. 68–69.

29. A. Gore, "Joel Kocher: Power COO Says It's Time to Evolve," *MacUser*, April 1997.

30. J. P. Kotter and L. A. Schlesinger, "Choosing Strategies for Change," *Harvard Business Review*, March–April 1979, pp. 106–14.

31. J. Moad, "Dupont's People Deal," *PC Week* 14 (September 29, 1997), pp. 751.

32. K. H. Hammonds, "Grassroots Leadership–Ford Motor Company," *Fast Company*, April 2000, p. 138; S. Wetlaufer, "Driving Change: An Interview with Ford Motor Company's Jacques Nasser," *Harvard Business Review* 77 (March–April 1999), pp. 76–88.

33. D. Tarrant, "Boss Aha!" *Australian Financial Review*, December 29, 2000, p. 24. For a discussion of employee involvement in change management, see J. P. Walsh and S-F. Tseng, "The Ef-

fects of Job Characteristics on Active Effort at Work," *Work and Occupations* 25 (February 1998), pp. 74–96; K. T. Dirks, L. L. Cummings, and J. L. Pierce, "Psychological Ownership in Organizations: Conditions under Which Individuals Promote and Resist Change," *Research in Organizational Change and Development* 9 (1996), pp. 1–23.

34. M. Evans, T. Hamilton, L. Surtees, and S. Tuck, "The Road to a Billion," *Globe and Mail*, January 6, 2000; R. Dyck and N. Halpern, "Team-Based Organizations Redesign at Celestica," *Journal for Quality & Participation* 22 (September–October 1999), pp. 36–40; "Celestica Nurtures Strong Corporate Culture Within," *Northern Colorado Business Report*, July 16, 1999, p. B5; K. Damsell, "Celestica Escapes from Its Cage," *National Post*, September 1, 1998, p. 9.

35. B. B. Bunker and B. T. Alban, *Large Group Interventions: Engaging the Whole System for Rapid Change* (San Francisco: Jossey-Bass, 1996); M. Emery and R. E. Purser, *The Search Conference: A Powerful Method for Planning Organizational Change and Community Action* (San Francisco: Jossey-Bass, 1996). For a description of Trist and Emery's first search conference, see M. R. Weisbord, "Inventing the Search Conference: Bristol Siddeley Aircraft Engines, 1960," in M. R. Weisbord, ed., *Discovering Common Ground* (San Francisco: Berret-Koehler, 1992), pp. 19–33.

36. R. Dubey, "The CEO Who Walked Away," *Business Today (India)*, May 22, 1998, p. 98.

37. R. E. Purser and S. Cabana, *The Self-Managing Organization* (New York: Free Press, 1998), chap. 7; "Making Organizational Changes Effective and Sustainable," *Educating for Employment*, August 7, 1998; R. Larson, "Forester Defends 'Feel-Good' Meeting," *Washington Times*, November 28, 1997, p. A9; W. Kaschub, "PECO Energy Redesigns HR," *HR Focus* 74 (March 1997), p. 3; A. Crombie, "Empowering People with Diabetes," in Weisbord, ed., *Discovering Common Ground*, pp. 249–64.

38. P. H. Mirvis and M. L. Marks, *Managing the Merger* (Englewood Cliffs, NJ: Prentice Hall, 1992).

39. R. Greenwood and C. R. Hinings, "Understanding Radical Organizational Change: Bringing Together the Old and the New Institutionalism," *Academy of Management Review* 21 (1996), pp. 1022–54.

40. T. Joyner, "Merger Toil Replaced Fun in Sun," *Atlanta Journal and Constitution*, August 5, 2001, p. A1.

41. J. Lublin, "Curing Sick Companies Better Done Fast," *Globe and Mail (Toronto)*, July 25, 1995, p. B18.

42. Nicolini and Meznar, "The Social Construction of Organizational Learning."

43. The importance of systems and structure in reinforcing change is discussed in W. F. Joyce, *MegaChange: How Today's Leading Companies Have Transformed Their Workforces* (New York: Free Press, 1999), chaps. 4 and 5.

44. E. E. Lawler III, "Pay Can Be a Change Agent," *Compensation and Benefits Management* 16 (Summer 2000), pp. 23–26.

45. R. H. Miles, "Leading Corporate Transformation: Are You Up to the Task?" in Conger et al., eds., *The Leader's Change Handbook*, pp. 221–67; Goodstein and Butz, "Customer Value," pp. 21–34.

46. C. L. Bernick, "When Your Culture Needs a Makeover," *Harvard Business Review* 79 (June 2001), pp. 53–61.

47. D. A. Nadler, "Implementing Organizational Changes," in D. A. Nadler, M. L. Tushman, and N. G. Hatvany, eds., *Managing Organizations: Readings and Cases* (Boston: Little, Brown, 1982), pp. 440–59.

48. B. McDermott and G. Sexton, "Sowing the Seeds of Corporate Innovation," *Journal for Quality and Participation* 21 (November–December 1998), pp. 18–23.

49. Callaghan, "Everything Old Is New Again. Really."

50. J. P. Kotter, "Leading Change: The Eight Steps to Transformation," in Conger et al., eds., *The Leader's Change Handbook*, pp. 221–67; J. P. Kotter, "Leading Change: Why Transformation Efforts Fail," *Harvard Business Review*, March–April 1995, pp. 59–67.

51. M. Beer, R. A. Eisenstat, and B. Spector, *The Critical Path to Corpo-

rate Renewal (Boston, MA: Harvard Business School Press, 1990).

52. R. E. Walton, *Innovating to Compete: Lessons for Diffusing and Managing Change in the Workplace* (San Francisco: Jossey-Bass, 1987); Beer et al., *The Critical Path to Corporate Renewal*, chap. 5; R. E. Walton, "Successful Strategies for Diffusing Work Innovations," *Journal of Contemporary Business*, Spring 1977, pp. 1–22.

53. J. Childs, "Five Years and Counting: The Path to Self-Directed Work Teams," *Hospital Materiel Management Quarterly* 18 (May 1997), pp. 34–43.

54. R. Beckhard, *Organization Development: Strategies and Models* (Reading, MA: Addison-Wesley, 1969), chap. 2. See also T. G. Cummings and E. F. Huse, *Organization Development and Change*, 4th ed. (St. Paul, MN: West, 1989), pp. 1–3. There is some debate about the distinction between OD and change management. For example, see N. A. M. Worren, K. Ruddle, and K. Moore, "From Organizational Development to Change Management: The Emergence of a New Profession," *Journal of Applied Behavioral Science* 35 (September 1999), pp. 273–86.

55. W. W. Burke, *Organization Development: A Normative View* (Reading, MA: Addison-Wesley, 1987), pp. 12–14.

56. L. Dickens and K. Watkins, "Action Research: Rethinking Lewin," *Management Learning* 30 (June 1999), pp. 127–40, J. D. Cunningham, *Action Research and Organization Development* (Westport, CT: Praeger, 1993). For a discussion of early applications of action research, see R. Sommer, "Action Research: From Mental Hospital Reform in Saskatchewan to Community Building in California," *Canadian Psychology* 40 (February 1999), pp. 47–55.

57. A. B. Shani and G. R. Bushe, "Visionary Action Research: A Consultation Process Perspective," *Consultation: An International Journal* 6 (1) (1987), pp. 3–19.

58. M. L. Brown, "Five Symbolic Roles of the Organizational Development Consultant: Integrating Power, Change, and Symbolism," *Proceedings of the Annual ASAC Conference, Organizational Behavior Division* 14, pt. 5 (1993), pp. 71–81; D. A. Buchanan and D. Boddy,

The Expertise of the Change Agent: Public Performance and Backstage Activity (New York: Prentice Hall, 1992); L. E. Greiner and V. E. Schein, *Power and Organization Development: Mobilizing Power to Implement Change* (Reading, MA: Addison-Wesley, 1988).

59. D. F. Harvey and D. R. Brown, *An Experiential Approach to Organization Development*, 5th ed. (Upper Saddle River, NJ: Prentice Hall, 1996), chap. 4.

60. M. Beer and E. Walton, "Developing the Competitive Organization: Interventions and Strategies," *American Psychologist* 45 (February 1990), pp. 154–61.

61. E. H. Schein, *Process Consultation: Its Role in Organization Development* (Reading, MA: Addison-Wesley, 1969).

62. For a case study of poor diagnosis, see M. Popper, "The Glorious Failure," *Journal of Applied Behavioral Science* 33 (March 1997), pp. 27–45.

63. M. Beer, *Organization Change and Development: A Systems View* (Santa Monica, CA: Goodyear, 1980), pp. 101–1.

64. K. E. Weick and R. E. Quinn, "Organizational Change and Development," *Annual Review of Psychology* 1999, pp. 361–86; D. A. Nadler, "Organizational Frame Bending: Types of Change in the Complex Organization," in R. H. Kilmann, T. J. Covin, and Associates, eds., *Corporate Transformation: Revitalizing Organizations for a Competitive World* (San Francisco: Jossey-Bass, 1988), pp. 66–83.

65. C. R. Hinings and R. Greenwood, *The Dynamics of Strategic Change* (Oxford, UK: Basil Blackwell, 1988), chap. 6; D. Miller and P. H. Friesen, "Structural Change and Performance: Quantum versus Piecemeal-Incremental Approaches," *Academy of Management Journal* 25 (1982), pp. 867–92.

66. P. Brabeck, "The Business Case against Revolution: An Interview with Nestlés Peter Brabeck," *Harvard Business Review* 79 (February 2001), pp. 112–18.

67. S. R. Olberding, "Turnaround Drama Instills Leadership," *Journal for Quality and Participation* 21 (January–February 1998), pp. 52–55.

68. Cummings and Huse, *Organization Development and Change*, pp. 158–61.

69. A. H. Church and W. W. Burke, "Practitioner Attitudes about the Field

of Organization Development," *Research in Organizational Change and Development* 8 (1995), pp. 1–46.

70. A. H. Church, W. W. Burke, and D. F. Van Eynde, "Values, Motives, and Interventions of Organization Development Practitioners," *Group and Organization Management* 19 (1994), pp. 5–50.

71. E. M. Van Aken, D. J. Monetta, and D. S. Sink, "Affinity Groups: The Missing Link in Employee Involvement," *Organization Dynamics* 22 (Spring 1994), pp. 38–54; G. R. Bushe and A. B. Shani, *Parallel Learning Structures* (Reading, MA: Addison-Wesley, 1991).

72. Breen, "How EDS Got Its Groove Back."

73. J. M. Watkins and B. J. Mohr, *Appreciative Inquiry: Change at the Speed of Imagination* (San Francisco: Jossey-Bass, 2001); G. Johnson and W. Leavitt, "Building on Success: Transforming Organizations through an Appreciative Inquiry," *Public Personnel Management* 30 (March 2001), pp. 129–36; D. Whitney and D. L. Cooperrider, "The Appreciative Inquiry Summit: Overview and Applications," *Employment Relations Today* 25 (Summer 1998), pp. 17–28.

74. The history of this and other aspects of appreciative inquiry are outlined in Watkins and Mohr, *Appreciative Inquiry*, pp. 15–21. For other descriptions of the appreciative inquiry model, see D. Whitney and C. Schau, "Appreciative Inquiry: An Innovative Process for Organization Change," *Employment Relations Today* 25 (Spring 1998), pp. 11–21; F. J. Barrett and D. L. Cooperrider, "Generative Metaphor Intervention: A New Approach for Working with Systems Divided by Conflict and Caught in Defensive Perception," *Journal of Applied Behavioral Science* 26 (1990), pp. 219–39.

75. G. R. Bushe and G. Coetzer, "Appreciative Inquiry as a Team-Development Intervention: A Controlled Experiment," *Journal of Applied Behavioral Science* 31 (1995), pp. 13–30; L. Levine, "Listening with Spirit and the Art of Team Dialogue," *Journal of Organizational Change Management* 7 (1994), pp. 61–73.

76. A. Trosten-Bloom, "Case Study: HunterDouglas Window Fashions Division," in Watkins and Mohr, *Appreciative Inquiry*, pp. 176–80. For more details about the HunterDouglas appreciative inquiry intervention, see

D. Whitely and A. Trosten-Bloom; *Positive Change @ Work: The Appreciative Inquiry Approach to Whole System Change* (Euclid, OH: Lakeshore Communications, 2002).

77. M. Schiller, "Case Study: AVON Mexico," in Watkins and Mohr, *Appreciative Inquiry,* pp. 123–26.

78. G. A. Neuman, J. E. Edwards, and N. S. Raju, "Organizational Development Interventions: A Meta-Analysis of Their Effects on Satisfaction and Other Attitudes," *Personnel Psychology* 42 (1989), pp. 461–89; R. A. Guzzo, R. D. Jette, and R. A. Katzell, "The Effects of Psychologically Based Intervention Programs on Worker Productivity: A Meta-Analysis," *Personnel Psychology* 38 (1985), pp. 275–91.

79. C-M. Lau, "A Culture-Based Perspective of Organization Development Implementation," *Research in Organizational Change and Development* 9 (1996), pp. 49–79.

80. R. J. Marshak, "Lewin Meets Confucius: A Review of the OD Model of Change," *Journal of Applied Behavioral Science* 29 (1993), pp. 395–415; T. C. Head and P. F. Sorenson, "Cultural Values and Organizational Development: A Seven-Country Study," *Leadership and Organization Development Journal* 14 (1993), pp. 3–7; J. M. Putti, "Organization Development Scene in Asia: The Case of Singapore," *Group and Organization Studies* 14 (1989), pp. 262–70; A. M. Jaeger, "Organization Development and National Culture: Where's the Fit?" *Academy of Management Review* 11 (1986), pp. 178–90.

81. For an excellent discussion of conflict management and Asian values, see several articles in K. Leung and D. Tjosvold, eds., *Conflict Management in the Asia Pacific: Assumptions and Approaches in Diverse Cultures* (Singapore: Wiley, 1998).

82. C. M. D. Deaner, "A Model of Organization Development Ethics," *Public Administration Quarterly* 17 (1994), pp. 435–46; and M. McKendall, "The Tyranny of Change: Organizational Development Revisited," *Journal of Business Ethics* 12 (February 1993), pp. 93–104.

83. G. A. Walter, "Organization Development and Individual Rights," *Journal of Applied Behavioral Science* 20 (1984), pp. 423–39.

84. Burke, *Organization Development,* pp. 149–51; Beer, *Organization Change and Development,* pp. 223–24.

CHAPTER SEVENTEEN

1. P. R. Chowdhury, "The Unbottling of Coke," *Business Today,* January 2001; P. O'Kane, "Coca Cola's Canny Man," *The Herald (Glasgow),* June 18, 2000, p. 3; "Debunking Coke," *The Economist,* February 12, 2000; "World Has Changed at Coca-Cola as 6,000 Lose Jobs," *National Post,* January 27, 2000, p. C10.

2. S. Ranson, R. Hinings, and R. Greenwood, "The Structuring of Organizational Structure," *Administrative Science Quarterly* 25 (1980), pp. 1–14.

3. J-E. Johanson, "Intraorganizational Influence," *Management Communication Quarterly* 13 (February 2000), pp. 393–435.

4. "Ford Motor Company Announces Consumer-Focused Organization for the 21st Century," *Auto Channel* (online), October 18, 1999.

5. H. Mintzberg, *The Structuring of Organizations* (Englewood Cliffs, NJ: Prentice Hall, 1979), pp. 2–3.

6. H. Fayol, *General and Industrial Management,* trans. C. Storrs (London: Pitman, 1949); E. E. Lawler III, *Motivation in Work Organizations* (Monterey, CA: Brooks/Cole, 1973), chap. 7; M. A. Campion, "Ability Requirement Implications of Job Design: An Interdisciplinary Perspective," *Personnel Psychology* 42 (1989), pp. 1–24.

7. A. N. Maira, "Connecting across Boundaries: The Fluid-Network Organization," *Prism,* First Quarter 1998, pp. 23–26; D. A. Nadler and M. L. Tushman, *Competing by Design: The Power of Organizational Architecture* (New York: Oxford University Press, 1997), chap. 6; Mintzberg, *The Structuring of Organizations,* pp. 2–8.

8. C. Downs, P. Clampitt, and A. L. Pfeiffer, "Communication and Organizational Outcomes," in G. Goldhaber and G. Barnett, eds., *Handbook of Organizational Communication* (Norwood, NJ: Ablex, 1988), pp. 171–211; H. C. Jain, "Supervisory Communication and Performance in Urban Hospitals," *Journal of Communication* 23 (1973), pp. 103–17.

9. V. L. Shalin, and G. V. Prabhu, "A Cognitive Perspective on Manual Assembly," *Ergonomics* 39 (1996), pp. 108–27; I. Nonaka and H. Takeuchi, *The Knowledge-Creating Company* (New York: Oxford University Press, 1995).

10. A. L. Patti, J. P. Gilbert, and S. Hartman, "Physical Co-location and the Success of New Product Development Projects," *Engineering Management Journal* 9 (September 1997), pp. 31–37; M. L. Swink, J. C. Sandvig, and V. A. Mabert, "Customizing Concurrent Engineering Processes: Five Case Studies," *Journal of Product Innovation Management* 13 (1996), pp. 229–44; W. I. Zangwill, *Lightning Strategies for Innovation: How the World's Best Firms Create New Products* (New York: Lexington, 1993).

11. For a recent discussion of the role of brand manager at Procter & Gamble, see C. Peale, "Branded for Success," *Cincinnati (OH) Enquirer,* May 20, 2001, p. A1.

12. D. Anfuso, "Core Values Shape W. L. Gore & Associates' Innovative Culture," *Workforce* 78 (March 1999), pp. 48–53; M. Kaplan. "You Have No Boss," *Fast Company* 11 (November 1997), p. 226; D. M. Price, "Gore-Tex Gets Hip," *Minneapolis (MN) Star Tribune,* May 5, 1997, p. D1.

13. Fayol's work is summarized in J. B. Miner, *Theories of Organizational Structure and Process* (Chicago: Dryden, 1982), pp. 358–66.

14. F. Jebb, "Rentokil Initial: A Place for Everyone and Everyone in Their Place," *Management Today,* August 1998, p. 46.

15. J. A. Conger, *Winning 'Em Over: A New Model for Managing in the Age of Persuasion* (New York: Simon & Shuster, 1998), Appendix A.

16. Y-M. Hsieh and A. Tien-Hsieh, "Enhancement of Service Quality with Job Standardization," *Service Industries Journal* 21 (July 2001), pp. 147–66.

17. J. H. Sheridan, "Lessons from the Best," *Industry Week,* February 20, 1995, pp. 13–22.

18. J. P. Starr, "Reintroducing Alcoa to Economic Reality," in W. E. Halal, ed., *The Infinite Resource* (San Francisco: Jossey-Bass, 1998), pp. 57–67.

19. J. Pfeffer, "Seven Practices of Successful Organizations," *California Management Review* 40 (1998), pp. 96–124.

20. D. D. Van Fleet and A. G. Bedeian, "A History of the Span of Management," *Academy of Management Review* 2 (1977), pp. 356–72; Mintzberg, *The Structuring of Organizations*, chap. 8; D. Robey, *Designing Organizations*, 3rd ed. (Homewood, IL: Irwin, 1991), pp. 255–59.

21. B. Simon, "Bank Leads by Example in Transformation," *Business Day (South Africa),* July 30, 1998, p. 17.

22. "Taking Care of the People," *Canadian Healthcare Manager* 6 (April–May 1999), pp. 5–9.

23. S. Ellis, "A New Role for the Post Office: An Investigation into Issues behind Strategic Change at Royal Mail," *Total Quality Management* 9 (May 1998), pp. 223–34; R. H. Kluge, "An Incentive Compensation Plan with an Eye on Quality," *Quality Progress* 29 (December 1996), pp. 65–68.

24. T. Peters, *Thriving on Chaos* (New York: Knopf, 1987), p. 359.

25. L. A. Bossidy, "Reality-Based Leadership," *Executive Speeches* 13 (August–September 1998), pp. 10–15.

26. Q. N. Huy, "In Praise of Middle Managers," *Harvard Business Review* 79 (September 2001), pp. 72–79; L. Donaldson and F. G. Hilmer, "Management Redeemed: The Case against Fads That Harm Management," *Organizational Dynamics* 26 (Spring 1998), pp. 6–20.

27. Mintzberg, *The Structuring of Organizations*, p. 136.

28. The number of layers at Microsoft is inferred from an example in F. Jebb, "Don't Call Me Sir," *Management Today,* August 1998, pp. 44–47.

29. P. Brabeck, "The Business Case against Revolution: An Interview with Nestlés Peter Brabeck," *Harvard Business Review* 79 (February 2001), p. 112.

30. Mintzberg, *The Structuring of Organizations,* chap. 5.

31. B. Victor and A. C. Boynton, *Invented Here* (Boston: Harvard Business School Press, 1998), chap. 2; M. Hamstra, "McD Speeds Up Drive-Thru with Beefed Up Operations," *Nation's Restaurant News,* April 6, 1998, p. 3; G. Morgan, *Creative Organization Theory: A Resourcebook* (Newbury, Park, CA: Sage, 1989), pp. 271–73; K. Deveny, "Bag

Those Fries, Squirt That Ketchup, Fry That Fish," *Business Week,* October 13, 1986, p. 86.

32. T. Burns and G. Stalker, *The Management of Innovation* (London: Tavistock, 1961).

33. A. Lam, "Tacit Knowledge, Organizational Learning and Societal Institutions: An Integrated Framework," *Organization Studies* 21 (May 2000), pp. 487–513.

34. Mintzberg, *The Structuring of Organizations*, p. 106.

35. Mintzberg, *The Structuring of Organizations*, chap. 17.

36. Robey, *Designing Organizations*, pp. 186–89.

37. M. Hamstra, "McD's to Decentralize US Management Team," *Nation's Restaurant News,* June 2, 1997, p. 1

38. "Microsoft Splits into Five Groups in Reorganization," *Reuters,* March 29, 1999; "Microsoft Plans Realignment to Focus on Customers," *Reuters,* February 8, 1999.

39. T. H. Davenport, J. G. Harris, and A. K. Kohli, "How Do They Know Their Customers So Well?" *Sloan Management Review* 42 (Winter 2001), pp. 63–73.

40. "Axa Executive Says Global Insurers Must Pool Local Expertise," *Best's Insurance News,* May 1, 2001. The evolution of organizational structures in global organizations is further discussed in J. R. Galbraith, "Structuring Global Organizations," in S. A. Mohrman, J. R. Galbraith, E. E. Lawler III, and Associates, eds., *Tomorrow's Organization* (San Francisco: Jossey-Bass, 1998), pp. 103–29.

41. Robey, *Designing Organizations,* pp. 191–97; A. G. Bedeian and R. F. Zammuto, *Organizations: Theory and Design* (Hinsdale, IL: Dryden, 1991), pp. 162–68.

42. K. Maddox, "Reinventing the Ad Agency," *B to B,* April 30, 2001, p. 1; C. Marshall, "The Kings of Madison Avenue," *Campaign,* April 27, 2001, p. 12; A. Baar, "Burnett USA Reorganizes, Names New Leaders," *Adweek,* October 25, 1999, p. 5; H. Shura, "Reorganization Positions Haupt to Lead Leo Group," *Advertising Age,* September 20, 1999, p. 25.

43. "Tearing Down Silos to Build a Corporate-wide Communication Plan," *PR News,* July 10, 2000.

44. R. Waters, "SAP America Faces Up to Challenge of Change," *Financial Times,* June 13, 2001.

45. R. C. Ford and W. A. Randolph, "Cross-Functional Structures: A Review and Integration of Matrix Organization and Project Management," *Journal of Management* 18 (1992), pp. 267–94.

46. J. Belanger, C. Berggren, T. Bjorkman, and C. Kohler, eds., *Being Local Worldwide: ABB and the Challenge of Global Management* (Ithaca, NY: Cornell University Press, 1999); M. F. R. Kets de Vries "Charisma in Action: The Transformational Abilities of Virgin's Richard Branson and ABB's Percy Barnevik," *Organizational Dynamics* 26 (Winter 1998), pp. 6–21; D. A. Nadler and M. L. Tushman, *Competing by Design* (New York: Oxford University Press, 1997), chap. 6.

47. H. F. Kolodny, "Managing in a Matrix," *Business Horizons,* March–April 1981, pp. 17–24; S. M. Davis and P. R. Lawrence, *Matrix* (Reading, MA: Addison-Wesley, 1977).

48. K. Knight, "Matrix Organization: A Review," *Journal of Management Studies,* May 1976, pp. 111–30.

49. C. Herkströter, "Royal Dutch/Shell: Rewriting the Contracts," in G. W. Dauphinais and C. Price, eds., *Straight from the CEO* (New York: Simon & Schuster, 1998), pp. 86–93.

50. G. Calabrese, "Communication and Co-operation in Product Development: A Case Study of a European Car Producer," *R&D Management* 27 (July 1997), pp. 239–52; J. L. Brown and N. M. Agnew, "The Balance of Power in a Matrix Structure," *Business Horizons,* November–December 1982, pp. 51–54.

51. C. A. Bartlett and S. Ghoshal, "Managing across Borders: New Organizational Responses," *Sloan Management Review,* Fall 1987, pp. 43–53.

52. G. Imperato, "Harley Shifts Gears," *Fast Company* 9 (1997). Harley-Davidson's team-based structure in the Kansas plant is described slightly differently in J. Singer and S. Duvall, "High-Performance Partnering by Self-Managed Teams in Manufacturing," *Engineering Management Journal* 12 (December 2000), pp. 9–15.

53. J. R. Galbraith, *Competing with Flexible Lateral Organizations* (Boston, MA: Addison-Wesley, 1994); J. B. Rieley, "The Circular Organization: How Leadership Can Optimize Organizational Effectiveness," *National Productivity Review* 13 (Winter 1993–1994), pp. 11–19; J. A. Byrne, "The Horizontal Corporation," *Business Week*, December 20, 1993, pp. 76–81; R. Tomasko, *Rethinking the Corporation* (New York: AMACOM, 1993); D. Q. Mills (with G. B. Friesen), *Rebirth of the Corporation* (New York: Wiley, 1991), pp. 29–30.

54. M. A. Brunelli, "How Harley-Davidson Uses Cross-Functional Teams," *Purchasing*, November 4, 1999, p. 148.

55. R. Bettis and M. Hitt, "The New Competitive Landscape," *Strategic Management Journal* 16 (1995), pp. 7–19; J. R. Galbraith, E. E. Lawler III, and Associates, *Organizing for the Future: The New Logic for Managing Complex Organizations* (San Francisco: Jossey-Bass, 1993).

56. P. C. Ensign, "Interdependence, Coordination, and Structure in Complex Organizations: Implications for Organization Design," *Mid-Atlantic Journal of Business* 34 (March 1998), pp. 5–22

57. L. Y. Chan and B. E. Lynn, "Operating in Turbulent Times: How Ontario's Hospitals Are Meeting the Current Funding Crisis," *Health Care Management Review* 23 (June 1998), pp. 7–18; M. M. Fanning, "A Circular Organization Chart Promotes a Hospital-Wide Focus on Teams," *Hospital and Health Services Administration* 42 (June 1997), pp. 243–54.

58. R. Cross, "Looking before You Leap: Assessing the Jump to Teams in Knowledge-Based Work," *Business Horizons*, September, 2000; W. F. Joyce, V. E. McGee, and J. W. Slocum, Jr., "Designing Lateral Organizations: An Analysis of the Benefits, Costs, and Enablers of Nonhierarchical Organizational Forms," *Decision Sciences* 28 (Winter 1997), pp. 1–25.

59. J. King, "Employers Quickly Hire Circuit Board Assemblers," *Detroit News*, October 15, 2000, p. 1; J-A. Johnston, "The Faces of Productivity," *Tampa (FL) Tribune*, September 4, 2000, p. 7.

60. R. Hacki and J. Lighton, "The Future of the Networked Company," *Business Review Weekly*, August 30, 2001, p. 58; A. M. Porter, "The Virtual Corporation: Where Is It?" *Purchasing*, March 23, 2000, pp. 40–48; J. A. Byrne, "The Corporation of the Future," *Business Week*, August 31, 1998, pp. 102–4.

61. J. R. Galbraith, "Designing the Networked Organization," in Mohrman et al., eds., *Tomorrow's Organization*, p. 102; C. Baldwin and K. Clark, "Managing in an Age of Modularity," *Harvard Business Review* 75 (September–October 1997), pp. 84–93; R. E. Miles and C. C. Snow, "The New Network Firm: A Spherical Structure Built on a Human Investment Philosophy," *Organizational Dynamics* 23 (4) (1995), pp. 5–18; W. Powell, "Neither Market nor Hierarchy: Network Forms of Organization," *Research in Organizational Behavior* 12 (1990), pp. 295–336.

62. T. W. Malone and R. J. Laubacher, "The Dawn of the E-lance Economy," *Harvard Business Review* 76 (September–October 1998), pp. 144–52.

63. T. Arsenault, "Return of the Rich Man," *Halifax-Chronicle Herald*, November 5, 1999; J. Hagel III and M. Singer, "Unbundling the Corporation," *Harvard Business Review* 77 (March–April 1999), pp. 133–41. For a discussion of core competencies, see G. Hamel and C. K. Prahalad, *Competing for the Future* (Boston: Harvard Business School Press, 1994), chap. 10.

64. D. Egbert, "Label Says 'Nortel,' but Somebody Else Probably Made It," *News and Observer (Raleigh, NC)*, June 15, 2000, p. D1.

65. R. Lieber, "Startups: The 'Inside' Stories," *Fast Company* 32 (March 2000), p. 284.

66. J. Matthews, " 'Baby Bills' Follow Leader to Success," *Baltimore Sun*, August 14, 1998; J. F. Moore, "The Rise of a New Corporate Form," *Washington Quarterly* 21 (Winter 1998), pp. 167–81.

67. L. Fried, *Managing Information Technology in Turbulent Times* (New York: Wiley, 1995); W. H. Davidow and M. S. Malone, *The Virtual Corporation* (New York: HarperBusiness, 1992).

68. P. Doyle, "Getting Their Act Together," *St. John's (Newfoundland) Telegram*, October 29, 1999.

69. G. Morgan, *Imagin-I-Zation: New Mindsets for Seeing, Organizing and Managing* (Thousand Oaks, CA: Sage, 1997); G. Morgan, *Images of Organization*, 2nd ed. (Newbury Park: Sage, 1996).

70. C. Meyer and S. Davis, *Blur: The Speed of Change in the Connected Economy* (Reading, MA: Addison-Wesley, 1998); P. M. J. Christie and R. Levary, "Virtual Corporations: Recipe for Success," *Industrial Management* 40 (July 1998), pp. 7–11; H. Chesbrough and D. J. Teece, "When Is Virtual Virtuous? Organizing for Innovation," *Harvard Business Review*, January–February 1996, pp. 65–73.

71. A. Gilbert, "Virtual Company Wins New Business," *InformationWeek*, April 2, 2001, p. 79.

72. Mintzberg, *The Structuring of Organizations*, chap. 13; D. S. Pugh and C. R. Hinings, eds., *Organizational Structure: Extensions and Replications* (Farnborough, UK: Lexington, 1976).

73. T. A. Stewart, *Intellectual Capital: The New Wealth of Organizations* (New York: Doubleday Currency, 1997), chap. 10.

74. Robey, *Designing Organizations*, p. 102.

75. C. Perrow, "A Framework for the Comparative Analysis of Organizations," *American Sociological Review* 32 (1967), pp. 194–208.

76. Mintzberg, *The Structuring of Organizations*, chap. 15.

77. Burns and Stalker, *The Management of Innovation*; P. R. Lawrence and J. W. Lorsch, *Organization and Environment* (Homewood, IL: Irwin, 1967); D. Miller and P. H. Friesen, *Organizations: A Quantum View* (Englewood Cliffs, NJ: Prentice Hall, 1984), pp. 197–98.

78. Mintzberg, *The Structuring of Organizations*, p. 282.

79. R. H. Kilmann, *Beyond the Quick Fix* (San Francisco: Jossey-Bass, 1984), p. 38.

80. J. Child, "Organizational Structure, Environment, and Performance: The Role of Strategic Choice," *Sociology* 6 (1972), pp. 2–22.

81. A. D. Chandler, *Strategy and Structure* (Cambridge, MA: MIT Press, 1962).

83. M. E. Porter, *Competitive Strategy* (New York: Free Press, 1980).

84. D. Miller, "Configurations of Strategy and Structure," *Strategic Management Journal* 7 (1986), pp. 233–50.

CHAPTER EIGHTEEN

1. M. Ruggeri, "Security Courtesy of Dan Schmitt and Company," Rich-mond (VA) Times-Dispatch, July 29, 2001; A. K. Smith, "Charting Your Own Course," U.S. News & World Report, November 6, 2000.

2. P. Cappelli, The New Deal at Work (Boston: Harvard Business School Press, 1999).

3. P. Sinton, "Double Disaster," San Francisco Chronicle, May 25, 2001, p. B1.

4. P. Kruger, "Betrayed by Work," Fast Company, November 1999, p. 182.

5. E. W. Morrison and S. L. Robinson, "When Employees Feel Betrayed: A Model of How Psychological Contract Violation Develops," Academy of Man-agement Review 22 (1997), pp. 226–56.

6. D. M. Rousseau, "Changing Obliga-tions and the Psychological Contract: A Longitudinal Study," Academy of Man-agement Journal 37 (1994), pp. 137–52; D. M. Rousseau and J. M. Parks, "The Contracts of Individuals and Organiza-tions," Research in Organizational Be-havior 15 (1993), pp. 1–43.

7. P. Herriot, W. E. G. Manning, and J. M. Kidd, "The Content of the Psy-chological Contract," British Journal of Management 8 (1997), pp. 151–62.

8. J. McLean Parks and D. L. Kidder, " 'Till Death Us Do Part . . .' Changing Work Relationships in the 1990s," in C. L. Cooper and D. M. Rousseau, eds., Trends in Organizational Behavior, vol. 1 (Chichester, UK: Wiley, 1994), pp. 112–36.

9. H. J. Van Buren III, "The Bindingness of Social and Psychological Contracts: Toward a Theory of Social Responsibil-ity in Downsizing," Journal of Business Ethics 25 (June 2000), pp. 205–19; P. R. Sparrow, "Reappraising Psychological Contracting: Lessons for the Field of Hu-man-Resource Development from Cross-Cultural and Occupational Psychology Research," International Studies of Man-agement and Organization 28 (March 1998), pp. 30–63.

10. L. Stevens, "Believers in the Mid-day Doze Are Stripping Away Stigma of Siestas," Fort Worth (TX) Star-Telegram, March 24, 2001; R. Hogan, "A Daytime Nap Could Make You More Produc-tive," Los Angeles Times, January 15, 2001; S. M. Handelsblatt, "Stressed Out and Stranded in Barcelona?" Wall Street Journal Europe, August 4, 2000, p. 32; R. Boudreaux, "Spaniards Are Missing Their Naps," Los Angeles Times, March 28, 2000.

11. S. L. Robinson, "Trust and Breach of the Psychological Contract," Admin-istrative Science Quarterly 41 (1996), pp. 574–99. For a discussion of the an-tecedents of trust, see E. M Whitener, S. E. Brodt, M. A. Korsgaard, and J. M. Werner, "Managers As Initiators of Trust: An Exchange Relationship Framework for Understanding Man-agerial Trustworthy Behavior," Acad-emy of Management Review 23 (July 1998), pp. 513–30.

12. R. D. Costigan, S. S. Ilter, and J. J. Berman, " A Multi-Dimensional Study of Trust in Organizations," Jour-nal of Managerial Issues 10 (Fall 1998), pp. 303–17.

13. D. M. Rousseau, S. B. Sitkin, R. S. Burt, and C. Camerer, "Not So Different After All: A Cross-Discipline View of Trust," Academy of Management Review 23 (July 1998), pp. 393–404; R. J. Lewicki and B. B. Bunker, "Developing and Maintaining Trust in Work Rela-tionships," in R. M. Kramer and T. R. Tyler, eds., Trust in Organizations: Fron-tiers of Theory and Research (Thousand Oaks, CA: Sage, 1996), pp. 114–39.

14. Whitener et al., "Managers As Ini-tiators of Trust"; W. Bennis and B. Nanus, Leaders: The Strategies for Taking Charge (New York: Harper & Row, 1986), pp. 43–55; J. M. Kouzes and B. Z. Posner, Credibility: How Leaders Gain and Lose It, Why People Demand It (San Francisco: Jossey-Bass, 1993). Knowl-edge-based trust is sometimes called history-based trust in the psychological literature. See R. M. Kramer, "Trust and Distrust in Organizations: Emerging Perspectives, Enduring Questions," An-nual Review of Psychology 50 (1999), pp. 569–98.

15. I. DeBare, "Keeping a Packed Bag at Work," San Francisco Chronicle, April 30, 1999.

16. S. L. Robinson and E. W. Morrison, "Psychological Contracts and OCB: The Effect of Unfulfilled Obligations on Civic Virtue Behavior," Journal of Or-ganizational Behavior 16 (1995), pp. 289–98.

17. D. M. Rousseau, "Changing the Deal While Keeping the People," Acad-emy of Management Executive 10 (Feb-ruary 1996), pp. 50–61.

18. C. Hendry and R. Jenkins, "Psy-chological Contracts and New Deals," Human Resource Management Journal 7 (1997), pp. 38–44; P. Herriot and C. Pemberton, New Deals: The Revolu-tion in Managerial Careers (New York: Wiley, 1995), chap. 3; W. H. Whyte, The Organization Man (New York: Simon & Schuster, 1956), p. 129.

19. J. C. Meister, "The Quest for Life-time Employability," Journal of Busi-ness Strategy 19 (May–June 1998), pp. 25–28; T. A. Stewart, "Gray Flannel Suit? Moi?" Fortune, March 16, 1998, pp. 76–82; A. Rajan, "Employability in the Finance Sector: Rhetoric vs. Real-ity," Human Resource Management Journal 7 (1997), pp. 67–78.

20. L. Uchitelle, "As Job Cuts Spread, Tears Replace Anger," New York Times, August 5, 2001; B. Moses, The Good News about Careers: How You'll Be Working in the Next Decade (Toronto: Stoddart, 1999).

21. P. Herriot and C. Pemberton, "Fa-cilitating New Deals," Human Resource Management Journal 7 (1997), pp. 45–56; P. R. Sparrow, "Transitions in the Psychological Contract: Some Evidence from the Banking Sector," Human Re-source Management Journal 6 (1996), pp. 75–92.

22. M. E. Podmolik, "Talkin' 'Bout My Generation," Crain's Chicago Business, June 4, 2001, p. E18.

23. "Towers Perrin Study Finds, Despite Layoffs and Slow Economy, a New, More Complex Power Game Is Emerg-ing between Employers and Employ-ees," Business Wire, August 30, 2001.

24. Facts about Manpower, Inc., are from its website (www.manpower.com). This observation is also noted in T. W. Malone and R. J. Laubacher, "The Dawn of the E-lance Economy," Har-vard Business Review 76 (September–October 1998), pp. 144–52.

25. M. Mallon and J. Duberley, "Man-agers and Professionals in the Con-tingent Workforce," Human Resource Management Journal, January 2000, p. 33; A. E. Polivka, "Contingent and Alternative Work Arrangements, De-fined," Monthly Labor Review 119 (Oc-

tober 1996), pp. 3–10. For further discussion of the meaning of *contingent work*, see S. Nollen and H. Axel, *Managing Contingent Workers* (New York: AMACOM, 1996), pp. 4–9.

26. S. Hipple, "Contingent Work: Results from the Second Survey," *Monthly Labor Review* 121 (November 1998), pp. 22–35.

27. For a discussion of contingent work, including estimates of the American workforce percentage in this category, see K. Barker and K. Christensen, eds., *Contingent Work: American Employment in Transition* (Ithaca, NY: ILR Press, 1998). Contingent work in Europe is discussed in G. Edmondson et al., "A Tidal Wave of Temps," *Business Week (International)*, November 24, 1997; Sparrow, "Reappraising Psychological Contracting."

28. C. von Hippel, S. L. Mangum, D. B. Greenberger, R. L. Heneman, and J. D. Skoglind, "Temporary Employment: Can Organizations and Employees Both Win?" *Academy of Management Executive* 11 (February 1997), pp. 93–104; A. E. Polivka "Into Contingent and Alternative Employment: By Choice?" *Monthly Labor Review* 119 (October 1996), pp. 55–74. A recent U.S. government study revealed that the percentage of contingent workers who want permanent employment is dropping. However, most of these people still prefer permanent employment. See "Gains in Job Security," *Monthly Labor Review* 121 (March 1998), pp. 74–75.

29. F. Buffini, "The Free Agent Nation," *Boss Magazine*, June 8, 2001, p. 38; D. H. Pink, "Land of the Free," *Fast Company*, May 2001, pp. 125–33; S. B. Gould, K. J. Weiner, and B. R. Levin, *Free Agents: People and Organizations Creating a New Working Community* (San Francisco: Jossey-Bass, 1997); von Hippel et al., "Temporary Employment," pp. 94–96; W. J. Byron, "Coming to Terms with the New Corporate Contract," *Business Horizons* 38 (January 1995), pp. 8–15.

30. P. Luke, "From Secretary to Cyber Queen," *Vancouver Province*, May 14, 2000; A. Daniels, "Virtual Assistant," *Vancouver Sun*, March 27, 2000, p. C10.

31. S. J. Hartman, A. C. Yrle, and A. R. Yrle, "Turnover in the Hotel Industry: Is There a Hobo Phenomenon at Work?" *International Journal of Management* 13 (1996), pp. 340–48; T. A. Judge and S. Watanabe, "Is the Past Prologue? A Test of Ghiselli's Hobo Syndrome," *Journal of Management* 21 (1995), pp. 211–29.

32. J. Walsh and S. Deery, "Understanding the Peripheral Workforce: Evidence from the Service Sector," *Human Resource Management Journal* 9 (1999), pp. 50–63; von Hippel et al., "Temporary Employment," pp. 93–104.

33. S. F. Matusik and C. W. L. Hill, "The Utilization of Contingent Work, Knowledge Creation, and Competitive Advantage," *Academy of Management Review* 23 (October 1998), pp. 680–97.

34. J. Larson, "Temps Are Here to Stay," *American Demographics* 18 (February 1996), pp. 26–30.

35. Malone and Laubacher, "The Dawn of the E-lance Economy."

36. For a recent survey on the complex array of problems and benefits of contingent work, see Mallon and Duberley, "Managers and Professionals in the Contingent Workforce."

37. J. Dionne-Proulx, J-C. Bernatchez, and R. Boulard, "Attitudes and Satisfaction Levels Associated with Precarious Employment," *International Journal of Employment Studies* 6, no. 2 (1998), pp. 91–114. The contingencies of contingent work attitudes are reviewed in M. Armstrong-Stassen, "Alternative Work Arrangements: Meeting the Challenges," *Canadian Psychology* 39 (1998), pp. 108–23. Potential organizational behavior problems with contingent work are discussed in J. Pfeffer, *New Directions in Organizational Theory* (New York: Oxford University Press, 1997), pp. 18–20.

38. L. Uchitelle, "As Job Cuts Spread, Tears Replace Anger," *New York Times*, August 5, 2001.

39. K. M. Beard and J. R. Edwards, "Employees at Risk: Contingent Work and the Psychological Experience of Contingent Workers," in C. L. Cooper and D. M. Rousseau, eds., *Trends in Organizational Behavior*, vol. 2 (Chichester, UK: Wiley, 1995), pp. 109–26.

40. Y-S. Park and R. J. Butler, "The Safety Costs of Contingent Work: Evidence from Minnesota," *Journal of Labor Research* 22 (Fall 2001), pp. 831–49; D. M. Rousseau and C. Libuser, "Contingent Workers in High Risk Environ-ments," *California Management Review* 39 (Winter 1997), pp. 103–23.

41. "Four Arrested as Campus 'Theft Ring' Is Exposed," *Simon Fraser News (Burnaby, BC)*, September 5, 1996.

42. Armstrong-Stassen, "Alternative Work Arrangements"; D. C. Feldman and H. I. Doerpinghaus, "Managing Temporary Workers: A Permanent HRM Challenge," *Organizational Dynamics* 23 (Fall 1994), pp. 49–63.

43. A. M. Saks, P. E. Mudrack, and B. E. Ashforth, "The Relationship between the Work Ethic, Job Attitudes, Intentions to Quit, and Turnover for Temporary Service Workers," *Canadian Journal of Administrative Sciences* 13 (1996), pp. 226–36.

44. J. Van Maanen, "Breaking In: Socialization to Work," in R. Dublin, ed., *Handbook of Work, Organization, and Society* (Chicago: Rand McNally, 1976), p. 67.

45. C. L. Adkins, "Previous Work Experience and Organizational Socialization: A Longitudinal Examination," *Academy of Management Journal* 38 (1995), pp. 839–62; T. N. Bauer and S. G. Green, "The Effect of Newcomer Involvement in Work Related Activities: A Longitudinal Study of Socialization," *Journal of Applied Psychology* 79 (1994), pp. 211–23.

46. E. F. Holton III, "New Employee Development: A Review and Reconceptualization," *Human Resource Development Quarterly* 7 (Fall 1996), pp. 233–52; G. T. Chao, A. O'Leary-Kelly, S. Wolf, H. J. Klein, and P. D. Gardner, "Organizational Socialization: Its Content and Consequences," *Journal of Applied Psychology* 79 (1994), pp. 450–63.

47. J. T. Mignerey, R. B. Rubin, and W. I. Gorden, "Organizational Entry: An Investigation of Newcomer Communication Behavior and Uncertainty," *Communication Research* 22 (1995), pp. 54–85.

48. K. Mieszkowski, "Get with the Program!" *Fast Company* 13 (February–March 1998), pp. 28–30.

49. B. E. Ashforth and A. M. Saks, "Socialization Tactics: Longitudinal Effects on Newcomer Adjustment," *Academy of Management Journal* 39 (1996), pp. 149–78; C. D. Fisher, "Organizational Socialization: An Integrative View," *Research in Personnel and Human Re-*

sources Management 4 (1986), pp. 101–45; N. Nicholson, "A Theory of Work Role Transitions," *Administrative Science Quarterly* 29 (1984), pp. 172–91.

50. C. C. Pinder and K. G. Schroeder, "Time to Proficiency Following Job Transfers," *Academy of Management Journal* 30 (1987), pp. 336–53; N. J. Adler, *International Dimensions of Organizational Behavior*, 2nd ed. (Belmont, CA: Wadsworth, 1991), chap. 8.

51. Van Maanen, "Breaking In," pp. 67–130; L. W. Porter, E. E. Lawler III, and J. R. Hackman, *Behavior in Organizations* (New York: McGraw-Hill, 1975), pp. 163–67; D. C. Feldman, "The Multiple Socialization of Organization Members," *Academy of Management Review* 6 (1981), pp. 309–18.

52. M. K. Gibson and M. J. Papa, "The Mud, the Blood, and the Beer Guys: Organizational Osmosis in Blue-Collar Work Groups," *Journal of Applied Communication Research*, February 2000, p. 68; Ashforth and Saks, "Socialization Tactics"; T. N. Bauer and S. G. Green, "Effect of Newcomer Involvement in Work-Related Activities: A Longitudinal Study of Socialization," *Journal of Applied Psychology* 79 (1994), pp. 211–23.

53. Porter et al., *Behavior in Organizations*, chap. 5.

54. D. M. Cable, L. Aiman-Smith, P. W. Mulvey, and J. R. Edwards, "The Sources and Accuracy of Job Applicants' Beliefs about Organizational Culture," *Academy of Management Journal* 43 (December 2000), pp. 1076–85.

55. J. Stites, "Going from the Corporate World to Silicon Alley Can Prove Tough," *New York Times*, August 31, 1998, p. 3.

56. M. R. Louis, "Surprise and Sensemaking: What Newcomers Experience in Entering Unfamiliar Organizational Settings," *Administrative Science Quarterly* 25 (1980), pp. 226–51.

57. E. Fitzmaurice, "A Hard Lesson," *Sun Herald (Sydney)*, March 11, 2001, p. 50.

58. C. A. Young and C. C. Lundberg, "Creating a Good First Day on the Job," *Cornell Hotel and Restaurant Administration Quarterly* 37 (December 1996), pp. 26–33; S. L. Robinson and D. M. Rousseau, "Violating the Psychological Contract: Not the Exception but the Norm," *Journal of Organizational Behavior* 15 (1994), pp. 245–59.

59. D. L. Nelson, "Organizational Socialization: A Stress Perspective," *Journal of Occupational Behavior* 8 (1987), pp. 311–24.

60. Morrison and Robinson, "When Employees Feel Betrayed," p. 251.

61. J. A. Breaugh, *Recruitment: Science and Practice* (Boston: PWS-Kent, 1992), chap. 7; J. P. Wanous, *Organizational Entry*, 2nd ed. (Reading, MA: Addison-Wesley, 1992), chap. 3; A. M. Saks and S. F. Cronshaw, "A Process Investigation of Realistic Job Previews: Mediating Variables and Channels of Communication," *Journal of Organizational Behavior* 11 (1990), pp. 221–36.

62. M. Truby, "Ford Romances Top Prospects," *Detroit News*, January 7, 2001.

63. J. M. Phillips, "Effects of Realistic Job Previews on Multiple Organizational Outcomes: A Meta-Analysis," *Academy of Management Journal* 41 (December 1998), pp. 673–90.

64. J. P. Wanous and A. Colella, "Organizational Entry Research: Current Status and Future Directions," *Research in Personnel and Human Resources Management* 7 (1989), pp. 59–120.

65. C. Ostroff and S. W. J. Koslowski, "Organizational Socialization as a Learning Process: The Role of Information Acquisition," *Personnel Psychology* 45 (1992), pp. 849–74; N. J. Allen and J. P. Meyer, "Organizational Socialization Tactics: A Longitudinal Analysis of Links to Newcomers' Commitment and Role Orientation," *Academy of Management Journal* 33 (1990), pp. 847–58; F. M. Jablin, "Organizational Entry, Assimilation, and Exit," in F. M. Jablin, L. L. Putnam, K. H. Roberts, and L. W. Porter, eds., *Handbook of Organizational Communication* (Beverly Hills, CA: Sage, 1987), pp. 679–740.

66. E. W. Morrison, "Newcomer Information Seeking: Exploring Types, Modes, Sources, and Outcomes," *Academy of Management Journal* 36 (1993), pp. 557–89; Fisher, "Organizational Socialization," pp. 135–36; Porter et al., *Behavior in Organizations*, pp. 184–86.

67. C. Goforth, "Still Recruiting Staff," *Akron (OH) Beacon Journal*, July 15, 2001; A. L. Stern, "Bridging the Workforce Shortage," *Trustee*, July 2001, p. 8; D. Francis, "Work Is a Warm Puppy," *National Post*, May 27, 2000, p. W20.

68. S. L. McShane, "Effect of Socialization Agents on the Organizational Adjustment of New Employees," Paper presented at the Annual Conference of the Western Academy of Management, Big Sky, Montana, March 1988.

69. "Employee Loyalty a Fading Virtue," *Canadian Press*, April 9, 2000.

70. M. B. Arthur, D. T. Hall, and B. S. Lawrence, "Generating New Directions in Career Theory: The Case for a Transdisciplinary Approach," in M. B. Arthur, D. T. Hall, and B. S. Lawrence, eds., *Handbook of Career Theory* (Cambridge, UK: Cambridge University Press, 1989), pp. 7–25.

71. M. B. Arthur, "The Boundaryless Career: A New Perspective for Organizational Inquiry," *Journal of Organizational Behavior* 15 (1994), pp. 295–306.

72. D. T. Hall, *Careers in Organizations* (Glenview, IL: Scott Foresman, 1976), pp. 93–97.

73. M. Hinkelman, "Loyalty Pays for Vanguard," *Philadelphia Daily News*, September 4, 2001.

74. T. Snyder, "Take This Job and Love It," *Chatelaine*, October 1999, p. 97.

75. J. Holland, *Making Vocational Choices: A Theory of Careers* (Englewood Cliffs, NJ: Prentice Hall, 1973).

76. G. D. Gottfredson and J. L. Holland, "A Longitudinal Test of the Influence of Congruence: Job Satisfaction, Competency Utilization, and Counterproductive Behavior," *Journal of Counseling Psychology* 37 (1990), pp. 389–98.

77. J. Arnold, "The Psychology of Careers in Organizations," *International Review of Industrial and Organizational Psychology* 12 (1997), pp. 1–37.

78. For example, see G. R. Cluskey and A. Vaux, "Vocational Misfit: Source of Occupational Stress among Accountants," *Journal of Applied Business Research* 13 (Summer 1997), pp. 43–54.

79. R. A. Young and C. P. Chen, "Annual Review: Practice and Research in Career Counseling and Development—1998," *Career Development Quarterly*, December 1999, p. 98.

80. P. R. Chowdhury, "The New Worker," *Business Today*, January 2001,

p. 68. For early discussion of lateral career development, see D. T. Hall and J. Richter, "Career Gridlock: Baby Boomers Hit the Wall," *Academy of Management Executive* 4 (August 1990), pp. 7–22.

81. B. Kaye and C. Farren, "Up Is Not the Only Way," *Training and Development* 50 (February 1996), pp. 48–53.

82. P. LaBarre, "The Company without Limits," *Fast Company* 27 (September 1999), p. 160.

83. P. Baker, "A Sideways Move Could Bring You out of Your Shell," *The Observer (UK)*, March 22, 1998, p. 8; "De-Layered Pay Systems Encourage Employees to Move Sideways," *Universal News Services*, January 24, 1997.

84. J. C. Meister, "The Quest for Lifetime Employability," *Journal of Business Strategy* 19 (May–June 1998), pp. 25–28.

85. Whyte, *Organization Man*.

86. M. B. Arthur and D. M. Rousseau, *The Boundaryless Career: A New Employment Principle for a New Organizational Era* (New York: Oxford University Press, 1996); Arthur, "The Boundaryless Career."

86. A. K. Smith, "Charting Your Own Course," *U.S. News & World Report*, November 6, 2000.

88. P. Oliver, "Shifting to Find a Job That Fits," *New Zealand Herald*, January 21, 2001. The backlash of job-hopping in Silicon Valley is discussed in J. Palmer, "Marry Me a Little," *Barron's*, July 24, 2000, p. 24.

89. Stewart, "Gray Flannel Suit? Moi?"

90. New York Times Staff, *The Downsizing of America* (New York: Times Books, 1996); R. J. Defillippi and M. B. Arthur,

"The Boundaryless Career: A Competency-Based Perspective," *Journal of Organizational Behavior* 15 (1994), pp. 307–24.

91. B. O'Reilly, "The New Deal: What Companies and Employees Owe One Another," *Fortune*, June 13, 1994, pp. 44–52.

92. J. P. Sampson, Jr., J. G. Lenz, R. C. Reardon, and G. W. Peterson, "A Cognitive Information Processing Approach to Employment Problem Solving and Decision Making," *Career Development Quarterly* 48 (September 1999), pp. 3–18.

93. "A Career with 'Karma,'" *ABC News*, May 3, 2001 (www.abcnews.com).

94. S. Terry, "Job Outlook for Grads: Off Peak, but Not Bleak," *Christian Science Monitor*, May 21, 2001.

95. B. Moses, "Give People Belief in the Future," *Workforce*, June 2000, pp. 134–41.

96. A. Zipkin, "Tough Bosses Don't Cut It in Today's Workplace," *San Jose (CA) Mercury*, May 31, 2000.

97. B. Moses, "Career Activists Take Command," *Globe and Mail (Toronto)*, March 20, 2000, p. B6.

98. F. T. McCarthy "Career Evolution," *The Economist*, January 29, 2000. The survey is reported in Drake Beam Morin, "1999 DBM Career Transition Study," November 2000 (www.dbm.com).

99. S. E. Sullivan, "The Changing Nature of Careers: A Review and Research Agenda," *Journal of Management*, May 1999, pp. 457–84; Moses, *The Good News about Careers*.

100. N. Beech and A. Brockbank, "Power/Knowledge and Psychosocial Dynamics in Mentoring," *Management*

Learning 30 (March 1999), pp. 7–24; S-C. Van Collie, "Moving Up through Mentoring," *Workforce* 77 (March 1998), pp. 36–40.

101. H. Handfield-Jones, "How Executives Grow," *McKinsey Quarterly*, January 2000, p. 117.

APPENDIX A

1. F. N. Kerlinger, *Foundations of Behavioral Research* (New York: Holt, Rinehart & Winston, 1964), p. 11.

2. J. B. Miner, *Theories of Organizational Behavior* (Hinsdale, IL: Dryden, 1980), pp. 7–9.

3. Miner, *Theories of Organizational Behavior*, pp. 6–7.

4. J. Mason, *Qualitative Researching* (London: Sage, 1996).

5. A. Strauss and J. Corbin, eds., *Grounded Theory in Practice* (London: Sage, 1997); B. G. Glaser and A. Strauss, *The Discovery of Grounded Theory: Strategies for Qualitative Research* (Chicago, IL: Aldine, 1967).

6. Kerlinger, *Foundations of Behavioral Research*, p. 13.

7. P. Lazarsfeld, *Survey Design and Analysis* (New York: Free Press, 1955).

8. This example is cited in D. W. Organ and T. S. Bateman, *Organizational Behavior*, 4th ed. (Homewood, IL: Irwin, 1991), p. 42.

9. Organ and Bateman, *Organizational Behavior*, p. 45.

10. R. I. Sutton and A. Hargadon, "Brainstorming Groups in Context: Effectiveness in a Product Design Firm," *Administrative Science Quarterly* 41 (1996), pp. 685–718.